AMERICAN CINEMATOGRAPHER MANUAL

TENTH EDITION

Volume I

REVISED 2014

EDITED BY

Michael Goi, ASC

THE ASC PRESS
HOLLYWOOD, CALIFORNIA

American Cinematographer Manual
Tenth Edition—Volume I

Copyright© 2013 by The ASC Press

Hollywood, California, USA
All Rights Reserved

ISBN 978-1-4675-6831-9

Cover design by Martha Winterhalter
Book design by Deeann j. Hoff
Production by Mark McDougal

Foreword

You hold in your hands the result of five years of thought, debate, and inspiration. When Stephen Burum, ASC, asked me to be the editor of this 10th edition of the venerable American Cinematographer Manual, the industry was in the birth throes of transition; digital intermediates were the exception and not the rule, we still used the term video rather than digital, and 4K as a viable production and post format was far beyond our reach. All these changes and many more came in rapid succession as we labored to bring this book to press. No sooner had we completed an article when it had to be updated due to sweeping advances in technology.

I am at heart a low-tech person. I like things simple. I questioned whether I was even the right person to be taking this book on. But in a strange way, it made sense. If I could design the manual in a manner that made sense to me, then the information it contained would be accesible to a wide spectrum of professional and prosumer image makers. Cinematographers today need to be closet scientists in order to decipher the tools they have at their disposal, but all those technologies need not be daunting; they can be fun to explore and exciting to utilize. Now more than ever, the dreams of a whole new generation can be made into real moving images. This edition contains some of the most comprehensive information on digital that you will find anywhere, but it doesn't leave behind the essential building blocks of film technology, which is at its highest level of development. Where we are now is really having the best of both worlds.

When you embark on a journey to a new world, it's best to take along a crew who know the territory. The contributors to this edition have proven to be the most helpful and dedicated group of scientists, artists and craftspeople one could possibly hope to assemble. Thanks go to Jim Branch, Curtis Clark, ASC; Richard Crudo, ASC; Dan Curry; Linwood G. Dunn, ASC; Richard Edlund, ASC; Jonathan Erland; Jon Fauer, ASC; Ray Feeney; Tom Fraser; Taz Goldstein; Colin Green and the Previsualization Society; Frieder Hochheim; Michael Hofstein; Bill Hogan; John Hora, ASC; Rob Hummel; Steve Irwin; Kent H. Jorgensen; Frank Kay; Glenn Kennel; Jon Kranhouse; Lou Levinson; Andy Maltz and the AMPAS Science and Technology Council; Vincent Matta; Tak Miyagishima; David Morin; M. David Mullen, ASC; Dennis Muren, ASC; Iain A. Neil; Marty Ollstein; Josh Pines; Steven Poster, ASC; Sarah Priestnall; David Reisner; Pete Romano, ASC; Andy Romanoff; Dr. Rod Ryan; Nic Sadler and Chemical Wedding; Bill Taylor, ASC; Ira Tiffen and Evans Wetmore.

Special thanks go to Iain Stasukevich for his assistance in research, Lowell Peterson, ASC, Jamie Anderson, ASC and King Greenspon for their proof-reading skills, and Deeann Hoff and Mark McDougal for handling the layout of the book.

Extra special thanks go to Brett Grauman, general manager of the ASC, Patty Armacost, events coordinator, Delphine Figueras, my assistant when I was handling being ASC president while trying to finish this book, Saul Molina and Alex Lopez for their expertise in marketing and events management, Owen Roizman, ASC, who is the heart, soul and inspiration for the organization, George Spiro Dibie, ASC, my mentor and friend, Martha Winterhalter, whose knowledge of what we do and how to convey it to the world knows no bounds, and Gina Goi, my wife, for her love and support during my many twilight editing sessions.

Enjoy the Manual. Go make movies.

Michael Goi, ASC
Editor

Table of Contents

Creativity,
your mind our
tools!
Let us help
you choose!

CLAIRMONT
CAMERA
FILM&DIGITAL

Providing you with the industry's widest selection of
film and digital cameras, lenses and accessories, backed with
superior service and legendary technical support.

www.clairmont.com

MODEL 7 MICROPHONE BOOM

AUDIO

J.L.Fisher

QUATTRO
CAMERA
PEDESTALS

VECTOR FLUID HEADS

MODEL 6E BASE

MODEL 21 JIB
CRA6 CROSSAR

VIDEO

WEAVER-STEADMAN FLUID HEAD

MODEL 11 CAMERA DOLLY

MODEL 10 CAMERA DOLLY

FILM

FULLY ARTICULATED
SKATEBOARD WHEELS
**Winner of the
cinecAward
"Special Award"**

Patents Pend

MODEL 23 SECTIONAL JIB & CENTER MOUNT   *AVAILABLE FOR* **24½"** *AND* **DEXTER TRA**

THESE AND OTHER PRODUCTS ARE AVAILABLE FOR RENTAL FROM:

J.L. Fisher, Inc.
1000 W. Isabel Street, Burbank, CA 91506 U.S.A.
Tel: (818) 846-8366   Fax: (818) 846-8699
Web: www.jlfisher.com e-mail: info@jlfisher.com

J.L. Fisher, GmbH
Emil-Hoffmann-Str. 55-59 50996 Köln, Germa
Tel: +49 2236 3922 0   Fax: +49 2236 3922
Web: www.jlfisher.de e-mail: info@jlfisher.de

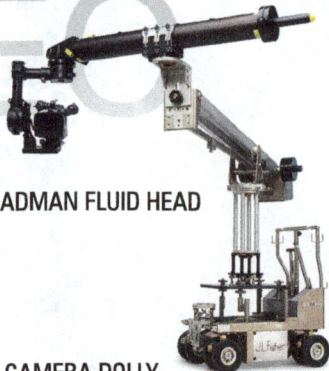

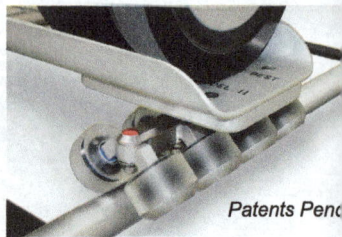

SONY

make.believe

what you get
is what you see

...ny TRIMASTER™ EL monitors.

...u believe black should actually be black. If you believe that moving pictures really
...'t benefit when the monitor adds motion blur. If you believe the only good color is the
...urate color. And if you believe high dynamic range is not only for cameras, Sony
...monitors you can believe in. Our award-winning TRIMASTER EL monitors change
...ything thanks to Sony Super Top Emission OLED technology. Choose the BVM-E Series
...igital cinema evaluation, BVM-F Series for broadcast evaluation or the surprisingly
...rdable PVM Series in 7.4, 17 and 25 inches* for picture monitoring. Seven models with
... standard of picture quality: the truth.

sony.com/TrimasterEL to arrange an on-site demo.

Sony Electronics Inc. All rights reserved. Reproduction in whole or in part without written permission is prohibited. Features and specifications are subject to change
...notice. Weights and measurements are approximate. Sony, TRIMASTER EL and the Sony make. believe logo are trademarks of Sony. Screen image simulated.
...ble area, measured diagonally.

CHAPMAN/LEONARD
Studio Equipment, Inc.
www.chapman-leonard.com

TELESCOPING CRANES

15',20',32',...Introducing the 73' Hydrascope
Equipment that works in any environment
Weather resistant and tough
With Stabilized Remote Camera Systems

Super PeeWee®
Part of The PeeWee® ser

DOLLIES....

Pedestals, Mobile Cranes, Arms & B

Hybrid
Part of The Hybrid ® seri

Time Saving Camera Support for All your nee

LOCATIONS: California: 888 883
New Mexico,Texas, Atlanta, Louisiana & Ohio: 888 758
Florida: 888 337
UK: +44 1 92 326
Ask about our Sound Stage in Fl

From Big Studios to the Smallest Indies

SAMY'S
DV & EDIT

Your Digital Cinema Headquarters

www.SamysDV.com

12636 BEATRICE ST. LOS ANGELES, CA 90066
(P)310.450.4365   (F)310.450.3079

SONY Canon Panasonic

 sachtler. oconnor ECARTONI PROFESSIONAL CAMERA SUPPORT FUJINON FUJIFILM

Schneider OPTICS ZEISS TiFFEN ARRI

STEADICAM SENNHEISER Chrosziel for optical excellence

 LITE PANELS  KINO FLO Lighting Systems TVLogic

codex AJA VIDEO SYSTEMS Blackmagicdesign

CAPTURE

PROCESS

ARCHIVE

SECURITY

MAKING YOUR WORK FLOW

codex

CODEXDIGITAL.COM

Samy's Camera

FOR ALL YOUR DIGITAL CINEMA NEEDS
Rent It or Buy It

FROM GRIP
TO LIGHTS
TO CAMERAS

STEADICAM.

Rental Department

Professional Cameras, Lenses, Studio Equipment & more...

Los Angeles **323-938-4400** I Playa Vista **310-450-7062** I Pasadena **626-796-3300**
Santa Barbara **805-963-7269** I Santa Ana **714-557-9400** I San Francisco

SALES

Los Angeles **323.938.2420** I Culver City **310.450.4551** Pasadena **626.796.3300**
Santa Barbara **805.963.7269** I Santa Ana **714.557.9400** I San Francisco

www•samys•com

Gemini 4:4:4™

nano3D™

nanoFlash™

FlashXDR™

Engineering
the NEXT Revolution

Each of Convergent Design's recorders was a
Revolution in digital video capture. When you
choose a Convergent Design product, you can
expect leading technology, field-proven resilience,
and world class customer service.

convergent
design

CREATIVE VISION
ANYWHERE. ANYTIME.

EC3 provides location services through the combined creativity, experience and technological infrastructure that is EFILM® and Company 3®; two of the industry's most trusted post production houses. Through custom configured hardware, software solutions and highly skilled field technicians, EC3 provides location services for all digital capture Features.

- On Location Dailies Deliverables including iPad® dailies and editorial media same day
- Color Correction On Location
- Instant Quality Control of your footage
- 2k /HD / 3D projector On Location

- Complete 3D capabilities including convergence On Location
- Data Management and Security
- Complete Engineering and Tech Support 24/7

323.308.3094 / 310.255.6643 / EC3ONLOCATION.COM

EC3, EFILM and Company 3 are Deluxe Companies
iPad is a registered trademark of Apple Inc.

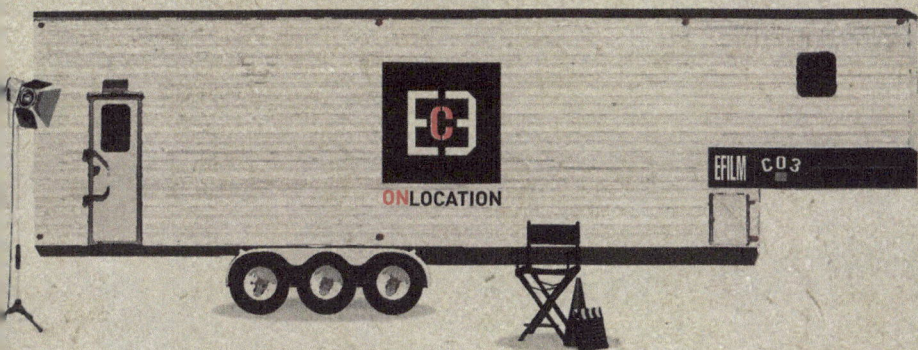

GLIDECAM
INDUSTRIES, INC. ®

THE NAME AND FUTURE OF CAMERA STABILIZATION.™

GLIDECAM X-10

For Cameras weighing up to 10 Pounds.

GLIDECAM X-22

For Cameras from 10 to 25 Pounds.

GLIDECAM HD-SERIES HAND-HELD STABILIZERS

www.Glidecam.com
1-800-600-2011

1-781-585-7900
or Fax us at
1-781-585-7903

STAGE 12

STAGE 3

STAGE 26

STAGE 34

LE BABLOUSE

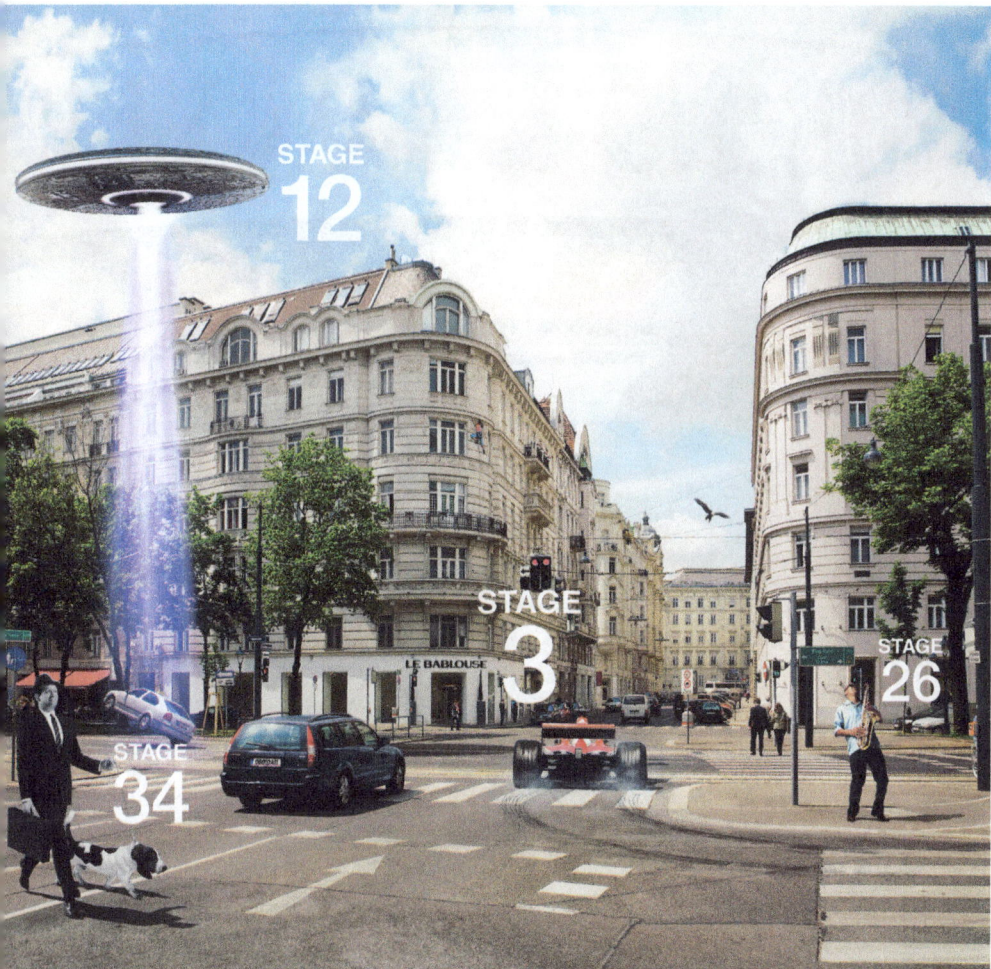

INTRODUCING THE CANON CINEMA EOS SYSTEM

GO WHEREVER THE STORY TAKES YOU.

Presenting a line of cameras designed to shoot anything at every level of production. From the C100 and C300, with their incredible low light performance, to the high resolution 4K image quality of the C500 and 1D-C. Cinema EOS delivers everything including a range of resolutions and recording options for optimized image capture, a Super 35mm CMOS sensor and compatibility with our full line of EF lenses, and new PL-mount and EF-mount Cinema lenses. The complete Canon Cinema EOS System. Now, the world truly is your stage.

GET STARTED. CONTACT US: 855.CINE.EOS - CINEMAEOS.USA.CANON.COM

CINEMA EOS

LEAVE NO STORY UNTOLD

Canon

EOS C100   EOS C300   EOS C500 4K   EOS-1DC 4K

© 2012 Canon U.S.A., Inc. All rights reserved. Canon and EOS are registered trademarks of Canon Inc. in the United States and may also be registered trademarks or trademarks in other countries.

BIRNS & SAWYER

Full Service

Camera – Lighting – Grip

Rentals – Sales

WWW.BIRNSANDSAWYER.COM

BIRNS & SAWYER
HOLLYWOOD

technicolor

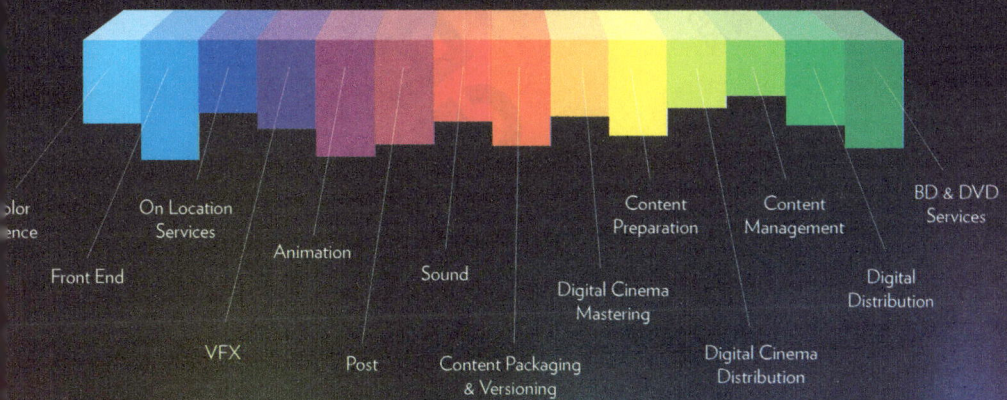

olor
ence

On Location
Services

Front End

Animation

Sound

VFX

Post

Content Packaging
& Versioning

Content
Preparation

Digital Cinema
Mastering

Content
Management

Digital Cinema
Distribution

BD & DVD
Services

Digital
Distribution

technicolor.com

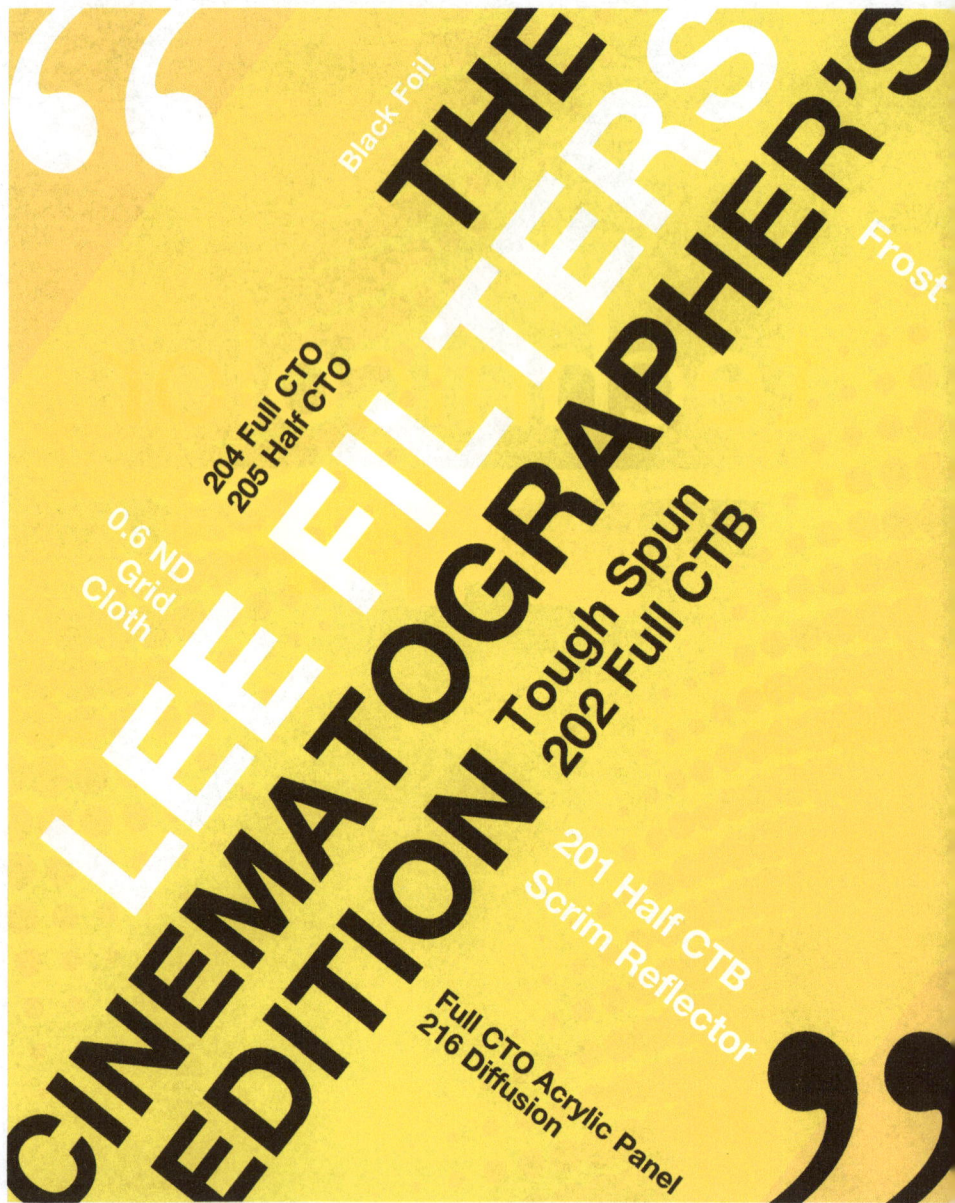

KINO FLO®
Lighting Systems

KINO FLO®
Lighting Systems
2840 North Hollywood Way
Burbank, CA USA
voice+1 818 767 6528
www.kinoflo.com

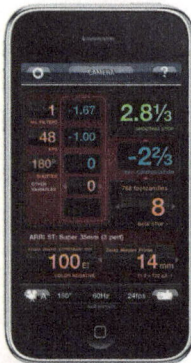

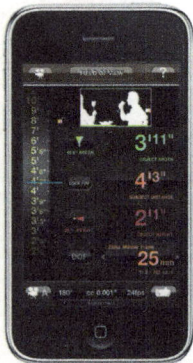

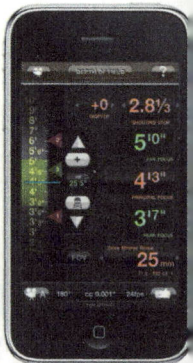

TOLAND
ASC DIGITAL ASSISTA
For iPhone and iPod Tou

GREGG TOLAND, ASC

For more than 70 years, the American Cinematographer Manual has been the key technical resource for cinematographers around the world. Chemical Wedding is proud to be partners with the American Society of Cinematographers in bringing you the Toland ASC Digital Assistant for the iPhone or iPod Touch.

Toland is an application that provides solutions to the technical concerns of cinematography in a unique multi-tasking interface. Combining a calculator and logging interface, it is designed to work with you throughout the process of cinematography.

Toland will track your photographic choices as you make them. As you change the camera speed, you will instantly get feedback on how this affects running time and exposure; when you change lenses, you will see Depth of Field and Field of View updates in real time.

KEY FEATURES

- Comprehensive database of cameras and lenses
- Exposure calculator covering camera speed, shutter angle & filter factor
- Running time and footage calculator
- 'Flicker Free' warning indicator
- Depth of Field calculator with clever focus marks
- Angle of View indicator with pretty picture
- Full camera data logging exportable for offline reporting

STEPHEN LIGHTHILL

" This app, named in honor of the legendary Citizen Kane cinematographer, Gregg Toland, is an indispensable, on-set, exposure management tool. And, in keeping with the educational role of the ASC, the app is also a teacher and mentor in its own right: as you learn the app, you learn the black art of exposure. "

MICHAEL GOI

" The combined intellectual and practical knowledge of the world's greatest cinematographers has been poured into this, the first app-based field tool worthy of carrying the ASC brand. The research and care that went into this was driven by our desire to make something innovative in design and function that would be a fitting tribute to the cinematographer whose name it bears. "

CHEMICAL
WEDDING

Available on the i
App Sto

POCKET ALCHEMY CAN BE FOUN
www.chemicalwedd

THE CLASSICS ARE
ALIVE

WHEN YOU CHOOSE TO ARCHIVE ON FILM, YOUR WORK LIVES ON.

Film is more than entertainment, it's history. Without it, countless classics would be lost.
Now, as digital storage becomes more seductive, modern classics could face extinction.
If it's worth shooting, it's worth saving. Protect your legacy on KODAK Asset Protection Films.

Find out more at www.kodak.com/go/archive

Kodak

© Kodak, 2012. Vision and Kodak are trademarks.

LEARN FILMMAKING
ACTING FOR FILM

PHOTOGRAPHY • PRODUCING • DOCUMENTARY
BROADCAST JOURNALISM • MUSICAL THEATRE
SCREENWRITING • CINEMATOGRAPHY • EDITING
GAME DESIGN • 3D ANIMATION • MUSIC VIDEO

NEW YORK
FILM ACADEMY

SCHOOL OF FILM & ACTING

The Most Hands-on Intensive Programs in the World

16mm • 35mm • Hi-Def • **RED EPIC®** • Super 16mm • HDSLR

1-800-611-FILM | WWW.NYFA.EDU

ONE & TWO-YEAR CONSERVATORY • TWO-YEAR MASTER OF FINE ARTS
BACHELOR OF FINE ARTS • ONE-YEAR MASTER OF ARTS
ASSOCIATE OF FINE ARTS • SHORT-TERM INTENSIVE WORKSHOPS

NEW YORK CITY • UNIVERSAL STUDIOS, CALIFORNIA • ABU DHABI, UAE • AUSTRALIA • FLORENCE
HARVARD UNIVERSITY* • DISNEY STUDIOS* • PARIS* • JAPAN* • KOREA* • CHINA* • INDIA* *SUMMER ONLY*

All credits and degrees are solely granted by the New York Film Academy California. All degree programs take place on the backlot of
Universal Studios, Hollywood. All workshops are solely owned and operated by the New York Film Academy and such workshops
are not affiliated with Universal Studios, Harvard University, or Disney Studios.

DISCOVER NEW TOOLS WITH ADORAMA AND

GET READY TO
MAKE
VIDEOS
LIKE NEVER BEFORE

ZACUTO   SONY   **Panasonic**   Blackmagicdesign   **Canon**   (T)STEADICAM   Convergent Design

It's not too late **CLICK BY 8**

Adorama's superior same-day shipping on orders placed by 8pm EST

ADORAMA.COM
800.223.2500
42 W 18 ST NYC 10011

ADORAMA
MORE THAN A CAMERA STORE

SCAN THIS CODE
TO ENTER OUR
MONTHLY DRAWING
for your chance at a
$200 gift certificate!

the **art** of film optics

optimo lenses transform light into the imagery of your story. Employing the finest optics and mechanics to capture images beyond every expectation. Available in 17-80mm, 24-290mm and now 19.5-94mm and 28-340mm.

angénieux

angenieux@tccus.com • www.angenieux.com

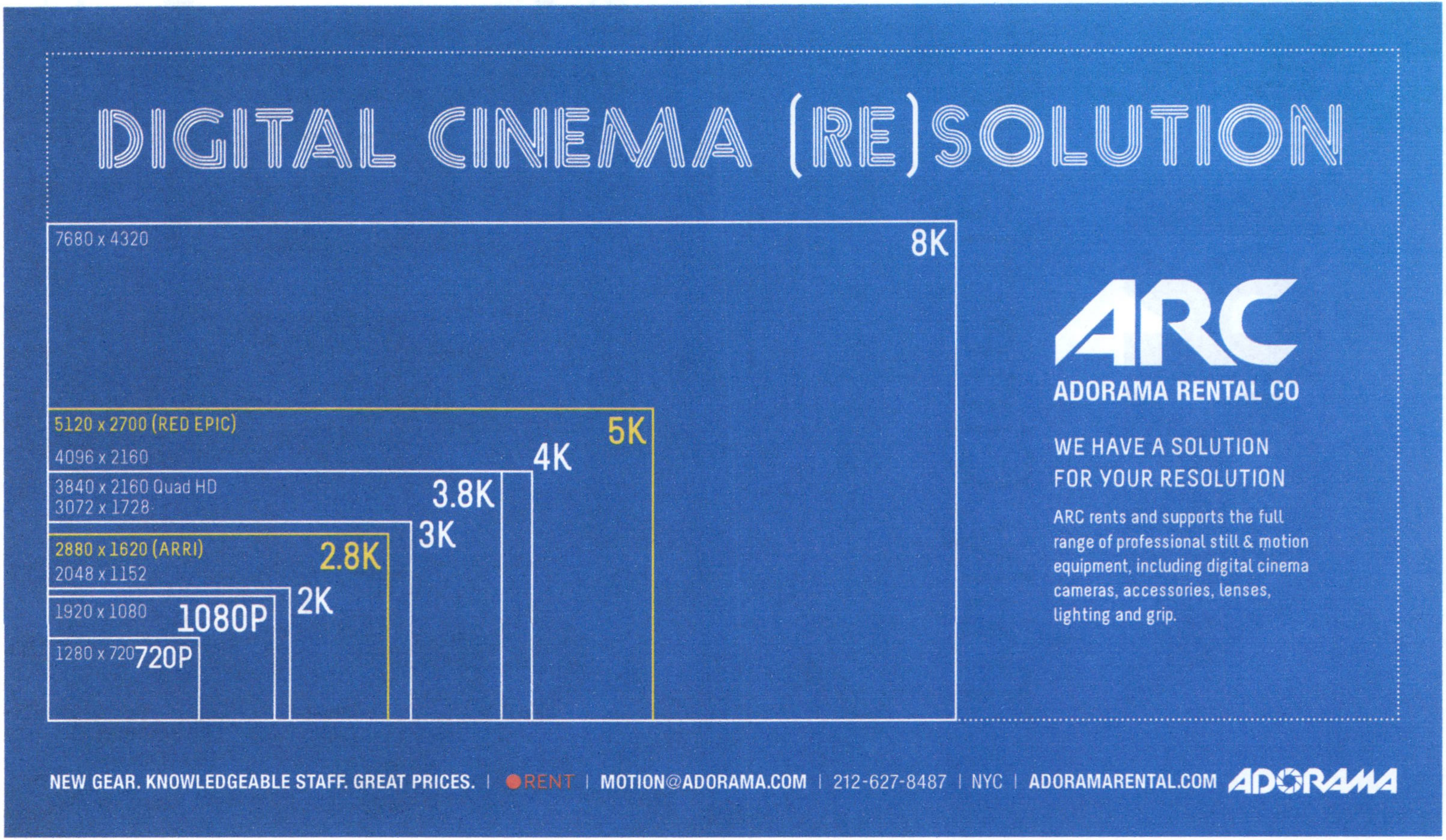
DIGITAL CINEMA (RE)SOLUTION
7680 x 4320
8K
5120 x 2700 (RED EPIC)
5K
4096 x 2160
4K
3840 x 2160 Quad HD
3.8K
3072 x 1728
3K
2880 x 1620 (ARRI)
2.8K
2048 x 1152
2K
1920 x 1080
1080P
1280 x 720
720P
ARC
ADORAMA RENTAL CO
WE HAVE A SOLUTION
FOR YOUR RESOLUTION
ARC rents and supports the full range of professional still & motion equipment, including digital cinema cameras, accessories, lenses, lighting and grip.
NEW GEAR. KNOWLEDGEABLE STAFF. GREAT PRICES. | RENT | MOTION@ADORAMA.COM | 212-627-8487 | NYC | ADORAMARENTAL.COM
ADORAMA

ARRI

Truly Cinematic

www.arri.com

Profile. Calibrate. Measure.

SEKONIC®
Sekonic.com

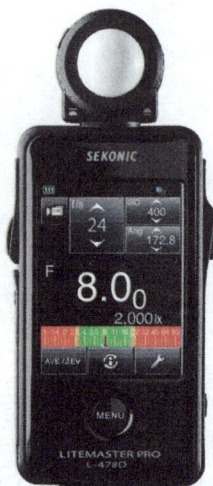

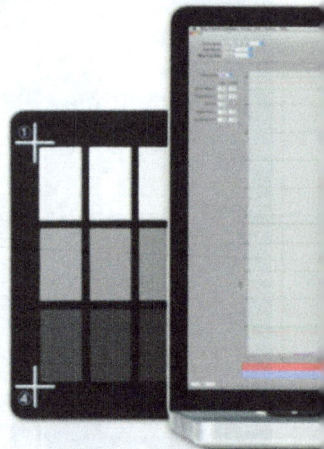

AAdynTech.™

Designed, Developed, Engineered & Assembled in the USA

LED'S ACCEPTED BY BROADCASTERS, NEWS AND SPORTS GROUPS

JAB HURRICANE
LED-IP65 RATED, "WEATHERPROOF"

Single Source & No multiple shadows, DMX compatible, AC/DC & output compatable to a 800 Watt HMI. Optional units Jab Daylight, Jab Variable & Jab Tungsten.

ECO PUNCH PLUS

4,044 foot candles @ 10 ft., Draws 4.8 Amps, Daylight 5600 K, Single Source & No multiple shadows, DMX Compatible & more output than a 2,500 Watt HMI.

FOR ALL UNITS ETL, UL, CE & CSA approved, RoHS Compliant, No Ultra Violet or Infra Red Rays, Cree LEDs, 60,000 hour warranty on LEDs, Green Technology, Universal power supply and much more.

JAB HURRICANE

IP65 Rated-Weatherproof

Total Protection against Dust and Low Pressure Water Jets

1,804 foot candles @10 feet

Daylight-Balanced at 5600°K

Draws 1.77 amps at max output

AC/DC Powered

SPACE LED LIGHT

Draws 6.5 Amps @ 120v AC

Up to 90% power savings

Tungsten – 3280° Kelvin

Over 52 foot candles @ 25 feet height

Even spread of light

High CRI – 95

Worldwide Distribution

LIGHTEQUIP
DIE LICHTWERKER
Germany & 20 Euro Countries

Schweizer AG
Professionelle Videotechnik
Switzerland

CINEQUIPWHITEINC.
A Comwork Group Member
Canada

PROKIT
U.K. & Ireland

interflo
Australia & New Zealand

TELETEC
Mexico, Brazil & Peru

...and LIGHTING s.r.l.
Professional Equipment for shows
Italy

www.AAdynTech.com

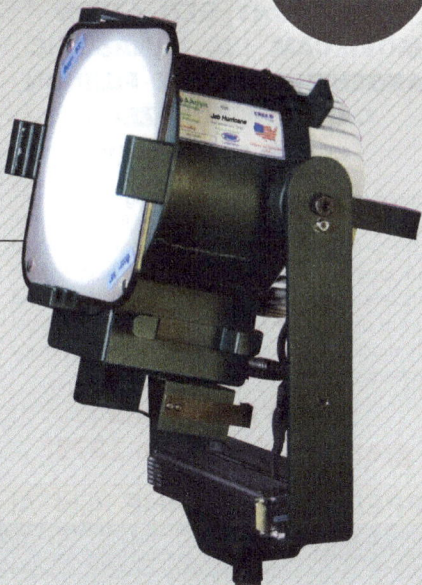

EVERYTHING YOU WANT IN A CAMERA RENTAL HOUSE

ARRI SONY RED AATON MOVIECAM JVC PANASONIC ANGENIEUX COOKE FUJINON CANON NIKON ZEISS
and so much more

Oppenheimer Cine Rental has long been the #1 choice for camera rentals in the Pacific Northwest. As the largest camera rental house north of LA, we work long and hard to maintain the best & most complete inventory, keep our technical skills at the top of their game, and provide the friendliest and most professional service, all at nationally competitive rates.

Great prices and great service since 1979!

20 Years of Service

Film & Digital SPECIALTY PRODUCTS

Oppenheimer Camera Products' offers OppCa Panhandle System, many LCD and OLED Monitor Yo Mounts, 60mm & 100mm Macro Lenses, ARRI ALEXA Sony F65 OB Power Supplies, On-Camera Viewfind Systems, Lens Carry Handles for Angenieux, Alu Canon and Fujinon zoom lenses.

OPPENHEIMER CINE RENTAL
Purveyors of Fine Cine Cameras

OPPENHEIMER CAMERA PRODUCTS

seattle 206-467-8666   toll free 877-467-8666   marty @oppcam.com   www.oppenheimercinerental.cor

---

We offer the largest inventory of professional lighting equipment and accessories!

Techni-Lux

Offering quality **light fixtures**, **consoles**, and **expendables** for over 20 years.

◁ **Stock ALL major brands over 6,800 different lamps**

◁ **Grip and Lighting Expendables**

◁ **Conventional and Intelligent Lights**

◁ **DMX Controllers and Dimmers**

◁ **Electrical Connectors and Cables**

Video & Film
HPL
LED
PAR
MSD MSR
Fluorescent
HMI
Color Media
MR16
Clamps
Tape
Haze/Fog Fluid

WE SHIP WORLDWIDE
SAME DAY DELIVERY AVAILABLE

Call 407-857-8770   www.techni-lux.com
SALES@TECHNI-LUX.COM

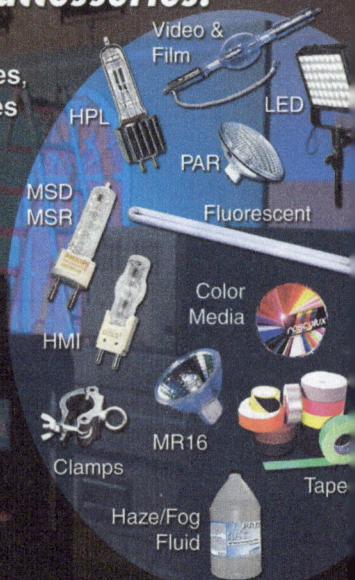

CINEMATOGRAPHERS PAINT THE MOOD
FOR MORE THAN 50 YEARS, PANAVISION HAS PROVIDED THE BRUSH

artistically
inspired

technically
advanced

*P*VINTAGE™

PANAVISION®
www.panavision.com

ZACUTO
U ★ S ★ A

INDUSTRY STANDARD FILMMAKING ACCESSORIES

INTERNATIONAL SALES
NATIONWIDE RENTALS

WWW.ZACUTO.COM

We Give New meaning to the Phrase "Best and Brightest"

NiLA

Environmentally
Sustainable
LED Lighting

Nila, Inc. 723 West Woodbury Rd., Altadena, CA 91001, 818-392-8370 Nila.co

RED EPIC/SCARLET RIG

TILTA
TILTA ARMED CAMERA
HIGH QUALITY WITH AFFORDABLE PRICE

SONY FS700 RIG

SONY F3 RIG

CANON C300/500 RIG

FILM DUAL FOLLOW FOCUS FF-T04

CARBON FIBER MATTE BOX
4x5.65 MB-T04

LIGHTWEIGHT
FOLLOW FOCUS FF-T03

CARBON FIBER MATTE BOX
4x4 MB-T03

BMCC RIG
BLACKMAGIC CINEMA CAMERA RIG

WWW.TILTA.TV   EMAIL:HUANG@TILTA.COM.CN

transvideo

Film & Digital Cinematography Equipment - S3D - Wireless

www.hd4dp.com

Technology Partner
imetadata.net

Technology by Dolby

CineMonitor HD, Creatively Connected
Connects /i lenses and CineTape to display essential informations

---

Enjoy AC on your iPad and iPhone!

Subscribe at the ASC Store, download our new app & enjoy free access to digital editions of *AC* from 2007 to the present on your computer, iPad or iPhone.

(Back issues exclusive to ASC Store customers only!)

Already a print subscriber? Access to the digital edition is included in your subscription for a limited time

www.theasc.com/store

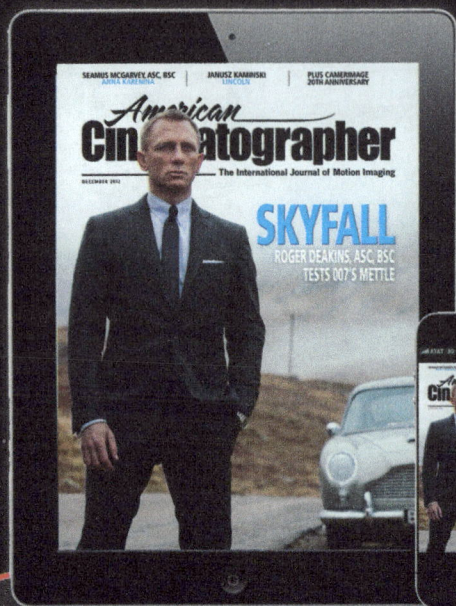

Lewis, Greg Marsden, Raigo Alas
I Vellekoop for the concept,
implementation of the Pictorvision
electronically stabilized aerial
tform.

vision Eclipse system allows
aphers to capture aerial footage
ng speeds with aggressive
neuvering.

THE ULTIMATE CHOICES
FOR ABOVE AND BEYOND
CINEMATOGRAPHY

eclipse

Find these and our latest inventory of cutting edge technologies at:

Pictorvision
Above & Beyond

WWW.PICTORVISION.COM   800.876.5583   818.785.9282

Eclipse

XR Series

Wescam System

Cineflex

ARTEMIS
DIRECTOR'S VIEWFINDER

- Completely updated engine
- Save images and notes to new internal image gallery
- Replicates popular motion picture cameras and lenses
- Add custom cameras for specific or exotic formats
- Available for iPhone, Android phones and the iPad

> I am working on a film called "Balls to the Walls" I use this app on every blocking rehearsal. I find the master and all the coverage and capture the frames and lens sizes in my photo library. Then I show the director. I can also start setting up the shot before the camera is in place. Great app and now an important tool for my work!
> **ROBERT REED ALTMAN**

> A lot easier and much more accurate than holding up your two hands to frame a shot. Much lighter than a heavy Director's Finder dangling from your neck. Every Director and DP should have this wonderful app.
> **FILM AND DIGITAL TIMES**

helios
sun position calculator

- Six tools to explore sun data
- Database of tens of thousands of locations around the world
- Email sun position data from within application
- Network connectivity not necessary for use

> I'm usually scouting for locations months before the DP comes on board and knowing precisely where the sun will be on the exact shoot date is essential. Helios is without doubt the best tool out there for DPs, production designers, location scouts and directors. Nothing comes even close.
> **RICHARD LONCRAINE**

> Simple. Elegant. Fast, Accurate... I love this!!!!
> **RUSSELL CARPENTER, ASC**

CHEMICAL WEDDING

Available on the iP
App Sto

POCKET ALCHEMY CAN BE FOUND
www.chemicalweddin

love Schneider One-Stop Linear
arizers for interiors. They allow
to handle the occasional cross-
t shine on complexions without
ing to deal with lighting."

Francis Kenny, ASC

"When shooting a multi-camera
series you are consistently cutting
back and forth between cameras.
I never worry about matching
because I always have Schneider
filters on each lens."

Don A. Morgan, ASC

'm a long-time fan of the
ssic Soft™. It is the best
nkle remover ever—and
s light enough to use on
ital and film."

Nancy Schreiber, ASC

"The Schneider ND
Attenuator is quite the
amazing tool, particularly
for digital sensors."

Bill Bennett, ASC

hneider came through for us
some of the first sets of their
t new Platinum IRNDs, and
ur color matching problems
ppeared."

owell Peterson, ASC

It starts with the glass...

...but it's nothing
without the
cinematographers
who use it.

Schneider OPTICS

Classic Filmmakers Choose Schneider

ww.schneideroptics.com   Phone: 818-766-3715 • 800-228-1254

HAWK ®

THE FINEST ANAMORPHIC GLASS

Origins of the American Society of Cinematographers

For over 93 years, the ASC has remained true to its ideals: loyalty, progress, artistry. Reverence for the past and a commitment to the future have made a potent and lasting combination in a world of shifting values and uncertain motives.

The American Society of Cinematographers received its charter from the State of California in January 1919 and is the oldest continuously operating motion picture society in the world. Its declared purpose still resonates today: "to advance the art of cinematography through artistry and technological progress, to exchange ideas and to cement a closer relationship among cinematographers."

The origins of the ASC lie in two clubs founded by cinematographers in 1913. The Cinema Camera Club was started in New York City by three cameramen from the Thomas A. Edison Studio: Phil Rosen, Frank Kugler and Lewis W. Physioc. They decided to form a fraternity to establish professional standards, encourage the manufacture of better equipment and seek recognition as creative artists. Meanwhile, the similarly conceived Static Club was formed in Los Angeles. When Rosen came to the West Coast five years later, he and Charles Rosher combined the clubs. The ASC now has more than 340 active and associate members.

The first ASC screen credit was given to charter member Joseph August when he photographed a William S. Hart picture in 1919.

American Society of Cinematographers' clubhouse.

The year after its charter, ASC began publishing American Cinematographer magazine, which ever since has served as the club's foremost means of advancing the art.

The ASC has been very active in recent years in expressing concern about choices for Advanced Television (ATV), ranging from the choice of aspect ratio to pushing for the abandonment of interlace displays. At the invitation of the House and Senate in Washington, D.C., members of the ASC have been asked to inform and advise legislators on these issues.

Currently our technology committee has created a standard test (StEM) for digital cinema. They are advising the industry on standards in both production and postproduction for digital capture, manipulation and presentation.

The ASC is not a labor union or guild, but is an educational, cultural and professional organization. Membership is possible by invitation and is extended only to directors of photography with distinguished credits in the industry.

—George E. Turner

Responsibilities Of The Cinematographer

DESIGNING THE LOOK

Filmmaking is a uniquely collaborative form of artistic expression with many people playing interlocking roles. Cinematographers require artistic sensibilities, exceptional organizational skills, the ability to master complex technologies that are constantly evolving, and a special talent for collaborating and communicating effectively.

The cinematographer's initial and most important responsibility is telling the story and the design of a "look" or visual style that faithfully reflects the intentions the director, or the producer/show runner if the project happens to be an episodic television series. It is mandatory for the cinematographer to accomplish that primary goal within the limitations of the budget and schedule. Other collaborators who are generally involved in this creative process with the cinematographer and director include the production designer, art director, and occasionally the visual effects supervisor and/or producer. The cinematographer must also provide guidance in all technical aspects of production. They offer advice regarding the choice of the most appropriate film or digital video format for creating the "look" within the restraints of the budget. There are many options today, ranging from anamorphic 35mm film to digital video. The cinematographer is responsible for explaining those options and the creative and financial trade-offs with precise clarity.

If the project is a feature film, the cinematographer can discuss the pros and cons of traditional timing at an optical lab versus a digital intermediate (D.I.) facility. If it is a film made for television, the cinematographer can address upfront and long-term issues linked to finishing in high-definition or standard definition formats. There are no textbook answers because technology is constantly evolving and every situation is different. It is essential for the cinematographer to have a thorough grasp of all technical options, including choice of film and digital cameras, lenses, cranes, dollies and other platforms for moving cameras, new emulsions, and such special techniques as aerial and underwater photography, blue and green screen and other visual effects, as well as the capabilities of equipment rental houses, labs and postproduction facilities.

PREPRODUCTION PLANNING

The cinematographer is frequently invited to watch rehearsals and offer suggestions for "blocking" scenes to provide artful coverage in the most efficient way. All aspects of production are planned at this stage, including how many cameras are needed, how to move them and whether older or newer prime or zoom lenses are best suited for each task. Cinematographers also frequently provide input to directors while they are developing storyboards and shot lists. They go on location scouts and make recommendations to the production designer and art director for dressing and painting sets based on the vision for the "look" of the film and requirements for lighting and camera movement. The cinematographer also confers with the director and assistant director about the best times and places to stage exterior scenes to take maximum advantage of available light. They must also plan for such variables as the weather and tides if they are going to shoot on the beach or at sea. The cinematographer consults with the production designer regarding plans for dressing stages and the space they need for rigging lights and moving cameras. This includes the use of wild walls, removable sections of ceilings, placement, sizes and angles of windows, practical lights, and the colors and textures of props and walls.

The cinematographer also organizes camera, electrical and grip crews, whose talents and skills are the right match for the tasks at hand. They work with the gaffer to plan placement and rigging lighting fixtures, including deciding whether a dimmer control console is needed. The cinematographer also confers with the key grip on issues related to camera movement, including what gear is needed. He or she also consults with the production manager regarding arrangements for rental of camera, lighting and grip equipment, and such specialized tools as insert cars, on the days it will be needed.

During preproduction, the cinematographer must establish rapport with the make-up, hair and costume designers, which frequently includes shooting tests with the actors. Using information gained by this testing, the cinematographer can then present a visual interpretation of the actor's character, helping to define and amplify the performance. They might also test new camera films, lenses and specialized photochemical or digital intermediate processes (DI) to determine the most efficient way to put the final touches on the visual design. In addition, the cinematographer establishes communications with the timer at the film lab or digital postproduction facility, which will provide dailies. They also make arrangements and check out facilities for viewing dailies, meet stand-ins for actors, and establish rapport and an open line of communications with the AD.

PRINCIPAL PHOTOGRAPHY

The cinematographer is responsible for executing the vision for the "look" of the film, while helping to keep production on budget and on schedule. On many feature films, the day begins with the cinematographer viewing dailies during early morning hours at the lab to verify that there are no technical problems and nuances in the "look" are working. They frequently watch rehearsals of the first scene with the director, and suggest whether modifications in lighting or coverage are needed. The cinematographer stays in touch with the production manager and AD regarding any changes in the anticipated schedule caused by unforeseen circumstances. In addition, the cinematographer approves the set up of lighting by the gaffer. Many directors want lighting and camera coverage to be "flexible" enough to give the actors the freedom to perform spontaneously.

Shots are often rehearsed with stand-ins. The cinematographer confers with the director regarding adjustments in plans for lighting and coverage and facilitates those changes with the grip, gaffer and lighting crews. They also work with the standby painter for any last minute touch-ups needed on sets, assist the AD in staging background action, and give the sound department the freedom to put their booms where they are needed to record great audio of the dialogue. If the director desires, a final walk-through or rehearsal is done with the actors. When cameras are rolling, the cinematographer assures that there are no technical glitches. They also provide an extra pair of eyes for the director on the set. The cinematographer might suggest retaking a shot because something didn't quite look or feel right, while assuring the director they will find a way to make up the time.

If a DI finish is planned, the cinematographer might be recording request that digital still images of the scenes be taken, which he or she later manipulates with a personal computer to give the dailies timer and colorist a visual reference for the "look."

The cinematographer, director and other key collaborators watch dailies together to judge how effectively the "look" is working. At the end of each day, the cinematographer discusses the first set up for the next morning with the AD and possibly the director. He or she also informs the script supervisor if there are special camera or lighting notes, makes sure that the camera, lighting and grip crews have all the information needed to rig their gear, provides any special notes and instructions required by the film lab and dailies timer, and works with the production manager regarding the need to return or acquire equipment.

POSTPRODUCTION

The cinematographer's role extends deep into postproduction with the goal of assuring that the "look" that he or she rendered is what audiences see on cinema and television screens. If possible, the cinematographer handles any additional photography required by changes in the script. They are also called on to supervise the seamless blending of visual effects shots with live-action footage. The cinematographer is responsible for timing the film for continuity and for adding nuances to the "look" in either a DI or optical lab environment. They also approve the final answer print in collaboration with the director and producer. In addition, the cinematographer verifies that what they approved is reflected in the release print. The final task for the cinematographer involves timing, and, if necessary, reformatting films for release in DVD, HD and other television formats. All of these final steps are meant to assure that audiences experience films on motion picture and display screens the way they are intended to be seen by the creators of the images.

Summary of Formats

compiled by Tak Miyagishima
ASC Associate Member

APERTURE SPECIFICATIONS

▶ **35mm Camera – Spherical Lens**

Academy Camera Aperture	.866" X .630"	22mm X 16mm

▶ **35mm Theatrical Release – Spherical**

1.37:1	.825" X .602"	20.96mm X 15.29mm
1.66:1	.825" X .497"	20.96mm X 12.62mm
1.85:1	.825" X .446"	20.96mm X 11.33mm

▶ **35mm Television Aperture and Safe Areas**

Camera Aperture	.866" X .630"	22mm X 16mm
TV Station Projector Aperture	.816" X .612"	20.73mm X 15.54mm
TV Transmitted Area	.792" X .594"	20.12mm X 15.09mm
TV Safe Action Area	.713" X .535"	18.11mm X 13.59mm
Corner Radii = .143"/3.63mm		
TV Safe Title Area	.630" X .475"	16mm X 12.06mm
Corner Radii = .125"/3.17mm		

▶ **35mm Full Aperture – Spherical Lens** (For Partial Frame Extraction) Prints (Super 35)

Camera Aperture (Film Center)	.980" X .735"	24.89mm X 18.67mm
Finder Markings		
35mm Anamorphic 2.4:1 AR	.945" X .394"	24mm X 10mm
70mm 2.2:1 AR	.945" X .430"	24mm X 10.92mm
35mm FLAT 1.85:1 AR	.945" X .511"	24mm x 12.97mm

▶ **35mm Panavision 2-Perf**

Camera Aperture (Film Center)	.980" X .365"	24.89mm x 9.27mm
Ground Glass 2.4:1 AR	.825" X .345"	20.96mm x 8.76mm

▶ **35mm Panavision 3-Perf**

Camera Aperture (Film Center)	.980" X .546"	24.89mm x 13.87mm
1.78:1	.910" X .511"	23.10mm x 12.98mm

▶ **35mm Panavision 4-Perf**

1.85:1 AR Spherical (FLAT) PROJ AP	.825" X .446"	20.96mm X 11.33mm
2.4:1 AR Anamorphic Squeeze PROJ AP	.825" X .690"	20.96mm X 17.53mm
5 perf 70mm 2.2:1 AR PROJ AP	1.912" X .870"	48.56mm X 22.10mm

▶ **Panavision 35 and Anamorphic Squeezed Negative**

Camera Aperture	.866" X .732"	22mm X 18.59mm
35mm Squeezed Print		
Finder Marking (2.2:1 70mm) & Proj AP	.825" X .690"	20.96mm X 17.53mm
16mm Squeezed Print	.342" X .286"	8.69mm X 7.26mm
	Max Proj. AP	
16mm Un-Squeezed Print (1.85:1)	.380" X .205"	9.65mm X 5.20mm
	Proj. AP matte	
70mm Unsqueezed Print Proj. AP	1.912" X .870"	48.56mm X 22.10mm

▶ **16mm Film Apertures 1.33:1 (4:3) Television Safe Area**

Camera Aperture	.404" X .295"	10.26mm X 7.49mm
TV Station Proj AP	.380" X .286"	9.65mm X 7.26mm
TV Transmitted Area	.368" X .276"	9.35mm X 7.01mm
TV Safe Action Area	.331" X .248"	8.41mm X 6.30mm
	Corner Radii R = .066"/1.68mm	
Safe Title Area	.293" X .221"	7.44mm X 5.61mm

▶ **Finder Markings for Enlarging to 35mm**

Camera Aperture	.404" X .295"	10.26mm X 7.49mm
Projector Aperture (1.37:1)	.380" X .286"	9.65mm X 7.26mm
Projector Aperture (1.85:1)	.380" X .206"	9.65mm X 5.23mm
(Enlarging ratio 1:2.105)		

▶ **Super 16mm (16mm Type W) for Enlarging to 35mm**

Camera Aperture	.486" X .292"	12.35mm X 7.42mm
Projector Aperture (1.66)	.464" X .279"	11.80mm X 7.10mm
Projector Aperture (1.85)	.464" X .251"	11.80mm X 6.38mm

▶ **65mm 5-Perf TODD-AO/PANAVISION 65mm Spherical Imaged Negative**

Camera Aperture	2.072" X .906"	52.63mm X 23.01mm
35mm 'Scope Extraction	1.912" X .800"	48.56mm X 20.31mm
35mm Projector Aperture	.825" X .690"	20.96mm X 17.53mm
		(with 2:1 squeeze)
70mm Projection Aperture 2.2:1	1.912" X .870"	48.56mm X 22.10mm
65mm 8-Perf		
Camera Aperture 1.35:1AR	2.072" X .1.485"	52.63mm X 37.72mm

▶ **65mm - 15-Perf IMAX/OMNIMAX**

Camera Aperture	2.772" X 2.072"	70.41mm X 52.63mm
Projector Aperture (computed from cut-off)	1.172" X 2.04"	29.77mm X 51.81mm
16mm Un-Squeezed Print (1.85:1)	.380" X .206"	9.65mm X 5.20mm
70mm Unsqueezed Print Proj. AP	1.912" X .870"	48.56mm X 22.10mm

▶ **VISTAVISION 8-Perf Horz. Pull Across**

Camera Aperture	1.485" X .981"	37.72mm X 24.92mm
35mm VistaVision		

▶ **Super 8mm**

Camera Aperture (1.33:1)	0.224" x 0.166"	5.69mm X 4.22mm
Projection Aperture (1.33:1)	0.209" x 0.158"	5.31mm X 4.01mm

MOST COMMON SCREEN RATIOS

 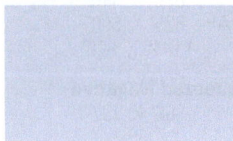 

1.37	**1.85**	**2.40**
(1.33 - TV)		

Basic Digital Concepts

by Marty Ollstein

A working understanding of digital theory is the foundation for success-ful use of all digital technology, from cameras to post-production hard-ware and software systems. Although the principles of photography still ap-ply, the cinematographer today should understand the relationship of digital to analog image acquisition.

1) ANALOG AND DIGITAL

The natural world is considered to be analog.[1] Human vision perceives continuously changing gradients of light from black to white, and color that spans the spectrum uninterrupted between infrared and ultraviolet. We model light and sound as waves whose shape varies by their amplitude and frequency in a continuously variable signal. An analog signal is understood to be composed of an infinite number of points. The scale used to measure light and color is infinitely divisible into smaller units. Film is an analog medium—it can record a continuous spectrum of color.

A digital representation of the world is finite. It uses numbers to approxi-mate analog physical phenomena. A digital signal is defined by a finite value in accordance with a predetermined scale. It may be hard to imagine using numbers to define and reproduce the subtle and random sights and sounds of our experience. But the more numbers we use, the closer we can come to reproducing the analog original.

In digital cinematography, light and color are represented by numbers organized in binary code. Each digit of binary code, a bit (b), defines only two values: 0 or 1. A single bit, then, can define a scale of only two levels. But two bits together can define four levels—two levels in each of the original two levels (2 x 2). Three bits define 8 levels, and four bits do 16. Eight bits are called a 'byte' (B). An 8-bit code defines a scale of 256 levels. The number of levels defined by a binary code can be expressed as 2^n, where n = number of bits. The more bits used, the more levels defined, and the more precision available to define values.

---

1 There is some debate as to this simple distinction. If light were modeled as discrete particles (photons) instead of analog electromagnetic waves, it could be considered digital. And although film grains are randomly distributed, they are separate, quan-tifiable (not infinite) particles, which might be described using some digital format. But for this discussion, we will consider the natural world as analog.

Film records an image by varying the density of silver or dye of the film emulsion in a continuous gradient from clear to opaque, black to white.

Digital imaging builds an image with numbers in a binary format. The detail displayed is limited to a scale with a discrete number of values, determined by the number of bits being used.

2) PIXELS AND CHIPS

Short for 'PICture ELement', a PIXEL is the building block of the digital image. It represents one sample of picture information. Pixels are grouped into fixed arrays of straight rows and columns. The pixels remain in the same position, frame to frame. All pixels in an array are the same size—usually square, but in some cases rectangular.

Instead of film behind the lens, digital cameras have chips that contain an array of light-sensitive sensors or photoreceptors that receive image data. The sensors convert light into voltage, an electrical charge proportional to the light striking it. The analog voltage is sampled, or measured at specified intervals, and converted to numbers on a scale—a digital code value. This process is called analog-to-digital conversion or A/D conversion. The resulting digital-code values determine the brightness of each pixel viewed on a display. The color of the pixel is defined by one of two general methods, determined by the chip design in the camera.

The two different sensor-array designs used in production cameras today include the three-chip design and the single-chip design. When HD video production first developed and became an industry standard, most professional cameras used a three-chip design. Some of the most common HD cameras in use were the SONY F900 and the Panasonic VariCam. These three-chip cameras contain a set of three $\frac{2}{3}$"-size chips, one each for measuring red, green and blue light. In most cases, a prism divides the light captured by the lens into separate red, green and blue rays, directing each ray to a dedicated chip. (See Figure 1.) The photoreceptors on these chips are grayscale devices that only measure light intensity. The color of a pixel is later determined by integrating the respective red, green and blue light values from the three chips.

The three-chip prism "block" system is precise and efficient. However, it takes up significant space in the camera. To keep production cameras small enough to be portable, the smaller $\frac{2}{3}$" chip size was used. Since the $\frac{2}{3}$" target is significantly smaller

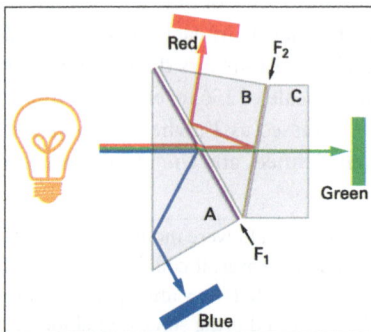

Figure 1. Three-chip prism system

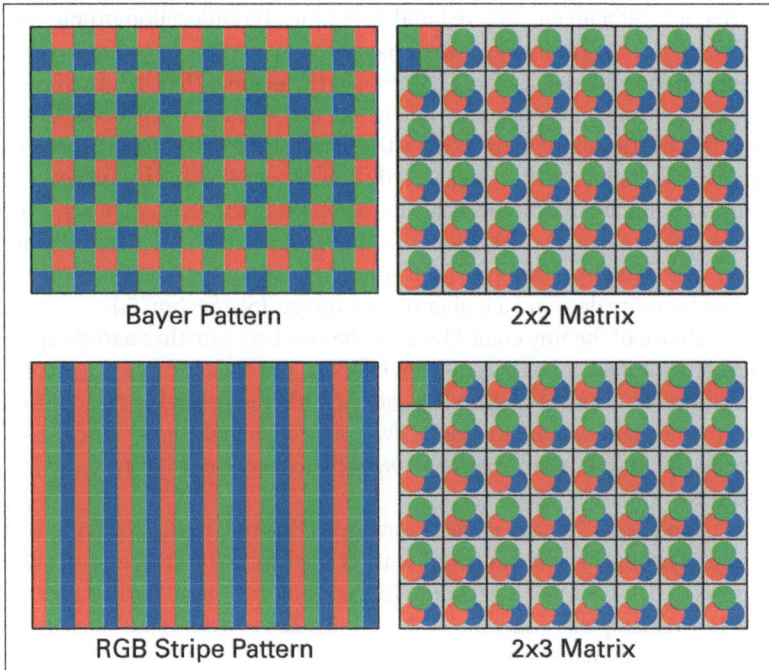

| Bayer Pattern | 2x2 Matrix |
| RGB Stripe Pattern | 2x3 Matrix |

Figure 2. Single-chip system configurations

than a 35mm film frame, different HD lenses were manufactured to optimize the optical path. Another requirement of this system is that the three separate chips in the block must be precisely registered to align their images with precision.

More recently, to enable the use of a larger chip (matching or exceeding the 35mm frame size) that would provide a reduced depth of field and allow the use of the large inventory of motion-picture lenses (optimized for the 35mm frame), camera manufacturers have moved to a single-chip format.

Single-chip cameras, such as the ARRI Alexa and RED Epic, contain a single large chip. No prism block is needed to separate the color rays from the spectrum. Image color is created by placing tiny red, green and blue filters over each sensor on the chip in a particular "mosaic" pattern, then using software matched to that pattern to calculate color values for each pixel. Each camera uses their own proprietary chip design, mosaic filter pattern, selection of filter color, and dedicated software—all of which have a significant effect on the characteristics of the image recorded.

The most widely used mosaic filter pattern for single-chip cameras is the Bayer pattern. (See Figure 2.) The ARRI Alexa and RED Epic both use the Bayer pattern for their chip. This pattern uses a series of square 2x2 matrices of filtered photo-receptor sites—two green, one red and one blue. Also called

RGBG, it is 50% green, 25% red and 25% blue. This allocation mimics the physiology of the human eye which is more sensitive to green light. The se groups of four filtered sensors are repeated throughout the chip. Dedicated proprietary softw are i nterprets t he s ignal (the d e-Bayering p rocess) f rom each sensor site, taking into account the particular spectral transmission of its' color filter along with the values of the adjacent sites in the matrix, and assigns a color and brightness value to each pixel of the recorded image. The image data can be recorded before this digital conversion (de-mosaic or de-Bayer process) is performed. Th is 'pre-conversion' format is called raw, and yields more data and a higher quality image. (See Section 6.)

The choice of the tiny color filters on the sensors—whether narrow spectrum or wide band—has a significant effect on the dynamic range and color saturation of the image captured. A wider-band filter leaves the sensor more sensitive to light, yielding a wider dynamic range and higher native ISO. But the color recorded by that wide-band filtered sensor is less true and less saturated.

The Panavision Genesis camera uses an RGB stripe mosaic pattern. This design uses a 2x3 matrix of filtered sensors (two each of red, green and blue) to measure the data that determines the value of each pixel. In this case, the data is "oversampled"—six sensors contribute data to define each single pixel in the recorded image.

The SONY F65 uses a new mosaic pattern that provides red, green, and blue data for every pixel of a recorded 4K image. The higher resolution 8K sensor array is rotated at a 45-degree angle so as to place the filtered sensors in position to measure all three color values for each pixel in a recorded image, producing a 'true' 4K RGB output image.

3) RESOLUTION

As the smallest element of a digital image, the pixel represents the limit of detail that can be displayed. An image composed of a small number of pixels can only show a rough approximation of a scene, with little detail. The more pixels used to display an image, the finer the detail that can be revealed. Resolution is the measure of the finest detail visible in a displayed image, and is defined numerically by the number of pixels recorded in the image raster—NOT by the number of sensors in the camera chip. This distinction has created some confusion and controversy in the resolution claims of some camera manufacturers.

Camera resolution is commonly defined by the number of lines of pixels (scan lines) it records. The standard HD camera records 1080 lines, although some cameras that record 720 lines are also considered HD. An increase in the pixel line count will produce a proportional increase in resolution and representation of fine detail. Image resolution is expressed by two numbers:

columns (or pixels per line) x lines. The HD standard image is defined as being 1920x1080 pixels.

A doubling of pixel lines and pixels per line (as the change from 2K to 4K), increases the total pixel count by a factor of 4, requiring four times the memory to store the image data. However, the MTF (modulation transfer function, an optical measure of line-pair resolution) only doubles.

Some of the most common image-resolution standards include:
- Standard definition analog NTSC = 640x480 (1.33:1)
- HD = 1920x1080 (or 1280x720) (1.78:1)
- 2K = 2048 pixels per line (line count varies with aspect ratio)
- 4K = 4096 pixels per line

Pixel count is not the only element in the imaging chain that affects picture resolution. Lens quality, precise registration of the chips in a three-chip camera, and image scaling and resizing conversions also affect image resolution.

4) EXPOSURE

Film has a greater dynamic range, or range of usable f-stops, than most digital formats. And due to the response of film dyes and silver to exposure extremes, which causes a gradual "rounding off" of values at either end of the tonal scale (highlights and shadows), there is a perceived extension of the dynamic range. Shadows merge smoothly into darkness, and highlights fade gradually (or "bloom") into white.

Digital images, however, "clip" at either end of the tonal scale—the shadows drop off abruptly into solid black, and highlights cut off into flat, white areas with no definition. Clipping occurs when the exposure moves beyond the specific threshold which is determined by the sensitivity and capability of the camera or recording device.

A cinematographer can avoid clipping a digital image by monitoring and controlling the light levels recorded in a scene. There are several useful digital tools available for monitoring exposure in a scene. A waveform monitor displays the exposure levels across a scene, read by the camera from left to right on a scale of 0–100 IRE (Institute of Radio Engineers). Generally, 0 IRE defines total black and 100 IRE defines total white, indicating the maximum amount of voltage that the system can handle. If the levels flatten out at either end of the scale (0 or 100), the image will clip, and no detail will be recorded in those areas. NTSC defines 7.5 IRE as black (called the "pedestal" in post, and "setup" on the set). The waveform monitor displays the pedestal and peak white levels, and indicates when clipping occurs.

Another tool is the Histogram, which graphically displays the distribution of light values in a scene, from black to white. Basically a bar chart, a histogram indicates the proportion of image area (y axis) occupied by each level of brightness from 0 IRE to 100 IRE (x axis). With a clear indicator of clipping at either end of the scale (often a red line), it is useful for determining whether the scene fits within the camera's dynamic range.

Some cameras record light levels up to 110 IRE. These brighter values can be used throughout the post-production process, then brought back down to a "legal" level to avoid being hard-clipped at 100 IRE when broadcast on television.

A handy exposure tool for digital production allows the user to quickly bring light levels in a scene within the safe range to avoid clipping. Developed by David Stump, ASC, the device consists of a hollow sphere (diameter about 1.5 feet) painted glossy white, with a hole in one side (diameter about 2 inches) that reveals a dark interior painted matte black. To use on the set, place the device in the brightest area of the scene, usually the position of the main subject. Adjust the lighting and camera exposure so that the specular (shiny) white highlight on the white ball registers under 100 or 110 IRE, and the black hole registers 0 IRE.

Some digital cameras have software tools that help protect the shadow and highlight detail or, if clipping is unavoidable, soften or round off the edge of the clipping. In the toe or shadow region, the technique involves the manipulation of the black pedestal (the level at which the image turns black) and black stretch. Black stretch flattens the curve of the Toe, lowering the contrast and putting more levels (and subtlety) into the lower part of the tone scale. The resulting effect of black stretch is to reveal more shadow detail. Going the opposite direction, "crushing the blacks" raises the slope of the Toe curve and compresses the tonal values in the shadows. Raising the black Pedestal turns more of the shadow area to pure black. In the highlight region, the "soft clip" or "knee" function compresses the values near 100 IRE, rounding off the exposure curve, allowing more highlight detail to be recorded, and giving a more pleasing shape to the edges of a clip in the very bright areas in the frame.

5) GAMMA AND LOG/LIN

Film dyes have a logarithmic response to exposure. The traditional sensitometric curve, used to describe the behavior of film stocks, plots density as the y coordinate and log exposure as the x coordinate. The resulting S curve, with a shallow slope in both the toe and shoulder regions, provides more shadow and highlight detail. Logarithmic code values are an important characteristic of what is considered film color space and the "film look." A logarithmic representation of light values is also typically used when scanning film material for digital intermediate or visual-effects work. And certain current digital-production cameras, such as the Arri Alexa and Sony F65, both provide log curves as a choice for image acquisition.

CRT (cathode ray tube) monitors have a nonlinear response to any input—the intensity of the image displayed is not directly proportional to the video signal input. This response is called gamma, contrast or a "power function" and is generally considered to be 2.6 for HD monitors.

Digital video cameras capture a scene as analog voltage and then digitize it with an A/D converter to create linear digital-code values. To view these unprocessed linear code values would require a linear display whose response was directly proportional to its input signal. But the CRT is not a linear display; its gamma or power function curve gives a nonlinear response to input signals. Linear digital code values do not display properly on a CRT monitor. The tones appear desaturated with very low contrast. To generate a video signal that will display properly on a CRT, video cameras apply a gamma correction equal to the reciprocal of the CRT power function.

To differentiate video color space from the logarithmic film color space, video is often referred to as "linear." This is inaccurate, however, due to the nonlinear gamma correction applied to the video signal. Video color space should more accurately be called a "power function" system.

As use of the CRT has decreased, new display devices have been developed that accept a wide range of input signals. No longer constrained by the limits of the CRT, digital cameras have been built to record image data without applying the gamma correction of video. Different input curves have been used in the cameras, often with some version of the log characteristic curve of film, such as ARRI's Log C or SONY's S-log. Image data recorded in these formats retains more information and can produce a higher quality image. Instead of applying the video gamma correction, these cameras convert the linear code values measured by the sensor into logarithmic code values which approximate a film gamma, resulting in a wider dynamic range and greater shadow detail.

6) VIDEO VS. DATA, RAW VS. DE-BAYERED
Video vs. Data

As described above, video cameras were designed to produce an image that displays correctly on a CRT monitor. To properly display on a CRT, a video signal uses a gamma correction that is the inverse (reciprocal) of the CRT gamma. The video format was also designed to limit the dynamic range of the light values it records in order to fit into the narrower brightness range that can be displayed by a CRT monitor. This conversion of light values into a video signal by the camera, which involves applying the gamma correction and limiting the dynamic range, reduces image quality and restricts its capacity to portray shadow and highlight detail. Another characteristic of video is that it records images in fields and frames, but stores them as clips—streaming clips that encode all frames of a shot (head to tail) into a single file.

The highest quality video-recording format used in production today is

HDCam-SR. Originally developed for recording on videotape cassettes, the HDCam-SR format can now also be recorded on dedicated hard drives or solid-state media. Other video recording formats in use include DVCPro-HD and HDCam.

More recently, digital data recording has been developed that records images in a frame-based format in which each frame is saved as a discrete data image file. This format allows direct access to any frame without the need to scroll through a video clip file to locate a frame. The camera and recording system selected determine the particular recording format used. Some file-based formats in use include .dpx, .jpg, .tiff and OpenEXR.

RAW vs. De-Bayered

As described in section (2), Pixels and Chips, single-chip cameras with mosaic patterns use software to immediately convert the light levels measured by their filtered sensors into RGB values. This conversion process (called de-Bayering, referring to the Bayer mosaic pattern) allows real-time viewing of the image. However, some quality is sacrificed by performing the de-Bayer process in real time.

A "raw" recording file format was developed to encode all the light-level data directly from the filtered sensors, before the de-Bayer process occurs. A raw recording of an image can result in a significantly higher quality image. A raw file will require de-Bayer conversion for viewing and most manipulation, but most professional systems used today provide that capability. Some DI (digital intermediate) color-correction systems allow raw files to be used seamlessly in their workflow. Others require a de-Bayer conversion to some RGB data format before proceeding. Cameras that record raw data use their own proprietary raw file format, such as Redcode Raw and ArriRaw.

7) VIDEO SCANNING— INTERLACE OR PROGRESSIVE

The video image is composed of a certain number of lines of pixels. A light or energy beam scans the lines to "write out" each frame. Since the beginning of television broadcasting, interlaced scanning was the standard. In this process, two vertical sweeps are made for each frame—one scans all the odd lines (1, 3, 5, etc.), the next scans the even (2, 4, 6, etc.). Each sweep produces a "field." The NTSC 30 fps television standard records 60 interlaced fields per second.

Progressive scanning is simpler—all lines are scanned sequentially in one vertical sweep. There are no fields, only complete frames, just as in motion-picture film photography. Computer screens use progressive scanning.

When broadcast standards were first being established, the bandwidth of the equipment was relatively small. That is, the throughput of the pipeline used to transmit image data, measured by the amount of data it could transmit over a given period of time, was very limited. The existing equipment was not capable of sending an entire (progressive) frame 30 times per second. It could, however, send 60 half-frames (the fields of interlaced frames) per second, since this requires transmitting only half the frame data at any given moment.

One benefit of interlaced scanning is that the higher frame rate (60 fields, instead of 30 frames) makes the portrayal of movement clearer and more accurate. At 24 progressive frames per second, or even 30, the shutter speed is slow ($\frac{1}{48}$ or $\frac{1}{60}$ second), and generates motion blur with any action. Camera movement can appear juddery over certain backgrounds. Interlaced fields, exposed at twice the shutter speed and frame rate, reduce these problems and give a sharper, more precise portrayal of movement. Subjectively, an interlaced image appears to have greater detail—an immediacy associated with television viewing.

Image flicker is also reduced with interlaced scanning. CRT monitors have a short persistence—the scanned image fades quickly, leaving a black screen. At 24 or 30 fps, there would be more black-screen time, causing noticeable flicker on the monitor. Interlaced scanning at 60 fields per second, refreshing the image twice as fast, greatly reduces flicker. Progressive computer monitors avoid the flicker problem by using a much higher frame rate.

The downside of interlaced scanning is a loss of resolution and steadiness when shooting movement. With subject or camera movement, the image changes from one field to the next. But those two consecutive fields perceptually merge to create each complete frame, even though the moving subject has changed position. Therefore, any movement will appear blurred and detail will be substantially reduced in areas of the frame that contain movement. This factor also creates difficulty for any image processing that involves spatial manipulation of the image, such as resizing or reframing.

A film release of interlaced material requires the creation of progressive frames from pairs of fields, so as to convert the interlaced video fields back to progressive film frames. There are various methods of doing this video-field-to-film-frame conversion. Some involve the interpolation of pixel values between the different fields. This merging of field pairs into frames reduces resolution wherever there is movement. For this reason, the progressive format is preferable for recording back to film.

Some cameras offer the option of recording in either a progressive or interlaced format. A key factor in deciding which format to use should be a consideration of the primary distribution goal of the project—be it theatrical screen, broadcast or DVD/Blu-ray.

8) COMPRESSION

One of the biggest challenges to creating high quality digital images is the handling of the large amounts of data they require. Compression is the means used to reduce the data content of an image source. The objective of compression is to reduce image file size with the least possible sacrifice in quality and detail.

A common method used by compression schemes or codecs is to analyze an image, identify redundant pixels in the picture, and remove them. For instance, a stationary solid blue sky is "redundant" and can be easily compressed. Conversely, subjects in motion change position every frame, are not redundant and are difficult to compress.

There are two categories of compression codecs—intraframe and interframe. The intraframe codec processes each frame individually, only removing redundant information from within that particular frame. The interframe codec uses a series of frames, or group of pictures (GOP), to compress the image data. Interframe compression compares consecutive frames within each GOP to remove redundancy from frame to frame and arrive at "difference" information. Although it's more efficient and can achieve a higher compression ratio, interframe compression can create challenges in editing and postprocessing due to the multiframe dependency.

Compression is quantified as a ratio, comparing the amount of data in the original noncompressed signal to that in the compressed version. The lower the compression ratio, the higher the quality of the resulting image. A format that uses a 2:1 compression ratio preserves more image information than one that uses a 4:1 compression ratio. Some cameras and recording systems offer several compression ratios, providing a choice between higher quality with larger image files and lower quality with smaller files.

Some compression codecs allow the original image to be fully reconstituted when decompressed. Such a codec uses "lossless" compression. However, a danger exists with certain codecs that claim to be "visually lossless." The claim may hold true for direct display of an original image that needs no manipulation in postproduction, but if it later requires significant color grading or visual effects, disturbing artifacts may appear that significantly reduce the quality of the image. Other codecs discard image information that cannot be subsequently retrieved. This is considered "lossey" compression.

9) COLOR SPACE

A color space is a framework that defines a range of colors within a color model. Most color-space systems use a three-dimensional model to describe the relationship among the colors. Each color space has a set of specific primary colors—usually three (a particular red, green and blue)—which shapes its color model.

The color space can be device-dependent or device-independent. A device-dependent system is limited to representing colors from a particular device or process, such as film. The RGB film color space describes the range of colors created by the color dyes used in film. A device-independent color space defines colors universally and, through a conversion process using a "profile" can be used to define colors in any medium on any device.

The color gamut is the range of colors a system can record or display. When a color cannot be correctly produced on a particular device, it is considered "out of gamut" for that device. Film has a different color gamut, for instance, than a CRT monitor. Some colors recorded on film do not properly display on a monitor. Likewise, some extremely saturated, high-intensity colors that can be displayed on a CRT monitor cannot be reproduced on film.

Different media and devices can have widely diverging color characteristics and gamuts. Yet the hybrid film/digital production workflow passes an image from one medium to another, and from device to device—shooting film, scanning it to digital files, viewing it on various monitors and projectors, then recording it back to film. Accurate format conversions are required at each stage to preserve image quality and color-space information. A device-independent color space is effective for accurately transferring and converting color information from one system, format or device to another. The challenge is to avoid losing data as the image is processed step-by-step through the workflow.

The CIE (Commision Internationale de L'Eclairage) XYZ color space has long been the industry's standard device-independent reference. Although this color space uses a three-dimensional model to represent colors, one can use it to plot the visible color spectrum on its flat chromaticity diagram. This diagram is actually a 2-D "slice" taken from the 3-D model of the color space. It has a horseshoe shape and leans left on the x-y axis. (See Figure 3.) All colors visible to human perception can be plotted on this graph. The colors of the spectrum lie along the horseshoe curve, left to right, blue to red. The specific red, green and blue primaries are specified as points on the graph. The neutral white point is nominally located where the three primaries are equal in contribution, but to accommodate different color temperatures, their respective white points are plotted along a curve across the center area of the model. Specific colors are identified in the 2-D space by a set of two numbers, called chromaticity coordinates (x, y), which specify their position on the diagram.

One method to compare media and devices is to plot their respective color gamuts as triangular shapes within the chromaticity diagram. The full horseshoe-shaped space represents the full range of human vision. A triangle within this colored shape approximates the gamut of digital cinema. A smaller triangle inside the digital-cinema triangle represents the more limited gamut of HD video color space (Rec. 709).

Color spaces have been developed to define color for many particular purposes, including film, video and digital-cinema display. The standard HD video color space (ITU-R BT.709 or Rec. 709) uses YCrCb space, which separates luminance (Y) and chrominance (Cr and Cb—red and blue color values). This separation allows for choices in color sub-sampling—for instance, the 4:2:2 sampling ratio measures color half as often as it does luminance, thereby saving memory space and time. (See section 12.) Film is represented by the RGB color space, in which the red, green and blue channels are sampled equally. Both the YCrCb and RGB color spaces are device-dependent.

The color space designated as the standard for Digital Cinema distribution is X'Y'Z,' a gamma encoded version of the CIE XYZ space on which the chromaticity diagram is based. A device-independent space, X'Y'Z' has

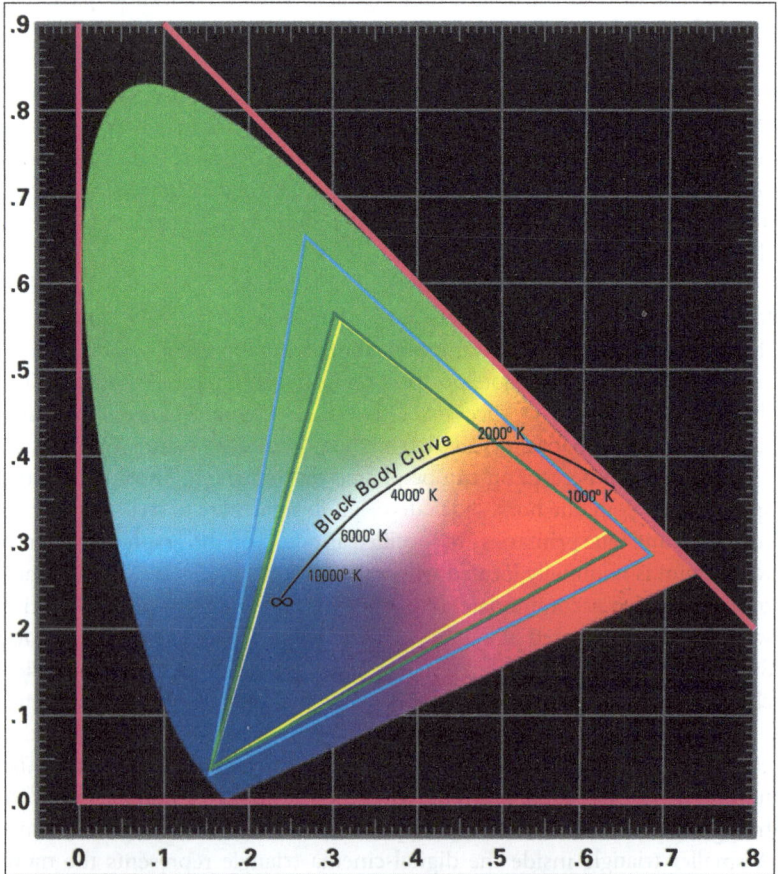

Figure 3. Chromaticity diagram: RED=ACES, BLUE=P3, YELLOW=REC 709.

a larger color gamut than other color spaces, going beyond the limits of human perception. All physically realizable gamuts fit into this space.

10) ACES

The digital workflow of a production today involves the passing of an image, with a particular Look attached, from facility to facility and system to system, requiring conversions and transfers to different formats and media. The risk of failing to achieve the intended result is significant—image quality (including resolution, exposure and color data) can be lost along the way. Look management and color management, discussed below, help reduce these risks, but a larger framework for the entire workflow has been missing.

The Academy of Motion Picture Arts and Sciences' Science and Technology Council developed ACES—the Academy Color Encoding System. ACES provides a framework for converting image data into a universal format. The ACES format can be manipulated and output to any medium or device. The system specifies the correct path from any camera or medium to ACES by using a dedicated IDT (input device transform). Camera manufacturers such as Sony and Arri have already generated an IDT for their camera systems. Display device manufacturers of projectors and monitors provide an ODT (output device transform) for their devices. Different ODTs are also needed for each distribution medium, including digital cinema projection, Blu-ray, and HD broadcast. A final color grading "trim pass" is still recommended for each master so as to insure fidelity to the intended look.

The most striking gain for the cinematographer is the ability for ACES to encode the full range of image information captured by any camera. Using a 16-bit floating-point OpenEXR format, ACES has the potential of encoding the full gamut of human vision, beyond what any camera can record today. It accommodates a dynamic range of 25 stops, far past the capability of any device. Highlights that were clipped and shadows that have been crushed using other formats and workflows now can re-emerge with surprising clarity. ACES empowers the cinematographer to use the full capability and range of the tools at his or her disposal.

11) BIT DEPTH

Bit depth determines the number of levels available to describe the brightness of a color. In a 1-bit system, there is only 0 and 1, black and white. An 8-bit system has 256 steps, or numbers from 0–255 (255 shades of gray). Until recently, 8-bit was standard for video and all monitors. Most monitors still have only 8-bit drivers, but several HD video camera systems support 10-bit and 12-bit signals through their image-processing pipelines.

A 10-bit system has 1024 steps, allowing more steps to portray subtle tones. A linear representation of light values, however, would assign a disproportionate number of steps to the highlight values—the top half of the full range (512–1024) would define only one f-stop, while leaving 0–512 to define all the rest. A logarithmic representation of code numbers, however, spreads equal representation of brightness values across the full dynamic range of the medium. In 10-bit log space, 90 code values are allocated for each f-stop. This allows for more precision to define shadow detail. For this reason, 10-bit log is the standard for recording digital images back to film. Some color publishing applications use a 16-bit system for even more control and detail. The cost of the additional bits is memory and disk space, bandwidth and processing time.

The consequence of too few bits can be artifacts, or flaws in the image introduced by image processing. Artifacts include banding, where a smooth gradient is interrupted by artificial lines, and quantization, where a region of an image is distorted. If image data were recorded or scanned in 10-bit color, down-converted to an 8-bit format for postprocessing, then up-converted back to 10-bit for recording back to film, image information (and usually quality) will have been lost and cannot be retrieved. Whenever possible, it is preferable to maintain the highest quality of image data and not discard information through conversion to a more limited format. Loss of image information can also result from reduction in color space and gamut, color sampling, and resolution.

12) COLOR SAMPLING

Color sampling describes the precision of the measurement of light and color by the camera system. It is represented by three numbers, separated by colons, and refers to the relative frequency of measurement, or sampling. The notation 4:4:4 represents the maximum possible precision, in which all values are measured at equal intervals.

In a video color space, where luminance and chrominance are differentiated, the first number represents how often the luma (brightness) signal is sampled (measured) on each line of sensors. The second number indicates how often the color values (red-minus-luma and blue-minus-luma signals) are sampled for the first line. The third tells how often the color values are sampled for the second line. The two lines are differentiated to accommodate interlaced systems. (See Figure 4.)

4:4:4 captures the most information, sampling color at the same frequency as luminance. 4:2:2 is the current standard on HD production cameras. The color information is sampled at half the frequency of the luminance information. The color precision is lower, but is adequate in most production situations. (Human vision is similarly more sensitive to brightness changes than it is to color variation.) Problems can arise, however, in postprocessing, such as in the compositing of greenscreen scenes, where color precision

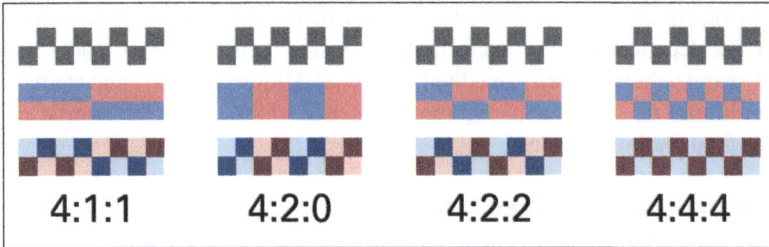

Figure 4. Color sampling ratios

is important. It is recommended that any visual-effects shots that require image processing be recorded in a 4:4:4 format.

13) LOOK MANAGEMENT
AND COLOR MANAGEMENT

The "look" is the visual style of the project. As author of the image, the cinematographer is responsible for the look. While supporting the director's vision of the script and integrating the contributions of the other creative members of the team, he or she should develop, execute and maintain the look throughout the Workflow of the project. This process is look management.

Understanding the fundamentals of digital technology and the production tools available empower the cinematographer to maintain the look and protect the creative intent of the filmmakers. Look-management software provides visualization tools that allow users to manipulate images to create a particular look. That Look can then be saved in a format that can be reliably and consistently shared with other team members. The software used ranges from photography apps, such as Adobe Photoshop, all the way to powerful systems created for motion-picture finishing, such as FilmLight's on-set app, Truelight. Other look-management systems in use include Technicolor's DP Lights, Assimilate's Scratch, Adobe's Speedgrade, Fujifilm's CCBox and Blackmagic Design's DaVinci Resolve.

Integrated throughout the Workflow

Look management starts from the very beginning of a project, and is active throughout the workflow, from previsualization of the look in prep through to the final grading of the distribution master. To start, test and scouting images can be gathered, discussed and processed with software to create a set of "hero" images or shots that encapsulate the look of the project. These images are saved along with their color-adjustment settings, and are used throughout the production workflow to communicate and maintain the look.

The hero images and look settings can be used on set during production, using look-management software, to support the crew as the set is dressed and lit to fulfill the look. Look management can then guide the dailies timer or Colorist as they embed the Look in the dailies they create. Visual-effects artists depend on look management to enable them to process shots that fit seamlessly back into the edited project. Additionally, look management communicates the cinematographer's intended look to the DI colorist for the final grading sessions.

A Universal Interoperable Format

To reliably communicate and reproduce the Look throughout the Work-flow, the instructions should be encoded into a format that can be understood universally and easily read by all the different applications, display devices and facilities that are used on the production. The laboratory printer timing-light number was the standard in existence before digital technology. Until recently, no such universal digital format existed to encode a look, leaving plenty of room for miscommunication and misunderstanding.

The ASC Technology Committee's Digital Intermediate Subcommittee took a significant step toward solving this problem with the ASC CDL (color decision list). Designed to advance the industry toward the goal of interoperability, the ASC CDL encodes basic color-correction instructions that can be read by many different software systems, facilitating communication and collaboration among the many artists and facilities working on a production. The ASC CDL uses 10 parameters to encode the Look of an image: slope, offset, and power for each of the three color channels (red, green, blue) plus a single value for saturation. Slope, offset and power cover a similar range of adjustment to the familiar telecine parameters gain, lift and gamma, but have a cleaner and purer logic and math. The telecine functions also tend to vary in definition from system to system. The ASC CDL format is now integrated into most professional look management and DI grading systems, and has become a reliable way to share and exchange Look information.

Working together with the Academy's Science and Technology Committee, the ASC Technology Committee has also developed a universal format for the look-up table (LUT), another digital tool often used to encode Looks and communicate visual choices.

Several camera systems have dedicated "LUT boxes" that generate and apply looks that were created either in-camera or imported from external media. A cinematographer can save encoded looks from one project and bring them to use on another.

The same industry committees have also been developing a standard for encoding and sharing of all metadata. Metadata encompasses all the nonimage data associated with a particular frame. It can be recorded within the frame's digital file header or, alternatively, in an external database. Metadata guides the processing of an image that is necessary to preserve the look as intended. This can include frame number, resolution, frame rate, motion-control data, as well as any look-management data, such as the ASC CDL values. As the production image is passed through the numerous postproduction steps in the digital workflow, it is important to preserve all metadata associated with an image and pass it on intact to the next stage.

This discussion of the look and look management describes a "nondestructive" process of creating a look and recording its parameters in metadata to a format such as the ASC CDL. The original photographed image is not altered until the final DI session, thereby preserving maximum image quality (resolution and color data) and full potential for post manipulation.

Another working style instead applies the Look modifications to the image on the spot during production, either using a LUT, a camera menu scene file, or an analog device, such as a glass filter. This style "bakes" the Look into the image, in effect marrying the look to the image. This workflow is often used by productions seeking to avoid extensive postproduction work. The disadvantage of baking-in a look, however, is significant. Depending on the modifications used to create the look, image quality may be reduced, whether in dynamic range, color record or resolution. The potential for later image manipulation in the DI may have been compromised, making it difficult or impossible to undo or alter the look already imposed upon the image.

Color Management, Calibration and Viewing Environment

An important requirement for successful look management is rigorous control and consistency of the display of the digital image. This involves color management, monitor or projector calibration, and control of the viewing environment.

With film, an image can be reproduced with reliable consistency—once correct printer lights are set for a given negative, the look of the resulting image is reasonably predictable. Digital images, however, require proper color management to assure their proper display. Particularly for the purpose of communicating a precise look, it is important that the image viewed display correct color, contrast and brightness.

When the cinematographer creates a look with camera and software, he or she views it on a particular monitor or projector. But when it is sent to the other members of the creative team, such as the director and production designer, it is likely to be viewed on different systems. How can the cinematographer ensure that the others see the same look—complete with the right colors, contrast and exposure?

First, the system (both hardware and software) that reads the image file must be able to understand the format in which the image is encoded, and be able to interpret all the metadata in the file. Next, the monitor or projector used to view the image must be properly calibrated to a shared standard (such as SMPTE bars) according to the device manufacturer's instructions. Finally, the image should be viewed in a controlled environment, considering both brightness level and the surrounding color. The same image viewed on a monitor in a sunny, warm room will look very different when viewed in a dim, blue environment.

With good color management, an image portraying a look can be successfully shared electronically, in an instant, around the world. Without color management, the exercise is pointless.

14) DIGITAL INTERMEDIATE

Although the term "digital intermediate" was originally defined as the entire digital postproduction process that comes between principal photography and the final distribution master, today the DI commonly refers to the color-grading session in which all visual elements of the production are brought together for the purpose of making the final adjustments, enhancements, effects and manipulations. (See Figure 5.)

Given the potential for reshaping the look of the picture in the DI session, the cinematographer needs to participate actively in the process, either in person or by remotely communicating his or her vision through images and software. The DP can use look-management software to generate a detailed set of instructions for the colorist. Taking representative frames from each shot in the EDL (edit decision list), he or she can adjust the color, contrast and density of each frame to create a scene-by-scene guide to the intended look for the picture. This process depends on precisely calibrated display devices and accurate digital format transforms. Format and color space must be coordinated so that the samples provided by the cinematographer use the same "palette" (determined by a color space's gamut and dynamic range) that is used by the colorist. Using ACES, this consistency is assured.

The best quality and highest resolution image material should always be used in the DI session. Since the editorial process is usually performed with a lower-resolution image, the EDL is used to conform the hi-res original to the low-res edit, generating a complete high-resolution copy of the project for use in the DI session. The final grading can be performed using any digital color-correction system, but several powerful systems have been developed to expand the creative potential of the DI session, including FilmLight's Baselight, Autodesk's Lustre, and Blackmagic Design's DaVinci Resolve.

Following are principal activities that can be performed by these systems in the DI session:
1) **Primary color correction**: Independently adjusting the lift, gain, and gamma of the RGB color channels .
2) **Secondary color correction**: Isolating specific colors in the spectrum, modifying their hue, saturation and brightness.

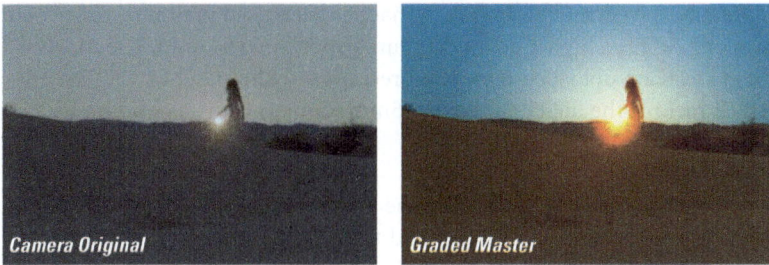

Figure 5. Digital intermediate color grading.

3) **Region-of-interest correction**: Using "windows" or articulated mattes to isolate specific areas of the frame (which may follow or track moving subjects) to make further primary and secondary corrections.
4) **Spatial corrections**;
    a) Repositioning the frame, zooming and panning.
    b) Applying digital filters to blur, flare or sharpen.
    c) Reducing (or amplifying) grain or noise.
5) **Stylized looks:**
    a) Emulating lab processes, as bleach bypass or ENR.
    b) Overall color-gamut manipulation.

15) MASTERING

Once the final grade is completed in the DI session, a digital source master (DSM) is rendered, creating new altered digital image files that encompass all the corrections and enhancements made during the DI. This master is the source for the versions or sub-masters that will be made for distribution in each format. Sub-masters are made for distribution in 35mm, digital cinema, HD and SD broadcast, Blu-ray, DVD, and for online streaming and down-loading. Creation of the sub-master in each medium requires a format conversion—and may then require supplemental color grading (a "trim pass"), so as to come as close as possible to matching the source master created in the DI session. Each medium, however, has different characteristics, including resolution, dynamic range and color gamut, and cannot exactly match the original DSM. To ensure that the look is preserved in each distribution format, the cinematographer should stay in the loop as the sub-master for each medium is created and, if possible, attend the grading sessions or trim-passes for each. The objective is to preserve the look—the original creative intent of the filmmakers.

Film

Creating a 35mm film master involves conversion of the source master to a digital format shaped to take best advantage of the capability of film. Traditionally, the Cineon 10-bit log format has been used in film recorders, but by using ACES, a higher quality output format could be used. The converted digital files are uploaded into a film recorder—either laser or CRT-based—which records the digital files onto 35mm film, exposing a new film master.

Digital Cinema

For the digital-cinema release, the DCI (Digital Cinema Initiatives—a joint effort of the major studios) and the SMPTE have established a set of universal format specifications for distribution—the DCDM and DCP. The specifications define the elements ("assets") used for digital-cinema display, and a structure by which the assets should be used for successful exhibition. The assets include the picture (Digital Source Master), soundtrack, subtitles, metadata and security keys.

The DCDM (digital cinema distribution master) incorporates all specified assets in an uncompressed format. The DCDM encodes the image in the device-independent CIE X'Y'Z' color space as TIFF files, with 12 bits per color channel. This color space accommodates the entire human visual color spectrum and gamut. It has two resolution formats: 2K (2048x1080) and 4K (4096x2160). Source images of other sizes and aspect ratios can be stored within the 2K or 4K image containers. The DCDM also accepts 3-D formats.

The DCP (digital cinema package) is a compressed, encrypted version of the DCDM. Using JPEG 2000 compression, the DCP is used for the efficient and safe transport of the motion-picture content. Upon arrival at the theater (or other exhibition venue), the DCP is unpackaged, decrypted and decompressed for projection.

16) ARCHIVING

Finally, all essential digital data should be properly archived for future generations. Secure storage should be arranged for the digital source master code (or ACES master data), and transferred periodically to fresh media to avoid any degradation or corruption of data. Digital data is vulnerable on all currently available media, whether it be magnetic tape, disk, hard drive or a solid-state medium. The frequency of transfer is dictated by the conservatively estimated life span of the medium being used. The only proven, long-term archive solution is film—black-and-white C/M/Y separations. Properly stored, black-and-white film negative can last at least 100 years.

CONCLUSION

With a working understanding of digital technology, the cinematographer can confidently choose the best methods and devices suited to any project in production. As new challenges arise and new technology becomes available, he or she can better know what issues to consider in making the technical and creative decisions that shape a career.

A working cinematographer, director and software designer, Marty Ollstein is a contributing member of the ASC Technology Committee, a Fellow of SMPTE, and member of the WGA.

He received his MFA in Film Production from UCLA, and developed Crystal Image, the first cinematography filtration software, used on Cineon and Flame visual-effects systems.

A Primer for Evaluating Digital Motion Picture Cameras

by Rob Hummel
editor of the 8th edition of
the American Cinematographer Manual

DIGITAL MOTION PICTURE CAMERAS

Suffice it to say that any aspect ratio is achievable with the current digital motion picture cameras available. Their capture format is generally that of HDTV (1920x1080) or what is commonly called 2K.[1] The aspect ratio of all but one or two of these cameras is the HDTV aspect ratio of 1.78:1 (16 x 9 in video parlance). This 1.78:1 aspect ratio is a result of the different camera manufacturers leveraging what they have built for HDTV broadcasting cameras. It's unique to find a digital camera that doesn't owe part of its design to television cameras.

When composing for 1.85, digital cameras generally use almost the entire 1.78 imaging area. When composing for the 2.40:1 aspect ratio, most digital cameras will capture a letterboxed 2.40 slice out of the center of the imaging sensor, which, in 1920 x 1080 cameras, results in the pixel height of the image being limited to only 800 lines (*Star Wars Episode 3, Sin City, Superman Returns*).

There is one digital camera that employs Anamorphic lenses to squeeze the 2.40 aspect ratio to fit within its sensor's 1.97 aspect ratio, utilizing the entire imaging area.

Yet another camera does creative things with the clocking of CCD pixels so that the entire imaging area is still utilized when shooting a 2.40 image, with a subtle compromise in overall resolution.

In the future, it is likely that more and more cameras will have imaging sensors with 4K pixel resolution.

1. When film resolutions are discussed, and the terms 2K or 4K are used, these refer to the number of lines that can be resolved by the film. In the case of 2K, that would mean 2048 lines or 1024 line pairs as photographed from a resolution chart. In the case of 4K, that would mean 4096 lines or 2048 line pairs (4096 lines) as photographed from a resolution chart. In digital imagery the term is applied a bit more loosely. While 2K and 4K still mean 2048 and 4096, respectively, with digital scanning and photography it refers to a number of photo sites on the scanner or camera chip. Numbers of pixels does not necessarily translate into actual image resolution.

In a 1920 x 1080 Digital Camera, only the center 800 lines are used for a "Scope" or 2.40:1 aspect ratio.

RESOLUTION VS. MEGAPIXELS

When it comes to determining which digital camera to choose, don't allow claims of "megapixels" to influence your understanding of what a

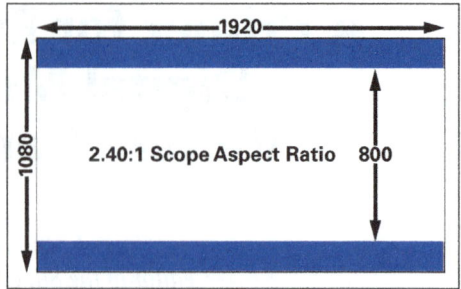

Figure 1. In a 1920 x 1080 Digital Camera, only the center 800 lines are used for a "Scope" or 2.40:1 aspect ratio.

camera is capable of. It is a term that is used loosely to indicate the resolution of a digital camera that doesn't follow any set guidelines. There are many factors that would have to be taken into account if you were going to evaluate the merits of a digital imaging device based on specifications alone.

The most straightforward way to understand a digital motion picture camera's capabilities is to shoot your own rigorous tests and evaluate them. In the same manner when a new film stock has been introduced, the best way to truly understand that emulsion's capabilities is to test it, rather than rely on the claims of the manufacturer.

Also, it will be less confusing if you focus your evaluations on the final image delivered by a given digital camera. Claims about a camera's imaging sensor can be influenced by marketing. If we concentrate on the final processed image that is delivered for projection, color correction, and final presentation, we will be evaluating a camera's true caliber.

SCANNER VS. CAMERAS

To clarify, at the risk of confusing, 2K and 4K film scanners generally capture more information than their camera counterparts; a 2K film scanner will usually have a CCD array of 2048 x 1556, while a 4K scanner will capture a 4096 x 3112 image. The lesson here is that one's definition of the dimensions of 2K or 4K can vary; the terms 2K and 4K are only guidelines, your mileage may vary.

It is important to understand these variables in characteristics, and the need to be very specific when describing the physical characteristics of film cameras, digital cameras, scanners and telecines. In the world of film cameras (and film scanners), 2K refers to an image which is 2048 pixels horizontally (perf to perf) and 1556 pixels vertically. This image captures the area of either the SMPTE 59 Style C full aperture frame (.981" x .735") or the SMPTE 59 Style B sound aperture frame (.866" x .735").

A 4K scan captures the same areas of the film frame as a 2K scan, but the image captured is 4096 x 3112. With both 2K and 4K scanners, each individual pixel contains a single unique sample of Red, Green and Blue.

In the digital camera world, 2K often refers to an image that is 1920 pixels horizontally and 1080 pixels vertically. Again, each individual pixel contains a single unique sample of Red, Green and Blue. This sampling of a unique Red, Green and Blue value for each pixel in the image is what is called a "true RGB" image, or in video parlance, a 4:4:4 image. While these cameras have an image frame size that corresponds to HDTV standard, they provide a 4:4:4 image from the sensor, which is not to HDTV standard; which is a good thing, as 4:4:4 will yield a superior picture.

FILL FACTOR

There is one area of a digital camera's specifications that is most helpful in determining its sensitivity and dynamic range. This is the statistic that conveys how much area of an imaging sensor is actually sensitive to, and captures light vs. how much of a sensor is blind, relegated to the circuitry for transferring image information. This is called the "fill factor." It is also a statistic that is not readily published by all camera manufacturers.

This is an area where not all digital cameras are created equal. The amount of area a digital imaging sensor is actually sensitive to light (the "fill factor") has a direct correlation to image resolution and exposure latitude. With the currently available professional Digital Motion Picture Cameras, you will find a range of high profile cameras where less than 35% of the sensor's total area is sensitive to light, to cameras where more than 85% of the sensor is light sensitive.

As film cinematographers, we are used to working with a medium where it was presumed that the entire area of a 35mm film frame is sensitive to light; in digital parlance, that would be a fill factor of 100%. When a digital camera has a fill factor of 40%, that means it is throwing away 60% of the image information that is focused on the chip. Your instincts are correct if you think throwing away 60% of image information is a bad idea. With this statistic, you can quickly compare camera capabilities, or at least understand their potential.

The higher the fill factor of a given sensor (closer to 100%), the lower the noise floor will be (the digital equivalent of film grain) and the better the dynamic range will be.

DIGITAL SENSORS AND AMOUNT OF LIGHT THEY CAPTURE

Since the imaging sites on a solid state sensor are arrayed in a regular grid, think of the 40% sensitive area as being "holes" in a steel plate. Thus, the image gathered is basically similar to shooting with a film camera through a fine steel mesh. You don't actually see the individual steel gridlines of the mesh, but it tends to have an affect on image clarity under most conditions.

In terms of sensor types with progressively more area sensitive to light, there are basically two categories: photodiodes (less area) and photogates (more area). Depending on the pixel size, cameras utilizing a single-chip photodiode interline transfer array (either CCD or CMOS) would be on the low end with less than 40 to 35% of its total area sensitive to light, up to a theoretical maximum of 50% for multichip (RGB) photodiode sensors. Next would be single-chip photogate based sensors that can, again, depending on pixel size, have anywhere from 70 to over 85% of its area sensitive to light.

In light sensitivity, as in exposure index, photodiode sensors will have a higher sensitivity than photogate sensors, albeit with an associated trade off in latitude and resolution.

In addition, solid state sensors tend to have various image processing circuits to make up for things such as lack of blue sensitivity, etc., so it is important to examine individual color channels under various lighting conditions, as well as the final RGB image. Shortcomings in automatic gain controls, etc. may not appear until digital postproduction processes (VFX, DI, etc.) begin to operate on individual color channels.

MORE ON MEGAPIXELS

Much confusion could be avoided if we would define the term "pixel" to mean the smallest unit area which yields a full color image value (e.g., RGB, YUV, etc., or a full grayscale value in the case of black and white). That is, a "pixel" is the smallest stand-alone unit of picture area that does not require any information from another imaging unit. A "photosite" or "well" is defined to be the smallest area that receives light and creates a measure of light at that point. All current Digital Motion Picture cameras require information from multiple "photosites" to create one RGB image value. In some

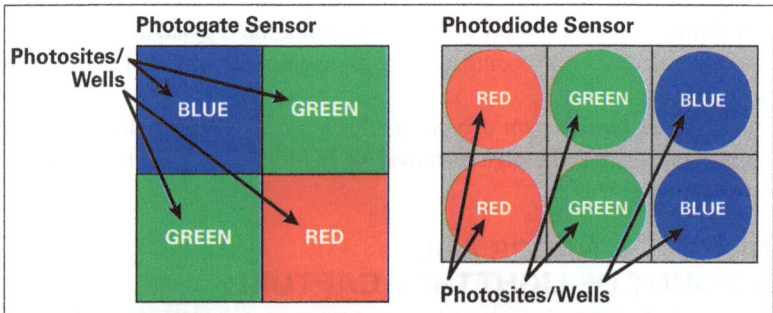

Figure 2a. A Bayer pattern Photogate sensor, where each photo site is transformed to yield one full color pixel value.

Figure 2b. A Photodiode "macrocell" design, where it takes six photosites to yield one full color pixel value.

cases three photosites for one RGB value, in others, six photosites to create one RGB image value, a then Bayer pattern devices that combine numerous photosites to create one RGB value.

These definitions inevitably lead us to define the term "resolution" as the number of pixels that yield a single full color or grayscale image value (RGB, YUV, etc.).

The images above are just two of many examples of photo sensors used by digital cameras. One illustrates a Bayer pattern array of photosites using a photogate sensor, and the other an interline transfer array of photosites employing a photodiode lenslet design.

SOUND COMPLICATED?

Perhaps, but all you need to understand is that product claims can, and will, be misleading. We've lost our way a bit when thinking that counting pixels alone is a way of quantifying a digital camera's capability. A return to photographing resolution charts, and actually examining what these cameras are capable of will serve you much better in understanding how a given camera will help you tell your story.

In short, do not be seduced by technical specification mumbo jumbo. Look at images photographed by the camera in question, and evaluate from a proper distance of screen heights from the image.

© 2007 Robert C. Hummel III • Special thanks to Stephen H. Burum, ASC, Daniel Rosen, Garrett Smith, Evans Wetmore, and Anne Kemp Hummel in helping bring greater clarity to this discussion.

Digital Cinematography on a Budget

by M. David Mullen, ASC

Before the year 2000, video technology had only been used sporadically for theatrical releases, mainly documentaries. For narrative fiction, milestones include Rob Nilsson's independent feature *Signal 7* (1985), shot on ¾" video, and *Julia and Julia* (1987), shot on 1125-line analog high-definition video. However, using video technology for independent features—primarily as a lower-cost alternative to film—didn't catch on until a number of elements fell into place: the introduction of digital video camcorders, desktop computer nonlinear editing systems, and the increase in companies offering video-to-film transfer work, all of which began to appear by the mid 1990s.

The major turning point came with the worldwide box office success of two features shot on consumer camcorders, the Dogma'95 movie *Festen* (*The Celebration*) (1998) and *The Blair Witch Project* (1999), proving that cinema audiences were willing to watch movies shot in video if the subject matter was compelling enough and the visual quality seemed to suit the content. However, with 35mm film being the gold standard for narrative feature production, many independent filmmakers have pushed manufacturers to develop affordable technology that would bring an electronic image closer to the look of 35mm photography.

24 fps progressive-scan (24P) digital video appeared in 2000 with the introduction of the Sony HDW-F900 HDCAM pro camcorder; then in late 2002, Panasonic released the AG-DVX100, a Mini-DV "prosumer" camcorder with a 24P mode that cost less than $5000. Not long after that, lower-cost high-definition video cameras appeared, starting with the JVC GR-HD1 HDV camcorder in late 2003. The next significant trend was the movement away from traditional tape-based recording, allowing greater options in frame rates and recording formats within the same camera. The first prosumer camera with this design approach was the Panasonic AG-HVX200, released in late 2005; it came with a standard Mini-DV VTR but could also record footage to P2 flash memory cards.

By 2009, there were HD video cameras being sold on the market for less than $1000, and now even phones and still cameras are capable of shooting HD video. Today many movie theaters are being converted to digital projection; this trend—combined with emerging online distribution schemes—

has diminished the need for a digital feature to be transferred to 35mm film (though there remains good archival reasons for doing this).

The term "prosumer" vaguely covers a range of lower-cost video products with a mix of consumer and professional features, often in a small-sized camera body. Prosumer cameras, by definition, are not only used by consumers but by professionals as well, either for cost reasons, or because their portability and low profile are better suited to a particular type of production. In fact, some of the cameras discussed in this article are actually made and sold by the professional division of the manufacturer and thus are not technically prosumer products.

Therefore, rather than separate cameras into debatable categories of "professional/prosumer/consumer," I will make the cut-off point for discussion any camera sold for under $15,000 and under that is capable of professional-quality video, preferably with a 24P or 25P option.

In this article, "SD" refers to standard definition video and "HD" refers to high definition video. "24P" refers to 24 fps progressive-scan video. "DSLR" refers to single-lens reflex still cameras with a digital sensor. "NLE" refers to nonlinear editing.

ASPECT RATIO ISSUES

Theatrical films are usually projected in 4-perf 35mm prints at 24 fps, either in the matted widescreen format (using a projector mask to crop the image, commonly to 1.85:1) or in the anamorphic widescreen format (the printed image is approximately 1.20:1 with a 2X horizontal squeeze, stretched to nearly 2.40:1 with an anamorphic projector lens). Current standards for digital cinema presentations follow the same conventions for aspect ratios.

In broadcast video, however, the standard aspect ratios are 4 x 3 (1.33:1) or 16 x 9 (1.78:1). Since most video cameras shoot in one or both formats, with 16 x 9 now becoming dominant, there are framing considerations for anything intended for theatrical release where the 1.85 and 2.40 ratios prevail.

In digital terms, the NTSC picture area is 720 x 480 (or 486) pixels; PAL is 720 x 576 pixels. An HDTV picture is either 1280 x 720 pixels or 1920 x 1080 pixels.

If you do some simple math, you'll realize that 720 x 480 equals a 1.50:1 aspect ratio, and 720 x 576 equals 1.25:1—neither is 1.33:1 (4 x 3). To confuse things further, the 16x9 option in NTSC and PAL share the same pixel dimensions as 4 x 3. The simple explanation is that the pixels in many recording formats are not perfectly square. You can see this right away when you capture a frame of SD video and display it on a computer monitor as a still image.

On a 16 x 9 monitor, a 16 x 9 SD recording displays correctly. But when played on a 4 x 3 monitor, it fills the screen but looks stretched vertically because of its nonsquare pixels, unless converted into a 4 x 3 signal with a 1.78 letterbox (a DVD player, for example, can be set-up to automatically do this but many tape decks cannot). This is why 16 x 9 SD is often called "anamorphic," not to be confused with the photographic process of the same name. HD, having a native 16 x 9 aspect ratio, does not use this anamorphic technique unless downconverted to 16 x 9 SD.

4 x 3 has given way over time to 16 x 9 as HD has become more commonplace in shooting, post, and distribution. Since HD cameras have 16 x 9 sensors, and the costs of these cameras have fallen to the same levels of SD cameras, there is little reason to deal with 4 x 3 SD camera issues anymore, even for SD distribution.

In terms of composing 16 x 9 for eventual 35mm 1.85 print projection, most prosumer cameras do not offer 1.85 framelines for the viewfinder. However, 16 x 9 is so similar to the 1.85 ratio that simply composing shots with slightly more headroom will be enough compensation for a later 1.85 crop. Many viewfinders can be set up to display a slightly smaller "safe area" inside the full frame that could serve as a rough guide for how much to protect the image. Also, one could point the camera at a 1.85 framing chart and tape-off any production monitors to match those framelines.

A recording of this framing chart would be useful in post as well.

If a film transfer is planned, it would be better to leave the final color-corrected master in 16 x 9 full-frame rather than letterbox it to 1.85. The entire 16 x 9 image would then be transferred to film within the 35mm sound aperture area (aka "Academy") with a 1.78 hard matte. The black borders of the hard matte would be just outside the projected 1.85 area. If you had transferred a 1.85 letterboxed image to film, then the 1.85 projector mask would have to be precisely lined up with the hard matte in the print or else the audience would see some of the matte on screen. A 1.78 hard matte allows some mild vertical misalignment during 1.85 projection, but not enough to allow the image to be clearly misframed by the projectionist. Also, since full-frame 16 x 9 and 1.85 are similar, keep the entire 16 x 9 frame clear of any film equipment (like mics and dolly tracks) when shooting. Odds are high that you will need to deliver a 16 x 9 full-frame version for HDTV broadcast, so protecting the entire frame will eliminate the need for expensive reframing and retouching in post.

Some filmmakers wish to shoot 16 x 9 video for transfer to 35mm 2.40 anamorphic. The most common solution is to simply compose the image for cropping to 2.40; for transfer to film, either a 2.40 letterboxed version or the 16 x 9 full-frame master can be used. You would instruct the transfer facility to crop the recording to 2.40 and transfer to the 35mm anamorphic ("scope") format. The cropping and stretching are usually done by the film recorder. If you submit a 16 x 9 full-frame recording, it is a good idea to add a framing leader showing the 2.40 picture area within 16 x 9.

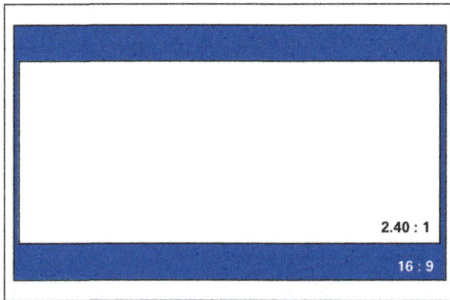

Figure 1. 1.85:1 format inside a 1.78:1 frame.

While it is easiest to just center the 2.40 composition vertically within 16 x 9, when the project is invariably broadcast in full-frame 16 x 9 on some HDTV channel, there will be an excess of headroom in the unmatted version. This may require some reframing in post when objectionable—but then it will be necessary to zoom into the picture slightly so you can raise the frame, at the loss of side information. A better solution would be to frame the 2.40 image higher up in the 16 x 9 frame, almost to what is called "common top" so that the headroom is similar between the full-frame and letterboxed version. Unfortunately, it's hard in many cameras to reposition 2.40 viewfinder framelines. Also, for the final 2.40 letterboxed master, you will have to vertically recenter the 2.40 image within 16 x 9.

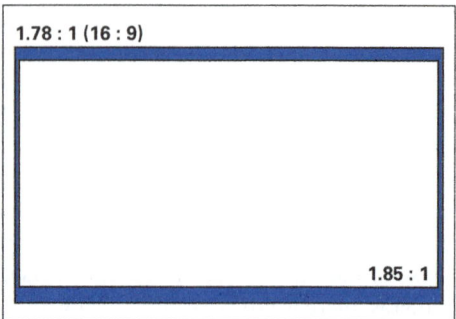

Flgure 2. 2.40:1 format centered inside a 1.78:1 frame.

A less common approach to achieve 2.40 is to use a 1.33X anamorphic lens attachment on a 16 x 9 prosumer camera. Normally these optical devices are used to squeeze a 16 x 9 image onto a 4 x 3 sensor, but they would also squeeze a 2.40 image onto a 16 x 9 sensor, more or less. Since a 16 x 9 recording with a 1.33X squeeze is nonstandard, you'll have to work carefully with the company doing the film recording to make sure they properly convert the 1.33X squeeze to a standard 2X squeeze. You'd also have to make an unsqueezed 2.40 letterboxed image for video distribution.

Another possibility is to use a 35mm groundglass adaptor that took PL-mount 35mm cine lenses; Vantage Film

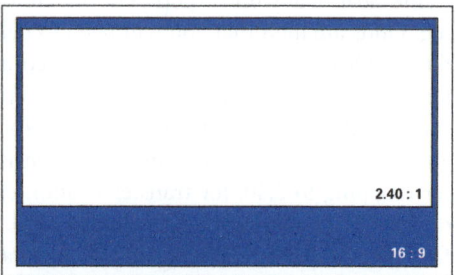

Figure 3. 1.85:1 format positioned near "common top" inside a 1.78:1 frame.

makes a 1.33X version of their Hawk anamorphic lenses that would have the correct squeeze ratio for a 16x9 sensor camera. And if you were using a B4-mount ⅔" video camera, Canon makes a rear-mounted lens attachment that adds a 1.33X squeeze.

Some cameras, particularly the large single-sensor ones, have cine lens mounts thus 35mm anamorphic lenses can be used directly. Keep in mind that the majority of anamorphic lenses made for cinema use have a 2X squeeze and were designed to fit a 2.40:1 image onto a 1.20:1 area of 4-perf 35mm film. Since most HD cameras have a 16 x 9 (1.78:1) sensor, once unsqueezed, the 2X anamorphic lens would create a 3.56:1 image and thus require as much cropping of the sides to make it 2.40:1 as would be involved in cropping a normal 16 x 9 HD image top and bottom to create the same aspect ratio.

After testing some of these options, you may end up preferring to just crop a normal spherical image to 2.40:1. The simplest solutions are often the best, especially in independent feature production.

FRAME RATE ISSUES

The 59.94 Hz rate used for television transmissions in 60 Hz North American countries started with the introduction of the color encoding for analog NTSC in the mid 1950s. For better or worse, it has remained today in digital ATSC broadcast rates for North America. In PAL countries, the rate is 50 Hz both for television and for household power.

In interlaced-scan video, each field contains every other line of video necessary to make up a whole frame; the second field contains the alternate lines. In a camera with an interlace-scan sensor, each field is captured sequentially and therefore a moving object appears in a slightly different position on each field. Thus when two temporally sequential fields are combined into a single frame, as for a film-out or for display on a progressive-scan monitor, the edges of the moving object have a "toothcomb" artifact and there is some loss of vertical resolution.

In a progressive-scan video camera, complete frames are captured by the sensor, whether or not this information is then stored that way or split into fields.

In 60 Hz countries, the interlaced-scan rate can be described as both 59.94 fields per second or 29.97 frames per second. It is can be expressed as "59.94i" (though often rounded to "60i"—which I will be doing often in this chapter). In 50 Hz countries, the interlaced-scan rate is 50 fields per second or 25 frames per second. It is expressed as "50i." If your camera could capture in progressive-scan, the frame rate would be expressed with a "P" after it, as in "24P" for 24 fps progressive-scan.

Broadcast HDTV for 60 Hz countries is either 720/60P or 1080/60i. In 50 Hz countries, it is 720/50P or 1080/50i. This means that, to some extent, the problems of NTSC and PAL are being carried over into HDTV, at least as far as the filmmaker attempting to use HD technology to create projects for transfer to 24 fps film. For example, if using an interlace-scan prosumer HD camera, it may be better to choose a 50i model over a 60i version since it is simpler to convert 50 fields into 25 frames than it is to convert 60 fields into 24 frames. 50i footage de-interlaced to 25P can be transferred 1:1 to frames of 35mm film for projection at 25 or 24 fps. However, with a 24P or 25P option becoming more prevalent in HD cameras, there is little reason to deal with conversions from interlace-scan photography anymore.

Since 60i is still used by broadcast video and many display devices, consumer cameras often convert 24P capture into a 60i recording using a "pull-down" scheme. This is particularly common for cameras that use an internal VTR for recording. Since some users want to simply edit and display the

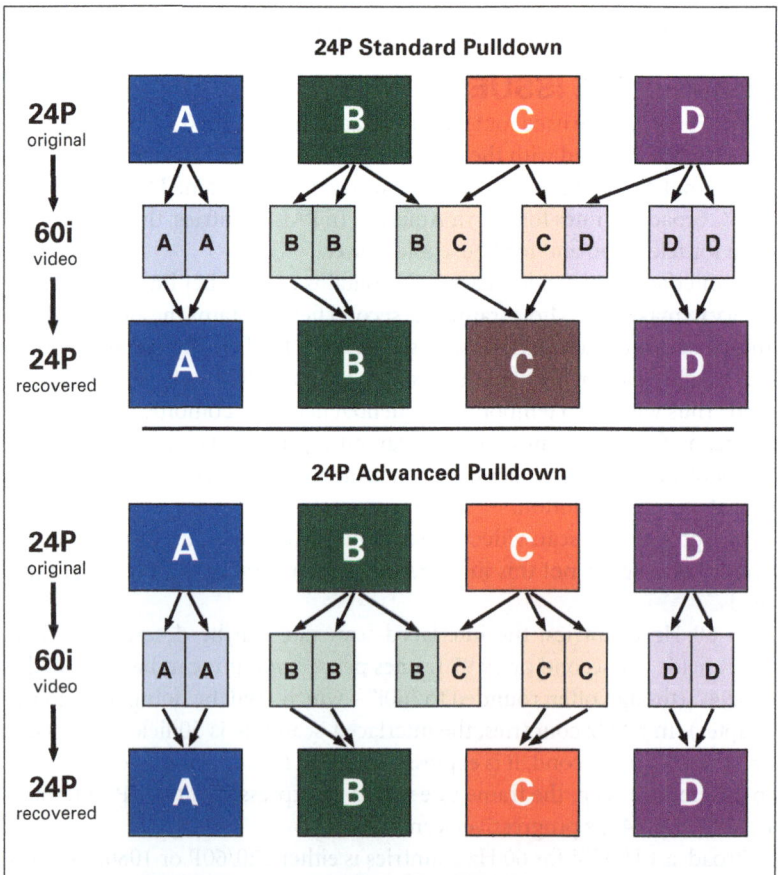

Figure 4. Two versions of pulldowns from 24 fps to 60 fps.

24P material in 60i, while others wish to edit the original progressive-scan frames, many 24P cameras offer two 60i recording modes: one using the standard 3:2 or 2:3 pulldown, and the other using an "advanced" pulldown. This is actually a more visible 2:3:3:2 cadence designed to make it easier to be removed at the editing stage.

In terms of motion artifacts during playback, the normal 3:2 pulldown cadence is designed to be as smooth as possible when viewing 24 fps material on 60i display devices; the scheme is more effectively "buried" but therefore also harder to extract in post. The advanced pulldown cadence is not as smooth but allows for a cleaner extraction of the original 24P frames. As you can see in the charts above, the original "C" frame is split between two different video frames when using normal pulldown; this means that in order to recover this frame, those video frames have to be decompressed and then recovered 24P frame recompressed back into the original codec. This can mean that the "C" frame will have suffered some possible degradation compared to the A, B, and D frames. As you can see in the chart for the advanced pulldown scheme, every third video frame is simply discarded in order to recover 24P in editing, and this discarded frame was the only one where each field came from a different original frame.

Due to its name, a number of people mistakenly believe that the advanced pulldown is "better"—either more film-like or better-looking. It's not. Its only purpose, in fact, is to be removed in post. If your edited 24P project needs to be converted back to 60i for broadcast applications, you'd then add a standard pulldown scheme to a separate 60i master.

While some interlaced-scan cameras offer a simulated 24 fps effect, this is really only intended to create film-like motion for 60i projects, not for transfer to 24 fps film. However, there are many consumer HD cameras now with progressive-scan sensors capable of true 24P capture, even if some of them record 24P to 60i with a pulldown. A number of these cameras are multi-format, with different frame rate options, particularly the ones using solid-state recording instead of videotape.

It is recommended that any pulldown be removed so that one can edit with the original progressive frames. This allows greater flexibility and quality in post for finishing the project to multiple deliverable formats. A progressive-scan master is optimal for a transfer to film as well distribution on DVD, Blu-ray, and the Internet. Otherwise, once you start editing a 24P-to-60i recording, you will be breaking up the pulldown cadence, making it harder to remove later.

Since many of these cameras record 24P in different ways, it would be prudent to find out what current editing software handles the particular camera and recording method you will be employing. Updates to current programs are constantly being released to accommodate these variations of 24P.

RECORDING FORMATS

This list is not all-inclusive because some formats and recorders fall outside the budget range that this article covers.

DV

This term describes both a recording codec (compression/decompression algorithm) and a tape format. Most lower-end SD cameras uses the DV25 codec, a 5:1 DCT intraframe compression at a fixed bitrate of 25 Mbit/sec. Chroma subsampling is 4:1:1 (NTSC) or 4:2:0 (PAL). The recorded video signal is 60i (NTSC) or 50i (PAL). Mini-DV and DVCAM cassettes are commonly used; the picture quality is the same for both tape formats. DVCAM uses a slightly wider track pitch and faster speed to reduce drop-outs and increase physical robustness. DVCPRO uses 4:1:1 worldwide but otherwise is still 25 Mbit/sec. DVCPRO50 is 50 Mbit/sec with 4:2:2 subsampling and roughly 3.3:1 compression.

HDV

This is an MPEG-2 recording format that uses both intraframe and interframe compression to reduce HD down to 25 Mbit/sec for 1080i, 19 Mbit/sec for 720P. Having the same bitrate, more or less, as DV, it can therefore use Mini-DV tapes for recording and the IEEE 1394 (FireWire) interface. The aspect ratio is 16x9; pixel dimensions are 1280 x 720 (720P) or 1440 x 1080 (1080i). The 720P format supports 60P/30P or 50P/25P recording with a 24P option; the 1080i format supports 60i or 50i recording with a 30P, 25P, and 24P option. Chroma subsampling is 4:2:0.

"Pro-HD" is JVC's name for their professional line of MPEG-2/HDV cameras.

DVCPRO HD

This is an HD codec and tape format developed by Panasonic. It uses DCT intraframe compression; the bitrate is 100 Mbit/sec when recording to tape. Chroma subsampling is 4:2:2. Aspect ratio is 16 x 9; the pixel dimensions of the recorded image are 960 x 720 (720P), 1280 x 1080 (1080/60i), or 1440 x 1080 (1080/50i).

AVCHD

This stands for Advanced Video Coding High Definition. This is an 8-bit 4:2:0 HD format that uses an MPEG-4 codec known as AVC/H.264. In prosumer HD cameras, it is recorded to nontape media such as memory cards, hard drives, and 8cm DVDs. It supports the same frame rates as HDV and DV. The bitrate is between 12 to 24 Mbit/sec. It uses long-GOP (group of pictures) interframe compression. The Panasonic name for their AVCHD pro camera line is "AVCCAM". Sony uses the name "NXCAM" for their line. AVCHD 2.0 allows bitrates to 28 Mbit/sec for 1080/60P and for 3-D applications.

AVC-Intra

Developed by Panasonic, this variation of MPEG-4/H.264 HD offers intraframe compression rather than interframe, at 10-bits using at higher bitrates, either 50 Mb/s (4:2:0) or 100 Mb/s (4:2:2).

XDCAM

Uses different codecs and compression methods (MPEG-2, MPEG-4, DV25). See above for DV recording specifications. The HD version of XDCAM uses MPEG-2 compression at bitrates of 18, 25, or 35 Mbit/sec. Recorded pixel resolution is 1440 x 1080. Chroma sub-sampling is 4:2:0. The Sony XDCAM EX "HQ" mode allows full-raster 1280 x 720 or 1920 x 1080 4:2:0 recordings at 35 Mbit/sec. "HD 422" mode allows 8-bit 4:2:2 at 50 Mbit/sec.

Canon XF

Similar to XDCAM HD, allows 8-bit 4:2:2 recording using MPEG-2 compression at 50 Mbit/sec, as well as 4:2:0 at 35 or 25 Mbit/sec.

Redcode

This is the name of the wavelet compression (JPEG2000 variant) scheme used by Red cameras to record RAW sensor data. Different bitrates are offered.

DTE (Direct To Edit)

Some cameras and recorders have the option to store data in the types of file formats used in nonlinear editing systems so that the footage can be edited immediately without transcoding. Examples include Apple ProRes and Avid DNxHD.

BEYOND VIDEOTAPE

Over the past few years, there has been a shift away from using videotape recorders inside camcorders. These are some alternative recording devices and mediums:

Optical Disk

SD and HD can be recorded using Sony's professional XDCAM optical disk system (similar to Blu-ray), but there are only some lower-end consumer DV cameras with built-in optical disk recorders, using the miniDVD format.

Solid-State Flash Memory Cards and Drives

Camera data can be recorded to different types of flash memory cards such as SD/SDHC (Secure Digital/High Capacity), CF (Compact Flash), ExpressCard, Panasonic's P2, and Sony's Memory Stick (though Sony has been moving away from that technology).

Panasonic's P2 cards are basically a RAID of SD memory cards in a PC (PCMCIA) card body. Multiple P2 cards can be used in slots in the cameras to increase recording times. Currently 16, 32, and 64 GB cards are available but capacity keeps increasing over time. One 16 GB card can record 40 minutes of 24P/720 material in DVCPRO HD.

The Sony XDCAM EX cameras record to SxS cards, a high-speed Express-Card SSD (solid-state drive) using PCIe interface specification. Current SxS cards are 16, 32 and 64 GB. A 16 GB card captures 50 minutes of 1080/24P at 35 Mbit/sec.

The Blackmagic Cinema Camera has an integrated recorder using 2.5" SSDs. The Red Scarlet has a side-mounted recorder using 1.8" SSDs.

External Recorders

There are portable recorders that can store larger amounts of video or data than the camera can internally; some of these external devices are small enough to be mounted directly to the camera. Some use an HDD (hard disk drive) or a SSD (solid-state drive); others use memory cards for storage. Some examples:

▶ Focus Enhancements makes a series of portable DTE recorders under the product name FireStore. Some units, like the FS100, record DV and Panasonic's DVCPRO50 and DVCPRO-HD; others record DV and HDV. Some are designed for specific camera models. The FS-200 records DV/HDV to CF cards. The units store footage as QuickTime or MXF files.

▶ Sony makes a solid-state device (HVR-MRC1K) for attachment to their tape-based cameras that can record HDV/DVCAM/DV to CF cards. Their PXU-MS240 mobile HHD storage unit is designed for use with the XDCAM EX cameras to transfer data from SxS memory cards for nearly continuous back-up or off-load of video clips in the field.

▶ Panasonic has a portable P2 recorder/player (AG-HPG20) that records 10-bit 4:2:2 AVC-Intra as well as DVPRO-HD, DVCPRO50, DVCPRO, and DV. They also make a handheld AVCCAM recorder/player (AG-HMR10).

▶ AJA's Ki Pro recorder can convert any camera's HD-SDI/HDMI/SD output to 10-bit Apple ProRes 422 QuickTime files; the footage is then stored on either a removable HDD or (optional) SSD storage module, or on ExpressCards. The smaller Ki Pro Mini records to CF cards.

▶ Convergent Designs' Flash XDR and NanoFlash devices can be mounted on a camera; they use multiple CF card slots to store footage as Quicktime or MXF files, compressed using MPEG-2 codec. Their Gemini 444 recorder can record uncompressed 10-bit 4:2:2/4:4:4 through single/dual-link HD-SDI to 1.8" SSDs. The Gemini Raw recorder can record Canon Raw, ARRIRAW, and CinemaDNG as well as 1080P.

▶ The Atomos Ninja and Samurai recorders capture HDMI (Ninja) or HD-SDI (Samurai) output to Apple ProRes on 2.5" HDD/SSDs.

▶ Fast Forward Video (FFV) offers the Sidekick HD camera-top recorder, recording Apple ProRes to 2.5" SSDs from HD-SDI or HDMI.

▶ Sound Device's PIX 220 and 240 recorders capture HDMI (220) and/or HD-SDI (240) to Apple ProRes or DNxHD to CF cards or 2.5" SSDs.

▶ Blackmagic Design's HyperDeck Shuttle records uncompressed HD-SDI output into 2.5" SSDs.

▶ A laptop computer can also be used during shooting to process signals for recording to an internal or external hard drive.

AVOIDING THE RECORDING CODEC

Some cameras can output a video signal before it gets processed and compressed by the codec used in the internal recorder. For example, an HDV camera often has an HDMI-out in order to send a picture to a consumer HDTV monitor; this is usually an 8-bit 4:2:2 HD signal that could be recorded using a computer (probably with a RAID array), an HDCAM-SR deck, or a data recorder. You probably will need to use an HDMI-to-HD-SDI converter in order to connect with these devices, though some devices accept HDMI directly. Some prosumer cameras already have an HD-SDI output. Single-link HD-SDI is limited to 1.5 Gbit/sec; an uncompressed 8-bit 4:2:2 1920 x 1080 59.94i signal is around 1 Gbit/sec. What comes out of these HDMI or HD-SDI connections is quite variable in quality, depending on the camera itself.

Though recording large amounts of uncompressed data at HD resolution for a feature-length project (sometimes 20 to 60 hours of footage) is somewhat inconvenient for many independent filmmakers, there may be reasons to do that for limited amounts of footage—for example, when doing chroma key vfx composites, or when mixing the footage with higher-quality formats. Again, testing is recommended to see if the results are significantly better, enough to warrant the difficulty or extra cost in using this approach. Over the years, it has become easier to manage larger and larger amounts of camera data, which means that filmmakers will be able to record hours of uncompressed HD without much effort.

DEPTH OF FIELD AND SENSOR SIZE

Small prosumer video cameras often have ⅓" sensors or even smaller (though a recent trend has been towards larger sensors.) This means that, in order to achieve the same field of view, the focal length used is much shorter than in 35mm cinematography—with a resulting increase in depth of field.

A ⅓" sensor is 4.8mm wide; a Super-35 film frame is 24mm wide. That's a 5X difference or conversion factor. Therefore you would need to use a 10mm lens on a ⅓" sensor camera to approximate the field of view of a 50mm lens on a 35mm movie camera. Practically-speaking, this means that ⅓" photography has about five more stops of depth of field compared to 35mm cine photography, once you match f-stop, distance, and field of view. The traditional solution to reduce this major increase in depth of field has been to use the widest aperture of the lens and then try to work in close-focus or at the telephoto end of the zoom in order to throw the background into soft focus. However, in smaller shooting spaces where wider-angle lenses need to be employed, this solution does not reduce depth of field appreciably.

There are some 35mm lens adaptors on the market that project the lens image onto a 35mm-sized groundglass screen, which is then rephotographed by the prosumer camera, thus retaining the field of view and depth of field of these lenses when used in 35mm photography. Since the groundglass screen has a surface pattern and texture, the more advanced adaptors either vibrate or rotate the groundglass while shooting, or use an extremely fine-grained material for the groundglass. The simplest devices simply leave the texture of the groundglass screen over the image. Since the image coming off of the 35mm lens is upside down, some adaptors will also flip the image; otherwise, either the camera itself has to be flipped upside down, or just the viewing monitors (leaving flipping the recorded image until later in post). A few cameras have an image flip feature. The first of these adaptors to hit the market was the P+S Technik Mini35, followed by many variations like the Letus35, MOVIEtube, Redrock M2, Cinemek Guerilla35, Agus35, Brevis35, etc.

In terms of larger sensors that come closer to 35mm in size, the Sony EX1 and EX3 cameras use ½" sensors (6.97mm wide). Most professional HD camcorders used for ENG/EFP work have ⅔" sensors (9.58mm wide). There is only an effective 2.5-stop increase in depth of field with ⅔" photography over 35mm cine photography, which is easier to compensate for by shooting at wider lens apertures—at least compared to ⅓" photography. The

Blackmagic Cinema Camera uses a sensor that is almost 16mm wide. The Panasonic AG-FS100 uses a Micro 4/3 sensor, which is about 80% as large as a 35mm motion picture frame (the sensor is about 18mm wide versus 24mm wide). Finally, there are now affordable models with 35mm-sized sensors in them—for example, the Canon C300 and Sony FS700U, NEX-FS100, NEX-VG10, and PMW-F3 all use a 35mm-sized sensor.

There are also digital still cameras with 35mm-sized sensors that shoot HD video. Some even have a "full-frame" (FF) 35mm sensor, 36mm x 24mm, which is the same size as the 8-perf 35mm VistaVision frame. With FF35 cameras, there is an effective 1.5-stop loss in depth of field over 35mm cine photography once you match field of view, distance, and shooting stop.

Today, the shallower-focus look of 35mm photography is no longer restricted to expensive professional cameras; however, keep in mind that with less depth of field comes greater difficulty in follow-focusing during a scene—and good focus is critical if the goal is projection on a large theatrical screen, or even on large consumer HDTVs.

SHOOTING HD VIDEO ON A DIGITAL STILL CAMERA

Digital still cameras have had limited video capabilities for years now, but recently, many have been able to shoot progressive-scan HD, either 720P or 1080P. This type of photography has been labeled "V-DSLR", "HD-DSLR", "HDSLR" or "DSLR Video" in various online forums and publications (though some of the still cameras being used are not actually DSLR's but are mirrorless.) Their small size, low cost, and high sensitivity have opened up new possibilities in cinematography.

Some issues to consider:

▶ *Sensor sizes.* Many cameras have an APS-C sensor, which varies from 22mm to 24mm in width, roughly the same size as the 3-perf 35mm cine frame. Because of this, sometimes this sensor size is referred to as "Super-35" (S35). The Canon EOS 7D and the Canon Rebels fall into this category, as well as the Nikon D90, D5000, and D300s. The Canon EOS 5D Mark III, Nikon D4 and D800 have a FF35 sensor (full-frame 35mm) comparable in size to the 8-perf 35mm VistaVision frame (36mm wide). Less common is the APS-H sensor used by the Canon EOS 1D Mark IV, which is between the APS-C and FF35 sizes, around 29mm in width. There is also the Micro 4/3 sensor used by cameras such as the Panasonic Lumix DMC-GH2, which is around 18mm in width, somewhere between Super-35 and Super-16 in size. Finally, more and more compact (a.k.a. "point-and-shoot") digital still cameras, most with small sensors, can now shoot HD, though usually 720/30P.

▶ ***Depth of field.*** The larger FF35 sensor, such as in the Canon 5D Mark III or Nikon D800, requires longer focal-length lenses be used to match the same field of view of shorter focal-length lenses on a 35mm cine camera, a 1.5X conversion factor. This will lead to a shallower-focus look unless compensated for by stopping down the lens. In practical terms, it's roughly a 1.5-stop difference in effective depth of field. The lower noise floor of the larger sensors help in this regard, giving you the flexibility of rating the camera at a higher ISO in order to shoot at a deeper stop. The APS-C sensor (such as in the Canon 7D) allows the same depth of field characteristics as 35mm cine cameras.

▶ ***Lens selection.*** Due to the flange depth of most PL-mount cine lenses, the mirror shutter in a DSLR can make it difficult to mount these lenses without risk of hitting the mirror. An increasingly popular aftermarket solution has been to remove the mirror shutter and add a PL-mount; still photography remains possible but would be limited to using the LiveView function. There are also some cine lenses made with a flange depth that does not interfere with the mirror function. Another option is to use a camera without a mirror shutter, such as the Panasonic Lumix DMC-GH2. Adaptors are made that allow a PL-mount lens to use the still camera's mount; however, these still camera mounts are not as robust as the PL-mount. Due to small variations in flange-to-sensor distances between still camera bodies, a cine lens shimmed to the correct depth for one still camera may be slightly off on another body, so test your set of lenses if you plan on sharing them between multiple bodies.

▶ ***Lens coverage.*** PL-mount cine lenses are normally designed to cover a Super-35 area, though many medium-to-long focal-length lenses will cover the larger FF35 area. Therefore the problem becomes finding the shorter PL-mount lenses that will cover FF35 for your wide-angle shots. However, if your frame of reference is Super-35 photography and you are trying to decide what short focal-length lenses you need, remember that a 50mm lens on a FF35 camera has approximately the same horizontal view as a 35mm lens on a Super-35 camera. There are also some PL-mount lenses on the market designed to cover FF35, such as the Zeiss Compact Primes. At the moment, however, it is more common to use still camera lenses on a FF35 camera shooting HD.

▶ ***Focusing still camera lenses.*** On most DSLR's, the Auto-Focus function does not work continuously in HD mode, unlike with many consumer video zooms (there are some exceptions like the Panasonic DMC-GH2 and Nikon D800.) While focusing the lens by hand is possible, many opt to add a bracket under the camera for holding standard 15mm rods, allowing a follow-focus unit to be attached, as well as a mattebox and various motors as needed. The still camera lens itself will need a toothed focus ring, either through conversion or attachment. The short barrel rotation of still camera lenses from minimum focus to infinity is one of the biggest challenges for focus-pullers, hence the interest in adapting cine optics to these cameras.

▶ *Recording.* Many of these cameras record 8-bit 4:2:0 1080P using AVC/H.264; others record 8-bit 4:2:0 720P using Motion-JPEG. Many of these cameras have a per-shot recording time limit of 5 to 12 minutes. Recently the recording time has been increased to just under 30 minutes in some models.

▶ *Storage.* Footage is recorded internally to CF and/or SD/SDHC cards. You will need to use an SD card with a higher class speed rating for recording HD video.

▶ *Frame rates for slow-motion.* While most of these cameras can shoot at 24/25/30 fps (or 23.98 and 29.97), 720P is often the highest resolution possible for 50/60 fps. However, 1080/60P is beginning to appear on the latest models.

▶ *Monitoring.* Most of these cameras have a mini-HDMI connection that can be fed to an external monitor; however, this usually disables the camera's LCD, requiring that the operator use an attached monitor which then is daisy-chained to other monitors. When not connected to an external monitor, some operators use a focusing loupe attached over the camera's back-panel LCD as a form of eyepiece. The Canon 7D always sends a 59.94 Hz interlaced signal through the HDMI port, whereas the monitor output of the Canon 5D Mark II drops to 480P while the camera is recording (the Mark III sends out a 720P signal however). The Nikon D90, on the other hand, allows you to select different formats for the HDMI-out; however playback is always 720P. While the D90 is recording, the resolution of the HDMI-out is reduced.

▶ *Bypassing the internal recorder.* There has been some interest in trying to record the HDMI-out from these cameras as a way of bypassing the highly compressed recording format; however, due to on-screen information (such as the red dot that appears in the top corner of the HDMI-out image during recording, or the white rectangle indicating the area used for Auto-Focus, or any letterboxing or pillarboxing), the usable picture information is somewhat limited even when the signal is 1080i. Also, 24P capture would have a pulldown added for a 1080/60i HDMI-out, and it may not be the type of pulldown designed for clean extraction in post back to 24P. The Nikon D800 does allow clean, uncompressed 8-bit 4:2:2 HD to be sent out by HDMI to an external recorder.

▶ *Audio.* These cameras lack XLR mic inputs and many only use AGC (Automatic Gain Control) for setting the audio levels, though some newer models are adding manual control. Of course, one could record the sound on a separate unit and sync it with picture in post—some people are using small portable recorders like the Zoom H4N and Tascam DR-100 alongside their DSLR. In the meanwhile, the biggest challenge for those wishing to record sound on a camera without manual audio controls has been to defeat the AGC. There are various devices on the market that do this by sending a tone to one of the two stereo channels, keeping the noise floor consistent during moments of quiet. For example, the Beachtek DXA-SLR and the JuicedLink DT454 have an AGC disabler, as well as XLR mic inputs, pre-amps and phantom power. Over time, more of these cameras will allow manual audio control but you may still need attached devices to allow XLR mic inputs and provide phantom power.

▶ *Picture quality.* These cameras do not offer a full-sensor RAW recording capability as of yet, because of limitations in processing power and data recording capacity needed to handle such large files (these cameras are primarily designed for still photography after all.) The Canon 5D Mark III, for example, has a 22MP sensor; a single frame of 1080P video, on the other hand, is only 2MP. To get around this problem, most of these cameras employ coarse downsampling techniques to reduce the amount of sensor data to be processed into HD video. This can reduce effective resolution and create aliasing and chroma moiré artifacts. Also, the reset rate of the rolling shutter creates a distortion called "skewing" during fast motion.

▶ *Postproduction.* H.264 and the other similar compression schemes, plus the color and luminance limitations of an 8-bit 4:2:0 recording, can have an impact on flexibility in color-correction. Also, the contrast of the DSLR video image was really designed for immediate viewing on a monitor, making it somewhat high for material to be color-corrected. The common solution has been to set the contrast level as low as possible through the camera's menu; some people are also loading custom gamma curves.

Future improvements in camera processing should reduce many of the artifacts, and more and more post solutions are being developed to maximize the quality of the footage. For now, however, the best solution is to shoot the best image you can in-camera, working within the more limited dynamic range of the recording and avoiding situations where aliasing and skewing can become a distraction. Also keep in mind that some of these still cameras do not have exposure aids common to video cameras such as zebras or histograms while rolling, nor focusing aids such expanded view or peaking.

A final note: some of the after-market alterations we are talking about, such as removing the mirror shutter and adding a PL-mount, plus buying a set of PL-mount lenses, not to mention all the desired accessories (mattebox, lens support, follow-focus unit, focusing loupe, handheld rig, remote focusing device, onboard HD monitor, etc.) may drive an initial investment of a few thousand dollars beyond the budgetary limit of $15,000 that this article is focused on.

BEYOND DSLR VIDEO

The popularity of using still cameras to shoot HD video has led manufacturers to start making video cameras with the larger sensors. One challenge for manufacturers is to create ENG-style electronic zoom lenses that cover the larger sensor while maintaining affordability for the consumer (not to mention, avoiding making physically larger lenses). Of course, adding standard video camera features and lenses generally means that the cost of ownership is going to be higher than with still cameras that have an HD mode; however, there may be a need for fewer accessories as a result of buying a product specifically made to shoot video.

A SELECTION OF CAMERAS

The breakdown is based around average retail prices for the body only. Please note that some of these cameras will need more accessories than others to become production-friendly, and some do not come with lenses at their base price. All of these factors can add dramatically to the cost of ownership. Keep in mind that it is possible to find deals on many of these cameras. Also, this is only a selection of what is available; new products are constantly being released, and existing products are constantly being updated with new features.

A few cameras allow a significantly better image, with attendant higher data rates, to be recorded using external recorders. However, some of these recorders are more expensive than the cameras mentioned.

High-end (in the $8,000-$15,000 range, or slightly higher)

▶ *Canon C300.* Single 35mm (S35) CMOS sensor. Records 8-bit 4:2:2 1080P using Canon XF codec at 50 Mbps to CF cards; Canon Log gamma option.

▶ *Canon EOS 1D C.* Still camera (DSLR) with FF35 18MP CMOS sensor. Capable of outputting 8-bit 4:2:2 Motion JPEG 4K video to a CF card at 24 fps (4K uses an APS-H crop of the sensor). Also records 8-bit 4:2:0 1080P video at either 24P or 60P using full-frame of the sensor, with option to use a S35 crop. Uncompressed 8-bit 4:2:2 signal output via the HDMI-out.

▶ *Canon XF305.* ⅓" 3-CMOS, 2.1MP full-res 1080P sensors. Records 8-bit 4:2:2 MPEG-2 (50 Mb/sec) to CF cards. Comes with Canon 4.1–738mm zoom.

▶ *Ikonoskop A-Cam dII.* 16mm CCD 1080P sensor. Sends uncompressed RAW in CinemaDNG format to integrated SSD recorder.

▶ *Panasonic AG-HPX370.* ⅓" 3-CMOS, 2.1MP full-res 1080P sensors. Records 10-bit 4:2:2 AVC-Intra (1080i, 1080P, 720P), plus 8-bit DVCPRO-HD, DVCPRO50, DVCPRO, and DV. 12–60 fps. P2 card recording (two slots). Comes with Fujinon 4.5-76.5mm zoom.

▶ *Red Scarlet.* 35mm (S35) CMOS sensor, 4K. Modular design; components sold individually. Records 4K RAW using Redcode compression to SSDs.

▶ *Sony NEX-FS700U.* 35mm (S35) CMOS sensor, 4K. Records 1080P using AVCHD to SD card/MemoryStick or via the FMU (flash memory unit) port, or it can output 8-bit 4:2:2 (with embedded timecode) via HDMI 1.4 or 3G/HD-SDI to an external recorder. High frame rates in short bursts (8 to 16 seconds) up to 240 fps at full resolution or 960 fps at reduced resolution. Future option allowing 4K output to external recorder.

▶ *Sony XDCAM PMW-EX3.* ½" 3-CMOS, full-res 1080P sensors. Records 8-bit 4:2:0 MPEG-2 (XDCAM, up to 35 Mbit/sec) & DVCAM, to SxS ExpressCards (two slots). 1–60 fps (720P); 1–30 fps (1080P). Time-lapse capability. Uses ½" EX Mount.

▶ *Sony XDCAM PMW-F3.* 35mm (S35) CMOS sensor. Records XDCAM HD to SxS cards. Optional 10-bit 4:4:4 S-Log out to external recorder.

Mid-range (in the $3000-8,000 range)
▶ *Blackmagic Cinema Camera.* Single CMOS sensor that is 15.1mm x 8.08mm. Records uncompressed 12-bit 2.5K RAW data (CinemaDNG) or compressed 1080P HD (ProRes or DNxHD) to 2.5" SSD's. EF & ZE lens mount.

▶ *Canon EOS 5D Mark III.* Still camera (DSLR) with a single FF35 22MP CMOS sensor. Records to CF or SD cards.

▶ *Canon XF105.* Single ⅓" CMOS sensor. Records 8-bit 4:2:2 MPEG2 (50 Mbit/sec) to CF cards.

▶ *JVC GY-HM750U.* ⅓" 3-CCD sensors. Records 8-bit 4:2:0 MPEG2 (1080P, 1080i, 720P), up to 35 Mbit/sec, to SDHC cards (two slots). Optional SxS card adaptor. 1–30 fps (1080P/i) or 1–60 fps (720P). Comes with detachable Canon f/1.6 4.4–61.6mm zoom.

▶ *JVC GY-HM250U.* ⅓" 3-CCD sensors. Records 8-bit 4:2:0 MPEG2 (720P, 480P/i), up to 35 Mbit/sec, to HDV tape. Optional SxS card adaptor. 1–30 fps (1080P/i) or 1–60 fps (720P). Comes with detachable Canon f/1.6 4.4–61.6mm zoom.

▶ *JVC GY-HM100U.* ¼" 3-CCD sensors. Records 8-bit 4:2:0 MPEG2 (1080P, 1080i, 720P), up to 35 Mbit/sec, to SDHC cards (two slots). 1–30 fps (1080P/i) or 1–60 fps (720P). Fixed Fujinon f/1.8 3.7–37mm zoom.

▶ *Nikon D800.* Still camera (DSLR) with FF35 36MP CMOS sensor. Records to CF or SD cards. Has clean 8-bit 4:2:2 HDMI-out for recording to external device.

▶ *Panasonic AG-AC160.* ⅓" 3-CMOS sensors. Records 1080P, 1080i, 720P using SD cards to MPEG-4 AVC/H.264. Switchable between 50Hz and 60Hz at variable frame rates.

▶ *Panasonic AG-AF100.* Single Micro 4/3 CMOS sensor. Shoots 12–60 fps; records 1080P, 1080i, and 720P using SD cards to MPEG-4 AVC/H.264. Has HD-SDI out. Micro 4/3 lens mount.

▶ *Panasonic AG-HMC150P.* ⅓" 3-CCD sensors. Records 1080P, 1080i, 720P using SD cards to MPEG-4 AVC/H.264 (up to 24 Mbit/sec). Fixed f/1.6 3.9–51mm zoom.

▶ *Panasonic AG-HPX250PJ.* ⅓" 3-CMOS sensors. Allows 10-bit 4:2:2 HD recording using AVC-Intra 100 format to P2 cards. Also records in AVC Intra 50, DVPRO HD, as well as standard def DV formats.

▶ *Sony HDR-AX2000.* ⅓" 3-CMOS 720P sensor, records 1080/24P to 60i using Sony Memory Stick or SD cards. MPEG-4 AVC/H.264 (up to 24 Mbit/sec). Fixed f/1.6 4.1–82mm zoom.

▶ *Sony NEX-FS100U.* Single APS-C 35mm CMOS sensor. Shoots 1–60 fps at 1080P. Records using Sony Memory Stick or SD cards to MPEG-4 AVC/H.264. Uses Sony E-mount lenses.

▶ *Sony NXCAM HXR-NX5U.* ⅓" 3-CMOS. Records 8-bit 4:2:0 ACVHD to Sony Memory Stick PRO Duo (two slots) or SDHC cards. Optional attachable 128GB flash memory unit (HXR-FMU128). Fixed Sony 4.1–82mm zoom.

▶ *Sony XDCAM PMW-EX1R.* ½" 3-CMOS, full-res 1080P sensors. Records 8-bit 4:2:0 MPEG-2 (XDCAM, up to 35 Mbit/sec) & DVCAM, to SxS ExpressCards (two slots). 1–60 fps (720P); 1–30 fps (1080P). Time-lapse capability. Fixed Fujinon f/1.9 5.8–81.2mm zoom.

Low-end (under $3000)

▶ *Canon EOS 7D.* Still camera (DSLR) with single 35mm (APS-C) 18MP CMOS sensor. Records 1080P/720P/480P using 8-bit 4:2:0 H.264 to CF cards.

▶ *Canon Vixia HF S21.* Single ½.₆" CMOS (3264 x 1840 pixels) sensor. Records AVCHD to SD cards (two slots) or internal 64GB flash drive. 24P/30P/60i. Fixed f/1.8 6.4–64mm zoom.

▶ *Canon XA10.* Single ⅓" CMOS sensor. Records to internal 64GB flash drive in 8-bit 4:2:0 MPEG-4-AVC H.264 (up to 17 Mbits/sec) Fixed f/1.8 4.25–42.5mm zoom.

▶ *Panasonic AVCCAM AG-HMC40.* ¼" 3-CMOS. Records 8-bit 4:2:0 AVCHD to SD/SDHC cards (two slots).

▶ *Panasonic Lumix DMC-GH2.* Still camera (mirrorless) with single Micro 4/3 16MP CMOS sensor. Records AVCHD to SD/SDHC cards.

▶ *Sony NEX-VG10.* Single APS-C 35mm sensor. Using Sony Memory Stick or SD cards, records 30P to 1080/60i using MPEG-4-AVC H.264 (up to 24 Mbits/sec). No 24P. Sony E-mount lenses.

The author would like to thank Adam Wilt, Randy Wedick, Charles Crawford, and Phil Rhodes for their technical advice.

M. David Mullen, ASC is a member of the Academy of Motion Picture Arts and Sciences. He has photographed more than thirty independent feature films and two television series. He has received two IFP Independent Spirit Award nominations for Best Cinematography, the first for Twin Falls Idaho *(2000) and the second for* Northfork *(2004).*

Putting the Image on Film

by Rob Hummel,
ASC Associate Member

The section on Exposure, together with the associated tables, is intended as a quick-reference condensation of material explained in more detail elsewhere in the manual. The section on Special Techniques contains additional information on many other photographic situations.

EXPOSURE

Most exposure meters incorporate some sort of calculator—some simple, some sophisticated. An exposure meter measures light, either incident or reflected. The calculator helps you decide how to use the light. There are six specific variables entering the calculation:

Variables	Expressed as:
Film exposure index	EI, ASA/ISO
Camera Speed	FPS (frames per second)
Shutter Opening	Degrees
Lens Aperture	T-stop/F-stop
Filter	Filter factor
Light	Meter reading: Footcandles, Footlamberts

T-STOPS

The "T" stop number is defined as being the true "f" stop number of a lens if it is completely free from all reflection and absorption losses. The T (transmission) number represents the f-stop number of an open circular hole or of a perfect lens having 100-percent axial transmission. The T-stop can be considered as the "effective" f-stop. It is from this concept that the means arises for standardization of T-stop calibration. T-stops are calibrated by measuring the light intensity electronically at the focal plane, whereas f-stops are calculated mathematically, purely on the basis of dividing the focal length of the lens by the diameter of the effective aperture (entrance pupil). Thus, f-stops are based on the light that enters a lens, while T-stops are based on the intensity of the light that emerges from the rear of the lens and forms the image.

There is no fixed ratio, however, between T-stops and f-stops that applies to all lenses. The difference actually represents light losses within the elements of a given lens due to reflection from the glass-air surfaces and from absorption within the glass itself. Consequently, this factor is variable and cannot be incorporated into an exposure meter, since the meter must function in connection with many different lenses calibrated in both f-stops and T-stops.

The reason why lens and exposure tables are presented in f-stops when all professional cine lenses are calibrated in T-stops, is that the f-stops are required for all calculations involving object-image relationships, such as depth of field, extreme close-up work with extension tubes, etc. Such tables are based on the size of the "hole" or diameter of the bundle of light rays that the lens admits to form the image. The diameter of the f-stop will normally be the same for all lenses of similar focal length set at the same aperture. The T-stop, however, is an arbitrary number that may result in the same T-stop setting varying in aperture diameter with different lenses.

It is recommended that all professional cine lenses be calibrated in both T-stops and f-stops, particularly for color work. T-stop calibration is especially important with zoom lenses, the highly complex optical design of which necessitates a far greater number of optical elements than is required in conventional lenses. A considerable light loss is encountered due to the large number of reflective optical surfaces and absorption losses. A zoom lens with a geometrical rating of f/2, for example, will transmit considerably less light than a conventional fixed-focal-length lens of similar rating with fewer elements.

Exposure tables are generally based on "effective" f-stops (which are, in fact, T-stops). Small variations in emulsion speed, processing, exposure readings, etc., tend to cancel out. Cinematographers should shoot tests with their particular lenses, meter, light and film to find the best combinations for optimum results.

Other variables such as direction and contrast of the light are factors calculated from the experience of the cinematographer, aided by such tools as photospheres and spot readings. Finally, manipulation of all the above, plus special negative processing to achieve a desired "look," is determined by the cinematographer.

The laboratory and choice of film are closely tied to exposure. It is important to keep exposure within limits satisfactory both to the selected film and to the printing range of the laboratory.

The tables on pages 812, 813 and 866 through 877 will aid exposure calculation for meters that lack settings for some of the factors, or will aid in calculating constant exposure control when one factor varies from another.

Comparisons of 35mm, 1.85, Anamorphic, Super 35 Film Formats

by Rob Hummel
Editor of the 8th edition
of the American Cinematographer Manual

INTRODUCTION

This chapter has always addressed creative aesthetic and technical differences depending on the choice of 35mm film format. The most salient change from earlier versions of this chapter is the impact of digital intermediate (DI) on final image quality.

While a DI can improve upon image quality that might degrade when created at a film lab, it does so at greater expense. On many films, that expense is trivial when compared to the overall cost of the film; on others, it may be a significant portion of the budget. In 2011, John Bailey, ASC saved a low-budget film substantially and was able to achieve everything desired from the image with a photochemical answer print. It is becoming increasingly rare to color correct a film in this manner, but it is still available.

Also, 2K DIs have made formats such as Super 35 and anamorphic appear almost equal in quality. Filmmakers often assume this is because the DI process makes the Super 35 image look so much better. While a 2K DI does improve the image quality of a Super 35 image, the only reason the image looks competitive with an anamorphic DI, is because a 2K DI sacrifices the image quality contained in the anamorphic frame. With the further rollout of 4K scanning and 4K DI workflows, the superior image quality of anamorphic imaging over Super 35 is now readily apparent again. 4K scanning begins to approach capturing all the resolution that the anamorphic image has to offer. While Super 35 benefits from 4K scanning, the improvements are not as dramatic.

Lastly, the focus of this piece has always been about image quality. That being said, I recognize, more than most, that we're not in the medical imaging business, we're in the motion picture business. When I reference grain, or noise in an image, I recognize that image quality may actually be what you desire in your picture. Where this chapter may talk about one format having superior image quality to another, you shouldn't take offense if the lower quality image is the preferred method for telling your story.

What's New

▶ A new section on how to evaluate images effectively, and discusses the importance of screen heights, complete with illustrations. (Page 60)

▶ For motion pictures that will enjoy an IMAX release, you will find a page briefly illustrating how that process works. (See Figure 11)

▶ If you are considering digital cameras instead of film, after the discussion of film formats and aspect ratios, you will find a new section with guidelines and information to help you understand what to look for when examining a digital camera. This should allow you to make an informed decision about what will most benefit your motion picture; whether comparing various digital cameras or comparing digital to film(see page 81).

Screen Heights are Critical!

When evaluating digitally captured or film originated imagery, it is important to examine the images at a proper distance from the screen, and on a screen of sufficient size. The distance one views an image is measured by multiples of the height of the image, or screen heights.

Using screen heights as a measurement of distance from the screen is all about quantifying the magnification of the image you are viewing. The closer you are to the screen, the greater the magnification, and the more demands are placed on the quality of the projected image. For example, the more you magnify an image in a printed magazine, the more you will start to discern the dots that make up the image; the further you hold the magazine away from you, the less likely you can see those dots. By way of example, you probably want to ensure you are evaluating the images you photograph from the same distance your audience will be viewing them. If you evaluate the image from too far away, you can be fooled into thinking the image is of better quality than it is.

In the case of today's state-of-the-art stadium seat theaters, that should be somewhere from 1 to 1½ screen heights from the screen. Most Stadium seat

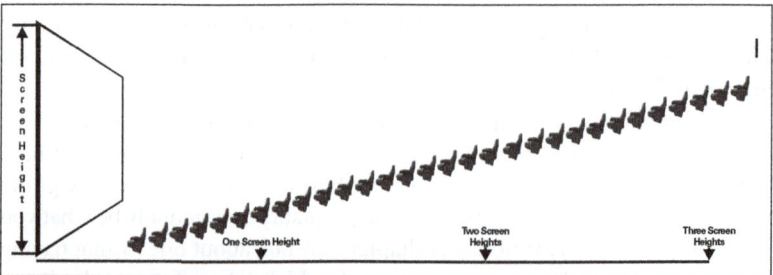

Figure 1: A typical stadium seat theater design, illustrating how many screen heights the audience is from the image.

Figure 2: As an example of how an image can improve with distance, hold the above image at arm's length and it will probably look just fine. Upon closer examination, you will notice the difference between the right and left sides of the picture.

theaters are no more than 3 to 3½ screen heights deep (see Figure 1).

When you are closer than seven screen heights away from your normal standard definition television set, you can resolve the pixels and scanning lines that make up the image. However, further than seven screen heights away, and it is impossible to resolve any of the picture elements that make up the image; basically, the image will appear as sharp as your eyes can resolve.

For example, if you were looking at an IMAX image and a standard definition TV image side by side, but you were evaluating the images from 7 screen heights away, both images would appear to have equal resolution. Once you got closer than 7 to 6 screen heights, the TV image would begin to exhibit its poor image quality, while the IMAX image would look exemplary at closer than ½ a screen height. If you have been in an IMAX theater, take notice that the back row of the theater is rarely much more than one screen height away from the screen; something IMAX can do because of the dramatically high resolution of IMAX photography.

At the risk of stating the obvious; the higher resolution the image, the closer you can get to the image before noticing pixels (in the case of digital) or grain (in the case of film).

In the case of HDTV, you have to get closer than three screen heights before you can start to see the pixels in the image. In current stadium seat theaters, our audiences are sitting no further than three screen heights from the images, and, in most cases, closer than two screen heights. For this reason, it's important we evaluate imagery from the same screen distance as our audience.

In the image above, your proximity to the image affects your perception of the image quality.

Most studios still have screening rooms that place you anywhere from six to eight screen heights from the image. Therefore, when sitting that far from the screen, you can fool yourself into thinking the image quality is adequate, perhaps even superb. Yet, when viewed from a distance of 1½ to 2 screen heights, your conclusions may be entirely different. Please make sure when evaluating image quality, you place yourself within 2 screen heights of the projected image. It is important that critical evaluation of image quality be viewed from where the audience will see the picture.

Also, the display medium must be taken into consideration as well. Many people evaluate high-definition (HD) or 2K images on HD displays that can resolve only 1400 of the 1920 horizontal pixels contained in an HD image. Those 520 missing pixels of resolution can hide artifacts that will show up clearly on a digital cinema projector, or a 35mm film out.

FILM FORMATS
History and a Definition of Terms

Currently, in the United States (and most of the world), the most prevalent motion picture film formats, or aspect ratios, are 1.85 and 2.40 (2.40 is still often referred to as 2.35).[1] As a point of reference, these ratios are determined by dividing the width of the picture by the height, which is why you will also see them written as 1.85:1 or 2.40:1. Verbally, you will hear them referred to as "one eight five" or "two four oh." 2.40 is also referred to as anamorphic, or "Scope," referring to its roots in CinemaScope.

An examination of films over the past sixty years shows that format is not automatically dictated by dramatic content. It is a creative choice, determined by the cinematographer and director. The full range of drama, comedy, romance, action, or science fiction can be found in both aspect ratios. The purpose here is to advise on the pros and cons of both aspect ratios and the photographic alternatives available to achieve them. This should help a filmmaker make an informed decision as to which format is best for a given project. Most importantly, you will be presented with the "conventional wisdom" arguments for and against the formats; this conventional wisdom will either be endorsed or countered with reality. This knowledge, in the end, will help you realize that, creatively, there are no technical obstacles to choosing any format. However, you will also understand the aesthetic impact those choices will have upon your production.

---

1. A historical note regarding 2.35 vs. 2.40 vs. 2.39. CinemaScope films with an analog soundtrack were originally an aspect ratio of 2.35:1. In the early 1970s, the height of the anamorphic aspect ratio was modified slightly by SMPTE to help hide splices, effectively changing the ratio to 2.40:1. Old habits die hard and many still refer to the format as 2.35:1. Also, in 1995, SMPTE again made a change in the size of the CinemaScope projection area to accommodate digital soundtracks. In both cases the math of the aspect ratio yields an aspect ratio number of 2.39 and continues on several places to the right of the decimal point. Cinematographers felt that rounding up to 2.40 ensured there would be less confusion with the 2.35 aspect ratio. The actual difference between 2.39 and 2.40 is so inconsequential that, from a compositional standpoint, they are the same.

As a clarification, the term full aperture refers to the entire image area between the 35mm perforations, including the area normally reserved for the soundtrack. In other literature you will find full aperture used interchangeably with camera aperture, silent aperture and full silent aperture. All four terms define the same area of the 35mm film frame.

In general, the term Academy aperture is used when referring to the imaging area of the negative excluding the analog soundtrack area. More properly, it would be referred to as the "sound aperture," the term used to indicate the area that remained when analog soundtracks were first added to 35mm film. However, throughout this chapter, we will follow convention, and use the term Academy aperture when referring to the imaging area excluding the soundtrack.

Academy aperture[2] is an aspect ratio of 1.37:1, centered within the sound aperture area, arrived at jointly by the American Society of Cinematographers and Academy of Motion Picture Arts and Sciences in the early days of sound to restore compositions closer to the 1.33 aspect ratio of silent films, and resolve the unpleasant composition produced by framing images within the narrow sound aperture.

All 1.85 composed films are achieved with "normal," spherical lenses. However, the 2.40 aspect ratio can be achieved two ways. One method is with the use of anamorphic[3] lenses that squeeze the image to fit within the Academy aperture (see Figure 6). The alternate method (see Super 35 in Figures 7, 8, and 9) uses normal lenses without any distortion of the image, and then is later squeezed for theatrical film release. Both methods will be discussed here.

The 1.85 and Super 35 formats can also be captured using cameras using a 3-perf pull-down movement. While all 35mm illustrations in this chapter use a 4 perforation frame, were you to use a 3-perf camera for 1.85 or Super 35, the advantages and disadvantages remain the same whether 3 or 4 perf.

3-perf camera movements do not provide adequate height for anamorphic photography.

Also, the film formats discussed here deal with general 35mm motion picture photography. Formats such as VistaVision and 65mm are most often

---

2. If you actually calculate the aspect ratio of Academy aperture from SMPTE specs, the math has always come out to 1.37:1. More often than not, people will refer to Academy aperture compositions as 1.33 (the original aspect ratio of silent films), and almost never is the ratio called 1.37. The compositional difference between the two is negligible.

---

3. Anamorphic comes from the word anamorphosis, meaning an image that appears distorted, yet under the proper conditions will appear normal again. Leonardo da Vinci is credited with first using the technique during the Renaissance.

used for visual effects and special event cinematography and would require an chapter of their own to discuss. However, Figures 10 and 11 illustrate how widescreen compositions are presented when converted to IMAX, and how films photographed in 65mm are released in 70mm.

At the end of this chapter, we'll cover current methods for achieving 1.85 and 2.40 aspect ratios with currently available digital cameras.

COMPOSITION

Before getting into specifics about the different formats, I want to point out the composition differences between the two aspect ratios 2.40 and 1.85, regardless of how they are achieved photographically.

Figure 3 is an image of the Taj Mahal with a 2.40 aspect ratio outlined in yellow.

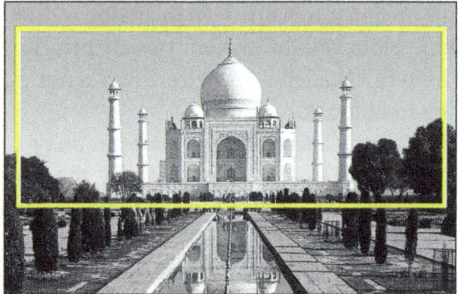

Figure 3: The yellow rectangle within the image outlines a 2.40:1 aspect ratio.

In Figure 4, two 1.85 aspect ratios are outlined by yellow rectangles. The larger of those two rectangles represents a 1.85 composition equal in its width to the 2.40 aspect ratio of Figure 3. The smaller 1.85 rectangle is equal in height to the 2.40 ratio of Figure 3.

The purpose here, is to illustrate that, depending on your framing, a 1.85 image has potential of encompass-

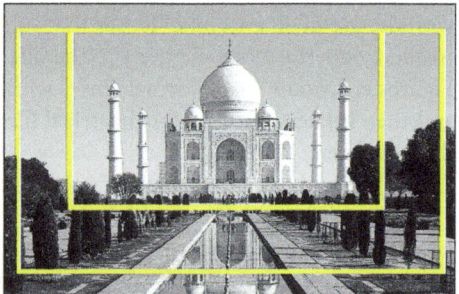

Figure 4: Two 1.85 compositions.

ing as much width as a 2.40 composition. Although 1.85 will take in the same width with greater height in the composition, it's important to realize that wide sets and vistas are not restricted to the 2.40 format.

PROS AND CONS – A CLARIFICATION

While this chapter addresses the pros and cons of these formats, it can appear contradictory upon reading when a disadvantage is countered with an opposite perceived advantage, and vice versa. This is because, in fact, many pros and cons are merely mythology about a certain shooting format, and are based on nothing other than conventional wisdom, or outdated production practices, rather than current practical experience.

I believe you will be able to sort the facts from opinions. That being said, nothing here is intended to dissuade you from choosing a given film format. Where there are possible true disadvantages to a format, it is presented so you have your eyes wide open to any potential challenges or creative compromises. We are working in a very artistic medium where there can truly be no absolute rights and wrongs. What one person may find an objectionable grainy image, another filmmaker may feel enhances the story being told.

Where possible, when listing outdated opinions, I immediately counter with the present fact, or contrary point of view. With this presentation, I want you to be able to draw your own conclusions and inform you with all the arguments and points of view about these formats. If you study it carefully, you will be able to effectively articulate your desire to photograph a film in the aspect ratio you feel will most benefit the story.

I. THE 1.85 ASPECT RATIO
Photographed in Normal Academy Aperture Photography

Until the early 1990s, 1.85 was far and away the most common aspect ratio for motion pictures filmed in the United States since the late 1950s. This trend shifted a bit in the 1990s with the advent of more and more films composed for the 2.40 aspect ratio. With the proliferation of films photographed in Super 35, in recent years, less then one third of the top 100 motion pictures are composed in 1.85. Around the world the spherical aspect ratio most commonly used swung between 1.85 and 1.66 depending on the country; however, in many countries that used to photograph exclusively in the 1.66 aspect ratio, 1.85 has become more common.

Figure 5 portrays how 1.85 films get from camera to screen. In the illustration, the red box indicates the 1.85 composition area of the frame. In actual practice, there is no indication on the exposed negative of the area composed for. The area above and below that area contains picture information, but is masked out when projected or eliminated entirely in the digital intermediate.

A. ADVANTAGES OF 1.85

1. **Intimate Format:** Many perceive 1.85 as more appropriate for pictures that lend themselves to a more compact visual. Since close-ups virtually fill the entire frame, it is often considered a more "intimate" format. However, it can be argued that many "intimate" films have been composed for the 2.40 aspect ratio.

2. **Interiors:** If a film is largely interiors, 1.85 is often argued as the preferred format, since they don't involve the wide panoramic vistas associated with 2.40. Conversely, many do not weigh interiors or exteriors in their choice of format.

Figure 5: Standard Academy 1.85:1

The image at left is a 1.85:1 aspect ratio, and is how that image might appear when composed in the viewfinder of a camera.

The workflow described here is a traditional film laboratory process, that can still be implemented. In a digital intermediate workflow, usually multiple printing negatives are recorded out, eliminating the IP and IN process.

Negative: Unless a hard matte is used in the camera, the entire frame is exposed with image information; including the soundtrack area to the left of the image. The 1.85 aspect ratio is achieved by masking off information above and below the composition. The red boundary delineating the 1.85 composition here are for illustration purposes only, and do not appear on the negative.

Interpositive (IP): To produce a release print, the standard 1.85 negative is first contact printed to a color interpositive The interpositive is similar in appearance to a color negative, yet contains a positive image.

Internegative (IN): The interpositive is then contact printed to a color internegative. This produces the dupe negative that enables mass release print manufacture without risking the original negative.

Release Print: The internegative is then contact printed to color positive print stock to produce the release print. When projected in a theater, the projector will mask out the unwanted image area above and below the 1.85 composition. If the film is not framed properly in the theater, unwanted information can be shown accidentally. Because of this, many filmmakers will use either a 1.66:1 hard matte in the camera, or have the lab build a hard matte into the printing internegative. In this illustration, we present a print that has been hard matted at the lab or DI facility.The Dolby d igital tracks are between the track side perforations; SDDS is outside the perfs; DTS is between the analog track and the picture area.

© 2012 Robert C. Hummel

3. **Depth of Field:** Greater depth of field (the total area in focus at a given distance). Since 1.85 uses shorter focal length lenses as compared with Anamorphic, greater depth of field is available.

    This advantage is often negated when lenses are shot "wide open," resulting in a little or no gain in depth of field.

4. **Composition:** Considered by many to be a "taller" composition. Lending itself to compositions with more emphasis on the vertical than horizontal. Cathedral interiors, or city skylines for example.

5. **Wide Sets:** An opinion often expressed is that sets don't need to be as wide on a 1.85 film as one photographed in 2.40, resulting in savings in set construction. However, there are many that would argue film format has no bearing on the width of set construction. As the examples in Figures 3 and 4 (page 64) point out, it's possible for 1.85 to require as wide a set as 2.40, depending on the composition.

6. **Least Complex:** 1.85 is the simplest format to execute from a mechanical/technical standpoint. The choice of photographic equipment is virtually unlimited, as any standard 35mm camera will accommodate this format. Plus, you have a choice of very wide and "fisheye" lenses not available in anamorphic.

7. **Expendable Cameras:** If a stunt camera mount is required that risks destroying a camera lens, spherical lenses can be used that are much more affordable than expensive anamorphic lenses.

8. **Video Transfers:** While they are effectively not manufactured any more, many production companies, are still concerned about accommodating the 1.33 (4 x 3) aspect ratio of Standard Definition television. With some effort on the shooting company's part, the 1.85 composition can protect for standard definition video so that a simple one-to-one transfer can be done without panning and scanning. While left and right image integrity remain virtually intact this way, there is an approximate 33% increase in the vertical height of the composition.

    Although many think it routine to protect the TV area from intruding objects (e.g., lights, microphones, etc.), it makes the cinematographer and soundman's job more difficult, by not being able to bring lights and microphones down close to the area of composition. This is why many cinematographers shooting 1.85 will request to shoot with a 1.66:1 aspect ratio hard matte. While the same width on the film, 1.66 is slightly taller than 1.85, closely approximating the height of the 1.33 (4 x 3) TV frame. This gives the cameraman more freedom to light his subjects without fear of a light or microphone showing up when transferred to video.

    Yet, in a world where 1.78:1 (16 x 9) aspect ratio video displays are now the norm, 1.85, for all intents and purposes, drops precisely into the HDTV frame. While not precisely the same aspect ratio, the 1.78:1 HDTV frame is only 42 pixels taller than the 1.85 aspect ratio. Meaning, if you did letterbox a 1.85 image in HDTV, you would have two 21-pixel lines above and below the image.

9. **Sharper Lenses:** Many people believe it is an advantage to shoot 1.85 because spherical lenses are sharper than anamorphic 2.40's lenses. This is a misconception. It is true that spherical lenses are often sharper than anamorphic; however, the much greater negative area used with anamorphic more than makes up for the subtle difference in resolution from spherical lenses. Properly executed camera tests comparing the two formats always reach this conclusion.

B. DISADVANTAGES OF 1.85

1. **Negative Area:** The principal disadvantage is the actual size of the 1.85 format on the negative. Because of the smaller area, 1.85 is noticeably grainier than anamorphic 2.40. This is not as noticeable in the original negative stage and projecting in small screening rooms, but becomes more pronounced when projected in large theaters.

   Graininess can be mitigated with digital grain reduction techniques in the DI; however, if not applied carefully, such techniques can render the images looking artificial, a loss of sharpness, and almost video like. When compared to 1.85, anamorphic 2.40 uses 55% more area on the negative. This is not insignificant.

2. **Composition:** Because of the greater height of the 1.85 aspect ratio, ceilings of sets are more prone to being photographed. This can be a restriction on how easily a cameraman can light an interior set (visible ceilings limit where a cameraman can hang lights). On some sets, it may require additional construction, and has been the experience on films shooting on studio back lots. Sound can also be compromised by the microphone having to be farther away.

3. **Magnification:** When projected, the area of the frame for 1.85 is subjected to much greater magnification on a screen than an anamorphic frame, resulting in more apparent grain in the image.

4. **Jump and Weave:** If your motion picture will be projected from a film print, film projectors always have some level of jump and weave, ranging from annoying to barely detectable. Because of 1.85's vertical height on the film frame, it is subjected to a 55% increase in visible jump and weave over an anamorphic image projected in the same theatre. This artifact is eliminated with digital projection.

5. **70mm:** Not truly compatible with standard 70mm: Although it can be done, there is a large amount of unused print on the sides when blown up to 70mm. Also, because of the greater magnification in 1.85/70mm

prints, grain is much more apparent than in anamorphic blow-ups to 70mm. While not generally an issue any more, this may be a choice for special events where a film is to be projected on a particularly large screen (e.g., stadiums or outdoor venues), and 70mm is chosen to mitigate jump/weave and gain more light on the screen. Less of an issue, with the proliferation of digital projection, but still an available option.

II. THE 2.40 ASPECT RATIO
Photographed with Anamorphic (Scope) Lenses

The following is a discussion of the 2.40 aspect ratio photographed with anamorphic lenses. A discussion of Super 35 composed for 2.40 will follow.

Anamorphic 2.40:1 (also known as CinemaScope®, Panavision®, Technovision®, or any other number of brand names), optically squeezes the width of the image to fit within the 35mm full aperture. While this discussion is about current state of the art 35mm anamorphic releases, we are now in an era of digital delivery where use of the area reserved for analog soundtracks could be employed again. For a film only presented digitally, a cinematographer could choose to use the entire full aperture width of the frame and compose for a 2.55 or 2.66:1 aspect ratio as when CinemaScope was originally conceived.

Figure 6 portrays how anamorphic 2.40 images get from camera to screen.

Many myths persist from the early days of CinemaScope when lenses distorted images, film speeds were slow, and sets required the use of arc lamps and their associated lighting crews. With today's sharper anamorphic lenses, combined with higher speed film stocks and more manageable lighting packages, the challenges of shooting anamorphically has all but disappeared.

A. ADVANTAGES of Anamorphic 2.40

1. **Negative Area:** The most salient advantage is the much larger negative area. A 55% increase in negative area over 1.85, results in finer grain, better opticals, and an increase in apparent sharpness (I say apparent, because while a similar image photographed in 1.85 may be sharper, the increase in grain and greater magnification actually make it appear less sharp). This difference becomes most apparent after going through dupe negatives.

2. **Composition:** Allows for complex compositions. Able to do a tight close up on two individuals simultaneously. Action can be spread across a wide expanse of the frame, or a subject can be placed at one extreme edge of the frame with an expanse of negative space emphasizing that subject. Objects can be used to occlude part of the frame, creating an artificially smaller aspect ratio for a given scene or camera angle. Gordon Wills, ASC's cinematography in *Manhattan* does this to great effect, as

Figure 6: Anamorphic 2.40:1

With its roots in CinemaScope, it is still referred to by many as 2.35:1. The anamorphic aspect ratio was actually modified slightly in the early 1970s to 2.40:1. The image at left is how a 2.40:1 composition might appear in the viewfinder of a camera equipped for anamorphic cinematography. Also called "Scope," and "Panavision."

Negative: In photography, anamorphic lenses "squeeze" the image to fit within the 35mm frame. The frame at left is how the "squeezed" image appears on the negative. The area to the left of the image is where the soundtrack is placed in the release print. In truth, image information is exposed in the soundtrack area; it is blank in this example to emphasize it is not normally used in anamorphic cinematography.

Interpositive (IP): To produce a release print, the anamorphic negative is first contact printed to a color interpositive. The interpositive is similar in appearance to a color negative, yet contains a positive image.

Internegative (IN): The interpositive is then contact printed to a color internegative. This produces the dupe negative that enables mass release print manufacture without risking the original negative. In a DI workflow, the IN would be recorded directly out on a laser film recorder, bypassing the IP step altogether.

Release Print: The internegative is then contact printed to color positive print stock to produce the release print. Upon projection in a theater, anamorphic projection lenses "unsqueeze" the image to appear as originally composed above. The Dolby Digital tracks are between the track side perforations; SDDS is outside the perfs; DTS is between the analog track and the picture area.

© 2012 Robert C. Hummel

well as using the wide 2.40 composition to photograph a very vertical city.

3. **Reason for Choice:** Traditionally the format and aspect ratio of choice for films with a lot of action or big production values. Conversely, many successful films have been photographed in this format that were intimate, dramatic interior pieces.

4. **Field of View:** Most closely approximates the normal field of vision.

5. **Lighting:** When shooting interiors, ceilings become obscured, potentially giving the cameraman more alternatives for placement of his lighting. The same applies to exterior city scenes with the possibility of less vertical set construction. However, these advantages rely on the chosen composition.

6. **Image Quality:** A clear advantage is realized when anamorphic negatives are scanned at 4K resolution for projection in digital cinema theaters. The area of negative used in anamorphic films means the grain structure at least equals the resolution of a 4K digital projector, and the benefits of the 4K scan are realized whether projecting in 4K digital cinema, 2K digital cinema, or displayed on a standard definition TV set. The "noisy" grain structure of many 1.85 and Super 35 films is readily apparent even on 2K projectors.

7. **70mm:** While generally only an issue for a special event presentation, anamorphic is more compatible with 70mm. Because of the original negative area, there is less of a blow up than 1.85 or Super 35, resulting in finer grain in the 70mm print. Also, the aspect ratio can more closely fill the entire 70mm print frame's 2.2:1 aspect ratio.

It must be said that poor quality anamorphic optical printing lenses can negate any advantage the anamorphic film element has. It is important that any lab implementing such a blowup uses state of the art optics. Or, in the case of digital film recorders, it is important that the facility executing the blow up uses advanced scaling algorithms.

B. DISADVANTAGES of Anamorphic 2.40

1. **Video Transfer:** Compromise of composition when transferred to standard definition's video aspect ratio. To extract a 1.33 (4 x 3) video image directly from the center of the 2.40 frame usually results in odd compositions and the loss of relevant action.

This is achieved with the "pan and scan" technique (panning the width of the 2.40 frame, following the most important action). While the technique is not more expensive to perform when doing the video transfer, it usually takes longer to perform because of the composition decisions required for each scene. Most importantly, many people feel it damages and compromises the original compositions.

Surprisingly, there still exist m ajor cable channels that transmit a 1.33 standard definition signal and present films panned and scanned.

The alternative is to release videos in letterbox format, where the 2.40 format is maintained by putting black mattes above and below the frame. This is a common practice in DVD releases of films. Letterboxing a 2.40 image with HDTV's 1.78 (16 x 9) aspect ratio isn't objectionable at all, yet there are still cable outlets that resist respecting a film's original composition.

Performing an HDTV 16 x 9 pan and scan can have just as many compositional compromises as those for standard definition TV.

The difficulty in video transfer is the most often stated disadvantage of the 2.40 format.

It has always been the position of the ASC that the original compositions of motion pictures should always be respected. Therefore, letterboxing of widescreen films is the preferred practice. When 1.33 motion pictures are presented on widescreen displays, the image should be presented with "side curtains" or in "pillar-box" format.

2. **Expense:** It is often said that Anamorphic is more expensive than 1.85. However, the difference in cost between an anamorphic lens package vs. a 1.85 lens package is negligible. Panavision 'C' series anamorphic lenses would be less than few thousand dollars more expensive over the course of a ten-week film schedule.

   Also, discussions with a number of prominent cameramen indicate they wouldn't increase the size of their lighting package significantly for the 2.40 aspect ratio. In fact, some say it wouldn't change at all.

3. **Composition:** Single close-ups result in wide areas on either side of a face, with potential for distracting objects in the frame. However, due to the nature of anamorphic's longer focal length lenses, usually anything in the background on either side of a face would be severely out of focus, tending to emphasize the subject.

4. **Set Construction:** Many feel that sets need to be built wider because of the wider aspect ratio. There are also many who feel it doesn't matter, and can be accommodated by choosing lenses carefully. See again Figures 3 and 4 and the discussion under Composition (page 64).

5. **Blocking:** Some directors have a hard time blocking action within the wider frame.

6. **Extras:** Expense of additional extras may be necessary for some crowd scenes.

7. **Valuable lenses:** Anamorphic lenses are far too valuable to risk in any risky stunt situation (Panavision's Primo lenses for example). Thus alternative forms of capture with a Super 35 type of setup must be used, risking the material may not cut well with the balance of the anamor-

phic originated material. Though, if used for a quick action shot, the difference in image quality will, most likely, not be detectable.

III. SUPER 35 FORMATS

The Super 35 formats, also sometimes referred to as Super Techniscope, Super 1.85, and Super 2.35, are all flat, spherical lens formats using similar equipment to that used in 1.85 photography.

When created in the film lab, all of the Super 35 formats require an optical step when making dupe negatives for 35mm release prints. When a digital intermediate is employed, the reformatting happens when a digital negative is created on a laser film recorder, resulting in a remarkably higher quality 35mm release element than one created optically. In digital cinema presentations this is not an issue, as the release element is effectively first generation.

At times, some will suggest shooting Super 35 composed for 1.85 (a.k.a. Super 1.85). The reason for this is the belief that the slight increase in negative area with Super 1.85 will yield a finer grained image for release. In tests with absolutely solid, perfect exposures this difference is almost imperceptible, and is hardly worth the effort for the subtle gain in resolution. The process of sending the image through interpositive and internegative, and repositioning for standard 1.85 release, negates any benefit from the small increase in negative area. In practice, when created photochemically, depending on the scene and how well it has been photographed, Super 1.85 can end up looking worse than standard 1.85.

In a film lab workflow, Standard 1.85 produces all dupe negatives and prints with contact printing, while Super 1.85 requires an optical step to reduce the image into the standard 1.85 area. Contact printing significantly reduces the appearance of grain, while any optical step precisely focuses the grain in a negative, effectively enhancing the appearance of grain.

While a digital intermediate eliminates any generational loss of quality in Super 1.85, the benefits are still not sufficient to justify the effort.

As for arguments that Super 1.85 yields a better 1.85 blow up to 70mm, the difference is subtle, and only noticeable in a direct A/B or side-by-side comparison, otherwise it is indistinguishable. If, however, a scene is already committed to an optical step (i.e., a visual effects shot), Super 1.85 may provide an improvement in negative area that results in a better image quality when compared with a standard 1.85 image going through the same VFX processes.

When people speak of the Super 35 format, they are usually referring to its use composed for a 2.40:1 aspect ratio, the same ratio as anamorphic 2.40.

Anamorphic 2.40 uses special lenses that squeeze the wide image to fit within the special anamorphic aperture frame (full aperture less the analog soundtrack area, a.k.a. the sound aperture). Super 35 composes for 2.40

Figure 7: Super 35/Super Techniscope 2.40:1

The image at left is how a 2.40:1 aspect ration might be composed in the viewfinder of a camer equipped for Super 35 cinematography.

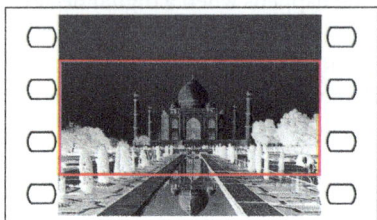

Negative: Super 35 is a full aperture format. This means the entire frame is exposed with image information, including the area normally reserved for the soundtrack. The desired aspect ratio is achieved by masking off information above and below the 2.40:1 composition. The lines delineating the 2.40 composition are for illustration purposes only; these do not appear on the negative.

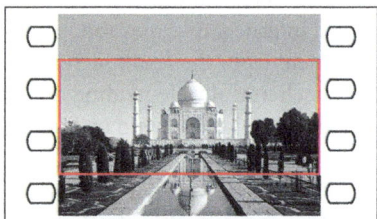

Interpositive (IP): To produce a release print, the general practice is for the full aperture negative to be contact printed to a color interpostive. The interpositive is similar in appearance to a color negative, yet contains a positive image. In a DI workflow, this step would be skipped, and an Internegative would be directly filmed out on a laser film recorder.

Internegative (IN): In order to make room for the soundtrack, the ultimate destination of a Super 35 film is an anamorphic release print. It is at this stage that the 2.40 composition is blown up from the interpositive and squeezed to conform to a standard anamorphic frame on the internegative. This internegative is the dupe negative that enables mass release print manufacture without risking the original negative.

Release Print: The internegative is then contact printed to color positive print stock to produce the release print. Upon projection in a theater, anamorphic projection lenses unsqueeze the image to appear as originally composed above. The Dolby digital tracks are between the track side perforations; SDDS is outside the perfs; DTS is between the analog track and the picture area.

© 2012 Robert C. Hummel

with standard lenses, making use of the full aperture area, extending the width of the frame into that area of the negative traditionally reserved for the soundtrack; yet the composition is just over 2 perfs high. Although most cameras already expose picture information in the soundtrack area, it normally goes unused. Figure 7 portrays how Super 35 composed for 2.40 gets from camera to the screen.

One version of Super 35 is where the image is centered on the frame of film, referred to as common center (see Figure 8). As the figure illustrates, information is exposed over the entire full aperture area of the film. The filmmaker decides what format he is composing for, and it is that aspect ratio the film lab or digital intermediate facility will eventually extract from the frame for theatrical presentation.

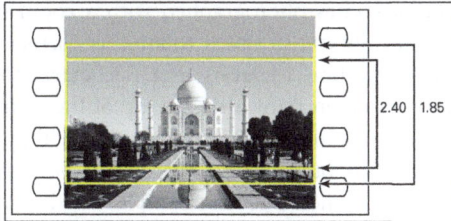

Figure 8: With common center, Super 35 images are aligned with the vertical center of the full aperture frame.

Another method of photography for Super 35 is referred to as common topline (see Figure 9). Common topline derives its name from the ground glass of the camera having multiple formats scribed on it, all having the same, or common, topline.

This variant of Super 35 was originally conceived with the notion that it could be a generic film format; shoot a movie with the option of releasing it in any aspect ratio you want. The common topline was supposed to lessen the effect of changing aspect ratios by maintaining the headroom and raising or lowering the bottom of the frame.

Figure 9: With common topline, Super 35 apect ratios share the same top, or headroom, for their compositions. Compositions other than 2.40:1 are obtained by the bottom of the composition.

However, most cinematographers find that composing for multiple formats neutralizes the effect of any one composition. In actual practice, it has mainly been used to mitigate conversion of Super 35 wide screen films to the 1.33 (4 x 3) aspect ratio of standard television. Yet, even in this application, the change in composition from 2.40 to television's 1.78 or 1.33 aspect ratios can rarely be achieved automatically (close-ups become medium shots, etc.), and usually requires the same care as an Anamorphic pan and scan.

Experience has shown, as most filmmakers will agree, just modifying a film's aspect ratio to fit within the video realm is a creative process. To assume that a generic format will automatically deliver pleasing compositions no matter what aspect ratio you choose will not hold up creatively.

That being said, there are several filmmakers that employ the common topline format with great success and feel it allows them to create a version for those venues still displaying a 4 x 3 image that is less objectionable than panning and scanning. Those most successful at the transformation are careful to evaluate each scene and camera angle on its own merits, and don't attempt a generic framing for an entire film.

Of course, the ideal is to view films in the composition they were originally intended to be seen, without any alteration in the composition.

The only other technical note with regard to the common topline format, is that scenes photographed with a zoom in common topline do not automatically transfer over to another format by just lowering the bottom of the frame line. Meaning, if a 1.33 extraction is performed, the zoom will still be centered towards the top of the frame, where the 2.40 composition is centered, and a 1.33 composition will appear to drift upwards during a zoom. Any other aspect ratios must be centered on that same point (1.33, 1.85, etc.) when a zoom takes place within a shot. For these shots, common topline must be panned and scanned.

The rest of this discussion will only deal with Super 35 composed for a 2.40:1 aspect ratio, and apply to either common center or common topline versions. Compositionally, Super 35's 2.40:1 aspect ratio has the same compositional benefits and constraints as anamorphic 2.40; here we discuss those qualities that are unique to the Super 35 format.

A. ADVANTAGES of Super 35 Composed for 2.40 Aspect Ratio

1. **Depth of Field:** A principal advantage of this format is its greatly increased depth of field over anamorphic 2.40 for the same field of horizontal view. To achieve a width of composition (field of view) the same as with an anamorphic lens, Super 35 will use a focal length half that of the anamorphic lens.

    For example, to capture the same composition as an anamorphic 50mm lens, a Super 35 setup (from the same nodal point) would use a 25mm focal length. As with all lenses, shorter focal lengths have greater depth of field; therefore, for a given composition, the Super 35 will have a greater depth of field vs. anamorphic.

    However, as stated in the advantages of 1.85, the potential for greater depth of field can be minimized if lenses are shot "wide open."

2. **Expense:** An often-stated advantage is the production savings in the lens/camera package over anamorphic. Yet the savings over the course of a production would amount to less than $20K per camera. This becomes even less relevant in a traditional lab workflow, as the expense

Figure 10: 65mm/70mm 2.2:1

This Image is composed to the 70mm aspect ratio of 2.2:1. While 70mm uses a substantially larger negative area than any of the 35mm formats, its aspect ratio is not quite as "wide" as anamorphic's 2.40:1.

Negative: The negative format for 70mm is 65mm. The extra 5mm added later to the print dimension was to accommodate the addition of magnetic soundtrack striping to either side of the perforations.

Interpositive (IP): To produce a large number of 70mm release prints, the 65mm negative is contact printed to a color interpositive. The interpositive is similar in appearance to a color negative, yet contains a positive image.

Internegative (IN): The interpositive is contact printed to a color internegative. This produces the dupe negative for producing large numbers of 70mm prints without risking the original negative.

70 mmRelease Print: The 65mm internegative is then contact printed to 70mm color positive print stock to produce the 70mm release print. The magnetic striping illustrated here, is only to indicate where they used to be. Magnetic tracks are not in use any more). The area outlined in yellow is the projection aperture of the 70mm frame.

© 2012 Robert C. Hummel

of optical Super 35 dupe negatives (needed for 35mm release prints) negate any cost savings in production.

When a digital intermediate is used for Super 35, the need for lab optical dupes is eliminated because a laser film recorder is able to produce remarkably high quality anamorphic negatives already optimized for 35mm release.

3. **Multiple Aspect Ratios:** Able to shoot a film composed for 2.40 and, if necessary, change directions and release in 1.85 by increasing the top and bottom of the frame. For most filmmakers, however, this would be a serious compromise of the original composition (see Figures 5 and 6 and Disadvantage #9 below).

4. **Size of Lenses:** Lenses are much smaller than anamorphic, resulting in a smaller, more lightweight and portable camera package. This smaller size allows the camera to fit in smaller places than some large anamorphic optics allow (this is one of the reasons it was chosen for *Top Gun*; the cameras were able to fit in the aircraft cockpits).

5. **Video Transfer:** Claimed to be a simpler 4 x 3 standard definition video transfer by just doing a full aperture extraction, resulting in a dramatic increase in the top and bottom areas over the original 2.40 composition (See Figures 5 and 6). In practice this never works, since a full frame extraction is such a distortion of the original composition (e.g., close-ups become medium shots). In actual practice, the best transfers are a combination of full aperture extractions where appropriate with variations of panning and scanning when required.

The word of caution here is that adapting a motion picture to the video domain always requires careful attention, and there are rarely any quick-fix ways to achieve that.

6. **70mm:** Often claimed to be more compatible with 70mm than anamorphic. Some have this impression because Super 35 is a straight blowup to 70mm, while anamorphic has to be unsqueezed when enlarged to 70mm.

This would be true if Super 35 had an equivalent negative area to anamorphic. As it stands, anamorphic's greater negative area makes up for any possible loss of resolution when unsqueezed to 70mm. The result is, 70mm prints from Super 35 appear noticeably grainier than those from anamorphic negatives. This holds true for both digital and optical blow-ups.

B. DISADVANTAGES of Super 35 Composed for 2.40 Aspect Ratio

1. **Negative Area:** Most notable is the small negative area. It has only slightly more negative area than standard 1.85 photography. When compared to anamorphic 2.40's projection aperture, anamorphic's negative

Figure 11: IMAX

IMAX photography photographs 65mm 15 perf film. When using the full area of the frame, the aspect ratio is 1.43:1. The dashed yellow reticle indicates the IMAX projection aperture. Other aspect ratios can be achieved with cropping the image in similar fashion to Super 35, yet with massively more image information. While previously limited to the domain of theme parks and science museums, films such as *The Dark Knight*, *Inception*, and *The Dark Knight Rises* (among others) have photographed significant portions of the films in IMAX to great effect. When presented in IMAX venues, the balance of material shot in 2.40 or 1.85 are converted as discussed below and intercut with the full frame IMAX material.

IMAX Conversions

IMAX Releases of Feature Films

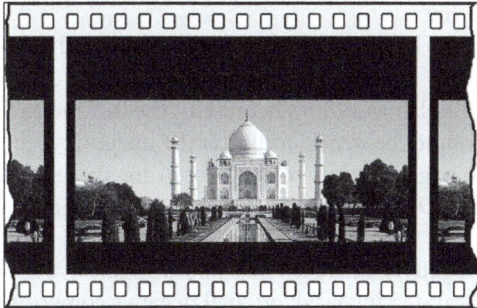

IMAX Releases of Feature Films: When 1.85 or 2.40 compositions are released in IMAX, the original composition can be maintained by letterboxing the image within the "taller" IMAX 1.43:1 projection aperture. In this example, the image is a 2.40:1 aspect ratio. IMAX also positions the letterboxed image slightly lower in the frame for a more pleasing position for the audience on the IMAX screen.

IMAX Pan and Scan

IMAX Pan and Scan: There have been times when films have been shown on the IMAX screen and enlarged to fill the entire IMAX image area. In this example, you can see how the original 2.40 composition from above is enlarged to fill the IMAX projection aperture, which results in 40% of the image not being seen. This method has compromises to composition very similar to "panning and scanning" for television.

© 2012 Robert C. Hummel

has over 53% more area. The difference in negative area becomes most pronounced after 35mm dupe negatives are made. Anamorphic dupe negs are made with contact printing, which in itself tends to lessen the appearance of grain. Super 35 dupe negs created in a film lab involve an optical step where the image is blown up, then squeezed to produce an anamorphic image for 35mm release prints. Because of this optical step, grain in the negative tends to be more sharply resolved. Combine that with magnifying a smaller area of negative to fill the same screen area, images become noticeably grainier than the same scene photographed anamorphically.

The most prevalent method for posting a Super 35 is to employ a digital intermediate. With a DI, the detrimental effects of the film lab's optical steps are eliminated. However, if negatives are scanned and projected at 4K, the differences between anamorphic and Super 35 negatives again become severe, with the anamorphic having much less apparent grain, greater sharpness and clarity of the image.

2. **Opticals:** If a film laboratory workflow is employed, all dissolves and fades must be done with double IP's or A & B printing, for best image quality. If traditional optical methods are employed, they become excessively grainy after being subjected to the second optical step required to produce the film release prints.

   Obviously, you will usually be using a digital intermediate, and these disadvantages vanish.

3. **Composite Prints:** In a film lab workflow, because of the full aperture image, composite prints cannot be struck until after the image has been repositioned into a dupe negative, thus making room for the optical sound track. If digital or HD previews are employed, this becomes a nonissue.

4. **Prints from Original Negative:** In traditional photochemical workflows, because of the optical step involved, original negative composite show prints cannot be struck. Actually, it is technically possible, but can only be done with complex procedures and such a high risk of failure, it doesn't merit subjecting the original negative to the handling involved.

   As you may have guessed by now, with a digital intermediate, a "new" negative will be created on a film recorder that will integrate the required anamorphic squeeze without introducing the grain found in traditional optical printing.

5. **Previews:** More difficult to preview a traditional film print, because of a special projection mask required for the full aperture work print. Since Super 35 uses the area reserved for a soundtrack in the workprint stage, many film theatres cannot be adapted to project the format. A nonissue for digital previews.

6. **Projected Image Size:** Not an issue in digital projection. However, when projecting the full aperture work print image, the 2.40 composition will be smaller than the same image projected from an anamorphic print. This is because the standard practice with Super 35 is to use a 1.85 lens when projecting the work picture. While possible to get custom lenses that enlarge the image to the same size as an anamorphic print, it isn't practical since you would need a special lens for each theatre where you would want to do this. Also, while a special lens may equal the size of an anamorphic projected image, the magnified image also means much greater magnification of projector jump and weave, and a loss in projection brightness.

7. **Editing:** On the rare occasion that a flatbed editing console would be used (KEM), it may require adaptation to reveal the image contained in the soundtrack area.

8. **Choice of Negative:** Because of the small negative area, cinematographers should limit choice of negatives to slower speed stocks, or overexpose high speed negatives a stop or more for better grain quality, often negating the advantage of the high speed negative.

    Because of the optical step involved, proper exposures are critical. Super 35 is not forgiving, should a negative be underexposed. In one instance, a film was so poorly exposed, that the film was altered from the 2.40 composition to a Super 1.85 composition as the reduction employed in Super 1.85 was less objectionable than the steps involved with creating an anamorphic element.

    Sometimes a DI can mitigate this problem, but not without some compromises.

9. **Pan and Scan:** 4 x 3 video transfers can involve panning and scanning of the widescreen aspect ratio. This is also a pan and scan of a much smaller negative area than anamorphic 2.40, resulting in a lower quality video transfer for 4 x 3 presentations. This becomes most evident in letterbox versions of a film and particularly in 16 x 9 pan and scans for HDTV.

10. **Visual Effects:** There is potential for more expensive visual effects, if a decision is made to have coverage beyond the 2.40 composition, allowing for full frame video transfers. Matte shots, miniatures, etc., might be compromised on full frame transfers if the image isn't protected completely to 1.33 (see Figure 5). However, the expense of coverage above and below the 2.40 composition for visual effects shots could add significant cost to those effects, making a pan and scan the more cost-effective option.

DIGITAL MOTION PICTURE CAMERAS

Suffice it to say that any aspect ratio is achievable with the current digital motion picture cameras available.

Up until the past few years, the capture format of most digital cameras has been that of HDTV (1920 x 1080) or what is commonly called 2K.[4] The aspect ratio of all but a few of these cameras is the HDTV aspect ratio of 1.78:1 (16 x 9 in video parlance). This 1.78:1 aspect ratio is a result of the different camera manufacturers leveraging what they have

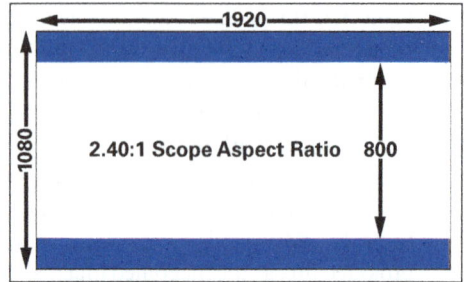

Figure 12: In a 1920 x 1080 digital camera, only the center 800 lines are used for a "Scope" or 2.40:1 aspect ratio.

built for HDTV broadcasting cameras. It's rare to find a digital camera that doesn't owe part of its design to television cameras.

More recently however, Arri, Red, and Sony have built cameras that have unique designs optimized for motion picture cinematography.

Previously, the photo chemical process of film put all the burden of imaging science on the film itself, allowing motion picture camera manufacturers to focus their tasks, when building cameras, on the functionality of everything that was required to get the image to the film; lenses, stable film transport, ergonomics, etc.

With the world of digital imaging, there has been a paradigm shift. Now the burden of the imaging science has been put on the camera manufacturers themselves; something once left to the likes of Kodak or Fuji.

When composing for the 2.40:1 aspect ratio, most digital cameras will capture a letterboxed 2.40 slice out of the center of the imaging sensor, which, in 1920 x 1080 cameras, results in the pixel height of the image being limited to only 800 lines.

Cameras with sensor aspect ratios approaching 2.0:1 or 1.33 sensors that can use anamorphic lenses mitigate the compromise of clarity when composing for 2.40:1.

---

4. When film resolutions are discussed, and the terms 2K or 4K are used, these refer to the number of lines that can be resolved by the film. In the case of 2K, that would mean 2048 lines or 1024 line pairs as photographed from a resolution chart. In the case of 4K, that would mean 4096 lines or 2048 line pairs (4096 lines) as photographed from a resolution chart.

In digital imagery the term is applied a bit more loosely. While 2K and 4K still mean 2048 and 4096, respectively, with digital scanning and photography it refers to a number of photo sites on the scanner or camera image sensor. Numbers of pixels does not necessarily translate into actual image resolution. Add to the confusion that many manufacturers have a curious habit of rounding up; which is how 1920 pixels gets called "2K."

Yet another camera does creative things with the clocking of CCD pixels so that the entire imaging area is still utilized when shooting a 2.40 image, with a subtle compromise in overall resolution.

We are already witnessing more and more cameras with imaging sensors with 4K pixel resolution. So, hopefully, we'll be back to movies having the highest fidelity imagery again.

Resolution vs. Megapixels

When it comes to determining which digital camera to choose, don't allow claims of "megapixels" or numbers of "K" to influence your understanding of what a camera is capable of. They are terms that are used loosely to indicate the resolution of a digital camera that don't follow any set guidelines. There are many factors that would have to be taken into account if you were going to evaluate the merits of a digital imaging device based on specifications alone. Two different cameras with precisely the same number of pixels/photosites can deliver images of dramatically different resolution, tonal scale, and dynamic range.

The most straightforward way to understand a digital motion picture camera's capabilities is to shoot your own rigorous tests and evaluate the images in a proper viewing environment (see "Screen Heights are Critical" on page 60). In the same manner when a new film stock has been introduced, the best way to truly understand that emulsion's capabilities is to test it, rather than rely on the claims of the manufacturer.

Also, it will be less confusing if you focus your evaluations on the final image delivered by a given digital camera. Claims about a camera's imaging sensor can be influenced by marketing. If we concentrate on the final processed image that is delivered for projection, color correction, and final presentation, we will be evaluating a camera's true caliber. This cannot be achieved looking at an on-set monitor.

Fill Factor

There is one area of a digital camera's specifications that is most helpful in determining its sensitivity and dynamic range. This is the statistic that conveys how much area of an imaging sensor is actually sensitive to, and captures light vs. how much of a sensor is blind, relegated to the circuitry for transferring image information. This is called the "fill factor." It is also a statistic that is not readily published by all camera manufacturers.

This is an area where not all digital cameras are created equal. The amount of area a digital imaging sensor is actually sensitive to light (the "fill factor") has a direct correlation to image resolution and exposure latitude. With the currently available professional digital motion picture cameras, you will find a range of high profile cameras where less than 35% of the sensor's total area is sensitive to light, to cameras where more than 50% of the sensor is light sensitive.

As film cinematographers, we are used to working with a medium where it was presumed that the entire area of a 35mm film frame is sensitive to light; in digital parlance, that would be a fill factor of 100%. When a digital camera has a fill factor of 40%, that means it is throwing away 60% of the image information that is focused on the chip. Your instincts are correct if you think throwing away 60% of image information is a bad idea.

Since the imaging sites on a solid state sensor are arrayed in a regular grid, think of the 40% sensitive area as being holes in a steel plate. Thus, the image gathered is basically similar to shooting with a film camera through a fine steel mesh. You don't actually see the individual steel gridlines of the mesh, but it tends to have an affect on image clarity under most conditions.

The fill factor is accurate only when it ignores lenslets, and only reflect the size of the actual photosite well that captures photons vs. the rest of the imaging area.

With this statistic, you can quickly compare camera capabilities, or at least understand their potential.

The higher the fill factor of a given sensor (closer to 100%), the lower the noise floor will be (the digital equivalent of film grain) and the better the dynamic range will be.

In addition, solid state sensors tend to have various image processing circuits to make up for things such as lack of blue sensitivity, etc., so it is important to examine individual color channels under various lighting conditions, as well as the final RGB image. Shortcomings in automatic gain controls, etc. may not appear until digital postproduction processes (VFX, DI, etc.) begin to operate on individual color channels.

Sound complicated? Perhaps, but all you need to understand is that product claims can, and will, be misleading. We've lost our way a bit when thinking that counting pixels alone is a way of quantifying a digital camera's capability. A return to photographing resolution charts, and actually examining what these cameras are capable of will serve you much better in understanding how a given camera will help you tell your story.

In short, do not be seduced by technical specification mumbo jumbo. Look at images photographed by the camera in question, and evaluate from a proper distance of screen heights from the image.

Scanner vs. Cameras

To clarify, at the risk of confusing, 2K and 4K film scanners often capture more information than their camera counterparts; a 2K film scanner will usually have a CCD array of 2048 x 1556, while a 4K scanner will capture a 4096 x 3112 image. The lesson here is that one's definition of the dimensions

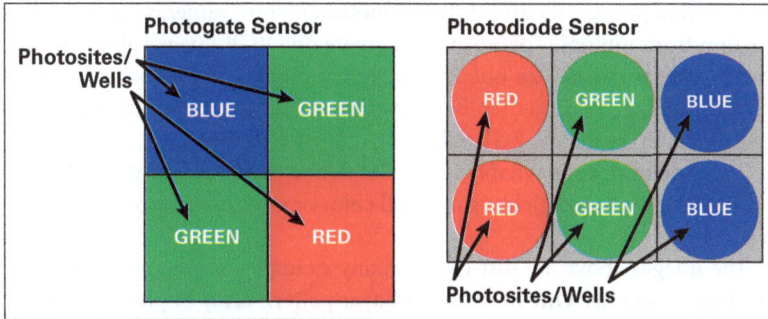

Figure 13: At left, a Bayer pattern photogate sensor, where each photosite is transformed to yield one full color pixel value. At right, A photodiode "macrocell" design, where it takes six photosites to yield one full color pixel value.

of 2K or 4K can vary; the terms 2K and 4K are only guidelines, your mileage may vary.

It is important to understand these variables in characteristics, and the need to be very specific when describing the physical characteristics of film cameras, digital cameras, scanners and telecines. In the world of film cameras (and film scanners), 2K refers to an image which is 2048 pixels horizontally (perf to perf) and 1556 pixels vertically. This image captures the area of either the SMPTE 59 Style C full aperture frame (.981" x .735") or the SMPTE 59 Style B sound aperture frame (.866" x .735").

A 4K scan captures the same areas of the film frame as a 2K scan, but the image yielded is usually 4096 x 3112. With both 2K and 4K scanners, each individual pixel contains a single unique sample of each of red, green and blue.

In the digital camera world, 2K often refers to an image that is 1920 pixels horizontally and 1080 pixels vertically. Again, each individual pixel contains a single unique sample of each of red, green and blue. This sampling of a unique red, green and blue value for each pixel in the image is what is called a "true RGB" image, or in video parlance, a 4:4:4 image. While these cameras have an image frame size that corresponds to HDTV standard, they provide a 4:4:4 image from the sensor, which is not to HDTV standard; which is a good thing, as 4:4:4 will yield a superior picture.

Pixels

Much confusion could be avoided if we would define the term "pixel" to mean the smallest unit area which yields a full color image value (e.g., RGB, YUV, etc., or a full grayscale value in the case of black and white). That is, a "pixel" is the smallest stand-alone unit of picture area that does not require any information from another imaging unit. A "photosite" or "well" is defined to be the smallest area which receives light and creates a measure of light at that point. All current digital motion picture cameras require information from multiple "photosites" to create one RGB image value. In some cases three photosites for one RGB value, in others, six photosites to create one RGB image value, a then Bayer pattern devices that combine numerous photosites to create one RGB value.

These definitions inevitably lead us to define the term "resolution" as the number of pixels that yield a single full color or grayscale image value (RGB, YUV, etc.).

The images above are just two of many examples of photo sensors used by digital cameras. One illustrates a Bayer pattern array of photosites using a photogate sensor, and the other an interline transfer array of photosites employing a photodiode lenslet design.

© 2012 Robert C. Hummel III

Special Thanks

To Stephen H. Burum, ASC, Daniel Rosen, Garrett Smith, Evans Wetmore, and Anne Kemp Hummel in helping bring greater clarity to this discussion.

Anamorphic Cinematography

by John Hora, ASC

A namorphic motion picture photography refers to a process by which an image is compressed or "squeezed" optically at the time of original photography. This geometrically distorted image is then expanded or unsqueezed in presentation by a complementary process of de-anamorphosis.

Beginning in the early 1950s, in response to competitive pressures from a growing television audience and reduced theater attendance, the motion picture industry moved to enhance the theatrical experience with large "widescreen" presentations with an aspect ratio wider than that of the previous standard of 1.37:1. The 20th Century Fox Corporation revolutionized the industry by introducing the "CinemaScope" process, which allowed the continued use of existing 35mm cameras and projectors. The CinemaScope process consisted of a system of 2X anamorphic compressed wide-angle photography and projection, a very large, curved, high-gain screen, four-channel discrete stereophonic sound, and specially perforated print stock. This special "Fox Hole" stock had smaller perforations, which allowed more area on the print for the magnetic striping that carried the special sound track.

In contrast to methods that simply masked the top and bottom of the Academy Aperture and required increased magnification in projection, the CinemaScope system increased the area of negative available for the photographic image. CinemaScope was able to use the full height of the available 35mm frame, simultaneously expanding the aspect ratio horizontally to 2.55:1 with anamorphic optics and reducing the magnification required to fill the large screen. This basic system has continued in use with various modifications.

In accurately controlled demonstrations, it has repeatedly been shown that the anamorphic photographic process produces an image quality that is superior to any other widescreen process where original photography is performed on 35mm film with standard 4-perf production cameras. One primary reason for this is that, compared to 1:85 or Super 35 (SuperTechniscope) methods, anamorphic photography is able to use a considerably greater area of the original negative, resulting in decreased grain, increased spatial resolution and increased fineness of tonal delineation.

High-quality anamorphic release prints can also be derived from "flat" (nonanamorphic) photography originated on larger negatives such as 65mm or VistaVision. This is often the preferred method for visual effects work. Anamorphic 35mm production photography also yields acceptable 70mm release prints.

Other systems of production photography such as Techniscope, Super-Scope and Super 35 (SuperTechniscope), attempt to emulate the wide aspect ratio of the "scope" image while using considerably smaller negative areas. In these systems, quality is lost when the image is converted to an anamorphic release print. The small image area requires slower and finer-grained film stocks to survive the blow-up, and many of the advantages sought by using the process are thus nullified. The high resolution use of the Digital Intermediate process can mitigate these losses.

The anamorphic optical system used for CinemaScope and Panavision processes are configured to compress the horizontal field of view by a factor of 2 times while leaving the vertical field unchanged.

There have been numerous methods to achieve this anamorphic capture of images, and some designs date to the nineteenth century. The original CinemaScope system was based on designs of Henri Chretien and consisted of a conventional prime lens that formed the image, and a supplementary afocal wide-angle attachment on the front. This attachment was essentially a reversed Galileon telescope, similar to viewing through a set of "opera glasses" in reverse. A large front concave negative element is seen through a positive convex element. This is essentially a supplementary wide-angle adapter. The anamorphic effect is achieved by grinding these lenses as sections of a cylinder rather than as sections of a sphere, as is the case with conventional optics. The power of this attachment is zero in the vertical axis and ½ in the horizontal, axis resulting in a "squeeze" factor of 2. Placed in front of a 50mm prime, for example, the lens system would behave as a 50mm in the vertical plane and as a 25mm in the horizontal plane. Thus, the lens behaves as if it were two different focal lengths simultaneously.

The anamorphic attachment had to be adjusted to bring the horizontal field into focus at the same plane as the vertical field which had been brought into focus by the spherical prime lens. With the introduction of integrated designs, these two focus adjustments are automatically done by precision mechanical coupling within the lens assembly. For example, when the focus is changed to a closer object, the prime lens which forms the image must be moved forward to obtain focus. Additionally, the anamorphoser's position and spacing must be simultaneously adjusted to bring the horizontal rays into focus at the same plane as the vertical.

However, since the spherical prime lens will have been racked forward from the film plane by the amount that a 50mm would demand, it will be forward of the position that a 25mm would need. When the anamorphic unit is adjusted to obtain correct focus, the effective focal length of this horizontal lens system will have effectively been increased in the horizontal, producing a larger image on that one axis. The result is that the squeeze ratio is now less than a full 2 times in the horizontal direction when compared to the unsqueezed vertical direction. Since the projection expansion remains constant at 2 times, close-up objects (such a human face) will be overly expanded horizontally by the projector lens, resulting in fat faces or "anamorphic mumps."

This can be avoided by leaving the lens at a more distant focus, even at infinity, and affecting focus by placing a lens of positive Diopter in front of the anamorphoser. A method of constructing anamorphics is to manufacture the lens pre-focused at some ideal distance for the particular lens and then use a spherical focusing lens system in front to do the actual focusing. This is similar to the methods used to focus most zoom lenses.

Panavision successfully eliminated the "mumps" problem by using counterrotating cylindrical elements. When the lens was set at infinity, these two elements were aligned to cancel each other and provided no cylindrical effect. As focus was placed on closer objects, the prime elements were moved forward to focus the vertical axis; at the same time, the horizontal axis would be brought to focus by the power obtained by rotating the two astigmatizers by appropriate amounts in opposing directions. With this design, rather than the image "pumping" horizontally with focus changes, the background will appear to stretch vertically. The lack of distortion on actor's faces quickly made the Panavision system universally favored in Hollywood.

On longer focal lengths, and on zoom lenses, a rear anamorphic unit can be fitted. This is equivalent to the familiar 2X extender attachment, except that it is again not a spherical lens but rather a cylindrical section. In this case, it cannot increase the angle of view of the spherical fore section, but rather is used to stretch the image vertically by a factor of 2 so that when expanded horizontally two times by the projection lens, images will have the correct geometry. Since the field of view is not increased horizontally but rather decreased vertically, the focal length is described as that which would be equivalent to a spherical lens with the same vertical field of view, i.e., equal to two times the lens' original focal length. Thus, a 20–100mm becomes a 40–200mm zoom. A 200mm prime would be labeled a 400mm. This keeps the terminology consistent. Also, the 2X vertical stretch will result in a loss of light of one stop, which is half what a conventional 2X extender would have required, since the expansion of the image is only along one axis, the vertical.

As a rule, short lenses are anamorphosed in front of the spherical components, and long lenses in the rear.

Other methods of compressing the image include the use of prisms and mirrors. Two wedge prisms may be placed before a spherical prime so that they will compress the image in one direction. This system allows the squeeze factor to be varied as the angle between the prisms is increased or decreased. To focus closer than infinity, a spherical focusing unit must be incorporated in front of the prisms, and it is possible to add the counter rotating astigmatizers. Traditionally, such prism systems were usually applied to lenses with narrow angles of view, and long lenses working at greater distances, such as those used in projection. Light losses are greater than with cylindrical lens systems. Prism systems have been used at lower squeeze ratios for original photography in the Ultra-Panavision and MGM Camera 65 systems with outstanding results.

Curved reflecting prism-mirror systems of very high quality have been constructed in the form of a periscope. Known as "Delrama," these optics were used with the Technirama system employing a moderate compression factor of 1.5.

All of these various methods are compatible and can be mixed as long as the long as the squeeze ratio remains consistent throughout the production and matches the expansion during the presentation.

USING THE LENSES

All anamorphic equipment must be manufactured and maintained to very close tolerances. As with all lenses, thorough inspection and testing should be performed before committing the equipment to a production. Lenses should be inspected on a lens projector and collimation and focus marks checked on the cameras to be used. Judging focus on the groundglass of the camera while in production is much more difficult for the camera operator with anamorphic lenses. The reliability of focus marks also takes on increased importance.

Film tests should be shot with every lens at full aperture, as well as at other apertures likely to be used. Due to the high (2X) power required of the anamorphoser, most anamorphic lenses will improve dramatically when stopped down from the maximum aperture by several stops. While very good results should be expected at even the widest apertures, test for improved quality at f/4 or f/5.6. Observe any differences in quality at the far right and left sides of the image. It is important to view tests projected on a *large* screen under optimal conditions. Anamorphic films are meant to be presented large.

The quality of the lens may change dramatically when focused at the closest distances, so test the lenses at these distances. In some cases it is possible to obtain better results using a +¼ or +½ supplementary diopter, rather than racking the focus to the closest range. Testing will reveal if this is the case.

Also test to observe how the depth of field falls off when focus is brought forward. The differing designs can give considerably different effects, even when set at the same focus and same f-stop.

When mounted on the camera or projector, the azimuth or vertical orientation is especially critical and must be straight north and south relative to the aperture or strange geometrical distortions will occur. This effect is sometimes used intentionally and rotating versions have been marketed as "Mesmerizers." (In the 1920s Bell & Howell sold just such a device for 16mm home movies.) Looking into the front of a front-anamorphosed lens while shining a flashlight or pocket laser pointer into it will quickly reveal if the vertical orientation is off. Lining the camera up exactly level and perpendicular to a chart with a vertical and horizontal grid on it, and shooting a film test, is recommended.

Over the years, differing generations of anamorphic lenses have found loyal adherents due to the specific "looks" or qualities of the particular lenses. Matching the lenses within a production is essential. The decision to choose lenses of a certain series or manufacturer has aesthetic as well as practical implications.

Anamorphic lenses have lots of glass, and much of it can be expected to move with changes in focus. Some elements may even rotate in opposing directions. The types of flare(s) that can be produced may be unique to a particular design. The rather dramatic horizontal line that can be caused by a light source such as a flashlight shining into the lens can be used for dramatic effect. Preparation should involve testing for flare and these possibly unique effects, whether or not they are desired.

As with all cinema lenses, depth of field should be calculated using the f-stop, and exposure set using the T-stop. Rather than being able to use a circle of confusion to calculate depth of field, anamorphic lens systems produce an "ellipse of confusion." The vertical and horizontal axes have differing depths of field. For example, a 50mm lens behaves as a 50mm vertically and as a 25mm horizontally. Between the vertical axis and the horizontal axis, the lens will exhibit the depth of field equivalent to various focal lengths between 25 and 50 millimeters. It is safe to use the most conservative value for calculating depth of field, which would be that of the spherical prime component. However, experience may show that the system can be quite forgiving. Again, testing and familiarity with the lenses being used is the best answer.

Despite what may at first seem to be formidable complications, anamorphic production photography remains the premier method of achieving large, high-quality images in 35mm production. The system frees the aspect ratio from the constraint of the shape of a predetermined camera aperture. The nearly square shape of the scope aperture is optically efficient. The undesired effects of higher speed films are reduced because of the large negative area, compensating for any need to work at a smaller aperture. The results on the screen at dailies is usually the clincher, and that quality can be depended on to hold to the release print, as no blowup or optical conversion is required.

John Hora is a member of the ASC Board of Governors. His many credits as a cinematographer include the feature films The Howling, Twilight Zone: The Movie, Gremlins *and* Honey, I Blew Up the Kid.

Exposure Meters

by Jim Branch

The usual final adjustment of a motion picture camera for exposure control is made with the iris diaphragm in the camera lens. While this is a very simple adjustment, a great deal depends upon its accuracy. Much thought has gone into the objectives to be attained by the adjustment of the diaphragm, and the means to obtain a correct adjustment.

It is recognized that a prime object of exposure control in motion picture photography is to obtain consistent and uniform images of the principal subjects. It is very important to obtain flesh tones that will be consistent from one scene to the next. It is undesirable to have flesh tones that are light in one scene, dark in the next without reason, and light again in the subsequent scene. Correct exposure control will provide negatives that are consistent from scene to scene, and that can be printed on a very narrow range of printer lights.

Modern exposure control is based on the use of a good light meter. The light meter measures the effective intensity of the light and takes into account the sensitivity of the film in the camera and the exposure time. The exposure time is a result of the frames-per-second rate at which the camera operates, and the angle of the shutter opening. Professional cinematographers usually think in terms of 24 frames per second and a 170- to 200-degree shutter, that give a basic exposure time of $\frac{1}{50}$ of a second. The light meter combines all of the foregoing factors to give an answer in terms of the appropriate camera lens stop.

Light meters are of two types. Some measure the incident light that illuminates the subject. Others measure the light that is reflected from the scene. The results obtained from these two different types of meters may be quite different. It is therefore important to understand the differences between the two types.

INCIDENT-LIGHT METERS

These meters are normally used at the location of the photographic subject. They measure the light that is effective in illuminating the subject, and provide an answer in terms of f-stop or T-stop for the camera lens. The camera lens diaphragm opening is then set to match the effective intensity of the prevailing illumination.

When the film is exposed, the various reflectances presented by the subject will then each fall into a given place in the film acceptance range. For example, a face tone of 30% reflectance will fall into the 30% reflectance position in the film acceptance range. This method thus provides consistently uniform face tones from scene to scene.

The incident-light meter accomplishes its purpose by doing two things. It measures the incident light intensity at the location of the photographic subject. It also takes into account the conditions of illumination geometry—that is, whether the subject has front key light, side key light, or a back key light. The meter combines these factors and gives an answer in terms of the correct setting for the camera's lens diaphragm.

There are several makes of incident-light meters that use a three-dimensional light collector. The hemispherical light collector allows these meters to automatically perform the dual function described above.

These incident-light meters are normally used at the position of the principal subject, with the hemisphere pointed at the camera lens. The hemisphere then acts as a miniature face of the subject. All illumination that will be effective on the subject, including key light, fill light, line light, hair light, eye lights, etc., will be received, evaluated and integrated by the meter. The meter will then indicate directly the correct f-stop or T-stop for the camera lens. Incident-light meters are particularly useful because they may be used on a scene before the principal subject appears. They may also be carried through a scene, with the hemisphere always pointed at the camera lens, to detect uneven illumination and particularly hot spots, into which the subject may move during the action. This allows the scene illumination to be suitably balanced before the principal subject is at hand.

In the case of outdoor photography, it is not always necessary to take the meter to the location of the principal subject. Under such conditions, the illumination is usually uniform over considerable areas. If the illumination is the same at subject location and at camera location, the meter may be used at camera location. Care should be exercised to point the meter in the proper direction, as though it were at the subject location.

In general, exposure meters are either analog (with a needle) or digital. The introduction of the analog incident meter with the 3-D light-collecting hemisphere revolutionized the method of determining proper exposure for the cinematographer.

Today, a number of companies throughout the world manufacture exposure meters that employ the basic incident-type principles in their design, but all due credit for the invention of this meter should be given to ASC Associate Member Don Norwood, who patented it, and Karl Freund, ASC, who was instrumental in its development. Most incident meters are provided with suitable adapters so that they may be converted for use as a reflected-light meter if the occasion should require it. The reflected-light adapter can be used in a situation where the cinematographer encounters difficulty in putting the meter into a position to read either the illumination directly on the subject, or illumination similar to that on the subject. For example, such a situation might be encountered when taking a picture out of the window of an airliner in flight. The reflected-light attachment can also be used in other situations to evaluate the relative brightness of a background.

SPECIAL EFFECTS

When a special effect is desired, the cinematographer may use the incident-light meter to first determine normal exposure for the subject. He may then deliberately modify that value, up or down, to achieve the desired effect. This can be done with considerable confidence, because the incident light meter will give a firm foundation upon which to base the desired modification.

SPECIFIC SITUATIONS

There are some situations, occasionally encountered in outdoor photography, that require special attention.

1. Unusually light or dark backgrounds are cause for consideration. When a scene includes an unusually light background, the cinematographer may wish to first use the meter as an incident-light meter to determine the basic exposure for the principal subject in the foreground. Then he can convert the meter to a reflected-light meter in order to measure the brightness of the unusual background. The second reading is then used to modify the basic incident-light reading somewhat. The same procedure could be followed in the case of an unusually dark background.

2. Outdoor scenes that include a subject in the foreground as well as distant objects, such as mountains, in the background, usually also include considerable aerial haze. This haze may be invisible or only partly visible to the eye, but strongly visible to the camera. A frequent photographic result is a recording of the aerial haze overlaid on the scene background, which gives the appearance of an overexposed background. In such a situation, a haze-cutting filter should be used to improve the background. In addition, use the procedure previously described for the case of an unusually light background.

3. Scenes consisting of a mixture of sunshine and shade areas, with the principal subject in a shade area, can be handled by: (a) using the meter in the sunshine area, or (b) opening up the lens by ½ to ⅔ f-stop from the meter indication.

REFLECTED-LIGHT METERS

A spot meter may be used at camera location and aimed at a selected spot in the scene. The effectiveness of the meter is heavily dependent on the operator's judgment in the selection of the spot. The selected spot must be precisely representative of the particular combination of elements in the composition of the scene. When using such a meter, the operator must be particularly careful when confronted with a scene that presents strong contrasts between the selected spot and the scene background. An example of such a situation would be a case where a person in the foreground is in front of a very light background, such as sky or white buildings, etc. In such a situation, the operator should modify the spot reading provided by the meter according to his own estimate of the situation. When the use of a reflected-light meter is required, the results of determining the exposure can be greatly improved by using a "Kodak Neutral Test Card."

This card is a piece of sturdy 8" x 10" cardboard that is neutral gray on one side and white on the other. The gray side reflects 18% of the light falling on it, and the white side reflects approximately 90%. Also, the gray side has a protective lacquer overcoat that reduces specular reflectance and resists damage due to fading, fingerprints, soil, etc. To a light meter, an average scene is one in which the tones, when averaged, form a tone brightness that is equivalent to middle gray—a tone that reflects 18% of the light illuminating it (the same tone and reflectance of the gray card). When a scene is not average, the gray card is a reference that helps you make the proper exposure judgments. A Kodak Gray Card is manufactured under close tolerances to provide a neutral gray-side reflectance of 18% (+ 1%) and white-side reflectance of approximately 90%.

TESTING

Small errors may exist in meters, lens calibrations, emulsion speeds and development. These small errors will frequently cancel out without undue harm to the final picture. It is when these errors add up in the same direction that their cumulative effect is serious. It is therefore wise to test equipment, film and meters under simulated production conditions so that errors may be detected and corrected before production begins. It is always a good idea to "tune up to the variables."

Much of the material in this section of the manual is basic, but reference should be made to ASC Associate Member Don Norwood and Eastman Kodak Co. for the gray card information.

EXPOSURE METERS
Gossen Starlite

Type: Handheld exposure meter for measuring ambient and flash and incorporating both incident and spot meter reading ability.

Light Sensor: 2 silicon photo diodes

Measuring Capability:

Measuring Range: *Ambient light:* Incident (at ISO 100/21°): EV -2.5 to +18; *Reflected with 1°:* EV 2.0 to 18; *Reflected light with 5°:* EV 1.0 to 18. *Flash Light:* Incident (at ISO 100/21°): f/1.0 to f/128; *Reflected light with 1°:* f/2.8 to f/128; *Reflected light with 5°:* f/1.4 to f/128.

Measurement Modes: lx, fc, cd/m2, fL, lxs, cds/m2, flLs
ISO Film Speeds: ISO 3.2/6° to 8000/40° (in 1° DIN increments)
Camera Speeds: 8–128 fps, additional Cine speeds can be adjusted.
Shutter Speeds: $\frac{1}{8000}$ sec. to 60 min.
Flash Sync Speeds: 1 to $\frac{1}{1000}$ sec.
F-Stops: f/1 .0 to f/128.
Power Source: 1.5V AA battery or 1.2V rechargeable.
Dimensions: 6½" x 2½" x 1"
Weight: Approximately 6.4 ounces.

Gossen Color-Pro 3F

Type: Handheld digital 3-color meter for ambient and flash; determines photographic color temperature of light sources and filtration required.
Light Sensor: 3 balanced silicon photodiodes for ambient and flash.
Measuring Range: 2000 to 40,000 degrees Kelvin.
Light Balancing Filters: -399 to 475 Mired Scale, switchable to corresponding Kodak Wratten filters.
CC filter Values: 0 to 95 Magenta and 0 to 06 Green.
Power Source: 9V MN1604 or equivalent.
Dimensions: 5" x 2¾" x 1"
Weight: Approximately 4.5 ounces.

Gossen Luna-Star F2

Type: Handheld exposure meter for measuring ambient and flash in both incident and reflected light (with 5° Spot attachment).
Light Sensor: sbc photodiode, swivel head
Measuring Range: Ambient light (at ISO 100/21°): EV -2.5 to +18; Flash Light (at ISO 100/21°) f/1.0 to f/90.
Measuring Angle in Reflected Mode: 30°
ISO Film Speeds: 3/6° to 8000/40°
Camera Cine Speeds: 8–64 fps, as well as 25 fps and 30 fps for TV.
Shutter Speeds: $\frac{1}{8000}$ sec. to 60 min.
Flash Sync Speeds: 1 to $\frac{1}{1000}$ sec., as well as $\frac{1}{90}$ sec.
F-Stops: f/1.0 to f/90.
Power Source: 9V battery.
Dimensions: 2¾" x 5" x 1"
Weight: Approximately 4.5 ounces.

Gossen Luna-Pro Digital

Type: Handheld exposure meter for measuring incident and reflected light.
Light Sensor: sbc photodiode
Measuring Range: Incident Light (at ISO 100/21°): EV -2.5 to +18.

ISO Film Speeds: 3/6° to 8000/40°
Camera Cine Speeds: 8–64 fps, as well as 25 fps and 30 fps for TV.
Shutter Speeds: 1/8000 sec. to 60 min.
F-Stops: f/1.0 to f/90.
Power Source: 1.5V battery.
Dimensions: 2½" x 4⅝" x ¾"
Weight: Approximately 3.5 ounces.

Gossen Luna-Pro Digital F

Type: Handheld exposure meter for measuring ambient and flash light.
Light Sensor: sbc photodiode.
Measuring Range: *Incident Light* (at ISO 100/21°): EV -2.5 to +18; *Flash Light* (at ISO 100/21°) f/1.0 to f/90.
ISO Film Speeds: 3/6° to 8000/40°
Camera Speeds: 8–64 fps, as well as 25 fps and 30 fps for TV.
Shutter Speeds: 1/8000 sec. to 60 min.
Flash Sync Speeds: 1 to 1/1000 sec., as well as 1/90 sec.
F-Stops: f/1.0 to f/90
Power Source: 1.5 V battery.
Dimensions: 2½" x 4⅝" x ¾"
Weight: Approximately 3.3 ounces.

Gossen Luna-Pro F

Type: Handheld analog exposure meter for measuring ambient and flash light.
Light Sensor: sbc photodiode.
Measuring Range: *Incident Light* (at ISO 100/21°): EV -4 to +17; *Flash Light* (at ISO 100/21°) f/0.7 to f/128.
ISO Film Speeds: 0.8/0° to 100,000/51°
Camera Cine Speeds: 4.5–144 fps.
Shutter Speeds: 1/4000 sec. to 8 hours.
Flash Sync Speeds: 1/60 sec.
F-Stops: f/0.7 to f/128.
Power Source: 9V battery.
Dimensions: 2½" x 4⅝" x ¾"
Weight: Approximately 3.3 ounces.

Gossen Luna-Pro S

Type: Handheld analog exposure meter for measuring ambient sun and moon incident and reflected light.
Light Sensor: Photoresistance (CdS)
Measuring Range: Incident Light (at ISO 100/21°): EV -4 to +17.
Measuring Angle in Reflected Light Mode: 30° (with Tele attachment).

ISO Film Speeds: 0.8 to 25,000
Shutter Speeds: $\frac{1}{4000}$ sec. to 8 hours.
Flash Sync Speeds: $\frac{1}{60}$ sec.
F-Stops: f/0.7 to f/128.
Power Source: Two 1.5V batteries.
Dimensions: $2\frac{3}{4}$" x $4\frac{1}{3}$" x $1\frac{3}{8}$"
Weight: Approximately 6 ounces.

Gossen Ultra-Spot 2

Type: Handheld Spot meter for measuring ambient and flash light.
Light Sensor: sbc photodiode.
Measuring Range: *Ambient Light* (at ISO 100/21°): EV -1 to +22; *Flash Light* (at ISO 100/21°) f/2.8 to f/90.
Measuring Angle of Reflected Light: Viewfinder (15°), metering field (1°).
ISO Film Speeds: 1/1° to 80,000/50°
Camera Speeds: 8-64 fps, as well as 25 fps and 30 fps for TV.
Shutter Speeds: $\frac{1}{8000}$ sec. to 60 min, as well as $\frac{1}{90}$ sec.
Flash Sync Speeds: $\frac{1}{8}$ sec. to $\frac{1}{1000}$ sec., as well as $\frac{1}{90}$ sec.
F-Stops: f/1.0 to f/90.
Power Source: 9V battery.
Dimensions: $3\frac{1}{2}$" x $2\frac{1}{4}$" x $7\frac{1}{2}$"
Weight: Approximately 12 ounces.

Gossen Mavolux 5032 C/B

Type: Handheld exposure meter.
Light Sensor: Silicon cell.
Measuring Modes: fc, lx, cd/m2, and fL.
Measuring Range: .01 to 199,900 lx in 4 ranges (MR I: 0.01 lx/0.001 fc; MR II: 1 lx/0.1 fc; MR III: 10 lx/1 fc; MBR IV: 100 lx/10 fc.), 0.01 to 19,990 fc.
Luminance Measurement with Luminana attachment: 1 to 1,999,000 cd/m2, 0.1 to 199,900 fL.
Power Consumption: Approximately 75 hours.
Power Source: 1.5V alkaline manganese AA (IEC LR 6).
Dimensions: Meter: $2\frac{1}{2}$" x $4\frac{3}{4}$" x $\frac{3}{4}$"
Sensor: $1\frac{1}{4}$" x $4\frac{1}{8}$" x $1\frac{1}{8}$"
Weight: Approximately 7 ounces.

Minolta Cinemeter II

Type: Handheld digital/analog incident meter.
Light Sensor: Large area, blue enhanced silicon photo sensor. Swivel head, 270 degrees.

Measuring capability: Direct readout of photographic exposures in full f-stops or fractional f-stops. Also measures illuminance level in foot-candles and Lux.

Measuring Range: Direct-reading multiple-range linear circuit incorporates a high quality CMOS integrated amplifier whose bias current is compensated against drift up to 70E° C.

Dynamic Range: 250,000 to one. Digital f-stop: f/0.5 to f/90 in $\frac{1}{10}$ stop increments. Analog f-stop: f/0.63 to f/36 in $\frac{1}{3}$-stop increments. Photographic illuminance: 0.20 to 6400 footcandles, 2 to 64,000 Lux.

Display: Vertical digital/analog bar graph that consists of 72 black liquid crystal bars (6 bars per f-stop), that rise and fall depending on the light intensity. The scale can be used in three different display modes (Bar, Floating Zone and Dedicated Zone), and in three different measurement modes (f-stops, footcandles and Lux).

Display Modes:
1. Bar mode is similar to a needle-reading meter, except that the movement is up and down instead of left to right.
2. Floating Zone mode: a single flashing bar forms a solid bar that graphically indicates the range of illumination in the scene. It can also be used for the measurement of flickering or blinking sources.
3. Dedicated Zone mode is used to save up to five separate measurements.

Display Range:
   ISO film speed: 12 to 2500 in $\frac{1}{3}$-stop increments.
   Camera speed: 2–375 fps
   Shutter Angle: 45E° to 90E° in $\frac{1}{9}$-stop increments, 90E° to 205E° in $\frac{1}{12}$-stop increments
   Filter factors: $\frac{1}{3}$-stop to 7 f-stops.
   Resolution: *Digital:* $\frac{1}{6}$ stop. *Analog:* $\frac{1}{6}$ stop.
   Accuracy: Digital $\frac{1}{6}$ stop.
   Additional Functions: Memory store and recall.
   Lamp: Electroluminescent backlit liquid-crystal display.
   Power consumption: Operating reading 5 mA with backlite on.
   Power Source: One 9V battery.
   Dimensions: 6⅝" x 3" x 1³⁄₁₆"
   Weight: Approximately 10 ounces.

Minolta Auto Meter IV F

Type: Handheld exposure meter for measuring ambient and flash light.

Measuring Modes: Ambient, flash.

Ambient Range (at ISO 100): *Incident:* EV 2.0–19.9.*Reflected:* Viewfinder 5 degrees EV 2.5–24.4

Display Range: ISO : 3–8000 in ⅓-stop increments
Shutter Speed (ambient): ⅛₀₀₀ sec.–30 min. in ½-stop increments.
Shutter Speed (flash): ⅟₅₀₀ sec.–1 sec. in ½-stop increments.
Camera Speeds: 8–128 fps.
F-Stops: f/1.0 – f/90 in ⅟₁₀-stop increments.
EV: -7.8 – 31.5 in ⅟₁₀-stop increments.
Power Source: 1.5V battery.

Minolta Auto Meter V

Measuring Modes: Ambient, Flash
Ambient Range (at ISO 100): EV-2.0 TO 19.9
Reflected: View Finder 5° EV 2.5 to 24.4.
Display Range: ISO 3 to 8000 in ⅓-stop increments.
Shutter Speed (Ambient): 30 min. to ⅟₁₆₀₀ sec.
Shutter Speed (Flash): 30 min. to ⅟₁₀₀₀ sec.
Camera Speeds: 8, 12, 16, 18, 24, 25, 30, 32, 64, 128 fps.
F-Stops: f/0.7 to f/90 +.09
EV: -11.8 to 35.5
Power Source: 1.5V battery
Repeatability: ±0.1 EV

Minolta Auto Meter VF/Kenko KFM-1100

Same stats as Auto Meter IVF - Except:
Measuring Range: EV: -17 to 40.8 in 0.1 stop increments
Minolta Luminance: ft-1E°, nt-1E° & nt-⅓E°
Type: Reflex-viewing spot-reading automatic/manual luminance meter.
Light Sensor: Silicon Photovoltaic cell with 1E° (⅓E° in model nt-⅓E°) angle of acceptance.
Viewing System: Focusing through-the-lens reflex type. Objective lens 85mm f/2.8. Angle of view: Circular 9E° with central 1E° (⅓E° in model nt-⅓E°) marked circle.
Magnification: 2.96X focused at infinity.
Measuring Capability: Direct readout of illuminance level in footlamberts or candelas.
Measuring Range: Model ft-1E°: 0.01 to 99900 ft-L (0.01step); Model nt-1E°: 0.1 to 99900 cd/m2 (0.1 step); Model nt-1/3E°: 1.0 to 99900 cd/m2 (0.1 step).
Display Range: Red (+) LEDs at the right of the number display indicates 10X and 100X the display reading.
Accuracy: Within +4% of C.I.E. standard +1 digit in last display position.
Screen-flicker accuracy: Within 1% of average luminance with projection cycle of more than 72 Hz and duty of 7% (projector at 24 fps).

Analog Output: Output voltage: 1v over full scale. Output impedance: 10 kilo-ohms.

Power Consumption: 6 mA in analog mode. Meter can monitor changes in luminance for a period up to 40 hours.

Power Source: 9V battery (Eveready 216 or equivalent).

Estimated Battery Life: Approximately 1 year with normal use.

Dimensions: 2⅞" x 6⅜" x 4¹¹⁄₁₆"

Weight: 18⅛ ounces, without battery.

Minolta 1-Degree Spot Meter

Type: Spot-reading reflex-viewing exposure meter for ambient or flash light.

Measuring Method: Reflected light by silicon photo cel detector masked for 1 degree angle of acceptance.

Measuring Range: *Ambient:* EV 1.0 to EV 22.5; *Flash:* f/2 to f/90.

Accuracy: ±¹⁄₁₀-stop repeatability.

F-Stops: F-numbers: f/0.7 to f/90 +0.9 stop in ¹⁄₁₀-stop increments.

EV numbers: -43 to +28 in ¹⁄₁₀-stop increments.

Brightness difference: -9.9 to +9.9 stops in ¹⁄₁₀-stop increments.

ISO range: 12 to 6400 in ⅓-stop increments.

Ambient Exposure Time: 30 min. to ¹⁄₈₀₀₀ sec. in 1-stop increments (cine ¹⁄₅₀ sec.).

Flash Exposure Time: 1 to ¹⁄₁₀₀₀ sec. in 1-stop increments.

Note: F-number, EV-number and brightness difference shown in both external and finder displays.

Memory: 2-measurement capacity, both indicated by pointers on analog display; digital recall possible.

Exposure Time Calculation: Analog/digital readout and recall of highlight, shadow or averaged (midtone) exposures automatically calculated for optimum correspondence of brightness range of subject with film latitude.

Power Source: 1.5V AA alkaline manganese (Eveready E91 or equivalent), carbon zinc or 1.2V nickel cadmium (Ni-Cad) cell.

Size: 1⅞" x 5⅞" x 3⁹⁄₁₆" (48 x 150 x 89mm).

Weight: 8½ ounces (240g) without battery.

Minolta Color Meter III-F/Kenko KCM-3100

Type: Three-color digital color meter for color photography; determines filtration required and photographic color temperature of light sources.

Film Type Settings: Daylight film balanced to 5500°K; Type-A tungsten film balanced to 3400°K; Type-B tungsten-balanced to 3200°K.

Measuring Range (ISO 100): *Ambient:* EV 3–16.3; *Flash:* f/2.8–180 (in two ranges).

Shutter Speed Setting Range (for flash measurements): 1 to ⅟₅₀₀ sec. in 1-stop increments.

Display Modes: LB index and CC index; LB filter number and CC index; photographic color temperature.

Display Range: LB index: -500 to 500 mireds; CC index: 200G to 200M; LB filter number: 80A + 80D to 85B + 81EF; Photographic color temperature: 1600 to 40,000°K.

Repeatability: LB index: 2 mireds; CC index: 2 digits.

Power Source: 2-1.5V AA batteries.

Pentax Spotmeter V

Measuring Range: EV 1–20 (100 ASA).

Film Speeds: ASA 6-6400

Shutter Speeds: ⅟₄₀₀₀ sec.-4 min.

F-Stops: f/1 to f/128.

EV Numbers: 1-19⅔; IRE 1-10.

Measuring Angle: 1 degree.

Measuring Method: Spot measuring of reflected light; meter switches on when button pressed; EV direct reading; IRE scale provided.

Exposure Read Out: LED digital display of EV numbers (100 ASA) and up to 2 dots (each of which equals ⅓ EV).

Photosensitive Cell: Silicon Photo Diode.

Power Source: 6V silver-oxide battery.

Pentax Digital 1 Degree Spot Meter

Measuring System: Spot measuring of reflected light; meter switches on when button pressed.

Exposure Read Out: LED digital display of EV numbers (100 ASA) and up to 2 dots (each of which equals ⅓ EV).

Photosensitive Cell: Silicon Photo Diode.

Measuring Angle: 1 degree.

Measuring Range: (ASA/ISO 100) EV 1-128 (EV 20 displayed as "0").

Film Speeds: ASA 6-6400.

Shutter Speeds: ⅟₄₀₀₀ sec.–4 min.

F-Stops: f/1 to f/128.

Camera Speed: 24 fps.

IRE: 1–10.

Power Source: 6V silver oxide battery (A544, PX28L or PX28).

Sekonic L508C

Type: Handheld exposure meter for ambient and flash incorporating both incident and spot meter reading ability.

Measuring Range: Incident Light: EV (-) 2 to EV 19.9 @ 100 ISO
Reflected Light: EV3 to EV 19.9 @ 100 ISO
Incident Reading Head: 270 Swivel Head
Measurement Modes: Footcandle 0.1 to 99,000, Lux 0.63 to 94,000, Foot-lambert 3.4 to 98,000
ISO Film Speed: ISO 3 to ISO 8000 (⅓-stops)
Camera Speed: 1, 2, 3, 4, 6, 8, 12, 16, 18, 24, 25, 30, 32, 36, 40, 48, 60, 64, 72, 75, 90, 96, 120, 128, 150, 200, 240, 256, 300, 360, 375, 500, 625, 750, 1000 fps
Shutter Angle: 5 to 270 at 5 stops + 144 and 172 degrees.
Shutter Speeds: 30 min. to ⅛₀₀₀ sec. (full, ½- or ⅓-stops)
F-Stop: f/1.0 to f/128.9 (full, ½- or ⅓-stops)
Accuracy: ±0.1 EV or less
Additional Functions: Digital f-stop and shutter speed readout in view-finder; Parallax-free rectangular 1–4 spot zoom; Retractable incident Lumisphere for dome or flat disc readings; Auto Shut-Off 20 min.
Lamp: Electro-luminescent auto illumination at EV6 and under for 20 Sec.
Power Source: 1.5V AA battery (alkaline, manganese or lithium)
Dimensions: 3.3" W x 6.1" H x 1.6" D (82mmW x 161mmH x 39mmD)
Weight: 8½ ounces (240g)

Sekonic L608C

Type: Handheld exposure meter for ambient and flash incorporating both incident and spot meter reading ability.
Light Sensor: Silicon photo diodes (incident and reflected)
Measuring Range: *Incident Light:* EV (-) 2 to EV 22.9 @ 100 ISO
Reflected Light: EV3 to EV 24.4 @ 100 ISO
Measurement Modes: Footcandle 0.12 to 180,000, Lux 0.63 to 190,000; Cd/m2 1.0 to 190,000; Foot-lambert 0.3 to 190,000
Display Mode: Digital f/0.5 to f/128.9 (in ⅓-stops); Analog f/0.5 to f/45 (in ⅓-stops)
ISO Film Speed: ISO 3 to ISO 8000 (1/3-stops)
Camera Speed: 1, 2, 3, 4, 6, 8, 12, 16, 18, 24, 25, 30, 32, 36, 40, 48, 50, 60, 64, 72, 75, 90, 96, 100, 120, 125, 128, 150, 200, 240, 250, 256, 300, 360, 375, 500, 625, 750, 1000 fps
Shutter Angle: 5–270 at 5 stops + 144 and 172
Shutter Speeds: 30 min. to ⅛₀₀₀ sec. (full, ½- or ⅓-stops)
F-Stops: f/0.5 to f/128.9 (full, ½- or ⅓-stops)
Filter Factors: 85, -n.3, -n.6, -n.9, -A3, -A6, -A9
Memory Function: 9 readings on analog scale (f/stop and shutter speed) with memory recall and clear feature
Accuracy: ±0.1 EV or less
Additional Functions: Digital f-stop and shutter speed readout in viewfind-

er; Parallax-free rectangular 1–4 spot zoom with digital display. Shutter speed and aperture are displayed in viewfinder; Retractable incident Lumisphere for dome or flat disc readings; Digital Radio Transmitter Module that eliminates the need for an additional external transmitter at the meter's position; 12 Custom Function Settings for advanced preferences and features.

Power Source: 3.0V (CR123A lithium battery)
Dimensions: 3.5" W x 6.7" H x 1.9" D (90mmW x 170mmH x 48mmD)
Weight: 9½ ounces (268g)

Sekonic L-308BII

Measuring System: Incident or reflected for flash and ambient light; Silicon photo diode.
Measuring Modes: Ambient and flash (cord, cordless) – incident and reflected (40 degrees)
Receptor Head: Nonrotating, noninterchangeable.
Aperture/Shutter Priority: Shutter speed priority.
Display Read-out: Digital LCD
ISO Range: ISO 3 to 8000 in ⅓-stop increments.
F-Stops: f/0.5–f/90 9/10
Shutter Speeds: *Ambient:* 60 sec.–¹⁄₈₀₀₀ sec.; *Flash:* 1 sec.–¹⁄₅₀₀ sec.
EV Range: (ISO-100) EV(-) 5 to EV 26.2
Camera Speeds: 8–28 fps.
Power Source: 1.5V AA battery.
Dimensions: 4.3" x 2.5" x .9" (110 x 63 x 22mm) WDH
Weight: 2.8 ounces (80 g) without battery.

Sekonic L-398M

Measuring System: Incident light type, reflected light measurement is also possible
Measuring Modes: Ambient incident and reflected
Receptor Head: Rotating, interchangeable receptor.
Display Readout: Indicator needle
ISO Range: 6 to 12,000; Measuring Range: EV4-EV17 (for incident light) EV9-EV17 (for reflected light)
F-Stops: f/0.7–f/128
Shutter Speeds: *Ambient:* ¹⁄₈₀₀₀ to 60 sec.; *Flash:* None.
EV Range: (ISO-100) EV 4 to 17
Camera Speeds: 8–128 fps
Power Source: Selenium photocell (no battery needed)
Dimensions: 4.4" x 2.3" x 1.3" (112 x 58 x 34mm) WDH
Weight: 6.7 ounces (190 g)

Sekonic L-358

Measuring System: Incident: Dual retractable lumisphere, Reflected: with included reflected light attachment; Silicon photo diodes

Measuring Modes: Ambient and flash (cord, cordless, multi flash)— incident and reflected (54 degrees).

Receptor Head: Rotating 270 degree with built-in retractable lumisphere.

Aperture/Shutter Priority: Aperture and shutter priority

Display Readout: Digital LCD plus LCD analog, (auto-backlit LCD at EV 3 and under for 20 sec.)

ISO Range: Dual ISO settings: 3 to 8000 (⅓-steps)

F-Stops: f/1.0 to f/90.9 (full, ½- or ⅓-steps)

Shutter Speeds: *Ambient:* ⅛₀₀₀ sec. to 30 min.; *Flash:* ¹⁄₁₀₀₀ sec to 30 min.

EV Range: (ISO-100) EV -2 to 22.9

Camera Speeds: 2–360fps

Exposure Memory: Capable of nine exposure measurement readings

Shadow/Highlight Calculation: Yes

Brightness Difference: Displays the difference in ¹⁄₁₀-stop increments

Flash To Ambient Ratio: Yes

Multiple Flash: Yes, unlimited

Exposure Calibration: ±1.0 EV

Power Source: One CR123A lithium battery

Dimensions: 2.4" x 6.1" x 1.46" (60 x 155 x 37mm) WHD

Weight: 5.4 oz (154 g)

Sekonic L-558

Measuring System: Dual function retractable incident lumisphere; 1° spot viewfinder; Two silicon photo diodes (SPD).

Measuring Modes: Ambient and flash (cord, cordless, multi-flash) – incident and spot (1°).

Metering Range: *Ambient Incident Light:* EV -2 to EV 22.9; *Reflected Light:* EV 1 to EV 24.4; *Flash Incident Light:* f/0.5 to f/161.2; *Reflected Light:* f/2.0 to f/161.2

Receptor Head: Rotating 270 degrees; with built-in retractable lumisphere.

Aperture/Shutter Priority: Aperture, shutter priority and EV metering value

Display Readout: Digital LCD plus LCD analog, (Auto-backlit LCD at EV 6 or under for 20 seconds)

ISO Range: 3 to 8000 (in ⅓-stop steps)

F-Stops: f/0.5–f/128.9 (full, ½- or ⅓-stops); Under and Overexposure indication.

Shutter Speeds: Ambient: 30 min. to ⅛₀₀₀ sec. (full, ½- or ⅓-stops, plus ¹⁄₂₀₀ and ¹⁄₄₀₀); Flash: 30 sec. to ¹⁄₁₀₀₀ sec. (Full, ½- or ⅓- stops; Special flash speeds: ¹⁄₇₅, ¹⁄₈₀, ¹⁄₉₀, ¹⁄₁₀₀, ¹⁄₂₀₀, ¹⁄₄₀₀)

EV Range: (ISO-100) EV -9.9 to 46.6 (in ¹⁄₁₀-stops).

Camera Speeds: 2–360 fps, (fps at a 180°).

Exposure Memory: Up to nine readings on analog scale with memory recall and clear feature.

Shadow/Highlight Calculation: Yes

Brightness Difference: ±9.9EV (in ¹⁄₁₀-stops) flash or ambient light evaluation.

Flash To Ambient Ratio: Yes; Displays percentage of flash in total exposure in 10% increments.

Multiple Flash: Unlimited readings.

Exposure Calibration: ±1.0EV for incident and reflected independently (in ¹⁄₁₀-stops); Exposure Compensation ±9.9EV for incident and reflected independently (in ¹⁄₁₀-stops); Filter compensation ±5.0EV for incident and reflected independently (in ¹⁄₁₀-stops).

Power Source: Lithium type, One CR123A; Auto "shut-off" after 20 minutes; Battery power displayed with a symbol in three status levels.

Dimensions: 3.5" x 6.7" x 1.9" (90 x 170 x 48mm) WDH

Weight: 9½ ounces (268 g)

Sekonic L-778 Dual Spot F

Type: Multi-function design light meter.

Incident: 270-degree swivel head with dual function retractable incident lumisphere.

Reflected: 1-degree to 4-degree parallax-free zoom spot viewfinder.

Photo Cells: 2 silicon photo diodes (SPD).

Measuring Range: *Ambient incident:* EV 0.2–EV 19.9; *ambient reflected:* EV 3–EV 19.9.

Film Speed: ISO 3-8000 in ¹⁄₃-stop increments.

F-stops: f/1.0–f/128 in ¹⁄₁₀-stop increments.

Shutter Speed Range: DIP Switch preselectable full speeds or ½-stop range.

Camera Speeds: ¹⁄₇₅, ¹⁄₈₀, ¹⁄₉₀, ¹⁄₁₀₀, ¹⁄₂₀₀, ¹⁄₄₀₀, 1, 2, 3, 4, 6, 8, 12, 16, 18, 24, 25, 30, 32, 36, 40, 48, 60, 64, 72, 96, 120, 128, 150, 200, 240, 256, 360 fps

EV Range: 0.9–36.1

Exposure Compensation: ±9.9EV in ¹⁄₁₀-stop increments.

Power Source: 1.5V AA penlight battery or 1.5V alkaline manganese or lithium battery.

Repeat Accuracy: ±0.1 EV or less.

Auto Shut Off: 20 minutes.

Tri Pod Socket: ¼".

Weight: 7.4 ounces (210 grams).

Dimensions: 3.3" x 6.1" x 1.7" (84 x 156 x 40mm).

Spectra Cinespot 1E Spot Meter

Type: Through-the-lens viewing, spot-reading auto-matic/manual luminance meter.

Light Sensor: Silicon Photovoltaic cell with 1E° angle of acceptance.

Viewing Optics: 1.6x magnification: erect system with focusing eyepiece.

Measuring Capability: Direct readout of illuminance level in footlamberts or candelas.

Measuring Range: Low Range 0–30 fL (or 0-100cd/m2) readings legible down to 0.5fL. High Range 0–300 fL (or 0–1,000 cd/m2), upper limit may be increased by use of accessory 10X or 100X attenuators.

Spectral Response: Within +4%(by area) of CIE Photopic Luminosity Function.

Accuracy: +1% of full scale or +5% of reading (whichever is greater).

Error Due To Chopped Light: +0.5 % at 24 cycles /second.

Power Source: 6V battery (Eveready 544 or equivalent).

Estimated Battery Life: Approximately 1 year with normal use.

Dimensions: 5" x 2" x 6.4".

Weight: 15 ounces.

Spectra Cinespot Footlambert Meter

Measuring Capability: Footlamberts or candelas/square meter; also measures illuminance with accessory reflectance standard.

Sensitivity: Low range, 0 to 30 footlamberts (0 to 100 cd/square meter on metric version); readings legible to 0.5 footlamberts. High Range, 0–300 footlamberts (0–1000 cd/square meter on metric version); accessory 10X and 100X attenuators increase upper limit to 3000 or 30,000 footlamberts (10,000 or 100,000 cd/square meter).

Angle of Coverage: 1-degree measuring field, 21-degree diagonal viewing field.

Viewing Optics: 1.6X magnification; focusing eye-piece; illiminated scale for low light reading.

Photodetector: Silicon photovoltaic cell.

Spectral Response: Matched to the human eye response (CIE 1931 photopic luminosity function) within +5% (by area), using computer-selected glass filter.

Accuracy: ±1% of full scale or ±5% of reading, whichever is greater, when measuring blackbody sources: traceable to the National Bureau of Standards.

Dimensions: 5" x 2" x 6.4"
(127 x 52 x 162mm).

Power Source: 6V battery (A544 or equivalent).

Warranty: One year, limited.

Spectra Professional IV

Type: Handheld exposure meter for measuring incident and reflected light.
Light Sensor: Silicon Photovoltaic cell, computer-selected glass filters tailored to spectral response of the film. Swivel head, 270 degrees.
Measuring Capability: Direct readout of photographic exposures. Also measures illuminance level in foot-candles and Lux.
Measuring Range: One million to one (20 f-stops) direct-reading multiple-range linear circuit controlled by microcomputer.
Display Range: ISO film speed: 3 to 8000 in ⅓-stop increments.
Camera Speeds: 2–360 fps.
Resolution: *Digital:* 0.1 f-stop. *Analog:* 0.2 f-stops.
Accuracy: Digital: 0.05 f-stop.
Additional Functions: Memory store and recall.
Lamp: Optional electroluminescent lamp for backlit liquid-crystal display.
Power Consumption: Operating (reading) 5mA. Data retention 5uA.
Power Source: 6V battery (A544, PX28L or PX28).
Estimated Battery Life: Approximately 1 year with normal use.
Dimensions: 5½" x 2½" x 2".
Weight: Approximately 6 ounces.

Spectra Professional IV-A
Advanced Digital Exposure Meter (ADEM)
Type: Measures both incident and reflected light; reflected light angle of acceptance is 42 degrees square.
Technology: Advanced front-end op amp, custom-sealed hybrid electronic circuitry, multiple-range linear-circuit-controlled by advanced microcomputer and custom liquid-crystal display with aviation green backlit electro-luminescent lamp.
Light Sensor: Silicon photovoltaic cell, computer-selected glass filters tailored to spectral response of the film; swivel-head assembly turns 270 degrees.
Measuring Capability: Direct readout of photographic exposures; measures contrast ratios and average in f-stop and illuminance modes; measures illuminance level in footcandles (fc) and lux (lx).
Measuring Range: One million to one (20 f-stop), widest sensitivity range available; digital f-stops: f/0.35 to f/128 in ⅒-stop increments; analog f-stop from f/0.7 to f/45 in ⅓-stop increments.
Photographic Illuminance: Footcandles 0.1 to 70,000 and lux 1 to 100,000.
Contrast Ratios: Contrast ratio of two readings – key plus fill to fill light alone from 1:1 to 999:1; f-stop difference: the difference in f-stop between a new reading and the last standard/memorized measurement is displayed in ⅒-stop increments up to ±12 f-stops.

Averaging: Average of two readings and or continuous averaging in f-stop and footcandle modes are made possible.

Film Speed: ISO 3 to 8000 in ⅓-stop increments.

Camera Speeds: 2–360 fps.

Exposure Time: 1/8000 sec.–30 min.

Accuracy: Digital: 0.05 f-stop; calibration is traceable to National Institute of Standard Technology, Washington, D.C.

Memory Recall: Recalls stored reading in memory (M1), second reading in memory (M2) and/or the ratio, average and f-stop of the two readings.

Instant Recall of All Measurement and Calculations: By pressing the recall (RCL) switch, the first stored/memorized reading (M1), the second stored\memorized reading (M2), contrast ratio or brightness (f-stop) difference, average footcandle or average f-stop can be recalled.

Immediate Update of All Exposure Calculations: If the film speed (ISO), fps/cine (fps) or exposure time/still (time) settings are changed, the f-stops are immediately recalculated and displayed in normal, f-stop difference or average modes.

Memory Erasure: You can erase the stored/memorized readings in memory (M1) and memory (M2) by pressing the store (STR) and recall (RCL) switch simultaneously.

Camera Shutter Angle: Complete list of shutter angles and equivalent compensation table conveniently provided.

Bright Green Display: Electro-luminescent lamp for viewing at very low light levels.

Power Consumption: Operating 5mA/reading; data retention 5uA.

Power Source: 6V battery, #s A544, PX28L, PX 28.

Battery Life: Approximately one year with normal use.

Dimensions: 5½" x 2½" x 2".

Weight: 6 ounces.

Supplied Accessories: Photosphere (for ambient light); photodisc (for key or directional light); leather carrying case; neck strap; 6V battery; instruction manual; warranty card (two-year limited warranty).

Lenses

by Iain A. Neil
ASC Associate Member

In the realm of cinematography, lenses form one part of a three-part camera system that comprises:
  i) **a light (or radiation) collecting and imaging device – the lens**
  ii) **a light (or radiation) detecting medium – the film**[1]
  iii) **a storage device – the film itself**[2]
The above sequence i), ii) and iii) follows the path of light from the object to the image and storage of many images over time (for later viewing). In essence, it technically describes the basic function of not only 100-year-old and modern film camera systems, but also future electronic camera systems. Interestingly, all of these past, present and future camera systems rely singularly on one image-forming device—the lens—which predates film and will probably outlast current silicon electronics (see Future Lenses section later in this chapter).

Yet the cine lens, with its centuries-old history of development, is generally not well understood. Indeed, the pedigree of contemporary cine lenses, bearing a descriptive title that is usually meaningless to anyone but the lens designer, has become a marketing tool. In a similar vein, "techno" terms such as modulation transfer function (MTF), which is common in defining military lenses, electronic and optical system performance, are now used to describe the overall performance of cine lenses. However, MTF is only one criteria for measuring cine lens performance; its real value lies in the lens designer/manufacturer domain.

In the field of cinematography, lens performance characteristics, both technical and artistic or aesthetic, are quite well known and appreciated to some degree, particularly by experienced and accomplished cinematographers. Therefore, considerable effort has been concentrated on providing useful, practical information regarding cine lenses in this chapter; for example, rules of thumb, tricks of the trade, special considerations, as well as some basic lens theory will be covered.

INTRODUCTION TO LENSES IN GENERAL

Before getting into any details about cine lenses, it is worth addressing some of the most commonly asked questions about lenses in general, which

---

1. Or, in the future, digital image detector, such as a charge-coupled device (CCD).

2. In the future, magnetic tape or magnetic/optical disk containing digital data.

apply both to cine and still-photographic lenses. The most common questions pertain to the basic formulation and function of lenses. For example:

  i) **What is a lens?**
  ii) **What does it do?**
  iii) **What is it made of?**
  iv) **Where and how does it fit into a cine camera system?**

To answer such questions, Figure 1 depicts a simple lens configuration, which may be referred to in the following brief discussion of the pertinent questions and other points of interest.

Essentially, a cine camera objective lens, or "taking lens," is tasked with collecting light (or radiation) emanating from object points in an object space (within a given field of view, which is dependent on lens effective focal length and size of image format) and forming image points in an image space; hence, the name objective lens.

Before we answer the above questions, some definitions are required. Because cine lenses are all tasked with collecting light (or radiation) from an object space and relaying this to an image space, and because the object and image are real and the light or radiation is almost always in the visible spectrum (as seen or nearly seen by the human eye), the following discussion of lenses refers to visible waveband objective lenses. Therefore, all cine lenses may be classified as objective lenses that collect visible light from a real object in front of the lens (anywhere from close to the lens to infinity distance) and form a real image of the light somewhere after the lens.

A lens is an image-forming device, normally refractive but sometimes reflective, which collects light emanating from a real object and, by virtue of its refracting or reflecting properties, forms a real image. Lens systems may be refractive or reflective or a combination thereof. Systems that are either partly or totally reflective, which are quite popular in long focal-length still-photography lenses and astronomical telescopes because of their compactness or efficiency at collecting light, are uncommon in cine lenses for one major reason. A reflective or partly reflective system (with coaxial optics) depends on at least two mirrors to change or reverse direction of the light from object space before it reaches a real image (see Figure 2a). To achieve this, such an optical system, with mirrors aligned on a common optical axis, must involve a central obscuration so that, in the central portion of light beams, light is vignetted and not transmitted to the final image (see Figure 2a). At first, this condition might not seem important to cinematography; however, the aesthetic result can be quite unacceptable to a cinematographer. To explain this, imagine a night scene with two street lamps, one at six feet and in focus, and one at 20 feet and considerably out of focus. With a refractive lens system, the result is as expected: one lamp sharp, and one lamp soft with a blurred image. However, in the case of a reflective or partly

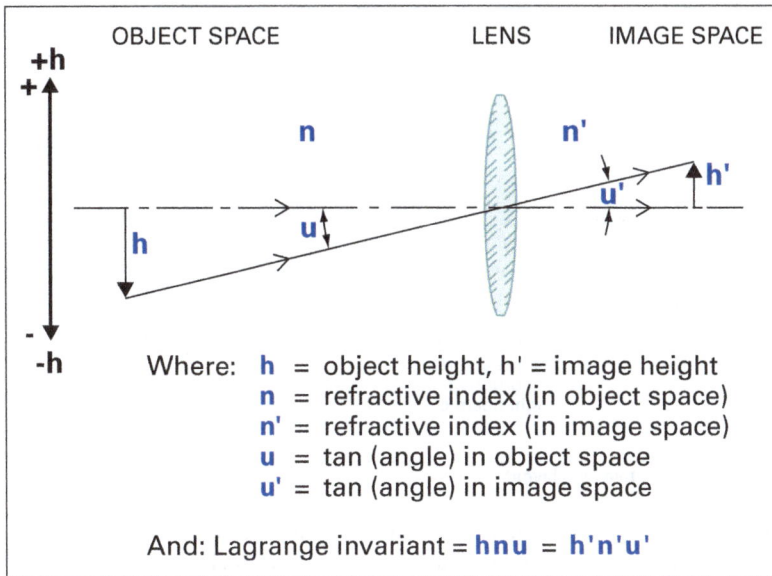

Figure 1a. Single lens definition

Where:
- h = object height, h' = image height
- n = refractive index (in object space)
- n' = refractive index (in image space)
- u = tan (angle) in object space
- u' = tan (angle) in image space

And: Lagrange invariant = $hnu = h'n'u'$

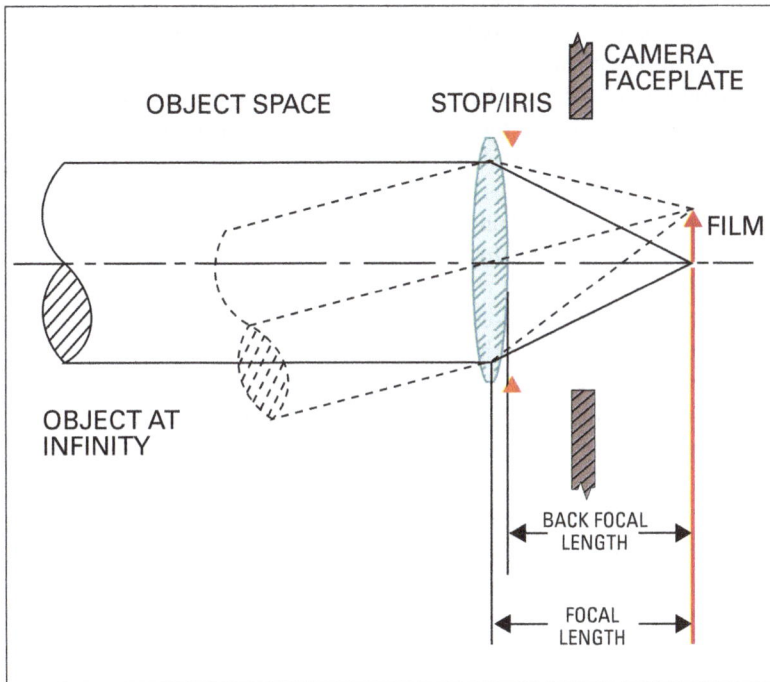

Figure 1b. Single lens illustration

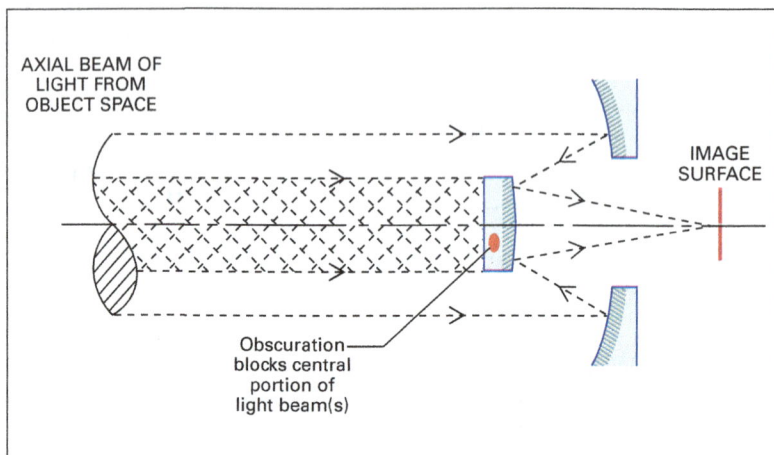

Figure 2a. Reflective lens layout

reflective system, one lamp is sharp and the other is soft, but in the form of a blurred, donut-shaped image that does not look normal or realistic (see Fig. 2b). Sometimes such a result is visually acceptable, maybe even appealing. However, for the majority of filming situations, this characteristic or effect of reflective (sometimes referred to as catadioptric[3] lens systems makes them unappealing to cinematographers).

The question "What is a lens made of?"(now restricted to refractive lens systems) is answered as follows: Objective lenses, including cine lenses, comprise one or more lens elements in a series that refract or "bend light" at their air-to-element surface interfaces. The lens element refractive materials can be glass, plastic, crystalline, liquid or even chemically vapor-deposited (CVD) materials (such as zinc sulfide, which transmits light from the visible to far infrared wavebands).

For the most part, glasses are the predominant refractive medium or substrate, mainly because their optical and mechanical characteristics are superior and consistently precise; this is extremely important in the field of cinematography, where lens-performance requirements are very demanding. Therefore, cine lenses are almost always made of glass elements,

---

3. Catadioptric still-photography lenses that utilize mirror surfaces (flat, spherical or aspherical), in addition to refractive surfaces, offer the intrinsic advantage of folding the optical path back on itself twice, making the lens compact in length, which is particularly attractive in narrow-angle, long focal-length lenses that otherwise would be large and cumbersome (see Figure 2a). Wide-angle, short focal-length catadioptric lenses are uncommon because of the presence of large field-dependent aberrations that are difficult to correct in a mirrored lens system.

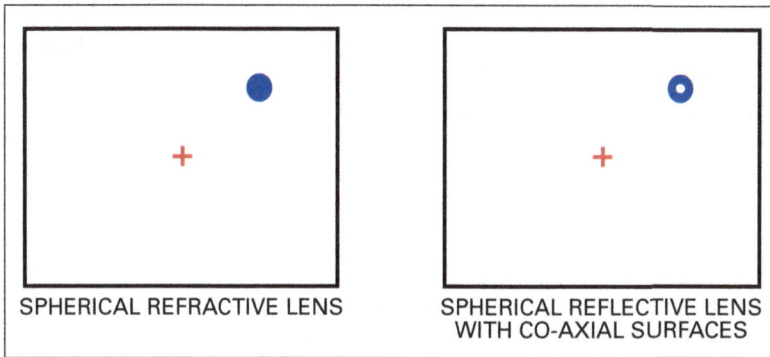

| SPHERICAL REFRACTIVE LENS | SPHERICAL REFLECTIVE LENS WITH CO-AXIAL SURFACES |

Figure 2b. Appearance of out-of-focus bright point objects at night

although occasionally they utilize calcium fluoride[4], a crystalline material (e.g., long focal-length telephoto Canon primes).

To answer the remaining lens question, "Where and how does it fit into a cine camera system?," it is first necessary to describe a couple of aspects about modern vs. old camera systems and how they, together with changing lens technology (both design and manufacture), have influenced the progressive design of cine lenses.

In the "old days," say, the first half of the twentieth century, all lens designs, including cine ones, had to be kept simple, employing up to five lens elements or five doublet components (i.e., two elements cemented together). This was simply due to the fact that anti-reflection coatings did not exist, thus causing tremendous light loss through a lens. For example, a 50mm f/2.8 focal-length lens containing five single lens elements and 10 refractive surfaces would typically experience a 5% loss per surface (i.e., 95% transmission or 0.95 normalized transmission), meaning that for 10 surfaces the overall transmission might be 60% (i.e., 0.95^{10}). Since T-stop = f-stop ÷ √ (normalized transmission), this 50mm f/2.8 lens would have a T-stop = 3.6. A f/2.8 lens working at T3.6 does not sound too bad, but consider a 10 or even 20 element f/2.8 lens with corresponding T-stops of 4.7 and 7.8. Fortunately, cine lenses of this era had one major advantage over later lenses: the film cameras they were attached to were predominantly nonreflex. Therefore, the lens could be placed quite close to the film, which made the lens-design task easier and the lenses less complicated. In fact, it is interesting to note that in

---

4. The use of calcium fluoride is best avoided in telephoto cine lenses because it is highly sensitive to temperature changes of even a few degrees Fahrenheit (or Celsius) and can be expected to produce significant defocusing that may be troublesome in obtaining and maintaining sharp focus of objects over a short period of time (1–5 minutes).

the case of old wide-angle, short focal-length lenses, their back focal length was normally smaller than their focal length, which would make them incompatible with modern reflex cameras. However, all of the light that is lost has to go somewhere, and even in the best lens designs, some of it would, by successive lens-element surface reflections, head toward the film, causing ghosting and/or veiling glare. To aggravate matters even more, these slow lenses of T3.6–T5.6 full aperture, coupled with the insensitivity of film stock, say ASA 50, meant that huge amounts of light were required to illuminate a scene—good for the lighting supplier but trouble for the cinematographer, especially in terms of ghosting and veiling glare. Still, the cinematographer benefitted from one great, indeed overwhelming advantage—a larger depth of field than he/she is accustomed to now. So these early cine lenses got close to the film, were necessarily simple in construction (no coatings), and due to their lack of speed (aperture) performed well (because of good aberration correction at their full aperture, albeit with careful lighting). A sampling of these old lens forms is depicted in Figure 3, which includes their well-known technical or inventor names.

Of course, modern cine cameras are virtually all reflex because of their need to provide continuous line-of-sight, through-the-lens viewing to the camera operator. What this means for the lens is that its rear element must be located some distance in front of the film as predicated by the reflex mirror design of the camera. Fortunately, by the 1950s the previously discussed transmission problem had been remedied by the introduction of thin-film technology that ushered in anti-reflection coatings. More complex lens configurations, containing anywhere from ten to twenty elements, were now considered practical, and the fixed focal-length lens (or prime) suddenly had a partner—the zoom lens. Both lens types still had to deal with a large back focal-length distance, but this was now easily managed because complex lens arrangements were feasible. Even those troublesome wide-angle lenses, now sitting at a film distance mostly exceeding their focal lengths, could be relatively easily constructed.

Even though the post-1950s cine lenses were substantially better than their predecessors, they had one additional demand—faster speed, i.e., greater aperture. Although film-stock sensitivity had gradually improved, low-light filming situations had increased, thus requiring cine lenses of full aperture T1.3-T1.4 and sometimes T1.0 or less. Fortunately, or perhaps with good timing due to demand, glass technology started to improve substantially in the 1960s. The first major effect on cine lenses was the realization that those fast-aperture lenses were now possible due to high refractive index glasses. However, aberration correction was still limited, especially at T1.3-T1.9 apertures. By the early 1980s, glass technology had improved so much that aberration correction, even in lenses of T1.9 full aperture and, to a lesser extent,

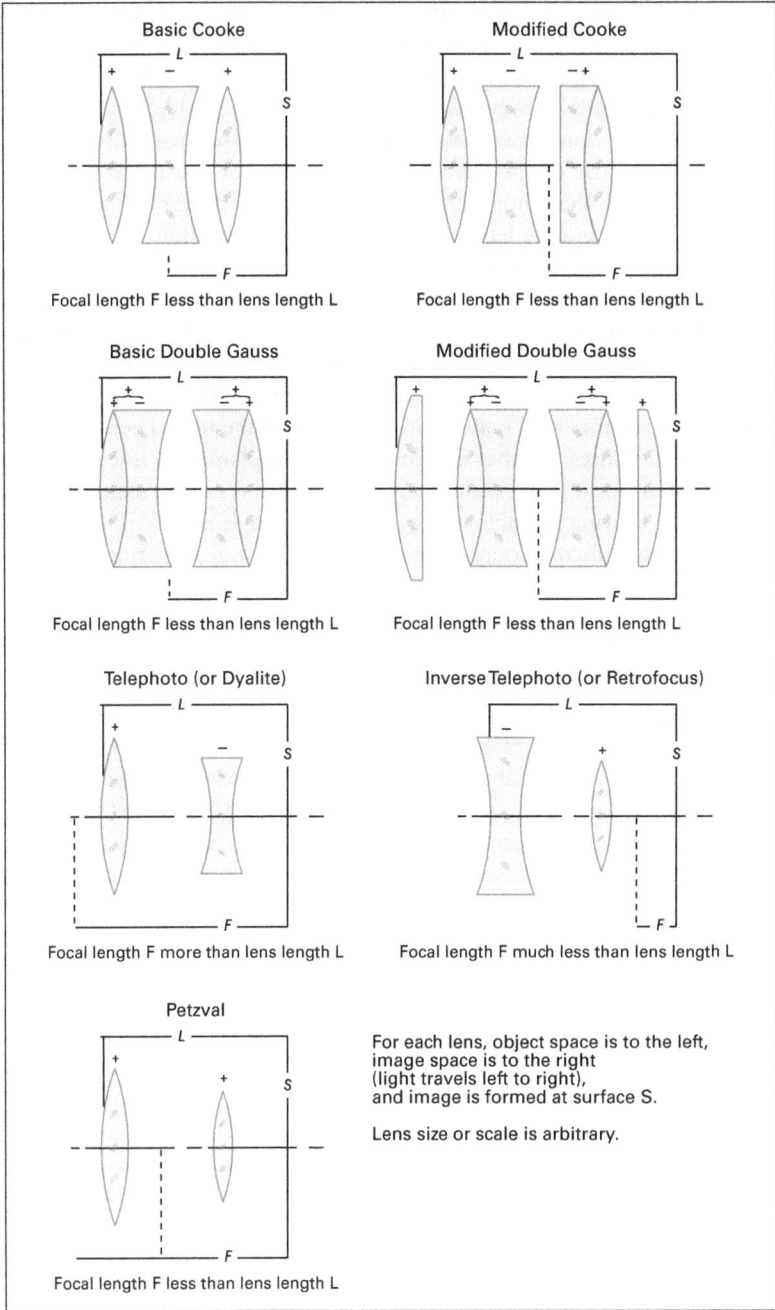

Basic Cooke

Focal length F less than lens length L

Modified Cooke

Focal length F less than lens length L

Basic Double Gauss

Focal length F less than lens length L

Modified Double Gauss

Focal length F less than lens length L

Telephoto (or Dyalite)

Focal length F more than lens length L

Inverse Telephoto (or Retrofocus)

Focal length F much less than lens length L

Petzval

Focal length F less than lens length L

For each lens, object space is to the left,
image space is to the right
(light travels left to right),
and image is formed at surface S.

Lens size or scale is arbitrary.

Figure 3. Basic "old" lens forms

T1.3, was approaching the maximum theoretical limit, even after allowing for all other lens design constraints such as length, diameter, weight, cost, etc.

Perhaps more significantly, zoom lenses could be designed to perform as well as prime lenses but were still of greater size, weight and cost. Of course, it is easy to draw comparisons with the still-photography market, but this is misleading because the performance requirements of that market are normally lower than than those of the cine arena. Nevertheless, advancements in the still-photography lens market are a good indication of where cine lenses might go. One important area of distinction between still and cine lenses is in the mechanical design. Whereas still lenses are intended for a consumer (amateur) market, cine lenses address an industrial (professional) market. The mechanical requirements placed on the latter dictate greater accuracy, reliability and higher cost than is necessary for the former. Precision lead screws (or threaded mated parts) have, for some time, been the norm in prime cine lenses, but they are slowly being supplanted by linear-bearing technology in some primes and many zooms. Zooms are the main benefactor of linear-bearing technology because they have at least two moving zoom groups and one focus group, all of high optical power requiring precision alignment and maintenance thereof. Just like in the still-photography market, the cost of all the technologies so far described means that in the field of cine lenses, zooms are likely to eventually dominate over prime lenses, except in extreme applications such as very wide-angle, fisheye, or long focal-length lenses.

Another optical technology in its infancy is the design and manufacture of cine lenses utilizing aspherical surfaces. These axially rotational, symmetrical, nonspherical surfaces, which have been used in infrared waveband military systems (e.g., thermal imagers) since the 1970s, are only now being introduced in cine lenses. Manufacturing and assembly techniques have improved to the extent that several cine zoom lenses employing one aspherical surface, and even one cine zoom lens employing two aspherical surfaces, are now available for use by the cinematographer. The aspheric technology utilized in cine lenses should not be confused with that used in inferior-performance still-photography lenses. Extremely high-precision, ground and polished glass aspherical surfaces are needed for cine lenses to achieve the high-performance imaging expected, but the much-advertised, aspherically surfaced still-photography lenses depend on essentially low-quality, low-cost, molded and replicated lens elements. Many other optical technologies that are perhaps relevant to cine lenses could be described, such as gradient index glasses (i.e., GRINS), diffractive or binary surfaces, and holographic elements, but for the time being aspherical-surface technology is the most promising (at least until, the next edition of the *ASC Manual*). Figure 4 illustrates several modern cine-lens optical designs.

To summarize what has been discussed so far, optical technology, along with camera equipment and customer requirements, have yielded the cine lenses commonly available today. Getting back to the question, "Where and how does a cine lens fit into a camera system?," the modern cine lens, be it prime or zoom, houses up to twenty-five lens elements and comprises high-technology glasses, coatings and mechanical components. Focal lengths from 6mm to 1000mm at working apertures from about T1-32 are available. All of these lenses fit onto reflex camera systems and generally perform admirably given all the physical constraints (length, diameter, weight) and cost imposed on their designs. Derivatives and other embodiments of these technology-driven lenses are available today in many forms. We will later discuss them in terms of function instead of technology via movie examples that indicate their purpose, versatility and limitations.

KINDS AND TYPES OF LENSES

In cinematography, three kinds of lenses are commonly used, providing wide, medium and narrow fields of view. For the dominant spherical (or so-called flat) format, 1.85:1, wide lenses have focal lengths from 10mm (or less) to 35mm, medium lenses have focal lengths from 35mm to 100mm, and narrow lenses have focal lengths from 100mm to 1000mm (or more). The above categorization is somewhat arbitrary, but it encompasses not only the preferred fields of view, but also the majority of lens constructional forms currently employed.

For the wide-angle lenses (as with the others), the exact constructional form varies depending on the source (designer, manufacturer, supplier). However, the form is almost always based on an inverse telephoto (i.e., ret-rofocus) arrangement of lens elements, which means that the front grouping overall is negatively powered and the rear grouping overall is positively powered. This arrangement is a prerequisite for obtaining the necessary back focal length or lens-to-film interface distance. Many variations within this power arrangement have been derived, but they all effectively do the same thing—suitably increase the back focal length while ensuring image-quality performance. A modern wide-angle lens design is shown in Figure 4a.

For the medium-angle lenses, the constructional form may vary from an inverse telephoto to a double Gauss and even a weak telephoto construction (Figure 3). This means that the power groupings may be quite different depending on the exact focal length, as well as size, weight, full aperture, cost, etc. Figure 4b shows a modern, medium-angle, double Gauss derivative lens design.

The narrow-angle lenses are dependent on "stretched" double Gauss and telephoto lens power constructional forms, with the latter dominating focal-length designs of 200mm or longer. Figure 4c gives an example of the former and Fig. 4d gives a zoom-lens example of the latter.

Anamorphic lenses contain a hybrid construction comprising either a spherical prime or zoom lens and either a front- or rear-integrated anamorphic lens usually containing mostly cylindrically surfaced lens elements. Due to the size of front anamorphic optics, they are most commonly used on prime lenses of focal length 25–200mm with full apertures of T2–T2.8; rear anamorphic optics, being relatively small in size, are usually found on large telephoto prime and zoom lenses with full apertures of T2–T4. With respect to anamorphic lens image-quality performance, a good rule of thumb is that front anamorph lenses are invariably better than rear anamorph counterparts even though they tend to be faster, offering full apertures of T2–2.8. In terms of focal length, anamorphic lenses usually afford twice that of spherical lenses. However, due to their horizontal squeeze, they still provide the same vertical field of view, per focal length, as spherical lenses.

Zoom lenses are highly complex, usually having upwards of fifteen elements. They may be telephoto or inverse telephoto in constructional form, but many times their form is not distinguishable. Figure 4d shows a modern, long focal-length, slightly telephoto zoom lens containing twenty-four elements. An even more complex inverse telephoto, macro-focus zoom lens is illustrated in Figure 7.

FORMATS AND LENSES

There are three film sizes currently in use: 35mm, 16mm and 65mm; the former two are the most popular. In terms of image formats, there are many, e.g., 16mm, Super 16mm, 1.85:1 35mm, 2.40:1 (anamorphic) 35mm, 1.33:1 (TV) 35mm, 8-perforation (VistaVision) 35mm, 65mm, 15-perforation (IMAX) 65mm, to name just a few of the more common ones. All of them require the film to be transported vertically through the camera (i.e., perforations traveling in a vertical direction) except for the 8- and 15-perforation ones, which require the film to travel horizontally through the camera (i.e., in a direction perpendicular to the other formats). The direction of movement is in itself not important to the lenses used, but the large difference in image format or negative area profoundly affects various aspects of the lenses to be used. In fact, the difference in area, or more exactly the diagonal dimension of any image format, is the parameter that directly relates to what the lens needs to cover in terms of field of view.

It must be unequivocally stated that the anamorphic format is defined as 2.40:1 and not 2.35:1, which has been popularized by well meaning but incorrect individuals or companies. To be exact, the universally used anamorphic film format is 2.39:1 at the film, which translates to 2.40:1. This anamorphic ratio has been around for nearly 30 years, and it is remarkable that other format ratios like 2.35:1 keep popping up to describe widescreen anamorphic movies. To be absolutely clear, the 2.35:1 anamorphic format first appeared in

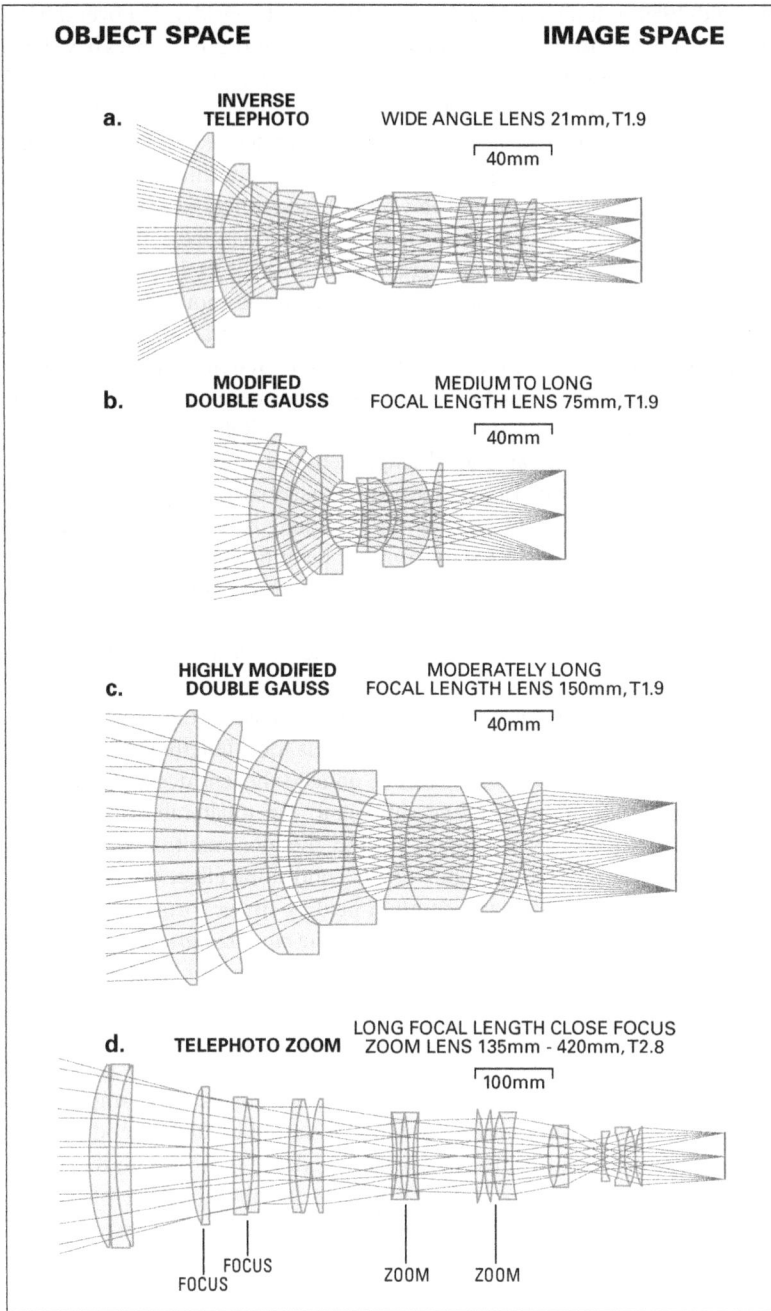

OBJECT SPACE — IMAGE SPACE

a. INVERSE TELEPHOTO — WIDE ANGLE LENS 21mm, T1.9 — 40mm

b. MODIFIED DOUBLE GAUSS — MEDIUM TO LONG FOCAL LENGTH LENS 75mm, T1.9 — 40mm

c. HIGHLY MODIFIED DOUBLE GAUSS — MODERATELY LONG FOCAL LENGTH LENS 150mm, T1.9 — 40mm

d. TELEPHOTO ZOOM — LONG FOCAL LENGTH CLOSE FOCUS ZOOM LENS 135mm - 420mm, T2.8 — 100mm

FOCUS FOCUS FOCUS ZOOM ZOOM

Figure 4. Variety of modern lens designs (29mm image size)

the mid-1950s but died out by the early 1970s. Just consider that over the last thirty years, the vast majority of 35mm format anamorphic movies have been shot using anamorphic lenses with a 2X horizontal squeeze covering a 1.2:1 film negative format, giving 2.40:1 presentation. The originator of the anamorphic format, CinemaScope, in the early 1950s defined it as an even larger 2.55:1, but this quickly disappeared when the 2.35:1 format was introduced. By the early 1970s, these anamorphic formats and others were superceded by the widely adopted 2.40:1 format, which became and is presently the de facto standard in anamorphic cinematography (see SMPTE 59-1998).

Before getting into format and lens specifics, it should be mentioned that detailed information about format image size, area, etc., can be found elsewhere in this manual (see Cinematographic Systems chapter). Also, to discuss the effect of specific formats on lenses, it is necessary to explain some elementary theory about film formats and lenses. Referring to Figure 5a, it can be seen that if the same focal-length lens, set at a constant aperture, is used in three widely differing image format diagonals, then the fields of view are entirely different. Now, let's say the focal lengths of the lenses (still at a constant aperture) are selected for constant fields of view as shown in Figure 5b. Then, upon projection of each image (after processing to a print) on a constant-size viewing screen, it would be apparent that the in-focus objects would look the same. However, for out-of-focus objects it would be clearly apparent that the depths of field are quite different. This result is extremely important to the cinematographer, not only because of the artistic impact, but also because apart from changing the lens focal length and hence field of view and perspective, nothing can be done to the lens design to alter this result. The optical term "Lagrange invariant" (an unalterable law of physics), has been defined (see Figure 1), and the aforementioned result is a direct consequence of it. In Figure 5b, its controlling effect on field of view (perspective), focal length and depth of field vs. image format size are self-evident. Only one real option is available to the cinematographer to alleviate this condition or even solve it—change the lens aperture. This seems quite simple until the practicalities of actual shooting are fully considered. How can you shoot in the 65mm format or, for that matter, the 16mm format and achieve the same look as for the 35mm format? Some remedies (not cures) can be implemented, and they are best understood by taking examples from old and new 65mm-format feature films. It should be understood that because the 65mm format intrinsically has less depth of field than the 35mm format for lenses of equivalent field of view, an abundant use of lighting combined with stopping down the lens enables a similar image to be realized (see *Lawrence of Arabia*, *Dr. Zhivago* and *Ryan's Daughter* all shot by Freddie Young BSC). Also, diffusion filters can help to increase the apparent depth of field, albeit with some loss of image sharpness. Another option to help the

a. Constant FOCAL LENGTH and f/2 aperture

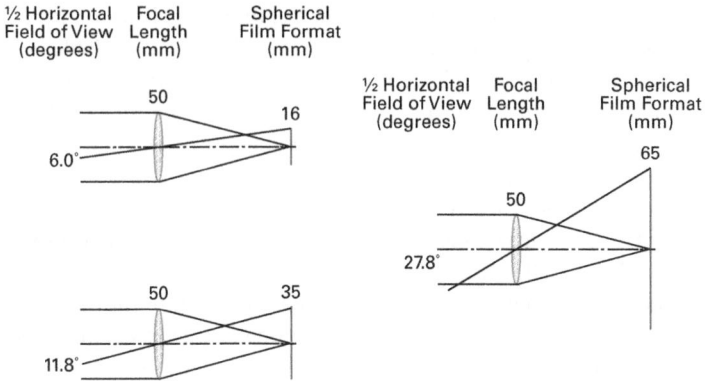

b. Constant FIELD OF VIEW and f/2 aperture

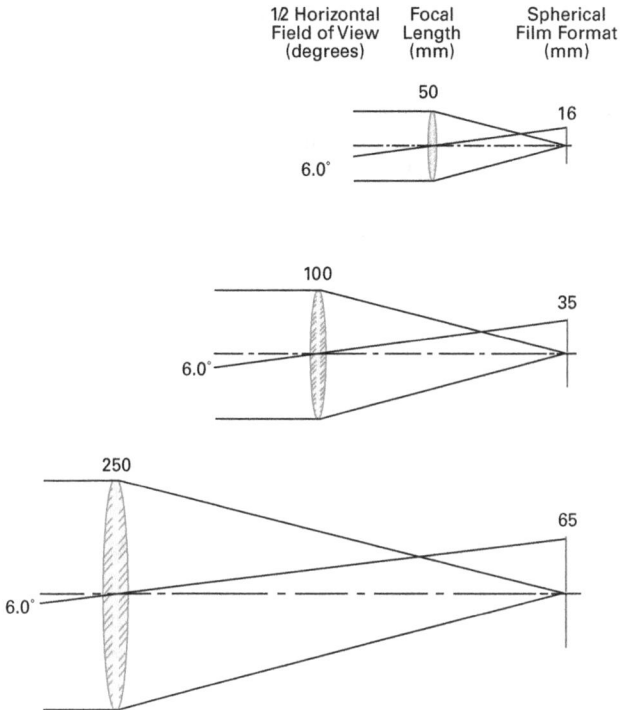

Figure 5. Formats and lenses.

65mm-format depth of field in certain scenes are slant-focus lenses (see the bar-top bar scene in *Far and Away,* shot by Mikael Salomon, ASC). In comparison, for the 16mm format the greater depth of field is more difficult to correct since this implies even faster lenses, which are not available because there is a minimum f-stop that cannot be gone below, f/0.5. Therefore, the only real solution for the 16mm format is to forego the preferred field of view and corresponding perspective by changing the focal length of the lens or working at lesser object distances. Using hard lighting is another approach that helps somewhat with 16mm format depth of field, but the overall look may suffer. Electronic enhancement in postproduction is another possibility, but again, the overall look may suffer.

To conclude, it is fair to say that for 35mm and 65mm film formats, just about anything can be successfully shot as long as one is willing to accept the costs involved for, say, lighting. For smaller formats, such as 16mm film or high-definition video cameras (with ⅔-inch detectors), the main limitation is too much depth of field in low-light-level situations where the lens aperture cannot realistically and practically be less than T1.2–T1.5. Only faster lenses or a retreat to larger formats, be they film or electronic, will completely solve the depth of field issue. Of course, what is or is not deemed acceptable in terms of the depth of field or look of the picture has so far been determined by what is expected. In other words, it is highly influenced by past results. Future results, especially with digital-video cameras and lenses, might look different, and over time might become quite acceptable. So maybe the depth of field concerns will disappear. In the meantime, the Lagrange invariant, just like Einstein's theory of relativity, cannot be broken, so lens depth of field, perspective and look is inextricably linked to and governed by the format size.

Anamorphic vs. spherical depth of field will be covered later in this chapter. Also, the deliberate omission of the circle of confusion in the preceding discussion about depth of field is because it has no bearing on different film formats that have similar resolution capabilities, especially when viewed eventually on a cinema screen. The circle of confusion is a purely mathematical value used to determine an estimate of expected or effective or apparent depth of field, but that's all, and it should only be used for that purpose.

SPHERICAL VS. ANAMORPHIC LENSES

Here we will discuss some of the differences between spherical and anamorphic lenses. There will be no attempt to suggest or imply which of these formats is better. Only lenses for the 35mm cine format will be described, but the same observations apply to other formats. Unlike the Super 35 pseudo-anamorphic format, both the true spherical (1.85:1) and anamorphic (2.40:1) 35mm formats require no anamorphic optics (i.e., special printer lenses) in the process of film negative to release print. Since the late 1950s, the anamorphic film format has been about 59% greater in negative film area than the spherical 1.85:1 film format. An often-asked question is, what happened to the original CinemaScope anamorphic lenses? Interestingly, the word "scope" has survived to this day, even though the terms spherical (i.e., flat) and anamorphic (i.e., widescreen) are best suited to describe the format difference. There are many reasons, mostly economic or business-related, as to why CinemaScope lenses disappeared by the mid-1960s. Some aspects of the early lenses did have technical deficiencies, and these are worth expanding upon.

Early anamorphic lenses produced one particularly disconcerting, focus-related image characteristic, which caused several problems with both actors (especially actresses) and the camera crew. The problem was "anamorphic mumps," a well-known term coined by movie production people. A good example of this is to consider an actress (speaking her lines) walking from, say, 20 feet to 5 feet (i.e., full-body to facial shot) while the camera assistant or focus puller does a follow focus to keep her in focus at all times. Assuming a high-quality anamorphic prime lens was used (CinemaScope circa 1955-1965), the face of the actress would naturally increase in size as she approaches the camera. However, due to lens breathing through focus (explained in detail later), and more specifically anamorphic lens breathing, not only did the face of the actress increase in size, but also the face would become fatter at the close focus. So the breathing effect, or increase in size of the object, is much greater in the horizontal direction as compared to vertical direction. Obviously, actors were unhappy about this phenomenon, so early anamorphic pictures had close-up shots at 10 feet instead of 5 feet (to alleviate the effect). Production companies and camera crews, particularly the cinematographer, did not like this, because with the old, slow film stocks, a ton (for lack of a better word) of lighting was required, and the perspective of the shot was not as it should be. Heat from the vast lighting required also produced problems, like sweat on the actors' faces and makeup meltdown. In 1958, a U.S. patent was issued for an anamorphic lens design that virtually eliminated this problem, and anamorphic lenses utilizing the patented invention have been used continuously for more than forty years. They are the predominant anamorphic lenses used to shoot the majority of widescreen movies to this day. The importance of these new anamorphic lenses was exemplified by the fact that Frank Sinatra the main actor, in the movie *Von Ryan's Express,* shot by William H. Daniels, ASC, demanded that these lenses be used. Before leaving this subject, an interesting piece of historical information: The first prototype anamorphic prime lenses with reduced "anamorphic mumps" were used in the 65mm-format film (2.75:1 with 1.25x anamorphic squeeze) *Ben Hur,* released in 1959 by MGM and shot by Robert Surtees,

ASC. A little-known anecdotal fact about these anti-anamorphic mumps lenses is that they can be specially designed to squeeze, or thin, an actor's face in close-ups; indeed, this was soon requested by a particular actress (who shall remain nameless) whose face had fattened with age.

An often-asked question about anamorphic vs. spherical lenses is, "What is the depth of field for each?" For a spherical lens, the answer is simple: look up published depth of field tables (provided in this manual; see page XXX). For an anamorphic lens, the answer is complicated; firstly, there usually are not any published depth of field tables, and, secondly, the depth of field is different depending on whether it is measured in the vertical or horizontal directions of the film format. What does this mean in reality? Taking an example of, say, two 50mm focal-length lenses, one spherical and one anamorphic, both set at the same aperture, two anamorphic scene compositions can be created, whereas only one is available spherically. Rather than dissect all possible compositions of a scene, a good rule of thumb is to allow for half the depth of field when comparing anamorphic to spherical lenses of equal vertical or horizontal fields of view and aperture. Although this covers a worst-case scenario of fitting an anamorphic scene horizontally into a spherical-format width, it does provide a good safety margin for all filming scenarios.

In terms of absolute or theoretical image quality and overall aberration correction, there is no doubt that spherical lenses are capable of superior performance over anamorphic lenses. However, in terms of practical image quality or what will be eventually viewed on the screen or on smaller presentation mediums (e.g., television), both easily provide adequate performance. For theatrical presentation on a fixed-width cinema screen, the anamorphic format will have a distinct advantage over the spherical format because there is more depth of focus at the film print in the projector, which means that constancy of film print position in the projector is less critical. Another consideration relating to image quality or residual aberration correction differences in spherical as opposed to anamorphic lenses is integration of visual effects (optical and computer-generated). Part of the reason why the Super 35 format (spherical-lens origination, anamorphic release) has recently become popular, even though the film negative is small—65% smaller than pure anamorphic 2.40:1—is because the aforementioned low residual aberrations may aid the effects community. Considering various aspects of spherical vs. anamorphic-lens residual aberrations, the latter lens tends to produce more field curvature, astigmatism and distortion. Because of this, the spherical lens has a sweet spot (i.e., excellent image quality) with a diameter roughly equal to 90% of the width of the format. In comparison, the anamorphic lens has an elliptical sweet-spot area bounded vertically within 80% of the format and bounded horizontally within 90% of the format (see Figure 6a). What this means practically for the cinematographer is that objects of principal impor-

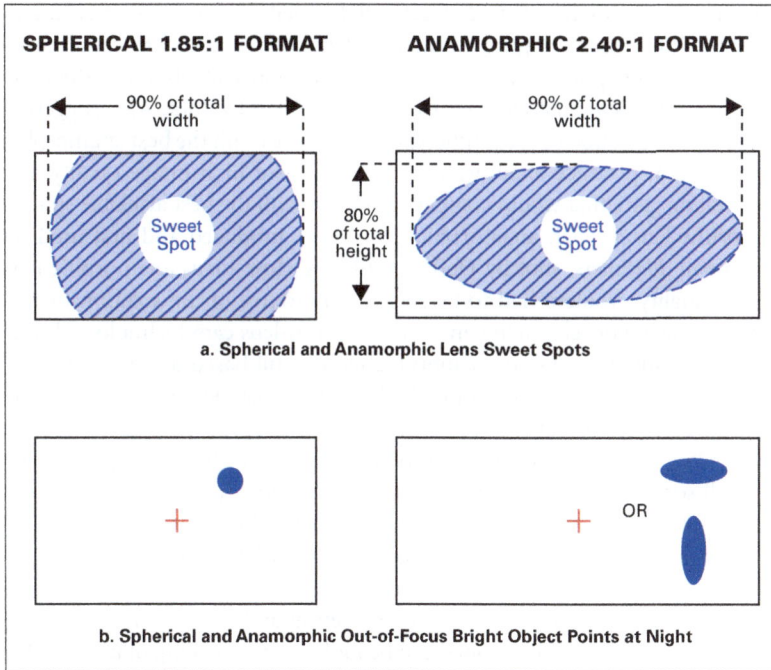

SPHERICAL 1.85:1 FORMAT   **ANAMORPHIC 2.40:1 FORMAT**

90% of total width

90% of total width

Sweet Spot

80% of total height

Sweet Spot

a. Spherical and Anamorphic Lens Sweet Spots

OR

b. Spherical and Anamorphic Out-of-Focus Bright Object Points at Night

Figure 6. Color sampling as a compression of image data

tance are best kept within these sweet spots (at lens apertures approaching full aperture). It should also be noted that all lenses, spherical and anamorphic, tend to perform best beginning at an aperture stopped down by at least one from their maximum aperture opening and up to, say, an aperture of T11 to T32 depending on lens focal length (i.e., T11 for very short focal-length lenses, T32 for very long focal-length lenses).

Until quite recently, a particular problem associated with anamorphic prime lenses has been their limited ability to provide good-quality imaging at close focus distances. In fact, all lenses, spherical and anamorphic, are usually designed to perform best at one distance, and gradually lose image-quality performance toward infinity focus and especially at close focus. Modern zoom lenses, spherical and anamorphic, are less afflicted by this problem because they incorporate complex, usually multiple, internal focus lens groups (described later). In the case of anamorphic prime lenses (as opposed to spherical prime lenses, which do quite well in this respect), there has always been a trade-off with regard to lens size, weight and image quality at close focus (6 feet to 3 feet). Indeed, compact, lightweight close-focusing anamorphic lenses of fairly low image quality have been around since the 1960s, but until recently no anamorphic lenses, large or small, could provide good image quality over a focus range from infinity to 2–3 feet with low veiling glare characteristics. In the mid-1980s, technological advances in lens coatings and fabrication techniques brought spherical prime lenses with the above attributes to the marketplace. Later, cinematographer (now director) Jan DeBont, ASC suggested that the combination of these spherical prime lenses with the best anamorphic optics might produce anamorphic prime lenses of high image quality and low veiling glare that would compete favorably with the best available spherical prime lenses. Such anamorphic lenses were produced and first used on the movie *Flatliners*, shot by DeBont. Still, the close-focus anamorphic lens image-quality problem had to be solved. The source of the solution turned out to be using developments in spherical zoom-lens cam technology. Using precision cams in modern anamorphic lenses, still based around that 1958 anamorphic lens patent invention, high-quality-imaging anamorphic prime lenses with substantially reduced veiling glare and close focusing down to 2½ feet or less were produced and are commonly used in the marketplace. They are still somewhat large and heavy, but they provide the main and preferred image-quality characteristics required for modern filmmaking.

Since anamorphic (widescreen) and spherical (flat) movies are no longer identified before being shown in theaters, and many times are not even presented in their full format ratio, what sets them apart lens-wise? Depth of field differences previously mentioned can be looked for. Streaking of hot (bright) objects, especially point objects such as a kick of sunlight off the chrome trim of a car, is usually more pronounced when anamorphic lenses have been used. Two good examples of films that purposefully use this characteristic to intensify the action are *Close Encounters of the Third Kind*,[5] shot by Vilmos Zsigmond, ASC, where the small alien spaceships with bright lights fly low along a twisty road at night; and *Speed*, shot by Andrezej Bartkowiak, ASC, where the underground runaway train with bright headlights hurtles along the tracks just before crashing. In both of these scenes, the streaking can be seen as blue, red, purple and white bright lines, mainly horizontally spread across the picture but also at other angles. To reduce streaking where bright point sources are unavoidable, one technique is to introduce a tiny amount of diffusion, say, by single fog or black Pro-Mist types of filters. Perhaps the definitive giveaway of an anamorphically lensed movie appears in a scene shot at night with a streetlamp well out of focus. In a spherical movie the lamp will be blurred and circular in shape, but in an anamorphic movie the lamp will be blurred and elliptical in shape. (See Figure 6b.)

In summary, the pace of development in spherical vs. anamorphic prime lenses has been greatest in the former, and yet the latter has benefited greatly

---

5. In some scenes, the streaking was introduced by visual effects using 65mm format lenses.

from some of the former's developments. The image-quality performance differences and depth of field considerations have been reduced from a technical level to that of artistic or aesthetic preference, which is good, because it involves interpretation of the storyline. To elaborate on this, it is worth considering a movie example concerning the practical issue surrounding anamorphic vs. spherical-lens depth of field. Dean Semler, ASC, ACS shot the feature film *Dead Calm* in the anamorphic format. Given the confined, if not claustrophobic, circumstances of filming almost entirely on a yacht on the open sea with many close focus distances, one might question the reason for choosing the anamorphic format. However, Semler had good reason: the cinematographer wanted to emphasize what was happening on the yacht during the movie, and not distract the viewer by drawing attention to things in the distance or not relevant to the scenes being enacted.

To conclude, it may seem that an excessive amount of attention has been placed on spherical vs. anamorphic lenses, but we wanted to thoroughly explain why the choice is artistic as well as technical.

PRIME LENSES VS. ZOOM LENSES

Earlier in this section, we discussed various technological developments relating to lenses in general. All of these and other developments have been instrumental in bringing zoom lenses to a point where today they rival or exceed prime lenses in virtually every aspect, be it cost, performance or versatility; their only drawbacks are still size and weight, but even those are being gradually eroded. In cinematography, where optical and mechanical performance requirements and expectations are traditionally higher, zoom lenses have seen a much slower acceptance than in other applications, (e.g., still photography—especially point-and-shoot cameras—photocopiers, video camcorders, etc). In the late 1950s to early 1960s, zoom lenses gained popularity with cinematographers mainly for their intrinsic zooming capability. Today, the most technologically advanced cine zoom lenses have become popular not only because of their zooming capability, but more importantly for their performance and versatility. They are used equally for zooming and as variable focal length primes.

Prime cine lenses, having a huge range of discrete focal lengths from about 6mm (fisheye) to 1000mm, full apertures starting at about T1.2 and close focusing to 1 or 2 feet, are commonplace. The overall performance of these modern prime cine lenses is usually excellent. In general, if you want more from a prime lens you can get it; you just have to pay more. The performance that can be achieved now closely approaches limits set by the laws of physics. Of course, good prime cine lenses still need proper optical design, mechanical design, manufacturing, assembly, testing and calibration, no matter how much development money is invested. Zoom lenses are controlled by the same factors. However, zoom lenses, apart from their zoom capabilities, can and already do offer considerable advantages over even the best prime lenses. Primarily due to their greater cost but far better return on investment, as well as their greater overall complexity, zoom lenses can readily incorporate advanced features, such as close-to-macro focusing (with virtually constant aperture throughout focus and zoom) and reduced breathing at short focal lengths. In particular, the breathing control offered in some modern cine zoom lenses is important to many cinematographers.

Optical breathing is a phenomenon peculiar to cameras that continually record images over time, i.e., film or video. It is not present in still photography. Breathing is well illustrated by considering a scene containing two persons talking intermittently with each other, one at 6 feet and one at 20 feet focus. Let's say the person at 20 feet (in focus and at the edge of the scene) first talks to the person at 6 feet (slightly out of focus but quite discernable, centered in the scene). Then let's say that during the conversation, the person at 6 feet (now in focus by refocusing the lens) starts talking to the person at 20 feet (now slightly out of focus), but the person at 20 feet, due to refocusing the lens, moves out of the scene. This means that the person at 6 feet is talking to nobody in the scene, thus ruining the take. In other words, breathing, through change in field of view during focusing, has moved objects at the edge of the scene into and out of the scene. Patents of zoom-lens inventions dating back to the late 1950s have addressed this problem, and several modern cine zoom lenses, sometimes using complex internal focusing arrangements, have successfully minimized this effect—especially at short focal lengths, where the larger depths of field make this effect more noticeable.

Modern cine zoom lenses are available in a variety of forms—lightweight (2-3:1 zoom ratio), variable prime (2.5:1 zoom ratio) and conventional. The latter comprises medium ratio (3:1–5:1), wide-angle and telephoto zoom lenses, e.g., 14.5–50mm T2.2, 17.5–75mm T2.3, 20–100mm T2.8, 135–420mm T2.8, 150–600mm T6.3, and large-ratio (10:1-11:1) wide to long focal length zoom lenses, e.g., 24–275mm T2.8, 25–250mm T3.5-4.0.

To conclude, prime and zoom lenses complement each other in the field of cinematography, and virtually all movies now feature prime lenses and one zoom lens. Many movies use prime lenses and more than one zoom lens; some movies use only a few prime lenses and are shot almost entirely with zoom lenses.

SPECIALTY LENSES AND SYSTEMS

In addition to prime and zoom lenses, the cinematographer has at his or her disposal a large variety of other lenses or lens systems (which contain primes or zooms) that provide different imaging characteristics or other features: specialty lenses. Some of these specialty lenses may be just prime

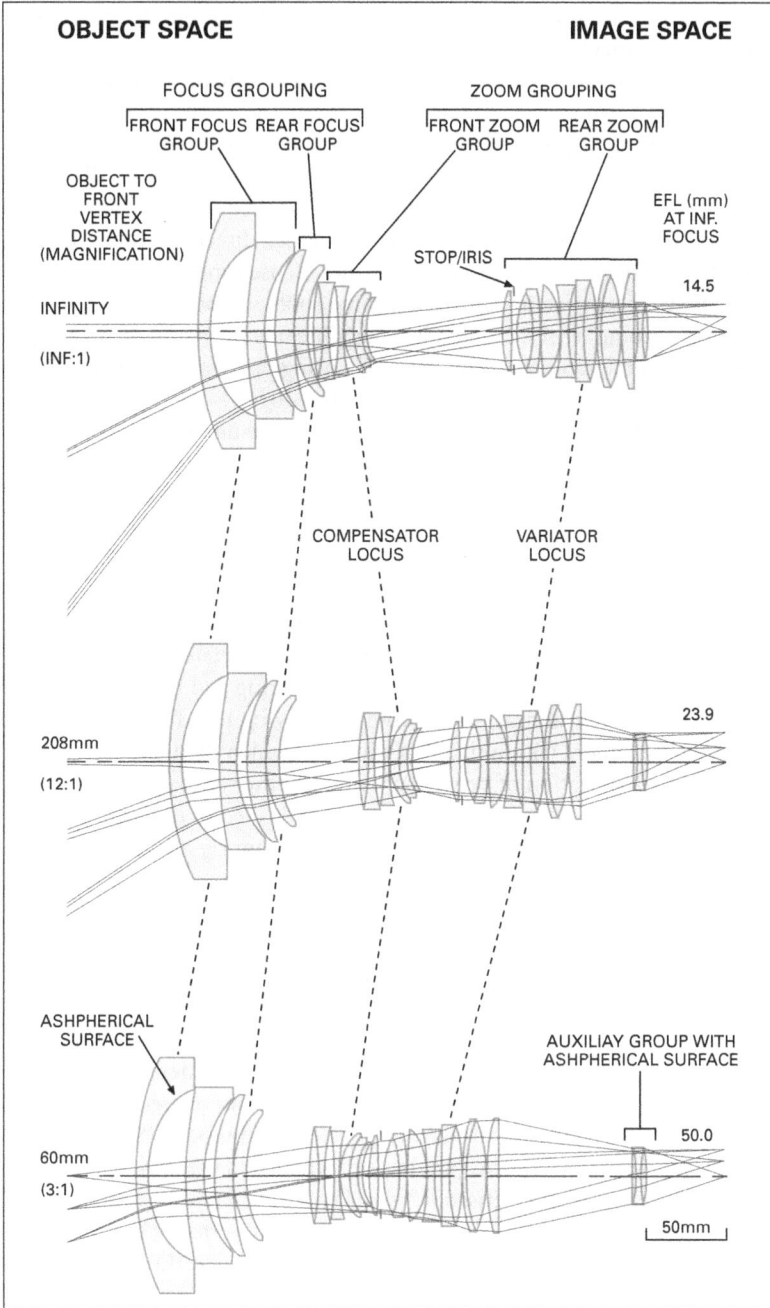

OBJECT SPACE   IMAGE SPACE

FOCUS GROUPING   ZOOM GROUPING

FRONT FOCUS   REAR FOCUS   FRONT ZOOM   REAR ZOOM
GROUP   GROUP   GROUP   GROUP

OBJECT TO
FRONT
VERTEX   EFL (mm)
DISTANCE   AT INF.
(MAGNIFICATION)   FOCUS

STOP/IRIS

INFINITY   14.5

(INF:1)

COMPENSATOR   VARIATOR
LOCUS   LOCUS

208mm   23.9

(12:1)

ASHPHERICAL
SURFACE   AUXILIAY GROUP WITH
ASHPHERICAL SURFACE

60mm   50.0

(3:1)   50mm

Figure 7. Color sampling as a compression of image data

lenses with unusual features, and some may involve an optical system that accepts attachment of a variety of primes or zooms.

The Cine Lens list, starting on page 65 3 in this manual, contains some of the best-known specialty lenses and systems and identifies their specific characteristics and possible applications. Some of them are dependent on folded optical configurations utilizing mirrors or prisms. They are all unique, but some have overlapping properties. None of them can be construed as front or rear lens attachments, because they attach directly to the camera.

By far the most significant aspect of these lenses and optical systems is their ability to achieve in-camera real-time shots not possible with regular primes and zoom lenses. Other advantages include provision of large depth of field, extreme close or even macro focusing, and maneuvering among objects (e.g., miniatures, models, forced perspective).

Some good examples of their shot-making capability can be seen in the following movie and TV sequences. In *Titanic*, cinematographer Russell Carpenter, ASC and visual-effects supervisor Erik Nash used a Panavision /Frazier lens system and camera, each under motion control, to shoot the beginning of the last sequence in the movie. Shortly after the woman drops the gemstone into the ocean from the back of the research ship, a dry-for-wet scene commences with the camera system approaching a model of the sunken Titanic hulk (in dark blue lighting), then traversing over the bow of the ship heading toward the port side, then entering and traveling through a covered outside walkway, and eventually slowing to a halt after turning left to see two doors with unlit glass windows, which then are lit and open to reveal a congregation of people collected together to toast the lead actor and actress. In this shot, which is far too complicated to describe fully (although it is worth noting that CGI and a Steadicam rig are also involved), the large depth of field, image-rotation control and pointing capability of the Frazier lens system are utilized up to the point where the doors open. Another movie, *The Rock,* shot by John Schwartzman, ASC, exemplifies the variety of shots that can be accomplished with the Frazier lens system and some other specialty lenses. Many of the shots are seen toward the end of the movie, when Nicolas Cage is being chased on the Alcatraz prison walkways while carrying the deadly green marbles and accidentally dropping, then grabbing, them on the parapet of the lighthouse tower. In this shot, the macro focus (close-up of his feet) to the infinity focus (San Francisco distant skyline) carry of focus (i.e., huge depth of field with no follow focus) is clearly illustrated. For periscopic specialty lenses, a good example can be seen in the introduction to public television's *Masterpiece Theatre* series, where the point of view given has the lens working its way through table-top memorabilia in a Victorian-era drawing room, eventually halting in front of a hardbound book with the title of the play about to be presented on its front cover. This particular shot combines the maneuvering, pointing, role and close-focus capabilities of the Kenworthy snorkel.

The above examples relate to specialty lens systems where different objective or taking lenses, primes and zooms, can be attached to an optical unit which basically relays the light through mirrors and prisms to form a final image, and wherein pointing and image-rotation means are housed. Many other lenses or lens systems, some under remote control, such as the pitching lens, can be used to achieve similar results.

Other specialty lenses, such as slant-focus lenses and bellows-type lenses, typically have fewer features than those afforded by the aforementioned lens systems. However, they do offer the cinematographer opportunities to capture other distinctive views of a scene. For example, the slant-focus lens permits reduced depth of field limitations to be overcome in low-light-level scenes where objects span across the field of view with continuously increasing focus distance or with continuously decreasing focus distance, such as is found in the typical car scene with the driver and passenger in conversation and the camera looking into the car from either the passenger or driver window. Bellows-type lenses can produce shots similar to slant-focus lenses, but because of their bellows dependency cannot easily be adjusted in shot. However, the real advantage of bellow lenses is their ability to produce a distorted field of view or perspective. In other words, even though the film-format shape remains constant, objects can be highly distorted and defocused differentially across the scene. For example, the well-known THX rectangular-shaped credit could be made trapezoidal in shape, with each corner defocused by different amounts.

All of these specialty lenses are currently very popular with cinematographers. Their attributes are quite well-suited to movie making, and they are used to great effect in TV commercials to get that difficult-to-obtain or different look.

LENS ATTACHMENTS

The most common cine lens attachments are placed before or after (and occasionally within) a cine camera lens, be it a prime or zoom, spherical or anamorphic.

Front lens attachments include diopter and split diopter close-focusing lenses, image stabilizers, image shakers, distortion optics and inclining prisms. Their main duty is to maximize the versatility of the lens to which they are attached. Most of these front attachments lose some light transmission and, in some instances, image quality, but their overall effect proves them to be worthwhile even though they have deficiencies.

Rear lens attachments mainly include extenders (to increase or decrease the overall lens focal length) and mesmerizers (rotatable anamorphic optics).

Extenders are well established in still photography. Their main property is to increase (or even decrease) the overall focal length of the lens. There are three disadvantages when using them: overall image quality may be somewhat degraded; aperture is reduced at the rate of one stop per each 1.4x multiplier (e.g., x2.0 extender = 1.4x1.4x, giving a two-stop loss); and the focus scale of the lens will be incorrect by approximately the physical length of the extender. In practical terms, the rule of thumb is that a good high-quality 1.4x rear extender will not substantially affect the overall image quality, but a 2x or greater extender will probably cause a significant reduction in image quality. Technically, rear extenders should only be employed if no alternative prime or zoom lens is available. Mesmerizers, due to their anamorphic nature, may degrade image quality even further. In TV commercials this is not a problem, but in moviemaking some caution should be exercised, such as stopping down the aperture at least one stop.

One front lens attachment, which is quite commonplace in the video-lens marketplace but has only recently been introduced in cine lenses, is the single or double aspherically surfaced element. The idea here is to take a single, negatively powered lens element with one or two nonspherical surfaces and attach it to the front of a wide-angle prime or zoom lens so that the focal length is decreased to 80% (or even as far as 66%) of its original value; correspondingly, the field of view is proportionally increased, the image quality is little changed. It should be pointed out that such attachments only work properly with prime or zoom lenses that have a minimum full field of view of about 75°. These front lens attachments offer an economical way to provide increased wide-angle, short focal-length lenses not available in a lens series and, by virtue of their aspherically surfaced lens design prescription, astigmatism, distortion and lateral chromatic aberrations are kept under control. The only real disadvantage of this wide-angle lens approach is the loss of focus capability, because the front attachment requires the principal lens to be set at the end of its close-focus range to reach the hyperfocal-focus distance of the overall system. However, such wide-angle lenses' large depth of field does not really warrant any focusability. Examples of these front lens attachments currently being used include a 6mm T2 prime covering the Super 16mm film format, which becomes a 4.5mm prime (using a 0.75x front lens attachment), and a 14.5mm T1.9 prime covering the Academy 35mm film format, which becomes an 11.5mm prime (using a 0.8x front lens attachment). Due to the simplicity of these front lens attachments, no significant stop loss is associated with their use.

FORMAT SIZE AND LENS ATTRIBUTES

Earlier, in Formats and Lenses, lens depth of field was discussed. There are some other important implications resulting from format size on lens size (volume and weight), image quality and aperture, as well as reflex mirrored camera considerations.

Perhaps the most noticeable effect is the tendency for lens size to increase almost linearly with each format size, assuming a constant focal length and constant full aperture. Of course, this must partly happen in reflex camera systems because the reflex mirror, size and position dictate the lens back-focal length. Since the size and distance of the mirror from the film (or image plane) increases mainly according to film-format size, this means that 65mm-format lenses tend to be larger than 16mm-format lenses, at least at their rears. However, the greater difficulty in covering a larger format, combined with the need for larger depth of field, makes 65mm-format lenses slower, T2.8–T5.6 full aperture, whereas 16mm format lenses are faster T1.4–T2.0. Unlike in still photography, where a larger-format lens is chosen to provide a larger print, in cinematography the 65mm, 35mm and occasionally 16mm prints are invariably shown on similarly sized cinema screens, roughly 20–50 feet wide. In summary, 65mm-format cine lenses are optically less complex, slower and have slightly less resolution per millimeter of film negative than 35mm- or 16mm-format lenses. Nevertheless, 65mm lenses perform as well as they need to, based on the size of the format. The key to the final presentation quality using large-format lenses, including 65mm, VistaVision and 35mm anamorphic, is, as it always has been, the larger format size and corresponding area of the negative.

SPECIAL APPLICATIONS OF LENSES

Special applications fall into the category of visual effects, which include special effects, computer-graphics imaging (CGI), digital effects, animation, etc. Most of these applications have one thing in common: they require principal photography with lenses and film to achieve about 2,000 pixels of usable information (and more recently up to 4,000 pixels) across the film format. Today, the most-used and best cine lenses perform adequately and can meet this requirement. Even anamorphic lenses, which get a bad name, are not pressed in meeting this requirement. In fact, until quite recently, film stocks, because of their chemical image processing for enhanced contrast in the negative, have proved to be more problematic than lenses, especially in blue or green matte screen applications.

Although modern cine lenses may be considered precision optical instruments that were designed, manufactured, tested and calibrated in a highly scientific manner, many of their characteristics, features and specific properties have not been made available publicly or accessible to people working in special applications. In the last five to 10 years, books or manuals containing some of this information have appeared; however, further dissemination of lens information is necessary.

To explain what some of this lens information is, a good method is to examine a recently made movie with many special effects, such as *Titanic*. After camera equipment was supplied to the production, the crew requested certain lens information. In particular, variations of distortion and field of view (see breathing earlier described) through focus and zoom and lens repeatability were topics that kept arising. Eventually, this and other kinds of information were released so that the desired special effects could be realized.

With the ever-increasing utilization of visual effects, a tremendous amount of lens information will be not only required, but also indispensable in the making of movies. Most of this information is not yet publicly available.

LENS DEPTH OF FIELD

Depth of field lens information is worth a special mention because until quite recently, its method of calculation, especially at close- to medium-focus distances (say 2–6 feet), has been somewhat inaccurate for wide-angle prime and zoom lenses; and its interpretation for wide-angle lenses in general needs clarification.

For modern, high-quality, wide-angle cine zoom lenses that are typically about 6–12 inches long, the lens length cannot be ignored when calculating the depth of field. To properly calculate the depth of field, the first nodal, or conveniently entrance pupil position of a wide-angle lens must be known. In most wide-angle zoom and prime lenses they are normally a few inches back from the front of the lens. So assuming that properly calculated depth of field tables for the lens in question are not available, a good rule of thumb for a short focal-length lens is to subtract the physical lens length (from front to flange/mounting point) away from the object distance (i.e., object to film), and then look up the depth-of-field table. It goes without saying that a lens at a close focus distance of 4 feet (object to film), after the subtraction of, say, one foot, will produce a significant difference in the depth of field from that expected—just look at any contemporary depth of field table to compare 4 feet and 3 feet at T2 for a lens of any focal length.

One common complaint about the depth of field observed for wide-angle primes or zooms: when the focus distance is 6 feet and the expected depth of field (according to the tables) is 4 to 9 feet, why is the defocused object at 4 feet almost as sharp as the focused object at 6 feet, while the defocused object at 9 feet looks comparatively very soft? The answer has nothing to do with the lens performance, the validity of the depth-of-field tables, or even lens physical length; it simply has to do with the magnification of objects at different focus distances. Since the object at 4 feet is only 1½X larger than the object at 6 feet, but the object at 4 feet is 2¼X larger than the object at 9 feet, then for the same object, (say, a person's face at all three focus distances, and all faces lit in a similar manner), it is to be expected that the aforementioned result will appear. In addition, it is worth noting that the introduction of even the weakest diffusion filters, as well as soft lighting, will further compound and exaggerate this condition.

LENS DESIGN AND MANUFACTURE

To the various suppliers of cine lens products, the design and manufacture (including assembly, test and calibration) of cine lenses have been, and still is, considered proprietary, as in intellectual property. A survey of cine-lens patents from the 1950s through today (few in number) confirms the secretive nature attached to cine-lens products by various suppliers. Quite a few technical and scientific publications on some of the above aspects of cine lenses are available and are listed under References toward the end of this manual. Most of them concentrate on the optical design of cine lenses.

Over the years, several different approaches have been used to provide suitable cine lenses to the cinematographic marketplace. More often than not, the best approach has been to design custom cine lenses from scratch. In this case, two substantially different lens development approaches have been chosen. The first, which for the sake of discussion will be called the old-world method, entails a company performing virtually all tasks in-house. The second, called a new-world method, has the design and development process controlled at one company (with the final assembly, testing and calibration performed there), but a large number of specialized suppliers being subcontracted for partial design and component manufacture—sort of like the way modern jet aircraft are produced. Both approaches have advantages, the first having everything totally controlled under one roof, and the second being better suited to exploit new technologies. In terms of which approach produces the best cine lenses, only the results can provide an answer. However, the latter approach is best suited to providing faster development of new lenses.

In such a limited space it is not realistic to discuss all the aforementioned aspects of cine lenses. The references we have mentioned, although mainly containing theoretical information, such as MTF performance, are very useful in gaining a fairly comprehensive understanding of optical aberrations and numerous other optical (e.g., veiling glare) and mechanical (e.g., use of linear bearings) considerations in the design of cine prime and zoom lenses. We suggest that the reader peruse the listed references for a more detailed account of this subject.

LENS ERGONOMICS

Unlike most still-photography lenses, which are purely driven by cost vs. image-quality requirements, cine lenses have a strong ergonomic component. This component is indirectly dependent on what the cinematographer expects of a cine lens, but is directly related to what his or her crew, specifically camera assistants, must do to obtain the desired shot. Since the assistant's job may depend on ergonomic aspects of the chosen cine lens, this little-discussed lens aspect is certainly worth noting.

It is often believed that the quickness of sharp focus being attained in a cine lens by rotation of the focus gear means that a sharp in-focus image of the object has been achieved. However, the opposite is true, because it is best (and this has been conclusively tested and will be verified by most camera assistants) for the lens to have a lengthened focus scale with many spaced-apart focus calibration marks (e.g., infinity, 60, 30, 20, 15, 12, 10, 9 feet, etc., continuing down to close focus) so that the sharpness of focus may appear more difficult to reach, but the likely error in focus is reduced. Camera assistants say that this ergonomic lens aspect of providing an extended, well-spaced and clear focus scale, usually on a large lens barrel, is crucial to providing a well-focused, sharp image.

The aperture or T-stop scale is also important, because it should have clear markings (e.g., T2, 2.8, 4, 5.6, etc.) spaced well apart and preferably linearly spaced for equal stop differentials. The ergonomics of the latter condition have become more important lately due to motion-control-powered iris practices including variable, aperture and frame-rate shots.

Zoom scales were until recently largely ignored in terms of the focal-length markings and spacing on the lens zoom scale. On modern zoom-lens scales, the normal cramping of long focal-length marks has been avoided through optimization of zoom cam data so that long focal-length zoom mark spacings have been expanded and short focal-length zoom markings have been compressed (but not to adversely affect selection of short focal-length settings).

Most modern prime and zoom cine lenses can be expected to offer expanded focus, aperture and zoom scales on both sides of the lens, i.e., dual scales. Also, all of these scales should not be obscured by matte boxes, motors or other ancillary devices.

Some other ergonomic or perhaps more practical aspects of cine lenses are worth identifying. In prime or zoom lenses, mechanical precision and repeatability of focus marks are important, especially in 35mm-format lenses of short focal length, say 30mm or less. Typically, in a high-quality, wide-angle prime lens, where the entire lens is moved to focus, the repeatability error due to mechanical backlash, slop, high spots, etc., should be less than a half-thousandth of an inch (i.e., 12 microns metrically). Correspondingly, in wide-angle prime or zoom lenses where internal or "floating" lens elements are utilized, a similar tolerance, sometimes smaller, needs to be achieved. The eventual tolerance required in this case may be larger or smaller than that mentioned, depending upon the focal length (or power) of the movable focus group(s).

Maintenance of line of sight or "boresight" in primes, but more so for zooms, is a major ergonomic consideration, especially in visual-effects and motion-control applications. The best quality zoom lenses today can be expected to provide a maximum, or, worst case, line of sight variation through zoom of less than one inch at a 12-foot focus distance.

In addition to what has been described, the camera assistant or any other lens user demands that a cine lens not only provide accurate focus, aperture and zoom control, but also the right feel. An analogous way to explain this is to consider the turning of the frequency-control knob on a radio. Any movement of the knob should be smooth, not rough or sticky, and yet require some force. The same applies to the feel of the focus, aperture, zoom or other gears on a cine lens. For the best cine lenses, this feel is taken for granted, but for many others an uncertainty and lack of confidence about the lens is built up in the camera assistant's mind, and this is not conducive to good filmmaking.

FUTURE LENSES

From conception to final use, all modern cine lenses are heavily dependent on computers. The complexity of modern cine lenses, whether optical, mechanical, electronic, some combination thereof, or otherwise, is so great that computers are not only needed, they are fundamental to producing high-quality cine lenses. The advancement and gradual inroad made by zoom lenses in many fields, including cinematography, is a testament to the importance of the computer in the whole zoom-lens design process, from initial idea to final application. Without computers, most modern zoom lenses would not exist.

A full series of prime lenses will still continue to be available for some time, but increasingly, the prime lens will need to become more complex, with features such as continuous focusing from infinity to close or even macro object distances; internal, optically generated filtration effects; and so on, so that their design and manufacturing costs, i.e., return on investment, remain economically attractive. Individual prime lenses do offer one valuable advantage over zooms: they fill niche or special lens requirements better, e.g. very wide angle and fisheye field of view, very long focal lengths, slant focus, bellows, etc. Therefore, in the future, cine lens complements will still include primes as well as zooms and specialty lenses, but the mix will undoubtedly change.

Technological advancements in raw glasses, aspherical surfaces, thin films (i.e., coatings), diffractive optics and other aspects of lenses will continue to fuel lens development. A recently introduced compact, wide-angle, macro-focus (continuously focusable from infinity down to almost the front lens element), constant-aperture (through focus and zoom) cine zoom lens indicates what is to come. This lens, which employs two aspherical surfaces, some of the most exotic glasses ever produced, five cams, two movable focus groups, two movable zoom groups, a movable iris and a total of twenty-three lens elements, is a good example of what is already possible (See Figure 7).

Given the high performance level achievable by such a zoom, whether it be image quality, breathing control, macro focusing or many other features, it is easy to understand why zoom lenses have gained and will gain ground over traditional primes.

A good footnote is to consider where lenses have come from and where they are likely to go in comparison to other technologies. Lenses were here before film and will be here after film. Lenses were here before silicon-based electronic computer processors and will be here after they are long gone! When optically based, electronic-like computer processors arrive in the not too distant future, lenses will still be around, and their development will still be thriving.

LENS DATA TABLES

The lens data tables provided in this manual have been compiled for many 35mm, 16mm, VistaVision and 8mm spherical cine lenses purely as a guide to what might be expected in terms of lens depth of field, hyperfocal distance and other characteristics. It is extremely important to note that only a real film test will determine the actual characteristics of any lens.

For lens depth of field, a conservative circle of confusion of .0010 inches ($\frac{1}{1000}$) has been consistently used throughout the lens data tables. However, with modern cine equipment, lesser circles of confusion may be necessary. There are two reasons for this. Firstly, most modern spherical cine lenses produce sharp images mainly due to their high-contrast capabilities, and, secondly, most modern film negative stocks exhibit similar high-contrast tendencies. So, for such a lens and such a film stock, with hard lighting and no filtration, the effective or apparent depth of field falls within a smaller range about the chosen focus distance than shown in the lens data tables. Although this lens depth of field scenario may be considered extreme, it seems to arise more and more often in modern filmmaking, and as most cinematographers and their film crews will attest, it is usually better to play it safe when dealing with lens depth of field. Therefore, it is recommended that a reduced depth of field, up to half of what is shown in the lens data tables, be adopted when extreme conditions arise.

In order to accommodate these needs (as indicated in the tables), the tables enable you to calculate a circle of confusion of .0005 ($\frac{5}{10,000}$), or half the size and twice as critical as listed under a given f-stop. Once you match your focusing distance to the chosen f-stop, merely move two columns to the left in order to see the depth of field value for a $\frac{5}{10,000}$ circle of confusion.

The hyperfocal distances provided in the lens depth of field tables in this manual indicate the focus distance to which a lens must be set so that the (defocused) image quality performance is nearly equal for objects placed at infinity and half the hyperfocal distance.

To conclude, it must be emphasized that no matter how rigorous the mathematical calculations of lens properties or characteristics (including depth of field) are, there will always be nonlens contributions, such as filters, film stock, lighting, etc., and these must be considered in the final outcome. Only the results of an actual film test can determine the depth of field that is acceptable to the eye of the beholder.

Iain A. Neil is an Optical Consultant based out of Switzerland. His company ScotOptix contracts globally with optical technology companies, providing technical, business and intellectual property expertise with specialization in zoom lenses, multi-configuration optical systems and new technology implementation. He has more than 100 worldwide optically related patents issued and applied for, has published and edited more than thirty papers and books and has garnered eleven Academy Awards, two Emmys and the Fuji Gold Medal. He has been active in the optics industry for over thirty-six years and is currently a fellow member of SPIE and SMPTE, an associate member of ASC, a member of OSA and a voting member of A.M.P.A.S.

Camera Filters

by Ira Tiffen
ASC Associate Member

Camera filters are transparent or translucent optical elements that alter the properties of light entering the camera lens for the purpose of improving the image being recorded. Filters can affect contrast, sharpness, highlight flare, color and light intensity, either individually or in various combinations. They can also create a variety of special effects. It is important to recognize that even though there are many possibly confusing variations and applications, all filters behave in a reasonably predictable way when their properties are understood and experienced. Most of these properties relate similarly to filter use in both film and digital imaging. The following will explain the basic optical characteristics of camera filters, as well as their applications. It is a foundation upon which to build by experience. Textual data cannot fully inform; there is always something new to discover for yourself.

In their most successful applications, filter effects blend in with the rest of the image to help get the message across. Use caution when using a filter in a way that draws attention to itself as an effect. Combined with all the other elements of image making, filters help make visual statements, manipulate emotions and thought, and make believable what otherwise would not be. When used creatively, with an understanding of their abilities, they can really get the viewer involved.

CHANGING TECHNOLOGY

More than ever, changes in technology have fostered new applications, considerations and formats for filters. Digital technology requires a new array of spectrum and sensitivity concerns as well as opening up new imaging opportunities, especially post-capture. Look for references to such changes throughout this section.

FILTER PLANNING

Filter effects can become a key part of the look of a production, if considered in the planning stages. They can also provide a crucial last-minute fix to unexpected problems, if you have them readily available. Where possible, it is best to run advance tests for preconceived situations when time allows.

SIZES, SHAPES AND ON-LENS MOUNTING TECHNIQUES

Lens-mounted filters are available in round and rectangular shapes and in many sizes. Round filters generally come supplied with metal rings that mount directly to the lens. Frugal filter users might find it preferable to use adapters allowing the use of a set of filters of a single size with any lenses of equal or smaller sizes. Round filters can also be supplied with self-rotating mounts where needed, as for polarizers or Star effects. They can be readily stacked in combination. Rectangular filters require the use of a special filter holder or matte box. They offer the additional benefit of allowing slidability for effects that must be precisely aligned within an image, such as graduated filters. In all cases, it is advisable to use a mounting system that allows for sturdy support and ready manipulation. In addition, the use of a lens shade at the outermost mounting position (from the lens) will minimize the effect of stray off-axis reflections.

FILTER FACTORS

Many filter types absorb light that must be compensated for when calculating exposure. These are supplied with either a recommended filter factor or a stop value. Filter factors are multiples of the unfiltered exposure. Stop values are added to the stop to be set without the filter. Multiple filters will add stop values. Since each full stop added is a doubling of the exposure, a filter factor of 2 is equal to a one-stop increase. Example: Three filters of one stop each will need three additional stops, or a filter factor of 2 x 2 x 2 = 8 times the unfiltered exposure.

When in doubt in the field about compensation needed for a filter that you have no information on, you might use your light meter with the incident bulb removed. If you have a flat diffuser, use it; otherwise just leave the sensor bare. Aim it at an unchanging light source of sufficient intensity. On the ground, face-up at a blank sky can be a good field situation. Make a reading without the filter. Watch out for your own shadow. Make a reading with the filter covering the entire sensor. No light should enter from the sides. The difference in the readings is the compensation needed for that filter. You could also use a spot meter, reading the same bright patch, with similar results. There are some exceptions to this depending on the filter color, the meter sensitivity, and the target color, but this method is often better than taking a guess.

Published filter-factor information should be taken as a starting point. Differing circumstances may call for deviations from the norm.

FILTER GRADES AND NOMENCLATURE

Many filter types are available in a range of grades of differing strengths. This allows the extent of the effect to be tailored to suit various situations. The grade numbering range can vary with the effect type; generally, the higher the number, the stronger the effect. Unless otherwise stated, there is no mathematical relationship between the numbers and the strengths. A grade 4 is not twice the strength of a grade 2. A grade 1 plus a grade 4 doesn't add up to a grade 5.

Another possible source of confusion is that the various filter manufacturers often offer filters with similar names, using terms such as "fog" and 'diffusion,' which may have different characteristics.

The oldest standard for naming filter colors was developed early in the 20th century by Frederick Wratten and his associate, C.E. Kenneth Mees. While at Kodak they sought to make early film capabilities more closely respond to customer requirements. In doing so, they created specifications for a series of filter colors that correspond to particular applications. They gave each color a number, what we have since called Wratten numbers. These will be referenced later in this article. Kodak makes gel filters that are the defining standard for the Wratten system. Other manufacturers may or may not reference the Wratten designations, even if they otherwise use their own numbering system.

Contact the various manufacturers for additional details about their filter products and nomenclature.

CAMERA FILTERS FOR BOTH COLOR AND BLACK-AND-WHITE

Ultraviolet Filters

Film often exhibits a greater sensitivity to what is invisible to us: ultraviolet light. This is most often outdoors, especially at high altitudes, where the UV-absorbing atmosphere is thinner, and over long distances, such as marine scenes. It can show up as a bluish color cast with color film, or it can cause a low-contrast haze that diminishes details, especially when viewing far-away objects in either color or black-and-white. Ultraviolet filters absorb UV light generally without affecting light in the visible region.

It is important to distinguish between UV-generated haze and that of airborne particles such as smog. The latter is made up of opaque matter that absorbs visible light as well as UV light, and will not be appreciably removed by a UV filter.

Since the amount of UV encountered changes often, some cinematographers find that they can obtain more consistent color outdoors through the regular use of a filter that totally removes UV, along with their other filters. Some manufacturers will offer combination UV absorbers with other effects on special order for this purpose.

Ultraviolet filters come in a variety of absorption levels, usually measured by their percent transmission at 400 nanometers (nm), the visible-UV wavelength boundary. Use a filter that transmits zero percent at 400nm for aerial

Figure 1a. NO FILTER: Digital cameras can be overly sensitive to light in the far red and infrared. Certain objects have the property of reflecting a disproportionate amount of light in this spectral region, which can result in dark objects like the four black fabric samples in the center and at the left of the chart appearing with a distinct reddish tint while the two samples on the right remain neutral.

and far-distant scenes; one that transmits in the 10%–30% range at 400nm is fine for average situations.

Digital imaging sensors typically are less sensitive than film to UV light and have less need of UV-attenuating filters.

Infrared Filters and Film Imaging

Certain special situations call for the use of black-and-white or color infrared-sensitive films. For aerial haze penetration, recording heat effects and other purposes, they are invaluable. Their color and tonal renditions are very different, however, from other film types (consult film manufacturers for further details). Various filters are used to reduce unwanted visible light. Red, orange and yellow filters, as used for panchromatic black-and-white film, can enhance contrast and alter color.

Filters that absorb all visible light, transmitting only infrared, such as the Wratten #87 or #89, can also be useful. Bear in mind that you cannot see through these filters, which makes their use more complicated. Results will vary with film type and other factors.

Since most lenses focus infrared wavelengths slightly differently than other colors, you may need to use a different focusing scale on your lens when using infrared film.

In general, for black-and-white imaging, heat-reflecting surfaces will appear lighter than they might ordinarily; for color imaging, the image will consist of artificial colors corresponding to the various levels of reflected heat. Prior testing for most situations is a must.

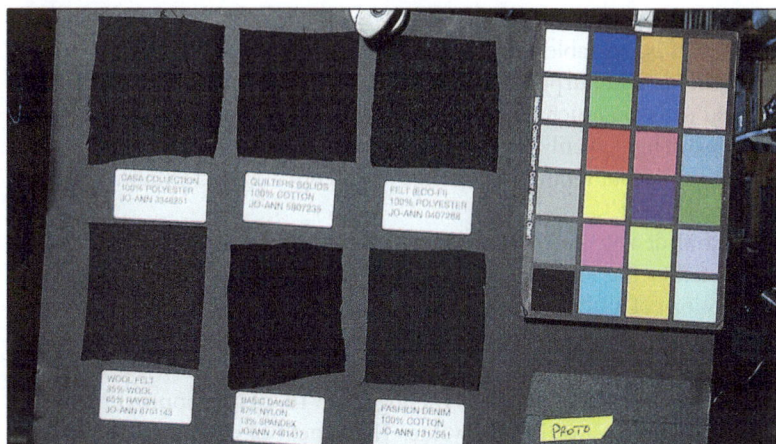

Figure 1b. WITH FAR RED/INFRARED FILTER: The addition of a filter that absorbs or reflects an appropriate amount of light in the far red/infrared region can eliminate the reddish cast and visually restore the objects to their proper neutral appearance, as seen in this image. Digital cameras differ by design so that the correction filter required by each will vary. It is best to check with the camera and filter manufacturers for what will work best with any given camera.

Infrared Filters and Digital Imaging

Digital imaging sensors have a greater sensitivity to far red and infrared than film. This part of the spectrum plays a more important part in the rendition of proper color, particularly for skin tones, than with film. However, this also raises some difficulties that can be mitigated by certain optical filters.

Black objects in particular can reflect varying amounts of far red and infrared light while often retaining a similar appearance to the eye. The difference is due to variations in the dyes used to color the objects. The extra sensitivity of the digital sensor to this light, though, can impart a color tint, often brownish-red, to the rendition of certain of the objects (and not to others) as captured by the camera. This can produce unacceptable color variations.

Using a filter that reflects infrared light, known as a hot mirror, is often the solution to this problem. Its dichroic coating equalizes the amount of far red and infrared light reflected from each object to a point where it does not exhibit a reddish color cast. Colors otherwise unsuitably tinted appear natural with this filter.

Some digital cameras already incorporate varying degrees of hot mirror capability in their internal design. It will be important to know what level, if any, of such attenuation of far red and infrared light is needed by the camera in use to avoid both the above effect and introducing any other unwanted color artifacts.

Another technique is the combination of certain color temperature control filters with hot mirrors. Examples include the 80C and the 80D Wratten colors. This has been found to be helpful for certain cameras.

Neutral-Density Filters

When it is desirable to maintain a particular lens opening for sharpness or depth-of-field purposes, or simply to obtain proper exposure when confronted with too much light intensity, use a neutral-density (ND) filter. This will absorb light evenly throughout the visible spectrum, effectively altering exposure without requiring a change in lens opening and without introducing a color shift.

Neutral-density filters are denoted by (optical) density value. Density is defined as the log, to base 10, of the opacitance. Opacitance (degree of absorption) of a filter is the reciprocal of (and inversely proportional to) its transmittance. As an example, a filter with a compensation of one stop has a transmittance of 50%, or 0.5 times the original light intensity. The reciprocal of the transmittance, 0.5, is 2. The log, base 10, of 2 is approximately 0.3, which is the nominal density value. The benefit of using density values is that they can be added when combined. Thus, two ND 0.3 filters have a density value of 0.6. However, their combined transmittance would be found by multiplying 0.5 x 0.5 = 0.25, or 25% of the original light intensity.

Neutral-density filters are also available in combination with other filters. Since it is preferable to minimize the number of filters used (see section on multiple filters), common combinations such as a Wratten #85 (daylight-conversion filter for tungsten film) with an ND filter are available as one filter, as in the 85N6. In this case, the two-stop ND 0.6 value is in addition to the exposure compensation needed for the base 85 filter.

There are two types of neutral-density filters in general use. The most prevalent type uses organic dyes to attenuate light. For situations where it is necessary to obtain the most even control from near-ultraviolet through the visible spectrum into the near-infrared, a metallic vacuum-deposition coating, often a nickel alloy, is ideal. For most situations, though, the silvered-mirror appearance of these filters imparts internal reflections that need to be addressed in use.

Special metallic coatings can also be employed for recording extreme bright-light situations, such as the sun during an eclipse. These filters are very dense and absorb substantially through the IR and UV range, as well as the visible, to reduce the potentially blinding level of light. The best have a density value of about 5.7, which allows less than 0.001% of the overall light through. Caution: Do *not* use any filter to aim at the sun unless it is clearly labeled as having been made for that purpose. Follow the manufacturer's directions and take all possible precautions to avoid accidental (and potentially permanent) blindness.

Variable Neutral Density Filters

While available for some time for use with film, the growth of digital imaging with its inherently greater light sensitivity has fostered a growing need for the variable ND filter. The most common version combines two polarizers in one assembly which, when rotated relative to each other, produce the desired variation in overall light transmission while retaining a mostly neutral color rendition. While you can produce your own version of this effect using two separate polarizers, particularly a circular one mounted on the lens and a linear one mounted onto that (away from the camera), there are reasons to obtain a purpose-built unit. Since polarizers can affect light of different wavelengths somewhat differently, they can generate a color cast, often deep blue, at the lowest transmission point, which is reached when both polarizers are positioned so their polarization axes are perpendicular to each other. Proper selection of polarizer foil characteristics for use by the manufacturers of variable ND filters will produce more neutral color balance, but even then, using these filters is usually better when not set for the lowest possible transmission.

For most current cameras that require circular polarization, it is important that the variable ND has a quarter-wave retarder on the side facing the camera, as with a traditional circular polarizer. In addition, if the variable ND assembly allows not only one filter element to rotate relative to the other (necessary to achieve the variable density effect) but also allows both elements to rotate together (while retaining their positions relative to each other) then the assembly can also function similarly to a traditional polarizer, where reduction of polarized reflected glare improves images of the sky, surfaces of bodies of water, and when imaging through windows. When using these remember to separately make rotational adjustments for both overall transmission as well as for polarized glare reduction.

Infrared-Neutral Density Filters

Digital camera sensors often have greater sensitivity to light than most film. This has prompted the need for increasing use of denser versions of neutral density filters for exposure control and for manipulating depth-of-field. An issue with these relates to the preponderance of infrared sources and reflecting surfaces as well as the manner in which neutral density filters are made, in reference to how ND filters handle light in the far-red and infrared regions of the spectrum.

Traditional ND filters made using dyes do not absorb light in the far red quite the same as elsewhere in the visible spectrum. When such a one-stop (0.3) ND filter is used it will allow a slightly greater percentage of light in the far red through than would be dictated by color neutrality. This percentage increases as the ND density increases, but is usually acceptable up through ND 0.9. Beyond that, the incremental increases in the relative amount of far red light passing through imparts an unwanted brownish-red color tint effect.

This can be handled by certain dyes in the glass that absorb specifically in the far red region. Another approach is to use strong dichroic coatings

IMAGES BY BRIAN AUSTAD

Figure 2a. NO FILTER: Midday scene as it appears without a filter. The underexposed foreground appears unnaturally dark when the exposure is set to properly render the sky.

that reflect such light, like the hot mirrors mentioned earlier. These can be made to various transmission percentages to match a particular camera's requirements. A characteristic of such a coating is that it is angle-dependent, meaning the color of light passing through it is different depending on the incident angle. In practical terms, light going straight through the center of the filter will be slightly differently tinted than light entering at a greater angle at the filter's edge. The stronger the effect of the coating, the greater this disparity between center and edge. In addition, this effect becomes especially prominent at wider lens angles. In some situations, you may find that this color shift is unacceptable. Testing is recommended.

Ultimately, what you need to know is that there are infrared-neutral density (IR-ND) filters made using various combinations of these techniques, the dichroic hot mirror coatings and the far-red-absorbing dyes, that are offered by various filter manufacturers that each work with a particular range of applicable cameras. A key concern to be aware of is that they may or may not be able to be stacked in combination depending on the specific filter types and application. The matching filter specifications can change with each new camera introduction. Keep abreast of developments in this area with your suppliers of cameras and filters.

A relatively new entry offering a unique approach in this field is the Tessive Time Filter. Essentially a controllable liquid crystal shutter panel that fits in a standard matte box, its primary use is to eliminate certain undesirable motion artifacts. Since it also acts as an electronically variable ND filter that attenuates IR it can function as a variable IR-ND filter.

Figure 2b. GRADUATED NEUTRAL DENSITY 0.6 FILTER: Taken at the same midday time as the unfiltered image, the filter absorbs two stops from the sky, allowing it to appear correctly while the exposure is adjusted to properly render the foreground through the clear half of the filter. The soft transition between the clear and the ND halves of the filter allow the effect to blend well together and make for a more balanced image.

Graduated ND Filters

Often it is necessary or desirable to balance light intensity in one part of a scene with another, namely in situations where you don't have total light control, as in bright exteriors. Exposing for the foreground will produce a washed-out, overexposed sky. Exposing for the sky will leave the foreground dark, underexposed

Graduated ND filters are part clear, part neutral-density, with a smoothly graded transition between. This allows the transition to be blended into the scene, often imperceptibly. An ND .6-to-clear, with a two-stop differential, will sometimes compensate the average bright-sky-to-foreground situation.

These filters are also available in combination colors, where the entire filter is, for example, a Wratten #85, while one half also combines a graded-transition neutral-density, as in the #85-to-85N6. This allows one filter to fulfill the need for two

Graduated filters generally come in three transition types. The most commonly used is the soft-edge graduation. It has a wide enough transition area on the filter to blend smoothly into most scenes, even with a wide-angle lens (which tends to narrow the transition within the image). A long focal length, however, might only image in the center of the transition. In this case, or where the blend must take place in a narrow, straight area, use a hard edge. This is ideal for featureless marine horizons. For situations where an extremely gradual blend is required, an attenuator is used. It changes density almost throughout its length.

The key to getting best results with a graduated filter is to help the effect blend in as naturally as possible. Keep it close to the lens to maximize transition softness. Avoid having objects in the image that extend across the transition in a way that would highlight the existence of the filter. Don't move the camera unless the transition can be maintained in proper alignment with the image throughout the move. Make all positioning judgments through a reflex viewfinder at the actual shooting aperture, because the apparent width of the graduation is affected by a change in aperture.

Graduated filters are best used in a square or rectangular format in a rotating, slidable position in a matte box. This will allow proper location of the transition within the image. They can be used in tandem; for example, one affecting the upper half, the second affecting the lower half of the image. The center area can also be allowed to overlap, creating a stripe of the combination of effects in the middle, most effectively with graduated color filters (see section on Graduated Color Filters).

Circular Gradient and Circular/Elliptical Center Spot ND Filters

Replicating the look of early lenses, which tended to go dark at the edges, or for other situations where such an effect is desirable, circular gradient filters can be made; they have a clear circular center that gradually darkens in a circular fashion out toward the edges. Center spot ND filters are similar in having a clear center, but there is no graduated transition: a clear circle or ellipse (or other shape, to order) with a razor-hard edge is surrounded by an even border of neutral density. In addition, subtly brightening a particular area of the image with these filters (relative to the darker edges) helps direct the viewer's eye toward action in the brighter area. This is especially useful when positioning the filter using a slidable, rotating mount such as a matte box so that the brighter area can be located almost anywhere within the frame.

Conversely, when using certain lenses with a design that produces a brighter center and darker edges, there are circular gradient filters that are darker in the center and clear toward the edges to compensate. These filters are usually offered by the same companies that manufacture these lenses.

Polarizing Filters

Polarizers allow color and contrast enhancement, as well as reflection control, using optical principles different from any other filter types. Most light that we record is reflected light that takes on its color and intensity from the objects we are looking at. White light, as from the sun, reflecting off a blue object appears blue because all other colors are absorbed by that object. A small portion of the reflected light bounces off the object without being absorbed and colored, retaining the original (often white) color of its source. With sufficient light intensity, such as outdoor sunlight, this reflected glare has the effect of washing out the color saturation of the object. It happens that for many surfaces, the reflected glare we don't want is polarized, while the colored reflection we want isn't.

The waveform description of light defines nonpolarized light as vibrating in a full 360-degree range of directions around its travel path. Polarized light in its linear form is defined as vibrating in only one such direction. A (linear) polarizing filter passes light through in only one vibratory direction. It is generally used in a rotating mount to allow for alignment as needed. In our example above, if it is aligned perpendicular to the plane of vibration of the polarized reflected glare, the glare will be absorbed. The rest of the light, the true-colored reflection vibrating in all directions, will pass through no matter how the polarizing filter is turned. The result is that colors will be more strongly saturated, or darker. This effect varies as you rotate the polarizer through a quarter-turn, producing the complete variation of effect from full to none.

Polarizers are most useful for increasing general outdoor color saturation and contrast. Polarizers can darken a blue sky, a key application, on color as well as on black-and-white film, but there are several factors to remember when doing this. To deepen a blue sky, the sky must be blue to start with, not white or hazy. Polarization is also angle-dependent. A blue sky will not be equally affected in all directions. The areas of deepest blue are determined by the following rule of thumb: when setting up an exterior shot, make a right angle between thumb and forefinger; point your forefinger at the sun. The area of deepest blue will be the band outlined by your thumb as it rotates around the pointing axis of your forefinger, directing the thumb from horizon to horizon. Generally, as you aim your camera either into or away from the sun, the effect will gradually diminish. There is no effect directly at or away from the sun. Do not pan with a polarizer without checking to see that the change in camera angle doesn't create undesirable, noticeable changes in color or saturation. Also, with an extra-wide-angle view, the area of deepest blue may appear as a distinctly darker band in the sky. Both situations are best avoided. In all cases, the effect of the polarizer will be visible when viewing through it.

Polarizers need approximately 1½ to 2 stops exposure compensation, generally without regard to rotational orientation or subject matter. They are also available in combination with certain standard conversion filters, such as the 85BPOL. In this case, add the polarizer's compensation to that of the second filter.

Certain camera optical systems employ internal surfaces that also polarize light. One example is the use of a videotap. Using a standard (linear) polarizer may cause the light to be further absorbed by the internal optics, depending on the relative orientation. This may interfere with the normal operation of the equipment. The solution in these instances is to use a circular polarizer. The term "circular" does not refer to its shape. Rather, it is a linear polarizer to which has been added, on the side facing the camera, a clear (you can't see it, you can only see what it does) quarter wave retarder. This corkscrews the plane of polarization, effectively depolarizing the light (after it has been through the linear polarizer, which will have already had its effect on enhancing your image), eliminating the problem. It is of critical importance, then, when using a circular polarizer that it be oriented in the proper direction. That is, the retarder layer must be on the side facing the camera. The filter must be either clearly labeled by the manufacturer as to the correct direction, or mounted in a ring that only threads on one way. Be careful when using a filter that mounts on the rear of a lens, as in some wide-angle designs. Some lenses will allow the threaded filter ring to mount in the wrong orientation. You can ensure the correct direction by seeing that the direction the camera views through the filter is the one where the filter functions as a normal polarizer. If turned the other way, it will not produce the polarization effect. The circular polarizer otherwise functions in the same manner as a standard linear one.

Polarizers can also control unwanted reflections from surfaces such as glass and water. For best results, be at an angle of 33 degrees incident to the reflecting surface. Viewing through the polarizer while rotating it will show the effect. It may not always be advisable to remove all reflections. Leaving some minimal reflection will preserve a sense of context to a close-up image through the reflecting surface. For example, a close-up of a frog in water may appear as a frog out of water without some telltale reflections.

For certain situations, it may be desirable to use a pair of polarizers to create a variable-density filter. Although the transmission will vary as you rotate one relative to the other, you should be aware of the resultant light loss, even at its lightest point.

For relatively close imaging of documents, pictures and small three-dimensional objects in a lighting-controlled environment, as on a copy stand, plastic polarizers mounted on lights aimed at 45 degrees to the subject from both sides of the camera will maximize the glare-reducing efficiency of a polarizer on the camera lens. The camera in this case is aimed straight at the subject surface, not at an angle. The lighting polarizers should both be in the same perpendicular orientation to the one on the lens. Again, you can judge the effect through the polarizer.

Polarization Filters and 3-D

The development of optical systems for capturing right and left eye stereoscopic views for 3-D productions uncovered new applications for polarization. A staple of 3-D production today, the beam-splitter rig positions two cameras at right angles to each other, each aimed at opposing sides of a partially silvered mirror. One camera sees through the mirror, the other images off the reflection. The reflected light will be partially polarized by the mirror; the transmitted light will only exhibit the partial polarization inherent in the scene that both cameras are recording. The differences in the two light paths can cause troublesome differences in brightness of particular details in the image that can disrupt the stereoscopic effect. One solution to this is to position a quarter-wave retarder plate, essentially a clear piece of glass that twists the polarization axis of the incoming light, in front of the mirror in the beam-splitter rig, effectively neutralizing the negative polarization effect.

SPECIAL EFFECT FILTERS
General Information
The following filter types are available in a wide range of grades useful in both color and black-and-white imaging. They have no recommended filter factors, but may require exposure compensation based on several things. Filters that lower contrast or create flare, where contrast and/or light intensity is higher, will do more for any given grade. The more light they have to work with, the more they can do. The same filter in two different lighting conditions may produce two different effects. With diffusion, or image-softening filters, higher contrast scenes appear sharper, needing more diffusion than scenes of lower contrast. Diffusion requirements will also vary with other conditions. Smaller film formats will allow less diffusion, as will large-screen projection. Color may allow less diffusion than black and white. Producing for television may require a greater degree of diffusion to survive the transition. These relationships should cause you to choose exposure and filter grade based on the situation and personal experience. Prior testing is always recommended.

Diffusion Filters
Many different techniques have been developed to diffuse image-forming light. Strong diffusion can blur reality for a dream-like effect. In more subtle forms, diffusion can soften wrinkles to remove years from a face. The optical effects all involve bending a percentage of the image-forming light from its original path to defocus it.

Some of the earliest portrait diffusion filters still in use today are nets. Fine mesh, like a stocking, stretched across the lens has made many a face appear youthful, flawless. This effect can now be obtained through standard-sized optical glass filters, with the mesh laminated within. These function through "selective" diffusion. They have a greater effect on small details, such as wrinkles and skin blemishes, than on the rest of the image. The clear spaces in the mesh transmit light unchanged, preserving the overall sharp appearance of the image. Light striking the flat surface of the net lines, however, is reflected or absorbed. A light-colored mesh will reflect enough to either tint shadows lighter, which lowers contrast, or its color while leaving highlight areas alone. The effect of diffusion, however, is produced by the diffraction of light that just strikes the edges of the mesh lines. This is bent at a different angle, changing its distance to the film plane, putting it out of focus. It happens that this has a proportionately greater effect on finer details than on larger image elements. The result is that fewer wrinkles or blemishes are visible on a face that otherwise retains an overall, relatively sharp appearance.

The finer the mesh, the more the image area covered by mesh lines and the greater the effect. Sometimes, multiple filters are used to produce even stronger results.

As with any filter that has a discrete pattern, be sure that depth of field doesn't cause the net pattern to become visible in the image. Using small apertures or short focal length lenses make this more likely, as will using a smaller film format such as 16mm vs. 35mm, given an equal field of view. Generally, midrange or larger apertures are suitable, but test before critical situations. When in need of net diffusion in circumstances where mounting it in front of the lens will cause the pattern to show, try mounting the filter in a suitable location behind the lens (if the equipment design allows). This should reduce the chance of the pattern appearing. Placing a glass filter behind the lens may alter the back-focal length, which may need readjustment. Check with your lens technician. A test is recommended.

When diffusing to improve an actor's facial appearance, it is important not to draw attention to the presence of the filter, especially with stronger grades, when diffusion is not required elsewhere. It may be desirable to lightly diffuse adjacent scenes or subjects not otherwise needing it to ensure that the stronger filtration, where needed, is not made obvious.

In diffusing faces, it is especially important that the eyes do not get overly soft and dull. This is the theory behind what might be called circular diffusion filters. A series of concentric circles, sometimes also having additional radial lines, are etched or cast into the surface of a clear filterThese patterns have the effect of selectively bending light in a somewhat more efficient way than nets, but in a more radial orientation. This requires that the center of the circular pattern is aligned with one of the subject's eyes—not always an easy or possible task—to keep it sharp. The rest of the image will exhibit the diffusion effect.

A variation on the clear-center concept is the center-spot filter. This is a special-application filter that has a moderate degree of diffusion surrounding a clear central area that is generally larger than that of the circular diffusion filter mentioned previously. Use it to help isolate the main subject, held sharp in the clear center, while diffusing a distracting background, especially in situations where a long lens and depth-of-field differentiation aren't possible.

IMAGES BY IRA TIFFEN

Figure 3a.
NO FILTER –
STANDARD EXPOSURE.
Midday scene as it appears
without a filter.

Figure 3b.
BLACK PRO-MIST 1
STANDARD EXPOSURE
Midday scene with highlight haze
more visually suggestive of the
sun's heat and the humidity by
the lake.

Figure 3c.
SUNRISE 3 GRAD PLUS
BLACK PRO-MIST 1,
one stop under.
Combining the hazy atmosphere
of the Black Pro-Mist with the
color of the Sunrise Grad, underexposure produces a visual sense
of early morning.

Figure 3d.
TWILIGHT 3 GRAD,
two stops under.
The cool colors of the Twilight
Grad plus a two-stop underexposure produces a visual sense of
early evening.

Another portrait diffusion type, long in use, involves the placement of small lenslets or clear refracting shapes dispersed on an otherwise clear optical surface. They can be round, diamond-shaped or otherwise configured. These are capable of more efficient selective diffusion than the net type and have no requirement to be aligned with the subject's eye. They don't lower contrast by tinting shadows, as light-colored nets do. These lenslets refract light throughout their surface, not just at the edges. For any given amount of clear space through the filter, which is relative to overall sharpness, they can hide fine details more efficiently than net filters.

The above types of filters, though most often used for portrait applications, also find uses wherever general sharpness is too great and must be subtly altered.

Some diffusion filters, notably called "dot" filters, can effectively combine image softening with the appearance of mild highlight flare and a reduction in contrast. Although perhaps more akin to mist and fog effects, they also fall into the category of diffusion filters.

Sliding Diffusion Filters

When attempting to fine-tune the application of diffusion within a sequence, it can be invaluable to be able to vary the strength of the effect while filming. This can be accomplished by employing an oversized filter that has a graduated diffusion effect throughout its length. It is mounted to allow sliding the proper grade area in front of the lens, which can be changed on camera. When even more subtle changes are required, maintaining consistent diffusion throughout the image while varying the overall strength, a dual opposing-gradient filter arrangement can be used.

Optical Diffusion in the Digital Camera

Unlike film, digital imaging records on discrete elements known as pixels. These are positioned as an array over the surface of the imaging sensor. The pattern of pixels can produce a distractingly animated moiré effect with details in the scene being recorded. To address this, digital cameras are typically provided with an optical low pass filter, or OLPF, placed in the light path just before the sensor. This alters the position and pattern of fine details striking the sensor so that the risk of generating unwanted moiré artifacts is substantially reduced or eliminated.

The OLPF will result in a typically minimal amount of image diffusion, but also a much improved image due to its effect on moiré.

Fog, Double Fog and Mist Filters

A natural fog causes lights to glow and flare. Contrast is generally lower, and sharpness may be affected as well. Fog filters mimic this effect of atomized water droplets in the air. The soft glow can be used to make lighting more visible, make it better felt by the viewer. The effect of humidity in, say, a tropical scene can be created or enhanced. In lighter grades, these filters can take the edge off excess contrast and sharpness. Heavier grades can create unnatural effects, as for fantasy sequences. In general, however, the effect of a strong natural fog is not produced accurately by fog filters in their stronger grades. Their look is too soft, with too much contrast, to faithfully reproduce the effect of a thick natural fog. For that, double-fog or graduated-fog filters are recommended.

Double-fog filters have milder flare and softening characteristics than standard fog filters while exhibiting a much greater effect on contrast, especially in the stronger grades. A very thick natural fog will still allow close-up objects to appear sharp. So will a double fog filter. The key to the effect is the much lower contrast combined with a minimal amount of highlight flare.

Graduated-fog filters, sometimes called "scenic," are part clear or light fog and part denser fog effect. Aligning the clear or weaker half with the foreground and the stronger half with the background will render an effect more like that of a natural fog, accumulating density with distance.

Mist filters generally produce highlight flare which, by staying closer to the source, appears more as a halo than will the more outwardly extended flare of a fog filter. They give an almost pearlescent glow to highlights. The lighter grades also find uses in toning down the excessive sharpness and contrast of modern film and lens combinations without detracting from the image. Black Pro Mist-type filters also create moderate image softening and modest-to-strong highlight flare, but without as much of a lightening effect on shadows.

Contrast Control Filters

There are many situations, such as bright sunlit exteriors, where proper contrast is difficult to maintain. Exposing for either highlights or shadows will leave the other severely under- or overexposed. Low-contrast filters create a small amount of localized flare near highlight areas within the image. This reduces contrast by lightening nearby shadow areas, leaving highlights almost unchanged. A variation, called Soft Contrast by its manufacturer, includes a light-absorbing element in the filter that, without exposure compensation, will reduce contrast by also darkening highlights. Use the Soft Contrast filter when lighter shadows are not desired and highlights are too bright. In both cases, the mild flare produced from bright highlights is sometimes used as a lighting effect.

Another type of filter reduces contrast without any localized flare. As named by Tiffen, the Ultra Contrast filter series uses the surrounding ambient light, not just light in the image area, to evenly lighten shadows throughout. Use it where contrast control is needed without any other effect on sharpness or highlight flare being apparent.

Star and Flare Effects

Making points of light in the scene more interesting has long been the purpose of star filters. These typically have patterns of parallel lines chemically etched into the filter's surface which act like cylindrical lenses, refracting the light into bright lines that appear to extend outward from the light source in a direction perpendicular to the lines on the filter. There will be two star points for each direction of parallel lines. Spacing the lines closely makes for a stronger effect; conversely wider spacing makes it more subtle.

A related flare effect originated with anamorphic lenses. When aimed into a bright point light source, it was possible to achieve a broad cyan-blue flare streak, often simply referred to as a "blue streak," due to the internal reflections in the nonspherical lens. More recently, lens accessories have been developed that achieve this effect with spherical lenses when desired. One is a mechanical device mated to a matte box that can produce two different strengths of this effect. Another approach embeds cylindrical lenses into the traditional glass filter format for use with standard matte boxes. This latter version also facilitates creating streaks in several strengths and a variety of colors besides blue.

FILTERS FOR BLACK-AND-WHITE

Tone Control Filters

Black-and-white imaging records only tonal differences between colored objects, which appear as black, white or different shades of gray. Proper rendition depends on your own desires and, for film, the differences between film sensitivity to colors and that of the eye. The latter is due to the fact that most panchromatic emulsions are more sensitive to blue, violet and ultraviolet than to other colors. Therefore, blue appears as lighter on film than it does to the eye. This can make a blue sky light enough to appear a similar shade of light gray as the clouds that are in it, making the clouds disappear. A more "correct" cloud presence is obtained through the use of a yellow filter, such as a Wratten #8, which can absorb blue light, darkening the sky to more closely match what the eye would see. The #8 also acts as a general compensator for most subjects, giving a tonal rendition similar to that of the eye. Deeper colors, closer to the red end of the spectrum, such as Wratten #15 deep yellow, #16 orange, and #25 and #29 red filters, will produce progressively deeper and artificially more dramatic renditions of blue sky.

Remember that since these filters act on color differences to produce tonal differences, the required colors must be present. The part of the sky you are recording must be blue to be affected. Areas of sky closer to the sun or nearer the horizon are generally less blue than elsewhere. Use of a graduated neutral-density filter can darken a sky relative to the foreground, but will not increase contrast between a blue sky and the clouds.

Using filters for contrast control can be a matter of artistic preference or of necessity. It is possible for two disparate colors, say, a certain orange and blue, to record as the identical tone, eliminating any visible difference between them. Filters will lighten objects of their own color and darken those of their complement. Complementary color pairs are: green-red, orange-blue, and violet-yellow. An orange filter in the above case will darken the blue and lighten the orange; a blue filter will perform the reverse.

A green filter, such as Wratten #11, can be used to lighten green foliage to show more detail. It may also be used to provide more pleasing skin tones outdoors, especially against blue sky.

FILTERS FOR COLOR
General Information

Recording color involves knowing more about light sources than is necessary for black-and-white imaging. Sunlight, daylight, exterior lighting at different times of day, incandescent, fluorescent, as well as other artificial sources, all have color characteristics that vary significantly. We see images through our eyes only after they are processed by our brain, which has the ability to make certain adjustments to the way we see color. White will still appear white to the eye in various types of lighting, as long as we don't have more than one type visible at a time. Film has no such internal compensation. It is designed to see only a certain type of light as white—all others will appear different to the extent of their difference. Filters are required to provide the necessary fine-tuning.

Knowing that light is a form of energy, we can theoretically view it as energy emitted from a hot object, usually termed a "black body," that gives off light as a function of its temperature. The color of that light can be measured in degrees Kelvin (°K). The normally encountered types of light can be categorized by certain anticipated color temperatures or can be measured with a color temperature meter.

Color in a Digital World

Optical filters for controlling color in digital imaging can yield different results than they do with film. The relationship between the light sensitive components and the techniques used to produce full-color images is sufficiently different between the two recording formats that it will help to learn more from their respective manufacturers about the important color rendition characteristics of the particular film stock or digital camera in use.

Film may be said to be chemically coordinated to expect light at a certain color temperature—using optical color filters will alter the spectral balance of incoming light in a manner that works well with this format.

Digital imaging combines optical as well as electronic manipulation of incoming light and its subsequent color rendition that may or may not react well to optical color filters depending on the particular design parameters of the equipment in use. It will be best to check with the camera manufacturer to determine their recommendation.

The following discussion of color control references those systems, film and digital, that react well to the use of optical color filters for attenuating the spectrum to yield desired color effects.

Color-Conversion Filters

Color-conversion filters are used to correct for sizable differences in color temperature between the film and the light source. These are comprised of both the Wratten #80 (blue, as used for daylight film in tungsten lighting) and the Wratten #85 (amber, as used for tungsten film in daylight) series of filters. Since they see frequent outdoor use in bright sunlight, the #85 series, especially the #85 and #85B, are also available in combination with various neutral-density filters for exposure control.

Light-Balancing Filters

Light-balancing filters are used to make minor corrections in color temperature. These are comprised of both the Wratten #81 (yellowish) and the Wratten #82 (bluish) series of filters. They are often used in combination with color conversion filters. Certain #81 series filters may also be available in combination with various neutral-density filters for exposure control.

Color-Compensating Filters

Color-compensating (CC) filters are used to make adjustments to the red, blue or green characteristics of light. These find applications in correcting for color balance, light source variations, different reversal film batches and other color effects. They are available in density variations of cyan, magenta and yellow, as well as red, blue and green filters.

Decamired® Filters

Decamired (a trademark of the manufacturer) filters are designed to more easily handle a wide range of color-temperature variations than the previously mentioned filters. Available in increments of both a red and a blue series, Decamired filters can be readily combined to create almost any required correction. In measuring the color temperature of the light source and comparing it to that for which the film was designed, we can predict the required filtration fairly well.

A filter that produces a color-temperature change of 100° K at 3400° K will produce a change of 1000° K at 10,000° K. This is because the filter relates to a visual scale of color. It will always produce the same visible difference. A color change of 100° K at the higher temperature would hardly be noticed.

To allow simple calculation of such differences, we convert the color temperature into its reciprocal, that is, to divide it into 1. Then, since this is usually a number with six or more decimal places, we multiple it by 106, or one million, for convenience. This is then termed the "mired value," for micro reciprocal degrees. It identifies the specific change introduced by the filter in a way that is unrelated to the actual temperature range involved.

To see this more clearly, let's look at the following changes in color temperature from both the degree and mired differences. Numbers are degrees Kelvin, those in parentheses are mireds:

9100 (110) to 5900 (170) = difference of 3200 (60)
4350 (230) to 3450 (290) = difference of 900 (60)
4000 (250) to 3200 (310) = difference of 800 (60)

From this, you can see that although the degree differential varies as the range changes, the actual filtration difference for these examples, in mireds, is the same.

To use this concept, subtract the mired value of the light source from that of the film (the mired value of the Kelvin temperature the film is balanced for). If the answer is positive, you need a reddish filter; if negative, use a bluish filter. Mired-coordinated filters are termed "Decamireds." Mired value divided by 10 yields Decamireds. The 60 mired shifts (above) would be produced by an R6 filter, where the higher values were that of the lighting. Sets of such filters come in values of 1.5, 3, 6 and 12 Decamireds, in both B (bluish) and R (reddish) colors. These numbers are additive; that is, a pair of R3s produces an R6. An R6 plus a B6 cancel each other out to produce a neutral gray.

Fluorescent and Other Discontinuous Spectra Lighting Correction

Since filters never actually add color but only absorb certain wavelengths to increase the relative proportion of others, the original light source must have the colors you want to start withSome sources are totally deficient in certain wavelengths, which cannot be added back using only filters. This is particularly true of many types of metal-halide lighting. With other lighting types, such as fluorescent, color-temperature measurements may not provide the correct filter requirements, because color-temperature theory is based on having a continuous spectrum, meaning light at all wavelengths. It is possible for a light source to have a sufficient spectral distribution to emulate a correctable color temperature when so measured, but its effect on film can be very different. (See section on Lighting for further details page 375.)

Fluorescent lighting generally produces a greenish color overcast. Each of the many lamp types varies in color, and it can be difficult to know the

Figure 4a. NO FILTER: Standard exposure/midday scene as it appears without a filter.

precise correction. Similarly named lamp types can vary with manufacturer, and lamps will also vary over time in use. Special filters are available, however, that are designed to yield good-to-excellent color under fluorescents, without the need for a color- temperature meter and a variety of CC filters.

Mixed Lighting Situations

A question often arises about what to do when there is more than one type of lighting used in a scene. The key to this is to first try to make all the light sources behave the same. That is, choose one that predominates, correct the camera for that, and correct the other lighting with gel filters made for them. You can convert daylight coming through a window with a gel placed over the window, which will make it a similar color temperature as the predominant tungsten, or even fluorescent, lighting inside. Then correct the camera for that type of light. There are many such combinations that will work; which one to choose is often a matter of economics. Filtering a factory of fluorescents with gels or filter tubes may cost far more than just gelling up the occasional window.

If there is no way to correct all the lights for one color temperature, try to minimize the intrusion of those for which you cannot correct to the camera. Sometimes, this can be used to advantage. The cool blue light from outdoors through a window can make the tungsten-lit interior seem that much warmer and cozier. Once "normal" color is within reach, frequently a variation can be even better. It all depends on your purpose and the story you are telling.

Graduated Color Filters

Similar to graduated ND filters, graduated color filters are also produced

Figure 4b. TAKEN AT THE SAME MIDDAY TIME AS THE UNFILTERED IMAGE: The filter absorbs two stops and is shown here with an additional one stop underexposure – a total of three stops under. The cool tones and underexposure produce a visual sense of evening under moonlight illumination.

in a wide range of standard and custom colors, densities and proportions for many applications. A blue-to-clear filter can add blue to a white, hazy sky without affecting the foreground. An orange-to-clear filter can enliven a tepid sunset. Color can be added to the bottom of the scene, as with a green-to-clear filter used to enrich the appearance of a lawn.

Stripe filters are another type of graduated filter, having a thin stripe of color or neutral density running through the center of the filter, graduating to clear on either side. These are often used to horizontally paint various colors in layers into a sky, as well as for narrow-area light balancing.

When seeking to gradually alter the color or exposure of a scene on-camera, an extra-long graduated (attenuated) filter, mounted to slide in front of the lens, can accomplish what might otherwise be a complicated task. For example, going from the appearance of daylight to that of twilight can be synthesized with a day-for-night filter in combination with a neutral density, both gradually altering density in the one filter. With careful lighting, this can achieve a realistic change-of-time look with a minimum of difficulty, as both exposure and color are altered together in a controllable manner

Coral Filters

As the sun moves through the sky, the color temperature of its light changes. It is often necessary to compensate for this in a variety of small steps as the day progresses, to match the appearance of different adjacent sequences to look as though they all took place at the same time. Coral filters are a range of graded filters of a color similar to a #85 conversion filter. From light to heavy, any effect from basic correction to warmer or cooler than normal is possible. Corals can also compensate for the overly cool blue effect of outdoor shade.

Sepia Filters

People often associate sepia-toned images with "early times." This makes sepia filters useful tools for producing believable flashbacks and for period effects with color film. Other colors are still visible, which is different from original sepia-toned photography, but appear infused with an overall sepia tint.

Didymium Filters

The Didymium Filter is a combination of rare earth elements in glass. It completely removes a portion of the spectrum in the orange region. The effect is to increase the color-saturation intensity of certain brown, orange and reddish objects by eliminating the muddy tones and maximizing the crimson and scarlet components. Its most frequent use is for obtaining strongly saturated fall foliage. It also enlivens brick and barn reds, colors that aren't bright scarlet to begin with, most effectively. The effect is minimal on objects of other colors. Skin tones might be overly warm. Even after subsequent color timing or correction to balance out any unwanted bias in these other areas, the effect on reddish objects will still be apparent. Prior testing should be done because film color sensitivities vary.

Underwater Color-Correction Filters

When imaging underwater, the light you are recording is filtered by the water it passes through. Longer wavelength reds and oranges are absorbed until only blue is left. The actual effect is determined by numerous factors, such as light source (sun or artificial), water quality and the water path. The latter is the distance the light travels through the water. In natural (sun)light, this is the depth of the subject from the surface plus the subject-to-camera distance. For artificial lighting, it is the light-to-subject-to-camera distance. The longer the water path, the greater the filtering effect of the water. In many cases, certain color-correcting filters can absorb enough shorter wavelengths to restore better color balance. For example, Aquacolor®, a patented system that precisely compensates for the light-filtering effects of water, comes in filter densities that match different water paths. The difference between corrected and uncorrected color can be dramatic. The use of faster speed films and lenses will facilitate the use of light-absorbing correcting filters.

Differences Between Camera and Lab/Post Correction

It is the job of the lab timer to fine-tune the finished color rendition of a film production. This accounts for variables in exposure, print stock and processing. Timing can also be used to impart certain color effects for densities available in the film emulsion to work with, and is limited to the range of variation of the optical printer. These are much more limiting than the multitude of colorants in the real world and the number of ways in which adjustments can be made at the camera. Filtering on the camera brings the lab that much closer to the desired result, providing a greater latitude of timing options. It can also center more creative control in the hands of the cinematographer.

There will be times when counting on the lab is either the only choice, or can produce some unusual effects. When faced with a low-light situation in daylight using tungsten film, it may be necessary for exposure reasons to pull the #85 filter and correct in the printing. When you do this, however, neutral gray tones will appear slightly yellow, even when all else looks correct. This effect can be used to artificially enhance lush green foliage colors through the addition of yellow. It may have other uses, but you will not achieve the same result as if you had used the 85 filter.

LL-D®

The LL-D was designed to help in the above situation. It requires no exposure compensation and makes sufficient adjustments to the film to enable the timer to match the color of a properly 85-filtered original. It is not an all-around replacement for the #85. Use it only where needed for exposure purposes, and for subsequently printer-timed work.

Digital Post Processing Options

There are many new options available that allow images to be manipulated after capture. Software now facilitates extensive control of color, contrast, sharpness, and other factors. There are numerous versions and platforms so it will be of benefit to find what applies best to the particular task at hand.

One variation among these produces digital filter effects that are close emulations of optical filter effects. These have special use in that they can more readily blend the looks of optically and digitally filtered scenes when combined in editing.

SPECIAL APPLICATION FILTERS

Contrast-Viewing Filters

Balancing lighting by eye is a matter of experience. Decisions can be aided through the use of contrast-viewing filters. These are designed to handicap the eye, with its much greater range of apparent densities, to resemble the range of the various types of film. Use contrast viewers to judge relative highlight and shadow densities. There are viewers for black-and-white film,

Figure 5a. WITHOUT THE SPLIT-FIELD LENS (1): The foreground here is out of focus when the background is sharp. You can't focus on both at the same time.

as well as various viewer densities for color film. A darker viewer is used for slower film speeds, where you would tend to use brighter lighting. Faster film, which can be used in dimmer settings, would require a lighter viewer. Further details can be obtained from the manufacturers.

There are also Green, Red and Blue viewing filters used to judge lighting effects when doing process work like greenscreen.

Figure 5b. WITHOUT THE SPLIT-FIELD LENS (2): The foreground here is sharp when the background is out of focus. You can't focus on both at the same time.

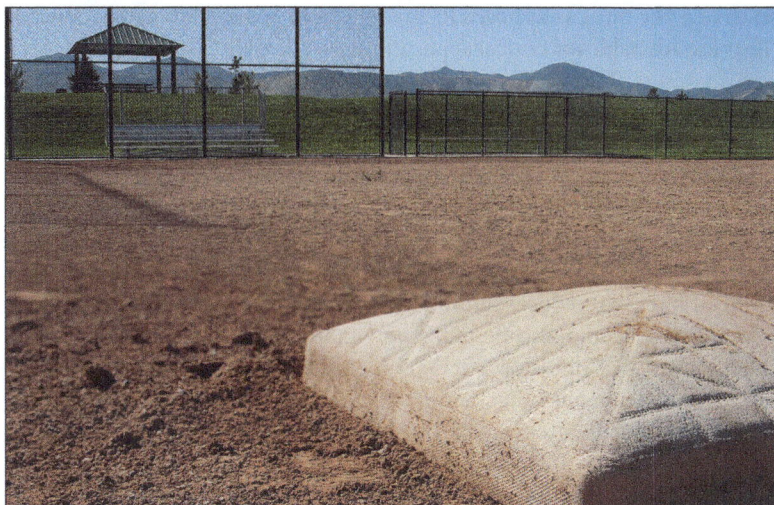

Figure 5c. WITH THE SPLIT-FIELD LENS: The close-up lens half allows sharp focus on the foreground while the camera lens is focused on the background. There is a soft transition between the two areas at the edge of the split-field lens at this middle-of-the-range lens opening.

Close-up and Split-Field Diopter Lenses

Close-up lenses allow for closer focusing than would otherwise be available with the unaided camera lens. Cutting such a lens in half produces the split-field lens. This can be used to have two fields of focus, one very near, the other very far, in one scene.

A more recent variation is to have a narrow linear sliver of lens that can be positioned in the middle region of the frame with clear spaces on either side. (See Extreme Close-Up Cinematography page 667.)

OTHER FILTER CONSIDERATIONS
Effect of Depth-of-Field and Focal-Length Changes

Standard color filters generally function without change through variations in depth-of-field and focal length. This may not be true of many of the special-effect filter types. There are no solid rules for predicting the variation in filter effect due to depth-of-field or focal-length changes. There are some things we can expect, however, especially when changing focal length. Let's look at a fog/mist type filter that causes a light to glow or flare. Take the example of a certain grade filter where we can see that the ratio of light diameter to glow diameter is, say, 1:3. As we view this through a changing focal length, we will see that the ratio remains the same, although the magnification will vary accordingly. So the decision to use a filter of a different grade to maintain a certain appearance at different focal lengths will be based on wanting to change the ratio, as opposed to any otherwise corresponding relationship. Tests are advisable for critical applications.

Multiple Filter Use

When any single filter is not enough to produce the desired results, use combinations. Choose carefully to minimize the number required. Try to get the job done with no more than three filters. Use filters that individually add to the final effect without canceling each other out. For example, don't use a polarizer, which can increase color saturation, in combination with a low-contrast filter that reduces saturation, unless it works for some other reason (the polarizer could also be reducing window reflections, for instance). It is important that diffusion filters be mounted closest to the lens with any additional filters going after. Some popular filter combinations may also be available in one filter to simplify their use.

Secondary Reflections

Lighting can cause flare problems, especially when using more than one filter. Lights in the image pose the greatest difficulties. They can reflect between filter surfaces and cause unwanted secondary reflections. Maintaining parallelism between filters, and further aligning the lights in the image with their secondary reflections where possible, can minimize this problem. In critical situations, it may be best to make use of a matte box with a tilting filter stage. Tilting filters of good optical quality only a few degrees in such a unit can divert the secondary reflections out of the lens axis, out of the image, without introducing unwanted distortion or noticeable changes in the filter's effect.

Custom (Homemade and Field-Ready) Filters

There will be times when you need an effect and don't have time to obtain one ready-made. Certain effects can be produced that, although different from factory filters, can be useful in a pinch or for unusual custom situations. Net-diffusion effects can be produced as they were originally by stretching and affixing one or more layers of stocking material to the lens end, held in place with a rubber band. (This is also an easier way of mounting net effects behind the lens.) There are also numerous things you can do if you have a clear filter (or several). Petroleum jelly can cause flare or diffusion, or even some star-like streaks, depending on its application on a clear filter, spread with a finger or cloth. The chief benefit here is that the effect can also be applied only to selected portions of the scene. Breathing on a clear filter can produce interesting but temporary fog-like results. Using cut gels can simulate certain graduated-filter effects. When doing this, be sure to keep the filter close to the lens, and use larger lens openings to keep the visible edge as soft as possible.

Rain Spinners

When rain or boat spray send distracting water drops onto the lens, you can mount a rain spinner, sometimes called a rain deflector, as you would a matte box on the front of the lens. A round filter, usually clear, spins at over 3000 rpm and flings off droplets before they form. This is very effective when filming the Tour De France in the rain.

Filtering for Digital Intermediate

When adding computer generated effects to filmed original, it may be best to minimize or eliminate the use of diffusion filters for image capture. Until digital software effects provide suitable correlated results as optical effects, it will be important to produce a suitable base for the digital post work.

It will still be best to record all of the important detail in the form that is closest to the desired finished result. Polarizing filters are perhaps the most useful in that they produce effects, such as reducing reflections from water and windows, that are unlikely to be done any other way. Contrast control filters can render shadow details visible that also may not be digitally added in later without a lot of effort if at all.

(For more information on filters see charts section pages 819-820 and 822-834.)

Ira Tiffen, ASC Associate Member, has created many of the important filter effects of the last forty years. He earned a 1992 Academy Technical Achievement Award for the development of the Ultra Contrast filter series and received a Prime Time Emmy Award in 1998. He was elected a Fellow of the SMPTE in 2002.

Camera Stabilizing Systems

There is good reason why the medium discussed in this manual is popularly known as "motion" pictures. Since the earliest days of the industry, cinematographers have been challenged to serve their stories by finding new and inventive ways of moving the camera. This section examines the latest devices that allow the operator to maintain control of the image while taking the viewer on a ride up, down or anywhere else.

BODY-WORN SYSTEMS

Modern camera-stabilizing systems enable a camera operator to move about freely and make dolly-smooth handheld shots without the restrictions or the resultant image unsteadiness encountered with prior methods. These systems transfer the weight of the camera unit to the operator's body via a support structure and weight distribution suit. This arrangement frees the camera from body motion influences. It allows the camera to be moved by the operator through an area, generally defined by the range through which his arm can move.

Camera smoothness is controlled by the "hand-eye-brain" human servo system that we use to carry a glass of water around a room or up and down stairs. Viewing is accomplished through the use of a video monitor system that displays an actual through-the-lens image, the same image one would see when looking through a reflex viewfinder. The advantage of these camera-stabilizing systems is that the camera now moves as if it were an extension of the operator's own body, controlled by his or her internal servo system, which constantly adjusts and corrects for body motions, whether the operator is walking or running. The camera moves and glides freely in all directions—panning, tilting, booming—and all movements are integrated into a single, fluid motion that makes the camera seem as if it were suspended in midair and being directed to move at will. These camera-stabilization systems turn any vehicle into an instant camera platform.

As with remotely controlled camera systems, servo controls may be used for control of focus, iris and zoom on the camera lens.

ADVANCED CAMERA SYSTEMS, INC.
BodyCam

The BodyCam camera support system moves the camera away from the operator's eye by providing a monitor for all viewfinding. Once separated that way, the camera is able to go into places and point in directions that would not be possible if the operator's head were positioned at the eyepiece. The lens can be placed anywhere the arm can reach. This also allows the operator's unblocked peripheral vision to see upcoming dangers and obstacles.

The BodyCam prevents unwanted motion from being transferred to the camera. With the average video camera, lens focal lengths up to 125mm are possible, and on 35mm film cameras, focal lengths up to 250mm are usable.

The Balance Assembly is suspended in front of the operator. It supports the camera, a viewfinder monitor and one or two batteries. The monitor is the green CRT-type. Batteries are brick-style and last two to three hours.

Adjustments allow precise balancing of the Balance Assembly around a three-axis gimbal. At this gimbal is an attach point where the Balance Assembly connects to the Suspension Assembly.

The Suspension Assembly consists of an arm supported and pivoted behind the left shoulder. The rear part of the arm is attached to a double-spring arrangement that counters any weight carried by the other end of the arm and provides vertical movement over a short distance. This arm isolates higher frequency motion. The front end of the arm attaches to the Balance Assembly with a hook. This hook is connected to a cable that travels from the front of the arm to the pivot point of the arm and an internal resilient coil.

The Suspension Assembly is attached to the Backbrace. The Backbrace is a framework that carries the load and transfers it to the human body.

Model L weighs 24 lbs (10.9kg) without camera or batteries and will carry up to 25 lbs (11.3kg) of camera package (not counting batteries). Model XL weighs 28 lbs (12.7kg) without camera or battery and will carry up to 40 lbs (18.2kg) without battery. Both models offer options for wired or wireless focus, zoom and iris control.

GLIDECAM INDUSTRIES, INC.
Glidecam V-20

The Glidecam V-20 professional camera stabilization system was constructed primarily for use with 16mm motion picture cameras and professional video cameras weighing 15–26 lbs.

The lightweight, adjustable Support Vest can be adjusted to fit a wide range of operators. High-endurance, closed-cell EVA foam padding and integral T-6 aluminum alloy create a vest which can hold and evenly distribute the weight of the system across the operator's shoulders, back and hips. For safety, quick-release, high-impact buckles allow the vest to be removed quickly.

The adjustable, exoskeletal Dyna-Elastic Support Arm is designed to counteract the combined weight of the camera and Camera Mounting Assembly (Sled) by employing high carbon alloy springs. The arm can be boomed up and down, as well as pivoted in and out and side to side. The spring force is field adjustable to allow for varying camera weights. For safety, dual-spring design is used to reduce possible spring failure damage.

The free-floating Three-Axis Gimbal, which incorporates integrally shielded bearings, creates the smooth and pivotal connections between the front end of the arm and the mounting assembly. A locking mechanism allows the gimbal to be placed at varying positions on the Central Support Post.

The Camera Mounting Assembly (Sled) is designed with a lower Telescoping Center Post which allows for vertical balance adjustment as well as varying lens heights. The center post can be adjusted from 22" to 32". The Camera Plate has both ¼" and ⅜" mounting slots to accommodate a variety of camera bases. For remote viewing, a LCD Monitor can be attached on the Base Platform, or either a LCD or a CRT Monitor can be attached to the base's adjustable monitor bracket. The base platform can also be configured to use counterbalance weight disks if a monitor and/or battery is not mounted on the base platform. The back of the base platform has threaded mounting holes for an Anton Bauer Gold Mount battery adapter plate.

Accessories include a low-mode camera mount, sled offset adapter, vehicle mount, and Vista Post 33" central support post extender.

Glidecam V-16

The V-16 is the same as the V-20 but designed to support lighter cameras weighing 10–20 lbs.

Glidecam Gold Series

The top-of-the-line Gold Series is made up of the Gold Vest and the Gold Arm. The Gold Vest offers no-tools adjustment with a breakaway safety system. It has a quick pressure-release dual-buckle design with positive locking buckles and fast-ratcheting adjuster buckles. The vest features integral black anodized T-6 aluminum with EVA foam padding, reversible and vertically adjustable arm mounting plate, and an industry standard arm connector. An optional V-series arm connector is available. Arm connectors are made of titanium.

The Gold Arm incorporates six titanium springs in order to handle a camera load of 13–38 lbs. Its combined camera and sled carrying capacity ranges from 31–56 lbs. Unique to the Gold Arm are its Hyper-Extension Hinges, which allow the arm more freedom of movement. The vest connectors are made of titanium.

GEORGE PADDOCK INC.
PRO-TM

The PRO-TM System's Donkey Box II camera mounting platform has linear slide bearings. The metal-on-metal design allows for smoother, easier movement fore/aft and side/side. Finer-thread lead screws and captured lead nuts enable the operator to make smaller, more accurate adjustments. A quick-release mechanism allows the camera to be mounted/dismounted with ease.

The PRO Gimbal is compatible with all 1.5" center posts and existing oversized grips. A locking mechanism achieves concentric clamping about the post, ensuring that all axes converge at the post's center.

The PRO Battery Module II batteries provide an independent and clean power supply to the monitor and video-related accessories while eliminating the need for a converter when running 24V cameras. The Sled can be configured to carry one to three batteries in multiple combinations to support a wider range of camera systems.

The PRO Arm, a departure from traditional tensioning methods has resulted in minimal friction and a force curve designed to complement an operator's instincts. It can be easily configured to accommodate a wide variety of load requirements ranging from 13–75 lbs.

The Post system was designed to eliminate all external cables except the monitor cable. The Upper Junction Box and the 17½"–26½" extendable post, which houses one internal cable, connects to the lower Junction Box via a quick disconnect/connect bayonet mount.

The Superpost allows the operator to achieve super hi/low-mode shots. It extends from 51"–60" (5') and is of the same design configuration as the PRO-TM Post.

The PRO Vest offers increased comfort due to improved load distribution. It is designed to conform anatomically to the individual operator and allows the operator a greater choice of hip and/or shoulder load distribution. A revolutionary latching system permits vest tension to be relaxed between takes without a change of settings.

The 5" Diagonal High Intensity Monitor II is a self-contained design that incorporates all electronic components within a water-resistant housing. The high-voltage, high-intensity screen features familiar onscreen graphics and indicators such as framelines, crosshairs and low battery and level indicators. Controls for brightness, contrast, image orientation, standard/anamorphic and graphics are all located on the faceplate for easy adjustment.

Nickel Metal Hydride Batteries deliver 14.4V @ 3.5A hours. A Fuel Gauge LED display on each battery provides immediate readout of battery condition. Weight is 1.9 lbs per battery.

The Pro Gyro Module is designed specifically for the PRO Battery Sled II. The new Gyro system increases the configuration possibilities of one to three gyros, while decreasing the time and complexity involved in transitioning to and from the use of gyros. Keeping one or two batteries on the sled leaves sled power in place, eliminating the need for an obtrusive umbilical cable.

The umbilical cable is replaced by a small, lightweight AC-only cable. A battery belt carries one battery and the DC/AC inverter.

MK-V

MK-V Evolution

The MK-V Evolution Modular Sled system can evolve with the operator. With the addition of optional extras, the basic MK-V Evolution rig can become a 24V 35mm sled. The base features a modular framework, allowing for customization in the field to any configuration and battery system and the addition of various accessories. It has a 4-by battery bar and clamp system for stability and universal battery compatibility. The modular base is also compatible with other leading stabilization systems. All battery systems, 12V and 24V, plug into the D-box distribution box. The D-box Deluxe has built-in digital level sensing and an onscreen battery display. MK-V's latest, highly configurable Nexus base is compatible with the Evolution.

The available carbon-fiber posts are two- and four-stage telescopic and available in three different lengths. The base has optional gyro mounts. The modular telescopic monitor works with CRT and LCD monitors. The V2 advanced, frictionless gimbal is compatible with leading sled systems, tools-free and designed to have no play in any axis. Front-mounting standard and advanced Xo vests are available. The Xo arm is frictionless and can support cameras of any weight with the change of its springs and features a modular front end.

SACHTLER

Artemis Cine/HD

The Artemis Cine/HD Camera Stabilizing System's post has a telescopic length ranging from 16.5"–27.5" (42–70cm). A variety of modules can be fixed to either end of the post to enable cameras, monitors and battery packs to be mounted. Scales on both tubes allow fast and precise adjustment. The gimbal's self-centering mechanism ensures aligned, precise position of the central bearing for easy system balancing.

The side-to-side module situated between post and camera gives the camera a sliding range of 1.18" (30mm) left, right, forward and back and includes a built-in self-illuminating level at the rear of the module. Two positions at the front and two at the rear enable mounting of remote focus brackets. All adjustments or locking mechanisms can be performed tool-free or with only a 4mm Allen wrench. The Artemis vest, made from materials such as cordura, has a full-length pivoting bridge made of reinforced aluminum alloy. It can be vertically adjusted independently of body size. Most of the weight is carried on the hips, reducing pressure on the operator's back. The arm is available with different spring sets that offer a load capacity ranging from

30–70 lbs (15–35kg). The two standard arm capacities are 44 lbs (20kg) and 57 lbs (25kg). It is fully compatible with all other stabilizer systems using the standard arm-vest connector and a ⅝" arm post.

TIFFEN STEADICAM
Universal Model III

The Steadicam system consists of a stabilizing support arm which attaches at one end to the camera operator's vest and at the other end to a floating camera mounting assembly which can accept either a 16mm, 35mm or video camera. The comfortable, adjustable, close-fitting camera operator's vest transfers and distributes the weight of the Steadicam system (including camera and lens) across the operator's shoulders, back and hips.

The stabilizer support arm is an articulated support system that parallels the operator's arm in any position, and almost completely counteracts the weight of the camera systems with a carefully calibrated spring force. The double-jointed arm maximizes maneuverability with an articulated elbow hinge. One end of the arm attaches to either side of the vest's front plate, which can be quickly reversed to allow the stabilizer arm to be mounted on the right or left side of the plate. A free-floating gimbal connects the stabilizer support arm to the camera-mounting assembly.

The camera-mounting assembly consists of a central support post, around which the individual components are free to rotate as needed. One end of the post supports the camera mounting platform, while the other end terminates in the electronics module. The adjustable video monitor is attached to a pivoting bracket. An electronic level indicator is visible on the CRT viewing screen. Electronically generated framelines can be adjusted to accommodate any aspect ratio. Positions of the components may be reversed to permit "low mode" configuration. The Steadicam unit is internally wired to accept wireless or cable-controlled remote servo systems for lens control. A quick-release mechanism permits the operator to divest himself of the entire Steadicam unit in emergency. A 12V/3.5A NiCad battery pack mounts on the electronics module to supply the viewfinder system and film or video camera.

Master Series

The cornerstone of the Steadicam family, this high-end production tool incorporates a new motorized stage, an enhanced Master Series vest, an advanced 5" monitor with artificial horizon and every state-of-the-art feature in the industry today.

System Includes: Camera Mounting Chassis (Sled), Motorized Stage, Low-Friction Gimbal, Composite Center Post and Covers, Advanced Monitor: 5" CRT w/16:9 aspect ratio switchable to 4:3, Artificial Horizon, Frameline Generator, On-screen Battery Display, Dovetail Accessory Bracket,

20–45 lbs camera capacity Iso-Elastic Arm, No-tools Arm Post, Master Series Leather Vest, four CP batteries with built-in Meter Systems, 12V/24V DC to DC Power Converter, Dynamic Spin & Docking Bracket, Long and Short Dovetail Plates, 12V power cable, 24V power cable (open-ended), two power cables for Panavision and Arri (24V) cameras, two power/video cables for Sony XC-75, soft case for the Arm, soft case for the Vest, hard case for the Sled, Owner's Manual.

Master Series Elite

With many of the same features as the Master Series, the Elite is a more basic and affordable Steadicam with a variety of upgradeable options.

System Includes: Camera Mounting Chassis (Sled), Low-Friction Gimbal, Composite Center Post and Covers, Monitor: 4" CRT w/4:3 aspect ratio switchable to 16:9, Frameline Generator, 20–45 lbs camera capacity Iso-Elastic Arm, No-tools Arm Post, Lightweight Master Series Vest, Dynamic Spin & Docking Bracket, two CP batteries with built-in Meter System, Long and Short Dovetail Plates, 12V power cable, 3' Lightweight video cable, hard case for the Sled, soft case for the Arm, soft case for the Vest, Owner's Manual.

Vector 12, Vector EL, Vector CN

Tiffen's latest system for film and video is surpassed only by the Ultra series. Each model offers no-tool arm technology that accommodates camera weights up to 45 lbs (20.5kg). The Vector Sled features carbon fiber post and covers, a three-post system that extends from 27"–48". The slim 2.75" wide sled has modular construction, 24V single battery system (Vector 12 is 13.2V only) and low-friction precision gimbal. Standard or compact lightweight vest.

The CN model includes the Tiffen HD UltraBrite Version2 color 8.4" LCD monitor that can display virtually all component high-definition and composite NTSC/PAL/SECAM signals (optional on 12 and EL models). The iso-elastic Vector arm has 24" of boom travel and utilizes titanium springs that can be adjusted while supporting the camera.

Ultra Elite, Ultra Cine

These models can configure quickly to the best advantage for each individual shot. The key component is a +20° head that maximizes use of extended posts, preserves dynamic balance in regular and long modes, helps with clearance reach and viewing, and enables whip pans with lens angled up or down. It features carbon-fiber telescoping posts, monitor, battery rods and brackets and a proprietary stiffening system.

The Ultra Cine system includes: Wireless motorized stage V.2.0, Dynamic Balance Calculator, Super Performance Monitor 4:3/16:9 switchable, Artificial Horizon, Frameline Generator, 20–40 lb camera capacity Iso-Elastic Arm, 24V battery, Onscreen Battery Display, No-tools Arm Post, Low-Friction Gimbal, Composite Post and Covers, Leather Vest.

HANDHELD STABILIZATION SYSTEMS
DOGGICAM SYSTEMS
The Doggicam
The Doggicam is a self-contained, lightweight and fully balanceable hand-held camera system. In low mode, shooting forward allows dynamic tracking free of tracks, and shooting backwards, the operator can view the monitor to see where he is going while leading the subject. High mode allows the operator to move the camera in an extremely dynamic fashion. Configuring from low mode to high mode takes 3–4 minutes.

At the heart of the Doggicam system is a lightweight, 6.5 lbs, highly modi-fied Arri 2-C with crystal speeds from 4–60 fps, PL or Panavision mounts and reflex viewing. The camera may be set up for Super 35 or anamorphic formats. It is easily adapted for 16mm cameras. Handheld bracketry is avail-able. The system is readily integrated for studio mode use by adding a riser block, rotating eyepiece and video door.

Robodog
This motorized version of the Doggicam allows the operator full-tilt con-trol of the camera by the handle-mounted motor controller. The inherent stability of the system is maintained by keeping the post vertical while allow-ing the full range of camera tilt within the yoke.

Doggimount
The Doggimount quickly secures the camera at any point in space using a compact aluminum framework similar to speedrail, yet much smaller.

Bodymount
Bodymount uses a specially designed vest and the standard Doggimount bracketry to allow easy and comfortable attachment of the camera to a per-son. The vest can be covered with wardrobe to allow framing to the middle of the chest.

Pogocam
The Pogocam is a small, weight-balanced handheld system that utilizes a converted 35mm Eyemo (100' daylight loads) with a videotap and onboard monitor. Nikon lenses are used. The compact size allows you to shoot where most stabilization systems would be too cumbersome to go.

MITCHELL-BASED PLATFORM-MOUNTED STABILIZATION SYSTEM

COPTERVISION
Rollvision

Rollvision is a lightweight, portable, wireless 3-axis camera system with 360° unlimited pan, tilt and roll capabilities and a gyro for horizon compensation. The dimensions are 14.5" x 19" x 19.5" with a weight of 16 lbs (camera system only). Rollvision works on numerous platforms including, but not limited to, cable systems, cranes, jib arms, camera cars, Steadicams, tracking and rail systems and much more. Mounting options consist of a 4" square pattern ¼"–20, Mitchell Mount adapter receiver ¼"–20 and two adjustable T-nuts sized from ¼"–20.

The Rollvision features electronic end stops, an hour meter with total system running time, lock for pan and tilt, removable sphere covers, film and video mode switch, and voltmeter.

Camera options include: Arri 435, 35-3, 2-C, 2-C SL Cine, 16SR-2 and 16SR-3, Aaton XTRprod and A-Minima plus multiple Sony and Panasonic High-Definition cameras.

Lenses up to 6 lbs can be used, including but not limited to, Panavision Primos from 17.5mm to 35mm, Ultra, Super and Normal Speeds; 35mm primes; and 16mm primes. Lens mount options include Arri standard, lightweight PL and lightweight Panavision mounts.

Several types of film magazines can be used including 400' SL Steadicam Mag, 200' Standard and 200' Steadicam Mag.

Remotevision, also designed by Coptervision, is the wireless, 4-in-1 radio control used to operate the Rollvision. Remotevision features a 5.6" color monitor and pan, tilt, and roll controls as well as camera zoom and iris controls. Gyro on/off and roll/record switches are included. The speed of the pan, tilt and roll is adjustable and a reverse switch allows the head to reset to the zero position.

The Rollvision fits in one to two ATA-approved size cases, and travels with the Rollvision operator as luggage.

GLIDECAM INDUSTRIES, INC.
Gyro Pro

The Gyro Pro camera stabilizer units liberate you to film while moving in any direction, even over rough ground, on rough rivers, in high seas or turbulent air. Accommodates most cameras weighing up to 100 lbs. Sets up in 20 minutes and features 360° pan, 60° tilt and 30° roll. 36V DC power is required. Ships in three cases totaling 310 lbs.

LIBRA HEAD, INC.
Libra III

The Libra III is a three-axis, digitally stabilized camera mount. It can be operated in either direct (digital) mode, or the operator can choose to stabilize one, two or all three axis at the flick of a switch. Custom-designed motors give it the precision of a well-tuned geared head that is extremely stable. Wet and muddy conditions are well tolerated. It fits on all industry-standard cranes and gripping equipment and either can be suspended or mounted upright. Fail-safe is comprised of two-systems-in-one electronics. It pans 350°, tilts 90° and rolls 90°. The Libra III comes with Preston FIZ remote-control system, a lens witness cam, 14" and 8" Sony color monitors, and AC and DC power supplies.

MOTION PICTURE MARINE
Hydro Gyro

A state-of-the-art digital-stabilization head that enables shot-making in the harshest of filming environments. The Hydro Gyro mounts under your pan/tilt head or camera. The result is a stable horizon without the pitch and roll generated by camera boats, cars, aircraft, dollys or other moving platforms. It weighs 32 lbs with a shipping weight around 70 lbs. It handles camera systems up to 150 lbs and can use lenses up to 500mm. The Hydro Gyro is waterproof up to 30'. Fine vibration can be reduced with a Hydro Gyro Shocksorber, a lightweight, 2" high, anti-shock and vibration damping system.

MINIATURE AERIAL SYSTEMS
COPTERVISION
CVG-A

The CVG-A is an autonomous, unmanned, small-scale helicopter platform and camera system. Possessing the same characteristics as Coptervision's line-of-sight, remote control helicopter (5' in length with a 6' blade span and weighing 40 lbs), the CVG-A incorporates a 3-D GPS waypoint navigation and flight-control system which is programmed through a computerized Ground Control Station (GCS).

Two different camera systems are available—the standard Coptervision three-axis, gyro-stabilized camera system that carries 35mm, 16mm and digital video cameras and/or a new smaller, three-axis, gyro-stabilized gimbal designed by the company called Flexvision that carries smaller video cameras. The 35mm camera package consists of a modified Arri 2-C and comes with either an Arri Standard mount, PL mount or Panavision mount. Lenses include 16mm and 24mm Zeiss prime lenses, with an optional 40mm anamorphic or Cooke S4 Wide Prime lens.

Any given flight plan can be preprogrammed, flown and repeated as many times as is necessary thus allowing flight patterns to be memorized. This feature allows for scalable shots that can be used in visual effects plates. A "return to home" command can be input into the flight parameters so that the helicopter will automatically return back to its starting position if necessary.

Like the Coptervision line-of-sight helicopter, the CVG-A is modular in design and has all of the same flight characteristics: up to 75 mph forwards, 45 mph backwards, 35 mph side to side, and hover. Since a digital microwave downlink is used to bring the signal down to the ground, the CVG-A camera operator can maintain precise framing while the helicopter is in motion. The system runs on aviation-grade fuel and does not emit smoke from the exhaust while flying backwards. The modular design allows for ATA-approved boxes so that a total of six cases travel with the crew as luggage. With the CVG-A, there is increased range (up to 3 miles and 450') and endurance (from 30–45 minutes).

Flying-Cam

The Flying-Cam is an unmanned aerial filming helicopter. The Flying-Cam aeronautical design, manufacturing quality, safety features and maintenance procedures are equivalent to those used in General Aviation. The vehicle has all the characteristics required for safe operation close to actors. The system is self-sufficient and combines the use of aeronautics, electronics, computer vision and wireless transmission technologies that are tailor made to fit in a 30 lbs take-off weight platform and a 6' main rotor diameter. Camera available are: 16mm, S16mm, 35mm, S35mm and various Video standards including HD and Broadcast live transmission.

The embedded Super 35mm 200' camera is custom made by Flying-Cam and mounted in a 1' diameter, three-axis gyro-stabilized remote head. The camera is the integration between an Arri 2-C and an Eyemo. The movement has been designed to achieve the same steadiness of an Arri 35-3 up to 30 fps and of an Arri 2-C up to 50 fps. The 200' magazine use standard core and is part of the camera body. When short reloading time is requested, the cameras are hot-swappable. The electric camera motor is crystal-controlled with two-digit precision. Ramping is optional. The minimum speed is 4 fps, the maximum 50 fps. Shutter is 160°. Camera trigger is remote. Indicators and readouts—timer, sync signal and roll out—are monitored from the ground control station. A color LCD monitor and a digital 8mm tape recorder are provided for monitoring playback on the ground. A color wireless video assist, used as parallax, gives peripheral information, allowing for anticipation in the camera remote head operation. A frameline generator is provided with prememorized ratio.

The mattebox used is an Arri 3"x3". ND3-6-9, 85ND3-6-9, Pola and 81EF filters are provided as standard. Aperture Plate is full and optical axis is centered on full. Available lenses are wide-angle: Cooke, Zeiss and anamorphic 40mm. Aperture is remote, focus remote is optional on standard lens and included on Anamorphic. Lens mounts are Arri Standard, PL, BNCR, and Panavision.

The HD Camera is a 3-CCD with HD-SDI output and onboard recording capability.

The Flying-Cam gyro-stabilized patented Remote Head includes one-of-a-kind top-shot horizon control. Pan: 360° unlimited, 180°/sec adjustable from ground. Roll: 360° unlimited, 60°/sec adjustable from ground. Tilt: 190° including 90° straight up and 100° down, 60°/sec adjustable from ground. On 90° tilt down with the 16mm Zeiss lens the front glass is 1" above ground. The maximum height above ground is 300' (100m) to respect FAA safety separation with general aviation. Flying-Cam provides the wireless Body-Pan® proprietary system: the camera operator has the option to take control of the tail rotor giving an unlimited unobstructed, gyro-stabilized 360° pan capability. The pilot has a transparent control and override authority if needed.

The Flying Platform has a top speed of 75 mph (120 kph) and can combine all the moves of a full-size helicopter. Take off weight of 30 lbs (15kg) reduces down wash to a minimum. Autorotation capability is enhanced by high rotor inertia. Tail rotor is overpowered for Body-Pan operation. The flight is controlled by a Flying-Cam licensed Pilot using a computer-base radiodensity. Density altitude is affected by temperature, humidity and pressure. The radio range is more than one mile. The maximum flight altitude is 14,000'. The practical range is the visual one. Pilot-in-relay operations are optional.

SUSPENDED CAMERA SYSTEM

SPYDERCAM

Spydercam is a suspended camera system that allows filmmakers to move their lens in safe, precise, multi-axis paths through space by combining highly specialized rigging components with computerized winch systems and an experienced crew.

- Speeds in excess of 70 mph
- Distances in excess of 4000' long, 600' high
- Compatible with most modern remote heads (Libra, Stab-C, Wescam, Flir, SpaceCam, etc.)
- Video, HD, 16mm, 35mm, VistaVision, IMAX
- Configurations for one-, two- or three-dimensional envelopes

- Seamless integration with previz systems
- Live fly or preprogram movements interchangeably on any axis. (X, Y, Z, pan, tilt, roll, focus, zoom)
- Small studio systems to giant outdoor runs
- Highly accurate (some 3-D systems are actually capable of double-pass motion control work)
- Modular, portable.

The system offers greater accuracy and allows closer proximity to sets, actors and crew than a helicopter can safely negotiate and offers a much greater speed and range of motion than can be provided by a standard camera crane. It a incorporates a 3-D GPS waypoint navigation and flight-control system which is programmed through a computerized Ground Control Station (GCS).

CABLECAM

A scaleable, multi-axis camera and stunt platform for film and HD. Cable-cam scales its rigs in interior and exterior locations. Truss, track, ropeways, towers, and crane attachments are modular.

Types of rigs include,

Basic: One-axis point to point.

Elevator Skate: Two-axis XZ travel.

Flying V: Two-axis XZ travel.

Traveling High Line: Three-axis XYZ travel using a gantry-like rail and rope rig.

Dual High Line: XYZ travel using parallel high lines.

Multi-V: Three-axis XYZ travel using four attachment points to construction cranes or high steel.

Mega-V: The upside down crane. XYZ flight of a 20' vertically telescoping pedestal. Attached to the bottom of the pedestal is a horizontal 12' extension/retraction arm which pans, tilts, and rolls. The camera head of choice is attached at one end of the arm.

Teathered Ballooncam: One-three-axis of aerial control over expansive distances.

Speed range of systems: 0–70 mph. Length, width, and height of rigs: 100– 5,000'. Propulsion: electronic or hydraulic. Software: Kuper and custom.

Cablecam's Kuper or custom, controlled servo-driven camera and stunt rigs are modeled in Maya and Soft image and exported to a previz model. "Virtual" Cablecam is flown in the previz milieu using teach and learn protocol.

Aerial platforms, balloons, and flying 3-D cranes support the Libra, Stab-C and XR as well as the Cablecam LP (low profile) stabilized HD head.

Lightweight, mobile operating stations. Repeatable motion control of both hydraulic and electric servos. Noise-free communications over long distances. Custom joystick control. Interfaces with other motion control systems for control of steppers, servos, relays, lighting, cameras and camera heads. Remote monitoring of servo drive functions. Mechanical and electronic braking.

Previsualization

by Colin Green

*(Incorporating material formulated and approved by the
ASC-ADG-VES Joint Technology Subcommittee on Previsualization
and adopted and maintained by the Previsualization Society)*

I. INTRODUCTION TO PREVISUALIZATION

Previsualization, also known as "previz," is a collaborative process that generates preliminary versions of shots or sequences, predominantly using 3-D animation tools and a virtual environment. It enables filmmakers to visually explore creative ideas, plan technical solutions and communicate a shared vision for efficient production. Filmmakers can leverage the previz process to effectively work out and convey the details of their vision to the people that will help execute it. The process allows sets, stunts, visual effects, sequences of action, story flow and other elements to be designed, developed, understood, refined and planned in advance using the visual power of 3-D modeling and animation and with a high degree of production-specific accuracy.

The prehistory of previsualization prior to the availability of computer-based imaging includes many years of creative solutions using a variety of physical tools. Popular techniques included mocking up shots and key elements with materials such as foam core and prefilming the "action" with lipstick video cameras. Digital previsualization first developed in the early 1990s in tandem with major milestones and enhancements in computer animation software and processing speed. Professionals around the industry quickly embraced these enhancements, with the majority utilizing the new 3-D animation capabilities towards creating stunning, never-before-seen synthetic creatures and imagery in visual effects. Concurrently, a smaller group was applying the same advancements to improve fundamental film design, planning and production techniques to create what is now called previz.

The earliest innovations in digital previz were made by pioneers at studios such as Sony Pictures Imageworks, Lucasfilm/ILM and The Trumbull Company. These innovators focused on large, visual effects-driven projects, paving the way for a wider use of previz with an expanding pool of previz-specific artists. Today previz is used on projects of all genres where a high degree of control over creative execution or advanced problem solving is sought. Previz continues to map to the needs of the market as the demands of shooting and shot completion become more challenging, time-critical and complex.

In 2009, the Previsualization Society, a permanent and ongoing previsualization organization inspired by groundwork from the interdisciplinary ASC-ADG-VES Joint Technology Subcommittee On Previsualization, was formed. The Previsualization Society provides an aggregate of resources on previz and offers membership to all disciplines that interface with the previz process. Materials maintained by the society and collected on its website, www.previssociety.com, include a library of previz examples, tips for using previz, best practice guidelines, professional forums and further links.

II. DEFINITIONS AND TYPES

The term "previz" has seen its fair share of differing meanings and usages over the years. The description in the first paragraph of section I above provides an accepted formal definition. A number of distinctive subtypes of previz have also been defined:

Pitchvis illustrates the potential of a project before it has been fully funded or greenlit. As part of development, these sequences are conceptual, to be refined or replaced during preproduction.

Pitchvis is often used with a more conceptual intention. Because it is typically created before a production staff is even assembled, pitchvis departs from the main definition of previz in that it is not specifically relevant to physical production or reflecting input and collaboration with key crew.

Technical Previz incorporates and generates accurate camera, lighting, design and scene layout information to help define production requirements. This often takes the form of dimensional diagrams that illustrate how particular shots can be accomplished, using real-world terms and measurements.

Technical previz may include virtual stage planning in which correct representations of actual shooting conditions can be defined, manipulated and studied to yield greater production efficiency and a more informed crew. This can include virtual representations of stages, blue- or greenscreens, camera cranes, motion control equipment and other gear. Technical previz can also provide motion control move exports, where data files containing the exact coordinates of the camera for each frame of the shot are exported and uploaded into motion control camera systems to precisely replicate the previsualized motions by the camera capturing the photography. The cinematographer should be consulted during this stage in order that the previz sequence has a harmonious flow with the project's visual objectives as a whole.

On-set previz creates real-time (or near real-time) visualizations on location to help the director, cinematographer, visual effects supervisor and crew quickly evaluate captured imagery. This includes the use of techniques that can synchronize and composite live photography with 2-D or 3-D virtual elements for immediate visual feedback.

Rather than delivering a specific end previz product or finished sequence, the purpose of on-set previz is to leverage previz assets to provide a quick mechanism for visualizing and evaluating any number of "what if?" scenarios. Decisions on trying out a specific setup can be made effectively, for example, before heavy rigging or equipment is moved. On-set previz can additionally serve a purely creative function as instant "postviz," with the video tap image being integrated into the previz sequence to immediately see how the shot footage works.

Postviz combines digital elements and production photography to validate footage selection, provide placeholder shots for editorial, and refine effects design. Edits incorporating postviz sequences are often shown to test audiences for feedback, and to producers and visual effects vendors for planning and budgeting.

Postviz is typically driven by the editorial process and is especially essential when there are key plot points, CG characters, etc. that are dependent on being realized through visual effects. Postviz, typically a combination of previz combined with principal photography, bridges the gap to provide immediate visual placeholders for storytelling purposes until final visual effects elements arrive. Postviz often also provides helpful information for visual effects completion and integration.

III. THE PREVISUALIZATION PROCESS STEP BY STEP

The typical previz workflow can be described by the following phases:

Asset Assembly

Working from a script, treatment, story outline or storyboards, key scene elements comprising the main visual subject matter of the sequence are constructed accurately in 3-D in the computer. The elements can include characters, sets, vehicles, creatures, props—anything that appears in the sequence being previsualized. The assets are ideally sourced through the Art Department (e.g., as concept art, from storyboards or from physical or digital models) and have already been approved by key creatives on the project. If specific assets, such as locations, are still being determined, best approximations are made.

Sequence Animation

The assets are laid out in space and time using 3-D software to create an animated telling of the story's action. The resulting previz sequence is reviewed by key creative personnel and is further tweaked until accurate and approved.

Virtual Shoot

Virtual cameras are placed in the scene. Previz artists ensure that these cameras are calibrated to specific physical camera and lens characteristics, including camera format and aspect ratio. This step allows the animated scene to be "seen" as it would from actual shooting cameras. These views can be based on storyboard imagery or requests from the director or cinematographer. It is relatively easy to generate new camera angles of the same scene or produce additional coverage without much extra effort.

Sequence Cutting

As previz shots/sequences are completed, they can be cut together to reflect a more cinematic flow of action, and are more useful as the entirety of the film is evaluated and planned. Changes required for previz sequences often are identified in the editing process.

Study and Review

The completed previz scene, with animation and virtual cameras, can be studied to consider many useful production aspects: configuration of the sets, speed of the action, frame composition, stunt planning, camera motion, rigging and equipment requirements and so forth.

The relevance of the previz is contingent upon including as many actual production specifications and limitations as possible. The previz process should inherently incorporate information from key collaborators, such as the cinematographer and art director, who influence the process and provide input to ensure the desired results can actually be achieved. In cases where information changes or new details come into play later in the process, the previz team may re-tool the sequence to fit within the new specs.

Crew Communication and Outreach

A key part of the previz process is distributing the previz sequences, once they have been approved by the director, to multiple production departments. The previz can be "communicated" in a number of forms—diagrams, documents, overview movies, stage layouts, visual effects breakdowns, etc. This information can be broken down by each department to ascertain the achievability of the previsualized shots.

Additional Problem Solving

During production, the previz team may take on a "rapid response" problem-solving role by working to address evolving planning and coordination needs that would benefit from on-set previz. This team can continue to be effective after the shoot is complete in a postviz capacity, using previz assets to make temp shots that accelerate the editing process and streamline the production of final visual effects.

IV. SOME BENCHMARKS FOR SUCCESSFUL PREVIZ

Taking into consideration the idea that previz by nature is a constantly evolving collaborative process, it is difficult to describe a particular previz sequence as specifically "finished" and successful. But there are some basic measures that are all equally important in measuring the success of previz for any given project.

1. The previz represents an approved creative road map. The director can watch a previz sequence and is confident that it expresses the film's intended story and creative vision.
2. The previz represents an approved technical road map. The previz is based on a foundation of the most accurate and current representations of sets, locations, production conditions and incorporates input from across many production departments.
3. The previz is distributed across the production and viewed as achievable. Previz sequences have been evaluated and provided as needed, and everyone on the production that the director has chosen to help realize the project feels it can be done as planned in both the practical and budgetary sense.
4. The previz is completed early enough to be effective. Previz sequences are done in time to affect the actual production of the shots.

V. PREVIZ AND THE CINEMATOGRAPHER

Input from the cinematographer, both from a technical and an aesthetic perspective, is a valuable part of making the previz process beneficial to a production. As early as possible, making the previz team aware of the shooting specs for the project, including the expected camera format, lens package and shooting aspect ratio, will help ensure that these critical parameters are incorporated into the previz work.

Previz serves a number of purposes for filmmaking, but it cannot simulate all aspects of motion picture photography. Previz in its normal form offers approximations of lighting conditions only in a general sense, not as the basis for determining lighting choices. Producers should note that, even though the cinematographer may be consulted for technical information during the previz process, previz sequences are not intended to represent the cinematographer's visual approach to the lighting, color and general aesthetic of the film.

3-D Stereoscopic Cinematography

by Robert C. Hummel III
Updated from the April 2008 issue of American Cinematographer *magazine*

The recent resurgence in stereoscopic motion pictures, more often called 3-D, is completely due to the application of digital technologies in both exhibition and production. As a result, they are being taken more seriously than ever before.

In exhibition, the advantage is digital projection that allows a single projector to project alternating left-eye/right-eye images at a fast enough frame rate that allows the images to be integrated by our brains into a continuous 24 fps 3-D motion picture. Also, because of digital imaging, it is allowing filmmakers to explore higher frame rates in 3-D. *The Hobbit* was photographed at 48 fps, and James Cameron has announced his *Avatar* sequel will be presented at 60 fps.

In production, the smaller form factor of many digital cameras allow for a more compact 3-D camera rig that was previously not possible. 35mm beam splitter rigs were virtually impossible for one person to lift, yet today's HD rigs are easily hand held by one person.

This chapter is intended as a primer on the basic constructs of this complex medium, and should give you a solid foundation from which to pursue further research on the subject. In order to save some ink, we will cave to convention and henceforth refer to stereoscopic cinematography as "3-D."

Before we begin the discussion, let's first define some terms.

Left Eye: Refers to photographed images that are intended to be seen only by a person's left eye. This term can refer to the lens or camera that is capturing the left-eye images, or the left-eye images projected in a theater.

Right Eye: Photographed images that are intended to be seen only by a person's right eye. In 3-D Cinematography, often called the master eye, or dominant eye.

Stereoscopic: Refers to the dual imagery obtained when viewed from two vantage points slightly offset horizontally from one another. Quite simply, it is what we observe when viewed with our left and right eyes, and gives a sense of dimensionality to objects closer than 19' to 23' (6 to 7 meters). Also called "binocular vision."

Monocular Depth Perception: Refers to depth perception not requiring dual image cues, or the depth perception that comes into play with objects farther than 19' to 23' away.

Convergence: What happens with the human visual system as two images seen with the left and right eyes become overlaid so they become one image. When looking at an object at infinity, your eyes are looking straight ahead (Figure 1).

Figure 1. When we look at something on the horizon, our eyes are focused at infinity and look straight ahead.

Convergence happens when stereoscopic depth perception comes into play, i.e., when objects you are targeting/focusing on are closer than 13'-16' (Figure 2). When focused at infinity, objects close to you appear as two transparent images; as you converge on those close objects, they become one solid image, and objects in the background become double images. Convergence in 3-D cinematography is when the two taking lenses are aimed to converge on a single point in space.

Figure 2. Eyes converging on a close object.

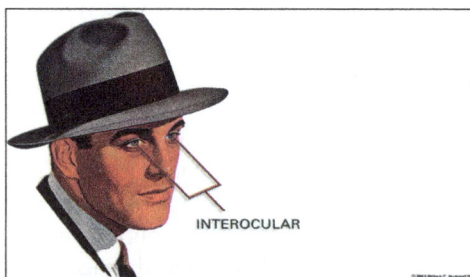

Figure 3. Interocular is the distance between the left and right eyes. In 3C Cinematography, the distance between the LEFT and RIGHT taking lenses is called the interaxial, and is the variable distance between the left and right taking lenses, adjusted for each scene.

Screen Plane: The position in a theater where the projection surface is located; a vertical plane coincident with the screen that helps define where objects appear in front of, behind, or on the screen.

Plane of Convergence: The vertical plane where your eyes are directed to converge on a 3-D object. If an object appears to be floating in front of the movie screen, the plane of convergence is where that object appears to be. The same would apply to objects appearing to be "behind" the screen.

Proscenium Arch: For our purposes, this refers to the edge of the screen when an object becomes occluded.

Interocular (also called Interaxial)**:** The distance between your eyes (Figure 3) is properly referred to as interocular. In 3-D cinematography, the distance between the taking lenses is properly called interaxial; however, more recently, you will find filmmakers incorrectly referring to the distance between taking lenses as the interocular. In 3-D cinematography, if done properly, the interaxial distance between the taking lenses needs to be calculated on a shot by shot basis. The interaxial distance between the taking lenses must take into account an average of the viewing conditions in which the motion picture will be screened. For large screen presentations, the distance is often much less than the distance between an average set of human eyes. Within reason, the interaxial can be altered to exaggerate or minimize the 3-D effect.

The 3-D cinematographer must weigh several factors when determining the appropriate interaxial for a shot. They are: focal length of taking lenses, average screen size for how the movie will be projected, continuity with the next shot in the final edit, and whether it will be necessary to have a dynamic interaxial that will change during the shot.

Because the interaxial distances are crafted for a specific theatrical presentation, a 3-D motion picture doesn't easily drop into a smaller home viewing environment. A movie usually will require adaptation and modification of the interaxial distances in order to work effectively in a small home theater display screen environment.

The facts presented in this chapter are indisputable, but once you become enmeshed in the world of 3-D, you will encounter many differing opinions on the appropriate ways to photograph and project a 3-D image. For example, when you're originating images for large-format 3-D presentations (IMAX, Iwerks, etc.), some people will direct you to photograph images in ways that differ from the methods used for 1.85:1 or 2.40:1 presentations. Part of this is due to the requirements for creating stereoscopic illusions in a large-screen (rather than small-screen) environment, but approaches also derive from personal preferences.

Many think stereoscopic cinematography involves merely adding an additional camera to mimic the left-eye/right-eye way we see the world, and everything else about the image-making process remains the same. If that were the case, this chapter wouldn't be necessary.

First off, "3-D" movies are not actually three-dimensional. 3-D movies hinge on visual cues to your brain that trigger depth stimuli, which in turn create an illusion resembling our 3-D depth perception. In a theatrical environment, this is achieved by simultaneously projecting images that represent, respectively, the left-eye and right-eye points of view. Through the use of glasses worn by the audience, th e left eye sees only the left-eye images, and the right eye sees only the right-eye images. (At the end of this chapter is a list of the types of 3-D glasses and projection techniques that currently exist.)

Most people believe depth perception is only created by the use of our eyes. This is only partially correct. As human beings, our left-eye/right-eye stereoscopic depth perception ends somewhere between 19' to 23' (6 to 7 meters). Beyond that, where stereoscopic depth perception ends, monocular depth perception kicks in.

Monocular depth perception is an acquired knowledge you gain gradually as a child. For example, when an object gets larger, you soon learn it is getting closer, and when you lean left to right, objects closer to you move side to side more quickly than distant objects. Monocular depth perception is what allows you catch a ball, for example.

3-D movies create visual depth cues based on where left-eye/right-eye images are placed on the screen. When you want an object to appear that it exists coincident with the screen plane, both left- and right-eye images are projected on the same location on the screen. When photographing such a scene, the cinematographer determines the apparent distance of the screen plane to the audience by the width of the field of view, as dictated by the focal length of the chosen lenses. For example, a wide landscape vista might create a screen-plane distance that appears to be 40' from the audience, whereas a tight close-up might make the screen appear to be 2' from the audience.

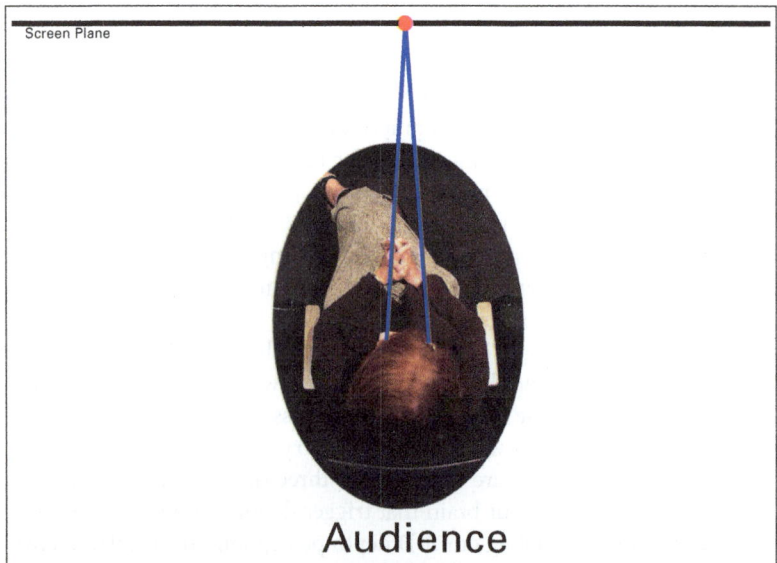

Figure 4. Eyes converging on an "on screen" object. As seen from above, as if viewing from the theater's ceiling, looking down on the audience and the screen plane.

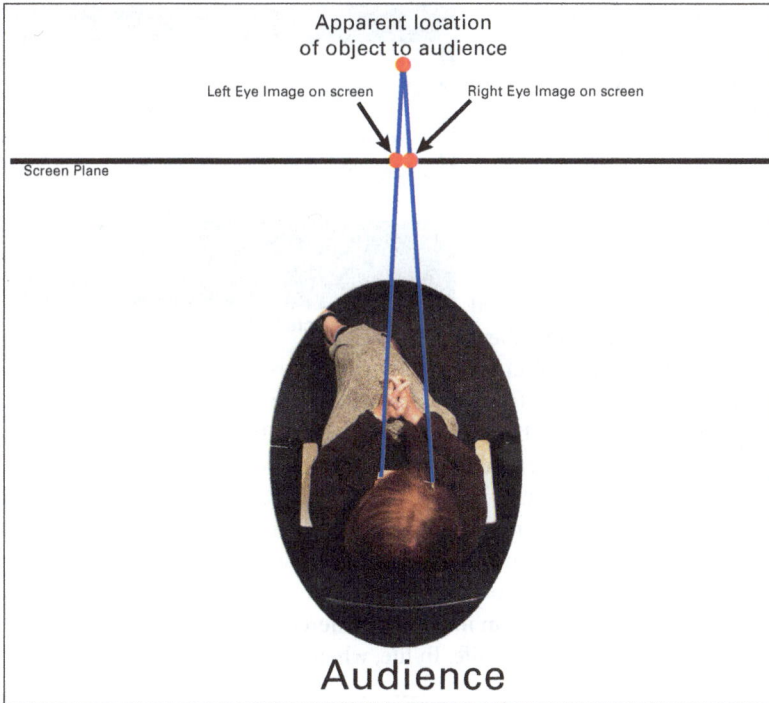

Figure 5. How a behind screen object is created.

Figure 4 illustrates when an object is at the screen plane and where the audience's eyes converge while viewing that object. (Figure 4 also effectively represents where your eyes converge and focus when watching a standard 2-D movie without special glasses).

If we want an object to appear behind the screen, the image is photographed with the lenses converged behind the screen plane. On set, the screen plane is an invisible plane that you establish to control where objects will be perceived by the viewer of the 3-D motion picture. In the theater, of course, the screen plane is a very real, physical object.

When the object you want to appear behind the screen is projected, it appears similar to what is presented in Figure 5.

In Figure 5, the right-eye and left-eye images are kept separated by the special glasses worn by the audience; in other words, the left eye sees only the left-eye image and the right eye sees only the right-eye image. If you were to remove your glasses, you would see both images simultaneously, as in the Figure 6 example of a behind-screen object viewed without special glasses.

Next, we want an object to appear in front of the screen plane so that from the audience's perspective, the object appears to be coming into the theater and closer to the viewer's face. This is achieved on set by adjusting the convergence of the left- and right-camera lenses so they are converging in front of the in theater screen plane. When projected, the images are viewed by the audience as illustrated in Figure 7.

Figure 6. A projected 3-D image viewed without special glasses.

This technique can be used to make audience members perceive that an object is very, very close to their faces. This creates a very effective 3-D illusion, but experience has shown that extreme examples of this effect should be used sparingly, if at all. Remember that while the viewer will be converging that object mere inches from his face, he will still be focusing on the screen plane many meters away. As a result, this type of 3-D "gag" (when properly done) always gets gasps from an audience yet, because of that disparity of focus, never quite matches reality.

This example illustrates an important difference between 3-D movies and what you experience in real life. In life, when an object is half a meter from

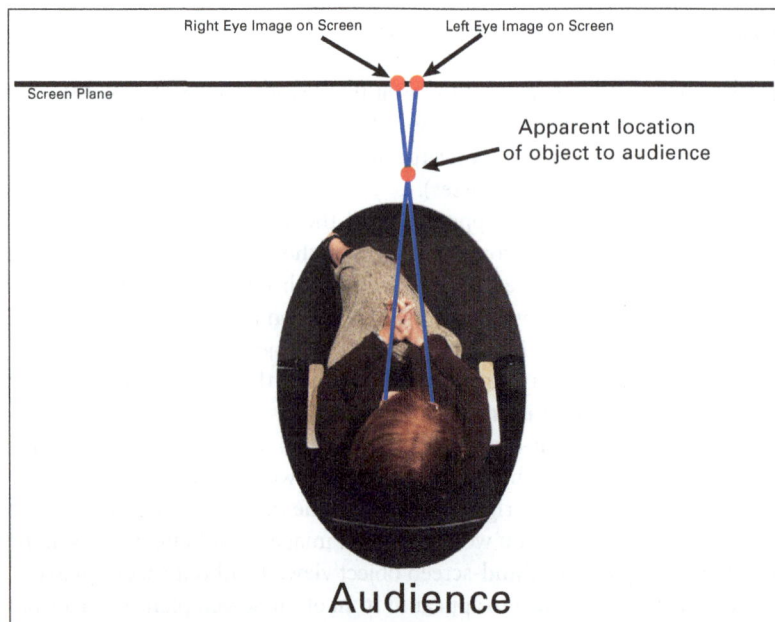

Figure 7. How an object appearing in front of the screen is created.

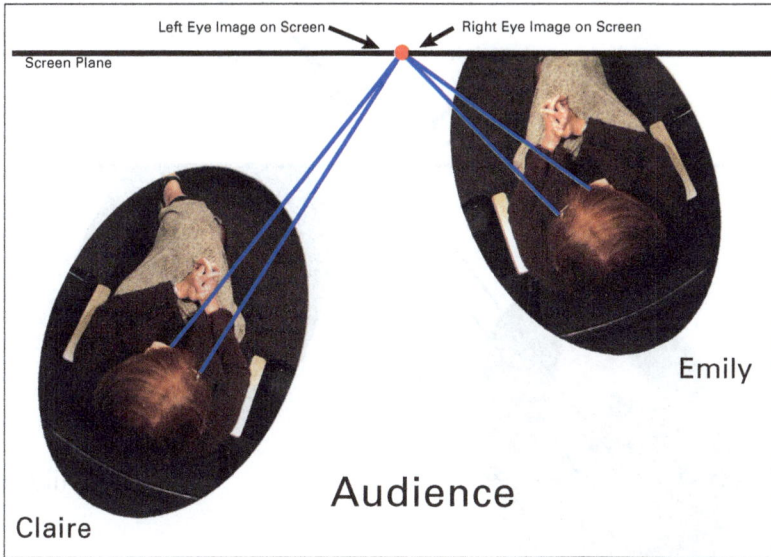

Figure 8. On-screen objects are seen in the same location by all audience members.

your face, your eyes converge and focus at half a meter from your face. In a 3-D movie environment, you can choose an angle of view and scale that, from your perspective, makes an object appear to be half a meter from your face even as your eyes are focused on the screen plane, which may be any-where from 5 to 30 meters away from you.

This doesn't mean the 3-D approach is "wrong;" it's just an example of why 3-D depth cues in a 3-D movie often seem to be exaggerated—why 3-D movies seem to be more 3-D than reality.

When an object appears on the screen plane, every member of the audi-ence sees the object at the same location on the screen because the left- and right-eye images appear precisely laid on top of each other (and thus appear as one image). Basically, the image appears the same as it would during a regular "2-D" movie projection (Figure 8).

Take a look at Figure 9, however, and see how things change when an object is placed behind the screen plane. As you can see, a person's specific location in the theater will affect his perception of where that behind-screen object is located. Also, how close that person is to the screen will affect how far behind the screen that object appears to be; the closer one's seat is to the screen, the shorter the distance between the screen and the object "behind" it appears to be.

Again, it is not "wrong" that this happens. Figure 9 simply clarifies the point that stereoscopic cinematography is not 3-D. Were it truly 3-D, every audience member would see these behind-screen objects in the same loca-

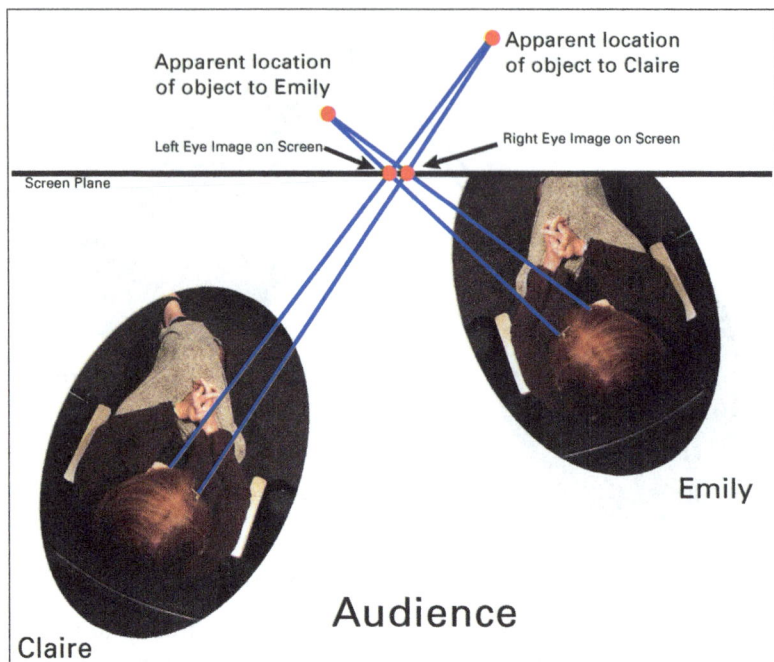

Figure 9. Audience position affects both lateral and depth convergence of behind-screen objects.

tion. When planning shots for a 3-D motion picture, the filmmaker should be conscious of how a dramatic moment might be received by viewers seated in various locations. Audience position will also affect the perceived location of off screen objects as well.

My next points concern the proscenium arch and "off-screen" objects. As mentioned earlier, the edges of the screen image (top, bottom, left and right) are collectively referred to as the proscenium arch. This is a nod towards live theater, where the term applies to that area of the stage in front of the curtain. In 3-D, the term is used when referring to objects that appear to be in front of the screen plane.

In short, the edges of the screen are relevant to objects appearing in front of the screen plane. Such an object can have very strong stereoscopic convergence cues that will make it appear to be "floating" very close to a viewer's face. A good example of this phenomenon occurs in the film *Muppet*vision 3-D*, during a scene in which the characters Waldo and Kermit the Frog appear to extend into the audience while clinging to the end of a ladder. Many recent 3-D motion pictures avail themselves of this 3-D principle, from *Beowulf*, when a spear is thrust toward Beowulf's face after he arrives on a beach, to dogs lunging towards the camera in *Hugo*.

However, if that floating object moves so close to the edge of the screen that it is occluded by that edge, your brain will quickly employ its knowledge of monocular depth cues, and your perception that the object is floating in front of the screen will diminish to the point of inconsequence. Your brain has learned that when one object is occluded by another, the occluded object must be farther away. In spite of all the stereoscopic depth cues, your brain knows that if that object is occluded by the edge of the screen, then it must be at, or behind, the screen plane. This scenario will be very noticeable to viewers as their brains attempt to sort out these contradictory depth cues.

Monocular depth perception overrules stereo depth cues because we are hard-wired to protect ourselves from danger. Because most danger (such as an approaching lion, bear or saber-toothed tiger) starts from outside our stereoscopic depth zone, it's easy to understand how the brain defaults to the depth cues that govern most of our life. The 3-D axiom to remember is that off-screen objects should never touch the edge of the screen, because if they do, the illusion will be disrupted. The illusion is most effective with objects that can float or be thrust toward the audience. You will also notice that when you experience these illusions, filmmakers are keeping the off-screen objects closer to the center of the screen in order to avoid the proscenium arch.

As with many axioms, however, there is sometimes an exception. There is a scenario in which an occluded object can still appear as though it is coming off the screen. Imagine a medium shot of a man who walks from behind the screen plane toward the screen plane, and then continues toward the audience until he is in front of the screen. Surprisingly, this shot will still work with the character apparently coming off the screen, even though the lower half of his body is cut off by the bottom of the projected image. The requirement for it to work, contrary to our earlier axiom, is that the viewer must have other audience members in front of him, with the bottom of the screen occluded by people's heads. When the bottom of an object is occluded by people very close to you, your brain will still believe the object is getting closer. However, even a clear view of the bottom of the screen will result in a fairly good effect of the man coming off of the screen; because we're programmed to look straight ahead, and often don't see, or focus on the lower half of a person coming towards us, obscuration of the lower half of a person usually won't entirely ruin the off screen effect.

One must also be aware of the constraints on editing in 3-D. This concept is relatively simple to grasp but is often disregarded to the detriment of a 3-D presentation. When editing for 3-D, it is important to consider the convergence extremes that the audience will experience in order to realize the stereoscopic illusion. For example, if the audience is viewing action that occurs behind the screen plane, it is inadvisable to then cut directly to an object in front of the screen. The average viewer will have difficulty converging the suddenly "close" object, to the point where he might see double images for several moments.

Experienced viewers of 3-D films won't have this problem, and this can lead to mistakes if you happen to be part of the creative team involved in a 3-D production. If you work extensively in post for 3-D movies, you become more and more adept at quickly converging disparate objects. However, your audience won't have the advantage of exercising their eyes as much as someone working on a 3-D film. If this disparity isn't taken into account, the resultant movie can cause problems for the audience. The filmmakers will have no trouble watching it, but the average viewer will find it difficult to converge 3-D images that cut between extreme positions in front of and behind the screen plane.

These extremes of convergence can mitigated to a great degree in the digital intermediate or by the post handling of the 3-D images. A technique of "handing off" the A side of cut to the B side by quickly easing the convergence between the two cuts can be very effective at making the cut much easier for the audience to watch.

Some 3-D films attempt to guide the viewer to converge objects in front of the screen. They do this by slowly bringing an object closer to the audience, allowing viewers to track the object as it comes farther and farther off the screen. The makers of the theme-park attraction *Captain EO* accomplished this with a shot of a floating asteroid that comes off the screen at the beginning of the film. In *Muppet*vision 3-D*, the effect is created with the simple gag of a "3-D" logo positioned at the end of a broomstick that is pushed into the audience's face; the effect is repeated at the end of the film with the shot of Kermit perched at the end of a fire truck's ladder. In *Terminator2*: *3-D*, Robert Patrick's molten head slowly comes out off the screen towards the audience.

THE GLASSES

Creating the illusion of true stereoscopic imaging requires that the left eye and right eye see unique left/right imagery. This is achieved with various kinds of glasses that perform the task for the viewer. It should be noted that all 3-D glasses—and projection systems—have an impact on the brightness of the projected image, generally a light loss on the order of 2–3 stops.

The first public use of polarized glasses for a 3-D motion-picture presentation took place at the 1939 New York World's Fair. Called linear polarizers, these glasses work by orienting the left- and right-eye polarizing material at right angles to each other. Though this is not actually visible to your eye, the effect is graphically illustrated in Figure 11.

In this system, the left- and right-eye projected images are each projected through linear polarizers that match the orientation of the glasses. This method is effective at separating the left and right image material; however, if the viewer tilts his head at an angle, there will be "leakage" of the image information, allowing the viewer to see both images simultaneously, which, of course, is not ideal. Polarizing glasses, and all glasses that do not require any electronics in order to function, are called "passive glasses." Polarized 3-D presentations always require projection onto a silver screen in order to maintain polarization of the projected image.

Figure 10. Linear Polarized Glasses

Glasses that employ circular polarization, with a casual observation, look just like their linear cousins in Figure 10, but perform quite differently. A simple explanation is that circular polarization can be oriented in clockwise and counterclockwise directions. The left- and right-eye projected images are polarized in opposing circular-polarization orientation, as are the respective lenses on the glasses. The circular-polarization effect is graphically illustrated in Figure 12.

Figure 11. Linear Polarizing Glasses, graphically illustrated.

A principle advantage of circular polarization is that the integrity of the left- and right-eye image informa-

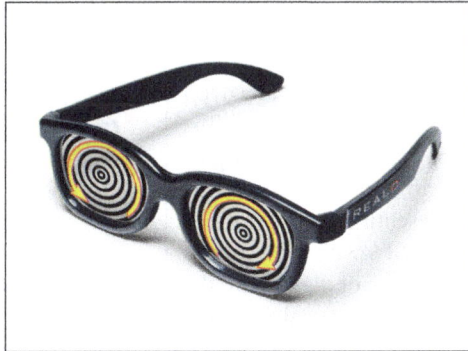

Figure 12. Circular Polarization Glasses, graphically illustrated.

tion is always maintained, no matter how much the viewer tilts their head. Circular polarization is the technique employed with the Real D "Z Screen" technique, used in conjunction with single-projector digital-cinema projection.

A variant on the passive-glasses front is Dolby 3-D technology (Figure 13). Developed in conjunction with Infitec GmbH, this system can use existing screen installations, as it doesn't require a silver screen. By shifting about half a dozen different RGB "primaries" of the projected image, the process is able to create separation of the left and right eye images. Dolby's glasses then filter these spectrums of light so each eye only sees its respective left and right image information. Dolby's color-spectrum technique could technically be described as anaglyph; yet it is actually a much more complex system that doesn't cause any of the color distortion usually associated with anaglyph.

Another type of passive glasses is the anaglyph system (Figure 14). The separation of left- and right-eye imagery is achieved by representing the left-eye material with the cyan spectrum of light and the right-eye material with the

Figure 13. DOLBY 3-D Glasses.

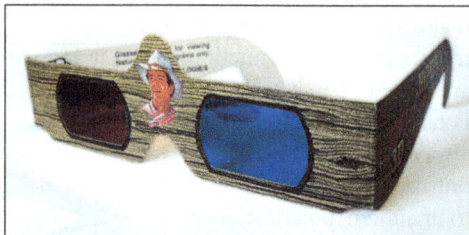

Figure 14. Anaglyph 3-D Glasses.

Figure 15. Liquid Crystal or Active 3-D Glasses.

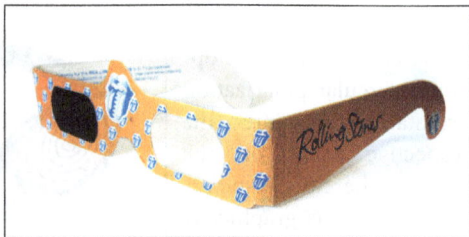

Figure 16. Pulfrich 3-D Glasses.

red spectrum. When the glasses are worn, those colors are directed to your left and right eyes, respectively. This system is often mistakenly thought to be how all 3-D films were viewed in the 1950s; actually, this method was not used very often, and almost all films in the 1950s utilized polarized projection and glasses. Over the past few years, it has been revived for some 3-D presentations, such as Spy Kids 3-D. This technique works on a standard white screen and does not require a silver screen.

Active glasses, also called "shuttered glasses," employ an electronically triggered liquid-crystal shutter in each lens (Figure 14). This method alternately synchronizes the left- and right-eye projected images with the respective liquid-crystal shutters contained in the glasses. An advantage of active glasses is that they do not require a silver screen. The glasses are electronic, require battery power to function, and usually operate in conjunction with a transmitted infrared signal that synchronizes the glasses with the projected left- and right-eye images.

Pulfrich glasses (Figure 16) are definitely the poor man's choice for 3-D, because they do not even produce true stereoscopic 3-D. The "Pulfrich Effect" was first documented by Carl Pulfrich in 1922. This passive eyewear has one clear lens and one lens that is significantly darker. It operates on the principle that it takes longer for your brain to process a dark image than a bright image. The resultant delay creates a faux 3-D effect when objects move laterally across the field of view. Objects "appear" 2-D until they move laterally across the frame, which causes an optical illusion that the brain interprets as a 3-D depth cue. This technique has usually been limited to broadcast-TV applications such as the short 3-D sequences in a 1990 Rolling Stones concert broadcast on Fox, and Hanna-Barbera's *Yo Yogi! 3-D.*

Is there more to 3-D production than the ground we've covered? You bet. But this chapter should gird you with a foundational understanding of the medium, allow you to converse in the vocabulary of 3-D, and enable you to begin to make the medium your own. I also hope you now appreciate that the complexities of 3-D stereoscopic cinematography should not be underestimated.

Day-for-Night, Infrared and Ultraviolet Cinematography

by Dr. Rod Ryan

DAY-FOR-NIGHT

The speed of modern color films makes it possible to shoot night-for-night scenes. However, there are night scenes that are impractical to illuminate artificially and actually film at night. Shooting such scenes day-for-night eliminates the additional problems and expense of night shooting and can deliver excellent pictorial results.

Techniques for filming day-for-night scenes in color or black-and-white vary greatly because of the many factors involved. Cinematographers naturally differ in their interpretation of what constitutes a night effect. The overall effect must be one of darkness. Processing laboratories differ in their negative preferences, although most prefer sufficient density on the original negative since it is always possible to "print down" for a darker effect, but impossible to obtain a rich, full-bodied print from a thin, shadowless original negative (if black shadows are desired, the scene must print at center scale or higher).

Choice of filters and degree of underexposure will vary according to sky conditions; color and contrast of subject and background; the strength, quality and direction of sunlight; and the particular effect desired. Very generally speaking, the most convincing day-for-night shots, in either color or black-and-white, are made in strong sunlight, under blue skies and with low-angle back-cross lighting.

Direct backlighting results in a "rim-light" effect which, although pleasing in a long shot, lacks the necessary three-dimensional, half-illuminated facial effects required in medium and close shots. Front lighting will flatten and destroy all shadows. Side and front-cross lighting is permissible but not as effective as back-cross illumination. Because production does not always permit shooting when conditions are exactly right, and since day-for-night shots must sometimes be made all day long, often the choice of sun angle must be compromised. Under these conditions, avoid front lighting as much as possible and stay with any sun angle that results in partial illumination, preferably with shadows toward the camera.

Skies give the most trouble, since they will invariably read too high and are difficult to balance against foreground action. Graduated neutral-density filters, which cover the sky area only, and Pola Screens, which will darken the sky with the sun at certain angles, are both useful for either color or black-and-white films because they do not affect color values and can be used in combination with other effect filters.

Neutral-density filters will tone down a "hot" sky even if it is bald white. A partial or graduated neutral-density filter covering only the sky will therefore be very useful for bringing the sky into exposure balance with the foreground. Care must be taken, however, that action does not cross the demarcation line between the filter material and the clear glass area. Pola Screens are most useful when the sun is directly overhead at right angles to the camera.

A Pola Screen should not be employed if the camera must be panned through a wide arc, since the polarization will vary and the sky tone will change in density as the camera revolves. Typical underexposure is 1½ to 2½ stops, rarely more. Brilliant sunlight will require greater underexposure, gray days less. The underexposure can be handled in several ways. One is by ignoring the filter exposure increase required, if it is close to the amount of underexposure desired. For instance, the filter being employed may require two stops increase in exposure for a normal effect. The increase is ignored and the diaphragm set for the exposure without the filter, thus delivering the necessary underexposure for the night effect. Or, a neutral density of the desired strength is employed and its exposure increase ignored.

Proceed as follows: insert the effect filter or combination of filters for the desired effect, and allow for their exposure increase as in normal filming. Add the desired neutral (a .30 for one stop, .50 for 1½ stops or a .60 for two stops). Ignoring the neutral filter's exposure increase will automatically underexpose the negative the necessary amount. This is a quick and effective method in fast production shooting where night effects are suddenly required and little or no time is available for computations.

If the sky is not sufficiently blue to filter properly, and if it is impossible to use a graduated neutral-density filter, try to avoid the sky as much as possible by shooting against buildings or foliage, or choose a high angle and shoot downward.

The contrast between the players and the background is very important because a definite separation is desirable. Dark clothing, for instance, will merge with a dark background, and the player will be lost. It is better to leave a dark background dark and players in lighter, although not necessarily white, clothing than to have a light background and players in dark clothing. The latter combination will result in a silhouette, rather than a night effect. This is the reason that back-cross lighting is preferable: so the background is not illuminated and the players have a definite separation through edge lighting, which also imparts shimmering highlights.

Black-and-White Film

The illusion of night in black-and-white cinematography is obtained by combining contrast filtering with underexposure. Since the sky is light by day and dark by night, it is the principal area of the scene requiring correction. Any of the yellow-orange or red filters may be used. A very popular combination is the light red Wratten 23A plus the green 56. This combination does everything the red filters accomplish—plus it darkens flesh tones, which are rendered too light by the red filters alone. When combining filters, remember that red filters add contrast but green filters flatten, so if a greater flattening effect is desired add a heavier green filter. Because flesh tones are not important in long shots, such shots are sometimes filmed with heavier red filters, and only the medium and close shots are made with the combination red-green filters. Care must be taken, however, that clothing and background colors do not photograph differently when filters are switched in the same sequence. If in doubt, shoot tests before production filming begins. Remember that only a blue sky can be filtered down. No amount of color filtering will darken a bald white sky. Use graduated neutral densities, or avoid the sky under these adverse conditions. The 23A-56 combination is usually employed with a filter factor of 6, rather than the 20 normally required (5 for the 23A and 4 for the 56, which multiplied equals 20). The factor of 6 automatically underexposes this filter combination approximately 1½ stops and achieves the desired effect without further computation. If a red filter is used alone, bear in mind that it will lighten faces, and use a darker makeup (approximately two shades) on close shots.

Reversal Color Film

Typical blue night effects can be obtained with reversal color films balanced for exposure with tungsten light by removing the Wratten 85 filter and under exposing 1⅓ stops. If the bluish effect is too great, an ultraviolet-absorbing filter can be used to filter out the excess ultraviolet. Flesh tones in closeups can be adjusted by using gold reflectors or 3200°K fill lights to light actors faces. Care must be taken that the actors are not overlit or that such lights appear as ambient light with the sun acting as a moonlight key.

Negative Color Film

A cameraperson shooting day-for-night with negative color film should check with his or her processing laboratory before the production begins. Laboratories have a far greater range of color correction available than the cinematographer has at his disposal during the original photography. They may add or subtract any color, or combination of colors, provided the original negative has sufficient exposure. Once the 85 filter is removed, however, it is often impossible to restore normal color balance to the film.

If the 85 filter is removed, it should be replaced with an ultraviolet filter, which will prevent overexposure of the blue sensitive layer and keep the negative within printing range. Warmer effects may be obtained by substituting a light yellow filter for the 85. A Pola Screen may also be used to darken a blue sky and provide the required underexposure (by ignoring its filter factor). It will have no effect on a bald sky, but it will act as a neutral-density filter and provide the needed underexposure. Remember that approximately ⅔ stop exposure is gained by removing the 85 filter. This must be included in exposure calculations.

INFRARED CINEMATOGRAPHY

Because cinematography by infrared light has had limited pictorial use, this will be a brief review. For more information, refer to Kodak publications number N-17 "Kodak Infrared Films" and M-28 "Applied Infrared Photography." Infrared for photographic purposes is defined as that part of the spectrum, approximately 700 to 900 nanometers (nm), which is beyond the visible red but not as far as would be sensed by humans as heat.

All infrared films are sensitive to heat and should be kept refrigerated before exposure and during any holding time before processing. While no longer listed as a regular catalogue item, Eastman Kodak still manufactures a black-and-white infrared-sensitive film, Kodak High Speed Infrared Film 2481, and modified color-sensitive film, Kodak Ektachrome Infrared Film 2236. Both of these films are on Estar base. Before deciding to use either film in a production, the manufacturer should be contacted regarding its availability, minimum order quantities and delay in delivery.

Black-and-White Films

For pictorial purposes, the greatest use of infrared-sensitive film for motion-picture photography has been for "day for night" effects. Foliage and grass reflect infrared and record as white on black-and-white film. Painted materials that visually match in color but do not have a high infrared reflectance will appear dark. Skies are rendered almost black, clouds and snow are white, shadows are dark but often show considerable detail. Faces require special makeup and clothing can only be judged by testing.

A suggested EI for testing prior to production is daylight EI 50, tungsten EI 125 with a Wratten 25, 29, 70 or 89 filter, or daylight EI 25, tungsten EI 64 with 87 or 88A (visually opaque) filter. Infrared light comes to a focus farther from the lens than does visual light. (Speak to your lens supplier for correct focus compensation for infrared photography.)

Color

No human can see infrared; color film can only record and interpret it. Kodak Ektachrome Infrared Film 2236 was originally devised for camouflage detection. Its three image layers are sensitized to green, red and infrared instead of blue, green and red. Later applications were found in medicine, ecology, plant pathology, hydrology, geology and archeology. Its only pictorial use has been to produce weird color effects.

In use, all blue light is filtered out with a Wratten 12 filter; visible green records as blue, visible red as green, and infrared as red. The blue, being filtered out, is black on the reversal color film. Because visible yellow light is used as well as infrared, focus is normal, and the use of a light meter is normal for this part of the spectrum. What happens to the infrared reflected light is not measurable by conventional methods, so testing is advisable. A suggested EI for testing prior to production is daylight EI 100 with a Wratten 12 filter.

ULTRAVIOLET CINEMATOGRAPHY

There are two distinctly different techniques for cinematography using ultraviolet radiation, and since they are often confused with each other, both will be described.

In the first technique, called reflected-ultraviolet photography, the exposure is made by invisible ultraviolet radiation reflected from an object. This method is similar to conventional photography, in which you photograph light reflected from the subject. To take pictures by reflected ultraviolet, most conventional films can be used, but the camera lens must be covered with a filter, such as the Wratten 18A, that transmits the invisible ultraviolet and allows no visible light to reach the film. This is true ultraviolet photography; it is used principally to show details otherwise invisible in scientific and technical photography. Reflected-ultraviolet photography has almost no application for motion-picture purposes; if you have questions about reflected-ultraviolet photography, information is given in the book "Ultraviolet and Fluorescence Photography," available from Eastman Kodak.

The second technique is known as fluorescence, or black-light, photography. In motion-picture photography, it is used principally for visual effects. Certain objects, when subjected to invisible ultraviolet light, will give off visible radiation called fluorescence, which can be photographed with conventional film. Some objects fluoresce particularly well and are described as being fluorescent. They can be obtained in various forms such as inks, paints, crayons, papers, cloth and some rocks. Some plastic items, bright-colored articles of clothing and cosmetics are also typical objects that may fluoresce. For objects that don't fluoresce, fluorescent paints (oil or water base), chalks or crayons can be added. These materials are sold by art-supply stores, craft shops, department stores and hardware stores. (Many of these items can also be obtained from Wildfire Inc., 10853 Venice Blvd., Los Angeles, CA, 90034, which manufactures them specially for the motion-picture industry.)

Fluorescence may range from violet to red, depending on the material and the film used. In addition to the fluorescence, the object reflects ultraviolet light, which is stronger photographically. Most film has considerable sensitivity to ultraviolet, which would overexpose and wash out the image from the weaker visible fluorescence. Therefore, to photograph only the fluorescence, you must use a filter over the camera lens (such as the Wratten 2B, 2E or 3, or equivalent) to absorb the ultraviolet.

The wavelengths of ultraviolet light range from about 10 to 400nm. Of the generally useful range of ultraviolet radiation, the most common is the long-wavelength 320 to 400nm range. Less common is the short to medium-wavelength range of 200 to 320nm. In fluorescence photography you can use long-, medium-, or short-wave radiation to excite the visible fluorescence depending on the material. Some materials will fluoresce in one type of ultraviolet radiation and not in another.

Certain precautions are necessary when you use ultraviolet radiation. You must use a source of short- or medium-wave ultraviolet with caution because its rays cause sunburn and severe, painful injuries to eyes not protected by ultraviolet-absorbing goggles. Read the manufacturer's instructions before using ultraviolet lamps.

Eye protection is generally not necessary when you use long-wave ultraviolet because this radiation is considered harmless. However, it's best not to look directly at the radiation source for any length of time, because the fluids in your eyes will fluoresce and cause some discomfort. Wearing glass eyeglasses will minimize the discomfort from long-wave sources.

There are many sources of ultraviolet radiation, but not all of them are suitable for fluorescence photography. The best ultraviolet sources for the fluorescence technique are mercury-vapor lamps or ultraviolet fluorescent tubes. If an object fluoresces under a continuous ultraviolet source, you can see the fluorescence while you're photographing it.

Since the brightness of the fluorescence is relatively low, the ultraviolet source must be positioned as close as practical to the subject. The objective is to produce the maximum fluorescence while providing even illumination over the area to be photographed.

Fluorescent tubes designed especially to emit long-wave ultraviolet are often called black-light tubes because they look black or dark blue before they're lighted. The glass of the tubes contains filter material that is opaque to most visible light but freely transmits long-wavelength ultraviolet. These tubes, identified by the letters BLB, are sold by electrical supply stores, hardware stores and department stores. They are available in lengths up to 4' and can be used in standard fluorescent fixtures to illuminate large areas. Aluminum-foil reflectors are available to reflect and control the light.

Mercury-vapor lamps are particularly suitable for illuminating small areas with high ultraviolet brightness. When these lamps are designed for ultraviolet work, they usually include special filters which transmit ultraviolet and absorb most of the visible light. Mercury-vapor ultraviolet lamps are available in two types, long-wave and short-wave. Some lamps include both wavelengths in the same unit so that they can be used either separately or together. If you use a light source that does not have a built-in ultraviolet filter, you must put such a filter over the light source. The filter for the radiation source is called the "exciter filter."

You can use a Kodak Wratten Ultraviolet Filter No. 18A or Corning Glass No. 5840 (Filter No. CS7-60) or No. 9863 (Filter No. CS7-54) for this purpose. Kodak Filter No. 18A is available in 2- and 3-inch glass squares from photo dealers. The dealer may have to order the filter for you. The Corning Glass is available in larger sizes from Corning Glass Works, Optical Photo Products Department, Corning, NY, 14830. The filter you use must be large enough to completely cover the front of the lamp. The scene is photographed on a dark set with only the ultraviolet source illuminating the subject. In order for the film to record only the fluorescence, use a Kodak Wratten gelatin filter, No. 2A or 2B, or an equivalent filter, over the camera lens to absorb the ultraviolet. When used for this purpose, the filters are called "barrier filters." Since the fluorescence image is visible, no focusing corrections are necessary. Focus the camera the same as for a conventional subject.

Determining Exposure

Many exposure meters are not sensitive enough to determine exposure for fluorescence. An extremely sensitive exposure meter should indicate proper exposure of objects that fluoresce brightly under intense ultraviolet, if you make the meter reading with a No. 2A or 2B filter over the meter cell. If your exposure meter is not sensitive enough to respond to the relative brightness of fluorescence, the most practical method of determining exposure is to make exposure tests using the same type of film, filters and setup you plan to use for your fluorescence photography.

Films

While either black-and-white or color camera films can be used for fluorescence photography, color film produces the most dramatic results. The daylight-balanced films will accentuate the reds and yellows, while the tungsten balanced films will accentuate the blues. Since fluorescence produces a relatively low light level for photography, a high-speed film such as Eastman Vision 3 500T (5219) or Eastman Vision 250D (5207) is recommended.

SPECIAL CONSIDERATIONS

Some lenses and filters will also fluoresce under ultraviolet radiation. Hold the lens or filter close to the ultraviolet lamp to look for fluorescence. Fluorescence of the lens or filter will cause a general veiling or fog in your pictures. In severe cases, the fog completely obscures the image. If a lens or filter fluoresces, you can still use it for fluorescence photography if you put the recommended ultraviolet-absorbing filter over the camera lens or the filter that fluoresces. It also helps to position the ultraviolet lamp or use a matte box to prevent the ultraviolet radiation from striking the lens or filter.

Aerial Cinematography

by Jon Kranhouse

A rudimentary understanding of basic aviation is essential for safe film-ing. When airborne, things can go wrong very quickly. Within respec-tive aircraft flight envelopes, altitude and speed provide an extra margin of safety; "low and slow" leaves little margin for error. The immutable laws of physics are unforgiving and must not be ignored, despite egos, budgets and schedules. Aerial filming can be exceptionally safe, or turn deadly with poor judgment.

Air-to-ground and air-to-air filming require the cinematographer to con-sider the proper type of helicopter or fixed-wing aircraft to use as a camera platform, as well as the appropriate camera mount. Factors include: match-ing air speeds of camera aircraft and story aircraft, total weight of people/equipment, top speed, low speed, range and time aloft, terrain to be flown over, working altitude, prevailing winds, precipitation, temperature and, of course, the budget.

While helicopters offer unobstructed views and outstanding maneuver-ability at low speed and/or very low altitude, they are much more expensive to operate per hour than most fixed-wing aircraft. Adequate results might be achieved from a small Cessna, if aircraft architecture doesn't block the required view. Many fixed-wing aircraft have greater range and altitude ca-pability than helicopters.

For maximum stability and safety, select a camera aircraft that will, during actual filming, be working near the middle of its flight envelope. There have been times when a Lear jet had to drop its landing gear and flaps during filming at altitude just to match speed with a slower story aircraft. In another example that I recall, a helicopter couldn't keep up with a race car; a fixed-wing aircraft should have been selected instead.

Sometimes the wrong aircraft is selected because a helicopter pilot doesn't want to lose a job to a fixed-wing pilot, or vice versa. At other times, the producer, director and cameraman were not envisioning the same shots; there's no substitute for good prep. Many variants of each aircraft type exist; if one variant is suitable for your needs, don't assume they all are. Blimps and hot-air balloons offer the most vibration-free mounting platforms, but they are the least maneuverable.

On-board cinematography is often accomplished with a handheld camera, onboard Steadicam, or by various methods of mounting the camera to the airframe (under guidelines of FAA #337 certificate; see FAA rules below).

Skydiving cinematography is a rare specialty of very experienced skydivers, usually working with helmet-mounted Bell & Howell 35mm Eyemo cameras or variants. Skydivers can be photographed from the ground with very long lenses, as well as from helicopters using various stabilization mounts.

Miniaturized radio-controlled helicopters bearing ultra-lightweight film cameras and video transmitters have yielded promising results. Depending on the shots desired, these might be the right tool for the job. Using these machines above crowds is illegal, their blades are as lethal as those of a full-sized helicopter.

AESTHETICS

Time of day: Of course, early morning and late afternoon light is desirable to reveal textures on the ground, and wind is usually calmest at these times. Consideration must be made for keeping aircraft shadow or reflection out of the shot. Midday heat can cause wind gusts, affecting stability. It is common for pilot and camera crew to be aboard a warmed-up helicopter, parked and "turning" on the ground, awaiting the earliest flyable light—it is not safe to fly low-to-ground in pitch-black night. Night filming is perfectly safe at altitude—above the power lines.

Metering: When the sky is clear, an incident light meter is quick and easy; the light hitting you is the same as that hitting your subject. When shafts of sunlight poke through stormy clouds, a spot meter is most useful. Lens hoods for spot meters prevent flare from biasing readings.

Filming speeds: To create shot dynamics, shooting at less than 24 fps is common. When viewed from the air, most inanimate air-to-ground subjects (e.g., city traffic, ocean waves and large ships) appear to move slowly; they can safely be shot at 18–22 fps and still appear quite natural. Exterior gyro mounts allow for exceptional stability at very slow framing rates (e.g., 2 fps), but usable pans and tilts must be pre-programmed. A door mount or handheld may be more appropriate if a less steady POV is called for. Conversely, in turbulent air with a door mount, slight overcranking (30–36 fps) can smooth results.

Choice of film stocks/T-stops: Geography and sun conditions may require changing the f-stop in-shot. It is not unusual to pull from T4 to T22 in one shot; the trick is hiding the change with shot choreography and a smooth remote aperture motor. Door mounts allow the changing of filters and magazines in mid-air, allowing for quick adaptation to changing conditions. Nose and exterior gyro mounts, however, require a smart compromise to be considered before take-off during sunrise/sunset periods of rapidly changing light intensity. You don't want to have to land to change filters or stocks just when the light is magic.

Exterior gyro mounts require focus to be a combination of estimations from the videotap finder, coupled with the estimations of a great assistant. But it doesn't hurt to have a T16 when doing air-to-air at 250mm. Low-speed daylight-balanced stocks with UV filtration are excellent for aerials if you have the light. When details in dark-green trees are important, some prefer tungsten-balanced film with No. 85 filter, or with only partial correction (e.g., Coral No. 1).

Creating dynamic action: Finding foreground elements to shoot through (e.g., trees, rock formations) can increase shot "energy." For air-to-air, plan intersecting vectors of the aircraft. If air-to-ground, utilize the horizon roll capability of a nose mount or the pirouette ability of a door mount. Exterior gyro mounts can combine zooms with helicopter motion to create tremendous approaches and reveals (peek-a-boo from behind hills/buildings), or can be undercranked for super-fast approaches. Most gyro-based systems don't tolerate panning as fast as fixed nose mounts, helicopter turns should not be too extreme. For example, long focal lengths with slower orbits around the subject can create a rapidly moving background behind a subject on a mountaintop. Because helicopters can't stop on a dime, some gyro-system approach shots are performed in reverse, rapidly climbing shots.

AVIATION BASICS
FAA Regulations for Camera Mounts

Federal Aviation Administration rules require that when any object is bolted or strapped anywhere to any airframe—Cessna or 747—the installation must be certified airworthy by a recognized FAA inspector. The inspector issues a temporary-use type 337 certificate specific to that aircraft. If you use the same mounting bracket on another aircraft of identical type, a new 337 must be obtained. Once granted, the 337 is added to a particular aircraft's manual, so future reinstallations don't require FAA recertification. Time must be allowed in the production schedule for this FAA field inspection, if required; the inspector is typically busy and backlogged.

Mounting hardware that has earned an STC (Standard Type Certificate) means that the equipment vendor has persevered through a costly process. STC installations do not require field inspection by an FAA examiner and are certified flight-ready by a more readily available A&P (airframe and power-plant mechanic).

Pilots

A truly qualified pilot is critical for both the safety and success of the production; it is obviously essential for the pilot to have many hours of "time-in-type" of similar aircraft. When filming in the United States, a pilot should be operating under his or her own (or company's) *FAA Motion Picture Manual*. This allows a pilot some latitude within the FAA guidelines, which restrict the activities of all other aircraft. A high level of expertise and judgment must be demonstrated before the FAA grants such manuals. Of course, many flying situations still require advance approval from the regional FAA office, as well as other local authorities. Preproduction consultation with pilots is strongly recommended.

Remotely operated gyrostabilized camera systems are often called upon for very close work with long lenses; precise camera positioning is absolutely critical. Few pilots have the skills necessary to hold a helicopter in a steady-enough hover for a shot with a tight frame size. While the gyro systems isolate the camera from helicopter vibration, an unstable hover causes XYZ spatial excursions, resulting in constant relocations of the film-plane—an undesirable parallax shift. The footage may appear as if the camera is panning or tilting; actually, the helicopter is wobbling about in the hover position.

A local pilot and helicopter may be the only option when on very remote locations. Some regional helicopter companies may not allow other pilots to fly their helicopter. These local pilots must understand that some filming maneuvers might require an exceptional degree of mechanical reliability from their aircraft; when hovering below 300 feet in calm air, a safe autorotate is impossible. Spend the minimum amount of time hovering low, and don't press your luck with unnecessary takes. If you must work with a helicopter pilot who has no film experience, try to choose one with many hours of long-line work (i.e., heavy cargo suspended by cable, or water-bucket fire suppression), as this type of flying requires both a high level of aviation skill and judgment.

Protocol, Planning and Nonessential "Payload"

For those new to aerial filming, getting swept up in the excitement of something new, combined with the typical rush of production, can distract one from safety. Always think before moving around aircraft—more than one crew member has died walking into spinning tail rotors. Never walk toward or around the rear of a helicopter!

Air-to-air shots must be choreographed so that one pilot can maintain visual contact with the other aircraft; the pilot with "visual" can switch off during filming, but never depend on a video monitor to determine safe spacing.

Ground locations that involve close helicopter work may require a wet-down to eliminate flying dust that might damage jet engines. Helicopter pilots should not be expected to land or fly low in unfamiliar terrain with no prior knowledge of electricity or telephone wires.

When a camera mount is installed aboard a helicopter under an STC or 337, that aircraft is put in a restricted category. Nonessential personnel are not allowed on board, according to FAA rules. Extra people cause the pilot to have less lift and agility. Unexpected wind gusts may require extra torque (or temperature demands of the turbine), which is not available when close to maximum payload. An extra person also means that less fuel can be carried.

Communication: Radios and Pilot Jargon

Handheld ground-to-air aircraft frequency radios are available and are most preferred. Tyler and Advanced Camera Systems (formerly Continental Camera) offer intercom boxes for helicopters, which allow communication to and from the helicopter using standard motion-picture walkie-talkie frequencies. For one-way communication with on-camera talent, an induction loop can be worn under wardrobe, which relays signals to an "earwig," a tiny wireless induction pick-up earphone (available from audio suppliers).

While flying in helicopters or fixed-wing aircraft, don't distract the pilot from his primary job. Theoretical conversations belong on the ground and should be kept to a minimum when airborne. In metropolitan areas, the pilot needs to listen for radio calls from air-traffic controllers and look for "Sunday fliers" who are "off" radar control.

Make things easy for your pilot; be specific and concise so he can anticipate his flight path. Pilots require a clear description of where the lens is pointing and what you're seeing. During a preflight briefing, learn each other's language. Usually when filming aboard a fixed-wing aircraft bigger than a small Cessna, the camera operator is positioned somewhere in the back, unable to communicate visually with the pilot and often relying upon headset communication. If the cinematographer cannot see out the front of the camera aircraft, the pilot might have to steer the plane off-course by 90° so the cinematographer can see what lies ahead.

Lining up a particular background behind a story aircraft can be tricky, even for experienced pilots. Getting story aircraft to enter an empty frame requires formation flying from very capable pilots. Military-trained pilots with high formation time are adept at such positioning.

Fuel Trucks

Helicopter agility suffers greatly as payload increases; having a fuel truck on location allows fuel weight to be kept to a safe minimum. Not all airports have jet fuel, which is required for the jet-turbine helicopters listed below. Not all fuel trucks are permitted to leave airports and travel on public roads.

Weather Basics

Aircraft performance suffers when air becomes less dense, which happens when heat and/or altitude is increased. Helicopters are most stable when moving forward faster than 20 mph air speed (translational lift). Therefore, steady breezes can be beneficial, allowing the helicopter to hover relative to the ground while actually flying forward in the airstream. Conversely, a strong, steady wind can make it impossible for a helicopter to maintain a hover in a crosswind or downwind situation. The types of helicopters used for filming are rarely intrumented to fly in heavy fog or clouds; they operate under Visual Flight Rules (VFR).

Choice of Sides for Mounting

All things being equal, it is best to mount the camera on the pilot's side of the aircraft, giving him or her the best visibility of the subject.

Max Speed

When an aircraft has any kind of exterior modification for camera mounts (i.e., door removed, nose/belly mounts or gyro mounts), a maximum allowable air speed known as VNE or "Velocity Not to Exceed" is determined through FAA certification. Be sure this VNE speed will match your subject. Air speed should not be confused with ground speed; prevailing wind conditions may help or hinder filming logistics.

Safety

See the related Industry-Wide Labor-Management Safety Bulletins at: http://www.csatf.org/bulletintro.shtml.

GLOSSARY OF FLIGHT PHYSICS

Awareness of these concepts, most of which are related to helicopters, will expedite communication and increase safety.

AGL: Above Ground Level altitude, expressed in feet or meters.

Flight Envelope: Published by the aircraft manufacturer, this term refers to the conditions in which a given aircraft can be safely operated. This takes into account air density (altitude, humidity and temperature) and allowable torque and temperature output of the engine/transmission/turbine.

Ground Effect: Condition of improved lift when flying near the ground. With helicopters, this is roughly within ½ rotor diameter, becoming more pronounced as the ground is approached.

Losing Tail-Rotor Authority: When helicopters attempt to hover or crab in a crosswind, especially when heavily loaded in thin air (close to the edge of their flight envelope), it sometimes happens that not enough power can be diverted to the tail rotor to maintain the sideways position relative to the wind direction. When the rudder pedal is maxed out, a wind gust can spin the helicopter on its mast like a weather vane. This causes an abrupt loss of altitude. If shot choreography requires such a position, have plenty of altitude above ground level for recovery.

Rudder Pedals: Cause an aircraft to yaw; if using a nose mount, the same as panning. Airplanes have a vertical rudder, though single-rotor helicopters use a tail rotor to control yaw. Helicopters change the pitch of the tail rotor blades to alter the force of the tail rotor, which counteracts the torque from the main rotor.

Settling with Power: When helicopters hover out of ground effect, but still near the ground in still air, prop wash can bounce off the ground and wrap back around the top of the helicopter as a cyclonic down-draft. A pilot can be fooled into applying more horsepower, which only increases the down-draft intensity. All pilots know of this phenomenon, but those who work infrequently in low-AGL situations may not be on guard. Try to change shot choreography to continuously move out of your own "bad" air.

Yoke/Control Stick: Makes the aircraft pitch and roll (stick forward = nose down, stick right = roll right). When using nose-mounts, coordinate with the pilot so aircraft pitch and camera tilts are harmonious.

COMMON HELICOPTERS
Aerospatiale A-Star/Twin-Star (AS350 and AS355 twin)
Pro: Very powerful engine(s) for superior passenger and fuel-range capacity. Extremely smooth flying with three-blade system. Accepts door and exterior gyro-stabilized mounts (gyro mounts require helicopter to have aft "hard points"). Tyler Nose Mount can fit if the aircraft is equipped with custom bracket by the helicopter owner. High-altitude ability is excellent.

Con: Costlier than Jet Ranger. Does not hold critical position well in ground-effect hover.

Aerospatiale Llama
Pro: Powerful engine mated to lightweight fuselage specifically designed for great lifting ability and high-altitude work. Accepts door and some gyro-stabilized mounts. Holds position quite well in ground-effect hover. Set the helicopter height record in 1972 at over 40,000'.

Con: Expensive; very few available.

Bell Jet Ranger (206)
Pro: Agile and relatively economical. Accepts door and nose mounts. Most variants will accept gyrostabilized mounts (must have external "hard points"); excellent close-hovering stability.

Con: Earlier models have low-power engines. Poor high-altitude performance; reduced range/payload for exterior gyro-mount work.

Bell Long Ranger (206L)

Pro: Excellent for both door and nose mounts. Very smooth and powerful; high-altitude performance is good.

Con: More expensive than Jet Ranger. Reduced inventory of external gyro-mount brackets from various vendors.

Bell Huey UH-1 (civilian version known as 204/205)

Pro: Accepts door mounts. Very powerful; high-altitude performance is good. Utilized more as a story ship than as a functional camera ship; camera often onboard with shots involving talent.

Con: Very bouncy, expensive. Requires permanent modification of airframe to fit external gyro mounts.

Hughes 500 series (A through E + NOTAR models)

Pro: Smoothest-flying (five rotor blades) and most agile of all helicopters; relatively economical. High-altitude ability OK.

Con: Extremely small rear compartment, impractical for door/side mounts; better for handheld. Custom-built (337 installation rules) bungee mount, "Outside Mount," or Spacecam bracket requires a permanent modification to the airframe. Earlier models have low-power engines.

COMMON FIXED-WING AIRCRAFT

But first another word about pilots:

The costs of operating a jet-turbine helicopter weeds out most "Sunday flyers." By comparison, many amateur fixed-wing pilots want to expand their experience, and some professional fixed-wing charter pilots may have low "time-in-type" of the aircraft most appropriate for your filming needs. Practically all fixed-wing pilots will be eager for a film job, but most underestimate how complicated piloting tasks can become while positioning for the camera. It's your life—choose wisely.

Cessna (many variants)

Pro: High-wing good for air-to-ground situations. Economical and ubiquitous. Some types may be flown with window/door ajar or removed with 337 waiver. Stability dramatically increased for short duration when flown in side-slip.

Con: Limited space for rigging mounting devices.

Twin (e.g. Piper Navaho, Cessna 414)

Pro: Higher speed, greater range. Some types may be flown with rear window/door ajar or removed with 337.

Con: Limited field of view to avoid aircraft structure for both air-to-air or and air-to-ground.

Customized Propeller aircraft
(e.g., B-24, B-25, Cessna 414, Pilatus Porter, Pitts)
Each offers unique capabilities: hard mounts on an aerobatic plane (Pitts); wide range of low to high speeds with harness to lower operator (protected by wind shroud) for wide field of view aft using door-mount type arm (Porter); unobstructed view through gun-port fuselage openings at speeds higher than the helicopter domain (B-24, 25). Nonpressurized aircraft become quite cold at altitude, which may create condensation problems for optics (see Arctic Cinematography page 239).

Customized Jet Systems (Learjet, L-39)
Pro: High-altitude and/or high-speed work. First choice for air-to-air of jet aircraft.
Con: Expensive.

TYPES OF CAMERA MOUNTS
A handheld camera may be adequate for wide perspectives with minimal pans/tilts for small cameras, but when more sophisticated shots are desired, there are three basic types of mounts.

Helicopter Nose/Belly Mounts
Abilities: Shoot straight forward or straight back, with tilting ability. Video-assist viewing. Very dynamic shots when used with a wide-angle lens, low to the ground, in narrow canyons or city streets and/or when the helicopter is making steeply banked turns. These mounts can tilt straight down or rearward, a position used when ferrying to protect the lens from bug strikes. Designed for Jet Rangers and Long Rangers, if equipped with standard or high skids.
Limitations: These systems do not pan; the helicopter must be yawed (steer left/right). No vibration isolation; smooth air and wider focal lengths required. Takes 400' of film at a time; landing to reload required. Bug strikes and moisture droplets cannot be cleaned in-flight, and if small might not be seen through the video viewfinder while in flight. These systems cannot be installed on helicopters with low skid gear. As the frontal area of the camera package exposed to wind-pressure increases, vibration increases; screw-on filters are recommended over matte boxes. Lens servo motors and the like should be kept to an absolute minimum. Vibration restricts use of focal lengths to no longer than 50mm in the best of conditions.

Helicopter Door/Side Mounts
(can be used from larger fixed-wing aircraft and camera cars)
Comprised of a platform attached to the aircraft floor with a vertical mast, which supports the camera arm. The rear of the camera arm extends behind the operator and forms a counterweight. Some arm systems may be attached to a Mitchell tripod plate for camera car use. Some mounts isolate the operator from vibration atop a sprung seat.

Abilities: Shoot fast pirouettes at radical down angle, either air-to-ground or air-to-air. Allows pilot to fly in a fairly normal manner, presenting the side of the aircraft toward the action. Takes 400' of film at a time; camera can be reloaded in the air. For optimal results, the camera should be allowed to float on the isolation mast, guided with slight fingertip pressure on hand grips, which contain servo focus/zoom controls. In general, the greater the mass of the vibration-isolated section of the mount, the better the image stability. Wind deflector fitted to the available aft doorhinge helps reduce wind pressure on front of lens. By ganging multiple Kenyon gyros on the camera arm and counterweight, using a 275mm lens is possible, if minimal panning and tilting is required.

Limitations: Fairly smooth air required. Slight overcranking may be required to steady the image. Shots for background plates may call too much attention to image chatter. Pan/tilt range is usually limited by the interior architecture of the aircraft cabin interfering with the swinging counterweight.

Exterior Gyrostabilized Mounts (a.k.a. Ball Mounts)
Offering ultimate image stability, a remotely operated camera housed inside a spherical wind shroud is bolted to the outside of the airframe with special brackets. All controls remain inside the helicopter; optical viewfinder is replaced with videotap. Most mounts attach to most Jet Rangers, A-Star/TwinStars and Llamas. These systems are also used on camera cars, cranes and boats. Some systems allow removal of wind-shroud sphere for use of wide-angle optics for ground applications.

Rate vs. Mass: The first gyro-stabilized aerial systems used heavy spinning wheels to generate angular momentum (mass gyros). Miniature solid state rate gyros and direct-drive motors, used in current military and video systems, have spawned a new genereation of on-the-ground stabilizing heads for film cameras (e.g., Flight Head, Libra, Stab-C, WescamXR); some of which are superior for longer focal lengths. Compared to mass-gyro systems offer superior operator response and allow far more aggressive helicopter maneuvering; gear wheels are optional.

Abilities: Complete isolation of the camera from all vibration; independent from pitch, roll and yaw movements of the vehicle. Frame rates below

4 fps yield perfectly stable images. Focal lengths in 35mm format up to 500mm can be used. As the helicopter yaws (steers left and right), the mount acts like a compass, keeping the camera pointed in the direction last panned. Shoot straight back, forward and down within one shot. Regardless of how bumpy the air, these systems deliver perfectly smooth images on days that would ground a door mount. Bugs and moisture droplets can be wiped off in flight in some configurations. Ideal for shooting background plates. All current gyro systems use a fourth vertical reference gyro to maintain a level horizon, regardless of helicopter bank angle. Some systems allow the camera to Dutch angle during helicopter turns if desired. All systems can be remotely operated at the end of very long tethers (e.g., 500 feet), some by radio link. All current systems allow camera speeds to be varied in-shot with automatic iris compensation. Magazines are 1,000' and require a full load for proper weight and balance. All current systems offer BNCR or Panavision mount cameras with choice of zooms or primes; 10:1 zoom is standard configuration.

Limitations: Mass-Gyro systems do not pan/tilt as fast as remote heads, and exhibit minor lag and over-shoot. They utilize a similar two-axis joystick control for pan/tilt, which takes time for operator skills to develop; no gear-wheel input available for on-the-ground application. All gyro systems require landing to reload and change filters; an experienced technician is required. Critical balance of these systems restricts their choice of lenses; lens changes between zooms and primes requires considerable time.

ALTERNATE STABILIZERS IN THE AIR
Bungee or Surgical Tubing Mounts

For filming inside-to-outside of a story aircraft, this is often the best solution. The camera is hung by a web of rubber shock cords that are secured to the airframe, so that the camera weight pulls the cords to the middle of their stretch range, thereby allowing for maximum excursions of the camera in any direction.

Limitations: Multiday custom design and fabrication; 337 inspection required.

Steadicam

Using a short center post between camera and sled and attached to an an appropriate vehicle mount (not worn), good results can be achieved as long as the camera is kept sheltered from the wind. Best for onboard a story aircraft, rather than as a substitute for a door mount.

Limitations: Wind pressure striking the camera causes gross instability. 337 inspections required.

Rigid/Hard Mounts (fixed-wing or helicopter)

Sometimes rigidly mounting the camera to the inside or outside of the aircraft achieves the best results. While the image of the background outside the aircraft may vibrate, the image of the airframe and passengers remains steady relative to the camera (think car-mount, but engineered for the FAA). **Limitations:** Multiday custom design and fabrication; 337 inspection required.

The Arriflex stabilizer (limited availability) is a small periscope box of two front-surface mirrors, one gyrostabilized. The Arri unit has somewhat limited pan/tilt ability due to gyro lag and is for small-diameter, longer focal-length primes (75–180mm in 35mm format).

Dynalens stabilizers, built in 1962, are liquid-filled prisms that are the predecessor to the "steadi-shot" found on modern home-video cameras. Two glass discs are coupled together with a bellows; sandwiched between the discs is a layer of high-index refractive fluid. Gyro motion sensors detect deviations in pitch and yaw, sending signals to servo motors which counter-pivot the appropriate "pan" or "tilt" disc. This counter-pivot creates a partial prism shape. The Dynalens can correct rapid vibration excursions up to 6° in either pitch (tilt) or yaw (pan); however, camera pan/tilt speeds must be reduced.

Only six units remain but have been refurbished; the maximum diameter available is 6″. Available from Steve Peterson in California: (714) 579-7857.

The Kenyon stabilizer is a small package containing two gyros to resist motion in two axes (typically pitch and roll). It mounts to the bottom of the device to be stabilized. Works best with ultralightweight handheld cameras with a videotap finder/mini-monitor replacing the optical viewfinder. Note that the gyro is useless if attachment to camera is not extremely rigid (bolted on). (800) 253-4681; http://www.ken-lab.com

CAMERA MOUNTS AND DEDICATED GYRO SYSTEMS

Advanced Camera Systems (formerly Continental Camera)
(Door and nose mounts; other ground based gear)
(818) 989-5222; http://advancedcamera.com

Door mounts for most common helicopters for video/16mm/35mm and specialty large formats. GyroMaster, Master and Magnum mounts handle cameras up to 46 lbs. GyroMaster uses up to four Kenyon gyros bolted to Master arm and counterweight.

Two belly mounts are available for Bell 206 A/B and L helicopters with standard or high skids. Megamount can be used on a crane arm as a three-axis head, or on the nose of a helicopter as two axis (no pan; tilt 225° and roll 360°). Megamount can handle large cameras up to 80 lbs and has the unique ability among nose mounts to look forward and rearward without having to land to change camera mounting. Megamount can also record 40-second moves for auto replay, and can be controlled by wheels or joystick. The Belly Mount accommodates 35mm cameras, no pan, 100° tilt. Can be mounted with camera looking fore or aft. Also Body-Cam stabilizer and various remote heads.

Gyron Systems (Dedicated Rate-Gyro System for Film and Video)

(626) 584-8722; www.gyron.com

Fiber optic rate-gyro coupled to active bearings allow for very rapid and precise pan, tilt and roll input during the most extreme helicopter maneuvering. Fast stabilized horizon roll possible (45° for film/90° for video); gear wheels available. Video system can be mounted on customized twin-eingine Cessna 337. Waterproofed components inside ball allow for windowless operation in most conditions; flies without shroud for extreme wide-angle film lenses.

Camera: Standard Arri 435, 1000' mags, lenses up to Panavision 11:1 Primo. Video systems use 36:1 lens (non-doubled).

Gyrosphere (Dedicated Mass-Gyro System)

(818) 787-9733; www.gyrosphere.com

Two Gyrosphere systems were built in the mid-1980s using earlier Wescam parts; the extensive upgrade and redesign work represented many "firsts." Vertical-reference gyros were added to automate level horizon; the speed-aperture computer was intergrated; improved stabilization and camera steering enabled faster and more accurate pans/tilts with less lag; improved ergonomics were made possible with hanheld joysticks; prime lens capability. Mixed analog and digital electronics. The vertical slit curved plexiglass window negates the use of a polarizing filter.

Camera: Modified Mitchell Mk-2 (3–36 fps) with underslung XR-35 magazine. Also available with Empireflex VistaVision camera from ILM (2–48 fps) or Vistacam from BCS (2–48 fps).

Pictorvision (Gyro-Stabilized Digital & Film Aerial and Ground Systems for Cinematographers)

(818) 785-9282; pictorvision.com

The original gyro-stabilized aerial systems were begun in the 1960s as Wescam systems—and Pictorvision is the original rental group from that Wescam era. Now Pictorvision offers all options of aerial systems—from the original Wescams, Cineflexes, the XR-Series for ground applications, and the most current and advanced technology—the Eclipse system. Revolutionizing a new generation of aerial camera systems, the Eclipse offers the most advanced steering, stability, and pointing capabilities available on the market. By partnering with some of the world's most creative and experienced DPs, Pictorvision's engineering team integrated user functionality with industry defining technology to produce the Eclipse—ushering in a NEW dawn of aerial cinematography.

Cameras: The open-architecture of the Eclipse & XR-Series allows for an unlimited choice in digital or film camera and lens combinations, including Arri 435, Alexa-Series, F65, Genesis, IMAX MSM, iWerks Compact, Phantom 65, Red One, RED Epic. The Wescam can support many of the current digital camera systems, or our own Mitchell Mk-2 (1–60 fps) all with a variety of cinema lens choices.

Spacecam (Dedicated Mass-Gyro System)

(818) 889-6060; www.spacecam.com

Unique gyro system using heavier gyro wheels spinning at greater rpms. Patented powered cardin joint allows more responsive and faster pans/tilts. Digital electronics allow many abilities (e.g., Dutching in sync with helicopter turns). The lens looks through a windowless port. Action-arm nose bracket for modified Hughes 500 helicopter allows steep banking; nose and tail position brackets for some other helicopters.

Camera: Customlightweight Mitchell Mk 2 (1–120 fps); VistaVision (1–48 fps); 65mm 5-perf

Underwater Cinematography

by Pete Romano, ASC

Underwater photography presents the cinematographer with a wide variety of situations not encountered in above water photography. Water is a dense medium and has certain light-absorption properties that cannot be changed. When working in open water, weather, current and visibility can change daily or sometimes even hourly and you have to be prepared for just about anything. Tank and pool filming present you with water temperature issues for talent comfort and visibility issues that might not work with the scenes to be shot. Locations might vary from a tropical reef to a frozen ice pack, from a backyard pool to a cement tank 200' in diameter and 60' deep, and water visibility could vary from 100' to less than a few feet. It is crucial to understand how to work with and around these factors. If you are an experienced diver and really understand the mechanics and optics of your underwater camera, you will be able to deal with most underwater filming assignments.

Buoyancy control is a very important consideration when shooting underwater. At certain times you will want to be neutrally buoyant so you can swim the camera like a Steadicam® and crane combined, or you might be stationed on a set of parallels or a ladder in a tank, without fins and be heavily weighted for stability and controlling the camera.

As the underwater specialist, your skills have to go beyond just dropping in the water and getting the shots. A lot of your assignments will have you as part of a first unit where your knowledge and experience will be called upon to explain the in's and out's of working underwater. Shots might be presented to you that might not be possible underwater or might be a safety concern. Your diplomatic skills will be called upon to explain the problems but you should have shot options to present to still be able to tell the story. Do not forget that you are there as a tool to record the director's vision while working closely with the film's director of photography.

When working with talent, who for the most part are in wardrobe without mask and fins and also holding their breath, your job is to get the shot as safely and quickly as possible. Your ability to move in to help make the shot happen instead of waiting for it to happen, could be the difference between getting or not getting the shot,

HD UNDERWATER

HD technology is constantly evolving. Although you can instantly see what you've recorded, at this time, HD is not as forgiving as film. The need to more accurately determine your underwater exposure will be essential. Relying on determining a working ASA/ISO setting for the HD camera you are using will not take into account the differences in color space and contrast between the various cameras available, and how those cameras will react to the lighting conditions underwater. You will most likely need a good HD engineer as part of your support crew. There are two camps on the best way to color correct for underwater HD. One camp white balances underwater, sometimes after every depth change. The problem with this scenario is when you tilt up your image goes orange because you have compensated for the lack of warm tones in the water. The other camp goes with the preset auto white balance and corrects the color in post. My advice is to keep it as simple for the operator/DP as possible. Most HD auto settings will deliver an adequately balanced image for color and exposure, and will save the underwater operator the hassle of trying to determine the proper settings while in an already abstracted environment.

Most HD cameras are sensitive to shifts in temperature and humidity. This can lead to problems with tape transport or back focus shifts. The sudden temperature change that can occur from the surface of the water to a few feet below the surface may in some instances be enough to impair a camera's normal function. Take adequate precautions to ensure that the camera is handled in a dry environment during tape or disc changes, and if filming in an area of cold depths, allow sufficient time while surfacing for the camera to gradually approach surface temperature in order to avoid moisture condensation.

HOW LIGHT IS CHANGED BY WATER

The intensity and quality of light available to the underwater cinematographer depends on many factors. Light rays from the sun, sky or motion picture lamps that strike the sea's surface or the surface of a pool or tank produce a number of phenomena that should be understood, so the undesired effects can be avoided or compensated for.

Reflection: Light is reflected back into the air at an angle equal to the angle of incidence. Light penetration is dependent upon the angle and intensity of the light source and water's surface conditions. Heavy seas and wave action will reflect much more light than a calm sea or pool and the waves will also affect the light intensity. Sunlight penetration in open water situations is best in the latitudes of the United States between 9 a.m. and 4 p.m. in the summer and 10 a.m. and 2 p.m. in the winter. This does not mean you cannot shoot film underwater before or after these times. It just means sunlight penetration is best during these times. With the latitudes of today's high speed films and HD's ability to capture images in low light, underwater cinematography can be accomplished successfully in low light situations.

Refraction: Light travels in a straight line, but light that penetrates the water undergoes a change in direction—it is refracted. For example, a pencil placed in a half-full glass of water appears to be bent at the place where it enters the water. Refraction is the source of most of the problems that are encountered in underwater photography.

Color Absorption: As light travels through water, the water acts as a filter reducing the spectrum of light that penetrates it. The long wave lengths of light—reds, oranges and other warm colors—are the first to be absorbed and the visible light is dominated by the blue-green (cyan) effects just a few feet below the surface. All water acts as a continuous filter and the water depth added to the distance of the subject to the camera equals the total water path that the light has to travel.

Scattering: Caused by suspended minerals, plankton, dirt, etc. The absorption and scattering of light rays reduces the intensity of light and the saturation of colors.

EQUIPMENT

The cameraperson and assistant should be completely familiar with the underwater camera equipment and have the ability to perform simple field repairs. In general, the camera housing should have provisions to adjust its weight for salt or fresh water and be slightly negative in buoyancy when submerged. Features to look for are: simplicity in design; easy-to-locate, bright reflex viewing; the ability to accept a variety of lenses; interchangeable flat and dome ports; external focus, iris and camera run controls; video assist to the surface; an underwater monitor; remote camera run capabilities; and the ability to mount the housing to a tripod. Servicing the housing for lens changes, fresh batteries and film reloads should be quick and easy so as not to eat up production time, and a spare parts kit for repairs is mandatory. Even though a water alarm might be incorporated into the housing's design, the assistant should have the ability to check the watertight integrity of the equipment before it goes into the water. Depending on the design of the underwater housing, you can check the sealing of the housing by either pulling a vacuum or adding slight positive pressure (approximately 2 to 3 pounds). Check with the underwater housing manufacturer as to whether a vacuum or positive pressure should be used.

CARE OF EQUIPMENT

At the finish of every shooting day, always rinse off the camera housing, lights and accessories with fresh water, especially when shooting in salt water. A daily clean and check of all exposed O-rings should be performed, as well as checking the external controls for camera run, iris and focus for ease of operation. In full sun, always cover the housing with a solar blanket or at least a white towel to avoid overheating the camera, batteries and especially the film. Do not overgrease any O-ring. The purpose of silicone on an O-ring is to keep the rubber supple, allowing it to lay comfortably in the groove. Too much silicone grease does nothing for the seal and actually attracts grit and debris, which can cause a leak.

In case of salt water exposure to any camera system, immediately disconnect battery power. Break down the entire camera system and rinse with fresh water. After the fresh water rinse, pour alcohol over the parts to displace the fresh water and allow the unit to dry. If there was fresh water exposure, go directly to the alcohol step and allow the unit to dry completely. These emergency steps might not get your camera system back on line, but will at least prevent much of the damage that would be caused to the camera if it were sent in for repairs while wet.

As a camera assistant caring for an underwater housing, one of the most important things to remember is that it's your responsibility to maintain the watertight integrity of the housing. No matter where the equipment comes from, no matter how recently it has been serviced or how thoroughly it was prepped, there are countless accidents, mistakes and oversights that can cause a potential leak. Every time a housing is opened for a magazine or lens change, careful attention must be paid while resealing the housing. No housing is 100 percent leakproof if safeguards are not applied.

In addition to the camera assistant's normal complement of tools, an underwater service kit will cover most of the problems that might arise. This kit should include a bottle of alcohol, a tube of silicone lube and spray, silicone adhesive, dental picks, Q-tips, a Scotch Brite pad, electrical tape, WD-40, soldering iron and solder, cotton towels, a multi-meter, spare O-rings, self-adhesive Velcro and an Allen wrench set.

FLAT OR DOME LENS PORTS

One of the most important and often misunderstood features of an underwater camera housing is the lens port. Flat ports were all that were available for underwater photography from its beginning in 1893 until 1931, when hemispherical dome ports were first used to correct for the refractive properties of water. Flat and dome ports both have their place in underwater photography and it is important to know the theory and practice of each. For underwater photography with wide lenses, the dome port is the best choice, but if the shot starts or ends above water, or if you need to shoot a close-up with a long lens, the flat port should be used. Glass is the best material for underwater ports. Be careful of plastic ports. They scratch easily and will cause flares on the image.

Flat Port

The flat port is unable to correct for the distortion produced by the differences between the indexes of light refraction in air and water. Using a flat port introduces a number of aberrations when used underwater. They are:

Refraction: This is the bending of light waves as they pass through different mediums of optical density (the air inside the camera housing and the water outside the lens port). Light is refracted 25 percent, causing the lens to undergo the same magnification you would see through a facemask. The focal length of your lens also increases by approximately 25 percent.

Radial Distortion: Because flat ports do not distort light rays equally, they have a progressive radial distortion that becomes more obvious as wider lenses are used. The effect is a progressive blur, that increases with large apertures on wide lenses. Light rays passing through the center of the port are not affected because their direction of travel is at right angles to the water-air interface of the port.

Chromatic Aberration: White light, when refracted, is separated into the color spectrum. The component colors of white light do not travel at the same speed, and light rays passing from water to glass to air will be unequally bent. When light separates into its component colors, the different colors slightly overlap, causing a loss of sharpness and color saturation, which is more noticeable with wider lenses.

Dome Port

The dome port is a concentric lens that acts as an additional optical element to the camera lens. The dome port significantly reduces the problems of refraction, radial distortion and axial and chromatic aberrations when the curvature of the dome's inside radius center is placed as close as possible to the nodal point of the lens. When a dome port is used, all the rays of light pass through unrefracted, which allows the "in-air" lens to retain its angle of view. Optically a "virtual image" is created inches in front of the lens. To photograph a subject underwater with a dome port you must focus the lens on the "virtual image", not the subject itself. The dome port makes the footage marks on the lens totally inaccurate for underwater focus. Therefore lenses should be calibrated underwater. The dome port offers no special optics above water and functions as a clear window.

UNDERWATER LENS CALIBRATION

To guarantee a sharp image when using either the flat or dome ports, it is best to calibrate the lenses underwater by placing a focus chart in a swimming pool or tank. Even on location, the hotel pool will offer a lot more control than an ocean or lake. Set the camera housing on a tripod and hang a focus chart on a C-stand. If possible, calibrate your lenses at night or in an indoor pool or tank. Crosslight the focus chart with two 1200 watt HMI'S, 2' in front at a 45-degree angle to the chart. Starting at 2', tape measure the distance from the underwater housing's film plane to the focus chart. Eye focus the lens and mark the housing's white focus knob data ring with a pencil. Slide the camera back to continue the same process at 3', 4', 5', 6', 8', 10', 12', and 14'. This should be done for all lenses. Once a lens has been calibrated, you must establish reference marks between the lens and data ring so that you can accurately sync up for underwater focus when lenses are changed during the shoot. After marking the data rings underwater with pencil, go over the calibration marks with a fine point permanent marker on the surface.

Dome Port

To calibrate a lens with a dome port, use this basic formula to determine the starting point for underwater focus: Simply multiply the inside radius of the dome by four. That number will be the approximate distance in inches from the film plane that the lens should be set on as a starting point for underwater eye focus calibration. The most commonly used dome radius is 4". Multiply the 4" dome radius times 4. That gives you a measurement of 16" at which to set your lens in the housing to begin calibration for underwater photography. If a lens cannot focus close enough to take advantage of the dome port, use a plus diopter to shift the lens focus back. Ultimately, your lens should be able to focus down to at least 10" to be able to follow focus from 1' to underwater infinity. When using most anamorphic lenses with the dome port, you will have to add a +3 diopter to the lens to shift close focus back in order to focus on the aerial image.

Flat port

The refractive effect of the 25 percent magnification produces an apparent shift of the subject towards the camera, to ¾ its true distance. As a general rule, for flat port underwater photography, if you measured your camera to subject distance at 4', you would set your lens at ¾ the distance, or around 3'. For critical focus, especially on longer lenses and when shooting in low light, underwater eye focus calibration is recommended. Shooting through a window or port of a tank or pool is the same as using a flat port. If you do shoot through a tank window and want to minimize distortion, the camera lens axis must be kept at 90° to the window's surface. Camera moves will be limited to dollying and booming to keep the lens perpendicular to the window's surface. Panning and tilting should not be done unless a distortive effect is desired.

LENS SELECTION

Wider lenses are usually the choice in underwater photography because they eliminate much of the water column between the camera and subject to produce the clearest, sharpest image. This is especially important in low visibility situations. Longer lenses, which are being used more and more underwater, usually will not focus close enough to take advantage of the dome port's "virtual image" (you need to focus down to 12") and a diopter will have to be added to the lens to shift the focus back, or you can switch to a flat port and allow for the 25 percent magnification. Most Zeiss and Cooke lenses between 10mm and 35mm can close focus on the dome ports "virtual image" without using diopters. When using Panavision spherical lenses, the close focus series of lenses allow the use of the dome port without using diopters. The commonly used anamorphic lenses for dome port cinematography are the Panavision "C" Series 30mm, 35mm and 40mm focal lengths. Because these anamorphic lenses only close focus to approximately 30", you will have to use a +3 diopter to shift minimum focus back to 12" to 14" to focus on the "virtual image" created by the dome port. When using longer lenses for spherical or anamorphic close-ups with the flat port, I set the lens at minimum focus and move the camera back and forth on the subject or a slate to find critical focus instead of racking the focus knob.

FILTERS

Filtering for film underwater, as in above water applications, is used to lower light levels, correct color balance and improve image contrast. Aside from the standard 85 filter used to correct tungsten film for daylight exposure, the use of color correction filters can be a very subjective issue. Water's natural ability to remove reds, oranges and other warm colors can be overcome by using underwater color correction filters. These filters alter the spectrum of light reaching the camera to reproduce accurate skin tones and the true colors of the sea. Because all water is a continuous filter, the deeper you go beneath the surface the more colors are filtered out. Also, the distance between the camera and subject must be added to the depth of the water to determine the correct underwater filter distance. UR/PRO™ and Tiffen AQUACOLOR® filters both provide color correction for underwater filming, and both manufacturers offer detailed information on the use of their filters. Polarizing filters can improve contrast where backscatter from artificial light is a problem but sunlight illumination underwater is not sufficiently polarized and makes polarizing filters ineffective.

EXPOSURE METERS

Both incident and reflected light meters can be used for reading your exposure underwater. In ambient light situations, the reflected meter is usually used because it measures the light reflected from the subject through the water column.

The most commonly used underwater light meters are the Sekonic L-164 Marine Meter and the Ikelite digital exposure meter. The Sekonic L-164, designed in 1969 specifically for underwater photography, was discontinued in

1993 but then reintroduced in 1998 because of demand. It is self-contained, needs no special housing, and is pretty straightforward in operation. The Sekonic L-164 has a reflected 30-degree acceptance angle and gives very reliable underwater exposures. The Ikelite digital is also a self-contained underwater meter and can measure incident or reflected light. It has a 10-degree acceptance angle in the reflected light mode. Both the Sekonic L-164 and the Ikelite digital meters can be used above water or down to 200' underwater. There are also commercially available underwater cases for the Spectra IV, Minolta IV, Minolta 1° Spot and the Minolta Color Temperature.

UNDERWATER COMMUNICATIONS

Communication between the director/AD and cameraperson and crew is critical. We've certainly come a long way since the days of banging two pieces of pipe together, so depending on your budget and shot list, there are different degrees of technology available.

A simple but effective means of communications between the cameraperson and the above water director/AD is a one-way underwater P.A. speaker system. Used in conjunction with video assist from the underwater camera, cues for roll, cut and talent performance can be instigated by the director on the surface. The cameraperson can also answer questions via the video assist with hand signals or a slate presented to the camera lens or by nodding the underwater camera for "yes" or "no".

For more complex set-ups where the cinematographer and the director need to talk directly to each other, or when the director works underwater with the crew, two-way communication is very efficient. While wearing full-face masks equipped with wireless communication systems, the underwater cinematographer can converse with the director and also talk to the underwater and surface crews via underwater and above water speakers.

LIGHTING

Specifics on lighting underwater, as in above water, will vary from cinematographer to cinematographer, and the following information is merely a guide. Experimenting and developing your own technique should be your goal. Today's underwater cinematographer has a wide variety of HMI, incandescent, fluorescent and ultraviolet lights and accessories from which to choose. Underwater lights designed for motion picture work should have the ability to control the light output by means of diffusion glass, filters, scrims, snoots and barndoors. Always check the condition of lampheads, connectors, plugs and cables before use. Become familiar with the lamp's lighting system and be able to perform simple repairs and maintenance.

Unlike air, even in the best water, the clarity is significantly reduced in distances as little as 10' to 20'. Artificial lighting is often needed to adjust light levels for exposure and vision, as well as to modify the color balance and image contrast of the subject. By incorporating supplemental lighting, the light's water path, from lamp head to subject to camera, can be kept relatively short, and the selective color absorption properties of water will be much less apparent than if the light had to originate at the water's surface.

HMIs light has a higher color temperature, approximately 5600 K (longer light wavelengths), and thus penetrates further, providing more illumination over a wider area.

The reflection of artificial light off suspended particles in the water is known as "back scattering". The effect is much like driving your car with your headlights on in heavy fog or a snowstorm. In addition to back scattering there is also side scattering and in some instances even front scattering. Light scattering can be greatly reduced if you separate the light source from the camera and by using multiple moderately intense lamps rather than using a single high intensity lamp. It is advisable to keep the light at a 45-degree to 90-degree angle to the lens axis of the camera. Generating a sharp light beam to help control the light and further reduce backscatter is done with the aid of reflectors, barndoors or snoots.

In addition to the basic effect of light intensity reduction in water due to absorption, the matter is further complicated by the fact that absorption is a function of color. Red light is absorbed approximately five times faster than blue-green light in water. This is why long distance underwater photographs are simply a blue tint without much color.

Fill lighting underwater on a moving subject is best accomplished by having the lamp handheld by the underwater gaffer. With the lamp being handheld, the underwater gaffer can maintain a constant distance between the lamp and the moving subject, keeping the exposure ratio constant. In a more controlled situation where the subject is confined to an area of a set, light can be bounced off a white griffolyn stretched on a frame or through a silk on a frame.

BLUESCREEN AND GREENSCREEN

There are different schools of thought on which color screen is best to use but both bluescreen and greenscreen have been used successfully underwater for many years. Backlighting a bluescreen underwater has been done successfully, but when the screen material is exposed to chlorine, it sometimes picks up density and requires more and more light to maintain its exposure reading. Front lighting fabric screens underwater has been very successful, and depending on the size of the screen, the logistics of the location and the budget, there are a variety of underwater lights to choose from. Underwater lamps also can be augmented with above water lamps. It is best to mount the screen on a movable frame, so it can be pulled out of the water and hosed off after every day of shooting. Chlorine bleaches the screen quickly, and rotating the screen 180° every day helps minimizes the color difference. From the bottom to the top, the frame should tilt back approximately 10°. Extending the screen above the surface of the water, even if only a few inches is very important. By extending the screen above the water, it allows the under surface of the water to act as a mirror and reflect the screens color on the surface. This extends the screens coverage and allows the cameraperson to tilt up to follow the shot while using the waters surface as an extension of the screen. It is also important to stop or at least reduce the agitation of the water to prevent a visible ripple effect on the screen.

LIGHTING SAFETY

From a safety standpoint, when using AC power in or near water or other potentially wet locations, it is essential (and in most cases, mandatory) to use a Class "A" UL approved GFCI (Ground Fault Circuit Interrupter) for actor and film crew protection.

The purpose of a GFCI is to interrupt current flow to a circuit or load when excessive fault current (or shock current) flows to ground or along any other unintentional current return path. The standard level of current needed to trip a "people" protection Class "A" GFCI is 5mA.

Class "A" GFCIs are designed for "people" protection. Other GFCIs are designed for various levels of "equipment" and "distribution" protection. In general, if you can't readily see the Class "A" marking on a GFCI, the device is probably not designed for "people" protection. To make sure that the GFCI being used is a Class "A" device, Section 38 of UL 943 (the standard for GFCIs) requires that the "Class" of the GFCI is clearly marked on the device in letters that are clearly visible to the user.

Today, Class "A" GFCIs are readily available for loads up to 100 Amps, single- and three-phase, for both 120v and 208/240v fixed voltage applications.

Certain special GFCIs can also operate on variable voltage power supplies (behind dimmers). If the device's label does not clearly state the working voltage range of the unit, check with the device's manufacturer before using the unit on dimmers (or other variable voltage applications), since conventional GFCIs may not operate correctly below their rated voltage.

Specialty GFCI manufacturers produce advanced GFCI devices that offer other important safety features, such as monitoring predictive maintenance, power supply phase and ground correctness.

Choose your GFCIs carefully, because if misapplied, these important safety devices may unknowingly fail to function and render your installation with a false sense of security.

Arctic and Tropical Cinematography

Most of the difficulties encountered when using motion picture equipment in the Arctic are caused by extreme cold and very low relative humidity. Average temperatures may vary from 45°F (7°C) to -45°F (-43°C), and temperatures as low as -80°F (-62°C) have been recorded. (Such low temperatures may also be encountered at very high altitudes.)

The lubricating oils usually used in photographic equipment in more temperate climates will congeal in an arctic environment so that moving parts of cameras or other equipment will not operate. Leather and rubber also become brittle at these temperatures. With motion picture films, loss of moisture from the film emulsion when the original packing material is opened may result in film emulsion shrinkage and brittleness, and subsequent film curl in the camera gate. Such difficulties are not minimized by using films with a polyester base unless these films (or those with a triacetate base) have a gelatin coating on the support to compensate for emulsion shrinkage. It is the effect of the very low relative humidity (less than 5%) and its emulsion-drying characteristics that produces film curl. (Small heaters are sometimes used in cameras to prevent film brittleness when working under conditions of extreme cold, but under certain conditions this practice could actually increase the chance of emulsion shrinkage by further reducing the relative humidity in the film chamber.)

The film speed is also lowered by extreme cold and may be about one lens opening slower at -50°F (-46°C) to -70°F (-57°C) than at 60°F (16°C). Film becomes progressively more brittle as the temperature drops below 0°F (-18°C), but there is no marked change at any one temperature. Even at subzero temperatures, film emulsion that retains its proper moisture content in the original package (equivalent to equilibrium at 40 to 60% relative humidity) is more flexible than film that has been allowed to become too dry. Film can also be bent with the emulsion side in with less chance of breaking than if bent with the emulsion side out. Whether the film emulsion cracks or the film support breaks at very low temperatures depends on 1) how soon the film is exposed after removal from the original package; 2) the care taken in handling the film; and, 3) on the type and condition of the camera in which it is used.

Temperatures generally encountered in the arctic will not cause polyester-base films to break.

PREPARATION OF EQUIPMENT

While the difficulties of photography under arctic conditions can be severe, they are by no means insurmountable. Careful advance preparation will pay rich dividends in the form of easier and more reliable equipment operation and better pictorial results. The first step in preparing for filming in the arctic, high mountain regions, or in unheated aircraft at high altitudes is to select the most suitable equipment with due regard for the work to be done and the results desired.

Each kind of camera has its adherents, and no one type seems to be outstandingly superior to the others. However, considering the working conditions, good judgment dictates that the camera or cameras selected should be compact, lightweight, easy to use, dependable, adaptable, and portable. In choosing a 16mm motion picture camera, many arctic explorers prefer the ease and convenience of magazine loading, threading roll film can be very difficult under conditions of extreme cold. Certain camera models are advantageous for low-temperature use because large-radius bends in the film path and low film accelerations help prevent broken film. For best protection of the film emulsion at extremely low temperatures, film-travel rollers should have a diameter no smaller than ½". (13mm). Electric power, if available from a reliable source such as a generator or vehicular power system, is more dependable than spring-driven or battery power. However, under field conditions, a spring-driven motor may prove more reliable than an electric motor drive that depends on portable or storage batteries, which can fail when subjected to extremely low temperatures.

Cameras should be winterized for satisfactory service under frigid conditions. Some camera manufacturers provide a winterizing service for cameras that are to be used at low temperatures over a long period of time. Winterizing is a highly specialized operation, best entrusted to the manufacturer or a competent independent camera service representative. Essentially, the procedure calls for dismantling the camera and removing the original lubricants. The shutter, lens diaphragm, film transport mechanism, and other moving parts are then relubricated with materials that will not thicken when the camera is exposed to extreme cold. In some cases, powdered graphite is still used for this purpose. However, so-called "broad-range" lubricants (such as Teflon and silicone) are becoming increasingly popular, not only because of their effectiveness at low temperatures, but also because they can be left in the camera permanently. In fact, such lubricants are being used in manufacture. Hence, a camera that has been lubricated with a broad-range lubricant, either in manufacture or as part of a winterizing operation, need not be dewinterized and relubricated when it is returned to use under normal conditions. When cameras are stripped down for winterizing, weakened or damaged parts may be discovered and should be replaced to avoid possible failure under the extra stress of severe arctic temperatures.

It is also sometimes necessary to machine parts to allow greater clearance between components. This is because aluminum and certain alloys have greater coefficients of thermal contraction and expansion than steel. Since small levers and knobs on cameras are difficult to operate when the photographer is wearing thick gloves, extensions can sometimes be added to levers, and small knobs can be replaced with larger ones.

It may be helpful to run even recently winterized motion picture cameras for a period of three or four hours to break them in thoroughly. A piece of film three or four feet long can be spliced end to end (to form a continuous loop), threaded into the camera, and allowed to run during the breaking-in. In cameras intended for use with film magazines, the loop should be formed in a dummy magazine. After the breaking-in period, the camera should be checked for speed and general behavior. It should be noted that, although magazine-type motion picture cameras can be winterized, the magazines themselves are not winterized and may jam under conditions of extreme cold. If film magazines are used, each day's working reserve carried into the field should be kept as warm as possible under the cinematographer's parka. Another possibility is to carry the film supply in an insulated thermal bag, along with one or two small hand warmers.

Before your location shoot, a test run should be made in a refrigerator or freezer capable of reaching temperatures as low as -30°F (-34°C) or -40°F (-40°C). Even "winterized" cameras can fail in use because some detail was overlooked in preparation, so this final test run is quite important. The film and camera should be cooled for at least 24 hours prior to the test. This long period of precooling is often overlooked, and the test becomes invalid.

Motion picture cameras should be given as much protection from icy winds as possible during use. When battery-driven motors are used on cameras, the motors and batteries should be kept as warm as possible. A flat black finish on the cameras has some advantage in the arctic because it absorbs heat when the sun is shining. Covers made from black felt material or fur and fitted with eyelets or other suitable fasteners protect the camera from frigid winds and help to retain its initial warmth for a time. Snaps and slide fasteners are not recommended for use in subzero temperatures. Small magazine-type motion picture cameras can be hung inside the coat to obtain some warmth from the body; you may even need to wrap a chemical heating pad around the camera. Inspect the camera's lens each time it is removed from the clothing to take a picture. The amount of "body static" generated under cold, dry conditions can cause the lens to attract lint from the clothing.

Tripods should also be conditioned properly for use in the arctic. When lubrication is required, there are oils available for use at temperatures down to -70°F. Tripod heads for motion picture equipment should be winterized if they include gyros, motors, or other revolving parts. As noted previously, extreme cold causes leather and rubber to become brittle. A wax leather dressing of good quality should be rubbed into leather carrying cases and leather-covered cameras to prevent the absorption of moisture. Rubber should be eliminated wherever possible.

Silk or lightweight cotton gloves under heavy woolen mittens are recommended. Gloves or mittens made from unborn lambskin are excellent for arctic weather. Silk gloves will keep the hands warmer and will afford considerable protection when the outside mittens are removed for loading the camera, adjusting the lens, etc.

EQUIPMENT AND FILMING TECHNIQUE

In the arctic or on mountain-climbing expeditions, as the altitude and the subsequent cold increase, breathing becomes difficult, and working normally involves a great effort. Reactions are slow. Therefore, everything pertaining to the use of the camera should be made as simple as possible. Exposure estimates may be poor when the faculties are dulled, so exposure and other data should be printed on a card and fastened to the camera or its cover in plain view.

Certain general cold-weather recommendations are in order for any camera, still or motion picture. Breathing on a lens or any other part of the camera to remove snow or other material will cause condensation that freezes instantly and is very difficult to remove.

An important factor to keep in mind is the ever-present danger of frostbite, a particular threat when hands or face come in direct contact with the metal of the camera body. Cameras that are used at eye level and must be brought close to the face for proper viewing and focusing should have their exposed metal areas covered with heavy electrical tape, plastic foam, or some other insulating material. Under no circumstances should the photographer touch the camera or other metal equipment with ungloved hands, because the skin will freeze to the cold metal almost instantly. A painful loss of skin almost always results.

A thoroughly chilled camera cannot be used in a warm room until its temperature equals the surrounding warmer temperature. Conversely, a warm camera cannot be taken out into a blizzard because the blowing and drifting snow will melt upon striking the warm camera, and soon the instrument will be covered with ice. Loading film, even during a driving snowstorm, can be accomplished with the use of a large, dark plastic bag, big enough to fit over the head and shoulders.

A deep lens hood is very desirable for filming in the snow. It will help keep the lens dry even during a fairly severe storm.

FILM

Great care must be used in handling film in subzero weather. The edges of cold, brittle film are extremely sharp, and unless caution is exercised, they can cut the fingers severely.

It is important that film be loaded and exposed promptly after removal from the original packing, not left in the camera for long periods of time. If motion picture film is allowed to stand in the camera for a day or so, the film may dry out and break where the loop was formed when the camera is again started. The film is adequately protected against moisture loss as long as the original packaging is intact. When loading the camera, make sure the film and the camera are at the same temperature—if possible, load the camera indoors.

Static markings are caused by an electrostatic discharge, and they appear on the developed film emulsion as marks resembling lightning, tree branches, or fuzzy spots. When static difficulties occur they can usually be traced to the use of film that has a very low moisture content.

Static markings are not likely to occur if the film is loaded and exposed within a short time after the original package is opened. In general, field photography under arctic conditions involves subjects of extremely low brightness scale and very high levels of illumination. Exposures should be held to a minimum and overexposure should be avoided.

STORAGE

If a cold camera is taken indoors where it is warm and humid, condensation may form on the lens, film, and camera parts. If the camera is then taken back outdoors before the condensed moisture evaporates, it will freeze and interfere with operation; the condensate can also cause metal parts to rust. One way to solve this problem is to leave the camera, when not in use, in a room at about 32°F (0°C).

If a camera is left in its case outdoors, the case should be made reasonably airtight. In the arctic, blown snow becomes as fine as dust or silt and can enter the smallest slit or crevice. If allowed to enter the camera around the shutter or other moving parts, the snow will affect the operation of the equipment. The speed and timing of motors should be checked frequently. Batteries should be checked every day and recharged at a base every night, if possible.

T. R. Stobart, who filmed the first conquest of Mt. Everest, preferred to seal the camera in an airtight polyethylene or rubber bag and then take the camera into the warmth of indoors. Any condensation takes place outside the bag, not inside, and the camera remains both dry and warm. This method has the advantage of keeping the camera from becoming "saturated in cold" for long periods of time. There is no problem in taking warm equipment back out into the cold, provided the snow isn't blowing.

TROPICAL CINEMATOGRAPHY

Heat and humidity are two basic sources of potential difficulty when using or storing photographic goods in tropical climates. Heat alone is not the worst factor, though it may necessitate special equipment care and processing techniques and may shorten the life of incorrectly stored light-sensitive materials. High humidity is by far the greater problem because it can cause serious trouble at temperatures only slightly above normal, and these troubles are greatly increased by high temperatures.

Associated with these conditions are several biological factors—the warmth and dampness levels encountered in the tropics are conducive to the profuse growth of fungus and bacteria and encourage the activities of insects. Many photographic and other related products are "food" for these organisms—gelatin in films, filters, leather, adhesives and so on. Even if fungus, bacteria or insects cannot attack materials directly, they can develop an environment that can. Fungus can also either directly or indirectly induce corrosion in metals, attack textiles and leather, change the color of dyes, attack glass, and cause a great variety of other forms of deterioration. The probability of damage is greater with frequent handling and transportation, especially under the difficulties met in hunting and scientific expeditions and in military operations. Exposure to harm is greater when equipment is used out of doors, on the ground or in makeshift facilities.

Atmospheric condition, with respect to moisture content, is usually described in terms of "relative humidity." This is the ratio, expressed as a percentage, between the quantity of water vapor actually present in the air and the maximum quantity that the air could hold at that temperature. Thus, if a given sample of air contains only half as much water as it would at saturation, its relative humidity is 50%.

When the temperature rises, a given space can accommodate more water vapor, and hence the relative humidity decreases, and vice versa. When air (or an object) is cooled sufficiently, a saturation point (100% relative humidity) is reached, and below this temperature drops of water or "dew" are deposited. In any locality, the temperature is much lower at high altitudes, so that dew is likely to form on objects following their arrival by air transport, especially when high relative humidity is present at ground level. In tropical climates, this "dew point" is often only a few degrees below the actual temperature during the day and is reached when the temperature drops at night.

The amount of moisture absorbed by films and by nonmetallic parts of equipment is determined by the relative humidity of the atmosphere. Therefore, the moisture absorption of photographic or other equipment can be reduced by lowering the relative humidity, either by removing some of the moisture with a desiccating agent or by raising the temperature of the atmosphere where the equipment is stored.

Extremes of relative humidity are a serious threat to all photographic materials, even at moderate temperatures. At high temperatures, the effects of high humidity are greatly accelerated, particularly if the relative humidity remains above 60%. Extremely low relative humidity, on the other hand, is not quite so serious, but if it falls below 15% for a considerable time, as is common in desert regions, an electric humidifier should be installed and set to maintain a relative humidity of 40% to 50% in the storage area.

Storage of Photographic Materials

Sensitized photographic materials are perishable products when stored under extreme conditions of high temperatures and high relative humidity. Proper storage is therefore important at all times. Fortunately, adequate protection of sensitized materials can be accomplished at relatively low cost and without extreme methods. Lightweight portable refrigerators or other cooling units are available from expedition outfitters and other similar equipment suppliers. Desiccants are available in bulk or kit form for reducing the moisture content of the atmosphere where film is to be stored. Further, portable electric dehumidifiers are also available to reduce the relative humidity in larger quarters, such as work rooms, to aid in the comfort of the occupants. And finally, the film packaging reduces the possibility of damage when the material is stored under recommended conditions. Usually, there will be little or no adverse effect to the film if it is stored and handled as described below.

Black-and-white films can be stored at normal room temperatures in an air-conditioned room. Color films should always be stored in a refrigerator at 55°F (13°C) or lower. To avoid moisture condensation on the chilled surfaces of the material, take film cans out of the cartons and allow 35mm rolls to warm up for three hours for a 20°F to five hours for a 75°F temperature rise above storage temperature. 16mm rolls take about one-third less time.

When the original packaging seal has been broken, films should be exposed and processed as soon as possible. Since the air in a refrigerator is moist, partially used packages should be returned to the refrigerator in a sealed container containing a desiccant to absorb the moisture within the container.

In general, do not keep more film than necessary in stock, particularly when good storage conditions are not available. Photographic materials can also be affected by the chemical activity of fumes and gases. Consequently, do not store films in newly painted rooms or cabinets. All films should be processed as soon as possible after exposure. If you are unable to do this for some reason, enclose the films in an airtight jar or can together with a desiccant and place them in a refrigerator. Exposed films can be kept for several days in this way.

Preparation and Protection of Equipment

To save time and avoid damage, cameras and other equipment should be readied well in advance of departure. It is well worthwhile to have the equipment thoroughly overhauled and cleaned, preferably by the original manufacturer, who should be advised as to the type of climate in which it will be used. Cases, packing material, and moisture-absorbing material (desiccant) should be obtained for the equipment and supplies. Protection during transportation and storage is readily obtained by the use of hermetically sealed cans or metal-foil bags or other water/vapor-proof containers and a suitable desiccating agent. If the containers have been properly sealed and contain an adequate quantity of desiccant, they will protect the contents practically indefinitely. There is, however, one reservation and caution: if precision instruments that require lubrication with certain types of light oils are subjected to high temperatures while in such packing, the oils may evaporate, leaving a gummy residue on the instrument bearings. This situation may prevent proper equipment functioning until the equipment can be cleaned and relubricated properly.

The protection of equipment that is in active use requires a somewhat different approach. The relative humidity can be lowered in an equipment-storage cabinet that is not used for film storage by burning electric light bulbs or operating an electric resistance heating unit continuously in the lower part of the cabinet. The number of lamps should be adjusted to keep the temperature about 10 degrees above the average prevailing temperature. Air spaces and small holes should be provided at the top and bottom of the cabinet and through the shelves to allow a slow change of air to carry off moisture introduced by the cameras and equipment. The positions of the holes should be staggered on the different shelves in order to produce a more thorough change of air. Since high relative humidity favors the growth of fungus on lenses, filters and other surfaces, storage in such a cabinet will help reduce fungus growth and may prevent it entirely.

Electric dehumidifiers are now appearing in stores in many of the larger cities in tropical regions. With these units, whole rooms and their contents can be dehumidified, provided they can be closed to outside air penetration. In dehumidified rooms, the humidity will not increase rapidly during short power failures, as it would in heated closets or cabinets. In a small, tightly sealed room, an average unit in operation for 12 hours out of 24 can keep the relative humidity below 60%. This should be checked about once a month with a relative humidity meter or sling psychrometer. When it is not practical to use a hot cabinet or electric dehumidifier, equipment should be stored in an airtight case containing plenty of desiccant. Two cans of silica gel the size of shoe-polish cans will do a very good job of drying equipment in a sealed 10-gallon paint can (one with a gasket and a "pound shut" lid).

A half-pound bag of silica gel works well in a gasketed 55-gallon "open top" drum that can be sealed with a cover. However, where shipment and handling are involved, or where the containers are to be opened briefly a few times, double or even triple the quantity of gel will provide a reserve of protection. Properly dehydrated containers will momentarily feel cool to an inserted hand due to rapid evaporation of the normal skin moisture. The sensation is brief but can be easily detected if one is looking for it. Its absence means the silica gel needs replacement or regeneration.

If none of these methods is practical, and the equipment must be left in an atmosphere of high relative humidity, the equipment should be opened and exposed to the sun at frequent intervals in order to drive out moisture. The exposures, however, should be kept short in order to avoid overheating. Cameras loaded with film should not be exposed to the sun any more than necessary.

Cameras should always be protected from excessive heat because many of the lenses used on cameras are composed of several elements of glass cemented together. Because some cements melt at 140°F (60°C) and begin to soften at 120°F (49°C), it is obvious that the lens elements might become separated or air bubbles might form if the lens were heated to such temperatures. Cameras should not be handled roughly or subjected to sudden jarring when used at high temperatures, because any slight shock might change the position of the lens components.

MAINTENANCE OF EQUIPMENT

One of the best protective measures that can be supplied in the tropics is to thoroughly clean every piece of photographic equipment at frequent intervals and expose it to air and sun whenever practical. This is particularly important for retarding the corrosion of metal surfaces and the growth of fungus or mold on lens surfaces and on leather coverings. Lens-cleaning fluids and papers now on the market are recommended for cleaning lenses. During the tropical dry season, or in any desert areas, dust should be removed from the lens surfaces with a sable or camel-hair brush before the lens tissue is used, to avoid scratches. Lens cleaning tissues containing silicones should not be used for coated lenses. They leave an oily film that changes the color characteristics of the coating and reduces its antireflection properties. This film is almost impossible to remove. Leather coverings and cases can best be kept clean by wiping them often and thoroughly with a clean, dry cloth. Frequent cleaning and polishing will minimize corrosion on exposed metal parts.

BLACK-AND-WHITE FILM

The exposure of black-and-white film in tropical areas is strongly influenced by the illumination in the subject shadow areas. The moisture and dust content of the atmosphere are important because shadows are illuminated only by light scattered by particles suspended in the air, except where supplementary lighting or reflectors are used. Thus where the atmosphere is very dry and clear, objects that do not receive the direct light of the sun appear, both to the eye and to the camera lens, to be in deeper than normal shadow. In regions like the southwestern United States or central Mexico, for example, the brightness range of average outdoor subjects is much greater than it is in less clear climates. In photographing people, this effect and the high position of the sun combine to put the eyes in deep shadow and even sometimes give the effect of backlighting. Therefore, it is best to avoid taking pictures, particularly close-ups of people, when the sun is overhead; if you must take close-ups of people, use reflectors or booster lights to soften the shadows.

Exposure meters should always be used with a reasonable amount of judgment and experience, and this is especially true in locations with such unusual atmospheric and lighting conditions. In the jungle areas of South and Central America, the local farmers often clear and burn large quantities of trees and brush during the dry season. The smoke, composed of solid particles, hangs in the lower atmosphere and is not easily penetrated even with filters. Also, at the height of the wet season in many localities, the water haze becomes almost as impenetrable as a heavy cloud. Distance photography is best done a few weeks after the close of the wet season and before burning begins, or a few weeks after the first rains of the wet season have settled the smoke particles and before the onset of the wet-season haze.

If extensive photographic work in the tropics is planned, the development of a few test exposures may prevent major failures. It is usually sufficient to determine a basic exposure that can then be modified to suit other films or conditions. Allowance should also be made for different types of subjects. Beach scenes, for example, generally require about one stop less exposure than an average subject.

COLOR FILM

In general, the exposure of color films should follow the same basic recommendations given for temperate zone exposure, with due regard to lighting and scene classification. There are, however, some differences in the lighting conditions and scene characteristics in the tropics that justify special considerations.

1. During the rainy season, a light haze is generally present in the atmosphere. When this haze is present, the disk of the sun is clearly discernible and fairly distinct shadows are cast. Under these conditions, the exposure should be increased by about one-half stop over that required for bright sunlight.
2. Frequently the brightness of beach and marine scenes is appreciably great-

er than encountered in temperate zones. With such scenes the camera exposure should be decreased one full stop from that required for average subjects. It should be remembered that the term "average subject" as used in exposure tables applies to a subject or scene in which light, medium and dark areas are roughly equal in proportion. It should not be taken to mean "usual" for a particular location or area. For instance, the usual desert scene is a "light subject" rather than "average subject," and should be exposed as such.

3. When the sun is high overhead, heavy shadows are cast across vertical surfaces, very much like those occurring in side-lighted subjects. Therefore, the exposure should be increased one-half stop more than normal, just as is recommended for side-lighted scenes. For close-ups having important shadow areas, a full stop increase in exposure is needed.

4. Many objects in the tropics, not only painted buildings and light-colored fabrics, but even the leaves of many plants and trees, have a high reflectance for direct lighting. Consequently, with front top- or backlighting they should be considered average subjects.

5. Very often the colors of nearby objects will be affected by the green light reflected from nearby bright green foliage. Similarly, in courtyards or narrow streets, the side that is in the shade gets much of its illumination from the opposite sunlit wall, which may be strongly colored. There is little that can be done to correct for this situation, but it should be recognized as a possible cause of poor results in color pictures.

Filming Television and Computer Displays

by Bill Hogan, Sprocket Digital and
Steve Irwin, Playback Technologies, Inc.

When filming television screens, video monitors or computer displays, there are two principal obstacles to achieving consistent and clear images on film. The two problems are the difference in frame rates between the film camera and the TV/computer display, and the color temperature difference between the film stock and the display technology.

Solutions for successfully photographing various display technologies, including televisions, computer monitors, LCD monitors, plasma screens and DLP projectors, vary depending on many factors. Are you shooting a feature film or episodic project where you must protect and deliver a 24-frame negative finish? Or are you shooting a commercial or documentary where you can run the film camera at nonstandard sync-sound speeds to match the refresh rate of the display?

We will first consider photographing display technologies based on standard CRT (cathode ray tube) displays, or more simply, glass picture tubes. This includes nearly all consumer televisions, broadcast and industrial video monitors and a majority of computer displays and consumer projection televisions. Flat-panel displays and projection technologies such as LCD, plasma, and DLP will be discussed later, along with color temperature.

FRAME RATES AND EXPOSURE TIME

North America and many other countries of the world have a television standard that displays 30 frames per second. Computer monitors can have refresh rates ranging from 50 to over 100 frames per second. The difference in frame rates is the predominant difficulty in photographing televisions and computers as part of a scene.

The basic concept to keep in mind is that of film camera exposure time based on the combined elements of film camera speed and shutter angle. To photograph clean, artifact-free images, the exposure time must be equal to or related by an even sub-multiple of the refresh rate of the display you are shooting. For example, standard 30 frame NTSC video (the actual frame rate is 29.97, but we will round off for ease of explanation) is composed of two separate images called fields. Each field is displayed by the video monitor every ¹⁄₆₀ of a second. With the film camera running at 30 frames per second with a 180-degree shutter, the exposure time is ¹⁄₆₀ of a second. This is exactly the right relationship we are looking for. Even though we have now matched the film camera's exposure time to our monitor, this still requires what is generically referred to as a "sync box." We must align the pulldown or shutter closed timing of the film camera to occur exactly during video's equivalent of pulldown, known as vertical blanking. This is the time interval, in video, which allows the scanning beam to jump up from the bottom of the screen to the top and start painting or scanning the next field. The sync box is fed a reference signal that is in exact speed and time as the video we are photographing. A phase control on the sync box allows us to adjust the shutter bar out of the image and precisely match the film camera's pulldown to the video's vertical blanking.

This basic example and explanation holds true whether you are shooting 30-, 25- or 24-frame video. Before we review some newer display technologies, let's discuss a few more ground rules for shooting "picture tube" type displays or projection systems.

OVER- AND UNDERCRANKING

Because it takes an interlaced video signal a full field to display a complete image on the monitor, it is not possible to photograph the monitor at any faster frame rates. Remember the concept of exposure time. For example, if we are running the film camera at 60-frames per second with a 180-degree shutter while photographing 30-frame video, our exposure time is only ¹⁄₁₂₀ of a second. The video monitor will only display of its image during this time. The film camera will only "see" of the image on one frame of film and the other half of the image on the next frame of film, creating a very drastic strobe effect. Undercranking on a monitor is possible by keeping one simple rule in mind. Shoot at even submultiples of the monitor's frame rate. For example, if shooting 24-frame video, you can shoot at 12, 6, or 3 frames a second and have a perfect image on the monitor. If shooting at 30 frames per second, you can shoot at 15 or 7.5 fps.

COMPUTER MONITORS

The same rules just discussed apply to standard computer monitors based on glass picture tubes. The images are still scanned top to bottom, and the frame rates must still be matched between the display and film camera.

When photographing a single computer monitor "insert style," and where you can shoot at nonstandard frame rates, a manual speed control and some way to measure the computer monitor's refresh rate are required. There are two well-known film industry optical frequency meters that allow you to measure a monitor's exact frame rate and then set that rate into the speed control.

Computer monitors are generally noninterlaced, but this has little impact on shooting them. Since some computer monitors can display very high refresh rates, it is possible to photograph them at high speeds. For example, a computer monitor with a 96 Hz refresh rate can be photographed at 48 frames a second. The exposure time of $\frac{1}{96}$ of a second matches the amount of time it takes the monitor to display one complete image.

Flat-panel displays

With display technology constantly evolving, there is now and will continue to be a large variety of new and constantly changing image display devices. Each one poses unique and technically challenging problems for successful photography.

LCD monitors and projectors

This is often referred to as the "easy one." A majority of LCD computer monitors and projectors can be photographed without regard to matching frame rates. The light sources and image forming technology known as "active matrix" creates a picture that is continuous and always on, as far as the film camera is concerned. Laptop computers fall into this category as well. There are some low-end LCD technologies, still in use today, known as "passive" or "dual scan." These are not part of the "active matrix" type and may photograph with some breathing or flicker in the image. While viewing angles are getting very good in high-end LCDs, you must be thoughtful of the viewing angles of any LCD laptops or monitors you are shooting. Being only 10 or 15 degrees off the monitor's sweet spot can cause the image to wash-out, darken, or shift colors. It is possible to over or undercrank to some degree on most LCD display technologies. Unfortunately, the only way to find the limits are to run a battery of tests on the exact model you are going to use.

Plasma displays

Often misunderstood, this display technology is a unique mix of both CRT and LCD science. The images are created by ionizing a gas which strikes a phosphor. The images are not always scanned like a traditional CRT display, but addressed pixel by pixel or row by row without regard for the input signal's refresh rate. This can create very annoying and different-looking artifacts from those seen when shooting standard monitors. Some manufacturers and other companies have taken steps to modify plasma panels that allow them to be used in film productions and photographed at 30, 25 and 24 frames per second. When presented with the task of shooting plasma screens, try to include them in a test day to work out syncing, exposure and color-temperature issues.

DLP DISPLAYS AND PROJECTORS

This fairly recent technology used in a wide variety of video and data projectors employs Digital Micromirror Devices (DMDs) as the fundamental image-creating component. Thousands of tiny mirrors acting as individual pixel or light-switching devices are fabricated using familiar semiconductor technology. DLP projectors are capable of extremely high lumen outputs and can deal with very high-resolution video and computer signals. Again, as in plasma displays, the way individual pixels are addressed and the rate at which they are turned on and off does not always relate exactly to the input signal's frame rate. Often, video and computer inputs are formatted or scan-converted onto part or all of the micro mirrors, depending on the input signal's resolution. When these displays are photographed, various artifacts such as image flicker and density breathing can occur. It is usually best to match frame rates between the DLP projector's input signal and your desired film camera speed. It is strongly recommended to also shoot your own tests when dealing with new or different projectors.

VIDEO WALLS AND LED DISPLAYS

Traditional video walls are based on either CRT monitors or CRT/LCD projection engines. These monitors or "projection cubes" are stacked into the desired size and shape and fed from a controller or processor that splits up the input signals across the individual monitors. When faced with a video wall, find out the underlying display technology and use the guidelines discussed earlier for them. Recently introduced as a large venue display technology is the LED video screen/wall. High brightness light-emitting diodes are used to create individual pixels. These displays are made to be viewed at long distances and are bright enough to be used outdoors in full sunlight. LED displays are now being used in sports arenas, at rock concerts, and at other special event venues, and can pose very unique problems to filming. With several manufacturers in the marketplace all designing their own control electronics, special research and film tests will be required to determine if they can be used practically.

COLOR TEMPERATURE

Once the frame rate and syncing issues have been worked out, the final important aspect to be dealt with is color temperature.

Regardless of the display technology you are photographing, most CRT, LCD, plasma and DLP devices are intrinsically daylight or near-daylight in color temperature. Most consumer televisions will be at or near 6000-8000°Kelvin. Broadcast and industrial video monitors should be close to 6500°K. Computer CRT and LCD monitors vary greatly between 5000°K to 9000°K; some are even as high as 12,000°K.

Since a majority of these devices will be photographed under tungsten lighting, some method of color correction/compensation will be required for proper grayscale reproduction. If an uncorrected display is photographed under tungsten lighting, the image will take on a very strong blue tone. You can use standard color temperature meters to determine the display's normal color temperature by measuring a known white area. This measurement can be used as a starting point to help in adjusting the display's internal color balance controls. A majority of computer monitors and projectors are now equipped with menu functions and presets to change the color temperature of the image. However, these internal controls will not always allow the display to reach 3200°K. A possible alternate solution is to gel the monitor or filter the projector, but these methods are not always practical.

CONCLUSION

A majority of productions will hire a specialist to be responsible for playback and/or projection. They will usually precorrect the playback material or display device to correct for tungsten photography. The playback specialist will also assist you in setting exposure and work with the 1st AC concerning film camera sync equipment setup and operation.

There is a large amount of misinformation circulating in the industry, and it is very difficult to keep up on all the display technologies as they evolve. Often, manufacturers will update or introduce new products several times a year, and what worked for you six months ago may not work the same way now. It cannot be emphasized enough to test any new or different display device when considering its use in your production.

Editor's note: For photography requiring synchronous sound recording that includes a TV screen, video monitor or certain computer displays, 24-frame playback is necessary. Refer to the American Cinematographer Video Manual *for further information.*

Digital Postproduction for Feature Films

by Glenn Kennel and Sarah Priestnall

Digital technology is used throughout the filmmaking process, from previsualization through origination, dailies, editing, conforming, color grading, to the generation of film, digital cinema and home video masters for distribution. The finishing processes of conforming, color grading and generating the various distribution masters are often grouped under the term "Digital Intermediate", which is illustrated in Figure 1.

In postproduction, the Digital Intermediate process offers expanded creative freedom and faster turnaround. Digital conforming allows the movie to be quickly assembled for market previews, and quickly recut to improve the audience response. Digital color grading is much more sophisticated than the traditional color timing tools of the film laboratory, offering localized control of color, contrast and detail through multiple windows and layers that effectively allow the cinematographer to "dodge and burn" the pictures. The color grading tools that have been available for finishing TV programs and commercials for many years are now available for finishing feature films.

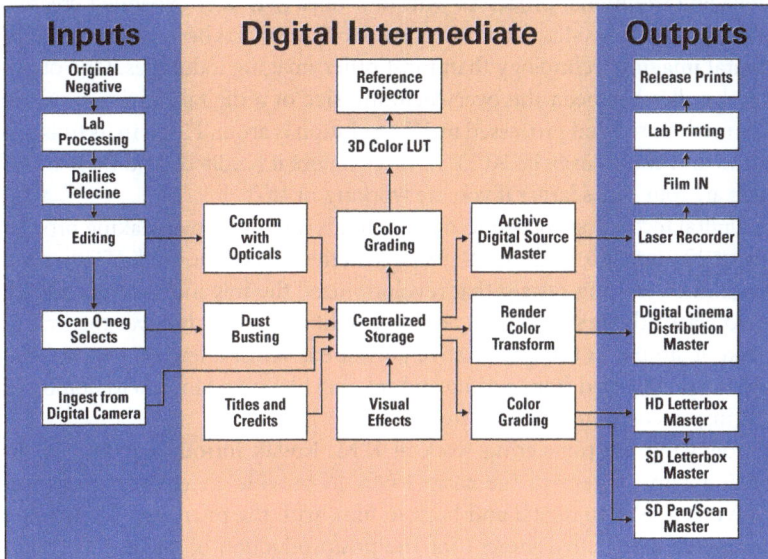

Figure 1. Digital Intermediate Process.

It is important to note here that digital technology is not a panacea and is not a substitute for good lighting and skilled cinematography. Although substantial creative control is provided by the selective and localized tools in today's color correctors, you have to start with a sharp and well-exposed image or the final results will be compromised.

Digital Intermediate also supports better picture quality. Digitally graded pictures can be more precisely tuned and more consistent than traditional film prints. Blowups from Super-35 to 2.39 anamorphic format, or from Super-16 to 1.85 format, are much cleaner and sharper than optical blowups. And, increasingly, multiple printing negatives are being created so that every print can be a first generation "show" print, eliminating the degradation of the traditional IP/IN analog duplication process.

In addition to making the film printing negative for traditional cinema distribution, the Digital Intermediate process produces a digital cinema distribution master, and the various home video masters. This consolidates the creatively supervised color correction steps, saving time and money. Digital Intermediate also enables the use of lower cost 3-perf 35mm and Super-16 film formats, as well as the mixing and matching various film and digital origination formats. All of which can represent substantial production cost savings over traditional 35mm film.

BRIEF DIGITAL HISTORY

Digital technology has changed the way that feature films are made, replacing traditional processes with new ones that offer expanded creative freedom, faster results, and lower costs. Hollywood has been slower to adopt digital imaging technology than most other imaging industries. One of the key hurdles has been the overwhelming size of a digital movie—a movie scanned, stored and processed in 2K resolution is around 2 TB in its finished form, and could easily be 50 TB or more before it is edited. And these numbers are four times larger if you are working in 4K.

Digital technology began to make inroads into the moviemaking process about 20 years ago. In the mid-1980s, Avid introduced the Media Composer, a nonlinear editing system that revolutionized the way movies were edited. Avid wasn't the first to offer a nonlinear editing system, but was the first to make it simple to use and relatively inexpensive. In a few short years, the industry converted from cutting and splicing film on a Moviola to nonlinear editing on computer-based systems.

Following the pioneering work at ILM, Kodak introduced the Cineon Digital Film System in the early 1990s to provide an efficient means of converting film to digital and back to film, with the intention of offering a computer-based environment for the postproduction of visual effects and for digital restoration. Kodak established Cinesite, a service bureau that offered film scanning and film recording services to enable the industry. Within a few short years, visual effects converted entirely from traditional optical printers and manual rotoscoping processes to digital compositing, 3-D animation and paint tools.

Kodak's original goal for Cineon was a complete "electronic intermediate system" for digitally assembling movies. In the early 1990s, it was not cost effective to digitize and assemble whole movies this way, but in choosing computer-based platforms over purpose-built (traditional television) architectures, these costs came down steadily, driven by the much bigger investments that other industries were making in computing, networking and storage technologies.

By the end of the 1990s, Kodak had discontinued the Cineon product line, but Apple, Arri, Autodesk, Filmlight, Imagica, Quantel, Thomson and other companies were offering products that provided the necessary tools for the digital postproduction of movies. Kodak chose to focus its energies on the demonstration and promotion of a new process dubbed "Digital Intermediate" that offered to revolutionize the traditional lab process of answer printing and release printing. The digital intermediate process provided digital conforming and color grading tools that opened up new creative opportunities, while improving the quality of the release prints. In 2000 Cinesite pioneered the digital intermediate process on the Coen Brothers' *O Brother, Where Art Thou* utilizing the Thomson Spirit Datacine and a Pandora color corrector, working in a digital, tapeless workflow at 2K resolution.

Since that early start, the supporting technology has evolved substantially with software-based color correctors offered from Autodesk, Filmlight, daVinci and others, and faster film scanners and recorders available. Within five years, the industry had embraced the digital intermediate process, with a majority of major Hollywood films, and many independent films, now finished digitally.

DIGITAL DAILIES

With the move to offline editing in the 1990s, and the increasing scrutiny of the production process by studio executives, video dailies were widely embraced. However, while the low-resolution, compressed video formats may have been good enough for editorial or continuity checking, they were not sufficient for judging focus, exposure and the subtleties of lighting. For this reason, most cinematographers demanded traditional film dailies although this was sometimes overruled for cost savings.

Now that HD infrastructure is widely available in postproduction, and the costs of the transfer, playback and projection displays have come down to reasonable levels, HD dailies are commonly used for the critical dailies review by the cinematographer and the director. Certainly, 1080/24p HDTV transfers with a Spirit Datacine represent a huge step up in resolution, making it possible to judge focus and detail in dailies.

However, high quality dailies require more than just HD resolution. Compression technology is generally used to reduce the cost of transport and playback. It is critical that the encoding bit rate be high enough to eliminate compression artifacts, so that the quality of the images can be judged. For 1080/24p this means a bit rate of at least 35 Mbps for MPEG2 or H.264 encoded content, and while this bit rate is supported by most servers, and HD media like Blu-ray disks, it is not artifact free.

High quality dailies also require a color-calibrated telecine transfer. Many facilities offer best-light or timed video transfers with the colorist making the picture look good on a traditional CRT monitor. While this produces good pictures for editorial or executive use, it does not produce a picture that looks like the final film product, and can create false impressions. Furthermore, this method provides no feedback on exposure level. A better approach that is now being embraced by some facilities is an extended range, best-light scan that protects the full range of the original negative, while displaying the picture through a look-up-table (LUT) that emulates print film. The picture can be "printed" up or down by applying offsets calibrated to match traditional printer lights. This provides the exposure feedback that a cinematographer needs, along with the capability of "printing" the picture up or down in the dailies playback to explore the range of the negative. Editorial and executive copies are created with the LUT burned in so that the pictures that they see include the print film characteristic.

For dailies review, it is important that a color-calibrated digital projector be used in a dark theatre or location trailer. Small HD monitors or consumer flat-panel displays are not acceptable for accurate color reproduction or visualization of the scale of the movie. Recently, several 1080p projectors have been introduced for the home theatre market that offer good contrast and stable calibration at a reasonable (under $10,000) price point. However, calibration and stability is critically important, so it is best to rent these from a facility that can provide experienced technicians for installation and calibration.

Communicating the creative intent is another challenge. Previsualization or "look management" products are available from Gamma and Density, Iridas, Filmlight and others that allow the cinematographer to capture a digital still and apply color correction on a laptop computer. Alternatively, some cinematographers use Adobe Photoshop. These systems can create a DPX or JPEG file to be sent to the dailies colorist as a proxy for guiding the color correction, along with notes or verbal instructions. However, this method takes an assistant to capture and catalog the digital pictures on the set, as well as time for the cinematographer to grade the pictures, so these tools see limited use.

Furthermore, the pictures still require interpretation and visual matching. Recently, the ASC Technology Committee has defined a format for interchanging simple color metadata, via a Color Decision List (CDL). Many of the color corrector manufacturers have implemented the ASC CDL, providing a means of translating the CDL into their internal color correction parameters. Facilities such as Laser Pacific (aIM Dailies), Technicolor (Digital Printer Lights) and E-Film (Colorstream) are early adopters of the ASC CDL into their internal workflows.

The ASC CDL information can be inserted into the Avid Log Exchange (ALE) files that are generated in telecine or video dailies, so that it can be carried through the editorial process and into the conformed DI. Here, the color correction decisions made on-set or in dailies can be used as the starting point for the final DI grading. This has been implemented in a few facilities for their internal workflows, but effective execution requires careful and continuous calibration of all telecines, scanners and reference displays.

DATA DAILIES

With modern scanners offering high speed scanning capabilities, and with the cost of storage coming down, it is now possible to forego traditional telecines and videotape workflows and scan dailies footage directly to data. This approach has been pioneered by E-Film in their CinemaScan process. Dailies are scanned to the SAN as 2K DPX files, where they are graded, synched and logged with software tools. The scanned files are archived to LTO4 tape and stored in a massive tape library, where the select shots can be pulled based on the editor's EDL, and conformed for the DI finishing step later.

SCANNING

Once the film has been edited and is "locked", the editor provides an Edit Decision List (EDL) to the scanning facility. There is no need to cut the negative. The EDL is translated to negative pull lists with keycode numbers marking the in and out points for scanning. The scanners provide automated scanning based on frame counts or keycodes, so it is actually easier to work with uncut camera or lab rolls, rather than compiling the select shots on a prespliced roll. And the negative is cleaner without this extra handling step.

Several manufacturers provide digital film scanners that are used for digital intermediate work. The Thomson Spirit Datacine, and its successor the Spirit4K scanner which provides real-time 2K scans, is widely used. The ARRIscan and Filmlight Northlight pin-registered scanners are also popular, but run at a somewhat slower rate. Since the Spirit4K is edge-guided, picture stability depends on clean film edges and tight transport velocity control. Steadiness is seldom a problem, but some people prefer pin-registration, which has always been used for visual effects shots. All of these scanners are calibrated to output logarithmic printing density in 10-bit DPX files.

Framing is a critical issue since camera apertures and ground glasses vary. It is extremely important to shoot a framing chart with each production camera and to provide that chart to the scanning facility for set up and framing of the scanner. In addition to defining the scan width, it is important to define the target aspect ratio. With the increasing use of Super-35 (full aperture) cameras, the target aspect ratio of 1.85 or 2.40 must be specified, as well as whether it is desired to scan the full height to use for the 1.33 home video version. Table A summarizes the typical camera aperture dimensions and scan resolutions for popular motion picture production formats including Academy, Cinemascope, Super-35 and Super-1.85, 3-perf 35mm and Super-16. All of these are transferred to 35mm inter-negatives for release printing.

		TABLE A:		
		Image Sizes, Scanned Dimensions and		
		Aspect Ratios for common film formats		
Film Format	**Camera Aperture Dimensions (H x V)**	**2K Scanned Dimensions (H x V)**	**Camera Aspect Ratio**	**Projection Aspect Ratio**
Academy	22.0 x 16.0 mm	2048 x 1332	1.37:1	1.85:1
Cinemascope	22.0 x 18.59 mm	2048 x 1556	1.18:1	2.40:1
Super-35	24.92 x 18.67 mm	2048 x 1536	1.33:1	2.40:1
Super-1.85	24.92 x 18.67 mm	2048 x 1536	1.33:1	1.85:1
3-perf 35mm	24.92 x 13.87 mm	2048 x 1144	1.79:1	1.85:1
Super-16	12.52 x 7.41 mm	2048 x 1234	1.66:1	1.85:1

2K OR 4K

One of the biggest debates within the technical community has been the question of what resolution to use for digital cinema mastering and distribution, which in itself is a continuation of a longstanding debate about the resolution of a frame of motion picture negative film. The studios are evenly divided between two opinions—2K (2048 pixels wide) is good enough and more cost effective, or 4K (4096 pixels wide) is better and will raise the bar. This debate raged for nearly a year, before DCI arrived at the grand compromise of supporting both 2K and 4K digital cinema distribution masters, using the hierarchical structure of JPEG2000 compression to provide a compatible delivery vehicle.

Today, most Digital Intermediate masters are produced at 2K resolution although more and more are being produced at 4K as costs come down.

Working in 4K requires four times the storage and four times the rendering time as 2K. The creative color grading process for 4K can be done in essentially the same time as 2K, because proxies are used to support interactive adjustment and display. The color correction can be rendered to the 4K images once the reel has been approved. Several of the software-based color correctors support this architecture, including products from Autodesk, Filmlight, Digital Vision, and DaVinci.

So what do you get for working in 4K? Does it produce pictures that are twice as good? If the original film format is 35mm and the release format is 35mm (the only viable film distribution format except for 70mm IMAX), then the answer is no. The difference between 2K and 4K is much more subtle, and very dependent on the quality of the camera lenses. A seminal paper by Brad Hunt of Kodak in the March 1991 *SMPTE Journal* describes the basis for Kodak's development of a 4K High Resolution Electronic Intermediate System in 1992 (which became Cineon), using a system MTF analysis to illustrate the effect of sampling resolution on the resulting images.[1] This is reproduced in Figure 2.

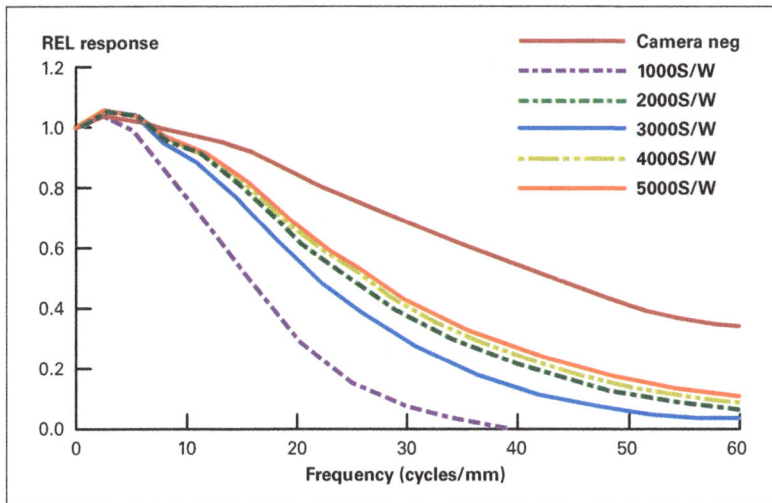

Figure 2. Modulation Transfer Function (MTF) a a function of sampling structure for Cineon digital file systems.

Kodak modeled the system modulation transfer function (MTF) as a function of sampling resolution in order to define the resolution requirements for its film scanners and recorders. Figure 2 shows the system MTF

1. B. Hunt, et al., "High Resolution Electronic Intermediate System for Motion Picture Film", *SMPTE Journal*, 100:156, March 1991.

responses for a sampling series of 1000 to 5000 samples per picture width on a 35mm Academy aperture. For reference, the MTF of a camera negative, which includes the negative film and camera lens, is also shown. MTF curves representing an analog photochemical system do not give you a single number to judge the resolution of film. If one takes a middle frequency of 25 cycles per mm as a basis, you can see that the system MTF response increases from about 15% at 1K to 40% at 2K and about 50% at 3K and 53% at 4K. So the system MTF improves significantly as the sampling resolution is increased from 1K to 2K, with diminishing returns beyond that. Kodak decided to design its Cineon system with a base resolution of 4K samples per picture width. With a nod towards practical and cost-effective postproduction work, however, Kodak also provided a direct 2K mode. Even today, more than fifteen years later, nearly all visual effects are done at 2K resolution.

Kodak's analysis included the input camera negative film and the output internegative element. It modeled the aperture response of the CCD film scanner and the Gaussian spot of the laser film recorder. It did not include the print film or the film projector, both of which further reduce the system MTF. Original negative films have improved substantially in the last fifteen years, now exhibiting higher speed and lower grain. However, the MTF has not improved much, and typical camera lenses are the same, and today's CCD film scanners and laser film recorders have similar MTF characteristics as the original Cineon conversion devices.

Even with an optically band-limited system like a camera negative (filtered by the camera lens and the MTF response of the film), it is still desirable to oversample the picture to avoid aliasing. In fact, scanning at 4K, then filtering and downsampling the image to 2K, produces sharper pictures with less aliasing than a direct 2K scanning process. So, even if the final digital master is produced at 2K resolution, there are good reasons to scan it at 4K and "down-rez" it for 2K manipulation.

Some studios are willing to pay a little extra for a 4K digital intermediate to deliver 4K digital cinema packages to those screens that are equipped with 4K digital cinema projectors. Although the initial installations of 5,000 digital cinema screens were all 2K systems, Sony introduced their 4K SXRD projectors in 2006, and Texas Instruments announced their support for 4K in 2009. There may also be some value in archiving a 4K digital master to protect for future release options.

DATA MANAGEMENT

With most digital intermediate processes, the scanned data is centrally stored in a Storage Area Network (SAN), where it can be accessed by various workstations performing dirt fix, conforming and color correction operations. Because of the bandwidth requirements of interactive adjustments and real-time playback, hardware accelerators and high performance disk systems and output cards are incorporated in many workstations.

In addition to the scanned shots, DPX files from VFX vendors are also loaded to the networked storage. OpenEXR is gaining support as an interchange file format for visual effects, particularly computer generated images (CGI). These files need to be converted into 10-bit printing density for subsequent conforming with the live action film scans.

DIRT FIX

All film images contain some dust or handling marks that have to be cleaned up. This process is called dirt fixing or "dustbusting." Basically, the process is to examine each frame for white marks caused by dirt, cinch marks or scratches and to remove these artifacts with a combination of automated and manual tools. Common tools include MTI's DRS and PF Clean by The Pixel Farm. The amount of dirt fixing varies with film format and handling. Typically, 16mm film requires more work than 35mm due to the higher magnification. Lab dirt and scratches are twice as big with 16mm format. Some scanners are now equipped with an infrared sensor that can detect dirt and either remove the dirt or provide a defect matte for later removal by software. Kodak licenses a technology called Digital ICE for this purpose, and it is now available on ARRI and Northlight scanners.

CONFORMING

The next step is to conform or assemble the shots to the EDL, and render the optical transitions (fades, dissolves etc.) to match the offline edit. As necessary, the data editor also generates subtitles and inserts visual effects shots, main titles and end credits.

COLOR GRADING

The color of the assembled shots is graded in a mastering suite equipped with a calibrated digital projector. DLP Cinema™ projectors from Barco, Christie or NEC are widely used as the reference display for mastering. Most facilities use a 3-D color display LUT to emulate a film print, implemented either in the color corrector or an external LUT box. This LUT is tuned for the characteristics of the specific print stock and lab that will be used for release printing.

Color grading is more than just adjusting or correcting the color from scene to scene to provide consistency and continuity. It also helps to impart the emotional context of the story, and complements the lighting and exposure used by the cinematographer to capture the scene. Color correctors provide a range of controls, generally grouped into primaries, secondaries and windows. The primary color correction controls adjust parameters that were originally implemented inside the telecine—these control the gain (white), gamma (midscale) and lift (black) in each of the red, green and blue records. The secondary controls mix the color primaries to create color difference signals that allow individual hues to be selected and rotated.

Although the first color correctors were analog processors, digital technology was incorporated in the 1980s, allowing much more control and flexibility with higher quality. One of the digitally enabled features was the introduction of user defined windows that allowed the colorist to draw mattes that applied selective color correction to the windowed region of the frame. These mattes can be tracked and animated as the subject or camera moves. Soft-edged mattes make the edges invisible. This powerful capability allows the cinematographer to digitally "dodge and burn" shots, brightening or darkening areas of the frame to enhance the original photography. In certain circumstances these tools can be used to save time in production, reducing the need for relighting or waiting for just the right natural light.

Color grading does have its limits, however. You can't enhance detail that wasn't captured on the original negative, so lighting and exposure are still critical. And creating mattes to selectively grade regions of the picture takes time and money. Extreme adjustments of color or contrast will amplify grain, so these color changes don't come free. It is always best to capture a sharp, well-lit image on the set, because you can always darken or defocus portions of the frame in post. It's much harder to go the other way. The larger the negative area, the finer the grain structure and the further you can push the color without artifacts. This means that Super-35 and Cinemascope negatives provide more creative flexibility over standard 35mm Academy or Super-16 formats.

COLOR GAMUT

DLP Cinema™ projectors were designed by Texas Instruments to support a wider color gamut than standard video (ITU Rec. 709). This wider gamut is commonly called P3, and was supported by DCI and SMPTE DC28 as the minimum color gamut for digital cinema. This extended gamut is based on practical mastering tests in which digital images were graded to match a film answer print, and has served the industry for several years. Figure 3 shows the color gamut of a SMPTE Reference Projector, compared to HDTV (ITU Rec. 709) and samples from Kodak Vision™ color print film. There are some film colors that fall outside of the gamut of the digital projector, particularly dark cyans, but most of the film gamut is enclosed. It is useful to note that the digital projectors are also capable of reproducing brighter primary colors (red, green and blue) since print film is a secondary color system with the image composed of cyan, magenta and yellow dyes.

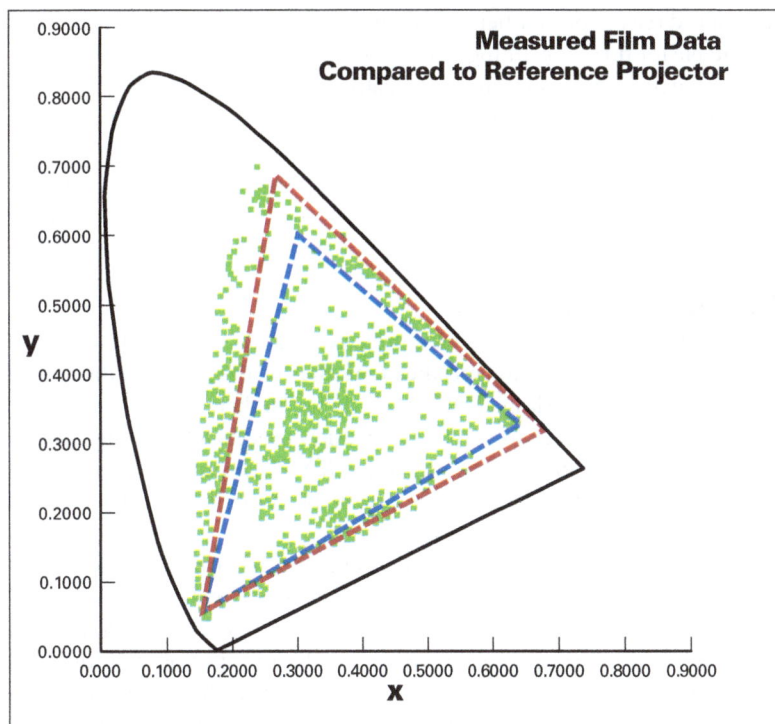

Figure 3. Color gamut of film compared to that of the digital cinema reference projector and ITU Rec. 709. A series of measured film samples are shown in green, with the reference projector gamut shown by the dashed redline and the ITU Rec. 709 gamut shown by the dashed blue line.

FILM OUTPUT

The finished digital master, called the Digital Source Master (DSM) in the DCI specification and some SMPTE digital cinema documents, is sent to a bank of film recorders for output to one or more inter-negatives for release printing. The widely used ArriLaser™ film recorder runs at about 2 seconds per frame, so a typical 20-minute reel requires 16 hours of continuous recording.

Color calibration is critical, and the 3-D color display LUTs that are used for the grading process must be built for the specific film stock and processing laboratory, because the variations between film stocks and labs are significant. Film processing is a chemical process that varies somewhat from day to day, and is a moving target that cannot be precisely matched. It is important to also recognize that the precision of digital color correction is much tighter than the process control and simple printer light adjustments of the film lab.

Each internegative can produce from 1,000 to 2,000 release prints on a high speed release printer before accumulating dirt or scratches that make it unsuitable for further printing. Therefore, a wide release (3000–5,000 prints or more) will require multiple internegatives. This can be accommodated by using the conventional IP/IN photochemical duplicating process, but this introduces another two generations of losses, which reduce the sharpness and steadiness of the image. The preferred approach is to generate multiple internegatives so that each release print is made directly from the digitally recorded internegative, so that each print is essentially a "digital show print".

DIGITAL CINEMA

Since the movie was graded on a projector that is calibrated to the DCI/SMPTE Reference Projector specifications, the creative work on the Digital Cinema Distribution Master (DCDM) is done. All that remains is to render the 3-D color LUT that was used in the preview process into the digital master, along with a simple color conversion to X'Y'Z'. This can be implemented as a software batch process, or if working in 2K, it can be a real-time output through an external 3-D LUT box.

The traditional practice in film scanning and recording is to scan and reproduce the full camera aperture, so that the image remains the same size on the internegative as the original negative without resampling, and the resulting print can be projected with a standard projection aperture. The standard film projection aperture is 5% smaller than the camera aperture, providing some margin for hiding the frame lines, covering any dirt caught in the camera aperture and also providing some "wiggle room" for picture weave (unsteadiness) introduced due to mechanical tolerances in printing and projection. The traditional practice works fine for film output. However, the Digital Cinema Distribution Master does not distinguish between the image structure of the master and the display. In fact, the DCI specification explicitly states that the projector must be capable of displaying the full DCDM, pixel for pixel, without any cropping.

If the same master is converted to a DCDM without resizing, the resulting digitally projected image will be 5% smaller than the film print shown on a projector with a standard aperture plate. While this may not be a big issue aesthetically, it does become a problem if the camera aperture is uneven or dirty, because now this distracting impairment may be visible on the digital projector, depending on the adjustment of the masking. With most theatres equipped with variable masking, it is standard practice to bring the masking into the picture area a little to provide a good clean black boundary to the picture. But this may not be enough.

Another option is to resize the picture for the DCDM, pushing in so that 95% of the original scan (1946 W) is resized to 2048 W, insuring that the digital picture is projected at the same size as the film print. However, this means that all DCDMs will suffer a small sharpness loss due to the 5% enlargement. Although this is probably acceptable operationally, it is inconsistent with the objective of optimizing the quality of the digital cinema presentation.

At the time of this writing, a proposal has been made to SMPTE to define a Safe Image Area for digital projection, similar in concept to the film projection aperture.

HOME VIDEO MASTERS

The next step is to generate the video masters for DVD and television distribution. Traditionally, home video masters were generated by transferring a color-timed IP on a telecine, with a colorist grading each scene on a calibrated video reference monitor, under the supervision of the cinematographer or director if they were available. This process often took an additional two to four weeks. With digital intermediate, much of the work of creating the various video masters can be automated, and that which requires supervision and approval can be accomplished quickly in a couple of days while the files are still on line and the cinematographer is still available.

Conversion to video for output requires two important processes. The first is framing and composition for the narrower video screen, which involves a panning operation to extract the appropriate part of the widescreen frame for the full-frame 4:3 standard definition video outputs. This process is called "pan/scan". With digital intermediate, this means overlaying a 4:3 framing rectangle and moving it as necessary to capture the most important part of the action.

The second process is to correct the color and tone scale of the picture for the very different characteristics and viewing conditions of a home video display. Remember that the movie was color graded on a digital cinema projector in a dark theatre. The home viewing environment typically includes some room light which fills in the shadows and increases the perceived contrast of the image. SMPTE RP166 defines a Recommended Practice for Critical Viewing Conditions for the Evaluation of Color Television Pictures that prescribes a dim surround that is 10% of the peak luminance of the monitor and matches the D65 color temperature of the monitor.

But grading for video is more than just a contrast correction for surround illumination that could be implemented with a simple color transform. The gamut of the HD video display (ITU-R Recommendation 709) is much smaller than that of print film or the Reference Display for digital cinema. So, it is necessary to map some colors that fall within the displayed color gamut of reference projector, but are outside of the color gamut of the video monitor. Although this could be implemented in a global 3-D LUT that compressed out of gamut colors, this compression must be implemented as a soft-clip or gradual ramp that also affects some of the in-gamut colors. So, it is always best to look at each scene and selectively apply the gamut mapping only when required. For these reasons, a color trim pass is often used to generate the video masters. However, this trim pass can typically be performed in a day or two, rather than the 2 to 4 weeks of the traditional mastering process.

ARCHIVAL ELEMENTS

As we move from a film to a digital world, the question of what materials to archive is stirring heated debates. The biggest problem is that there is no accepted archival digital medium today, due to both media deterioration and software and hardware obsolescence. Magnetic tape formats are not expected to last for more than ten years or so, requiring an expensive migration strategy to protect the data. The lowest risk approach today to archive the finished digital master is to make black and white film separations that have a proven shelf life of over 100 years (if stored properly) and can either be reconstructed photo-chemically or redigitized.

Which elements should be saved for the future? With traditional film production, it is common practice to store the original camera negative, a timed IP, and an answer print in addition to the black and white separations. A HD 1080/24p master tape is also stored as the home video master. A similar approach should be taken in the digital world. A comparison of archival elements for film and digital postproduction is shown in Table B.

TABLE B: A comparison of archival elements for traditional film and digital processes.		
Element	**Film Process**	**Digital Process**
Original	Original negative (o-neg)	Original tapes
Color corrected master	Timed Interpositive (IP)	Digital Source Master (DSM)
Reference picture	Answer Print	Digital Cinema Distribution Master (DCDM)
Video master	HD 1080/24p	HD 1080/24p
Long term storage	Black and White Separations	Black and White Separations

The original negative or original digital tapes should be stored. The conformed and graded Digital Source Master (DSM) is the equivalent to the timed IP. Although the color grading has been applied, it preserves much of the range of the original photography if the movie needs to be remastered in the future for a high dynamic range display. The most common file format is DPX, with the data stored as 10-bit printing density. In the future, the Open EXR file format may also be used, storing linear RGB data in floating point form. It is important to tag the data with the color characteristics of the Reference Projector used in mastering, and the 3-D color LUT used to emulate print film.

Although the various distribution formats can easily be regenerated from the DSM, it is also worth saving the output Digital Cinema Distribution Master (DCDM) in TIFF-16 file format, storing 12-bit X'Y'Z' color data, as well as the HD 1080/24p home video master. The DCDM serves as the answer print for color reference in future releases or restorations as well as the master from which additional copies can be made. The HD 1080/24p format is the master from which all other home video formats can be made.

ADDITIONAL CONSIDERATIONS FOR DIGITAL CAMERAS

Digital cameras are increasingly being embraced for motion picture origination. Just as with film, it is important to run preproduction camera tests to explore the range of the camera and to optimize the setup. Calibration is important with both the camera setup and the post facility that is generating the dailies or Digital Intermediate. Pioneered by the Panavision Genesis, Thomson Viper and ARRI D-21 cameras, many cameras now offer a film-style logarithmic storage mode, that captures an extended dynamic range that provides grading flexibility in postproduction, much like negative film.

Data storage decisions affect production and postproduction. It is critical that you consult the postproduction facility that will be supporting your dailies and finishing work. Many digital cameras store the pictures on HDCAM-SR tape which is efficient to unload and reload on the set, as well as quick to load into postproduction. However, this does require the rental of relatively expensive HDCAM-SR recorders.

Another option is to temporarily store the pictures as data files on portable flash cards, flash magazines or disk packs. Both compressed and uncompressed storage solutions are available, but it is important to understand the tradeoffs. Later, these digital files may be transferred to tape, or transferred directly to working storage in the postproduction facility.

S.two and Codex offer uncompressed HD data storage on their disk-based field recorders, which can be tethered to the camera via dual HD-SDI cables. In 2009, S.two introduced the OB-1, providing dockable onboard storage of uncompressed HD data via flash magazines. Also in 2009, Panavision introduced their dockable Solid State Recorder SSR-1 for the Genesis camera.

The S.two and Codex field recorders also support the ARRI D-21's ARRIRAW format, which stores the full 12-bit signal range and full 1.33 frame area in a packed data format that can be transmitted across dual HD-SDI cables, a proprietary mode that ARRI calls T-LINK. This means that the ARRI D-21 camera can support traditional anamorphic lenses for widescreen photography without compromising vertical resolution. ARRI supplies a free software utility, the ARRIRAW Converter (ARC), which allows the ARRI-RAW files to be converted to full frame 1.33 DPX files in postproduction.

Several cameras also support compressed data storage with onboard flash cards or disk drives, including the RED One (r3d), Panasonic 3700 (P2), and Sony EX-3 (XD-CAM) cameras. The RED camera uses a proprietary wavelet compression codec, which produces reasonable results at a compression ratio of about 10:1. RED also provides software utilities for high quality rendering to DPX files for finishing. The P2 and XD-CAM formats use much higher compression ratios, and while the resulting artifacts are not a problem for editorial, they are not the best solution for finishing.

With any of these data formats, the production company must consider the need to backup or archive the production footage to tape for storage. The most widely used approach is LTO3 or LTO4 tape. For uncompressed data, this tape backup takes about 3:1 run time and can be performed on location or back at the post house that is providing dailies support.

ASC Color Decision List

by David Reisner and Joshua Pines
ASC Associate Members

In most modern workflows, images—whether originated on film or with digital cameras—spend most of their time and are processed in digital form. Often, multiple facilities, with different color correction systems, are involved in creating and processing elements for a show.

The American Society of Cinematographers Technology Committee, DI subcommittee—with participants from the ASC, color correction system vendors, postproduction facilities, and color scientists—created the ASC Color Decision List (ASC CDL) to allow basic primary color correction data to be interchanged between color correction systems made by different manufacturers. This standardized interchange, when accompanied by good communication and consistent viewing conditions, can create the same results on multiple systems, substantially improving the consistency and quality of the resulting images while also increasing efficiency and reducing cost. The ASC CDL is widely used in motion picture production, television production and visual-effects. The ASC CDL is the primary Look Modification Tranform used to express artistic intent in the wide gamut, high dynamic range Academy Color Encoding System (ACES).

The ASC CDL defines a small set of operations—*transfer functions*—that provide the most basic set of color correction operations—operations that can be implemented in all color correction vendors' systems. They are *Slope, Offset,* and *Power* which are applied to each of the R, G, and B signals independently, and *Saturation* which operates on R, G, and B in combination. Thus, ten parameters describe any ASC CDL color correction.

Most color correction systems natively provide vendor-specific *Lift, Gain,* and *Gamma* functions. *Slope, Offset,* and *Power* are similar but mathematically purer functions. In most cases, vendor-specific *Lift, Gain,* and *Gamma* can be easily translated into some combination of *Slope, Offset,* and *Power* for interchange between systems.

The ASC CDL defines mathematical operations that are applied to all image data, regardless of the format/encoding of that data. The ASC CDL defines the math, not the encoding-specific interpretation of that math. Each of the operations will have quite different results on log data than on "linear" data. For example, a *Slope* of 2.0 multiplies the image code values by 2.0. If the image data is linear, that will brighten the image by one stop. If the image data is log, a *Slope* of 2.0 will double the contrast of the image.

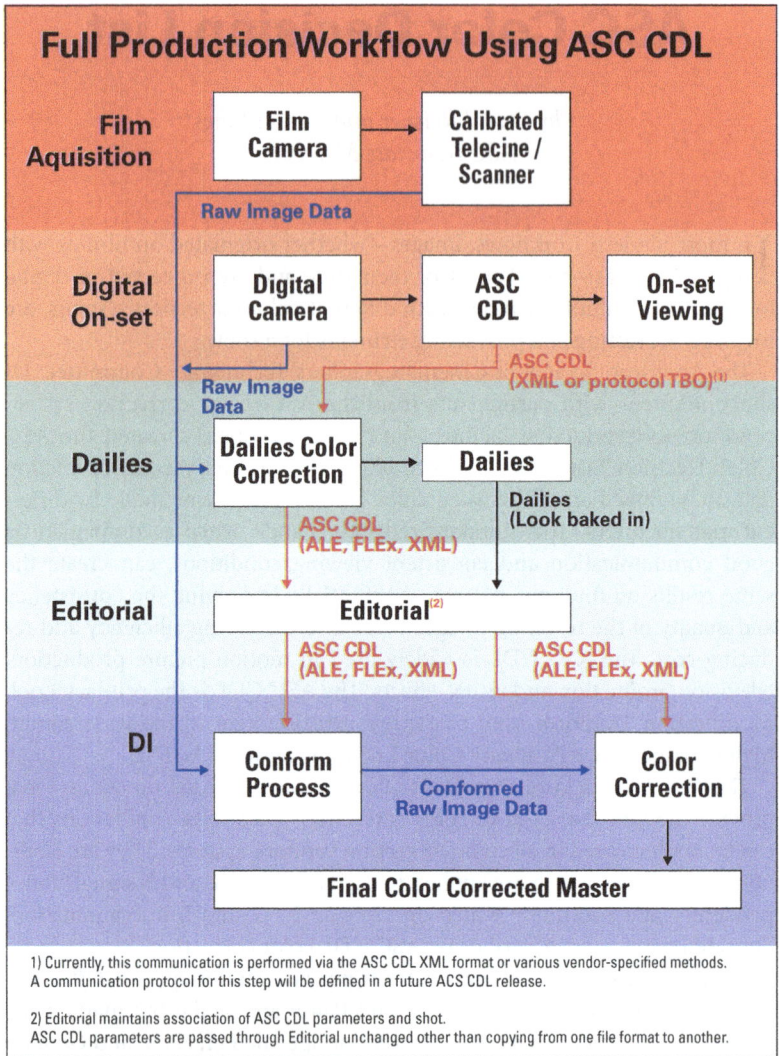

Figure 1. ASC CDL production workflow chart

The application of the ASC CDL provides no "interpretation" of the underlying metric of the image code values. A given correction applied on two systems that are assuming data in different formats, and therefore apply different input or viewing transforms, will almost certainly produce inconsistent results. But awareness of the data metric and encoding-customized operation is outside the scope addressed by the ASC CDL.

And a correction applied to the right data in the right way on two systems must still be viewed on calibrated displays with the same characteristics and in very similar viewing conditions to communicate the intended look. Co-ordination of data metrics and viewing conditions is also outside the scope of the ASC CDL and must be handled elsewhere in a project's workflow.

Although the ASC CDL functions are intended for purposes of inter-change—to communicate basic color correction operations from set to facility and between systems from different vendors—many vendors also provide user level controls that operate on ASC CDL functions directly.

In a workflow, the set of ten ASC CDL parameters for a correction is interchanged via ASC CDL-defined XML files, by new fields in ALE and FLEx files, or special comments in CMX EDL files. Most often the formats shown in Fig. 1 will be used, but the exact methods used will be facility- and workflow-dependent.

ASC CDL corrections are metadata that are associated with shots. Unlike LUT corrections, the ASC CDL corrections are **not** baked-in to the image. Because of this approach, corrections later in the workflow can be based on earlier ASC CDL corrections without modifying the image data multiple times—yielding highest possible image quality. And sharing an ASC CDL correction gives information about how the earlier corrector was thinking about the look. Corrections implemented with LUTs are fixed—they can be viewed, or additional corrections can be layered on, but they cannot practi-cally be adjusted or tuned.

The ASC CDL supports only the most basic color correction operations. Not all operations of interest (e.g., log/linear conversions, 3D LUTs, window-ing, tracking) can be expressed with these operations. It is possible that future releases will support a somewhat expanded set of interchangeable operations.

The ASC CDL does not handle everything necessary to communicate a look. A project must manage and communicate basic and critical information like color space, data representation format, display device, and viewing en-vironment. To communicate a look between on-set and post or between post facilities absolutely requires that information be shared and used intelligently.

ASC CDL TRANSFER FUNCTIONS

Although generally similar to the common *Lift*, *Gain*, and *Gamma* operations (which, incidentally, vary in detail from system to system and manufacturer to manufacturer), the ASC CDL defines a set of three transfer functions with unique names and simple definitions.

The ASC CDL's three basic transfer functions are *Slope*, *Offset*, and *Power*. They are applied in that order—*Slope*, then *Offset*, then *Power*—and are sometimes referred to collectively as *SOP*. The transfer functions are in RGB color space and are applied independently to each color component. These three transfer functions for the three color components (assuming the cur-

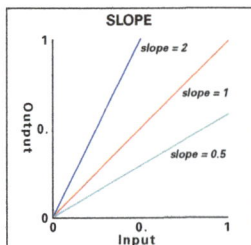

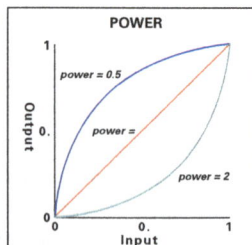

| Figure 2. Slope | Figure 3. Offset | Figure 4. Power |

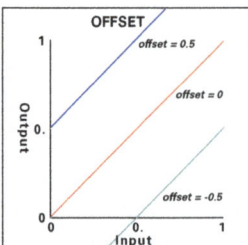

rent trichromatic systems) can collectively be described by nine parameters.

The vendor-specific *Lift*, *Gain*, and *Gamma* operations found on most systems, individually or in combination, can be translated into *Slope*, *Offset*, and *Power*.

The *Saturation* function was added to the ASC CDL in release 1.2. Unlike the *Slope*, *Offset*, and *Power* functions, *Saturation* operates on all three color channels in combination. The ASC CDL uses a common industry definition for *Saturation* ("Rec. 709" weightings). Saturation is applied after *Slope*, *Offset*, and *Power*.

Vendors may still have their own proprietary saturation algorithms, but they must support the ASC CDL Saturation algorithm when they are operating in "ASC CDL mode".

Slope

Slope (see Figure 2) changes the slope of the transfer function without shifting the black level established by *Offset* (see next section). The input value, *slope*, ranges from 0.0 (constant output at *Offset*) to less than infinity (although, in practice, systems probably limit at a substantially lower value). The nominal *slope* value is 1.0.

$$out = in * slope \quad 0 \le slope < \infty$$

Offset

Offset (see Figure 3) raises or lowers overall value of a component. It shifts the transfer function up or down while holding the slope constant. The input value, *offset*, can in theory range from -∞ to +∞ although the range —1.0 to 1.0 will fit most traditional use. The nominal *offset* value is 0.0.

$$out = in + offset \quad -\infty < offset < \infty$$

If the underlying data is log, then *Offset* is an interpretation of *printer points*—the most common method of color correction in film lab work.

Power

Power (see Figure 4) is the only nonlinear function. It changes the overall curve of the transfer function. The input value, *power*, ranges from greater than 0.0 to less than infinity. The nominal *power* value is 1.0.

$$out = in \wedge power \quad (where \wedge is \text{ "raised to the power"}) \quad 0 < power < \infty$$

Saturation

Saturation provides a weighted average of the normal color (*saturation* 1.0) and all gray (fully desaturated, *saturation* 0.0) images. The saturation operation modifies all color components. Color components are weighted by the values used in most Rec. 709 implementations of saturation. *Saturation* values > 1.0 are supported. Values > 4 or so will probably only be used for special purposes.

Saturation is applied after the *SOP (Slope, Offset, Power)* operations.

sat is the user input saturation parameter. *inR* is the input red color component value, *G* green, and *B* blue. *outR* is the output red color component value, *G* green, and *B* blue. *gray* is the fully desaturated gray value, based on the color compo nent weightings.

$$gray = 0.2126 * inR +$$
$$0.7152 * inG +$$
$$0.0722 * inB$$
$$outR = Clamp(gray + sat * (inR - gray))$$
$$outG = Clamp(gray + sat * (inG - gray))$$
$$outB = Clamp(gray + sat * (inB - gray))$$
$$0 \leq sat < \infty$$

BEHAVIOUR FOR DIFFERENT IMAGE ENCODINGS

The ASC CDL operations perform the same math regardless of the encoding of the image data to which they are being applied. The resulting modifications to the image will vary a great deal for different image data encodings. Management of the image encoding and appropriate application of the ASC CDL operations is the responsibility of the project/show and outside the scope of the ASC CDL.

VIDEO-GAMMA AND LINEAR (GAMMA 1.0)

ASC CDL operations will have similar effects on images in the common encodings that are generally linear. Those encodings include linear light (photon count or energy) often used in CGI; Academy ACES scene-referred linear which will be showing up more often in both film and digitally originated material; and video signals which are linear but always have a gamma (power function) applied—nominally 2.2 but numbers vary in practice. Some custom "linear" encodings may have special handling near toe (blacks/crush) or shoulder (whites/rolloff). In those cases, the interaction of ASC CDL operations and the non-linear regions will have to be evaluated on a case-by-case basis.

Slope

For linear encodings, Slope controls the brightness of the image while maintaining contrast—like adjusting the f- or T-stop.

Offset

For linear encodings, Offset controls the overall "base fog" of the image. The values of the entire image are moved up or down together, affecting both brightness and contrast. This is not traditionally a common operation for linear data.

Power

For linear encodings, Power controls the contrast of the image.

Saturation

For all encodings, including linear, Saturation controls the saturation—intensity of the color of the image.

The old telecine Lift function—raising or lowering the darks while holding the highlights constant—can be achieved via a combination of Offset and Slope. Similarly, the telecine Gain function can also be achieved via a combination of Offset and Slope.

Log

ASC CDL operations will have similar effects on images in the common encodings that are generally log. Those encodings include printing density (e.g.

Figure 5a and b.

**Video Gamma Examples:
a) Slope**

Slope: RGB all 0.5

Slope: RGB all 1.0

Slope: RGB all 1.5

b) Offset

Offset: RGB all -0.2

Offset: RGB all 0.0

Offset: RGB all 0.2

Cineon, DPX), commonly seen from film scanners and created or imitated by other sources; and the various log modes output by various digital cameras to present a more filmlike response with a wider dynamic range (at least until cameras put out the high dynamic range Academy ACES "scene-referred linear" floating point format). Some "log" encodings have special handling near the toe (blacks/crush) or shoulder (whites/roll-off). In those cases, the interaction of ASC CDL operations and the special regions will have to be evaluated on a case-by-case basis.

In digital intermediate, log images will usually have a film print emulation applied as an output display transform in order to see the color corrected images as they will be theatrically projected. For this workflow, the ASC CDL is applied before the film print emulation. (This procedure was applied to the example log images shown here.)

Slope

For log encodings, Slope controls the contrast of the image.

Offset

For log encodings, Offset controls the brightness of the image while maintaining contrast—like adjusting the f- or T-stops. This is essentially the same as Printer Lights but with different values/units.

Power

For log encodings, Power controls the level of detail in shadows vs. highlights. This is not traditionally a common operation for log data.

Figure 5c and d.

Video Gamma Examples:

c) Power

Power: RGB all 1.5

Power: RGB all 1.0

Power: RGB all 0.5

d) Saturation

Saturation: 0.5

Saturation: 1.0

Saturation: 2.0

Saturation

For all encodings, including linear, Saturation controls the saturation—intensity of the color of the image.

ASC CDL INTERCHANGE FORMATS

The ASC CDL allows basic color corrections to be communicated through the stages of production and postproduction and to be interchanged between equipment and software from different manufacturers at different facilities. The underlying color correction algorithms are described above.

When ASC CDL color correction metadata is transferred from dailies to editorial and from editorial to postproduction, provided that data representation, color space, and viewing parameters are handled consistently, the initial "look" set for dailies (perhaps from an on-set color correction) can be used as an automatic starting point or first pass for the final color correction session. ASC CDL metadata is transferred via extensions to existing, commonly used file formats currently employed throughout the industry: ALE, FLEx, and CMX EDL files. There are also two ASC CDL-specific XML file types that can be used to contain and transfer individual color corrections or (usually project-specific) libraries of color corrections.

ALE and FLEx files are used to transfer information available at the time of dailies creation to the editorial database. New fields have been added to these files to accommodate ASC CDL color correction metadata for each shot.

CMX EDL files are output from editorial and used primarily to "conform"

Figure 6a and b.

Log Examples:
a) Slope

Slope: RGB all 0.75

Slope: RGB all 1.0

Slope: RGB all 1.25

b) Offset

Offset: RGB all -0.1

Offset: RGB all 0.0

Offset: RGB all 0.1

the individual shots into the final edit. As there is a convention to include shot specific metadata as comment fields after the associated "event" in the EDL file, it made sense to use this mechanism to attach ASC CDL parameters to each "event". There are two ways of specifying this in an EDL file—either "inline" or "via XML reference."

Many vendors are currently using XML to support their internal data structures. The ASC CDL includes a hook so that CDL parameters can reside in simple XML text files that can be referenced by the CMX EDL format or other vendor-specific formats. The two types of XML files are:

1. **Color Decision List (CDL):** files that contain a set of color decisions (a color correction with a reference to an image) and that may also include other project metadata.

2. **Color Correction Collection (CCC):** files which solely contain one or more color corrections.

Each and every color correction defined in these files has a unique Color Correction id. Any specific color correction defined in these XML files can be referenced by its unique ColorCorrection id.

FOR IMPLEMENTORS

The ASC CDL release documents are intended for implementers and vendors. The release includes details on the interchange formats as well as example code and test images. To get instructions on how to get the current release, send an

Figure 6c and d.

Log Examples:
c) Power

Power: RGB all 1.25

Power: RGB all 1.0

Power: RGB all 0.75

d) Saturation

Saturation: 0.5

Saturation: 1.0

Saturation: 2.0

e-mail to asc-cdl@theasc.com.

The ASC CDL was created by the American Society of Cinematographers Technology Committee, DI subcommittee. Participants included ASC members, color correction system vendors, postproduction facilities, and color scientists.

Discussion and questions may be directed to: Lou Levinson, ASC Technology Committee, DI sub committee chair: joe.beats@yahoo.com; Joshua Pines, ASC Technology Committee, DI subcommittee vice-chair: jzp@technicolor. com; David Reisner, ASC Technology Committee and DI subcommittee secretary: dreisner@d-cinema.us.

The Academy of Motion Picture Arts and Sciences Academy Color Encoding System

by Curtis Clark, ASC and
Andy Maltz, ASC Associate Member

OVERVIEW

The Academy Color Encoding System (ACES) is an image and color management architecture designed primarily for the production, mastering and long-term archiving of motion pictures, although it is being successfully used in television production as well. Developed by the Academy of Motion Picture Arts and Sciences in collaboration with many motion-picture production and color science experts, ACES provides a set of digital image encoding specifications transforms and recommended practices that enable the creation and processing of high fidelity images. It offers a larger dynamic range of scene tones, a wider color gamut and greater mathematical precision than is possible with 10-bit Cineon encoding or High Definition Television standards such as ITU-R Rec. BT.709.

ACES also resolves ambiguities frequently linked to transforms between so-called "log" and "linear" image encoding,[1] as well as those associated with using a variety of display devices during production, postproduction and mastering. ACES supports flexible image pipeline development for many different processes including film and digital acquisition, digital intermediate, visual effects production, remastering and on-set color management. For cinematographers, ACES provides the following benefits:

▶ Eliminates uncertainty between on-set look management and downstream color correction through standardized viewing transforms and equipment calibration methods

---

1. The terms "log" and "linear" as currently used in motion picture production are loosely defined. "Log" can refer to some form of printing density values or log-encoded RGB values, and "linear" can refer to some form of video code values or linear-encoded RGB values. While the use of these terms is deprecated in ACES-based workflows, it should be noted that log-encoded forms of ACES data are being developed for use in certain color correction operations and for realtime transmission of ACES data over HD-SDI.

▶ Preserves the full range of highlights, shadows and colors captured on-set for use throughout postproduction and mastering

▶ Preserves the ability to use traditional photometric tools for exposure control rather than having to compensate for custom or proprietary viewing transforms in conjunction with a video monitor

▶ Simplifies matching of images from different camera sources

▶ Enables future expansion of the creative palette by removing the limitations of legacy workflows

Key components and features of ACES include:

▶ A standardized, fully-specified high high-precision, high dynamic range, wide color gamut color encoding specification (SMPTE ST2065-1:2012 Academy Color Encoding Specification) encompassing the full range of image color and detail captured by current and future digital cameras

▶ A standardized, fully-specified high precision and high dynamic range printing density specification (SMPTE ST2065-3:2012 Academy Density Exchange and the related SMPTE ST2065-2:2012 Academy Printing Density) encompassing the full range of image color and detail captured by modern motion picture film stocks

▶ Standardized file formats for colorimetric and densitometric data based on the popular OpenEXR and DPX data containers

▶ A methodology for display device-independent mastering that produces higher quality images than are possible with legacy workflows

▶ Recommended best practices for interfacing digital motion picture camera "raw" data and film scanner output data to ACES

▶ Support for ASC CDL in on-set color management systems

The full benefits of ACES are achieved when cameras, color correctors, image creation and processing tools, and display devices correctly implement the ACES specifications and recommended practices.

ACES Technical Description

The standardized Academy Color Encoding Specification (which also is referred to as "ACES") is a core component of the ACES architecture. It defines a high-precision wide color gamut digital image encoding appropriate for both photographed and computer-generated images. From image capture to theatrical presentation and/or other forms of display, ACES encodes the image data in a manner that makes it available for downstream processing, which ultimately allows more flexible and creative color grading. This is in contrast to legacy 10-bit systems such as Cineon and ITU-R Rec. BT. 709, whose precision, color gamut and dynamic range capabilities are below those of modern digital motion picture cameras and film stocks.

ACES is capable of encoding all colors viewable by the human visual system (see Figure 1). This greatly exceeds the range covered by HDTV and Digital Cinema projectors.

ACES is derived from a hypothetical ideal recording device, designated as the Reference Input Capture Device (RICD), against which actual recording devices' behavior can be compared (see Figure 2). As conceived, the RICD can distinguish and record all visible colors, as well as capture a luminance range exceeding that of any current or anticipated physical camera. The RICD's purpose is to provide a documented, unambiguous, fixed relation-

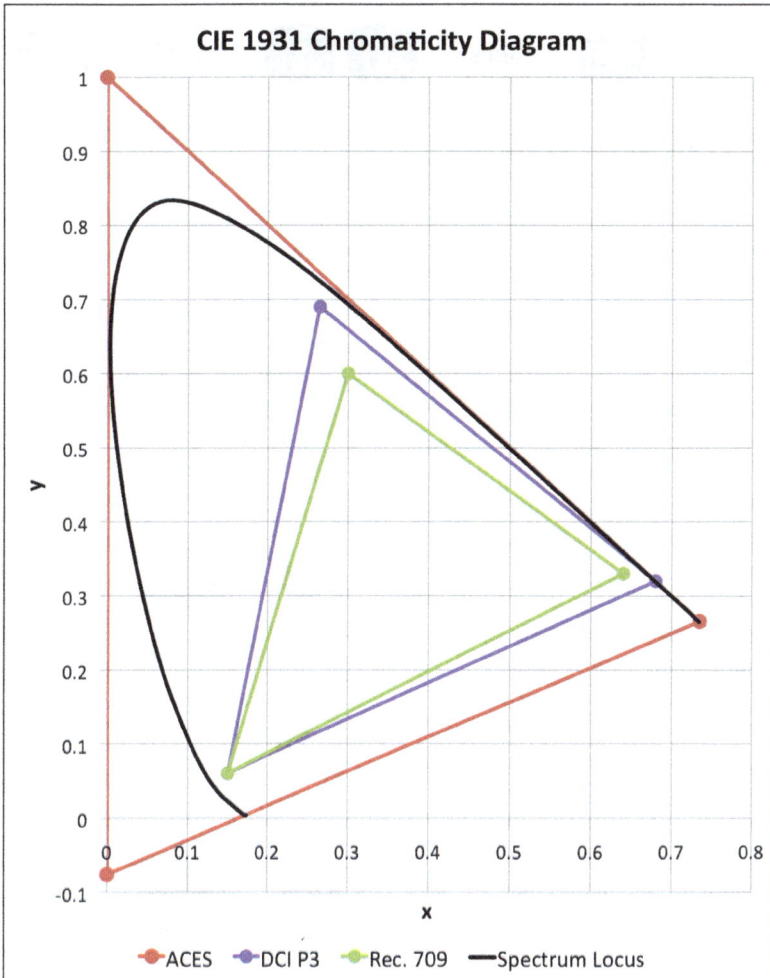

Figure 1. CIE 2-Degree Chromaticity Diagram with Gamuts showing ACES primaries compared to other color encoding specifications

ship between scene colors (also called "relative scene exposure values") and encoded RGB values. This fixed relationship is integral to a fully specified imaging architecture, as it provides a reference point for bringing any form of image source data into the system.

Because ACES encodes scene colors, ACES values must be adjusted for the target display environment and device characteristics to faithfully represent the recorded images. These adjustments are performed by the Reference Rendering Transform (RRT) and a display device-specific Output Device Transform (ODT) that are, in practice, combined into a single transform.

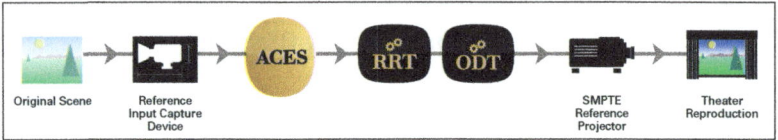

Figure 2. ACES Reference Signal Chain

Figure 2 also shows the combined RRT and ODT along with the SMPTE Digital Cinema Reference projector, a common configuration for mastering theatrical motion pictures.

When an actual camera records a physical scene, or a virtual camera (e.g., a CGI rendering program) constructs a virtual scene, a camera-specific Input Device Transform (IDT) converts the resulting image data into the ACES relative exposure values as though the subject had been captured by the RICD (see Figure 3).

As noted earlier, ACES images are not appropriate for final color evaluation or direct viewing; like film negative or digital files containing scanned images encoded as printing density they are only intermediate representations. ACES images can be examined to identify image content, cropping region, sequencing, the amount of shadow or highlight detail and other qualities. For final color evaluation, the RRT must be used in conjunction with a specific display device's ODT to produce

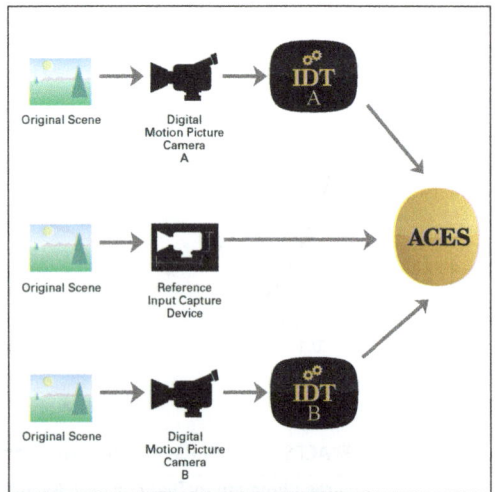

Figure 3. Input Device Transforms (IDTs)

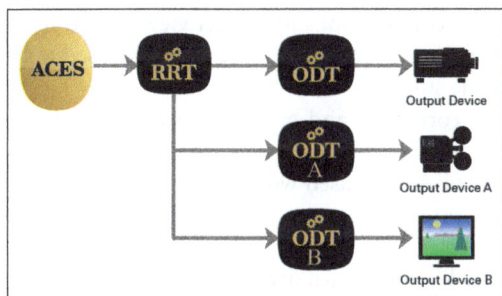

Figure 4. The Referencing Rendering Transform (RRT) and Output Device Transforms (ODTs)

a "color correct" viewable image (see Figure 4).

Figure 5 shows the full ACES block diagram.[2]

Using the full range of color corrector tool sets, Look Modification Transforms (LMT - not shown for clarity) can be applied to camera and/or CGI images in ACES to record basic color adjustments (using ASC CDL, for example) or to achieve preferred creative looks during color grading. Examples of preferred creative looks include bleach bypass and film stock-specific looks, or any custom look that serves the visual storytelling.

Using ACES in practice, as with any production pipeline, requires advance preparation and sufficient technical support to achieve satisfying results. Key issues to consider when using ACES include:

▶ If shooting with digital cameras, selection of appropriate IDTs to produce well-formed ACES-encoded images

▶ If shooting film, proper calibration of film scanners to produce well-formed ADX-encoded images

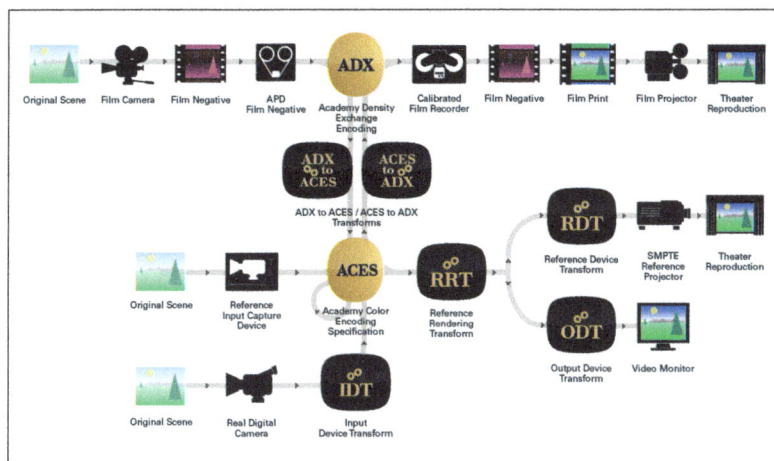

Figure 5. Academy Color Encoding System Block Diagram.

---

2. RDT (Reference Device Transform) is the ODT for SMPTE Reference Projector Minimum Color Gamut (Nominal) (see SMPTE RP431-2-2007 Reference Projector and Environment, Table A. 1).

▶ Use of appropriate RRT/ODT combinations for on-set viewing and mastering, as well as consideration of any LMTs that might be used both on-set and in the mastering suite

▶ Use of ACES-enabled color correctors and other ACES-enabled image-processing equipment

With a correctly implemented ACES-based workflow, cinematographers can rely on properly exposed source images as the best starting point for visual effect integration and mastering.

For more information on ACES, please visit oscars.org/aces

Curtis Clark, ASC currently chairs the ASC's Technology Committee and has done so since it was revitalized in 2002.

Andy Maltz serves as the director for the Academy of Motion Picture Arts and Sciences's Science and Technology Council.

The Cinematographer and the Laboratory

revised by Rob Hummel
ASC Associate Member

The relationship between a cinematographer and the laboratory processing his or her film can mean the difference between the revelation of
seeing exactly the images conceived upon exposing the film, or a defensive,
frustrating time spent constantly seeking to achieve the right look. Remarkably, and not surprisingly, this all rests on effective communication between
the cinematographer and that person at the laboratory responsible for handling your dailies. Since the production process begins with dailies and principal photography, that's where we'll begin this discussion.

When working with a laboratory for the first time, it is advisable to contact the lab well in advance of principal photography or any tests to be shot.
Upon locating the individual who will be handling your dailies, you should
discuss the film to be shot, the looks you are trying to achieve, and learn
from the lab what procedures they employ to ensure that your dailies are
delivered with a consistent look. At this time, you should find out what light
points the lab considers to be normal from a properly exposed piece of film,
and whether the lab utilizes RGB or YCM color-timing methods. Ideally,
this process begins with a visit to the lab for a face-to-face meeting.

For reasons discussed below, it should be understood that for the same
piece of film, light point values can vary many points one way or another
depending on where a lab has trimmed their printers. This needs to be understood so as not to be alarmed when using a lab for the first time and
discovering that your printer lights are 8 points lower than the lab you are
accustomed to using.

Laboratories routinely use the film manufacturers' recommended specifications for processing, modified to meet their particular equipment. (The
entire system—type of film, manufacturers' EI recommendation, laboratory printing and processing range—is calibrated to produce a pleasing
rendition of fully lighted flesh tones under normal projection conditions.)
In addition to producing normal results on the screen, most laboratories
are able to offer several techniques that can modify the look of a film to a
certain degree; these processes would include flashing of negative or positive, push/pull processing, ENR and bleach bypass. You should speak to
your lab representative to understand all of the techniques that are available to you.

Figure 1. LAD color chart

PRINTER POINTS

The laboratory controls print density and color balance by increasing or decreasing the intensity of each primary color of light in steps called printer points. Since the development of the B&H Model C printer, most manufacturers have standardized on a range of 50 light points in 0.025 Log E increments. In addition to the light points, each printer usually also has 24 trim settings (0.025 Log E), providing an available total of 74 lights.

When a lab changes the brightness/darkness of a print, they will say they are adjusting the density of the print (which, quite literally, they are). Density is adjusted by moving the values of all three light points (RGB or YCM) in unison. Individual adjustment of the colors is obviously used for specific color correction, or timing.

This means that at some laboratories, just because your light point is up at 50, it may not mean there isn't any more room to go. Sometimes you may have the ability to go up to the equivalent to a 65 light point. That being said, at some laboratories it can also mean that when you are at a 50 light point, there isn't any more room at all. Again, you must consult the lab you are using and get advice about the flexibility of their light point scale.

One could argue that the ideal settings for scene-to-scene timing would be at mid-scale (Trim 12 + Tape 25 = 37 lights). In actual practice the available range is considerably less. Printer lamps are usually operated under their rated voltage. This reduces the light intensity in all three colors. For example, lowering the voltage from 120 to 90 volts on a BRN-1200 watt lamp results in a relative change in printer points equal to minus 12 Red, 13 Green, 17 Blue. The trims are usually used to balance the printer for a given print-film emulsion. A typical emulsion might require 16 Red, 13 Green, 10 Blue or, in terms of the ideal, plus 4 Red, plus 1 Green, minus 2 Blue. Other factors influencing the available printer points are the operating speed of the printer, and the use of neutral-density filters in the individual channels and the main light beam.

The sum of these variables explains why a given negative might be printed 28 Red, 29 Green, 22 Blue at one laboratory and 36 Red, 32 Green, 36 Blue at another laboratory to produce matched prints. It is important to understand that printer points relate only to how the printer exposes film. A one-stop .30 Log E change (12 printer points x .025 Log E) is equal to a one-stop exposure in the camera only if the film in the camera has a gamma of approximately 1.0.

The current negative films, both black & white and color, have gammas of approximately .65. Therefore, in correlating camera and printer exposure, one stop equals ⅔ x 12 = 8 printer points per stop. Much testing has borne out the fact that one camera stop change in exposure equals 8 points of printer density. At extreme ends of the printer scale it may vary a point or so from that, but using 8 points is always the best rule to follow.

MONITORING THE PROCESS

It must be pointed out that all manufacturing processes are subject to variables and, as such, acceptable tolerances are set to ensure success without being unreasonably demanding. The same principal applies to the processing of film.

Through the use of a device called a densitometer, labs can measure the processing of film and determine how far off of a predetermined standard the negative is printing. By measuring a photographed gray scale, the accuracy of original negative exposure can be measured. Most major laboratories have the ability to expose a 21-step gray scale into an original negative, which, when each step is measured and plotted, can produce a curve that will illustrate a negative's characteristics (sensitivity, gamma/contrast, highlight/sshadow detail, etc.).

Labs have control departments whose principal purpose is to constantly monitor the negative and positive processes, and calibrate the printers. Printer calibration is, in fact, one of the areas most subject to drift, as the lamp in each printer is constantly migrating color and brightness as it ages. Through exposing predetermined exposure strips through the printers, the control department can keep the printers on target by adjusting their trims.

While film manufacturers can always provide you with the characteristic curve of any specific emulsion batch, if you're uncertain about an emulsion (due to age, transport conditions, possible exposure to radiation, etc.), the lab will happily expose a section of your negative with a 21-step gray scale, process the negative and plot the negative's curve, so you will immediately be able to see what condition your emulsion is in. When compared with the curves supplied by the manufacturer of that emulsion batch, you can precisely determine if this batch has shifted.

I'd like to make a comment here about professional motion picture negatives. It is always assumed that motion picture negatives will be used within six months or so of manufacture, and once exposed, will be processed within 72 hours. Negatives older than six months run the risk of a high base fog density that will result in milky blacks in your print. Motion picture films don't remotely have the latent image stability of still-camera films, which is why they need to be processed promptly or refrigerated at very low temperatures when timely processing isn't possible.

For consistent tracking and monitoring of processing from lab to lab, the industry came up with Laboratory Aim Density, or LAD.

With LAD, film laboratories can determine how far off of a reference standard they are when printing. We are principally concerned with LAD for color positives printed from original negative; however, there are LAD values for interpositives and internegatives as well. Again, a densitometer is used to read a predefined "LAD patch" on a print. The RGB/YCM LAD value is the same for all Eastman Kodak Motion Picture negatives. Fuji elements have their own LAD values.

LAD values for all Kodak negatives are: 0.80 Red, 1.20 Green and 1.60 Blue.

Cutting in of a LAD reference frame is standard operating procedure for answer printing at film laboratories. This enables the answer-print timer to know exactly where any given print stands vs. the LAD reference point. Reading of the LAD patch lets the timer know if the print is leaning one way or another in color or density. It's always advisable before beginning a screening of any answer print to ask the timer how the print is, or "What's the chart reading?" The timer will then express to you the values for each color and how far off of standard, plus or minus, the print is.

While not standard, it's not out of the question to ask to have a LAD patch cut into your dailies each day, and have the patch read so you can know how far off of standard your daily prints may be. If this is requested, also understand that it adds one more part to the delivery of your print dailies, and will delay their delivery ever so slightly. When printing one-light dailies, an advantage of a LAD patch cut into your dailies is you will know immediately if color drift is the cause of the laboratory or your own cinematography.

As for tolerance in LAD readings, understand that for camera negative, 0.025 Log E equals one point. For release prints, the lab should be allowed a swing of 0.05 Log E (two points) on any individual color; however, you shouldn't have to be tolerant of anything more than 0.05 Log E sway in any of the readings (especially for answer prints), but how tolerant you want to be is at your discretion.

An example of how this procedure is implemented at a lab might be as follows:

You travel to the laboratory to screen a reel of your movie with the answer print timer. As you settle into your seat, you ask, "How did this print come up?," "What's the chart reading for this print?" or "How are we doing today?"

While the timer is provided the precise Log E value plus or minus from the standard, he or she will usually do some quick math and express its values in light points. For example, you might hear, "It came up plus one, zero, minus a half," which would translate into plus one point red, on target for green and minus a half point of blue (unless you are at a lab that uses subtractive colors, where they would be referring to yellow, cyan, and magenta). That being said, they will happily provide you with the precise Log E values if you request it, remembering that 0.025 Log E translates into one printer point.

EXPOSURE REPORTING

It used to be normal practice for laboratories to furnish one-light rather than timed daily rush prints. However, most labs today find that, to be competitive, they must offer scene-to-scene timing of dailies. That being said, timed dailies usually yield an inconsistent workprint since they end up being timed on an individual basis each day.

The term "one-light dailies" doesn't mean that all negatives are printed at the same light points. The laboratory establishes a day exterior, day interior, night exterior and night interior light points for each film stock a cinematographer may choose when he or she starts a picture, based on the first few days of shooting. Each laboratory establishes its own method, but basically all try to keep usable negative within the 1 to 50 light point scale (laboratories do not necessarily agree on the numerical value of the preferred mid-scale light point, but this is not critical as long as you know which system your laboratory uses). A conference with your laboratory representative will establish methods that fit your style of photography. After that, variation in your exposure will show up as variation in the density of your solid black in any area of the print; exposure must be kept at or above what the laboratory tells you is their average light point for a well-exposed piece of film.

Should you feel uncomfortable committing to one-light dailies, at least instruct your dailies timer/grader to try and use the same color and density ratio light point, should you be shooting the same scene for several days at a time. This will mitigate color shifts from timing the dailies on their own merits each day.

Negative raw stock from different manufacturers may or may not have the same base density, maximum density or density/exposure characteristic (curve shape), although these differences are usually small. A daily print made by the LAD control method shows the density and color ratio at mid-scale on the printer. Negative from two manufacturers, both exposed correctly, may or may not look the same at this printer point. If necessary, an adjustment to the printer point may be made for the difference in raw stock, and this new light point can be used for printing dailies on the subject.

SPECIAL PROCESSING

If special processing is requested, a conference with the laboratory representative and experimentation (or experience) is desirable. If special processing is requested, or the cinematographer is using high or low exposure for effect, it is desirable to test the effect by going through the entire release-print technique, including the interpositive/duplicate negative generations, and to view the result as nearly as possible under the anticipated release-print viewing conditions. If the scene to be photographed will be used in an optically printed visual-effect, it is wise to confer with the appropriate visual-effects experts.

RELEASE PRINTING PROCEDURES

After the picture negative and soundtrack negative have been assembled in their final form, the laboratory will analyze the picture negative for scene-to-scene color and density variations and make a print known as the first trial answer print. As many trial prints are made as are necessary to resolve all printing data. The final approved timing is also often known as a final answer print. With the data thus obtained, one or more intermediates are printed and from these the release prints are made. Modern film stocks used to make the interpositives and internegatives or intermediate negatives are of excellent quality, but they do entail added printing generations. The appearance of scenes involving effects such as off-normal film exposure or processing can suffer if they exceed the extremes the system can handle. (See also Testing and Evaluation.)

COLOR REVERSAL FILMS

Most of the above also applies to color reversal films; however, color reversal films are now usually used only when it is intended to project the original, or for a desired visual effect. Exposure latitude is short compared to that of color negative films. Proper exposure is therefore critical in order to keep all scenes at a usable density.

BLACK-AND-WHITE NEGATIVE AND REVERSAL FILMS

The above also applies to black-and-white reversal films. Black-and-white negative films, however, are an exception. Both their contrast and density are more strongly affected by developing time than are color negative films.

While there is much more latitude in exposure with black-and-white negative films as compared to color negative films, both grain and acutance are affected by exposure variations. Deviation from the manufacturers' recommended EI (exposure index) should be tested and evaluated.

FORCED DEVELOPMENT OF COLOR FILMS

With the color films most commonly used today, it is possible to compensate for underexposure by extended development, or "pushing." Similar to the principles of traditional black-and-white sensitometry, forced development of these color films increases their contrast, graininess and the fog level.

Therefore, forced development can never yield the same image quality possible when films are exposed and processed strictly according to the manufacturer's recommendations. In many instances, however, the image quality obtained with underexposure and overdevelopment is entirely satisfactory, and a cinematographer may want to take advantage of this fact when shooting under adverse light conditions. What pushing means, in effect, is that the cinematographer can deliberately underexpose the film (sometimes by as much as two stops) and request that the laboratory compensate in development.

With the introduction of high-speed color negative emulsions, there is less call for pushing the moderate-speed films, except for a special "look" or when underexposure is unavoidable and high-speed negative is not at hand. It is possible to push one stop in development without appreciable loss in image quality. The scenes produced in this manner can be intercut with scenes exposed and processed normally.

If color negative is pushed two stops in development, the increase in the graininess and the fog level is substantial, but the results are acceptable for scenes involving night-for-night photography or available-light photography under exceptional circumstances.

Extending development beyond two stops does not appreciably contribute to the image; rather, it increases the grain and fog level and should not be attempted even as an emergency measure. It should be realized that with color films the sensitometric balance of the three emulsion layers is only achieved with normal processing and that forcing the development does not accomplish a true compensation for underexposure. Forced development does not result in a substantial increase in the exposure index of the negative as measured by accepted scientific methods. Nevertheless, it cannot be denied that the technique proves to be of some practical value if it brings the underexposed negative into an acceptable printing range.

Reversal films, unlike negative, derive their projection density from the camera exposure. Forced processing of underexposed film can bring up the projection density to normal. Eastman Ektachrome Films 7240 and 7285 (tungsten balanced), can be pushed one stop with acceptable results. In emergency situations they can be pushed up to three stops with some loss in quality. The ability to underexpose these films and still obtain on film a usable image should by no means be regarded as a suitable substitute for additional lighting when it can be provided.

If a cinematographer anticipates the need for deliberate underexposure during a production, he or she should, if possible, shoot careful tests in advance using the same emulsion that to be used for the production and have them processed by the lab that will be processing the production film. The results can then be analyzed with the help of a laboratory representative. Needless to say, underexposed rolls should be clearly marked with instructions as to how much they should be pushed when they are sent to the laboratory.

FLASHING

Even before discussing flashing, it must be said that one lab's measurement of a flash is not likely to match how another lab measures it. Thus, don't base a request for a type of flash on an experience at another lab; testing is critically important.

Flashing may be described qualitatively as subjecting the negative film to a weak, controlled, uniform fogging exposure prior to development—either before, during or after photographing the desired subject. There is no measurable difference in the effect if the flashing takes place before or after the principal exposure. As a result, because of various unfavorable factors (such as not being able to control the time interval between the flash exposure and the time that development will actually take place, and not knowing the actual conditions of photography in advance), preflashing is generally avoided in favor of postflashing.

Simultaneous flashing during actual photography by means of a special device attached to the front of the camera lens is described shortly under the heading Lightflex. However, if not properly controlled, flashing on the camera in the field runs the risk of an imprecise and improperly color-balanced flash.

Since color negative consists basically of three emulsion layers sensitive to red, green and blue light, the spectral composition of the light used for flashing can be a neutral equivalent to tungsten light (3200°K) or daylight (5500°K) which, depending on the film, would affect all three emulsion layers equally. The fundamental reasons for using a neutral flash are to reduce the contrast of the image and to increase shadow detail. This effect is accomplished because the flashing exposure affects principally the shadow region of the negative image.

Another reason for flashing is to achieve certain creative effects by using a nonneutral flashing exposure that would then alter the normal color rendition of the developed negative.

Flashing is also used sometimes to reduce contrast of positive or reversal films when such films are to be used for special effects duplication purposes, such as projection backgrounds or aerial image compositing with animation.

Some good examples of negative flashing can be seen in the films *McCabe and Mrs. Miller, Heaven's Gate* and *Deliverance*, all shot by Vilmos Zsigmond, ASC. In *Heaven's Gate*, Vilmos combined a 10% negative flash with a 30% positive flash (as measured at Technicolor).

LIGHTFLEX

Lightflex (and Arriflex Varicon) is an on-camera accessory, mounted in front of the lens, which overlays a controlled amount of light on the scene to be photographed at the time of exposure. It allows the cameraperson to modify the gamma curve of the film in the camera during shooting. This can extend the photometric range of the film, and provide more detail in the shadow areas without affecting grain.

Lightflex works exactly the same with video cameras, providing more shadow area detail with no increase in noise. A filter tray between light sphere and reflector permits colored light overlay for special effects. The system's lamphouse holds three quartz bulbs that operate selectively or simultaneously to hold color temperature stable over the widest possible range. Compound curved reflectors cover all standard 16mm and 35mm fixed lenses and zooms.

Intensity control is by a handheld electronic dimmer with a digital $\frac{1}{10}$-volt line indicator. The lamphouse front features a built-in Obie light, with changeable masks for direct or diffused light. The unit housing is mounted on a swing-away bracket to facilitate lens changes and maintenance. There are two front-mounted matte box shades for wide angle or normal lenses. There are two lens filter stages: one for two 3" x 3" filters and one for two 4" x 4" or 4" x 5.6" filters or grads (rotatable). A single 4" x 5.6" filter may be mounted inside the Lightflex housing.

Panavision's Panaflasher achieves similar results with an internal device.

Emulsion Testing

by Steven Poster, ASC

The object of these series of tests is to determine the best working exposure index and the dynamic range for your original camera negative. This system takes into account any processing techniques, print stocks, further duping of the original camera negative and the effects of scanning and digital output.

Judging these tests should be done visually, although densitometer readings should be taken for later reference. It is more important to train your eye to see the various characteristics of the chain of events that result in the presentation of images that we create during production than to know scientifically all of the sensitometry that goes into the imaging system.

PREPARING BENCH TEST NEGATIVE

The basic physical nature of the film stock (i.e., how much density there is in the negative without any exposure) must be calibrated.

If you are going to test or use other film stocks and/or processing techniques, these should also be calibrated at this time. If the negative is going to be push- or pull-processed, or if it is going to be flashed, or skip-bleach processed, or if you create a negative by cross-processing reversal stock, these special treatments should also be done in the prescribed way at this time. You can measure the specific densities of the base density plus fog levels on a densitometer for reference. (This reference can be used later if there is a change of emulsion or lab, or just as a simple check on your standard emulsion.)

We know that this specific density will be used to reproduce a black tone on the final print. If this density on the negative is not printed deep enough to reproduce a desirable black on the print stock, there will be no black tones in the final print, and the images will be appear to have been underexposed. If this is the case, the images can also develop a grainy appearance and will not dupe well.

The lab should process a short length of unexposed negative no less than 50' in length. At this point you have a piece of unexposed, processed negative that reflects any pre-exposure or special processing techniques done to that negative. You should also have noted reference densities of that negative. This leads us to the second part of the test.

PRINTED BLACK TEST

In order to determine the specific amount of light needed to print your test negative to a desirable black tone, you must test the print stock and any printing techniques (flashing the print stock, ENR, CCR, optical printing, digital scanning or print skip-bleach processing for example). This is done by printing your piece of unexposed processed film stock at a succession of printer lights increasing by 2 to 4 points of density (the equivalent of ⅓ of a stop of printer exposure at your lab). If you are planning to use any unusual printing techniques or print processing techniques, they should be applied at this point. Any subsequent printing for these series of tests should have these techniques applied as well.

A trick that I have often used to help me judge my optimum black density is to punch a hole in the negative with a single-hole paper punch before it is printed. This will give you a reference to zero density in the frame, which can help determine the optimal visual black tone that you want. Your desired black tone will never be as black as the portion printed through the hole, but the reference helps to determine what density you will want to achieve with your processing and printing techniques.

If your lab has film-strip projectors that they use for timing purposes, this is a very good way to view these tests. Two identical prints can be made which can be viewed side by side on these projectors, allowing you to study the results and compare different densities. If no filmstrip projectors are available, the length of each exposure should be long enough to allow you time to view it sufficiently on the screen during projection.

Once you have determined which density you would like to represent black in your final print, this should be read on the densitometer and used for later reference. You can also read the densities of each level of printer lights to see where reciprocity sets in, although this is not actually necessary because this density will probably be deeper than you will actually be using to print.

A test for no-density print highlights can also be done at this time by printing a piece of opaque leader at the determined printer lights and reading the resulting density. The difference between your chosen black density and the resulting white density will determine the dynamic range of the print stock. In order to determine the speed and working range of your negative in relation to that print stock, further testing is necessary.

You should now have an optimum black density and a reference to the intensity of the printer lights that will be required at your lab to achieve that density with your chosen negative stock, as well as any unusual processing methods and any variation in printing techniques that you choose to use. This brings us to the third part of the test.

EXPOSURE CALIBRATION

This will be the first camera test that will provide the working speed or exposure index (EI) that will allow you to judge the exposure necessary to represent the values photographed as normal tones on the final print, when that print is made using the recommended density arrived at during the first two parts of these tests. You must determine the amount of light that it will require to properly photograph a midgray tone when the negative is printed to the benchmark density.

There are several things I would like to mention at this point about testing methods. Everybody has their own method of measuring light values. There are probably as many methods as there are people taking exposure readings. If your meter and method of reading works for you, it is correct.

I prefer to use a spot meter and take my neutral readings off of a Permanent Gray Card. I feel that this gives me a consistent and accurate way of judging not only the light falling on a subject but the reflectance of that subject as well. For these tests I also like to vary the amount of light falling on the subject rather than changing the T-stop on the lens. I feel that this method gives me a more accurate series of exposures because there is no reliable way to vary the stop by fractions due to the variables and tolerances of the lens iris. As you see later extreme exposures will be needed. In these cases I may vary exposure speed but never T-stop.

The lighting for these tests require flat, even illumination over the surface of the subject like copy light (light from two sides of the subject, at a 45° angle from the camera). The color temperature of the light should be as close to 3200° Kelvin as you can get, except in tests of daylight film, when 5500° Kelvin should be used.

If you are planning to use filtration (such as diffusion of some kind), these filters should be used in all subsequent tests. This is because some of these filters can tend to absorb light. Even though this effect will be very slight, it can affect the results of your tests by as much as ⅔ of a stop when you use heavy filtration.

Make a series of exposures of an 8" x 10" gray card and a face with neutral skin tone at a series of stops based on variations in the manufacturer's recommended exposure index. Start the series at one stop under the EI and decrease the exposure by ⅓ of a stop until you reach one stop over the recommended speed.

For instance, if you were testing an emulsion with a recommended speed of 500, you would start your test at an EI of 1000 and proceed to an EI of 250 in ⅓-stop increments, resulting in seven different exposures.

Remember, don't vary the T-stop. Change the amount of light to give the proper exposure at the T-stop you are using.

Print the negative at the benchmark density arrived at in the second part of the test, adjusting the printer ratio (color balance) to reproduce a neutral gray. Read the print density of the gray in each exposure. A proper midgray print density for theater viewing should be R/1.09, G/1.06 and B/1.03 (status A filters).

LABORATORY AIM DENSITY				
	RED	**GREEN**	**BLUE**	
Color Negative	.80	1.20	1.60	0
2383/2393 Color Print	1.09	1.06	1.03	0
5242 Master Positive	1.15	1.60	1.70	± 0.10 Aim
2242 Dupe Negative	1.0	1.45	1.55	± 0.10 Aim

View the print to determine which print is closest to that recommended density. Look carefully at the quality of the color balance of the skin tones in relation to the gray card. If an emulsion cannot reproduce skin tones properly when the gray card is printed correctly (or vice versa), this is a good indication that there are problems with either the emulsion or the lab processes that have taken place. If this is the case when the skin tones are printed properly in the final print, there will always be problems getting the proper color balance in the shadows.

The print that is chosen as the best representation of the gray card and skin tone will become the midpoint in the dynamic range of your negative. Check which exposure index was used for this test. This EI will become your empirical emulsion speed. Most often I have found that the EI that is derived will be within ⅓ of a stop of the manufacture's recommended speed unless some form of processing modification is used (such as push- or pull-processing).

TESTING FOR DYNAMIC RANGE

This is the part of the testing process that will determine the usable dynamic range of your negative when exposed, processed and printed using the information gathered in the previous tests.

Make a series of exposures using a Macbeth Color Checker color chart, an 8" x 10" gray card, a small gray scale and a face with neutral skin tone. Mount the color chart vertically with the gray card in the middle and the scale vertically next to the gray card all on one piece of card. Mount this card on a grip stand and place it over the head of the model. This allows you to fill the frame with the cards and then tilt down to see the face. Shoot the chart and the face each for a minimum of 10 seconds (more if you can afford the film) so that you will have enough time to study the results on the screen. If you are comparing emulsions or processing techniques, repeat these tests for each variation.

Using the EI that you derived from the last test, start the series of exposures at normal and underexpose successively until you reach five stops underexposed. Do the same with overexposure.

For example:

First Series	Second Series
Normal	Normal
1 Stop Under	1 Stop Over
1⅓ Stops Under	2 Stops Over
1⅔ Stops Under	3 Stops Over
2 Stops Under	3⅓ Stops Over
2⅓ Stops Under	3⅔ Stops Over
2⅔ Stops Under	4 Stops Over
3 Stops Under	4⅓ Stops Over
3⅓ Stops Under	5 Stops Over
4 Stops Under	
5 Stops Under	

The reason for the uneven increments of exposure is based on experience. I know that the first shadow detail will fall somewhere in the range of 2 and 3 stops underexposed and that the last highlight detail will fall between 4 and 5 stops over. I also know from experience that the increments between 1 and 2 are very useful shadow densities to have as a visual reference.

Print these tests again at the benchmark densities. View the work print to make sure the color ratios are correct. At this point, if possible, an interpositive, dupe negative and final print should be produced using any special printing techniques or digital manipulation intended for the final release (such as ENR, flashing the interpositive, or scanning). This will allow you to view the results as they would be viewed in the theater. If this is not possible, enough useful information can be gleaned by viewing the work print.

When you view the results projected, either in motion or on strip projectors, you will begin to see the effects of exposure on different tones and colors. If you are comparing different emulsions or processing techniques, the results should be viewed side by side for proper comparison.

The exposure difference between first shadow detail and last highlight detail and their relation to midgray will determine the empirical dynamic range of the negative, processing and printing combination.

CONCLUSION:
TRUST YOUR EYE MORE THAN YOUR METER

It is important to remember that these tests are not scientific but empirical. They are meant to train your eye to the dynamic range of your emulsion under working conditions. The tests should be a good working reference. In fact, I have often taken frames of each exposure and mounted them in slide mounts for viewing on the set if I want to know exactly where to place a specific tone on the scale so that it will be represented exactly as I want in the final print. To do this, you will need a small light box properly color-corrected and with an illumination of 425 FC ±10%.

It is most important to learn to trust your eye rather than relying upon too many exposure readings. These tests should give you a better understanding of the results of exposing, processing and printing your original camera negative so that you can predict exactly what the images you make will look like. With this knowledge, you should be able to make more consistent, dramatic images that will help tell the story of your motion picture.

Steven Poster, ASC is President of the International Cinematographers Guild and a vice chair of the ASC's Technology Committee. He is a current member of the committee for the Nicholl Fellowship of the Academy of Motion Picture Arts and Sciences and a former member of the Executive Board of the International Documentary Association.

Finding Your Own Printer Light

by Richard Crudo, ASC

Among the numerous tests to be performed before starting a project destined for theatrical presentation, perhaps the most valuable one is the test that establishes a single printer light setting to be used in dailies printing. Although not connected to lighting in the literal sense, a direct relation does exist in that a consistent printer light precisely determines how lighting will be rendered on screen, and by extension influences the final release print's texture. The use of a single, predetermined set of numbers takes the guesswork out of the laboratory's dailies printing protocol and places total control of the film's look where it belongs—in the hands of the cinematographer.

Each night, dailies timers scroll an incredible amount of negative through their color analyzers. These tens of thousands of feet are culled from a wide range of productions shot under a variety of circumstances. Very often, their only guidance in determining what information gets sent to the printer is an unintelligible scrawl at the bottom of a camera report—print cool, print warm, day-for-night, dawn effect and so on. While lab technicians are pretty good at drawing meaning from the indefinable, when using a single printer light setting—arrived at through one's own choosing—the problems caused by relying on vague, highly personal and subjective written or verbal descriptions are eliminated. In addition, working in this manner allows the cinematographer to introduce any amount of variation in color and density to the image in a quantifiable and repeatable way. Whether these changes are effected through filtration used on the lens, gels over the lamps or by ordering a measured shift in the printer light itself is a matter of taste and experience. Then, when a deviation from the norm occurs or a new batch of raw stock brings a shift in the film's look, the anomaly becomes easy to isolate and correct. Assuming the lab's chemistry is up to code, the immediate payoff is day-to-day image consistency on par with the still photographer's vaunted "previsualization." For the long term, answer and release printing are much simpler affairs, since making corrections is a matter of fine-tuning rather than a complete rebalancing of the entire film.

PREPARATIONS FOR AN EMULSION TEST TO ESTABLISH A SINGLE PRINTER LIGHT (TUNGSTEN)

First, understand that the one-light print enabled by this test is markedly different in concept from what dailies personnel commonly refer to in the same words. Left to its own devices, any lab can deliver a one-light print every day. The difference is that since the dailies timer is making color and density choices on his or her own, the lab's version will inevitably change its R-G-B Hazletine values from negative roll to negative roll or even among different shots and setups within each roll. The printer light that ultimately results from the following procedure is something chosen by the cinematographer, and is meant for use in all situations matching the lighting conditions under which the test is performed. Thus, it is possible—indeed preferable—to shoot an entire feature film on the same printer light. That said, it is also viable to establish printer lights for defined situations, (i.e., day/exterior, day/interior, night/exterior, night/interior, etc.).

Preliminaries

A. Make sure that camera body and lens tests are already completed and approved.

B. Secure a pair of showcards flat against a wall, end-to-end in a horizontal fashion. The black side of one of the cards should be placed on the left, the white side of the second card on the right.

C. Recruit a model with a representative fleshtone. The term "representative" is somewhat ambiguous in its use here, but that is part of what this test is trying to determine. Avoid extreme complexions or coloring of any kind unless you anticipate dealing with them during principal photography. Also, make sure that your model dresses in neutral shades rather than solid blacks or whites or any heavily saturated colors.

D. Using a lens from your tested, matched production set, compose the shot so that the two showcards completely fill the frame. Place your model directly facing the lens, just slightly in front of the center seam where the two showcards meet. In 1.85 format, a 40mm lens works well at a distance of about eight feet and renders a pleasingly medium close-up of the model.

E. Create a series of individual flash cards that the model will hold within the frame to clearly indicate the exposure information relevant to each take:

NORMAL	+1½	-½	-2
+½	+2	-1	NORMAL
+1	NORMAL	-1½	

F. In addition to a gray card, the following information should be mounted in a plainly readable fashion somewhere within the frame but not in such a way as to impede sight of the model:
  - emulsion type and batch/cut numbers
  - ASA/Exposure Index
  - lens focal length

- T-stop
- development information (normal, push, pull, ENR, CCE, etc.)
- print stock type
- optional: color temperature of the light source you're using

Lighting

A 2K fresnel is an ideal unit to use with this test. Placed at an angle of about 20 degrees off camera right, make sure the light is evenly spread at full flood across both the model and the two showcards—with no hot spots or dropoff of any kind. From this position, the lamp serves a dual purpose by not only properly illuminating the model but by throwing the model's shadow onto the black-sided showcard that covers the left half of frame. The deep, rich, velvety darkness this provides will serve as an important point of reference when judging the projected print.

Do not use any diffusion on the lamp and do not add any light to the fill side.

ASA/Exposure Index

Since film speed is a relative concept, the best starting point is to rate the negative at the manufacturer's suggested value. Besides providing the information necessary to choose a single printer light for the run of the show, this test will also allow the setting of an effective ASA/EI rating for the manner in which the film is to be exposed.

T-Stop

In the interest of contrast uniformity and the elimination of as many variables as possible, lock the iris ring at a predetermined T-stop and leave it alone for the length of the test. It should rest precisely at or close to the primary setting intended for use across much of the shoot. Measured exposure shifts will be carried out through adjustments in lighting intensity and a combination of neutral-density filters and shutter-angle changes. (For the purpose of this article, the working stop for the test will be T2.8.)

Filters

If plans for principal photography include the use of filters in front of or behind the lens, slip the appropriate grade into the matte box or filter slot before you begin the test.

Laboratory Instructions

The camera report should prominently display the following orders:

▶ Develop—(normal, push, pull, ENR, CCE, etc.)
▶ Print this negative roll two times.
▶ First pass: print on best light for gray card/normal exposure only.

▶ Second pass: correct each take back to normal in ½ stop (4 points each)* increments.

▶ Note well: normal exposures should all print at the same light in all cases.

▶ Do not join these rolls together or to any other roll.

By keeping the two test rolls separate, you will be able to view them in rapid succession without having to deal with any other distracting material.

Basically, the one-light printing of the gray card and normal takes—and thus the timing of the entire first roll—allows the dailies timer a fighting chance at showing his or her interpretation of what will look best onscreen with respect to the lab's processing standards and the conditions set up by the cinematographer. The second uncorrected printing pass insures that you will see the effect over- and underexposure will have on the emulsion in its purest state—without any assistance or augmentation from the lab. Examining both rolls together essentially defines a place from which the lab timer and cinematographer can begin to deviate.

Note: For purposes of this test, it is given that the laboratory's system is calibrated so that 8 printer points equal one T-stop on the lens.

Miscellaneous

▶ Beware of ambient light or anything else that might compromise the test's integrity.

▶ Be meticulous with meter readings. If you choose an iris setting of T2.8, your normal exposure should read precisely T2.8 at the model's face. Measuring the increase in light level needed to support the overexposure parts of the test should be handled with equal care.

▶ Do a separate test for each emulsion you plan to use and each lighting condition you plan on encountering.

▶ Be sure the model clearly displays the placards indicating the proper exposure for the take being photographed.

▶ Don't rush.

The Test

First, fill the frame with a gray card. Light it to T2.8 and expose 20 feet at the same value.

Next, recompose to fill the frame with the black and white showcards, featuring the model at the center seam.

Following the notations in each column, expose 30 feet for each step as noted:

(Note that after the first normal exposure the light level increases from T2.8 to T5.6. This is done to facilitate the overexposure takes. The standard iris setting here is T2.8, so before starting the test, simply light the model to T5.6 and then use two double scrims on the 2K Fresnel to knock down the intensity to T2.8 when needed.)

If overexposure is to be carried as far as +3 stops, the basic light level must be increased to T8 to accommodate that portion of the test. Proportional changes should then be made to the scrims and shutter angle/neutral density filter combinations.

The Results

When viewing the projected film, refer to the lab's printer-light notation sheet that corresponds to the test exposures.

You should speak to your lab contact as to what is considered a "normal" printing light for the lab you are using; however, we will assume for this article that a "normal" printer light would read 25-25-25. Roll 1 will now obviously play all the way through at light 25-25-25. Any exposure changes noted on screen will thus be a direct result of what was done at the lens. This pass is especially helpful in gauging color drift as it relates to exposure. It is also a good indicator of the emulsion's ability to hold detail at the noted extremes.

Roll 2 is merely a second printing pass of the same negative but with the identical series of exposures corrected back to normal in measured increments by the Hazletine timer. Based on the concept of 25 across being normal, refer to the following boxed chart for the progression of printer lights (assuming a laboratory printing scale of 8 points = 1 stop).

In this instance, the dailies timer has "helped out" by correcting "mistakes" in exposure. The second pass thus provides an idea of how far the emulsion can be stretched before it falls apart. Special attention should be paid to the white and black showcards that make up the background behind the model. Grain, color shift and variation in detail will be most readily apparent in these areas. This pass can also provide information about contrast. If necessary, it may be requested that the laboratory print "over scale" in order to achieve correction on an overexposure.

Conclusion

Now that the data needed to decide all critical concerns has been revealed, decisions that will directly affect the film's look can be made in an informed manner. Subjective judgement once again comes into play, but the difference is that the cinematographer is the one doing the judging.

Usually, the model's fleshtone will need some tweaking regardless of which test exposure is most pleasing. Let's say that Eastman 5213 was used at its recommended ASA/EI rating of 200. While viewing results of the corrected Roll 2 on screen, it is decided that the grain structure and shadow detail of the take indicating ½ stop overexposure (printed back to normal) looks best. By referencing the lab's printer light notation sheet, this would render a printer light of 29-29-29 to start and therefore an effective ASA/EI rating of 160. A desire for a different sort of fleshtone might lead the cinematographer to order a small adjustment in the addition of perhaps 1 point red and 2 points yellow. The resulting printer light of 28-29-31 would then be the one to use during principal photography. To verify the effect, it would be advisable to shoot an additional test under identical conditions with the same model, while printing it at these new numbers.

Hereafter, by having the assistant cameraperson stamp 28-29-31 in the camera report's printing instructions box, the cinematographer can be certain of two things. Besides meeting a specific standard that depends solely on the effort put into each shot, such items as silhouette effects will indeed come back from the lab as silhouettes—each and every time. Instead of communicating with such agonizing vagaries as "print for highlights," this simple set of numbers conveys to the dailies timer exactly what is needed in a way that will stand up in court. This isn't to say, however, that the printer lights are by any means sacrosanct. Over the long haul of shooting a feature, modifications are inevitable.

Ultimately, however, what is most important is that the cinematographer is always the one who chooses how and when to do the modifying.

Richard Crudo, ASC currently serves on the Academy of Motion Picture Arts and Sciences Board of Governors, and is a former ASC President and current ASC Vice President. He has photographed the feature films Federal Hill, American Buffalo, American Pie *and* Down to Earth.

Adjusting Printer Lights to Match a Sample Clip

by Bill Taylor, ASC

Here's a low-tech but usefully accurate method for modifying printer lights "in the field" to match the color of a film clip, using CC Wratten filters.

You'll need a light box with a color temperature around 5400°K, a cardboard mask with two closely-spaced, side-by-side frame-size holes cut into it and a set of color correction filters of .05, .10, .20, .30, .40, and .50 values in Yellow, Cyan, Magenta, and Neutral Density. (Kodak Wratten CC filters are expensive and fragile to use as viewing filters, however they will last a long time if handled carefully. PC filters retired from darkroom or still photo use are just fine. You may be able to find less-expensive plastic substitutes.) You'll also need a loupe with a field big enough to see at least part of both frames.

Put the mask on the light box, put the sample print film clip (the one to match) over the left-hand mask aperture. Put the target print (to be reprinted) over the right-hand aperture. (The mask keeps your eyes from being dazzled by white light leaking around the film frame.)

It's a two-step process.

MATCH OVERALL BRIGHTNESS

Looking at the midtones of the two prints, add ND filters under one clip or the other until the brightness is an approximate match. It's much easier if there's a similar subject in both frames!

COLOR ADJUSTMENT

Estimate the color shift needed to bring the color of the target clip around to match the sample. For example if the sample is a too blue, add yellow filters. If it's too cyan, add yellow and magenta. If the target clip now looks too dark with the color filters added, remove some ND from the target (or add it to the sample). With practice, you'll be able to get a reasonable match. From time to time, look away for a moment at a neutral color so your eyes will not get tired.

Now add up the color filters (ignore the ND's for now). Let's say you added a total CC .15 magenta and .30 yellow to the target print. Consult the table below for the correction needed in printer points.

ADJUSTING THE PRINTER LIGHTS

Make the first correction of the printing lights, adjusting color only. The printer lights are usually listed in Cyan, Magenta, Yellow order on the light card, or the corresponding printer filters Red, Green and Blue, respectively. But don't think about Red, Green and Blue when you're dealing with color print! The layers in color print produce Cyan, Magenta and Yellow dye, so if you think in those terms, you can't get confused.

Let's say the hypothetical target print, which needs 2 printer points of Magenta and 4 points of Yellow to bring it around, originally printed on C 25, M 22 and Y 34.

Adding 2 points of Magenta and 4 points of yellow yields an adjusted printer light of C 25, M 24 and Y 38.

Now let's get back to the ND's. Assume you wound up with .30 ND over the target print, which was too light as well as needing the color correction. Per the table, you should add 4 printer points across. So the new, final printing light is C 29, M 28, and Y 42.

If you had to lay the ND filters over the sample print instead, that meant that the target print was too dark. So subtract the neutral printer point adjustment instead of adding. If it needs to be .30 daarker, subtract 4 printer points across, and so forth.

This method requires mid-tones in both clips. If the target clip is mostly highlights (on the "toe" of the print curve), it will take more correction to "move" them to where you want. Obviously a burned-out specular highlight on the print will not change at all from a modest printer light correction.

A very dark scene is also hard to correct. Adjust the lightest detail you can find, preferably a skin tone.

With experience the filter adjustments will become second nature easy and the arithmetic automatic; you'll be calling lights like a film lab timer.

PRINTER POINTS = CC CHANGE					
1	=	.10	5	=	.35
2	=	.15	5	=	.40
3	=	.20	6	=	.45
3	=	.25	7	=	.50
4	=	.30	8	=	.60

Why it works: color print stock has a gamma of about 3, meaning, as an exmple, that a CC .10 (log E) change in exposure produces a change of .30 density. Each printer point equals CC .025 change in exposure, so it takes 4 printer points to produce that .30 change. The table shows calculations to the nearest whole printer point.

Cinemagic of the Optical Printer

by Linwood G. Dunn, ASC

Lin Dunn, the author of this article, is one of the motion-picture industry's most accomplished pioneers. Involved with the design and origins of the first optical printers, Dunn remained vibrantly active in the industry throughout his life and applauded the introduction of CGI techniques that, in many ways, obviated many of the needs for his optical printer. Dunn is responsible for the effects you can and can't see in Citizen Kane, *and literally hundreds of film projects after that. He was always on the cutting edge, and in his nineties founded of one of the first companies to develop digital cinema,* Real Image Digital. *Dunn's passing in May 1998 was a loss to all who were fortunate enough to be on the receiving end of his generous knowledge and skill; his was also the loss of one of our remaining links to Hollywood's earliest days. Winner of the Gordon E. Sawyer Academy Award from the Motion Picture Academy of Arts and Sciences, and a past President of the ASC, Dunn penned an article that is as relevant today as when he first wrote it. — Editor*

The earliest optical printers were custom-built by the major studios and film laboratories, and were usually designed and made in their own shops to fit their particular requirements. Modern standardized optical printing equipment, capable of creating the innumerable effects heretofore possible only in the major studios, became available to the entire motion picture industry in 1943 with the introduction of the Acme-Dunn Optical Printer, designed and built for the United States Armed Forces Photographic Units. Later the Oxberry, Producers Service, Research Products and other optical printers appeared on the market. Commercial availability of this type of equipment greatly stimulated and widened the scope of the special-effects field. Even the smallest film producers could now make motion pictures with special effects limited only by their imagination and budgets, utilizing the services of growing numbers of independent special-effects laboratories which could now operate competitively using equipment available to all.

Developments over the years of more sophisticated equipment, new duplicating films, special-purpose lenses and improved film-processing techniques, as well as skilled technicians, have increased the use of the optical printer to a point where its great creative and economic value is common knowledge in the motion-picture industry. In more recent years, the adaptation of computer technology to the optical-effects printer has basically simplified the control and accuracy of some of its important functions, thus making it much easier to produce certain complex visual effects at lower cost, as well as to greatly expand its creative scope. This has made it possible to program, record and repeat the movement of certain of its devices with such a degree of accuracy that area-blocking functions can now produce traveling matte composite scenes heretofore highly impractical, if not impossible. One can truly say that the creative capability of the modern visual-effects optical printer is only limited by the creative talent and technical skills of the operator. In recent years, such major film productions as *Star Wars, The Black Hole, The Empire Strikes Back* and *Cocoon* have all utilized the full capabilities of the modern optical printer to create a whole new world of imaginative creativity through their extensive use of very sophisticated motion-picture visual effects. The following list of some of the work that is done on the modern optical printer will illustrate its vast scope and tremendous importance to modern filmmaking.

TRANSITIONAL EFFECTS

Employed to create a definite change in time or location between scenes. The fade, lap dissolve, wipe-off, push-off, ripple dissolve, out-of-focus or diffusion dissolve, flip-over, page turn, zoom dissolve, spin-in and out, and an unlimited variety of film matte wipe effects are all typical examples of the many optical transitional effects possible.

CHANGE OF SIZE OR POSITION

May be used to eliminate unwanted areas, obtain closer angles for extra editing cuts, reposition action for multiple-exposure framing, including montages and backgrounds for titles.

FRAME SEQUENCE MODIFICATION

Screen action may be sped up or slowed down in order to: convert old 16 fps silent films to standard 24 fps sound speed; change speed of action and length of certain scenes or sections of scenes; provide spot frame modification to give realism to specific action in fights, falls, chases, etc.; hold a specific frame for freeze effects and for title backgrounds; add footage for comedy effects; reverse direction of printing to lengthen action and for special effects use; extend scenes through multiple-frame printing for action analysis in instrumentation, training and educational films.

OPTICAL ZOOM

Optical zoom is used to change frame-area coverage and image size during forward and reverse zooming action in order to: produce a dramatic or impact effect (according to speed of the move); counteract or add to the speed and motion of camera zooms or dolly shots; reframe by enlargement and/or add footage to either end of camera zooms or dolly shots by extending the range of moves; momentarily eliminate unwanted areas or objects by zooming forward and back at specific footage points (such as when a microphone or lamp is accidentally framed in during part of a scene); add optical zoom to static scene to match camera zoom or dolly in a superimposure. The out-of-focus zoom also is effective to depict delirium, blindness, retrospect, transition, etc.

SUPERIMPOSURE

Superimposure is the capability used to print an image from one or more films overlaid on one film. This is commonly done in positioning title lettering over backgrounds. Also used for montages, visionary effects, bas relief; adding snow, rain, fog, fire, clouds, lightning flashes, sparks, water reflections and a myriad of other light effects.

SPLIT SCREEN

Employed for multiple image, montage effects, dual roles played by one actor, for dangerous animals shown appearing in the same scene with people (as in *Bringing Up Baby,* which shows Katharine Hepburn working with a leopard throughout the picture), where such split screens move with the action. Matte paintings often utilize this technique when live-action areas require manipulation within an involved composite scene.

QUALITY MANIPULATION

The quality of a scene, or an area within a scene, may be altered in order to create an entirely new scene or special effect or to match it in with other scenes. There are innumerable ways to accomplish this, such as adding or reducing diffusion, filtering, matting and dodging areas, and altering contrast. Often library stock material must be modified to fill certain needs, such as creating night scenes from day; reproducing black-and-white on color film through filtering, printed masks or appropriately coloring certain areas through localized filtering; and the combining of certain areas of two or more scenes to obtain a new scene, such as the water from one scene and the terrain or clouded sky of another.

ADDING MOTION

Employed to create the effect of spinning or rotating, as in plane and auto interiors and in certain montage effects; rocking motion for boat action, sudden jarring or shaking the scene for explosion and earthquake effects; distortion in motion through special lenses for drunk, delirious and visionary effects.

GENERAL USES OF THE OPTICAL PRINTER

The preceding represent some of the special categories of effects that can be produced on the optical printer. The following are a few of the more important general uses employing this useful cinematic tool.

Traveling Mattes

Used to matte a foreground action into a background film made at another time. The various matte systems in use today require the optical printer in order to properly manipulate the separate films to obtain a realistic-quality matching balance between them when combined into a composite. Use of this process has greatly increased as modern techniques produce improved results at reduced costs. Motion control, referred to earlier, has greatly widened the scope of this visual-effects category.

Blow-Ups and Reductions

The fixed set-up optical printer is used for 16mm reduction negatives and prints, and for certain limited release printing from 35mm originals. This is utilized when small volume makes this procedure more economical than through a converted negative, and when maximum quality is of greatest importance. Enlarging from 16mm to 35mm color or black-and-white is a very important function of the optical printer. Many fine theatrical films, such as the Academy Award-winning *The Sea Around Us, The Living Desert* and *Scenes From a Marriage,* have been photographed in 16mm, and have enjoyed great financial success through 35mm release prints made from 35mm blow-up internegatives.

Special new lenses, raw stocks and immersed-movement printing have enhanced the overall quality to a point where the 16mm–35mm blow-up medium is presently enjoying very successful commercial usage. Conversions between 65mm and 35mm are also an important function of the optical printer. Productions made in almost any film format are being release-printed in different types to meet certain theatrical distribution requirements. *The Concert for Bangladesh* was the first feature-length film to be enlarged from 16mm color internegative directly to 70mm theater prints.

Anamorphic Conversions

The standard optical printer equipped with a specially designed "squeeze" or "unsqueeze" lens can be used to produce anamorphic prints from "flat" images, or the function reversed. The possibility of the "flat" or spherical film being converted for anamorphic projection without serious loss of quality has greatly widened this field of theatrical exhibition. The manipulations available on the optical printer also make it possible to scan and reposition any scenes that require reframing when converted to or from widescreen proportion.

DOCTORING, MODIFYING AND SALVAGING

Some of the important uses of the optical printer are not recognized as special effects in the finished film, and often are not apparent as such even to skilled motion-picture technicians. One of these applications is the field of "doctoring" by modifying scenes that, for a variety of reasons, may not be acceptable for use. This includes salvaging scenes that are completely unusable due to some mechanical failure or human error during photography; and also the modification of stock film material through the various methods noted to fit specific requirements. Many expensive retakes have been avoided by the ingenious application of such optical-printing reclamation techniques. The liquid, or immersion, film gate produces dramatic results in the removal of scratches.

Citizen Kane is an excellent example of scene modifications created on the optical printer during the postproduction period. New ideas were applied to existing production scenes for which new supplementary scenes were photographed and integrated to enhance and create various new concepts.

In *It's A Mad, Mad, Mad, Mad World,* an important scene was photographed in which a truck was supposed to back into a shack and knock it over. The breakaway shack was rigged to collapse when wires were pulled on cue. Signals became crossed, and the shack was pulled down well before the truck touched it. A very costly retake was indicated, so the optical printer was called to the rescue. The task of correcting the error through a split screen seemed relatively simple until it was discovered that the camera panned with the falling shack. It then became necessary to plot and move the split matching point frame-by-frame on the optical printer to follow the pan. Through this traveling split-screen technique, the progress of the shack's falling action was delayed until the truck had reached the point of impact. Perhaps the entire cost of the optical printer was saved by this salvaging job alone. Such clever techniques have been used many times to bring explosions close to people working in a scene, such as in *One Minute to Zero,* where a line of so-called refugees were "blown to bits" by artillery shelling. Split screens in motion and trick cuts, with superimposed smoke and flame, did the job in a most effective manner.

NEW SYSTEMS

The optical printer is being used to develop new horizons in the creation of special camera moves within an oversized aperture. This is particularly effective in the creation of camera movement in a composite scene, such as one involving a matte painting, thereby giving a greater illusion of reality.

VistaVision and various 65mm negative formats, including 15-perforation IMAX and 8-perforation Dynavision as well as standard 5-perforation frames, lend themselves to this technique.

Copying onto 4-perforation 35mm makes possible spectacular pans, zooms, dolly shots, etc., without sacrificing screen quality, and with full control over such movements, all of which are created on the optical printer in the internegative stage and made during the postproduction period. Use of this technique makes it possible to avoid time-consuming and complicated setups during production, with the added advantage of flexibility in later change of ideas.

Probably the most exciting new optical-printing development has been in the field of electronics. The adaptation of video image transfer through sophisticated high-resolution scanning systems, in conjunction with the new developments in cathode-ray tubes, lenses, film-moving mechanisms, special-purpose film stocks and the latest research in electronic image compositing, have opened up exciting new vistas in special visual effects. The modification of filmed color motion-picture images through computerized electronic transfer back to film is making it possible to create photographic effects on film or tape faster, more economically, and with a scope of creativity heretofore not possible. The ability to easily and quickly transfer areas or moving objects from one film to another through their instantaneous electronic isolation and self-matting will be of tremendous economic benefit in this area of film production, as well as in stimulating creativity in the wider use of special effects.

Motion-Control Cinematography

by Richard Edlund, ASC

In the 1970s the modern technique of motion-control liberated the long locked-off effects camera from its tripod, giving it freedom to move, becoming an inseparable part of film grammar. Digital image tracking has pulled out the remaining stops, giving complete freedom to the director of photography who wants no restriction of camera movement.

Prior to the advent of digital technology, repetitve control of motion had been attempted with various degrees of success by using analog wire recorders, Selsyn motors and gears, even by hand-cranking mechanisms using a metronome for synchronization. Finally, solid-state digital electronics made it possible to accurately record and play back motion with sufficient reliability to achieve the robotic camera systems necessary to produce the dog-fight and space sequences in *Star Wars*. How appropriate that this technology was born of the space race in the late 1960s. The phenomenal success of *Star Wars* brought on the modern renaissance of motion-picture visual effects, and since that time, a clear majority of the top boxoffice grossers are "effects films" that have relied on motion-control and image tracking for crucial scenes.

To define it, motion control comprises an electromechanical system that allows for the physical motions of a camera and/or other objects—such as models mounted on motorized gimbals, tracks, etc., to be digitally recorded, enabling successive passes to be photographed "on the fly" with the corresponding motion blur characteristics of normal motion picture cameras.

Thus, in combination with traveling matte systems of varying kinds, foregrounds and backgrounds of differing scales can be combined using a moving camera. Composites became possible that could combine separately photographed actors, miniatures, lighting effects, background paintings, pyrotechnics, and myriad other creative possibilities. With the use of synchronized video playback systems, actors could perform within virtual or separately photographed sets and locations, or can interact with themselves, other performers, creatures or miniatures shot previously or subsequently.

Several companies have developed hybrid field motion-control systems. These incorporate specially built or modified gearheads and dollies, which have differing and various facilities, such as panning, tilting, booming, follow-focus, remote operation, preprogrammability, ease of set-up, quietness of operation for sound, high tracking speed, long distance of travel, and adaptability to various production cameras and visual effects cameras.

A visual effects supervisor who is familiar with this paraphernalia should be available to collaborate with the director, director of photography, first assistant director, production designer, and other appropriate crew members to achieve the proper set-up for any given plate. Of course there is responsibility to achieve any given plate within reasonable and predictable set-up time, and for this reason careful preproduction planning is necessary between the contracted visual effects facility and the unit production manager. When shooting bluescreen or greenscreen scenes involving actors within the principal production schedule, the wardrobe should be discussed with the visual effects supervisor to make an attempt to avoid certain colors that might cause matting problems in postproduction.

MOTION-CONTROL EXTENDS
Cinematic Capabilities

Motion-control systems are useful in many ways for visual effects. The following list is certainly not exhaustive:

1. The ability to program model shots so that the motion of objects in an effects scene is believable, and to preview these moves and modify them as needed for approval.
2. The ability to repeat these scenes for front-light/back-light or front-light/ front-light matte passes if needed.
3. The ability to repeat these scenes for enhancement effects such as engine passes, running lights, smoke-room effects, filtration, etc.
4. Precision flyby and extremely close approaches to objects can be accomplished smoothly and in perfect (programmable) focus.
5. Stop-motion and other forms of animation can be subsequently included in live-action scenes that have field recorded moving camera data.
6. Massive rig removals on stage or on location can be easily accomplished with moving split-screen techniques by shooting a clean pass of the background once the director is satisfied with any given take.

Motion Tracking Further Extends Cinematic Capabilities

Modern digital tracking systems have emerged which enable the use of a normal (nonmotion-control) production camera on set, and even Steadicam, which enable the precise camera moves to be mathematically recaptured in a digital post production environment. This technique, while not inexpensive, offers much greater creative freedom on set and saves the production time cost of setting up motion-control cameras, gearheads, dollies, etc. It is also a technique which is in constant development by various effects houses and equipment and software vendors, and that continues to advance. When this technique is to be deployed, it is necessary to shoot geometrically perfect grids, noting focus setting and object to camera distances to aid the computer graphics technicians in discovering the precise distortion characteristics and actual focal length of the particular taking lens that was used.

In most cases, the prospect of using such techniques requires a survey of the set, and/or the use of precisely spaced witness points placed in the set. On long shots, for example, red tennis balls are placed within the shot, and will be painted out during the composite process. The exact positional relationship of these markers must be recorded for use in the mathematically intensive move regeneration process during post-production.

There are production cranes and gearheads available which have encoders on the movement axes which enable the recording of move and position data only for scenes that will have subsequent computer graphic enhancements.

In practice, the production company is best advised to contract with a visual effects supervisor and/or visual effects company to aid production in the carrying out of specific shots and sequences that require these approaches.

Motion-Control Equipment: Visual-Effects Studio

An ideal motion-control system for photographing miniatures consists of a steady pin-registered camera with a motorized follow-focus system mounted on a pan-tilt-roll gearhead (wherein the nodal point of the lens can be situated at the vertex of all three axes) attached to a rotatable boom arm that rides on a track of at least 50 feet in length.

Various model movers, rotators, or pylons are usually mounted on another track of 20 feet or so set perpendicular to the camera track. There are many variations on this basic theme incorporating various levels of engineering prowess within the industry and the precision and reliability of such systems provide the operators with different levels of creative freedom. An electronic control system runs the motors, then stores the motion files created by the operator. Usually stepping motors are used unless considerable speed or power is needed, in which case DC closed-loop servo motors are used.

Studio motion-control equipment often has provisions to control the camera shutter angle over a wide range in order to control the motion blur of objects being photographed. The exposure range is from about ¼ second to extremely long. Most systems have several ways to program moves and any or all of the following methods may be used.

Joysticks (usually potentiometers or rotary optical shaft encoders) are often used to manually program the motors that operate the various parts of the system. The joystick might be used to program one motion-controllable motorized function at a time, (i.e., pan, tilt, track, model rotator, etc.), and as the programming proceeds, these motion files are recorded one at a time and played back in concert until all of the functions necessary to the particular shot are completed. The result is similar to remote controlling a model airplane or car and making an exact record of what happened.

Using another programming technique, the joystick can be used to move the components of the system to a series of start and end positions while a record is made of these key positions, then subsequently commanding the system to generate a mathematically smooth path through these points. Much more complex methods of move generation are available using computer graphics. There are many bells and whistles available which include move-smoothing programs, even the use of a digital graphics tablet which enables visual modification of graphically displayed motion curves; and other specialized software ad infinitum.

The move files can be edited and modified in as many ways as there are motion-control systems. A few commercial electronic motion-control systems are available, as well as mechanical systems, the most ubiquitous being the Kuper system which recently received a Scientific and Engineering Oscar®.

Motion-Control Equipment: Field

If it is necessary to use motion-control in the field (defined here as outside the walls of a visual effects studio, with the camera operating at sound speed), there are different requirements. The director will almost always need a moving camera, and if this is to be done, much of the following will be required:

1. A steady camera, which is slavable to the motion-control electronics, which will provide frame/shutter position accuracy in successive passes. Though not always imperative, the camera should be silent so dialogue can be recorded. It should have a synchronized videotap and playback system that can be slaved to the motion-control electronics.

2. A reliable motion-controlled follow-focus system. Double-pass shots must exactly repeat.

3. A pan-tilt motion-control gearhead, which by any of a variety of techniques can provide scaleable lens entrance-pupil positions for postproduction use on less than full-scale props or miniatures. This pan-tilt head must have a remote operating console with hand-wheels and video monitor, and in practice it is little different than using a remote head. Usually such a head will use DC servo motors to provide a normal to high-speed pan-tilt range. Again, silence of operation is often important.

4. A dolly with track, having a powerful tracking motor, and a motorized boom, with positional encoders on both axes which enable dolly grip control as in normal shots, or remote operation, or pre-programmed moves. Ideally, the above equipment should be as standard as possible in appearance and operational characteristics, and operate on quickly deployable dolly track.

5. A motion-control electronics console, operated by a technician who can efficiently log and store motion files shot-by-shot, and do this as invisibly as possible to the rest of the production crew.

6. A videotap flicker-free system, which can store shots as they are made, and play them back instantly for directorial scrutiny. It is often necessary that this system be able to provide on-the-spot video composites for comparisons of A to B scene action, and the ability to playback A while recording B, etc. The video requirements will vary with the shot requirements.

7. A bookkeeping detail which can log actors' positions, distances, etc.; camera and track positions within the set; and other mathematical and geographical information for use in postproduction. Again, this should happen systematically and invisibly to the rest of the production crew.

Motion-Control Technique

When working on *Star Wars,* we started with an empty building and had to amass, modify and build our motion-control equipment before we could produce any images. We had created visual "violins" and had to learn to play them. Fortunately, the picture hit and a large audience showed up for our motion-control recitals. Since then, many innovations have come about in the equipment and many excellent motion-control cinematographers have appeared, and with many specialty techniques. In the studio there are two main techniques for programming motion files: one is to use start and end positions for each axis of motion and have the computer generate the moves; the other allows the cameraperson to generate the move by joystick. It is my opinion that the computer-generated method is superior for graphics and animation purposes, and the human interface is best for most miniature and model photography. If shots are created using a computer, the moves will have mathematically perfect curves, slow-ins, slow-outs, etc., and will have no heartbeat or verve, especially in action sequences, therefore becoming subliminally predictable and less interesting to the audience. The human operator is not interested in mathematical perfection, rather, they tailor the camera move moment by moment to what is interesting in their viewfinder. This human sense of curiosity is present in the work of a talented operator, and it transfers to the audience.

Richard Edlund, ASC currently serves on the Academy of Motion Picture Arts and Sciences Board of Governors and is a chairman of the Academy's Scientific and Technical Awards Committee as well as the Academy's Visual Effects Branch. He has been awarded Oscars® for visual effects in Star Wars, The Empire Strikes Back, Raiders of the Lost Ark *and* Return of the Jedi.

Greenscreen and Bluescreen Photography

by Bill Taylor ASC and Petro Vlahos

OVERVIEW

Greenscreen and bluescreen composites begin with foreground action photographed against a plain backing of a single primary color. In a digital postproduction process, the foreground action is combined with a new background. The new background can be live action, digital or traditional models, artwork or animation, or any combination.

For the sake of simplicity, we'll refer to "greenscreen" shots, with the understanding that the "screen" or "backing" can instead be blue or even red.

These composites (and others using related technology) are also called "traveling matte" shots because they depend on creating an Alpha-channel silhouette "mask" or "matte" image of the foreground action that changes and travels within the frame.

The final composite is usually created in postproduction, although real-time, full resolution on-set compositing[1] is possible in HD video.

FIX IT IN POST

Production and post-production are not only separated in the budget, they are too often separated by a huge cultural gulf. The driving force of production is time, and in the name of speed it's very easy to take shortcuts that have a disastrous downstream impact. "Fixing in post" can cost hundreds of thousands over the scope of a film and jam up an already tight post schedule. Furthermore there is no "post fix" possible for some on-set mistakes. We describe here what have proven to be the best practices, materials and equipment available for this work.

For ease of reference, we'll deal with the most-requested topic first:

HOW TO EXPOSE A GREENSCREEN SHOT, AND WHY
Balancing Screen (Backing) Brightness to the Shooting Stop

Let's assume that the camera choices are optimal, screen materials and lighting are ideal, and the foreground lighting matches the background lighting perfectly. (All these topics are dealt with later in this chapter.)

---

1. In live composites, full-bandwidth HD video is fed to an HD Ultimatte hardware device with a second camera, an HD deck or a digital wor kstation providing the background.

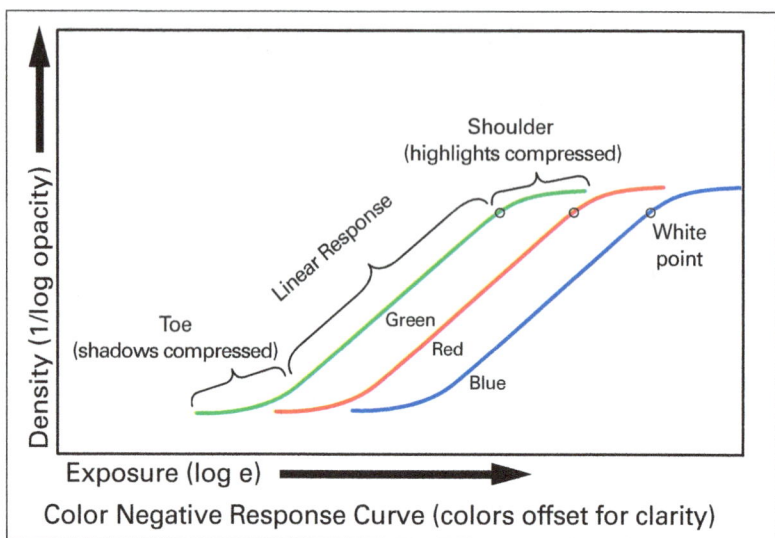

Figure 1. Schematic H&D curve

A common misconception is that backing brightness should be adjusted to match the level of foreground illumination. In fact, the optimum backing brightness depends only on the f-stop at which the scene is shot. Thus, normally lit day scenes and low-key night scenes require the same backing brightness if the appropriate f-stop is the same for both scenes. The goal is to achieve the same blue or green density on the negative, or at the sensor, in the backing area for every shot at any f-stop.

The ideal blue or green density is toward the upper end of the straight-line portion of the H and D curve, but not on the shoulder of this curve, where the values are compressed. Figure 1 shows an idealized H&D curve, a graph which shows how the color negative responds to increasing exposure. In film, each color record has a linear section, where density increases in direct proportion to exposure, and a "toe" and a "shoulder" where shadows and highlights respectively can still be distinguished but are compressed. Eight stops of exposure range can comfortably fit on the H&D curve, a range only recently achieved by digital cameras. The "white point" is shown for all three records: the density of a fully exposed white shirt which still has detail.

Imagine a plume of black smoke shot against a white background. It's a perfect white: the measured brightness is the same in red, green, and blue records.

The density of the smoke in the left-hand image ranges from dead black to just a whisper. What exposure of that white backing will capture the full range of transparencies of that smoke plume?

Obviously, it's the best-compromise exposure that lands the white backing at the white point toward the top of the straight line portion of the H&D

IMAGE COURTESY OF BILL TAYLOR ASC

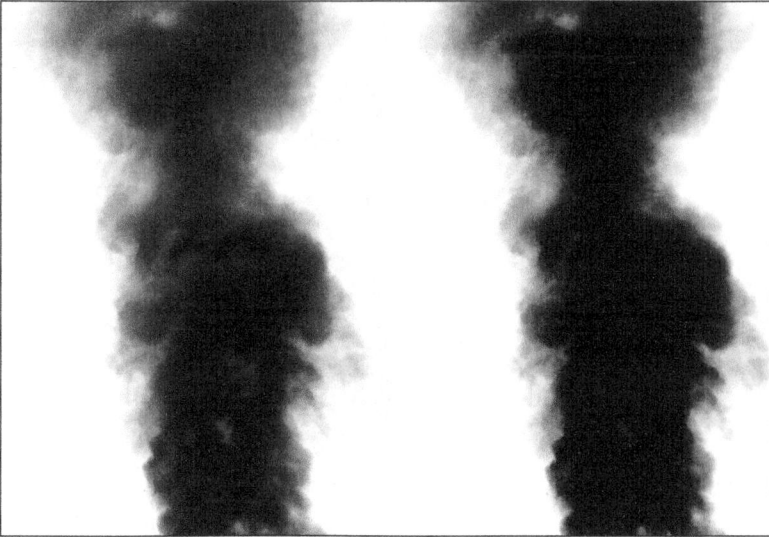

Figure 2. Normal and underexposed smoke plumes

curve in film (a white-shirt white) or a level of 90% in video, and brings most of the dark values in the smoke up off the toe. If the backing was overexposed, the thin wisps would be pushed onto the shoulder and compressed (or clipped in video) and pinched out by lens flare. If the backing was underexposed (reproduced as a shade of grey), detail in the darkest areas would fall on the toe to be compressed or lost entirely.

You could make up for underexposure by boosting the image contrast or making a levels adjustment (remapping the brightness range to a wider gamut). As the right hand image in Figure 2 shows, boosting contrast makes the backing white (clear) again, but tonal range is lost (the dark tones block up), the edges of the smoke become harder, and noise is exaggerated. The effect of a levels adjustment is subtler, (and preferable), though extreme levels adjustments betray the missing tonal values with banding or blocking.

Now imagine that instead of a white screen, we're shooting the smoke plume against a greenscreen and that the measured green brightness is the same as before. What's the best exposure for the greenscreen? Obviously, it's the same as before. The only difference is that the red and blue-sensitive layers aren't exposed.

Just like the smoke plume, greenscreen foregrounds potentially contain a full range of transparencies, ranging from completely opaque to barely there. Transparent subject matter can include motion blur, smoke, glassware, reflections in glass windows, wispy hair, gauzy cloth, and shadows.

To reproduce the full range of transparency, the greenscreen should be fully but not overexposed. In other words, its brightness should match the green

Figure 3. White card in set, lit to shooting stop (incident reading)

component of a well-exposed white object like a white shirt; roughly defined as the whitest white in the foreground that still has detail. (We don't want to expose that white shirt as top white, because we want to leave some headroom for specular reflections, on the shoulder in film, 100% and over in video.)

SETTING SCREEN BRIGHTNESS

Meter readings of blue- and greenscreens can be misleading. Some exposure meters respond inconsistently to monochrome color, especially blue, and some are affected by the high levels of UV coming from green and blue tubes. A waveform monitor on a digital camera is the most accurate and informative source of exposure information available. For film shoots, or if a waveform monitor is not available, the most reliable method for balancing a blue or green screen is still by eye, with the White Card Method:

White Card Method for Screen Balancing

1. Choose the f-stop at which the scene is to be shot. Let's say it is f4. Position a 90% reflectance white card in the acting area and light it to an incident light reading[2] of f4, keeping the spill light off the backing. The white card

---

2. Incident Light Reading is usually measured with an incident light meter. The meter measures the light that is illuminating or falling on the subject. Incident light meters typically add up all the sources falling on the surface of a white hemisphere, which must therefore be shielded from the lights one does not want to include in the measurement. Using the flat disk on the meter held parallel to a flat surface will give a more accurate reading of the light falling on that surface than the meter's sphere. takes into account the angle, or geometry, of the light—what direction it is coming from—and averages these two things together into a single reading.

is now lit to the brightest tone that still has detail (white shirt white) even though the actual set lighting may not reach that level.

2. View the white card against the screen through a Wratten No. 99 green filter. (Use a Wratten No. 98 blue filter for a blue backing.) In a pinch, Primary Green or Primary Blue lighting gels, folded to several thicknesses, will serve.

3. Adjust the backing brightness so that the white card blends into the backing. The circle overlay in Figure 3 shows the view through the filter. When the edges of the card are invisible or nearly invisible, the green light coming from the screen is now the same brightness as the green light component coming from the f4 white card. (If you were to photograph the white card now, the red, blue and green components coming from the card would reproduce near the top of the straight line portion of the curve. Since the greenscreen matches the brightness of the green component coming from the white card, the green layer will also be exposed near the top of the straight line portion of the curve, without overexposure.) The backing will now expose properly at f4.

If it is easier to adjust set lighting than backing brightness, the procedure can be reversed. Adjust the white card's light until the card blends in, then take an incident reading. Light the set to that f-stop.

The white card procedure needs to be done only once for a given screen and illuminator setup. For the rest of the shoot, a quick spotmeter reading will confirm the brightness and exposure needed. Once the backing brightness is set, the spot meter may be calibrated for use with the appropriate color filter to read f-stops directly: Wratten No. 99 + 2B for green; Wratten No. 98 (or 47B + 2B) for blue. (The UV filters—built into the No. 98—ensure that UV from the tubes does not affect the reading.) Simply adjust the meter's ISO speed setting until the reading from the screen yields the target f-stop (f4 in the example above). It's advisable to use the same individual meters (not just the same models) for the shoot as was used for testing.

Just as in the smoke plume example, more exposure is counterproductive; it pinches out fine detail due to image spread and pushes the backing values into the nonlinear range of the film or video sensor. Slight underexposure is preferable to overexposure, but more than a stop of underexposure is also counterproductive; the software will have to make up matte density by boosting contrast or a levels adjustment.

LEVELS FOR DIGITAL ORIGINAL PHOTOGRAPHY

Most of the same considerations apply as in film photography. It's particularly important that none of the color channels be driven into highlight nonlinearity or "clip", allowing some headroom for specular highlights. If the screen lighting can be adjusted independently of the set, light the screen to

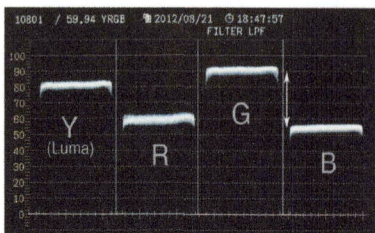

Figure 4. Waveform display showing Green at 90%

Figure 5. Greenscreen with white strip in same light

an IRE video level of about 90% in the appropriate channel, as shown on the waveform monitor.

The waveform display Figure 4 show the 4 channels of the image of a greenscreen displayed in "parade mode": Y or Luminance (brightness), Red, Green and Blue. The display tells us a lot about the subject, which is a greenscreen filling the width of the frame and exposed to a level of 90% IRE. (Note that 100% IRE represents the full scale of brightness from black to white. IRE values are expressed as a relative percentage because a video signal can be any amplitude.) The traces are flat in all channels, showing that the screen was evenly illuminated across its width. Since this screen was lit with white light, there is a substantial level of Red and Green contamination present, and the relative amount is shown clearly. (Had it been lit with Kino Green fluorescents, the Red and Blue values would be close to 0.)

The difference in level between Green and Blue (indicated by the white double-headed arrow in Figure 4) is the headroom that the software exploits to create the Alpha channel. The greater the difference, the less the software will need to boost the contrast of the Alpha channel. The waveform monitor makes it a simple matter to compare paints and materials,

However If the screen and the action must be lit together, a value of about 80 IRE on the waveform monitor is the maximum level at which the screen can be exposed without clipping the whites in the foreground. Including a strip of white card lit to the same level as the green screen, as in Figure 5, and the corresponding waveform display Figure 6 shows why. With Green at 80, the white card (indicated by the three white arrows in Figure 6) is at 90; more exposure would push the white into clip. In practice a slight underexposure is preferable to overexposure.

Too much underexposure is undesirable. In Figure 7, the Green level has been set to IRE 45. There is now significantly less difference between Green and Blue levels available to create the matte image in the Alpha channel.

Digital cameras like Arri Alexa and Sony F65 have even greater dynamic range than film, with more latitude for exposure in the linear (nonclipping) range. In these cameras the waveform monitor can be set to read the "log C"

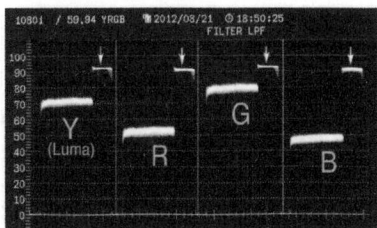

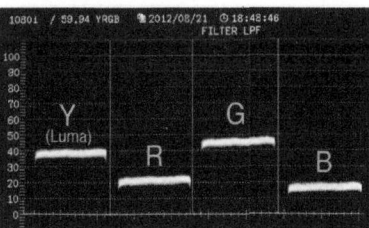

Figure 6. Waveform display showing Green at 80%, White at 90%   Figure 7. Waveform display showing Green at 45%

transform (preferable to Rec. 709) of the camera's "Raw" or data mode. Lacking a waveform monitor, it's a safe bet to set exposure for these cameras as you would a film negative.

FUNCTION OF THE BACKING – GREEN, BLUE OR RED

The purpose of the blue or green backing is to give the software an unambiguous distinction between the color hues and values in the foreground and the monochromatic backing. White and black backgrounds are used in special circumstances to create "luminance masks" or "luma keys" but since it is likely that similar luminance values will be found in the foreground, these backings have limited use.

The degree to which the compositing software "sees" the backing determines the degree of transparency of the foreground in the final composite. That transparency can be expressed as a percentage: Where the backing value is zero in the Alpha channel image, the foreground is completely opaque; where the backing value is 50% the foreground will be partly transparent, and so forth for all values to 100%, the areas of the frame where the foreground image is either not present or completely transparent. The goal is to retain the foreground subjects' edge transitions (including motion blur), color and transparency in the final composite.

HOW THE SOFTWARE CREATES THE COMPOSITE

The software uses the difference between the backing color and the colors found in the foreground to accomplish four tasks:

1. Optimally it will correct nonuniformity in the backing (the screen correction function, not available in all software packages).
2. It must create a silhouette matte (the alpha channel) of the foreground action.
3. It must create a processed foreground in which all traces of the backing color are suppressed (turned black or neutralized), while the foreground color is carried through unchanged.
4. Finally, it must bring all the elements together into a believable composite.

Figure 8a & b. Orignal photography, silhouette (Alpha) matte

THE ALPHA CHANNEL

The alpha or matte channel (the channel which carries transparency information) is a gray scale image in which the foreground image is a silhouette. The silhouette may be imagined as black against clear (and all the values in between) (Figure 9b) or with its values inverted, clear against black.

The alpha channel represents the difference in color between the backing color and the colors in the foreground subject. The matte's numerical level at any pixel is proportional to the visibility of the backing.

The Processed Foreground

The original image contains the green backing and the foreground subject. Green is limited so that it cannot exceed red or blue, which has the effect of turning the screen into a dark, near-neutral tone. The green backing is further reduced to a black backing by subtracting a proportion of the Alpha (matte) signal equal to the RGB content in each channel where the green backing shows. All of the screen color seen through transparent and translucent subjects likewise disappears. The subject appears to have been photographed against a perfectly black backing. This is the processed foreground image (see Figure 10a).

If the foreground subject (actor) is close to the backing or standing on a green floor, the subject will have a green color cast due to reflected (bounce) light from the floor and from lens flare. (This reflected light from the screen is sometimes called "spill," but it should not be confused with the spill light from the subject's lighting falling on the screen.) No attempt should be made to remove this color with filters on the lights or camera, or with color correction in transfer. All backing contamination is removed from the subject by the compositing software's white, gray and black balance controls.

Blue bounce is much harder to see on the set than green, but just as troublesome in the composite. There is no difference between greenscreens

IMAGE COURTESY OF BILL TAYLOR ASC

Figure 9a & b. Background image, background image multiplied by silhouette matte

and bluescreens of the same brightness as far as bounce is concerned. A dark blue or green will bounce less, but dark colors have too little color saturation to make a high-quality matte.

The order in which the foreground is processed is important. Noise reduction to the foreground should be applied when the processed foreground is made, before the Alpha is created, while color correction should wait until the final composite.

THE COMPOSITE

Once the Processed Foreground and the Alpha Channel are made, the final composite is a straightforward two-step operation. First the values in the Alpha Channel image are multiplied pixel-by-pixel with the background image. The result is a silhouette of the foreground combined with the background image (see Figure 9b).

Then the processed foreground is added pixel-by-pixel to the combined Alpha and background. If good practices have been followed, the final result is a seamless combination of foreground and background images (see Figure 10b).

IMAGE COURTESY OF BILL TAYLOR ASC

Figure 10a & b. Processed foreground, final composite

DISTINCTIONS FROM OTHER COMPOSITING METHODS

Projection Composites

Rear projection or front projection creates a projected background on-set behind a live action foreground. No postproduction work is needed. Creating a high quality background image with projection is challenging. (Incidentally, a green or blue backing can be created by front-projecting the appropriate color.) All the issues of projection such as shadow lines and screen uniformity apply.

Rotoscoping

"Rotoscoping" or "roto" is another method for making alpha-channel composites. The alpha-channel masks are created by hand-tracing the outline of the foreground action frame-by-frame. This technique of tracing live action (named by its inventor, the pioneer cartoonist Max Fleischer) is now more refined and widely used than ever, because 3-D conversion depends on it. It is extremely labor intensive but very flexible, since no special backing or lighting is required.

Present-day computer-assisted rotoscoping can produce excellent composites. Nearly all the composites of foreground actors in *Flags of Our Fathers* (2006) were created by rotoscoping. Good planning was the key to avoiding difficult foreground subjects. It helped a lot that many of the actors wore helmets, simplifying their silhouettes.

Some foregrounds are poor candidates for rotoscoping. For example if the foreground has a bright, burned-out sky behind it, it will flare into and even destroy the edge of the foreground. Flare can be very difficult to deal with (unless of course the final background is also a bright, burned out sky.) Fine detail and blurred motion are also difficult or impossible to roto, often requiring paintwork replacement. The skill of the artists is the single most important factor.

Rough roto masks ("G mattes") are often used with green screen compositing, to clean up contaminated areas of the backing, remove unwanted supports, and so forth.

SCREEN CHOICES: FABRIC, PAINT AND PLASTIC MATERIALS

The best materials currently available are the result of years of research to create optimal combinations of lamps. dyes and pigments.

Fabrics

Even an indifferent backing can give good results if it is lit evenly with narrow-band tubes or LEDs to the proper level (within plus or minus ⅓ f-stop) Spill from set lighting remains a concern.

Composite Components Co.[3] offers a fabric that is highly efficient, very light, stretchy and easy to hang. It must be backed by opaque material when there is light behind it. The green fabric is fluorescent, so it is even more efficient under UV-rich sources like skylight. CCC also make a darker material for direct sun use,.

Following Composite Components' lead, many suppliers now provide "digital-type" backings of similar colors. While similar in appearance, some of these materials are substantially less efficient, which can have a great cost impact when lighting large screens. Dazian Tempo fabric, a fuzzy, stretchy material, has a low green or blue saturation when lit with white light, so it isn't recommended for that application. Dazian's Lakota Green Matte material is a better choice for white-light applications like floor covering; it is resistant to fading and creasing, and can be laundered. Another major supplier, The Rag Place in North Hollywood, CA, supplies Optic Green Tempo Fabric, which has a built-in opaque backing. Its reflective value is between that of Digital Green© and chroma-key green.

Measured reflective values relative to an 18% gray car (N) are: chroma-key Green = N, Optic Green =N+⅔, Digital Green© +1⅔ EV.

When using fabric backings, minimize the seams and avoid folds. Stretch the fabric to minimize wrinkles All green materials will sun-fade with time. If a day-lit screen must be kept up for several days it should be protected when not in use.

Paint

Composite Components' Digital Green© or Digital Blue© paint is the preferred choice for large painted backings. As with fabrics, there are other paint brands with similar names that may not have the same efficiency. Equivalent paints made specifically for this purpose are also available from Rosco. Paints intended for video use, such as Ultimatte chroma-key paints, can also be used with good illuminators (lights). A test of a small swatch is worthwhile with materials whose performance is unknown.

Plastic Materials

Plastic materials are a good alternative to fabric or paint for floor covering. Fabric can be hazardous if loose underfoot. Painted floors scuff easily and quickly show shoe marks and dusty footprints.

ProCyc's Pro Matte plastic material is a good choice for floors or for entire limbo sets. The material is a good match to Digital Green© and Digital Blue©

---

3. A noted researcher and pioneer in the field, Jonathan Erland of Composite Components Co. in Los Angeles, won an Academy Award for CCC's line of patented Digital Green© and Digital Green© lamps, fabric and paint.

Figure 11a & b. Unevenly lit Blue set, actor in the set with shadows and reflections

paint and fabric. It is tough, scuff-resistant and washable. It is available in sheets, preformed coves and vertical corners in several radii. It is relatively costly, but the cost is at least partly offset by time and materials saved in shooting.

Great American Market in Hollywood, CA supplies GAMFloor, a self-adhesive vinyl which is more durable than paint and easily cleaned and repaired.

BACKING UNIFORMITY AND SCREEN CORRECTION

Since the luminance level and saturation of the backing determines the level of the background scene, it is important to light the backing as uniformly as is practical, ideally within plus or minus ⅓ f-stop.

While a perfectly uniform backing is desirable, it may not be achievable in the real world. (Please refer to screen lighting section.) If the backing itself is irregular in brightness, the background image seen "through" the irregularities will become equally irregular in the composite.

In Figure 11b, an actor appears in a "Virtual Set" reclining on unevenly lit blue steps. She casts shadows on three of the surfaces and is reflected in the bottom plane. In the final composite, the actor, her shadow and her reflection will appear on some marble stairs; for demonstration purposes, we will substitute a gray limbo for the background stairs that the blue set was built to match.

In Figure 12a, the software has faithfully reproduced the actor shadows and reflections, along with the unevenly lit set. It is possible to clean up the Alpha channel by increasing the contrast (gamma) in the nonuniform areas until those values are pushed (clipped) to 1.0 (see Figure 12b). Although clipping the alpha values eliminates the nonuniformity in the backing, the same values on the subject and her shadows are clipped, too, resulting in hard edges and lost shadows, reflections and transparencies.

Virtual sets like these often contain set pieces that correspond to objects in the final background, so that the actor can climb stairs, lean against a

IMAGE COURTESY ULTIMATTE CORP.

Figure 12a & 12b. Straight composite, composition with clipped Alpha

doorway, and so forth. The props all cast shadows on themselves and the blue or green floor, and the actor casts shadows on everything. With lighting alone it's impossible to eliminate set piece shadows without washing out the actor's shadow.

Several software packages have features to cope with nonuniform backings. Ultimatte Screen Correction software can compensate for backing luminance variations as great as two stops.

Screen correction is easy to use: After lighting the set, shoot a few seconds before the actors enter. This footage is called the "clean plate" or "reference plate". All the backing and lighting imperfections are recorded on those few frames. Now shoot the actors as usual.

When making the composite, the artist selects a well-lit reference point near the subject. Software derives a correction value by comparison with the clean plate and corrects the rest of the backing to the measured level. Software compares the clean frames pixel by pixel with the action frames, and inhibits the correction process in the subject area (the actor) and proportionately inhibits the correction in transparencies. Even though the set had a wide variation in color and brightness, the fine hair detail, the actor's shadows,

IMAGE COURTESY ULTIMATTE CORP.

Figure 13a & b. Alpha with screen correction, composite

her reflections and the full range of transparencies in the shawl have been retained in the Alpha (Figure 13a) and in the composite (Figure 13b).

Backing defects such as scuffed floors, set piece shadows, and color variations in the backing as well as minor lens vignetting all disappear. Note that the actor's shadows reproduce normally, even where they cross over shadows already on the backing.

There is a significant limitation: if the camera moves during the shot, the identical camera move must be photographed on the empty set for the length of the scene. While it is reasonably quick and simple to repeat pan-tilt-focus camera moves with small, portable motion control equipment, that equipment is not always available. Fortunately top camera operators have an almost uncanny skill at repeating previous moves. Skilled match movers can bring a "wild" clean pass into useful conformance around the actor, and remove discrepancies with rotoscoping. Some matchmovers prefer the clean footage to be shot at a slower tempo to improve the chances that more wild frames will closely match the takes with the actors.

When it's not possible to shoot a clean plate, Ultimatte AdvantEdge software can semiautomatically generate synthetic clean frames. The software can detect the edges of the foreground image, interpolate screen values inward to cover the foreground, and then create an alpha using that synthetic clean frame. There are some limitations; it's always best to shoot a clean plate if possible.

ILLUMINATORS

The best screen illuminators are banks of narrow-band green or green fluorescent tubes driven by high-frequency flickerless electronic ballasts.[4] These tubes can be filmed at any camera speed. The tube phosphors are formulated to produce sharply cut wavelengths that will expose only the desired negative layer while not exposing the other two layers to a harmful degree. These nearly perfect sources allow the use of the lowest possible matte contrast (gamma) for best results in reproducing smoke, transparencies, blowing hair, reflections, and so forth.

Kino Flo four-tube and eight-tube units are the most widely used lamps. They are available for rent with "Super Green" or "Super Blue" tubes from Kino Flo in Sun Valley, CA, and lighting suppliers worldwide. The originators

---

4. Flickerless electronic ballasts prevent the light from being unevenly exposed on film at speeds that are faster or slower than 24 frames per second. If one does not use them and shots at any other speed than 24 frames per second the image will appear to flicker. At 180° shutter, other frame rates which are evenly divisible into 120 will be flicker free with standard balasts, assuming 60 Hz AC power. For 50 Hz, divide fps into 100. For frame rates that are not evenly divisble, other shutter angles that eliminate lighting flicker can be confirmed by testing.

of narrow-band tubes, Composite Components still supplies Digital Green© and Digital Blue© tubes tailored specifically to film response. Mac Tech and others have introduced extremely efficient LED sources with similar characteristics to narrow-band fluorescent globes.

All these lamps have very high output and can be set up quickly. The light from these tubes is nearly perfectly monochromatic; there is almost no contamination. Flickerless power supplies run these units. Some high frequency fluorescent ballasts and all the LED sources can be dimmed, a great convenience in adjusting backing brightness.

Large lightweight fixtures like Kino Flo make it easy to evenly illuminate large backings, and the doors built into most units simplify cutting the colored light off the acting area.

A good scheme for front-lit backings is to place arrays of green fluorescents above and below the backing at a distance in front equal to approximately ½ the backing height. The units may be separated by the length of the tubes, or brought together as needed to build brightness. The lamps must overlap the outer margins of the screen. Keep the subjects at least 15 feet from the screen. The goal is to eliminate direct green light falling on the actor. Figure 14b shows side and top views of an actor standing on a platform that serves to hide the bottom row of lights. If the actor's feet and shadow are to be in the shot, the platform may be painted green or covered with green cloth or plastic material.

Note that if a platform is not practical, mirror Plexiglas or Mylar on the floor behind the actor can bridge the gap from the acting area to the screen, extending the screen downward by reflection.

A backing can be evenly lit entirely from above by placing a second row of lamps about 30% further away from the screen and below the top row. The advantage of lighting from above is that the floor is clear of green lamps. Lighting from above requires careful adjustment to achieve even illumination. The overhead-only rig requires about 50% more tubes and spills substantial green or green light onto the foreground in front of the screen. To film 180-degree pan-around shots on Universal's *The Fast and the Furious* (2001), the ace rigging crew lit a three-sided backing 30 feet high and more than 180 feet long entirely from above.

The number of tubes required depends on backing efficiency, the film speed and the desired f-stop. As an example, six four-tube green lamps are sufficient to light a 20 by 20 foot Composite Components Digital Green© backing to a level of f4 at ISO 200. Eight four-tube blue lamps yield f4 with a 20 by 20 foot blue backing from the same maker.

ALTERNATIVE LIGHT SOURCES

In a pinch, commercial daylight fluorescent tubes or Kino Flo white tubes wrapped with primary green or primary blue filter sheets can produce good

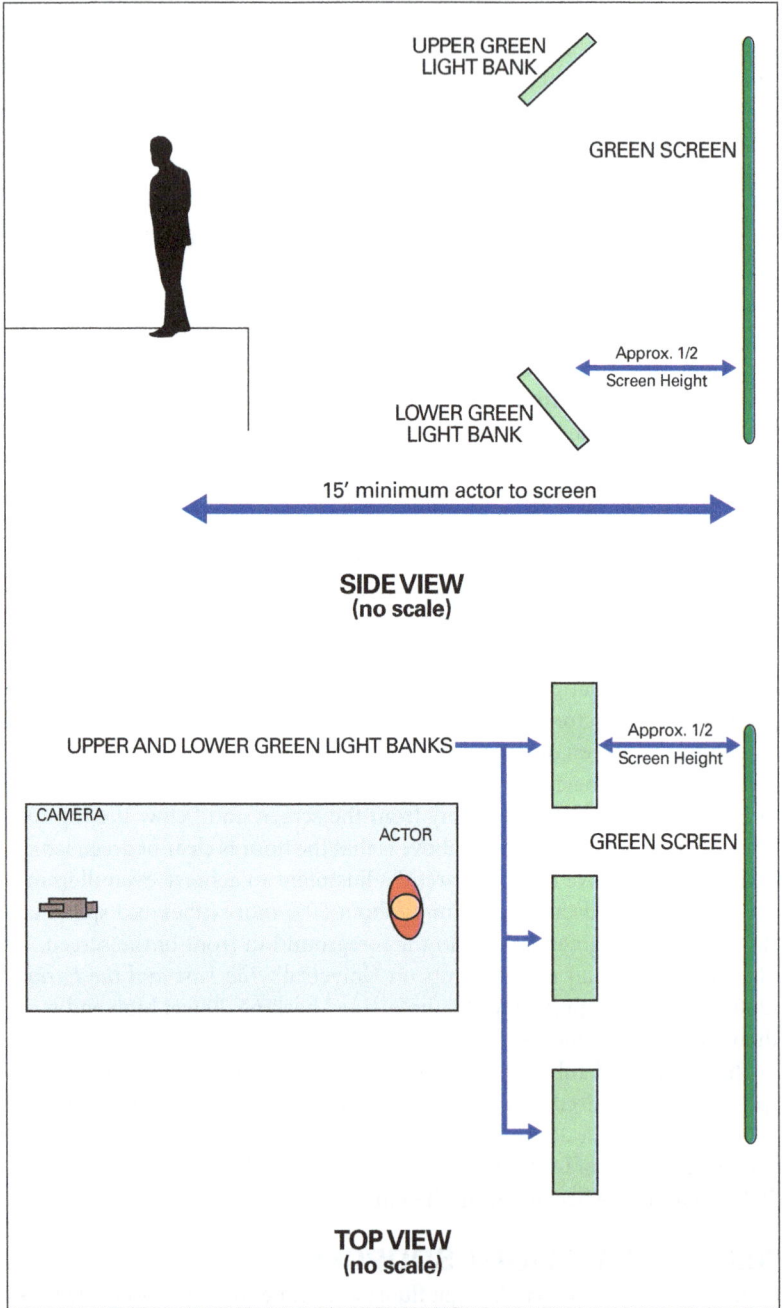

UPPER GREEN
LIGHT BANK

GREEN SCREEN

Approx. 1/2
Screen Height

LOWER GREEN
LIGHT BANK

15′ minimum actor to screen

SIDE VIEW
(no scale)

UPPER AND LOWER GREEN LIGHT BANKS

Approx. 1/2
Screen Height

CAMERA

ACTOR

GREEN SCREEN

TOP VIEW
(no scale)

IMAGE COURTESY OF BILL TAYLOR ASC

Figure 14a & b. Side view and top views of screen lit with 6 light banks

results. The Rosco CalColor line of primaries works best. Balance to the desired brightness in the screen color as described below. The downside is great loss of efficiency; it takes about four filtered daylight tubes to equal the output from one special-purpose tube.

Regular 60Hz ballasts can be used with commercial tubes at the cost of weight and power efficiency. As with any 60Hz fluorescent lamps, 24 fps filming must be speed-locked (nonlocked cameras are fortunately rare) to avoid pulsating brightness changes, and any high-speed work must be at crystal-controlled multiples of 30 fps. These tubes are somewhat forgiving of off-speed filming because of the "lag" of the phosphors.

Backings can also be front-lit with Primary Green or Primary Blue-filtered HMI lamps. The only advantage is that the equipment is usually already "on the truck" when a shot must be improvised. Getting even illumination over a large area is time-consuming, and filters must be carefully watched for fading. Heat Shield filter material is helpful. Because of high levels of the two unwanted colors, HMI is not an ideal source, but it is better than incandescent.

In an emergency, filtered incandescent lamps can do the job. They are an inefficient source of green light and much worse for blue (less than 10% the output of fluorescents) so they are a poor choice for lighting large screens. Watch for filter fading as above.

A green or green surface illuminated with white light is the most challenging, least desirable backing from a compositing standpoint. White light, however, is required for floor shots and virtual sets when the full figure of the actor and his shadow must appear to merge in the background scene. Advanced software can get good results from white-lit backings with the aid of Screen Correction and a "clean plate" as described above. Difficult subjects may require assistance with hand paintwork.

EYE PROTECTION

A word about eye protection: Many high-output tubes produce enough ultraviolet light to be uncomfortable and even damaging to the eyes. Crew members should not work around lit banks of these fixtures without UV eye protection. It is good practice to turn the tubes off when they are not in use. The past practice of using commercial blueprint tubes was dangerous because of their sunburn-level UV output.

CHOOSING THE BACKING COLOR

The choice of backing color is determined by the wardrobe or subject color. The range of permissible foreground colors is wider when the backing can be lit separately from the actor, rather than when the actor must be photographed in a white-lit green set (a "floor shot") for example.

A blue backing is satisfactory for most colors except saturated blue. Pastel blues (blue eyes, faded blue jeans, etc.) reproduce well. The color threshold can be adjusted to allow some colors containing more blue than green (such as magenta/purple) into the foreground. If too much blue is allowed back into the foreground, some of the blue bounce light will return. Therefore, if magenta wardrobe must be reproduced, it is prudent to take extra care to avoid blue bounce and flare. Keep the actors away from the backing, and mask off as much of the backing as possible with neutral flats or curtains. Saturated yellows on the subject's edge may produce a dark outline that requires an additional post step to eliminate. Pastel yellows cause no problems.

A green backing is satisfactory for most colors except saturated green. Pastel greens are acceptable. Saturated yellow will turn red in the composite unless green is allowed back into the subject, along with some of the green bounce or flare from the original photography. The same precautions as above should be taken to minimize bounce and flare. Pastel yellow is acceptable. Figure 15 shows a test of green car paint swatches against green screen. The hue and saturation of the "hero" swatch was sufficiently distinct from the screen color to pose no difficulties in matting or reproduction. Bounce light from the screen was carefully flagged off in the actual shot. Note that none of the colors in the MacBeth chart are affected except for two saturated green patches, which have become semi-transparent.

High bounce levels are unavoidable where the actor is surrounded by a green floor or virtual set: one should not expect to reproduce saturated magenta or saturated yellow on a green floor without assistance in post.

If the foreground subject contains neither saturated green nor saturated blue, then either backing color may be used. However, the grain noise of the green emulsion layer on color negative and the green sensor in a digital camera is generally much lower than the grain noise of the blue layer. Using a green backing will therefore result in less noise in shadows and in semi-transparent subjects. Black smoke in particular reproduces better against a green backing.

Obviously, it is important for the cinematographer and his ally the vfx supervisor to be aware of wardrobe and props to be used in green screen and blue screen scenes. Sometimes a difficult color can be slightly changed without losing visual impact, and save much trouble and expense in post. If in doubt, a test is always worthwhile. Video Ultimatte Preview (see below) can be invaluable.

Some visual effects experts prefer blue backings for scenes with Caucasian and Asian actors, finding it somewhat easier to achieve a pleasing flesh tone without allowing the backing color into the foreground. Those skin tones reflect mostly red and green and relatively little blue. For dark-skinned actors, either backing color seems to work equally well.

IMAGE COURTESY OF BILL TAYLOR ASC

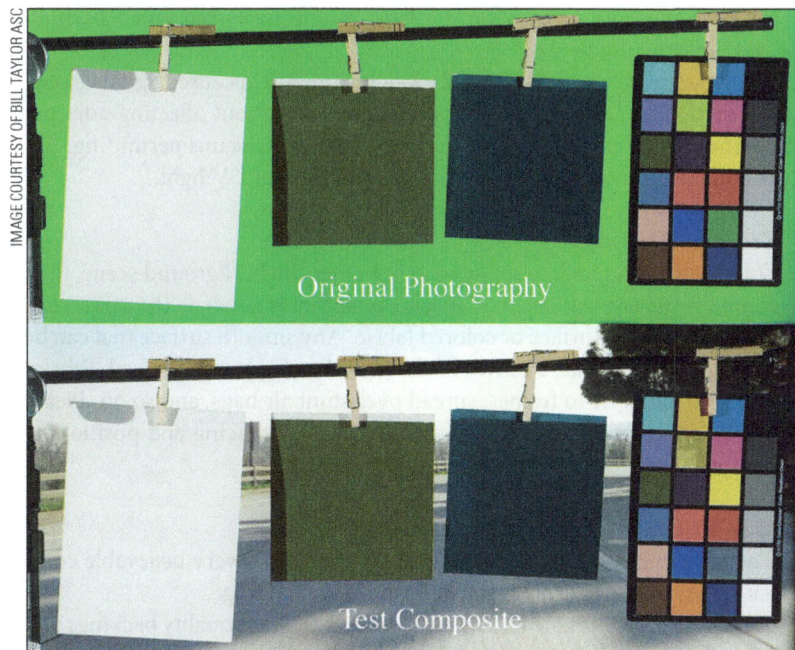

Figure 15. Green paint swatch test against greenscreen, composite

In extreme cases (for example if the foreground contains both a saturated green and a saturated blue, troublesome foreground colors can be isolated (with rotoscoping if necessary) and color corrected separately.

BACKING TYPES AND LIGHTING

The color and illumination of the backing are crucial to a good result. A perfect green backing would expose only the green-sensitive element of the color negative or digital sensor. Cross-color sensitivity in the negative or sensor, imperfect illuminators and spill light from the set all compromise this ideal. It's no surprise that the best combinations of backing, illuminators and camera type yield the best quality composites.

Back-lit Backings

Backings can be backlit (translucent) or front-lit. Big translucent backings are almost extinct due to their high cost, limited size and relative fragility. Translucent Stewart blue backings gave nearly ideal results and required no foreground stage space for lighting. Due to lack of demand, Stewart has never made translucent greenscreens. Front-lit backings are more susceptible to spill light, but with careful flagging they can produce a result every bit as good as back-lit screens.

Translucent cloth screens can be back-lit effectively but when back-lit, seams limit the usable size.

Fluorescent fixtures with UV (black light) tubes will cause Digital Green© and Digital Red© fabrics and paint to fluoresce without affecting adjacent sets. The fabric can be lit from the front or the back, seams permitting. Actors and crew should not be exposed to high levels of UV light.

Front-lit Backings

If the actor's feet and/or shadow do not enter the background scene, then a simple vertical green or green surface is all that is needed. The screen can be either a painted surface or colored fabric. Any smooth surface that can be painted, including flats, a canvas backing, and so forth, can be used. Fabrics are easy to hang, tie to frames, spread over stunt air bags, and so on. Please see the section on Illuminators in this chapter for spacing and positioning of lamps.

Day-Lit Green and Blue Backings

For big exterior scenes, authentic sunlight makes a very believable composite that can only be approximated with stage lighting.

Daylight is the ultimate challenge, requiring the best quality backings and Screen Correction compositing for good results. Thanks to those advances, there are no limits to the size of a traveling matte foreground aside from the size of the backing.

Figures 16a and 16b show the first daylight green screen shot made for a feature film. Every trick in the book including Ultimatte Screen Correction was used to achieve this result. Original photography was on 8-perf VistaVision. The two reflector boards shown plus a third out of frame on the right foreground are the only supplementary lighting.

Coves are to be avoided; as seen in Figure 16a, there is usually a wide band of overexposed, desaturated glare in the cove. Later experience has shown that a clean, straight line is much easier to deal with in post. A raised platform, painted or covered with backing material, with a separate vertical backing well behind it is ideal.

If a platform is not practical, the cinematographer of *Journey to the Center of the Earth*, Chuck Schuman, recommends a flat 45-degree join between green floors and walls.

When the screen is to be lit by direct sunlight, using the darker of the Digital Green© fabrics or chromakey green fabric or paint makes it easier to avoid overexposure. When the actors are in backlight and the screen is lit by skylight, the lighter, standard Digital Green© fabrics (which fluoresce in UV light scattered from the sky) are the best choice. Tipping the screen back about 15° will help catch skylight. In some cases the screen must be used in

IMAGE COURTESY OF UNIVERSAL STUDIOS

Figure 16a & b. Daylight greenscreen shot from *Greedy* (1993)

both front light and back light. In that instance the more reflective Digital Green© material is the best compromise, with exposure controlled carefully to avoid overexposure.

Limits of Day-Lit Backings

Because the green backing set must be oriented to achieve the sun direction matching the background plates, one can shoot relatively few set-ups in a day. At some times of year, the sun on the set may never get high enough to match the background sun, thus requiring a replacement source.

FLOOR SHOTS, VIRTUAL SETS

If the actor must be composited head-to-toe into the background scene, then the floor must also be the color of the backing. (Green is preferred for floor shooting since the shadows will be less noisy.) The same type of white light and lighting fixtures that light the actor are also used to light the floor and backing. A shadow cast on a green-painted wall or floor by the subject can be transferred (when desired) into the background scene together with the subject.

Floors may be painted or covered with fabric. Fabric can be hazardous if loose underfoot. Painted floors scuff easily and quickly show shoe marks and dusty footprints.

Pro-Cyc's Pro Matte plastic material is a good alternative for floors. The material is a good match to Digital Green© and Digital Green© paint and fabric. It is tough, scuff-resistant and washable. It is available in sheets, pre-formed coves and vertical corners in several radii. Permanent sets are good candidates for this material, due to cost.

Lighting uniformity problems (within plus or minus one f-stop), color contamination of the floor, scuff marks and green set piece shadows can be dealt with in compositing when Screen Correction frames are available.

Sheets of 4' x 8' mirrored Mylar or mirrored Plexiglas may also be used as a walking surface. (Please see Illumination and Reflections from the Backing section). Of course no shadow is cast on a mirror surface, and the reflection must be dealt with.

The choice of fabric and paint affects not only the quality of the composite, but also lighting cost. Some screen materials are much more efficient than others, and require many fewer lamps to light to the correct level. In general, green screens and tubes are more efficient than blue screens and tubes. Savings on lamp rentals can amount to tens of thousands of dollars per week on large backings.

Limitations of Floor Shots and Virtual Sets

Floor shots and virtual sets are both difficult and rewarding, because the actor can walk or sit upon objects in the background, climb stairs, and walk through doorways, even when the background scene is a digital model or a miniature. When the actor's shadow appears in the background scene, it adds believability to the shot. To help tie in foreground action to the plate, screen-colored shapes can be used to either cast a shadow of something in the plate, or to catch an actor's shadow so that it conforms appropriately to a shape in the plate.

Alpha channel (matte) contrast must be high in a floor shot to achieve separation from the contaminated color of the floor. Even the finest green pigment or dye reflects significant quantities of red and blue The problem is often compounded by glare from backlighting. Since the matte is created by the difference between the backing color and the colors in the subject, and since there is inherently less difference because of red and blue contamination, the alpha values must be multiplied by some factor to yield an opaque matte that will prevent the background from showing through. This multiplication raises the gamma (contrast) of the matte image.

If the real shadow can't be reproduced, it can sometimes be simulated within limits with a distorted copy of the alpha channel. If necessary, the shadow can be hand animated.

UNDERWATER PHOTOGRAPHY

In addition to underwater diving or swimming shots, underwater green-screen photography creates a zero-G environment for actors with an all-axis freedom of motion impossible on wire rigs.

The biggest challenge is keeping the water clear of sediment and particulates. Underwater diffusion causes the screen to flare into the foreground and vice-versa; It's ruinous to the matte edges. High capacity pumps, good water circulation and a multistage filter are necessary to keep the water clear. It's also important that all personnel have clean feet when they enter the tank.

Composite Components' green material stretched on a frame works well under water in a swimming pool or a tank. Tip the screen back to catch light from above, with Rosco diffusion material floating on the water surface to kill caustic patterns on the screen. Build up the screen lighting level with green fluorescent units above the water. Underwater Kino Flo lamps are also available.

High chlorine levels common in swimming pools bleach out the screen quickly; pull the screen out of the tank daily and rinse it off with tap water.

FOREGROUND LIGHTING ON THE STAGE
Creating the Illusion: Lighting to Match the Background
Inappropriate lighting compromises a shot the instant it appears on screen, while imperfect compositing technique may be noticeable only to experts.

Obviously, the foreground photography must match the background lens and camera positions, but lighting considerations are just as important. This is why it is generally preferable to shoot live action backgrounds first. (If the background hasn't been shot yet, the job depends on everything from careful map-reading to educated guesswork. Even the best guesses can be defeated by unexpected weather.)

Foreground lighting must match the background in direction, shadow hardness and key-to fill ratio. True sunlight has nearly parallel rays coming from a single point at a distance that's optically equivalent to infinity. To simulate the sun, use the hardest source available, as far away as the shooting space will allow. Multiple sources cast multiple shadows—an instant give-away. Sometimes folding the light path with a mirror will allow the hard source to be further away, and a better representation of the parallel rays of the sun. Skylight fill and environmental bounce light must be shadowless. Therefore surrounding the actors with the biggest, broadest sources of light available is preferable. The perfect skylight source would be a dome like the real sky, which can be approximated on stage with big silks or white bounces.

To help in lighting the foreground subject while the screen is lit, a contrast viewing glass of the complementary color can be used to "black out" the screen area. The viewing glass also reveals spill light on the screen.

ENVIRONMENTAL BOUNCE LIGHT
Since the software drops out the backing and the backing reflections from the foreground object, the subject is "virtually" surrounded by black. The black surroundings cause no problem if the composite background is an essentially dark night scene.

However, if the eventual background is a light day scene, and if the subject had really been in that day environment, the environmental light would light up the hair and provide the normal edge brightness along arms, sides of the face, and so forth. The cinematographer must restore the light that the environment would have provided from the sun, the sky, the ground and so forth. Large, white bounces are useful in creating back cross reflection sources just outside the frame. Otherwise, edges of arms, legs and faces will go dark causing the foreground to look like a cutout.

Simulated light from the environment can be added digitally to replace the suppressed screen color with color derived from the background. It's a slight glow around the edges that can look good when tastefully applied. The real thing is to be preferred.

High levels of fill light in wide day exteriors while sometimes desirable for esthetic reasons, hurt the believability of day exterior composites. Movie audiences are accustomed to seeing more fill in close-ups, a common practice in daylight photography.

Local Color

Of course, skylight is intensely blue, so fill light supposedly coming from the sky should be blue relative to the key. Likewise, if actors and buildings in the background are standing on grass, much green light is reflected upward into their shadows. If the actor matted into the shot does not have a similar greenish fill, he will not look like he belongs in the shot. Careful observation is the key. In a greenscreen shot, the bounce light from grass is low in both brightness and saturation compared to the screen color, so that color cast can be allowed in the composite foreground while still suppressing the screen. The same is true of sky bounce in a bluescreen shot.

A day exterior shot will often shoot in the f5.6 to f11 range or even deeper. Fortunately, efficient lighting and high ASA ratings on films and sensors permit matching these deep f-stops on the stage. In a day car shot, for example, holding focus in depth from the front to the rear of the car contributes to the illusion.

Figure 17 shows a 28'-wide screen lit with 16 four-tube Kino Flo lamps, plus two HMI "helper" lamps with green filters on the sides. This combination made it possible to film at f11 with 200 ASA Vision 2 negative. Curtains at left, right, and top made it easy to mask off portions of the screen outside the frame.

Of course, when it's possible to film foregrounds like this one in daylight, so much the better.

Color Bias in Foreground Lighting

In the past, some cinematographers used an overall yellow or magenta color bias in foreground lighting to "help" the composite, with the intent that the bias be timed out later. This practice is counterproductive, resulting in false color in blurs and transparencies. If an overall bias is desired, it's easy to achieve in post.

Illumination and Reflections from the Backing

Colored illumination and reflections from the backing on the subject must be minimized for top-quality results. Illumination and reflection are separate issues!

IMAGE COURTESY OF BILL TAYLOR ASC

Figure 17. Greenscreen lit to f 11

Green illumination from the backing can be made negligible by keeping the actors away from the backing (at least 15 feet, 25 feet is better) and by masking off all the backing area at the backing that is not actually needed behind the actors. Use black or neutral flags and curtains (The rest of the frame can be filled in with window mattes in compositing.) Any remaining color cast is eliminated by the software.

Screen reflections are best controlled by reducing the backing size and by tenting the subject with flats or fabric of a color appropriate to the background. In a common worst case, a wet actor in a black wetsuit, the best one can do is to shoot the actor as far from the screen as possible, mask the screen off as tightly as possible, and bring the environmental bounce sources fully around to the actor's off-camera side, without, of course, blocking the screen. A back cross light will of course wipe out any screen reflection on

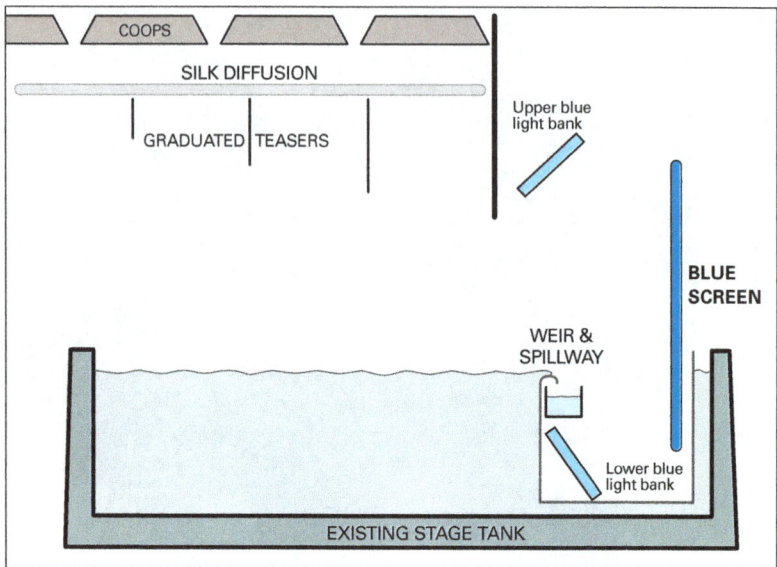

Figure 18. Water tank diagram

the actor but it will look false if it's not justified by the background lighting.

Big chrome props and costumes present similar challenges. Since they present the whole crew with a huge headache (every light shows, and sometimes the camera crew as well) it is usually not too difficult to arrange modifications to these items. When the visual effects team is brought in early on, problems like these can be headed off in the design stage.

A common reflection challenge is a Plexiglas aircraft canopy or a compound-curve spacesuit helmet which, depending on the lighting angle and camera position, can show every lamp and bounce source. A bounce source for a canopy shot must be uniform and surround the canopy 180 degrees on the camera side. Sometimes the best solution is to shoot without the Plexiglas and track a CG model back in, in the composite. An advantage to CG Plexiglas is that it can reflect the composited background.

Reflections can be disguised with dulling spray, but sometimes they cannot be eliminated. In the worst case, reflections make "holes" in the matte that must be filled in digitally in post. Pay particular attention to the faces of perspiring actors, which can be very reflective. Of course, when the actor must stand in the middle of a green-painted virtual set, some green contamination is unavoidable; it will be removed by the compositing software.

Sometimes reflections are desirable: Sheets of mirror Mylar or Plexiglas can extend a screen by reflection, even below the stage floor. Actors can walk on mirror Plexiglas to be surrounded by the screen's reflection. (Of course their own reflection must be dealt with.)

IMAGE COURTESY UNIVERSAL STUDIOS

Figure 19. Water tank in use

In a scheme devised by the late Disney effects wizard Art Cruickshank, ASC, an actor on a raft in a water tank was shot against a Sodium matte backing. The backing and the actor reflected strongly in the water. This enabled the Disney optical department to matte the actor and his reflection into ocean backgrounds. Cruickshank's method was revived and used effectively in blue screen shots in *Daylight* (1996) and more recently in greenscreen shots in *Bruce Almighty* (2003) where Jim Carrey and Morgan Freeman seem to be walking on Lake Erie, while actually standing in a shallow water tank on the back lot.

The spillway at the back of both tanks ensure a seamless transition between the screen and its reflection in the water.

Controlling Spill Light

Attentive use of flags and teasers on set lighting and black cloth on bright surfaces outside the frame will eliminate most spill light on the backing. (To see spill light when the backing is lit, look through a red filter.) A small amount of white spill light from the set inevitably hits the backing. It usually comes from the large, nearly unflaggable soft sources that simulate skylight. Since the skylight is typically two or three stops down from the key light, the spill has little effect on the backing. Realistic lighting should be the paramount concern.

If there is white light contaminating an area of the backing, a higher level of the alpha channel can be applied in post to darken it. Since there is no difference in color between, say, transparent white smoke or mist, and white light of the same brightness falling on the backing, it's clear that the less white light contamination there is to be cleaned up, the better. Otherwise, as

IMAGE COURTESY BRUCE ALMIGHTY, ©UNIVERSAL STUDIOS

Figure 20. Bruce Almighty water tank composite

the contamination disappears, so do all the transparent foreground pixels of the same color. Screen Correction is invaluable in extracting the maximum detail from smoke and spray shot against white-lit backings.

If the foreground must be flat-lit to simulate overcast, a good approach is to bring most of the light in from overhead through a large, translucent silk. On stage, much of the overhead soft light may be kept off the backing with a series of horizontal black teasers hung directly beneath the silk, running its entire width parallel to the backing. The teasers are progressively longer top to bottom as they get near the backing, preventing the backing from "seeing" the silk (see Figure 18 above).

LIGHTING VIRTUAL SETS

Inescapably, if one is lighting an actor and the surrounding floor with white light, there is no way to control the floor brightness independently of the actor, other than changing the floor paint or floor fabric. The only control available is the balance between the actor's shadow and the rest of the floor and backing.

Lighting Procedure for Holding the Shadow (Petro Vlahos Technique)

1. Turn on the key light so as to cast the desired shadow.
2. Measure the brightness on the floor just outside the shadow (use a spot brightness meter and green filter assuming that it's a green floor).
3. Light all the rest of the green floor to this measured brightness while adding as little light as possible to the shadow area.
4. Light the green walls to achieve the same brightness as the floor.
5. Shadow density may be increased by blocking fill light from the shadow area, or lightened by adding fill light to the shadow area.

Shadow density is controlled by adjusting the fill light, not by adjusting the key light. Outside the shadow, the entire green set should appear to have equal and uniform intensity as seen from the camera position. Strive to stay within ±⅓ f-stop; Screen Correction can deal with brightness variations as great as plus or minus one f-stop.

Figure 21. Blue virtual set lit to retain shadow

The human eye quickly compensates for small light changes; it is not a good absolute measuring device. (It is however superb at comparisons.) It is necessary to use a spot brightness meter and green filter to check for uniform brightness. A digital camera with a computer display is also useful for making a quick check of lighting uniformity in the three color channels.

In backlight, because of the shallow angle between the camera and floor, the floor will not appear as green as the back wall. A diffused, polarized white-light "glare" component is reflected by the floor because of the shallow angle. For holding good shadows in backlight it is essential to use a polarizing filter over the camera lens. The HN38 is recommended. Rotate the filter until the floor glare is canceled. Ideally, the backlights should be polarized too, but it is rarely done. Large sheets of polarizing plastic are available up to about 19" wide; they can be protected against heat with Heat Shield reflecting filter material. Of course, HMIs emit less heat than tungsten lamps to begin with.

The composite in Figure 21 might be improved by adding a slight greenish density and image shift to the background where it is seen through the thick glass table top

LIGHTING TO ELIMINATE THE SHADOW (VLAHOS TECHNIQUE)

1. Light the entire green set uniformly with large area diffused light sources.
2. Check uniformity as noted above.
3. Place the actor in position. If he casts a shadow, add additional low-level lighting to return the light level in the shadow to its original level.
4. Add a modest key light to create the desired modeling, and ignore the shadow it casts. The added key light will cause a shadow to be visible to the eye, but because the key light did not affect the green intensity of the floor in the shadow it has created, the shadow can be made to drop out in compositing.

Tracking Markers

When the foreground camera moves, the background must move appropriately. Unless foreground and/or background can be photographed

IMAGE COURTESY
UNIVERSAL STUDIOS

Figure 22. Three frames from "Bruce Almighty" Steadicam shot

with a motion-control camera, tracking data must be extracted from the foreground image and applied to the background during compositing. This process is called Matchmoving.

Tracking marks applied to the otherwise featureless screen give the matchmovers fixed points to track. These marks must obviously show in the photographed scene, but ideally they should clear the foreground actors, or at least avoid their heads, since they must be removed in the composite. Marks are typically laid out in a rectangular pattern, with about 3' to 5' between them—depending on the lens used, the action and the distance to the backing. Black or white tape crosses will usually suffice, though uniquely identifiable markers are very helpful if there is much tracking to do.

Figures 22 shows the continuation of the elaborate Steadicam shot that begins in Figures 8 through 10 earlier in this chapter that includes a pan of about 140 degrees The black tape marks on the screen provided the data to track in the panoramic background (Figure 23), which was seamed together from three static BeauCam VistaVision plates shot from a tugboat with a gyro-stabilized head. In the process the American Falls and the Canadian Falls were moved closer together.

If camera shake or other sudden motion is required in the foreground photography, motion blur can obliterate the tracking marks. The Aerocrane Strobe Tracking System created by Alvah Miller provides target arrays of LED lamps which strobe in sync with the camera shutter, giving well-defined marks on every frame even if they are not in focus. Cylindrical LEDs have uniform brightness even when viewed off axis.

Sometimes it is desirable to light the tracking LEDs continuously, allowing them to blur in motion. Valuable tracking information can be derived from the length of the blur. Consult the tracking team for their preference.

ON-SET PREVIEW

On-set preview composites made with a still camera and calibrated monitor, like the Kodak/Panavision Preview System, or a live composite made with a hardware Ultimatte device will alert the crew to problems before they are committed to film. A few video assist companies provide this specialized service.

Using the digital Ultimatte previewer (hardware device or software on a computer) on the motion picture set eliminates much guesswork and un-

IMAGE COURTESY BRUCE ALMIGHTY, ©UNIVERSAL STUDIOS

Figure 23. Panoramic background from three VistaVision plates

certainty. It's a great assist in photographing actors who must be realistically integrated with people and objects in the background scene. Previewing with Ultimatte also immediately identifies the acceptable limits in lighting irregularities and wardrobe color.

If it's a digital shoot, an output video stream must be available that's compatible with the Ultimatte. An outboard processor may be needed. This yields the best preview available with all the foreground-background relationships visible at full quality.

For film shoots, a small, outboard color camera feeds the previewer. (Film camera color taps, even when they can be switched to 100% video, are so starved for light that they usually cannot make good composites, although if their geometry is properly adjusted, they are fine for alignment purposes.) Playback from disk or tape provides the background scene.

TV Monitors

It's often necessary to matte TV images into monitors when the desired on-screen material is not available before shooting. When the monitor is live, the best approach overall is to feed it a pure green signal and adjust its brightness to match the shooting stop. With this approach the room reflections in the monitor surface can carry over believeably into the composite, the camera can operate freely, and actors can cross over the screen without difficulties in post. Watch for reflections of the screen on actors. Where the monitor is just a prop, it's often possible to rig a backlit green fabric screen in or behind the monitor. If set lighting permits the monitor to be front-lit to a sufficiently high level, the monitor can be painted green or covered with green fabric behind the glass face plate. The edges of the monitor usually provide all the tracking data needed in operated shots; no on-screen markers required.

COSTS AND CONSEQUENCES

Film Photography: Choosing a Camera Negative

Some camera negatives are better suited to composite work than others. Ideally, one would choose the finest grained, sharpest film available. It is also important to have low cross-sensitivity between the color layers. Foreground and background film stocks do not have to match, but of course it's helpful if they have similar grain and color characteristics.

Kodak Vision 2, 100T and 200T (tungsten balance), films are ideal for green and blue backing work. The dye clouds are very tight and well defined. Vision 3, 500T, the latest in a series of remarkable fine-grain high-speed films, as one would expect is still grainier than the lower speed films. While the 500T film is not ideal, a well-exposed 500T negative is much better than a marginally exposed 200T negative!

An interlayer effect in these films produces a dark line around bright foreground objects (such as white shirts) when they are photographed against a green screen. Software can deal with this effect.

Kodak Vision 2, 50-speed daylight film produces superb results in sunlight, with very low shadow noise, but require high light levels on stage.

If these 100T and 200T films cannot be used for aesthetic reasons, one should still pick the finest grain emulsion compatible with lighting requirements. Be aware that additional image processing (and cost) may be required. A few negative emulsions have so much cross-sensitivity between the color layers that they should not be used.

Film emulsions are constantly evolving. As an example, recent improvements in red sensitivity in some emulsions have been accompanied by more sensitivity to infra-red reflected from costumes, altering their color noticeably. This effect is easily dealt with by filtration—if you know it's there. A quick test of actors and costumes is always worthwhile.

Digital Photography: Choosing a Camera

Since all three color channels are used in creating the composite, an ideal camera would have high resolution and uncompressed color (bandwidth) in each channel.

There are there are thee major factors affecting color recording:

1. Spatial resolution
2. Captured bit depth
3. Recorded bit depth and compression

Spatial resolution

Spatial resolution is broadly related to the number of photosites (light-sensitive elements) available for each color. In single-chip cameras, the green, red, and blue photosites are on a single plane in a mosaic geometry. Depending on the camera, groups of four to six adjacent photosites are sampled and interpolated to create each full-color pixel. (The variation in sampling methods is the reason that there is not necessarily a relationship between pixel count and actual resolution of a given camera.) Most digital cameras use a mosaic called a Bayer Array on which there are half as many blue photosites as there are green photosites. Likewise there are half as many red photosites as green photosites. The "missing" values are derived through interpolation from adjacent pixels in the "de-Bayering" operation. Since human visual acuity is greatest in the green wavelengths, Bayer's array gives excellent visual results from an optimally small number of photosites.

Even in the best high-resolution Bayer arrays the blue and red image is still half the resolution of the green image, which limits the resolution and fine detail of the mask image.[5] To address this and other image quality issues, a few high-end single-sensor cameras (Panavision's Genesis, Sony F35) have a 35mm-film-sized sensor with full resolution in all three colors. (Although the sensors in the two cameras are nearly identical, at this writing the F35 has the edge in dynamic range.)

In three-chip cameras like Sony F23, the color image is split into green, red, and blue images by a beam-splitter behind the lens. Each component color is imaged on one of three full-resolution chips, so there is no resolution loss in the red and blue channels, and no need to interpolate color values. The F23 uses ⅔" HD resolution sensors, smaller than 35mm film, which results in greater depth of field (similar to that of 16mm), which some filmmakers love and others find undesirable. F23's native output is a 4:4:4 pixel-for-pixel uncompressed image, which when correctly processed yields first-class composites.

"4:4:4" does not refer directly to RGB bandwidth, but rather to "YUV". The Y channel carries the luma or brightness information while U and V are the channels from which the color information is derived (similar to Lab color space in Photoshop). In a 4:4:4 recording, every channel is recorded at the full color depth. "4-4-4" is actually a misnomer, carried over from standard definition D1 digital video. Because it's well understood to mean full bandwidth in all three channels, its use has continued into the high-definition-and-higher digital cinema world.)

Arri Alexa, with a 35mm-film-sized Bayer Array sensor, on paper isn't the winner of the Pixel Count contest. Nevertheless Alexa has produced some of the best composite results to date, thanks to dynamic range at least the equal of present-day film negative and extremely high quality on-board image processing.

RED Epic and Sony F65, examples of a new generation of 4K-and-higher Bayer Array cameras, have produced state-of-the-art composite work. F65's huge dynamic range is particularly useful. At 4K and above, detail loss due to de-Bayering is less of a factor. Any untried camera should of course be tested with the actual subject matter.

---

5. It should be noted that film builders use a roughly equivalent compromise: green- and red-sensitive negative layers have more grain and less resolution than the green layer.

Color Bandwidth and Compression

Assuming your camera can produce a full-bandwidth, uncompressed RGB signal, much information can be lost when that signal is compressed and recorded. Many HD VCRs are limited to 4:2:2 recording, which includes rolling off the green channel's high frequencies and applying half-bandwidth MPEG compression to blue and red.

Just as the classic Bayer array has a negligible effect on images intended for viewing but can adversely affect composite quality, well-compressed images designed to look good on screen can have serious limitations when composited. Good software engineering can recover some of the lost bandwidth, but edge detail (fine hair and so forth) and shadow noise still suffer from compression artifacts. A laundry list of compression artifacts includes dark or light lines trailing or leading moving objects, banding in dark areas, and so forth. These problems are even more pronounced in DV and SD cameras. With new cameras constantly coming on line, testing on the actual subject matter is always worthwhile.

Edge Enhancement/Sharpening/Detail Settings

Camera edge enhancement/sharpening should be turned off. The artificial edges that sharpening produces will otherwise carry into the composite. If sharpening is needed, it can be done during compositing.

Recording

Recording in "data mode" gives maximum flexibility and best quality in post. "Data mode" records the uncompressed data (as directly off the camera sensor as the camera's design allows) to a hard disk. This is often called "Raw" mode, but beware: at least one camera's (RED) "Raw" mode is in fact compressed. Since Raw data cannot be viewed directly, a separate viewing conversion path is required to feed on-set monitors.

If recording in data mode is not possible, shoot material intended for postcompositing as uncompressed 4:4:4 full-bandwidth HD (or better) video onto a hard drive or a full-bandwidth VCR, such as Sony's 4:4:4 SR format machines. While Arri Raw is the preferred output from Alexa cameras, Alexa can also record in Apple ProRes 4444, a remarkably high quality compressed format that has produced good composite results.

To sum up, resolution numbers are not the whole story, since some cameras trade off resolution for color depth. Test your available camera and recorder choices.

An Imperfect World

You may have no choice but to shoot or record with 4:2:2 equipment. While 4:2:2 is not ideal, don't forget that the last two *Star Wars* films were shot with ⅔" 4:2:2 cameras, cropping a 2.40 slice from the center, including thousands of green screen composites. Test the camera on the subject matter. 4:2:2 can produce a satisfactory result in greenscreen (since the green channel has the highest resolution in these cameras), but one should not expect the ultimate in fine edge detail. (Consumer cameras typically record 4:1:1, and are not recommended for pro visual effects use.)

Whatever the camera, it can't be overemphasized that any edge enhancement or sharpening should be turned off. The artificial edges that sharpening produces will otherwise carry into the composite and cannot be removed. If sharpening is needed, it can be added during compositing.

FILTRATION

In general no color or diffusion filters other than color-temperature correction should be used on the camera when shooting green or blue screen work. Compositing can be called "the struggle to hold edge detail"; obviously low-con, soft effects or diffusion filtering that affects the edge or allows screen illumination to leak into the foreground will have an adverse effect. For that reason, smoke in the atmosphere is not recommended; it can be simulated convincingly in the composite.

To ensure that the filter effect you desire will be duplicated in the composite, shoot a short burst of the subject with the chosen filter, making sure it is slated as "Filter Effect Reference".

Negative Scanning and Digital Conversion

The film frames, data recording, or video recording must be converted into frame-based digital files the software can use. It's important not to lose information at this step.

The three layers of the color negative are sensitive exclusively to the red, green and blue portions of the color spectrum. When the negative is scanned, the RGB densities of each pixel in the image are translated into red, green and blue numerical levels in a digital memory. The three color records of each frame are referred to as the red, green and blue channels. They are usually recorded as Cineon or DPX frames, which are uncompressed formats.

Video and data must be similarly converted into frames. This step is sometimes called "digitization", really a misnomer since the source is already digital. These frames are usually recorded in the DPX format. The Academy ACES format, a universal format which is coming on line at post facilities around the world, can accommodate DPX and any future wider-gamut color space.

COLOR CORRECTION

Color correction at the scanning/conversion stage can be a major source of data loss. It should not be built-in to image files intended for compositing.

On the other hand, a few frames recorded with the desired color and filtration will be invaluable reference in the composite step.

WORKING WITH THE VISUAL EFFECTS SUPERVISOR

The vfx supervisor is the cinematographer's ally on the greenscreen set. So much depends on the quality of the original photography. Befriend that person early in the game, and keep him or her in the loop!

The supervisor will help you achieve the photographic result you desire. Be sure he or she understands the final look required, if (for example) you need to shoot without diffusion on the lens. Be sure to shoot properly slated reference with the desired diffusion, filtration and so forth, so that it can be matched in the composite stage.

For more information, refer to the *Visual Effects Society Handbook*, which has a similar chapter on this topic, with an expanded sections dealing with setting up large greenscreens on location.

APPENDIX: COMPOSITING SOFTWARE

While it's rarely necessary for cinematographers to create composites themselves, it's very useful to be aware of the tools in common use.

The software described below is in wide use. All save Nuke IBK are available as "plug-ins" for most of the leading digital compositing packages, including After Effects, Nuke, Flame/Inferno, Shake, and so on. All contain filters to deal with less-than-ideal video like DV.

Each package has individual strong points; all are capable of first class results with well-shot photography. Sometimes the best results come when two programs are used on a single shot. This list is by no means inclusive.

Keylight

At this writing, Keylight is the most-used package, thanks to its bundling into After Effects Professional and Nuke. A straightforward interface makes it very easy to use.

Keylight was developed originally at London's pioneering Computer Film Company by Wolfgang Lempp and Oliver James. It is marketed worldwide by The Foundry.

Ultimatte

Ultimatte and Ultimatte AdvantEdge, are still the tools of choice for difficult shots. AdvantEdge borrows from Ultimatte's knockout concept by processing the edge transitions separately from the core of the foreground image, blending them seamlessly into the background without loss of detail.

The deep and rich user controls require an experienced operator to get the most from the software. The interface works as a "black box" within the compositing package, which can complicate workflow. One benefit of this architecture is that the interface is identical in the wide range of supported software packages. In 2010, Ultimatte AdvantEdge software was bundled into Nuke, the first implementation in 32-bit color depth.

Ultimatte software was the first of its kind; it was derived from the original film Color Difference logic created by Petro Vlahos. The digital implementation won multiple Academy Awards. Ultimatte real time video hardware compositing devices are also available from the company.

Primatte

Primatte was orginally developed at Imagica Japan by Kaz Mishima. The unique polyhedral color analysis allows fine-tuned color selections between foreground and background. The user interface is intuitive and uncomplicated while offering many options.

Nuke IBK (Image Based Keyer)

The Nuke IBK was developed by Paul Lambert at Digital Domain. It employs Ultimatte code carried over from earlier Cineon and Rays compositing software packages. Like Ultimatte, it can deal with a wide variance in backing color by creating a synthetic clean plate

DEDICATED WITH GRATITUDE TO PETRO VLAHOS

This document draws heavily on the Traveling Matte chapter that Petro Vlahos and I wrote for previous editions of the ASC manual. Mr. Vlahos, a multiple Oscar® winner, perfected traveling matte systems for film with several revolutionary inventions, including the Color Difference blue screen technique in 1958. In the years that followed, he created analog and then digital hardware and software versions of Ultimatte, the first high-quality electronic compositing tools. At their core, all digital bluescreen and greenscreen compositing software employs variants of the original Vlahos algorithms.

With thanks to:

Chuck Schuman, Cinematographer of "Journey to the Center of the Earth", whose detailed notes on the previous version have been incorporated into this article.

Paul Vlahos for images from Ultimatte Corp.

Jon and Kay Erland of Composite Components Corp. for decades of friendship, advice and their tireless efforts to improve visual effects composites.

Petro Vlahos is the inventor of the film Color Difference Travelling Matte System, and both video and film Ultimatte compositing. He has won three Oscars® for his work.

Bill Taylor ASC is a cinematographer specializing in visual effects and co-owner of Illusion Arts, Inc.

Persons interested in details of the purely photographic travelling matte process should consult the 7th edition of the American Cinematographer Manual.

Photographing Miniatures

by Dennis Muren, ASC

The recent increase in the use of miniatures in motion pictures means that live-action cinematographers may now be called upon to photograph miniatures, an area usually handled by specialists. Today's pinpoint-sharp lenses, very fine-grain color negatives and crystal-clear film stocks can reveal flaws, and the solutions require the utmost attention to detail by every member of the effects team. The effects cinematographer should talk to the director, the live-action director of photography and the effects crew. He or she should look at as much footage from the job as possible, especially immediately preceding and following the miniature shot. Based on this material, he should then visualize how the shot would have been photographed had it been built full size and apply that information to the following:

1. The notion that miniatures look big when photographed with wide-angle lenses from a low viewpoint is somewhat true. But when cut into a sequence filmed from above or with long lenses, the shot may look out of place.
2. A small f-stop is usually necessary to hold the depth of field needed to keep the model in focus.
3. The entire model and set must appear to be in focus, as it probably would have been if the scene had been built full size.
4. When shooting a fully miniature shot, a diffusion filter on the camera can give an artificial atmosphere that enhances the sense of reality.
5. Match the preceding and following live-action photography as closely as possible. Lighting units should be placed at the scaled distance from the model to duplicate natural light falloff. Small units help the scale.
6. Artificial smoke can be used to slightly cloud the atmosphere in a miniature and give a realistic aerial haze. In instances where more control is needed, bridal veil material can be tightly stretched within a set and separately lit.
7. Panning, tilting, trucking, and even jolts and shakes can add greatly to a shot if they are appropriate to that moment.
8. High-speed film stocks allow for extra stopping down. Perforation size and location can be checked on each roll to help ensure rock-steady images, if necessary.
9. For high-speed shooting, rental cameras should be loaded and tested by the assistant who will use them. Registration steady tests should be made at the chosen speeds, if necessary.

MODEL SIZE

Water, fire and exploding models should be as large as the budget and safety allow, even half size if possible and shot high-speed. Intense wind can help break up out-of-scale water droplets and, in some cases, fire. Exploding models should be prebroken, reassembled and exploded within slow-moving, low-powered and colorful pyrotechnics, preferably with two or more blasts. Other types of models can be built just big enough to be adequately detailed and still carry depth of field.

Miniature explosions and fire can be dangerous because the camera may need to be in close proximity to the miniature. Plan accordingly.

SHOOTING SPEEDS

If there is no motion on the miniature, it can be photographed at any speed. Water, fire, explosions and falling effects are usually done with large models and camera speeds of up to 360 fps. The exact speed depends upon the scale of the model and the effect desired. The chart on page 896 is a starting point, but for the best results, tests should be made.

High-speed shots can often be expensive and unpredictable events because of the uncertainty of required camera speeds, pyrotechnics, winds, mechanical equipment, human error and the need to sequence events in much faster succession than they will be viewed. It is not unusual to shoot miniature explosions at 300 fps to achieve a huge scale. One second of shooting time will be seen as 12.5 seconds of screen time ($^{300}/_{24}$). If the pyrotechnician wants to sequence many explosions, he may ignite the charges using a computer and be able to specify each timing by the millisecond. Movements of the camera and any objects in the shot will need to move 12.5 times faster than in real time. This can make for some very fast-moving riggings. Be sure to work closely with the rigging crew so that they will understand your problems (reaching speed, operating, event timings, aborting, etc.). Achieving an adequate level of good-looking lighting can be very difficult if shooting high-speed at a small f-stop. If using HMIs, make sure that there will be no flicker at the filming speeds. Scenes which are supposed to take place outdoors should be shoot outdoors if weather permits.

With stop motion, shooting is accomplished at one frame at a time with the object being slightly moved by hand between each frame. One fourth-second exposures or more per frame allow for great depth of field in low light levels. Stop-motion photography is used to give a freedom of movement and expression to an object or figure.

Motion-control photography is used when the camera or an object or figure is moved by computer-controlled motors at very slow speeds. Long exposure times per frame allow for very small f-stops. The computer can repeat the movements of the motors, which allows for multiple exposures. Any facet of a shot can be isolated and wedged for intensity, color, filtration and atmosphere. The image can be built up through multiple exposures made from the chosen wedge frames, while the computer repeats the same motions each time.

Go-motion shooting is used when shooting animal or creature models. The major body parts are attached to rods that are moved by computer-controlled motors. Detail movements are animated by hand each frame. Single-frame shooting allows for small f-stops at long exposure times. Coverage at various angles and camera speeds is especially useful to help cushion the risks on high-speed shots.

CALCULATING CAMERA SPEED
Explanation of table (Page 896)

The scale of the model may be stated as "inches per foot," or as a fraction of full size. In photographing a miniature, portraying any motion when the speed of that motion depends on gravity, the frame rate of the camera is governed by the scale. This includes falling objects or water, wave action, fire or smoke, explosions in which objects are thrown into the air, etc. On the other hand, any object (for instance, an automobile) moving at a controllable speed can be related to the selected camera speed; the camera frame rate is increased as the inverse square root of the scale fraction (the square root of the relation of full size to miniature). For instance, for a miniature $1/16$ full size ($3/4$ inch = 1 foot), the inverse of the fraction is 16. The square root of 16 is 4 and the frame rate should be: 4 x normal = 96 fps.

In the same set, an automobile portrayed as traveling 60 mph should move $1/16$th that speed because of the scale, but increased four times because of the frame rate.

$$\frac{(Scale\ fraction)\ x\ (portrayed\ speed)\ x\ (frame\ rate)}{(normal\ frame\ rate)}$$
$$1/16\ x\ 60\ x\ {}^{96}/_{24} = 15\ mph\ (or\ 22\ ft./sec.)$$

Dennis Muren, ASC is the senior visual-effects supervisor at Industrial Light & Magic. Recipient of eight Academy Awards for Best Achievement in Visual Effects, Muren is actively involved in the design and development of new techniques and equipment.

In-Camera Compositing of Miniatures with Full-Scale Live-Action Actors

by Dan Curry
ASC Associate Member

"Hanging" or "Foreground" miniatures have been a valuable method of creating production value since the earliest days of filmmaking. In-camera compositing makes the use of miniatures an attractive alternative when postproduction compositing may not be possible. These techniques may be of special interest to student filmmakers working with microbudgets.

With the exception of 3-D, photographed images are two-dimensional. The camera, and the audience, cannot tell how far or near an object may actually be. The only clues are linear perspective, aerial perspective (caused by natural atmospheric haze) and focus. Filmmakers can take advantage of this by placing a miniature within the frame to create the illusion that it is part of the full-scale world being photographed. There are many ingenious ways to incorporate live actors into foreground miniatures using platforms, ladders, and devices to cast shadows. Once the basic principles of photographing miniatures are understood, filmmakers can expand upon them to suit their specific needs.

Some advantages of hanging miniatures

▶ In-camera compositing eliminates postproduction costs.
▶ One miniature can be photographed from many different angles, and therefore used for different shots.
▶ Good miniature builders are easier to find than matte painters.
▶ When shot in daylight, light on the miniature will naturally match the light in the scene.
▶ Nodal pan/tilts can be utilized.
▶ When carefully aligned, people can be positioned "inside" or "on" the miniature.

Important considerations when photographing hanging miniatures

▶ Scout and shoot reference photos of location in advance and prepare miniature for specific location requirements.
▶ Adequate depth of field must be established.

Illustration is not to scale

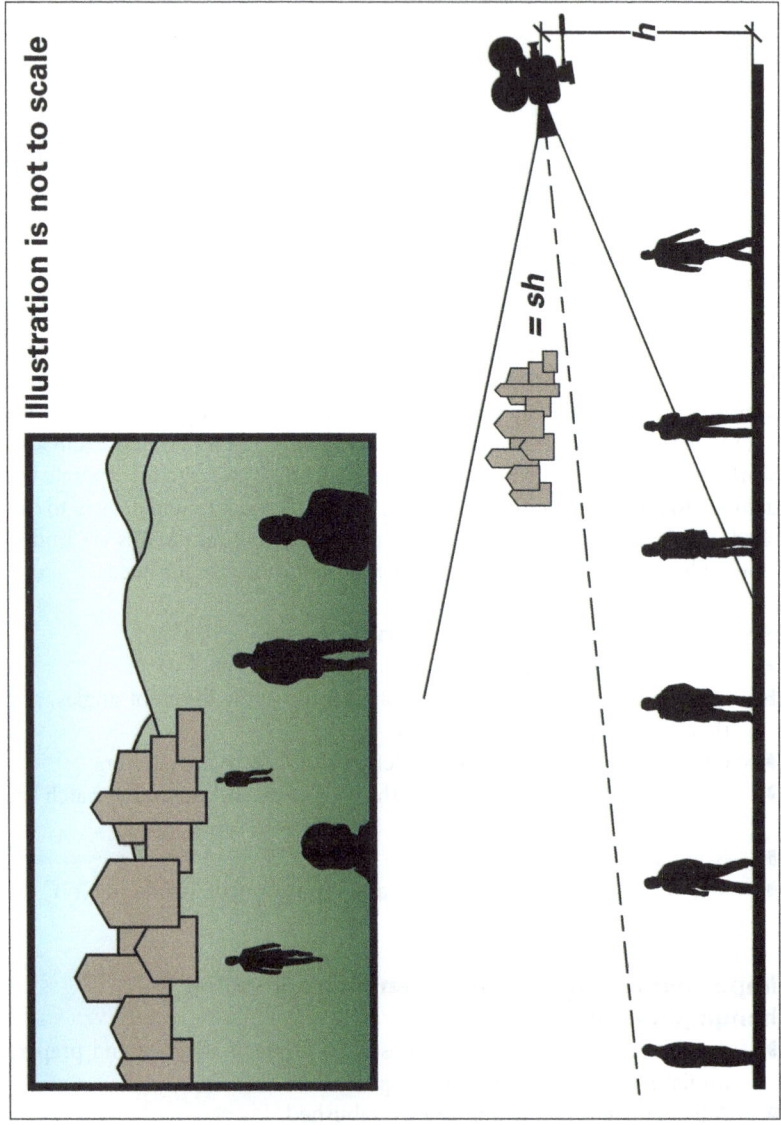

Figure 1.
The actual height of the lens above ground level should be the same as the height in scale above the ground level miniature.

E.g., If the actual lens height is 8 feet, and the scale of the model is ½ inch equals 1 foot, then the lens height above the miniature's ground level should be 8 feet in the scale of the miniature: (½" x 8 = 4").

Depth of field must be sufficient to carry focus from the nearest point on the miniature to infinity. Use the Depth of Field Chart in this manual to determine the aperture needed.

h = actual height above ground

sh = equivalent scale height

Figure 1a. Approaching distant structures

▶ Plan proper set-up for accurate perspective and miniature stability.
▶ Make sure that light angles and cast shadows work with the illusion. A backlit structure that would naturally cast a shadow on the ground in front of it (which it cannot do unless the ground is built into the miniature set) will shatter the illusion of reality. Key light should be forward of the miniature. When scouting locations note time of day for the best light angle.
▶ If actors are to appear "inside" or "on" the miniature, provisions must be made to cast shadows on them where needed.
▶ Short focal length lenses offer the greatest depth of field.
▶ Aerial perspective (natural atmospheric haze) can be simulated with diffusion sprayed onto a foreground glass in the appropriate areas. Clear Krylon spray works well.

It is impossible to predict every situation that may arise, but the following examples may provide useful guidelines:

Example 1: Actors approach a distant city or structure.
▶ If the actual height of the lens is 10', the ground level on the miniature must be set below the lens an equal distance in scale. If the scale of the miniature is ½" = 1', then ground level on the miniature should be 5" below the lens.
▶ Depth of field must be determined (use the chart elsewhere in this manual) to carry focus to include the miniature. If the nearest point on the model is 4' from the camera and an 18 mm lens (on a 35 mm camera) an f-stop of 5.6 with focus set at 6½' will carry focus from 3' 6" to infinity.

Example 2: Using a miniature as a foreground cutting piece.

Example 3: Perspective from a tall structure.

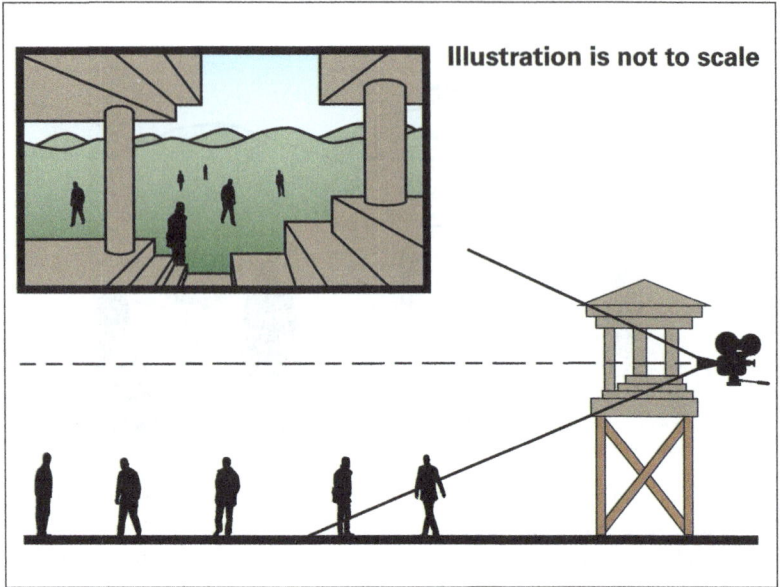

Figure 3. Floor level of the miniature should be the same elevation it would have if full scale. E.g., If the set was full sized and the floor was supposed to be 25' above ground level, the floor of the miniature should also be 25' in elevation to keep the people on the ground scale with the miniature. The lens should be the correct scale height above the model's floor.

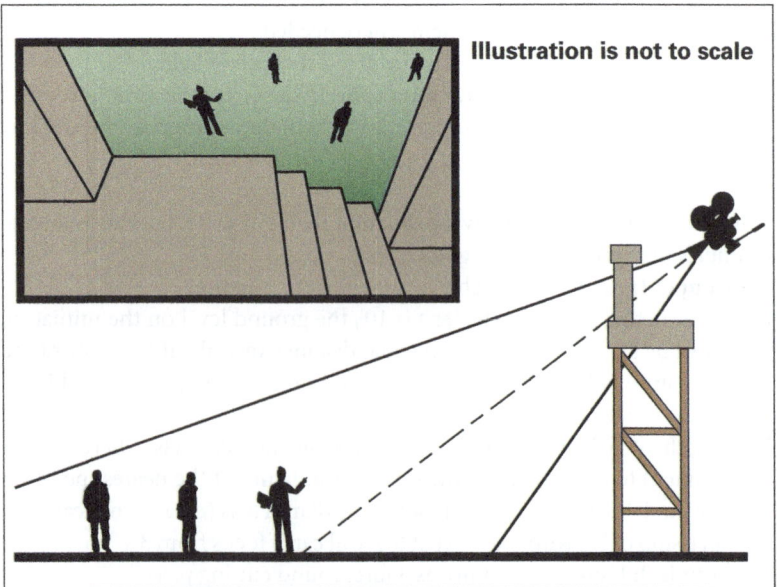

Figure 4. The same guidelines apply as in Figure 3

Example 4: Hanging miniature as a ceiling extension.
▶ This can be useful on soundstages where lighting grids must be used to illuminate set and there is no room for a practical ceiling.

NODAL PANS AND TILTS

Pans and tilts are possible if the camera is mounted so that the pivot point is set at the nodal point of the lens. A simple way to confirm that the camera is properly mounted at the nodal point is to set two objects (c-stands, stakes, human stand-ins, etc.) directly in line with one another in front of the camera. Try a test pan. If the foreground object appears to move in the opposite direction of the pan, then the camera is mounted in front of the nodal point, slide it back on the head until the two objects remain in alignment when the camera pans.

FORCED PERSPECTIVE

Situations may arise where forced perspective or constantly changing scales may provide the best solution to production needs. If this is the case, close coordination between director, director of photography, visual effects supervisor, production designer, and a highly skilled model maker is required, as there is no room for error.

MIXED SCALES

To gain a greater illusion of distance, elements within a miniature scene can be built, working from larger scale in the foreground to smaller scale the farther away objects are intended to appear.

ADJUSTING SPEEDS OF MOVING OBJECTS

Useful for situations such as moving miniature trains to be photographed as an in-camera composite with full-scale elements at 24 fps.

Example:
▶ A miniature elevated train, scale ¼" = 1', is to pass through frame as part of a live-action scene.
▶ At 4 (¼" units) per foot 4 x 12" = 48 (¼" per second)
▶ The fractional equivalent of this scale is ¹⁄₄₈. (scale expressed as a fraction) x (depicted speed) = scale speed
▶ If the speed depicted is 30 mph, then ¹⁄₄₈ x 30mph = .625mph
▶ The speed of the miniature must be ¹⁄₄₈ of the desired speed or .625 mph.
▶ It is more practical to calculate in feet per second.
(5280'/3600 sec) x .625 = .92 ft/sec
▶ In a practical situation, mark off as many .92 ft increments as is convenient, and adjust the speed of the miniature train to match. If you mark

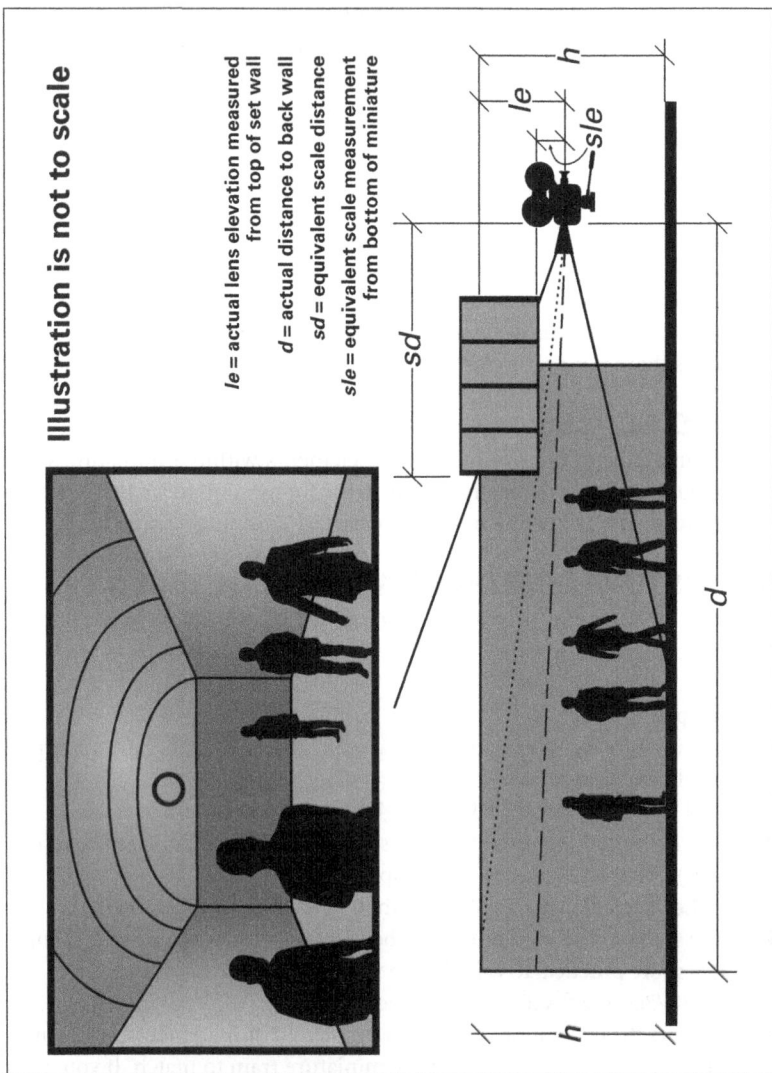

Figure 5.

The actual elevation of the lens below the level of the top of the set wall should be the same as the distance in scale below the level of the equivalent part (bottom) of the miniature.

The actual distance to the back wall of the set should equal the scale distance to the back of the miniature.

E.g., If the actual lens height is set 6' below the top of the set wall, and the scale of the model is ½" equals 1', then the bottom of the miniature shoudl be set 6' in scale above the lens height (½" x 6 = 3").

Depth of field must be sufficient to carry focus from the nearest point on the miniature to the back wall. Use the Depth of Field Chart in this manual to determine the aperture needed. Set lighting and lighting within the miniature must be matched to create a successful illusion. The miniature can be suspended by any means invisible to the camera.

Illustration is not to scale

le = actual lens elevation measured from top of set wall

d = actual distance to back wall

sd = equivalent scale distance

sle = equivalent scale measurement from bottom of miniature off four .92 increments, then it should take 4 seconds for your train to cover the distance.

(Please refer to "Calculating Camera Speed" on pages 365, 682-683 and 896.)

Dan Curry is an Emmy-winning master of visual effects. Working as an art director, matte painter, effects supervisor and producer on more than sixty television productions. He has many classic shows under his belt, including Star Trek, Deep Space Nine *and* Star Trek Voyager. *He holds a MFA in film and theater.*

Drawing Photographic Perspective

There is only one horizon line.

All vanishing points are on the horizon line.

All elements must fall parallel to the rays of the vanishing point.

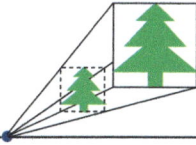

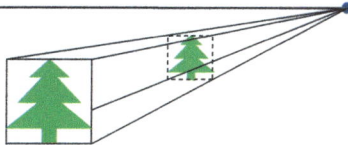

Light Sources, Luminaires and Lighting Filters

COLOR TEMPERATURE

Color temperature describes the "true" temperature of a "black-body radiator" and thereby completely defines the spectral energy distribution (SED) of the object. When the object becomes luminous and radiates energy in the visible portion of the spectrum, it is said to be incandescent. Simply stated, this means that when an object is heated to an appropriate temperature, some of its radiated energy is visible.

The color temperature is usually described in terms of degrees Kelvin (°K). The first visible color when an object is heated is usually described as "dull cherry red". As the temperature is increased, it visually becomes "orange," then "yellow," and finally "white" hot.

One of the most important features of incandescent radiators is that they have a continuous spectrum. This means that energy is being radiated at all the wavelengths in its spectrum. The term "color temperature" can only be properly applied to radiating sources that can meet this requirement. When the term "color temperature" is applied to fluorescent lamps (or other sources that do not meet the criteria for incandescence), it really refers to "correlated color temperature."

CORRELATED COLOR TEMPERATURE

The term correlated color temperature is used to indicate a visual match where the source being described is not a black body radiator. The term is often abused, an example being its application to such light sources as mercury-vapor lamps.

From a photographic standpoint, the correlated color temperature can be extremely misleading. It is important to keep in mind that its connotations are visual. It is a number to be approached with extreme caution by the cinematographer.

See the Correlated Color Temperature chart on page 821.

THE MIRED SYSTEM

When dealing with sunlight and incandescent sources, the MIRED system offers a convenient means for dealing with the problems of measurement when adjusting from one color temperature to another. This system is only for sources that can truly be described as having a color temperature. The term MIRED is an acronym for Micro Reciprocal Degrees. The MIRED number for a given color temperature is determined by using the following relationship:

Sunlight should not be confused with daylight. Sunlight is the light of the sun only. Daylight is a combination of sunlight and skylight. These values are approximate since many factors affect the correlated color temperature. For consistency, 5500°K is considered to be Nominal Photographic Daylight. The difference between 5000°K and 6000°K is only 33 MIREDs, the same photographic or visual difference as that between household tungsten lights and 3200°K photo lamps (the approximate equivalent of ¼ Blue or ⅛ Orange lighting filters).

$$\text{Mired Value} = \frac{1{,}000{,}000}{\text{Color Temperature (degrees Kelvin)}} = \frac{10^6}{°\text{K}}$$

As a convenience, refer to page 835 to determine the MIRED values for color temperatures between 2000°K and 10,000°K in 100-degree steps.

Filters which change the effective color temperature of a source by a definite amount can be characterized by a "MIRED shift value." This value is computed as follows:

MIRED shift values can be positive (yellowish or minus blue filters) or negative (blue or minus red/green filters). The same filter (representing a single MIRED shift value) applied on light sources with different color temperatures will produce significantly different color-temperature shifts. Occasionally, the term "decamireds" will be used to describe color temperature and filter effects. Decamireds are simply MIREDs divided by 10.

$$\text{Mired Shift Value} = \left(\left[\frac{10^6}{T2} \right] - \left[\frac{10^6}{T1} \right] \right)$$

COLOR RENDERING INDEX

The Color Rendering Index (CRI) is used to specify the stated characteristic of a light source as it might be used for critical visual color examinations, such as in color matching or inspection of objects. The CRI is established by a standard procedure involving the calculated visual appearance of standard colors viewed under the test source and under a standard illuminant. The CRI is not an absolute number, and there is no relative merit to be determined by comparing the CRIs of several sources.

The CRI is of importance photographically only when it is between 90 and 100. This is accepted to mean that such a source has color-rendering properties that are a commercial match to the reference source. For example: the

HMI lamps have a CRI of 90 to 93, referred to the D55 standard illuminant (D55 is the artificial match to standard daylight of 5500°K).

DEALING WITH ILLUMINATION DATA

1. Lighting Quantities — Intensity

There are two ways that intensity information is normally shown. Most lighting manufacturers supplying instruments to the motion-picture industry tend to present their data in a rectangular format. The polar presentation is more likely to be encountered with commercial/industrial-type fixtures.

Where the intensity distribution of a lighting source is known, the illumination produced by the unit can be calculated using the inverse square law. This is expressed as follows:

$$\text{Illumination (footcandles)} = \frac{\text{Intensity (candelas)}}{D^2 \ (D=\text{distance in feet})}$$

$$\text{Illumination (Lux)} = \frac{\text{Intensity (candelas)}}{D^2 \ (D=\text{distance in meters})}$$

Example: A fixture is described as having a center intensity (or center beam candlepower) of 50,000 Candelas. What is the illumination at 25 feet? (What is the illumination at 10 meters?)

(a) at 25 feet:
$$\text{Illumination} = \frac{50,000}{25 \times 25} = \frac{50,000}{625} = 80 \text{ footcandles}$$

(b) at 10 meters:
$$\text{Illumination} = \frac{50,000}{10 \times 10} = \frac{50,000}{100} = 500 \text{ LUX}$$

2. Lighting Quantities — Coverage

Beam Coverage: This is described as the limit of the area covered to within 50% of the maximum intensity.

Field Coverage: This is described as the area covered to within 10% of the maximum intensity.

Of the two areas described above, the beam coverage is the more important photographically. It describes the area that is illuminated at a level that is not lower than one stop down from the center intensity. The assumption is made, where a single distribution is shown, that the distribution pattern is essentially circular.

Calculating Coverage from Beam Angle: The following expression allows the computation of the coverage diameter (W) for any distance (D) and a given beam angle. (See tangent function table on page 679.) The expression is:

W = 2 x (D) x [Tangent (¹/₂ Beam Angle)]

Example: For a distance of 50 feet and a known beam angle of 26 degrees, what is the coverage diameter of the beam (50% of the center)?

D = 50 feet;   Beam Angle = 26 degrees
¹/₂ Beam Angle = 13 degrees
Tangent of 13 degrees = .231

W = 2 x 50 x .231 = 100 x .231 = 23.1 feet

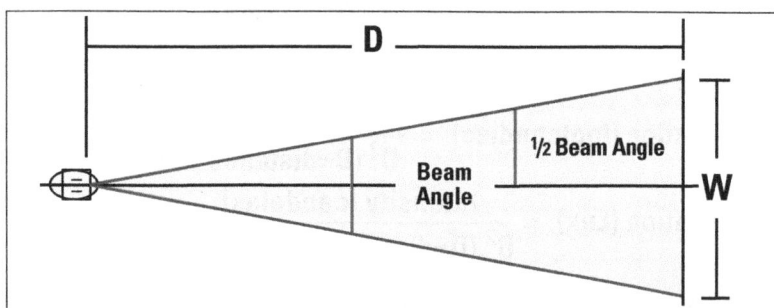

Fig. 1. Lamp Beam

3. General Comments on Calculations

In the event that it is necessary to convert from footcandles to Lux, the value of footcandles should be multiplied by 10.76. To convert Lux to footcandles, divide Lux by 10.76. Lux is the metric measurement of illumination, whereas footcandles is the English method.

PHOTOGRAPHIC LIGHT SOURCES

The sources covered in this section include the more familiar types, such as incandescent, and the AC and DC types of discharge lamps. The initial section deals with the properties and characteristics of natural daylight.

The general characteristics of each type are delineated in moderate detail, including spectral energy distributions and electrical characteristics. In addition, any special considerations for the cinematographer are noted. (See the chart on page 837 for characteristics of typical photographic light sources.)

NATURAL DAYLIGHT

Daylight conditions are highly varied from a photographic viewpoint and are based on the local atmospheric conditions, location on the earth, altitude, time of year, hour of the day and the amount of atmospheric pollutants that may be present. A brief summary of some of the possibilities are presented in the Correlated Color Temperature chart on page 821.

Least Diffuse – In clear cloudless sunlight, the sun as the main lighting source (key) is truly a point. This produces the hardest, most distinct shadows. The incident light level from the sun on such a day can be as much as 10,000 footcandles. The skylight contribution (fill) is about 1,500 footcandles. This produces a lighting ratio of about 7:1 (key to fill). Lighting control in these situations may require booster lighting or the use of certain grip devices such as large overhead scrims.

Most Diffuse – A completely overcast day is essentially shadowless lighting. The entire sky, horizon to horizon, becomes the light source. The incident level may be as low as 200 footcandles.

FILTERS FOR CONTROL OF NATURAL DAYLIGHT

A family of materials supplied as deep-dyed polyester films are made in a variety of subfamilies for application in a number of different lighting situations. One of these subfamilies is designed to deal with natural daylight situations. The materials are supplied in rolls ranging from 48" (122cm) to 60" (152cm) wide, and in rigid acrylic panels ⅛" (3mm) thick and in the same widths as noted and 8' (244cm) to 10' (305cm) high.

When properly applied, image clarity is maintained through windows treated with either the plastic film or rigid panel filters. The panels are particularly useful where wind or strong air movement may cause the plastic film to move and produce visible highlights.

There are three kinds of filters available in these materials: neutral density filters, color-correction filters, and combination filters. (See the filters for daylight correction on page 829.)

INCANDESCENT LIGHT SOURCES

All incandescent light sources consist of a tungsten filament in a sealed bulb which is designed so that the terminals of the filament are accessible. By applying a voltage across these terminals, a current flows through the filament and raises its temperature to a level that results in the production of visible light.

For many years, the standard incandescent globe has been replaced in motion-picture photography with tungsten halogen incandescent lamps that have a longer life and more consistent color temperature.

INCANDESCENT LAMP
OPERATIONAL CHARACTERISTICS

Filters for Incandescent Lamps

These filters are placed in front of incandescent sources to change the color temperature to an approximation of daylight. The filters may be plastic film types, or dichroic filters. The dichroics are usually only utilized as filters which fully convert 3200°K sources to an approximation of daylight (approximately 5500°K). Where the conversion is to be used for fill lighting, the final color temperature would usually be 5000°K, which permits a higher light transmission level.

Care must be exercised in the use of dichroic filters because they do not have uniform filtering characteristics. When used on some types of focusing lights (particularly some of the open reflector tungsten halogen types) as well as wide beam floodlights, there may be color shifts at the outer edges of the field. There also may be sufficient difference between dichroics so that if used on multiple keys in the same scene, there could be significant differences in the various areas being lit. A color-temperature meter should be applied in these situations.

A broad range of very good conversion filters are available. The blue filters (CTB) are used to convert 3200°K sources to higher color temperatures. There is a range of conversion levels. The ⅛, ¼, ½ and full CTBs will allow for adjustment in light sources due to voltage variations and to correct the standard incandescent source to an approximation of 3200°K. The full CTB correct 3200°K to daylight (5500°K). The orange filters (CTO) are used to lower the color temperature. The full CTO will convert daylight (5500°K) to 3200°K. The ⅛, ¼, ½ and ¾ complete this set of filters. However, the primary reason for their existence is to permit the cinematographer to achieve artistic effects.

In order to maintain these artistic effects, the importance of testing any filter conversion system, cannot be over emphasized. There are many small variations that can add up to disappointment. The use of a carefully calibrated three-color color temperature meter is essential. Variations that could cause trouble include: incorrect voltage, lamp globe, lamp reflector, lamp lens, lamp filters, bounce surfaces, atmospheric conditions (open shade, overcast, sunset, sunrise), camera lens, camera filters, negative and positive processing, and finally poor exposure.

DC Carbon Arc Sources

The open carbon arc remains in use, in particular the 225 ampere "Brute" Fresnel lens spotlight. The tables on pages 833 and 838 summarize the various carbon arc units, as well as the type of carbons necessary for each type. There is also a summary of the electrical characteristics of these arcs when properly operated.

Boosted Voltage Operation

It is possible to overvoltage a wide range of standard 120-volt, 2800°–2900°K lamp types and convert them effectively to photographic lamp types. This system ("Colortran" boosting) was widely used in many places around the world until the advent of the tungsten-halogen lamp. Little used in the United States now, it is still in wide use in other parts of the world and offers some interesting advantages. There are many situations in which this system may be both cost-effective and functionally desirable.

Typically, when 120-volt lamps are operated at 165 volts, the color temperature should be approximately 3100–3200°K. It is possible to continue the boosting operation, and some lamp types will actually yield 3300–3400°K when operated at approximately 185 volts. Due to the low pressure in the standard incandescent, long-life lamps, this is a safe type of operation.

A further advantage of this system is that the standard incandescent types utilized in it tend to be much less expensive than the photographic lamp types rated at 3200°K at the operating voltage. Further, the expected life of many of these lamps at 3200°K operation is directly comparable to the life that can be expected from 3200°K-type photographic lamps operated at their rated voltages.

Fluorescent Lighting

There is now a considerable selection of professional lighting fixtures, some of which are very portable and compact, that utilize a range of fluorescent lamps which closely approximate 3200°K and 5500°K lighting. These utilize high frequency (25,000Hz) electronic ballasts which completely eliminate any concerns regarding possible "flicker" problems from operation at usual line frequencies. This system was perfected by Kino Flo. The fluorescent tubes used in these systems have a typical life of 10,000 hours.

Noncolor-correct fluorescents may be corrected by using a series of either minus green (magenta) or plus green filters on the lamps or camera. Some color-correct fluorescent tubes still may have some green spikes in their output when they get too hot. This can be easily taken care of with these filters. (See charts pages 832 and 839.)

Enclosed AC Arc Lamps

Most of these lamps are operated from alternating current sources only and require the use of a high-voltage ignition device to start and restrike them when hot, as well as a ballasting device to limit the current.

AC Arc Lamp Flicker Problem

The potential for a flicker problem exists when simple inductive or reactive-type ballasting is used at line frequency, and where there is no provision for modifying the modulation characteristics of the light source. In such cases, it is necessary to be sure the power source is precisely at 50Hz or 60Hz, and the frame rate and shutter angle of the camera are held in certain specific relationships.

Lamps that can exhibit flicker problems include: fluorescents, mercury-vapor, metal-halide additive types and high-pressure sodium, as well as photographic types such as HMI, CID or low-pressure AC Xenon arcs.

All of the lamps listed require the use of a ballasting system to provide current limiting after the arc is struck. In the past few years, an increasing number of reliable, electronic "flicker-free" ballasts have become available for all HMI wattages. However, a significant number of inductive (magnetic) ballasts are still in rental.

The time-related factors involved in ensuring a uniform exposure from frame to frame using these types of light sources (i.e., flicker-free) are the following:

1. Stability of the power frequency to the lamp ballast
2. Camera frame rate
3. Stability of camera speed
4. Camera shutter angle
5. Phase of shutter relative to light (particularly at high camera speed)

Simply stated, it is necessary to be sure that the same number of light pulsations are present during each exposure interval of the film. The amount of variation permitted is different for different values of the parameters noted above.

The light output of an HMI lamp modulates 83%. This means that the light output is pulsing from 100% to 17% at two times the line power frequency. The result is that there are two light pulsations for each full cycle of the power line fundamental frequency (for 60Hz systems there are 120 pulses per second; for a 50Hz system there are 100 light pulses per second). For 60Hz power, the only valid shutter speeds are any that can divide into 120 evenly (e.g.1, 2, 3, 4, 5, 6, 8, 10, 12, 15, 20, 24, 30, 40, 60, 120). For 50Hz power, the shutter speed must divide into 100 evenly (e.g.1, 2, 4, 5, 10, 20, 25, 50, 100).

HMI™ Lamps

The most widely used of the new types of photographic enclosed AC discharge lamps are known as HMIs. They are made in wattages ranging from 125–18,000. The chart on page 836 illustrates the various versions of this light source.

These are considered medium-length arc types and are fundamentally mercury arcs with rare earth halide additives. The color-temperature range is normally quoted as being between 5600°K and 6000°K with a tolerance of ±400°K. The CRI of all these types is 90 or more, and they are dimmable and capable of being restruck hot.

As the power to the lamp is reduced further, color temperature increases and the CRI decreases. Where the light output needs to be reduced, it is preferable to use neutral density filters on the luminaire in order to avoid any possibility of a shift in color characteristics.

CalColor™ Filters

Rosco Laboratories in conjunction with Eastman Kodak has recently created a family of filters for motion-picture lighting for which they were jointly awarded an Academy Award for Scientific and Technical Achievement. This is Rosco CalColor™, the first system of lighting filters specifically related to the spectral sensitivity of color negative film.

These filters are very precise equivalents to the established range of the very familiar "CC" filters. The Series I colors include the primaries blue, green and red, along with the secondaries yellow, magenta and cyan. The Series II will include six intermediaries, two of which are available at this writing, pink and lavender. All colors are produced in the familiar 15, 30, 60 and 90 designations (½, 1, 2 and 3 stops).

All of the colors are produced on a heat-resistant base. During manufacture the CIE references are continuously monitored by online computerized colormetric equipment, which ensures the consistency of product from run to run. The CalColor™ products are available in sheets (20" x 24") and rolls (48" x 25').

The principle of this system is that each color enhances the individual color elements at each light source to which they are applied. For example, CalColor™ 90 Green selectively enhances green transmission by reducing the blue and red transmission by three stops. A CalColor™90 Magenta enhances the blue and red transmission by reducing the effective green transmission by three stops. See CalColor chart on page 834.

Another feature of the CalColor™ system relates to the colorant, selections that were made with concern for the purity of each color. The colors finally presented are so "clean" that they can be combined with fully predictable results (i.e., combining 30 Cyan (-30R) and 15 Blue (-14G, -16R) results in a Light Steel Blue filter (-14G, -46R)).

High-Pressure DC Short Arc Xenon Light Sources

These are the best commercially available light sources for use in projection systems. The excellent color-rendering properties of this nominal 6000°K source (CRI = 98), its very compact source size and very high luminance (often referred to as "brightness" or "brilliance"), and the stability of the arc location due to the DC operation make it the light source of choice for motion-picture projection.

Xenon has recently found application in spotlights for motion-picture photography due to its long throw capability.

A feature of these lamps is that the color temperature is virtually inde-

> **OF NOTE...**
>
> The SMPTE standard for motion picture projection is 5600°K at 16 Footlamberts, ±2Fl. Unless you are using a dedicated Footlambert meter to measure the screen brightness, you should use an analog reflective spotmeter (digital meters will be fooled by the flickering display). Set the meter to 100ASA for 1/50 of a second.
>
> 32Fl = f/4.8 or EV 10 16Fl = f/3.2 or EV 9 12Fl = f/2.8 or EV 8 ⅔
> 10Fl = f/2.5 or EV 8 ⅓ 4Fl = f/1.5 or EV 7

pendent of lamp type, lamp current, wattage, dimming or boosting, lamp voltage or the age of the lamp.

Low-Pressure AC/DC Xenon Arc Lamps

These are low-pressure long arc light sources. DC units are available in fixtures at power levels of 1.1K, 2.2K, 3.3K and 10K.

The AC Lamps represent the highest-powered modules available in the arc discharge field (AC or DC operated), with modules ranging from 10K to 50K.

It is claimed the DC units do not have any flicker problems, while the AC units require the same caution as with AC discharge lamps.

SPECIAL PURPOSE PHOTOGRAPHIC LIGHTING EQUIPMENT AND SYSTEMS

Lightning and Other Flashing-Type Lighting Effects

Several companies now supply electronically controlled Xenon flash tubes for simulating lightning and other types of flashing effects.

The lightning-effect fixtures range from a handheld unit (20K) used to simulate strobe flashes associated with still photography, up to a 2,000,000 watt unit. These sources all produce light at 5600°K, which is dimmable from 100% to approximately 20%. An attractive feature of this equipment is that it is not necessary to synchronize the flashes because the shortest flash duration of any of the heads is 1/24 of a second.

A broad range of functions can be accomplished with the control devices that are available. The simplest and most often used is one that will vary the light intensity of a unit down to 20% of maximum and control the flash duration up to 1.5 seconds per flash. This unit also permits random intensity changes of up to 3 f-stops in level as many as 24 times per second to approximate the look of natural lightning. Another unit with the same functional controls manages up to four lighting units.

A number of other specialized controllers are available. These include a precision fader that allows programming of flash time and intensity frame by frame up to 99 frames, and has four stored programs, "Photoflash," "Ex-

OF NOTE...

CAUTIONS: Xenon lamps have high internal pressure, even when cold (cold, the internal pressure can be up to approximately 150 psi, and in operation this pressure can be as high as 450 psi). The lamps are supplied with a protective jacket over the bulb, and this should not be removed until the lamp is fully installed. It is required that suitable face shield, body jacket and gauntlets be used any time that the protective jacket is removed. The protective jacket should be installed before steps are taken to disconnect and remove a lamp.

A further caution must be considered relative to the characteristically high luminance of the arc in these sources. Direct viewing of the arc can result in serious damage to the retina.

Xenon lamps produce a considerable ultraviolet component (up to about 6% of the total lamp energy output). This can result in the production of ozone which is harmful to health if breathed for extended periods or in poorly ventilated spaces. This caution should be observed even when using "ozone-free" versions of these sources.

plosion," "Machine Gun" and "Undulate". Custom programs can be created and stored in memory. Optical and acoustic triggers initiate the flash effect by sensing a bright light or by a loud sound. Another device allows timing flashes by triggering from standard SMPTE time code. There is yet another that can be programmed to chase up to sixteen lights and can be preset for each light for number of frames on and frames off.

Synchronized Stroboscopic Lighting

These typically utilize Xenon flashtubes, which produce a good approximation of daylight (about 6000°K) and a relatively stable color temperature throughout life.

The strobes must be synchronized to the camera shutter. It is imperative that the units flash when the shutter is fully clear of the gate; otherwise a partially exposed frame will result. To check camera synchronization, the lens should be removed and the cavity illuminated with the strobe with the camera turned on. The shutter should appear to be frozen in one position.

OF NOTE...

CAUTION: People with photosensitive epilepsy should be informed that strobe lighting will be in use.

The control equipment for these strobes permits the addition of delay to the pulse in degree increments. The position of the shutter will move either forward or backward in relationship to the gate until it is in the proper position. For reflex cameras the strobe fires twice for each frame, once to illuminate the subject and a second time to illuminate the viewfinder.

COMMERCIAL/INDUSTRIAL LIGHT SOURCES

With today's readily available color-corrected light sources, it is much more cost-effective to change out the globes at a location rather than struggle with correcting the existing sources with gels and filters.

However, most filmed television shows transferred and corrected electronically require only that the location illumination is the same color temperature; correction to "normal" can happen in the telecine suite.

LUMINAIRES
Fresnel Lens Spotlights

Fresnel spotlights are made for standard incandescent and tungsten halogen incandescent sources, and also for the range of HMI, CID and CSI arc discharge lamps. The range of wattages, taking into account all types, is from 100–24,000.

These luminaires represent the most widely used motion-picture lighting units. They provide the

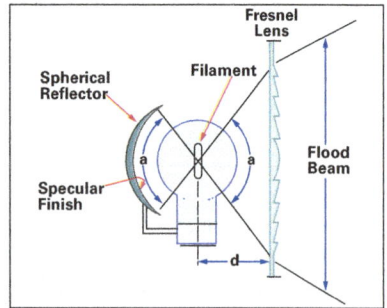

Fig. 2. Optical system of standard Fresnel spot light when in full flood position

means for changing the beam diameter and center intensity through a relatively broad range. Using standard incandescent lamps, the spot-to-flood ratio may be 6 to 1 or so, and with a tungsten-halogen lamp it may be possible to extend this ratio to 8 or even 9 to 1 under some circumstances.

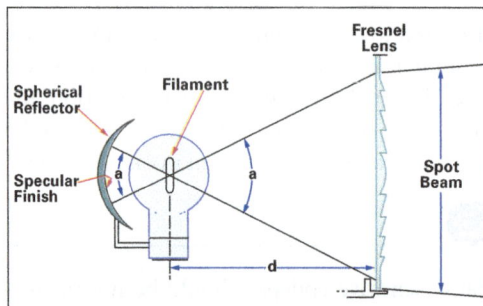

Fig. 3. Optical system of standard Fresnel spot light when in spot position

The optical system of these luminaires is the same for all the variations that may be presented. The light source and a spherical reflector are located in a fixed relationship to one another. This combination of light source and back reflector is designed so that the spherical reflector reflects the energy being radiated toward the back of the housing through the filament and toward the lens. The effect intended is that the energy radiated to the lens appears to come from a single source. The combination of reflector and light source is moved in relation to the lens to accomplish the focusing.

One of the most important features of the Fresnel lens spotlight is its ability to barndoor sharply in the wide flood focus position. This property is less apparent as the focus is moved toward a spot (at spot focus it is not effective at all). The barndoor accessory used with this spotlight provides the cinematographer with the means for convenient light control. The sharp cutoff at the wide flood is, of course, due to the fact that the single-source effect produces a totally divergent light beam. The action of the barndoor, then, is to create a relatively distinct shadow line.

Occasionally it may be desirable to optimize the spot performance of these units, and for this situation "hot" lenses are available. These tend to produce a very narrow beam with very high intensity. It is important to remember that the flood focus is also narrowed when these lenses are used.

Open Reflector Variable-Beam Spotlights

These are typically the tungsten-halogen open reflector spotlights. There are also some low-wattage HMI-types available. These nonlens systems provide "focusing" action, and therefore a variable diameter beam, by moving the light source in relationship to the reflector (or vice versa). These types of units are available for sources ranging from 400–2,000 watts. One of the drawbacks of this system, when compared with the Fresnel lens spotlights, is that there are always two light sources operative. The illumination field produced by these systems is the sum of the light output directly from the bulb and the energy reaching the field from the reflector. The use of the barndoor accessory with these lights does not produced a single shadow due to this double-source characteristic. Typically a double shadow is cast from the edge of the barndoor.

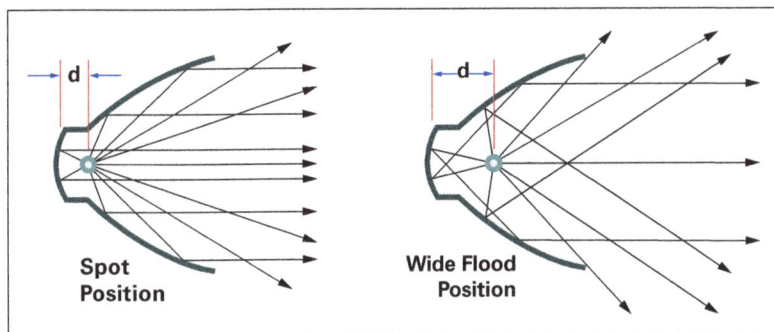

Fig. 4. Non lens, variable beam spotlights

The great attraction of these luminaires is that they are substantially more efficient than the Fresnel lens spotlights. Typical spot-to-flood intensity ratios for these types of units is between 3:1 and 6:1.

Tungsten-Halogen Floodlights

A variety of tungsten-halogen floodlighting fixtures take advantage of these compact sources. Two of the more typical forms are treated here. These fixtures are available in wattages from about 400–2,000.

There are types of "mini" floodlights using the coiled-coil, short-filament, tungsten-halogen lamps, which provide very even, flat coverage with extremely sharp barndoor control in both directions. Due to the design of the reflector in this system, the light output from this fixed-focus floodlight appears to have a single source. This accounts for the improved barndoor characteristics.

Cyclorama Luminaires

These lighting fixtures were originally developed for lighting backings in theater but have broad application in similar situations in film. Because of the design of the reflector system, it is possible to utilize these fixtures very close to the backing that is being lit and accomplish a very uniform distribution for a considerable vertical distance. Typically these units are made for tungsten-halogen linear sources ranging from 500–1,500 watts.

Based on the variations in design, some of these may be used as close as 3' to 6' from the backing being illuminated. The spacing of the luminaires along the length of the backing is in part determined by the distance of these fixtures from the backing itself.

Soft Lights

Soft lights, which attempt to produce essentially shadowless illumination, are made in wattages from 500 up to about 8,000 and typically utilize multiple 1000w linear tube tungsten-halogen lamps. The degree of softness is determined by the effective area of the source.

The Aurasoft™ is unique, in that it produces a greater area of coverage than a comparable conventional unit, at a full stop advantage in light level and with comparable "shadow-casting" character. These units can be quickly converted in the field between tungsten-halogen and HMI light sources.

Also available is a plastic tubular diffuser with a reflector at the closed end which is fitted at the open end, with a tungsten-halogen spotlight. The configuration allows for the unit to be easily hidden or placed in a corner to provide soft light that can be used very close to the actors.

The helium filled balloons are designed to contain either tungsten-halogen or HMI sources in various combinations. These balloons are tethered and can be used up to an altitude of about 150 feet (45 meters). They range in

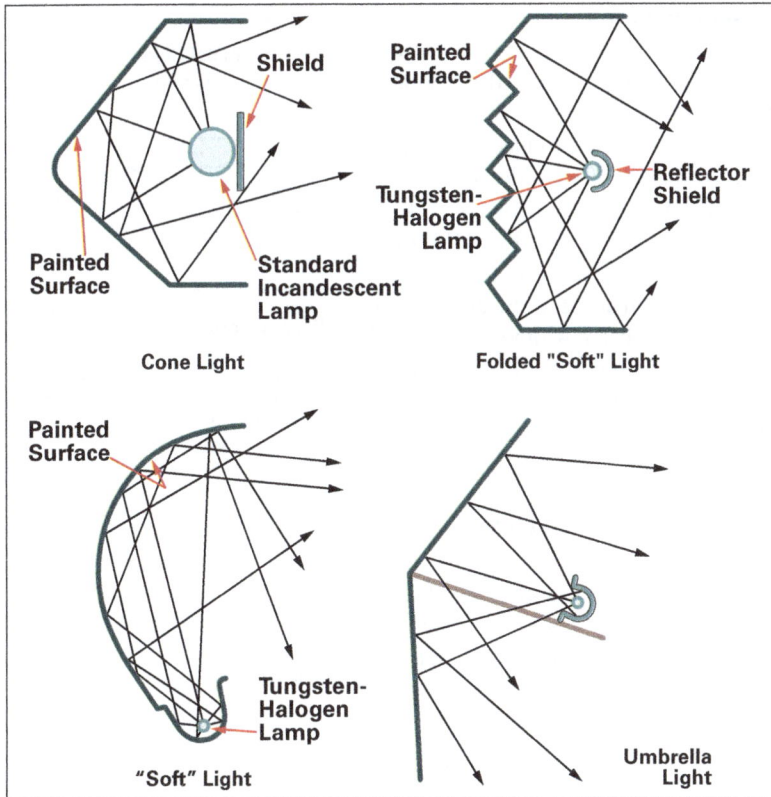

Fig 5. Reflector systems of various "soft" lights

size from approximately 4 feet in diameter (1.2 meters) to tubular shapes as much as 22 feet long (6.6 meters) by 10 feet in diameter (3 meters). There is a range of power levels, with tungsten halogen lights up to 16,000 watts and HMI lights up to 32,000 watts.

"Par" Fixtures and Lamps

The most popular of these are the Par64 and Par36 configurations. These lamps have a parabolic reflector that has a high-reflectance aluminized coating and a prismatic type of front lens. Typically they are supplied in VNSP (very narrow spot), NSP (narrow spot), MFL (medium flood) and WFL (wide flood) lens systems. They are extremely efficient optical systems.

Fixtures are available which assemble multiples of these types of lamps for daylight fill applications or for long-throw stadium and arena lighting requirements. Both 3200°K and dichroic coated versions (approximately 5000°K) are available.

Beam Projectors

A luminaire consisting of a large parabolic mirror with the globe filiment placed at the focal point of the mirror, so as to produce a parallel beam of light. Sizes are described by the diameter of the mirror: 18", 24", 36". The lamp source is either HMI or tungsten. In by gone years the source was the carbon arc, thus the old name "sun arc". The beam width can be varied a small amount. A series of baffle rings are placed to cover the filament area to eliminate nonparallel rays of light.

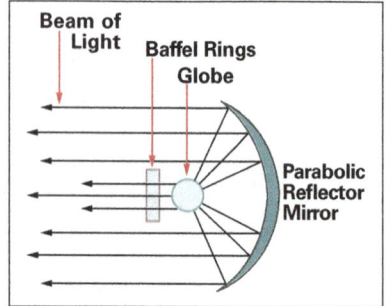

Fig. 6. Beam projector

Optical Lens System Lights

The most commonly used is the ellipsoidal spotlight. It consists of an ellipsoidal reflector and two plano convex lenses of various focal lengths that project very sharp shadows. Various shadow-making devices can be introduced on the focal plane in the interior of this light to create sharp shadows (e.g., variable iris, cutter blades, and pattern holder).

A variant of this design is the Dedo light and the Focal spot attachment, which can be placed in the barndoor holder of Fresnel spotlights.

The biggest option is the theatrical follow spot. The size and intensity of the beam can be varied by an internal lens and reflector system. Sources for shorter throws are either tungsten or low wattage HMIs. For stadium use HMI, Xenon or Carbon arc source are used. Many types of internal and external accessories are available: color changers, pattern holders, irises and motorized wheels for moving effects.

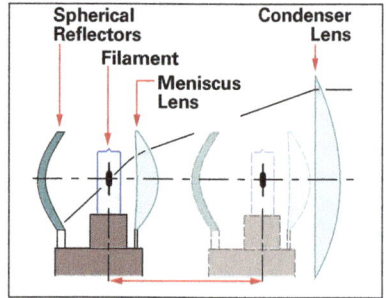

Fig. 7. Dedolight

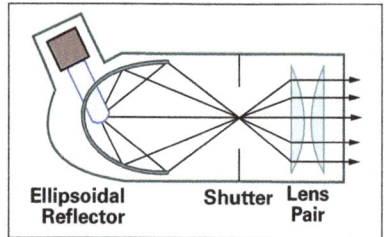

Fig. 8. Ellipsoidal Spotlight

LED (Light Emitting Diodes)

Flat panels consisting of colored or white LEDs that simulate tungsten or daylight color temperature. They may be programmed via computer to produce most colors in constant or chasing mode.

LIGHT-CONTROL ACCESSORIES

Barndoors

The purpose of this accessory is to prevent the illumination beam from the fixture from reaching certain portions of the set. A relatively well-defined edge can be established that delineates the end of an illuminated area and the beginning of an unilluminated zone.

Barndoors are most effective when used on Fresnel spotlights when the spotlight is in the wide flood position. The effectiveness of the barndoor is reduced as the focus is moved toward spot and is totally without effect at the spot focus.

The effectiveness of the barndoor as an accessory on other types of luminaires varies sharply with the design of the specific item. In a number of the open reflector tungsten-halogen systems (particularly floodlights), barndoor effectiveness is limited to the edge of the barndoor that is parallel to the source.

Snoots

This is a funnel-shaped device used to limit the beam of a Fresnel spotlight. Available in various diameters.

Scrim

The type of scrim referred to here is placed directly in the accessory-mounting clips on a luminaire. This type of scrim is normally wire netting, sometimes stainless-steel wire, which is used as a mechanical dimmer.

The advantage of the scrim is that it permits a reduction in light intensity in several steps (single and double scrims) without changing the color temperature or the focus of the luminaire. Contrary to popular belief, it is not a diffuser.

The half-scrim permits the placement of scrim material in only half of the beam and is widely used on Fresnel spotlights. It overcomes the problem encountered when the Fresnel is used at fairly high angles. The portion of the beam striking the floor or objects near the floor closest to the luminaire produces intensities that are too high to match the desired level at the distance associated with the center of the beam. The reason for this, of course, is the substantial variation in the distances that the illumination energy travels. The half-scrim applied on the portion of the beam impinging on the nearest objects can overcome this problem.

Gel Frames

Different forms of these holders are made and designed to fit into the accessory clips on the front of most luminaires. They permit the use of various types of plastic filter materials to modify the characteristics of the beam. Color media may be put in these holders to affect color, and a wide range of diffusion products are available.

Electrical Dimmers

The old-fashioned resistance and autotransformer dimmers have given way to the solid state SCR dimmer systems. Computer management DMX controllers cannot only control the intensity of each luminaire, but can switch cues, replug circuits, precisely control the duration of a dim, and control many other accessories (color wheels, lamp movement and focus). All of these cues can be recorded and stored in the computer for replayability. With arcs, mechanical shutters are motorized to execute the dim.

GRIP ACCESSORIES FOR LIGHT CONTROL

Diffusers

There are various diffusion materials sewn on wire frames of different types and size which permit the diffusion of both artificial and natural sources.

They are translucent materials (various textiles) that truly act as diffusion. When supplied in very large sizes and supported from a single point, they are called butterflies; when the frame becomes extremely large and is supported from two or more points, it is called an overhead.

Solids, Gobos, Flags or Cutters

These all come in the same form as the various scrims, dots, fingers, butterflies and overheads but are opaque. They are utilized to keep light from falling in a given area and permit very fine adjustment of the lighting in a large area.

The cucoloris is a cutout pattern placed in the path of the spotlight in order to cast a shadow that might be comparable to the light coming through the leaves on a tree.

Reflectors

Reflector boards are widely used for redirecting sunlight and modifying its characteristics so that it is suitable for use as set illumination and fill light. These boards have been surfaced with various reflecting media, usually sign-painter's leaf, either silver or gold.

Most reflectors have two sides, a soft side and a more mirror-like surface, commonly referred to as the "hard" side.

Egg Crates

Large, fabric egg crates can be stretched in front of soft diffusion material to control spill light.

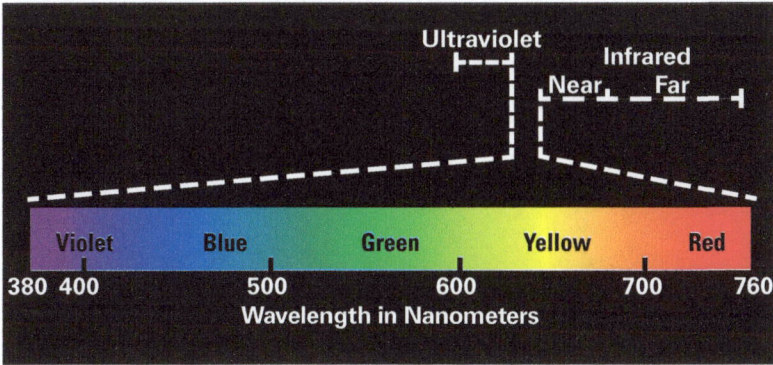

Fig. 9. Visible Light Spectrum
Violet: 380-430nm; Indigo: 430-450nm; Blue:450-480nm;
Green: 510-550nm; Orange: 590-610nm; Red: 610-760nm

LED Lighting for Motion Picture Production

by Frieder Hocheim
ASC Associate Member

Over the last four years LED lighting fixtures have been working their way into the motion picture industry. Lead by companies such as Litepanels Inc., products have been introduced that effectively exploit the inherent characteristics of LED technology: low DC power and amperage draw, low heat, and dimmable without color shift. LEDs are primarily powered by low-voltage DC with low-energy demands. This has enabled the design of some innovative battery-operated fixtures. Untethered from a power cable, the instruments have provided a handy, easy-to-rig fixture well suited to the fast-paced shooting styles of today's production environments. The use of multicolored LEDs based on RGB principles or the newer multicolored LED mixing allow for products that expand the potential for accurate spectral displays.

LEDs display a number of advantages over conventional lighting technology:
▶ Low power requirements, allowing for battery operation
▶ High Lumens per watt efficiency
▶ Color mixing
▶ Video Imaging display capability
▶ Full range dimming without shift in color

A number of companies have emerged over the past few years that are providing innovative LED products: Color Kinetics, Litepanels, Mole-Richardson, Gekko Technologies, Element Labs, Kino Flo, Zylite, Nila, LEDz among others.

Challenges however remain in this new technology. For a cinematographer it is all about the light. If a fixture's light characteristics aren't correct for the scene, it will be passed over. Cinematographers strive for clean edge shadows or soft light sources that display diffuse shadow lines. The LED will have to deliver light as good as or better than existing tools provide. Energy savings alone will not be the reason to embrace the LED.

The introduction of the LED has presented lighting designers with somewhat of a predicament as it pertains to motion picture lighting. The LED is a point source much like Thomas Edison started with back in the 1880s. Edison's source was wrapped in a clear glass envelope. One bulb alone provided little light. Numerous light bulbs needed to be combined to provide adequate light levels.

The same challenges that the early designers of lighting instruments dealt with are now being addressed again in the twenty-first century. Given the number of patent filings the U.S. patent office has seen over the LED, you would think that Thomas Edison had never existed. We are essentially reinventing the light bulb.

LED design challenges can be broken down to a number of issues:
- Glare
- Multiple shadows
- Loss of efficiency when diffused
- Color rendering
- Heat management

GLARE

As a bright point source the LED is very glaring when viewed on axis. Large quantities have to be assembled to provide adequate levels of illumination.

When an LED fixture is in the direct eyeline of an actor they tend to complain of discomfort.

There is not much you can do to reduce glare if you need the light output.

Adding a diffuser to the fixture will reduce the glare but leads us into the next problem: substantial light loss and loss of efficiency.

DIFFUSION AND LIGHT LOSS

In order to soften the light and reduce the glare from an LED, it needs to be diffused. Diffusion breaks down the optical characteristics of the LED and dramatically reduces its light output. Most of the heralded advantages of lumens-per-watt efficiency are gone, along with any advantage over existing technologies.

MULTIPLE SHADOWS

Depending on the spacing of the LEDs, the light characteristics can display multiple shadow lines. Much like the number of pixels per inch determines the resolution in a digital image the density of LEDs in a fixture will define the shadow line characteristics of an LED fixture. The tighter the spacing of the LED, the more homogenous and clean the shadow. Open faced fixtures without diffusion can give off very distracting multiple shadows from a barn door.

COLOR

Early adoption of LEDs was hampered by their spectral output. LED manufacturers specified their color space as dictated by the demands of general lighting applications or a larger customer such as the automotive industry. Lumen-per-watt efficiencies dictated the color point targets. This inevitably resulted in light that resembled that of early fluorescents. They were green and did not render images on film or digital accurately. The introduction of color binning or measuring and sorting LEDS according to their specific color performance enabled fixture manufacturers to provide a better color more suited for the imaging industry. This is an approach that adds more cost and reduces the yields of each manufacturing run.

HEAT MANAGEMENT

Although the lamps are highly efficient it comes at the cost of heat. Put a few 2 watt or 5 watt LEDs on a matrix and heat builds up rapidly. The lightweight LED now has to be linked to a much heavier and bulkier heat management system or heat sink. This gives the designers challenges as to how to exploit the LED's advantages of size and light output against the weight and size of the heat-sink requirements. So if it ends up as hot and bulky as a 1 K Fresnel and the color is not as good as an incandescent, will the industry care to work with it?

The challenges are being addressed in innovative ways and are resulting in new and useful lighting tools. Together with the inherent advantages of the LED, we can expect it to play a major role in providing lighting solutions to the motion-picture industry.

TYPES OF LED FIXTURES AVAILABLE TO THE CINEMATOGRAPHER

A number of companies are offering LED products that have found acceptance by cinematographers. Some of the companies are designing fixtures specifically for the imaging industries and some are hybrid offerings that have been designed primarily for event lighting or architectural applications. Architectural and event products for the most part do not display color correct or high CRI illumination.

Companies such as Litepanels, Gekko Technologies, Kino Flo, Nila and Zylight are marketing directly to the motion picture and TV industry. Color Kinetics and Element Labs come from a strong architectural and event lighting market.

Litepanels – www.litepanels.com

Product names: *Micro Series, Mini-Plus Series, 1 x 1, 2 x 2, 4 x 4, Ringlite Series, SeaSun*

One of the first successful companies to exploit the advantages of LEDs was Litepanels. Founded by industry gaffers, they have provided innovative lighting tools for on camera lighting as well as more general set lighting applications. Their battery operated Micro, Mini-Plus and Ringlite products are designed to mount onto the camera as eye-lights or fill light. Their 1 x 1 fixtures provide a lightweight lighting tool that can operate on battery power or AC. By carefully binning their LEDs they have been able to provide a high CRI light quality essential for good imaging.

Color Kinetics – *www.colorkinetics.com*
Products: *ColorBlast, iColor Cove, ColorBlaze,*
Intelliwhite Lighting systems
Color Kinetics has had great success in the architectural markets and has a substantial intellectual property portfolio relating to LED color controls. Products such as the Blast series and Cove fixtures have found applications incorporated into motion picture set lighting. RGB color mixing does not provide high color rendering light but is widely used in color changing applications such as backgrounds or effects lighting. Color Kinetics also features a white light product range. These systems incorporate special binning techniques in selecting their LED components to ensure high color rendering white light.

Gekko Technology Ltd. – *www.gekkotechnology.com*
Product names: *K-lite, Kicklite, kuelite lenslite,*
kisslite, george, Kelvin Tile, karesslite
Founded by cinematographer David Amphlett, Gekko Technology has introduced a very successful line of high color rendering LED lighting instruments. Taking advantage of the low DC power requirements and the lightweight nature of the LED, Gekko produces a range of portable lighting instruments that can be mounted to the camera or used for small area set lighting applications.

Element Labs – *www.elementlabs.com*
Product names: *Stealth Display, Versa Tile, Versa Ray,*
Versa Tube, Helix Screen, Versa Tile T100, Helix P1 Screen, Cobra
Element Labs comes from a strong background in large area video displays for concert/event lighting and architectural applications.

The Stealth Display, Helix Screen, Versa Tile, Versa Ray and Cobra are all variations on a means of creating large area architectural displays that incorporate video images and patterned color changes.

The Versa Tube looks like a color changing fluorescent tube that can be assembled into a large video wall. Individual tubes can be rigged into set designs and controlled through a standard DMX512 protocol from a dimmer board.

The Versa Bank is a portable panel of LEDs designed for motion picture and TV production. It has been effectively used in rendering sophisticated color changing light effects for process shots. The Versa Bank can simulate the ever changing source light in synchronization with a process background plate.

Nila – *www.nila.tv*
Product names: *Nila JNH series*
Founded by gaffer/grip Jim Sanfilippo, Nila offers a high powered LED lighting system consisting of a module that interconnects to form larger fixtures. Interchangeable lenses vary the beam angles in 10-, 25-, 45- and 90-degree increments as well as vertical and horizontal Elliptical beam options. Other accessories such as yokes and gels flesh out the system. The module is dimmable through a DMX protocol and is available in either daylight or tungsten equivalents. The units operate on a universal 90-240 AC/DC power supply.

Zylight – *www.zylight.com*
Product names: *Zylight IS3, Z90 & Z50, Remote using Zylink protocol.*
Founded by Charlie Collias a veteran of video and documentary production and his brother Jim from an electrical engineering background, Zylight produces a range of color-changing RGB portable lights well suited for on-camera and general studio lighting applications. An innovative wireless remote-control system, ZyLink offers control over numerous fixtures at one time. The units operate on AC or DC power. Given the high density of LEDs on the light emitting surface the shadow characteristics are very clean not multiples of shadow lines.

LEDz – *www.led-z.com*
Product names: *Mini-Par, Brute 9, 16, and 30.*
Founded by veteran HMI designer Karl Schulz, LEDz offers a range of small portable lighting instruments.
The Mini-Par is a 12VDC on-camera light that offers various beam angles using a set of accessory lenses. The Brute fixture family consists of fixtures from 30 watts, 50 watts, and 90 watts. The fixtures are available in Daylight, 5500°K or Tungsten 3000°K.

An Introduction to Digital Terminology

by Marty Ollstein
and Levie Isaacks, ASC

What follows is much more than a simple glossary of terms. This is a comprehensive overview of the science behind motion imaging and a cornerstone in forming a working knowledge of digital technology and how it relates to analog image capture.

ANALOG – The natural world is analog. Light and sound are described as waves whose shape varies with their amplitude and frequency in a continuously variable signal. An analog signal is understood to be formed by an infinite number of points. Analog human vision perceives light as a continuous gradient and spectrum from black to white. Film is an analog medium and can record a continuous spectrum. Digital video cameras capture a scene as analog voltage and then digitize it with an A/D (analog-to-digital) converter to create linear digital code values.

A/D CONVERSION – Analog-to-digital conversion transforms analog data (such as light intensity or voltage) into a digital binary format of discrete values. Referred to as digitization or quantization.

ANAMORPHIC – An optical process in which a widescreen (wide aspect ratio) image is recorded onto a narrower target (film or sensor) using an anamorphic lens to squeeze the image horizontally. An anamorphic lens will squeeze a 2.40:1 'Scope scene onto a 1.33:1 negative frame or 4 x 3 camera chip. The format uses almost the entire image area with no waste (of pixels or negative area), resulting in a higher-resolution image. For display, an anamorphic projector lens is needed to unsqueeze the image.

ARTIFACT – A flaw or distortion in an image—a result of technical limitation, incompatibility or error. An artifact can be introduced at any step in which an image is altered or converted to another format.

ASPECT RATIO – Ratio of screen width to height.
Common ratios:
1.33:1 (4 x 3) Standard TV—*or*
35mm Full Aperture (Silent)
1.37:1 Academy Aperture—*or*
Regular 16mm Full Aperture
1.66:1 European Theatrical Standard

1.66:1 Super-16mm Full Aperture

1.78:1 (16 x 9) HDTV

1.85:1 American Theatrical Standard

2.40:1 Anamorphic or 'Scope

BAKED IN – Changing or re-recording recorded images to integrate a particular look. This action limits options in postproduction but insures that the look is preserved.

BANDING – A digital artifact caused by digital processing in which lines or bands appear in an image that previously displayed a smooth unbroken gradient between light and dark or two different color values. Banding can be caused by the down-conversion of the bit-depth or sampling ratio of an image that results in a loss of data.

BANDWIDTH – Literally, the range between the lowest and highest limiting frequencies of an electronic system. Commonly used to refer to the size of the "pipeline" employed to transmit data, quantified by the amount of data that can be transmitted over a given period of time, such as megabits per second. Compression techniques are used to reduce the size of image files to facilitate real-time display of high-quality images in systems with limited bandwidth.

BAYER PATTERN – A chip design that allows a camera to record full color using a single chip. The pixel array employs a pattern of 2 x 2 matrices of filtered photoreceptor sites—two green, one red and one blue. Three-chip cameras record red, green and blue on three separate chips. (See Figure 7.)

BINARY CODE – The mathematical base of digital systems that uses combinations of only 0 and 1 to represent all values. A mathematical representation of a number to base 2.

BIT – The smallest increment of digital information. A bit is a digit of binary code which can define only two states—0 or 1, on or off, black or white.

BIT DEPTH – Bit depth determines the number of steps available to describe the brightness of a color. In a 1-bit system, there is only 0 and 1, black and white. An 8-bit system has 256 steps, or numbers from 0–255 (255 shades of gray). Until recently, 8-bit was standard for video and all monitors. Most monitors still have only 8-bit drivers, but many HD video systems support 10-bit signals through their image-processing pipelines.

A 10-bit system has 1024 steps, allowing more steps to portray subtle tones. A linear representation of light values, however, would assign a disproportionate number of steps to the highlight values—the top range of 512–1024 would define only one f-stop, while leaving 0–512 to define all the rest. A logarithmic representation of code numbers, however, gives equal representation across the full dynamic range of film negative—in 10-bit space, 90 code values for each f-stop. This allows for more precision to define shadow detail. For this reason, 10-bit log is the standard for recording digital images back to film. Some publishing color applications use a 16-bit system for even more control and detail. The cost of the additional bits is disk space, memory, bandwidth and processing time.

The consequence of too few bits can be artifacts—flaws in the image introduced by some image processing. Some artifacts include banding, where a smooth gradient is interrupted by artificial lines, and quantization, where a region of an image is distorted. If image data is recorded or scanned in 10-bit color, converted to an 8-bit format for postprocessing, then converted back to 10-bits for film recording, image information (and usually quality) is lost and cannot be retrieved. Whenever possible, it is preferable to maintain all of the image data and not discard information through conversion to a more limited format.

BLACK STRETCH – Flattens the curve of the toe to put more steps or values in the lower part of the tone scale. Reveals more shadow detail.

BYTE (B) – A digital "word" composed of 8 bits which can describe 256 discrete values.

- **KB** = Kilobyte (100 bytes)
- **MB** = Megabyte (1,000 bytes)
- **GB** = Gigabyte (1 million bytes)
- **TB** = Terabyte (1 billion bytes)

CALIBRATION – The adjustment of a display device, such as a monitor or projector, that prepares a device to produce accurate, predictable and consistent results in accordance with a standard. Calibration is an essential factor in color canagement and look management. It enables two people, in two different locations, to look at the same digital image and see the same look.

CCD – (charge-coupled device) A type of light-sensitive chip used in cameras for image gathering, either as a single chip or in a three-chip array. Basically a grayscale device that measures light intensity, a CCD records color in a single-chip camera by using color filters on each photoreceptor site (see Bayer pattern). CCDs are analog sensors that convert light intensity into voltage. An A/D converter then transforms the analog voltage value to digital data.

CHIP – A device aligned behind the lens that contains an array of photoreceptor sites, or light-sensitive sensors, for capturing image data. The sensors convert light intensity into voltage levels, an electrical charge proportional to the intensity of the light striking it. The voltage is then sampled and converted to a digital code value—one for each pixel of the image.

CHROMATICITY DIAGRAM – The two-dimensional plot of visible light, commonly used to represent the three-dimensional 1931 CIE XYZ colorspace standard. It is effectively a 2-D "slice" out of a 3-D model. The horseshoe-shaped plot defines the range of human color vision, independent of brightness. More limited color gamuts (ranges) of media (such as film or HD video) or display devices can be clearly portrayed in the diagram. Individual colors are defined as points in the diagram with chromaticity coordinates (x, y). Color saturation is greatest at the outer rim of the color plot; the neutal white point area is near the center of the plot.

CHROMATICITY COORDINATES – (x, y) Chromaticity coordinates define specific color values in the CIE XYZ color space. They describe a color quality (hue and saturation only) independent of luminance (brightness value).

CIE XYZ COLOR SPACE – The color space originally defined in 1931 by the Commission Internationale de L'Eclairage. (The CIE standard has been updated, and is currently being re-evaluated.) CIE XYZ uses a

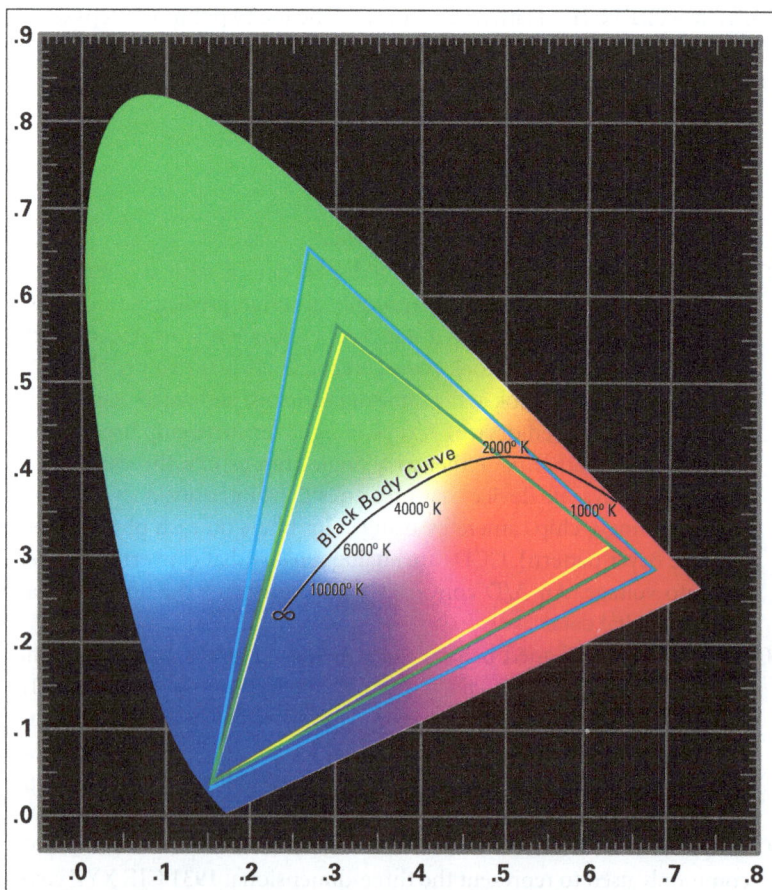

Figure 1. Triangles within CIE chromaticity chart define limits of color gamuts

three-dimensional model to contain all visible colors. It defines a set of three primaries (specific red, green and blue colors) and a color gamut to describe the range of human vision.

CINEON FILE – a 10-bit log image file format based on film density. Designed to capture the full dynamic range of the motion picture negative, it is an industry standard for film scanning and recording.

CLIPPING – The total loss of image detail at either end of the scale—highlight or shadow. Clipping occurs when the exposure moves beyond the threshold determined by the capability of a camera or recording device. On a waveform monitor the exposure thresholds for clipping are usually 0 and 100 IRE.

CMOS (Complementary High-density Metal Oxide Semiconductor) – A category of chip with an array of photoreceptor sites. Its integrated circuitry has both digital and analog circuits. Unlike CCDs, where the charge is actually transported across the chip and read at one corner of the array, CMOS chips have transistors at each pixel that amplify and move the charge using traditional wires. This approach is more flexible because each pixel can be read individually; however, CMOS chips are less sensitive to light because many of the photons hit the transistors instead of the photodiode. The distinguishing characteristic of the CMOS chip is that it allows a large number of camera processing functions while using less power and generating less heat than other types of chips. It can perform at various frame rates and perform either progressive or interlaced scans. The Arri D-20 uses a CMOS chip, while the Panavison Genesis uses a CCD chip.

CMY (cyan, magenta, yellow) —The additive secondary colors. Combining two additive primary colors (R, G, B) produces an Additive Secondary color.

CODEC – A compression/decompression algorithm. The software that executes the compression and decompression of an image.

CODE VALUE – The digital representation of the brightness and color of a pixel.

COLOR DECISION LIST (ASC-CDL) – Designed by the ASC as the beginning of a universal color-grading language, the CDL is a standardized limited expression of how an original image has been graded in digital post. Currently addressing only lift, gamma and gain parameters, the CDL can facilitate working in multiple facilities on the same production, and allow basic color-correction data to be interchanged between color-correction systems from different manufacturers. Within the areas addressed, using color-correction systems that accommodate the CDL code, the CDL will process an original image and produce the same results on different systems and in different facilities. It is a useful tool for the cinematographer in look management.

COLOR GAMUT – The range of colors a system can display or record. When a specific color cannot be accurately displayed in a system, the color is considered "out of gamut" for that system. The standard HD video color space, defined by ITU-R BT.709 (aka. Rec. 709), is an example of a device-dependent color space. It uses a YCrCb space, which separates luminance (Y) and chrominance (color – described by Cr and Cb), and allows for color subsampling, another means of compression.

One method to compare media and devices is to plot their color gamuts on the chromaticity diagram. The CIE XYZ color space is the standard device-independent reference. Although the color space uses a three-dimensional model to represent its colors, it plots the visible colors on a flat chromaticity diagram, actually a 2-D "slice" taken of the 3-D model, usually represented as a colored horseshoe-shaped area, leaning left on a 2-dimensional x-y axis. All colors visible to human perception are plotted on the graph. The colors of the spectrum lie along the horseshoe curve, left to right, blue to red. Red, green and blue primaries are specified. The white point is nominally located where the three primaries are equal in contribution, but to accommodate different color temperatures, their respective white points are plotted along a curve across the center area of the model. Specific colors are identified in the 2-D space by a set of two numbers, called chromaticity coordinates (x, y), which specify their position on the diagram.

COLOR MANAGEMENT – Maintaining the accuracy and consistency of color throughout the digital workflow from capture to final release.

COLOR SAMPLING – Describes the precision of the measurement of light and color by a camera system. It is represented by three numbers, separated by colons, and refers to the relative frequency of measurement (sampling) of color values. The first number represents luminance (Y, commonly associated with green) and the second two numbers represent chroma or color as red and blue difference values (Cr, Cb).

4:4:4 captures the most information, sampling color at the same frequency as luminance. 4:2:2 is the current standard on HD production cameras. The color information is sampled at half the frequency of the luminance information. The color precision is lower, but is adequate in most production situations. (Human vision is more sensitive to brightness changes than it is to color variation.) Problems can arise, however, in post-processing, such as in the compositing of greenscreen scenes, where color precision is important. It is recommended that any visual effects shots that require image processing be recorded in a 4:4:4 format.

Sampling can also be understood as a type of compression of image data: 4:4:4 sampling is uncompressed, 4:2:2 sampling compresses color values by a factor of 2, 4:1:1 compresses color 4:1.

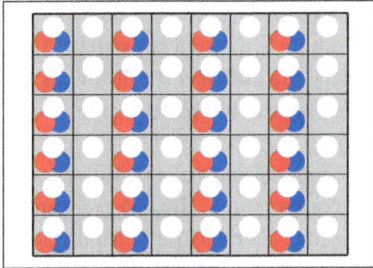

Figure 2. 4:2:2 color sampling   Figure 3. 4:4:4 color sampling

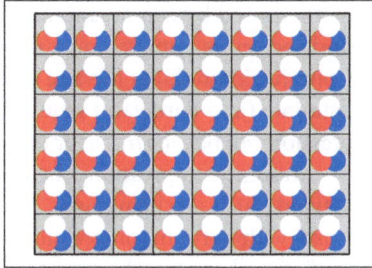

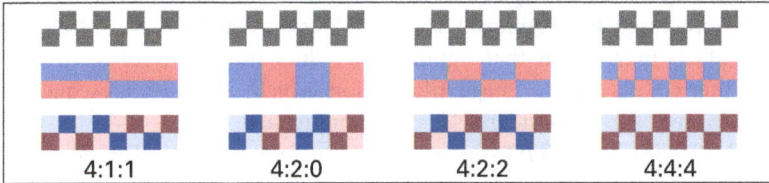

4:1:1   4:2:0   4:2:2   4:4:4

Figure 4. Color sampling as a compression of image data

COLOR SPACE – A color space is a structure that defines colors and the relationships between colors. Most color-space systems use a three-dimensional model to describe these relationships. Each color space designates unique primary colors—usually three (a defined red, green and blue)—on which the system is based. The system can be device-dependent or device-independent. A device-dependent system is limited to the color representation of a particular device or process, such as film. The RGB color space that describes film is representative of the range of colors created by the color dyes used in film. A device-independent color space defines colors universally, which through a conversion process using a profile, can be used to define colors in any medium on any device.

The color space designated as the standard for digital-cinema distribution is X'Y'Z,' a gamma-encoded version of the CIE XYZ space. A device-independent space, X'Y'Z' has a larger color gamut than other color spaces, going beyond the limits of human perception. All other physically realizable gamuts fit into this space.

COMPONENT VIDEO SIGNAL – A video format in which luminance and chrominance remain as separate entities and have separate values.

COMPOSITE IMAGE – An image created by the combination of two or more source images. Compositing tools include matte-creation software, and chroma-key hardware.

COMPOSITE VIDEO SIGNAL – A video format in which luminance and chrominance are combined.

COMPRESSION – Compression is the process used to reduce the size of an image file with the least sacrifice in quality or usable information. One method used by compression schemes is to analyze image material, and find and remove any redundancy, such as blue sky with a consistent color. Compression reduces the size of the image file and as a result lowers the data rate (and hardware) required to display the file in real time. Compression can be *interframe* or *intraframe*.

In some compression schemes, the original image can be fully reconstituted. Such a scheme uses "lossless" compression. However, a danger exists with certain compression codecs that claim to be "visually lossless." The claim may be true for the direct display of an original image that requires no manipulation in postproduction, but if it later needs to be processed for significant color grading or visual effects, disturbing artifacts may appear that significantly reduce the quality of the image. Other codecs discard image information, which cannot be subsequently retrieved. This is considered "lossey" compression.

COMPRESSION RATIO (uncompressed to compressed) – The ratio that compares the image file size of the original noncompressed image to the compressed version. The lower the ratio, the lower the compression, and usually the higher the quality of the resulting image. A format that uses a 2:1 compression ratio preserves more image information than one that uses a 4:1 compression ratio.

CRT (cathode-ray tube) – The traditional TV monitor. Cathode rays are streams of electrons produced by the heating of cathode inside a vacuum tube. The electrons form a beam within the cathode-ray tube due to the voltage difference created by two electrodes. The image on the screen is formed by the manipulation of the direction of this beam by an electromagnetic field that sweeps across the surface of the phosphorescent screen. Light is emitted as the electrons strike the surface of the screen.

CRUSHING THE BLACKS – Raises the slope of the toe, which reduces the number of steps or values in the lower part of the scale. Darker shadow details are lost in black.

DATA – Information stored in a digital file format. Digital image data is assumed to be raw, unprocessed and uncompressed, retaining all original information, as opposed to video, which has been processed and compressed, thereby losing some information.

DCDM (digital cinema distribution master) – The distribution standard proposed by DCI: uncompressed and unencrypted files that represent moving image content optimized for direct electronic playback on a projector and sound system in a theater. The DCDM's files contain the master set of raw files that produce high-resolution images, audio, timed text (subtitles or captions) and metadata—auxiliary data that can include data to control room lights and curtains.

DCI (Digital Cinema Initiative) – DCI was founded in March 2002 as a joint venture of Disney, Fox, MGM, Paramount, Sony, Universal and Warner Bros. DCI's purpose was to create uniform specifications for digital cinema projection, and establish voluntary specifications for an open architecture for digital cinema to insure a uniform and high level of technical performance, reliability and quality control.

Some of the specs in the standard: 12-bit, 4K or 2K, JPEG 2000. The DCI system specification defines a life cycle in which content exists in a succession of states:

• **DSM** – Content originates as a digital source master; format not specified.
• **DCDM** – Content is encoded into a digital cinema distribution master, according to the specification (12 bit, 4K or 2K, X'Y'Z' color space).
• **DCP** – Content is compressed and encrypted for transport to the theater as a digital cinema package, covered by the specification (JPEG 2000).
• **DCDM** (again) – Content is unpackaged, decrypted and decompressed at the theater for exhibition.

DCP (digital cinema package) – The compressed, encrypted DCDM (digital cinema distribution master) When the DCP arrives at the theater it is unpackaged or decoded—decrypted and decompressed—to make a DCDM ready for display or projection.

DEAD (dark or bright) **PIXEL** – A pixel that is either permanently bright (either white, red, blue or green) or dark (black) on the screen. It can occur in either recording devices (as cameras) or display devices (as monitors or projectors). Some cameras have systems to correct for dead pixels, filling in the space with values from adjacent sensors.

DEVICE-DEPENDENT COLOR SPACE – A color space that is limited by the performance of a particular device or process, such as film. Film reproduces a particular range of color (color gamut). The RGB color space that describes film is representative of the gamut of the color dyes used in film. It is only accurate for describing colors in the film medium.

DEVICE INDEPENDENT COLOR SPACE – A color space that defines colors universally. Through a process of conversion or translation specific to the application, medium or device being used, its values can be used to specify colors in any medium on any display device.

DIGITAL CONFORM – The process of editing the full-resolution digital image material to match the EDL (edit decision list) which was created in the editorial process.

DIGITAL INTERMEDIATE – The conversion of a film image into digital media for all postproduction processes, including the final color grading, as an intermediate step for distribution, whether by film or digital media. Common usages of the term:

• The entire digital postproduction process that comes between principal photography and the production of the final distribution master.

- The digital version (image files) of the production, used during post-production.
- The final color-grading process (which may take weeks for a feature) that integrates all visual elements and determines the final look of the production.
- The product or result of the final color-grading process (digital master).

DIGITAL MASTER – The completed output or result of the final color-grading process, subsequently used to create the distribution masters. Or, the full digital version of the camera-original production.

DIGITAL SIGNAL – A signal represented by discrete units (code values), measured by a sampling process. A digital signal is defined by a finite code

Figure 5a. Camera Original   Figure 5b. Graded Master

value in accordance with a predetermined scale.

DISCRETE – Discrete values use a finite scale of whole integers.

DLP (Digital Light Processing) – Texas Instruments' micromirror technology is a display solution that manipulates light digitally. It uses rectangular arrays of up to two million hinge-mounted microscopic mirrors that reflect light onto the screen. In a three-chip DLP system, light generated by the lamp passes through a prism, which divides it into red, green and blue streams, each aimed at a DLP mirror chip assigned to that color. The digital signal operates the hinges of the mirrors, controlling the degree of reflection of each mirror. The colored light reflects selectively off the micromirrors, combines into a single stream, and passes through the projection lens to project an image.

DPX FILE – A 10-bit log image file format. The current standard format for recording digital image data back to film, it is the digital input format required by the ARRI laser recorder. It is a versatile file format used for the processing and storage of resolution-independent, pixel-based (bit-mapped) images.

DYNAMIC RANGE – The range of light values from black to white that a medium or device can record or display.

EDIT DECISION LIST (EDL) – A frame-accurate description of every cut in a production, including digital effects and titles.

ENCODING – The recording of information into a particular digital format, or conversion of digital data from one format to another.

FIELD – An image composed of either the even or odd scan lines of an interlaced video frame. Two fields displayed sequentially make up a video frame.

FILE FORMAT – The software structure that records digital data. The file format determines the organization of data within the file. File formats often determine the spacial resolution and color depth of an image.

FILE-FORMAT CONVERSION – The transformation of an image file from one format to another. A conversion may be required at various steps in the workflow, depending on the devices and processes used. Conversion is usually required for distribution on different media. Depending upon the resolution and color parameters of a particular format, resolution and color information can be lost in a file-format conversion. Referred to as downconverting, image information is lost when converting to a smaller, more limited format.

FLASH MEMORY – A storage scheme that records data on a chip and retains that data when the host system has been shut off. Secure digital and compact flash memory cards use flash memory. The Panasonic P2 system uses flash memory.

FLOATING POINT – A numbering system that uses "real" numbers, rather than integers. The decimal point of a real number floats, or moves, according to its exponent component. A floating-point number consists of two parts: the mantissa, which is a decimal value between 0 and 1, and a multiplier of 10^n. For example, $<.123456 \times 10^3>$ is a floating point number with a value of 123.456.

This system is capable of defining a much wider range of values than a fixed-point integer with the same number of bits. When used to create digital image files, the greater range afforded by floating-point numbers allows for finer shadow detail (small values) while still accommodating the many stops (large values) required to display highlight detail. It creates the capability to store, process and display images closer to a continuous tone scale, reduce artifacts, and produce a more faithful rendition of the original photographed scene.

FRINGING (COLOR) – A digital artifact resulting from errors in compositing one image into another. An imperfect matte can cause a foreground element to acquire an exaggerated (usually bright) color outline.

FTP – (file transfer protocol) A language used for file transfer from computer to computer on the Internet.

GAIN – The process of manipulating a digital image by holding the black value constant and raising or lowering the value that creates white, affecting the apparent brightness of an image. On a video camera, the gain control adjusts the CCD sensor's sensitivity to light.

GAMMA – The slope or contrast of an image. In color-correction terms gamma refers to the contrast affecting only the midtones of an image. Adjusting the gamma changes the brightness of an image without dramatically changing the shadows and highlights. Film dyes have a logarithmic response to exposure. This is why the traditional sensitometric curve, used to describe the behavior of film stocks, plots density as the y coordinate and log exposure as the x coordinate. The resulting S curve, with a lower slope in both the toe and shoulder, provides more information about shadow and highlight detail. A logarithmic representation of light values is typically used when working with scanned film material for digital intermediate or visual-effects work. Logarithmic code values are an important characteristic of what is considered film color space.

GAMMA CORRECTION – The gamma adjustment applied to a video camera's signal to allow correct display of the video image on a CRT monitor. This is necessary because of the nonlinear response, or power function, of the CRT monitor. Cameras that can record raw data do not apply this gamma correction, and avoid the loss of information caused by a gamma correction.

GRADING – The process of color correction, enhancement and manipulation used to alter a recorded image. A tool in look management, a key objective of grading is to maintain a consistent look throughout the entire workflow of a production.

HDRI (high dynamic range image) – An image that records pixel values spanning the full dynamic tonal range of a real-world scene. An HDRI can encode the high contrast ratios that occur in nature—a 100,000:1 ratio is common in the natural world. The values of an HDRI image are linear and remain proportional to actual light values. An HDR image must be encoded in a format that allows a large range of values, such as one that uses floating-point values stored with 32 bits per color channel.

HEADER – The location in a digital image file where metadata (any relevant information, such as frame number and image size) can be recorded.

HIGH DEFINITION (HD) – A video format consisting of either 720 active lines of progressive video or 1080 active lines of either progressive or interlaced video.

The standard HD frame is 1920 x 1080 or 1280 x 720. The aspect ratio is 16:9, or 1.78:1.

HISTOGRAM – A graph that displays the distribution of light values in a scene. Basically a bar chart, a histogram indicates the proportion of image area (y axis) occupied by each level of brightness from 0–100 IRE, black to white (x axis). With a clear indicator of clipping at either end of the scale, it is useful for determining whether the values in a scene fit within the camera system's dynamic range.

HUE – A specific color in the spectrum, independent of saturation or luminance.

HYBRID FILM/DIGITAL WORKFLOW – A production workflow that integrates digital technology into the traditional film workflow. A system that mixes traditional silver-halide technologies with digital imaging technologies.

IMAGE FILE – A recording of a single image frame in a particular file format.

IMAGE PROCESSING – The process of altering a digital image with software and hardware. Examples include color grading, compression and color-space conversion.

INTERFRAME CODEC – The interframe codec uses series of frames, or groups of pictures (GOP), to compress the image information. Interframe compression compares consecutive frames to remove redundancy or common elements and arrive at "difference" information. Although it's much more efficient and can achieve greater compression, this scheme creates significant challenges in editing and postprocessing due to the interframe dependency.

INTERLACE SCANNING – Since the beginning of television broadcasting, interlaced scanning has been used. Two vertical sweeps are made for each frame—one to scan the odd lines and the other to scan the even lines. Each individual sweep is called a field.

The downside of interlaced scanning is a loss of resolution and steadiness when shooting movement. With subject or camera movement, the image changes from one field to the next. Two consecutive fields must be perceptually merged to create each complete frame, even though the moving subject has changed position. Therefore, any movement will appear blurred, and detail will be substantially reduced in areas of the frame that contain movement. This factor also creates difficulty for any image processing that involves spatial manipulation of the image.

A film release of interlaced material requires the creation of progressive frames from pairs of fields, so as to convert the interlaced video fields back to progressive film frames. There are various methods of doing this video-field-to-film-frame conversion. Some involve the interpolation of pixel values between the different fields. This merging of field pairs into frames reduces resolution wherever there is movement. For this reason, the progressive format is preferable for recording back to film.

INTERPOLATION – Connecting the dots or estimating in-between values. A process of creating new data based on a set of existing data, such as inserting new material between existing material; estimating missing values by taking an average of known values at neighboring points; an estimation of a value between two known values in a sequence of values. Interpolation can be used by software to increase apparent resolution by adding pixels based on the value of surrounding pixels.

INTRAFRAME CODEC – A compression scheme that processes each frame individually. It is limited to removing redundant information from within each frame. Generally the result is higher quality, but less-compressed than interframe compression.

ITU (International Telecommunications Union) – An international broadcast-standards committee that replaced the CCIR.

ITU-R BT. 601.5 – Commonly referred to as Rec. 601. The standard for standard-definition television. The international standard for component digital television from which the SMPTE 125 M standard was derived. This ITU recommendation defines the sampling systems, matrix values and filter characteristics for both Y/ B-Y/R-Y and RGB component digital television.

LASER RECORDER – A device used to record digital image data onto motion-picture film. It uses red, green and blue lasers to write directly to each color layer of the film. The brightness of the lasers allow the use of fine grain, low sensitivity intermediate stock.

LCD (liquid crystal display) – Used for the viewfinder of most digital cameras.

LIFT – The process of altering an image by holding the white point constant and raising or lowering the value that creates full black, affecting shadow detail. The slope of the transfer function is changed, affecting the contrast of the image.

LINEAR CODE VALUES – A linear representation of light assigns code values directly proportionate to the intensity of the light. Double the light intensity (as from 100 to 200 foot candles) and the linear code value doubles. The ISO/ASA measurement scale is linear. The disadvantage of using a linear scale in digital photography is that a disproportionate number of code values end up assigned to the highlight values. In a 10-bit linear scale of 0–1023, the top range of 512–1023 defines only one f-stop, leaving 0–512 for all the rest of the f-stops.

LINEARITY – The degree to which the input of a signal is proportional to the output.

LOGARITHMIC CODE VALUES – The system that uses a logarithmic formula (log2) to encode light values. The logarithmic representation of light assigns an equal number of code values to each f-stop. This scale allows more precision in defining values, particularly in the toe region, and is consistent with the photographic f-stop scale, zone system and human visual perception.

LOOK – The look expresses the visual tone of a project, supports the director's vision and integrates the contributions of the creative members of the team.

The cinematographer develops and maintains the look throughout the production.

LOOK MANAGEMENT – The process of creating, communicating, protecting and maintaining the agreed-upon look of the picture throughout the digital workflow.

LOSSLESS COMPRESSION – A compression scheme in which all image information can be reconstituted when the image is decompressed.

LOSSY COMPRESSION – A compression scheme in which discarded image information is lost, and cannot be retrieved.

LUMINANCE – Lightness or brightness. Measured as the average of the brightest and darkest of the three individual RGB channels that define the value of a pixel.

LUT (look-up table) – A software tool for manipulating the color of an image; a method of mapping input colors to output colors. Used in color management and look management to create a particular look or convert an image to be read or display properly on a device.

MPEG (Motion Pictures Expert Group) – A digital compression standard.

METADATA – All data associated with a specific image, recorded in the digital image file header (or alternatively, in an external database), to facilitate some aspect of the processing the image to realize the project.

MOIRÉ PATTERN – Usually seen as a wavy, vibrating pattern in an image, a moiré pattern is an artifact that appears when one repeating pattern interferes with another repeating pattern. It often occurs in scenes with fine repetitive detail, such as on a herringbone fabric design or an old screen door. The moiré pattern appears when the level of detail (frequency) in the scene exceeds the recording capability (resolution) of the recording device (camera or scanner).

MOTION-CONTROL DATA – Metadata documenting camera placement and movement, including lens height, position, pan and tilt data, and all pertinent camera information.

NOISE – Noise appears like randomly placed "snow" or film grain in an electronic image. Caused by electronic error or signal interference in a camera, noise can represent irregular level fluctuations of a low order of magnitude. Some noise is present in all analog video signals. The level of noise is a function of the efficiency of the sensors (such as CCD or CMOS) and signal processing of the camera. Noise levels can vary by color channel when sensors are more sensitive to particular colors.

Digital signal compression is another common source of noise, where it can appear as high-frequency signal fluctuation.

NONLINEAR EDITING – A system that allows random access to all images in a database. An edited sequence can be rearranged without re-recording the images from the beginning of the sequence, as a linear system requires.

NTSC (National Television Systems Committee) – The color television standard format that uses 525 lines, 30 interlaced frames (60 fields) per second.

OPEN EXR – An image file format capable of recording extremely high dynamic range images (HDRI) far beyond the capability of human perception. Developed by ILM, it stores data as 16- or 32-bit floating-point values. It is also capable of recording metadata, such as camera position and color balance information. It supports several lossless compression schemes and is extensible, capable of integrating new compression schemes. Open EXR files record images as *scene-referred data*, documenting the actual light values in the physical scene that was photographed. It is a good candidate for archival image storage.

OVERSAMPLING – The process of using multiple measurements of a particular value to arrive at a more accurate, higher quality result. An example is the use on a chip of multiple photoreceptors to define each individual pixel.

PANALOG – A transfer curve used in software developed by Panavision that extends the dynamic range of their Genesis camera by up to 3 stops. The curve transforms the camera's internal 14-bit linear digital signal (with a range of 0–16,383) to a 10-bit "quasi-log" signal (with a range of 64–1,019).

Designed to capture and preserve the entire range of the camera's signal, the Panalog scale creates a perceptually equal grayscale in which each stop increment is expressed by the same number of code values, providing more values in the darker regions of an image than the linear scale provides. The white point is placed at 680 on the log scale (about 70% up the 10-bit scale), allowing for more highlight detail, and helping to avoid clipping.

PERSISTENCE OF VISION – The perceptual process of the brain or the retina that retains an image for a period of time. Motion blur in each image helps create the illusion of motion which results when a series of images are displayed in quick succession.

PEDESTAL – The light level at which a pixel turns black. The pedestal can be raised or lowered to change the level at which an area of an image turns black, thereby crushing to black or increasing shadow detail.

PHOTOSHOP – A software program that can be used to grade and manipulate digital images.

PIXEL – Short for "picture element," a pixel is the building block of the digital image. It represents one sample of picture information. Pixels are grouped into fixed arrays of straight rows and columns. The pixels remain in the same position frame to frame. All pixels in an array are the same size, usually square, but in some cases, rectangular.

POWER FUNCTION – The nonlinear gamma of a CRT. In order to properly view video on a CRT, a nonlinear gamma correction has to be applied to the video.

PRIMARIES – The specific colors that define a color space or are specified to calibrate a display device. Most systems today use three primaries—a specified red, green and blue. But some systems are now experimenting with the use of more than three primaries in order to improve color display.

PRIMARY COLOR CORRECTION – Independently adjusting the lift, gain and gamma of the three additive color channels (red, green and blue).

PROGRESSIVE – The method of sequentially scanning all lines of a pixel array to create a frame in one vertical sweep. There are no fields as there are in interlaced scanning—only complete frames. Computer screens use progressive scans.

QUANTIZATION ARTIFACT – Where a region of an image is distorted as a result of some form of image processing. Loss of image information can result from reduction in color space, bit depth, color sampling or spatial resolution. A common example: downconverting an image from 10-bit color to 8-bit color.

RAID ARRAY (Redundant Array of Independent Disks) – A group of hard-disk drives, linked by a system that enhances speed, increases storage capacity and performs automatic backup of data. A RAID array writes to multiple disks simultaneously and backs up data in the process. Often used in film production, the benefits of the RAID system include increases in data integrity, fault tolerance, throughput, speed and storage capacity. There are different RAID levels, including 0 (no redundancy or backup capability) and 5 (most common, with redundancy) through level 10 and "RAID S."

RAW FILES – The digital recording of images without applying the gamma correction of video. This unprocessed data retains more information and can potentially produce a higher-quality image. Instead of applying the video gamma correction, they convert the linear code values it captures into logarithmic code values which approximate a film gamma and color space, resulting in a wider dynamic range and greater shadow detail.

REDUNDANCY – Values that are repeated in an image.
Compression codecs find and compress redundant values in an image in order to reduce the size of the file. An example of visual redundancy is a blue sky with consistent color.

REGION-OF-INTEREST CORRECTION – Using "windows" or articulated mattes to isolate specific areas of the frame to make alterations.

REGISTRATION (COLOR) – The alignment of the three-color sensors or sources (red, green, blue) on a three-chip recording or display device. Poor alignment can create color ringing artifacts. Registration charts can be used to insure that the camera is in precise registration.

RENDER – The process of re-recording a digital image in accordance with certain specifications or adjustments.

RESOLUTION – The measure of the finest detail visible in an image. The resolution of an image is measured by the number of pixels in the image display, not by the number of sensors in the camera chip.

Camera resolution is commonly referred to by the number of lines of pixels (scan lines) it records. An increase in the pixel line count will produce a proportional increase in resolution and representation of fine detail. Image resolution is expressed by two numbers: (pixels per line) x (number of lines). A doubling of pixel lines and pixels per line (as the change from 2K to 4K), increases the total pixel count by a factor of 4, requiring four times the memory to store the image data. However, the MTF (an optical measure of line pair resolution) only doubles.

Some of the most common resolution standards:

Standard Definition Analog NTSC = 640 x 480
(1.33:1)
High Definition = 1920x1080 or 1280x720
(1.78:1)
2K = 2048 pixels per line
(line count varies with aspect ratio)
4K = 4096 pixels per line

Pixel count is not the only element in the imaging chain that affects picture resolution. Lens quality, registration of multiple chips in a three-chip camera and image scaling conversions also affect image resolution.

RGB (Red, Green, Blue) – The additive primary colors. Combining all three primary lights in equal intensities produces white. The RGB color space is widely used to encode scanned film material.

RINGING – An artifact that appears like an outline or halo on the edge between bright and dark areas of an image. An exaggerated transition often caused by excessive sharpening.

SCAN – The process of reading and converting an analog image into a digital file.

SCENE-REFERRED DATA – Device-independent data that documents the light values in the physical scene that is photographed. Most image data is *output-referred data* that depends on the limited dynamic range and gamut of a particular output device or display. Scene-referred data does not have these limits, but can be tone-mapped or converted for display on any output system or device—including systems yet invented.

SECONDARY COLOR CORRECTION – Isolating specific colors in the spectrum, then modifying their hue, saturation and brightness.

SENSOR – A photoreceptor site on a chip. The two most common types are known as CCD (charge coupled device) and CMOS (complementary metal oxide semiconductor).

SOFT CLIP – Software functions used to compress values as they approach the top of the scale. This effect keeps some detail in the bright areas, or at least softens the edge where the clipping begins.

SPACIAL CORRECTIONS – Examples include: frame repositioning, digital filter blur, flaring, sharpening and adding grain or noise.

SPACIAL RESOLUTION – Actual detail recorded. Sharpness and contrast, dynamic range of exposure, highlight detail and shadow detail; the accuracy, subtlety and character of color; the smooth portrayal of motion including the capability to alter speed or frame rate and the degree to which you will be able to manipulate the image in post.

STANDARD DEFINITION – Refers to an NTSC, PAL or SECAM video format. NTSC uses of 480 active lines of interlaced video.

SUBTRACTIVE COLOR – Primaries: cyan, magenta, yellow—the complements of the additive primaries: red, green and blue. Used as filters that absorb discrete color values, the three subtractive colors will absorb all color, resulting in black.

TC – Time code.

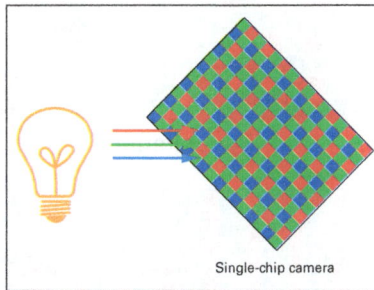

Single-chip camera

Figure 6. Single-chip camera – A chip design in which an array of filtered photoreceptor sites on a single chip record a full-color image. Proprietary chip designs have different designs of color-filtered sensors.

TIFF FILE (tagged image file format) – An industry standard raster file format developed for universal transfer between many digital imaging applications and devices.

TONAL MAPPING – Converting the tonal (brightness and color) values of an image from one system to another with a different dynamic range and color gamut. For example, converting a high dynamic range 12-bit image to a much more limited 8-bit format that can be displayed on a standard CRT monitor. The challenge of tonal mapping is to preserve the quality and character of the original image on the more limited system.

VECTORSCOPE – A vectorscope is an oscilloscope that measures the accuracy of color recorded by a camera and facilitates the adjustment of the camera to record accurate color. It does not measure the brightness or luminance of a signal. The vectorscope screen has a marked scale (graticule) inscribed with a circle marked in degrees (0–360), a center crosshair, and six individual boxes distributed around the circle (one for each primary and secondary color).

The direction of the "vector" (measured by degrees) pointing from the center to a point on the circle, indicates the *hue* (phase) of a color in the scene. The length of the vector, starting at the center and extending toward the circle, indicates the *saturation* (amplitude) of the color. The center point is considered 0 saturation or neutral (as gray, black or white).

The color boxes correspond to the SMPTE/NTSC specifications for the hue and saturation of that particular color in the standard color-bar

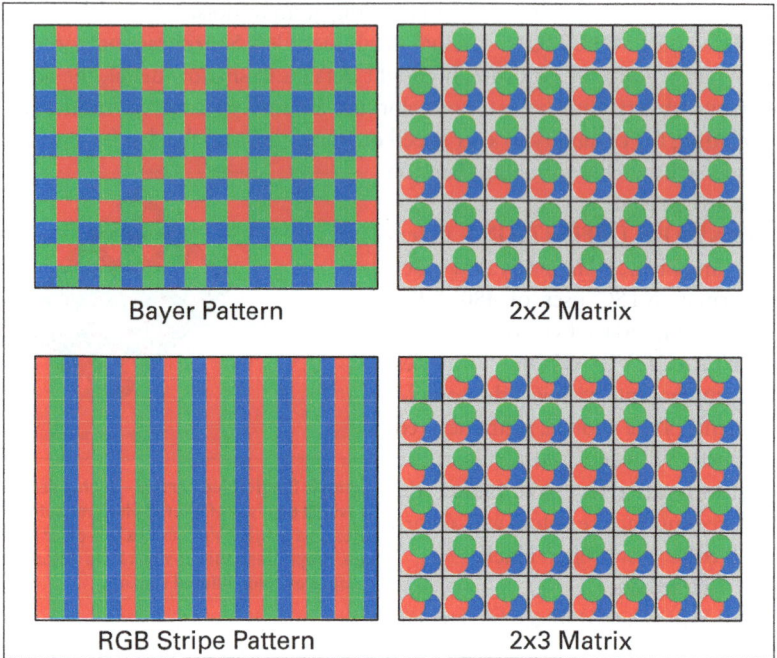

| Bayer Pattern | 2x2 Matrix |
| RGB Stripe Pattern | 2x3 Matrix |

Figure 7. Single-chip systems using a color filer array mosaic

test signal. 0 degrees is at the 9 o'clock position. The color boxes, clockwise from 0 degrees, are labeled YL (yellow), R (red), MG (magenta), B (blue), CY (cyan) and G (green).

VFX (Visual-effects material) – Plates, composites, CGI, etc.

VISUALLY LOSSLESS – A compression scheme that claims to be lossless and may appear to be lossless without manipulation (or color correction). However, when it must be manipulated for color grading or visual effects, artifacts often appear.

WATERMARK – A security scheme in which bits are altered within an image to create a pattern, which constitutes proof of ownership.

WAVEFORM MONITOR – An oscilloscope adapted to display luminance or brightness light levels across a scene, from left to right, as recorded by a camera, as well as other video signal levels. It measures voltage levels from the camera and displays them on a screen in a scale of 0–100 IRE (black to white). If the levels flatten out at either end of the scale (at 0 or 100, with some exceptions), the image will clip and record no detail in those areas.

WHITE POINT – The white reference, expressed in chromaticity coordinates, that determines the white balance, or color temperature, of a system. An important parameter in color management and device calibration.

Devices such as monitors and projectors can be calibrated to a given white point, usually designated by color temperature, such as D65 (6500°K).

WYSIWYG (Wizee-wig: "What You See Is What You Get") – An acronym describing the situation in which the image displayed on a monitor closely resembles the final image output for display.

XYZ COLOR SPACE (and X'Y'Z') – A color space using a linear representation of light values in a scene. The values can be output-referred (based on the capability of a particular display system) or scene-referred (based on the values measured in the physical scene). The <'> indicates that the values are encoded with a 1/2.6 gamma function. The X'Y'Z' color space has been designated by DCI as the standard for digital cinema.

YCrCb – the standard HD video color space that converts RGB by encoding luminance (Y) and color-difference signals (Cr, Cb) separately. One reason for this separation is that the human eye is less sensitive to chrominance than luminance. Compression algorithms take advantage of this phenomenon.

YCM (yellow, cyan, magenta: the subtractive colors) – Refers to the black-and-white separation film negatives that are created to archive a color motion picture. Three monochrome negatives are made from the original color negative, separating out the contribution of each color layer in the negative. This process was developed to take advantage of the much longer lifespan of black-and-white film.

Further References

3-D

Spottiswood, Raymond, *Theory of Stereoscopic Transmission*, Berkeley, CA; University of California Press , 1953.

Aerial Cinematography

Wagtendonk, W.J., *Principles of Helicopter Flight*, Aviation Supplies & Academics, Newcastle, WA, 1996.

Crane, Dale, *Dictionary of Aeronatical Terms*, Aviation Supplies & Academics, Newcastle, WA, 1997.

Spence, Charles, *Aeronautical Information Manual and Federal Aviation Regulations*, McGraw-Hill, New York, NY, 2000.

Padfield, R., *Learning to Fly Helicopters*, McGraw-Hill, New York, NY, 1992.

Industry-Wide Labor-Management Safety Bulletins at: http://www.csatf.org/bulletintro.shtml

Arctic Cinematography

Eastman Kodak Publication: *Photography Under Artic Conditions*.

Fisher, Bob, "Cliffhanger's Effects were a Mountainous Task," *American Cinematographer*, Vol. 74, No. 6, pp. 66-74, 1993.

Miles, Hugh, "Filming in Extreme Climactic Conditions," *BKSTS Journal Image Technology*, February 1988.

Moritsugu, Louise, "Crew's Peak Performance Enhanced Alive," *American Cinematographer*, Vol. 74, No. 6, pp. 78-84, 1993.

Biographies and Interviews

Almendros, ASC, Nestor, *A Man With a Camera*, New York, Farrar, Straus, Giroux, 1984.

Bitzer, ASC, Billy, *Billy Bitzer – His Story: The Autobioagraphy of D.W. Griffith's Master Cameraman*, New York, Farrar, Straus, Giroux, 1973.

Brown, ASC, Karl, with Brownlow, Kevin, *Adventures With D.W. Griffith*, New York, Farrar, Straus, Giroux, 1973.

Cardiff, BSC, Jack, *Magic Hour*, London, Faber and Faber, 1996.

Challis, BSC, Christopher, *Are They Really So Awful?: A Cameraman's Chronicle*, Paul & Co. Publishing Consortium, 1995.

Clarke, ASC, Charles G., *Highlights and Shadows: The Memoirs of a Hollywood Cameraman*, Metuchen, NJ; Scarecrow Press, 1989.

Eyman, Scott, *Five American Cinematographers: Interviews with Karl Struss, Joseph Ruttenberg, James Wong Howe, Linwood Dunn and William H. Clothier*, Metuchen, NJ; Scarecrow Press, 1987.

Higham, Charles, *Hollywood Cameramen: Sources of Light*, Indiana University Press, 1970.

Kalmus, Herbert T. and Eleanor King, *Mr. Technicolor*, Abescon, NJ; Magic Image Filmbooks, 1993.

Lassally, BSC, Walter, *Itinerant Cameraman*, London, Murray, 1987.

Laszlo, ASC, Andrew, *Every Frame a Rembrandt: Art and Practice of Cinematography,* Boston, MA; Focal Press, 2000.

Laszlo, ASC, Andrew, *It's A Wrap!,* Hollywood, CA; ASC Press, 2004.

LoBrutto, Vincent, *Principal Photography: Interviews with Feature Film Cinematographers,* Westport, CT; Praeger, 1999.

Maltin, Leonard, *The Art of the Cinematographer: A Survey and Interviews with Five Masters,* New York, Dover Publications, 1978.

McCandless, Barbara, *New York to Hollywood: The Photography of Karl Struss, ASC,* Albuquerque, NM; University of New Mexico, 1995.

Miller, ASC, Virgil E., *Splinters From Hollywood Tripods: Memoirs of a Cameraman,* New York, Exposition Press, 1964.

Rainsberger, Todd, *James Wong Howe Cinematographer,* San Diego, CA; A.S. Barnes, 1981.

Rogers, Pauline B., *More Contemporary Cinematographers on Their Art,* Boston, MA; Focal Press, 2000.

Schaefer, Dennis and Salvato, Larry, *Masters of Light: Conversations with Contemporary Cinematographers,* Berkeley, CA; University of California Press, 1985.

Sterling, Anna Kate, *Cinematographers on the Art and Craft of Cinematography,* Metuchen, NJ; Scarecrow Press, 1987.

Walker, ASC, Joseph, *The Light On Her Face,* Hollywood, CA; ASC Press, 1984.

Young, BSC, Freddie, *Seventy Light Years: An Autobiography as told to Peter Busby,* London, Faber and Faber, 1999.

Camera

Adams, Ansel, *The Camera,* New York, Morgan and Morgan, Inc., 1975.

Fauer, ASC, Jon, *Arricam Book,* Hollywood, CA; ASC Press, 2002.

Fauer, ASC, Jon, *Arriflex 16 SR Book,* Boston, MA; Focal Press, 1999.

Fauer, ASC, Jon, *Arriflex 16 SR3 the Book,* Arriflex Corp., 1996.

Fauer, ASC, Jon, *Arriflex 35 Book,* Boston, MA; Focal Press, 1999.

Fauer, ASC, Jon, *Arriflex 435 Book,* Arriflex Corp., 2000.

Samuelson, David W., *Panaflex Users' Manual,* Boston, MA; Focal Press, 1990

Camera Manufacturers

Aaton, +33 47642 9550, www.aaton.com

ARRI, (818) 841-7070, www.arri.com

Fries Engineering, (818) 252-7700, www.frieseng.com

Ikonoskop AB, +46 8673 6288, info@ikonoskop.com

Panavision, (818) 316-1000, www.panavision.com

Photo-Sonics, (818) 842-2141, www.photosonics.com

Pro8mm, (818) 848-5522, www.pro8mm.com

Camera Supports

A + C Ltd., +44 (0) 208-427 5168, www.powerpod.co.uk

Aerocrane, (818) 785-5681, www.aerocrane.com

Akela: Shotmaker, (818) 623-1700, www.shotmaker.com

Aquapod, (818) 999-1411

Chapman/Leonard Studio Equipment, (888) 883-6559, www.chapman-leonard.com

Egripment B.V., +31 (0)2944-253.988, Egripment USA, (818) 787-4295, www.egripment.com

Fx-Motion, +32 (0)24.12.10.12, www.fx-motion.com

Grip Factory Munich (GFM), +49 (0)89 31901 29-0, www.g-f-m.net

Hot Gears, (818) 780-2708, www.hotgears.com

Hydroflex, (310) 301-8187, www.hydroflex.com

Isaia & Company, (818) 752-3104, www.isaia.com

J.L. Fisher, Inc., (818) 846-8366, www.jlfisher.com

Jimmy Fisher Co., (818) 769-2631

Libra, (310) 966-9089

Louma, +33 (0)1 48 13 25 60, www.loumasystems.biz

Megamount, +44 (0)1 932 592 348, www.mega3.tv

Movie Tech A.G., +49 0 89-43 68 913, Movie Tech L.P., (678) 417-6352, www.movietech.de

Nettman Systems International, (818) 623-1661, www.camerasystems.com

Orion Technocrane, +49 171-710-1834, www.technocrane.de

Pace Technologies, (818) 759-7322, www.pacetech.com

Panavision Remote Systems, (818) 316-1080, www.panavision.com

Panther, +49 89 61 39 00 01, www.panther-gmbh.de

Spacecam, (818) 889-6060, www.spacecam.com

Strada, (541) 549-4229, www.stradacranes.com

Straight Shoot'r, (818) 340-9376, www.straightshootr.com

Technovision, (818) 782-9051, www.technovision-global.com

Wescam, (818) 785-9282, www.wescam.com

Cinematography

Brown, Blain, *Cinematography,* Boston, MA; Focal Press, 2002.

Campbell, Russell, *Photographic Theory for the Motion Picture Cameraman,* London, Tantivy Press, 1970.

Campbell, Russell, *Practical Motion Picture Photography,* London, Tantivy Press, 1970.

Carlson, Verne and Sylvia, *Professional Cameraman's Handbook,* 4th edition, Boston, MA; Focal Press, 1994.

Clarke, ASC, Charles G., *Professional Cinematography,* Hollywood, CA; ASC Press, 2002.

Cornwell-Clyne, Major Adrian, *Color Cinematography,* 3rd edition, Chapman Hall LTD 1951.

Malkiewicz, Kris J. and Mullen, M. David, *Cinematography: A Guide for Filmmakers and Film Teachers,* New York, Fireside, 2005.

Mascelli, ASC, Joseph V., *The 5 C's of Cinematography,* Beverly Hills, CA, Silman-James Press, 1998 (c1965).

Wilson, Anton, *Anton Wilson's Cinema Workshop,* Hollywood, CA; ASC Press, 1983, 1994.

Color
Albers, J., *Interaction of Color,* New Haven and London; Yale University Press, 1963.

Eastman Kodak Publication H-12, *An Introduction to Color,* Rochester, 1972.

Eastman Kodak Publication E-74, *Color As Seen and Photographed,* Rochester, 1972.

Eastman Kodak Publication H-188, *Exploring the Color Image,* Rochester.

Evans, R. M., *An Introduction to Color,* New York, NY; John Wiley & Sons, 1948.

Evans, R. M., *Eye, Film, and Camera Color Photography,* New York, NY; John Wiley & Sons, 1959.

Evans, R. M., *The Perception of Color,* New York, NY; John Wiley & Sons, 1974.

Friedman, J. S., *History of Color Photography,* Boston, MA; American Photographic Publishing Company, 1944.

Hardy, A. C., *Handbook of Colorimetry,* MIT, Cambridge, MA; Technology Press, 1936.

Hunt, R. W. G., *The Reproduction of Colour,* Surrey, UK, Fountain Press, 1995.

Itten, J., *The Art of Color,* New York, Van Nostrand Reinhold, 1973.

National Bureau of Standards Circular 553, *The ISCC-NBS Method of Designating Colors and A Dictionary of Color Names,* Washington D. C., 1955.

Optical Society of America, *The Science of Color,* New York, NY; Thomas Y. Crowell Company, 1953.

Society of Motion Picture and Teclevision Engineers, *Elements of Color in Professional Motion Pictures,* New York, NY, 1957.

Wall, E. J., *History of Three-Color Photography,* New York and London, Boston, MA; American Photographic Publishing Company, 1925.

Film
Adams, Ansel, *The Negative,* New York, Little Brown, 1989.

Adams, Ansel, *The Print,* New York, Little Brown,1989.

Eastman Kodak Publication H-1: *Eastman Professional Motion Picture Films.*

Eastman Kodak Publication H-23: *The Book of Film Care.*

Eastman Kodak Publication H-188: *Exploring the Color Image.*

Eastman Kodak Publication N-17: *Infrared Films.*

Eastman Kodak Publication: *ISO vs EI Speed Ratings.*

Eastman Kodak Publication: *Ultraviolet and Fluorescence Photography.*

Hayball, Laurie White, *Advanced Infrared Photography Handbook,* Amherst Media, 2001.

Hayball, Laurie White, *Infrared Photography Handbook,* Amherst Media, 1997.

Film Design

Affron, Charles and Affron, Mirella Jona, *Sets in Motion,* Rutgers University Press, 1995.

Carrick, Edward, *Designing for Films,* The Studio LTD and the Studio Publications Inc, 1941, 1947.

Carter, Paul, *Backstage Handbook,* 3rd edition., Broadway Press, 1994.

Cruickshank, Dan, *Sir Banister Fletcher's A History of Architecture,* 20th edition, New York, NY, Architectural Press, 1996.

Edwards, Betty, *Drawing on the Right Side of the Brain,* revised edition, Jeremy P. Tarcher, 1989.

de Vries, Jan Vredeman, *Perspective,* Dover Publications, 1968.

Heisner, Beverly, *Studios,* McFarland and Co., 1990.

Katz, Stephen D., *Shot by Shot – Visualizing from Concept to Screen,* Boston, MA; Focal Press, 1991, pp. 337-356.

Preston, Ward, *What an Art Director Does,* Silman-James Press, 1994.

Raoul, Bill, *Stock Scenery Construction Handbook,* 2nd edition, Broadway Press, 1999.

St John Marner, Terrance, *Film Design,* The Tantivy Press, 1974.

Film History

The American Film Institute Catalog: *Feature Films 1911–1920,* Berkeley and Los Angeles, University of California Press, 1989.

The American Film Institute Catalog: *Feature Films 1931–1940,* Berkeley and Los Angeles, University of California Press, 1993.

The American Film Institute Catalog: *Feature Films 1921–1930,* Berkeley and Los Angeles, University of California Press, 1997.

The American Film Institute Catalog: *Feature Films 1961–1970,* Berkeley and Los Angeles, University of California Press, 1997.

The American Film Institute Catalog: *Within Our Gates: Ethnicity in American Feature Films 1911–1960,* Berkeley and Los Angeles, University of California Press, 1989.

The American Film Institute Catalog: *Feature Films 1941–1950,* Berkeley and Los Angeles, University of California Press, 1999.

Belton, John, *Widescreen Cinema,* Cambridge, MA; Harvard University Press, 1992.

Brownlow, Kevin, *Hollywood the Pioneers,* New York, NY; Alfred A. Knopf, 1979.

Brownlow, Kevin, *The Parade's Gone By,* New York, Knopf, 1968.

Coe, Brian, *The History of Movie Photography,* New York, Zoetrope, 1982.

Fielding, Raymond, *A Technological History of Motion Pictures and Television,* University of California Press, 1967.

Finler, Joel W., *The Hollywood Story,* New York, Crown, 1988.

Ryan, R.T., *A History of Motion Picture Color Technology,* London, Focal Press, 1977.

MacGowan, Kenneth, *Behind the Screen: the History and Techniques of the Motion Picture,* New York, Delacorte Press, 1965.

Rotha, Paul and Griffith, Richard, *The Film Till Now: A Survey of World Cinema,* London, Spring Books, 1967. (New York, Funk & Wagnalls, 1951.)

Schatz, Thomas, *The Genius of the System: Hollywood Filmmaking in the Studio Era,* New York, Pantheon, 1988.

Turner, George E., *The Cinema of Adventure, Romance and Terror,* Hollywood, CA; ASC Press, 1989

Film Processing

ACVL Handbook, Association of Cinema and Video Laboratories.

Case, Dominic, *Motion Picture Film Processing,* London, Butterworth and Co. Ltd. (Focal Press), 1985.

Eastman Kodak publications: H-1, H-2, H-7, H-17, H-21, H-23, H-24.07, H-26, H-36, H-37, H-37A, H-44, H-61, H-61A, H-61B, H-61C, H-61D, H-61E, H-61F, H-807 and H-822.

Happe, L. Bernard, *Your Film and the Lab,* London, Focal Press, 1974.

Kisner, W.I., *Control Techniques in Film Processing,* New York, SMPTE, 1960.

Ryan, R.T., *Principles of Color Sensitometry,* New York, SMPTE, 1974.

Filters

Eastman Kodak Publication B-3: *Filters.*

Harrison, H.K., *Mystery of Filters-II,* Porterville, CA; Harrison & Harrison, 1981.

Hirschfeld, ASC, Gerald, *Image Control,* Boston, MA; Focal Press, 1993.

Hypia, Jorma, *The Complete Tiffen Filter Manual,* AmPhoto, New York, 1981.

Smith, Robb, *Tiffen Practical Filter Manual.*

Tiffen Manufacturing Corporation Publication T179: Tiffen Photar Filter Glass

Journals, Magazines and Associations

ANSI Standards, American National Standards Institute, www.ansi.org.

American Cinematographer, ASC Holding Corp.,www.cinematographer.com.

BKSTS Journal, "Image Technology," British Kinematograph, Sound and Television Society, www.bksts.com.

SMPTE Journal, Society Of Motion Picture and Television Engineers, www.smpte.org.

Lenses

Angenieux, P., "Variable focal length objectives," U.S. Patent No. 2,847,907, 1958.

Bergstein, L., "General theory of optically compensated varifocal systems," JOSA Vol. 48, No. 9, pp. 154-171, 1958.

Cook, G.H.,"Recent developments in television optics," *Royal Television Society Journal,* pp. 158-167, 1973.

Cox, Arthur, *Photographic Optics, A Modern Approach to the Technique of Definition,* expanded edition, London, Focal Press, 1971.

Kingslake, R. "The development of the zoom lens," *SMPTE* Vol. 69, pp. 534-544, 1960.

Mann, A., Ed., "Zoom lenses," *SPIE Milestone Series* Vol. MS 85, 1993.

Neil, I.A. and Betensky, E.I, "High performance, wide angle, macro focus, zoom lens for 35mm cinematography," *SPIE* Vol. 3482, pp. 213-228, Kona, Hawaii, U.S.A., 1998.

Neil, I.A., "First order principles of zoom optics explained via macro focus conditions of fixed focal length lenses," *SPIE* Vol. 2539, San Diego, California, U.S.A., 1995.

Neil, I.A., "Liquid optics create high performance zoom lens," *Laser Focus World,* Vol. 31, No. 11, 1995.

Neil, I.A., "Uses of special glasses in visual objective lenses," *SPIE* Vol. 766, pp. 69-74, Los Angeles, California, U.S. A., 1987.

Zuegge, H. and Moellr, B., "A complete set of cinematographic zoom lenses and their fundamental design considerations," Proceedings of the 22nd Optical Symposium, pp. 13-16, Tokyo, Japan, 1997.

Lighting

Adams, Ansel, *Artificial Light Photography,* New York, Morgan and Morgan, Inc., 1956.

Alton, John, *Painting With Light,* Berkeley and Los Angeles, University of California Press, 1995.

Bergery, Benjamin, *Reflections – 21 Cinematographers at Work,* Hollywood, CA; ASC Press, 2002.

Box, Harry, *Set Lighting Technician's Handbook,* Boston, MA, Focal Press, 2003.

Malkiewicz, Kris J., *Film Lighting: Talk with Hollywood's Cinematographers and Gaffers,* New York, Touchstone, a Division of Simon & Schuster, 2012.

Millerson, Gerald, *The Technique of Lighting for Television and Film,* Boston, Focal Press, 1991

Miscellaneous

Arnheim, Rudolf, *Art and Visual Perception,* Berkley, CA, University of California Press, 1974.

Darby, William, *Masters of Lens and Light: A Checklist of Major Cinematographers and Their Feature Films,* Metuchen, NJ, Scarecrow Press, 1991.

Houghton, Buck, *What a Producer Does,* Silman-James Press, 1991.

Kehoe, Vincent J. R., *The Technique of the Professional Makeup Artist,* Boston, MA, Focal Press, 1995.

Kepes, Gyorgy, *Language of Vision,* New York, MA, Dover Publications, 1995.

Moholy-Nagy, L., *Vision in Motion,* Wisconsin; Cuneo Press, 1997.

Nilsen, Vladimir, *The Cinema as a Graphic Art,* New York; Garland Pub., 1985.

Waner, John, *Hollywood's Conversion of All Production to Color Using Eastman Color Professional Motion Picture Films,* Newcastle, ME; Tobey Publishing, 2000.

Photography

Evans, R.M., W.T. Hanson Jr., and W.L. Brewer, *Principles of Color Photography*, New York, John Wiley & Sons Inc., 1953.

Mees, C.E.K., *The Theory of the Photographic Process*, New York, Macmillan, 1977.

Thomas Jr., Woodlief, *SPSE Handbook of Photographic Science and Engineering*, New York, John Wiley & Sons, 1973.

Woodbury, Walter E., *The Encyclopaedic Dictionary of Photography*, New York, The Scovill and Adams Company, 1898.

Traveling Matte Composites

Composite Components Corp. (323) 257-1163, www.digitalgreenscreen.com

Curious Software (gFx roto)
UK: Tel: +44 (0)20 7428 0288   Fax: +44 (0)20 7428 5811
US: Tel: +1 505 988 7243, Fax: +1 505 988 1654
Email: info@curious-software.com
Web: www.curious-software.com

Dazian Theatrical Fabrics: East Coast (877) 232-9426 or East Coast Design Studio (212) 206-3515, West Coast (877) 432-9426 or West Coast Design Studio (818) 841-6500.

Flo Co (818) 780-0039 or (661) 269-2065, www.flo-co.com

Keylight (650) 326-2656, www.thefoundry.com

Kino Flo (818) 767-6528, www.kinoflo.com

Pinnacle Systems, (Commotion, Primatte) www.pinnaclesys.com

Primatte: Phototron USA, Inc. (530) 677 9980, www.primatte.com or www.phototron.com

Red*D*Mix [Ray McMillan, Flo Co Distributor] (416) 879-3761
email: mcmillan20@cogeco.ca

RFX (compositing software and hardware) (323) 962-7400, www.rfx.com

The Science and Technology Council of the Motion Picture Acadamy (310) 247 3000, www.oscars.org/council/index.html

Stewart Filmscreen Corp. (310) 784-5300, www.stewartfilm.com

Ultimatte Corp. (818) 993-8007, www.ultimatte.com

Underwater Cinematography

Mertens, Lawrence, *In Water Photography: Theory and Practice*, Wiley Interscience, New York, John Wiley & Sons, 1970.

Ryan, R.T., *Underwater Photographic Applications – Introduction*, SMPTE Journal, Vol. 82, No. 12, December 1973.

Industry-Wide Labor-Management Safety Bulletins at: http://www.csatf.org/bulletintro.shtml

Visual Effects

Abbott, ASC, L.B., *Special Effects with Wire, Tape and Rubber Bands,*
Hollywood, CA; ASC Press, 1984.

Bulleid, H.A.V. (Henry Anthony Vaughan), *Special Effects in Cinematography,*
London, Fountain Press, 1960.

Clark, Frank P., *Special Effects in Motion Pictures Some Methods for Producing Mechanical Effects,*
New York, SMPTE, 1966.

Dunn, ASC, Linwood, and Turner, George E., *ASC Treasury of Visual Effects,*
Hollywood, CA; ASC Press,1983.

Fielding, Raymond, *The Technique of Special Effects Cinematography,* Boston, MA;
Focal Press, 1985.

Glover, Thomas J., *Pocket Ref,* Littleton, CO, Sequoia Publishing, 1997.

Harryhausen, Ray, *Ray Harryhausen: An Animated Life,* New York, NY, Billboards Books, 2004.

Rogers, Pauline B., *The Art of Visual Effects: Interviews on the Tools of the Trade,*
Boston, MA; Focal Press, 1999.

The Nautical Almanac, commercial edition, Arcata, CA, Paradise Cay Publications (yearly).

Vaz, Matt Cotta and Barron, Craig, *The Invisible Art: The Legends of Movie Matte Painting,*
San Francisco, CA; Chronicle Books, 2002.

INDEX

Page numbers followed by an "f" refer to a figure or illustration

Raw versus de-Bayered, digital basic concepts, 16
REC. 709, 20
Recorders, external, 46–47
Recording formats, digital, 44–45
Recording HD video on digital still camera, 51
Red Epic camera, 358
Red Epic digital camera, 617–618
Red One digital camera, 619–620
Red Scarlet camera, 46, 54
Red Scarlet-X digital camera, 618–619
Redcode raw format, 16, 45
Redundancy definition, 417
Reflected-ultraviolet photography, 211
Refraction and underwater cinematography, 231, 232, 233, 234
Reflection(s)
  polarizing filters and, 171
  secondary, 170
  underwater cinematography and, 230
Reflector boards, 393
Region of interest correction definition, 417
Registration (color) definition, 418
Releases handheld apps, 848, 849
Remotevision, 181
Render definition, 418
Rental orders handheld app, 848
Resolution, digital basic concepts, 12–13
  common image standards, 13
  definitions, 12, 34, 86
Resolution definition, 418
Resolution versus megapixels and digital motion picture cameras, 32
Responsibilities of cinematographers, 3–6
  designing look, 3
  postproduction, 5–6
  preproduction planning, 3–4
  principal photography, 4–5
Reversal color film and day-for-night cinematography, 209
RGB (red, green, blue)
  definition, 418
  stripe pattern, 11f, 12
Rigid/hard mounts (fixed wing or helicopter), 226
Ringing definition, 418
Robodog, 180
Rock and Frazier lens system, The, 132
Rollvision stabilization system, 181
Rosco
  CalColor line of primaries, 341

diffusion materials, 347
lighting filers, 383
Rotoscoping (roto), 334, 338, 343

S

Safety on the set, 423–425
Salvaging, doctoring, and modifying with optical printer, 317
Scan definition, 418
Scanner versus cameras and digit motion picture cameras, 32–33, 84–85
Scanning and digital postproduction for feature film, 261–262, 262f
Scanning video—interlace or progressive, 16–18
Scattering and underwater cinematography, 231
Scene-referred data definition, 418
Screen heights importance, 60–62
Screen ratios, most common, 8
Scrim, 391, 392
Secondary color correction definition, 419
Sekonic exposure meters
  L 164 Marine meter, 235–236
  L 308 BII, 105
  L 358, 106
  L 398M, 105
  L 508C, 103–104
  L 558, 106–107
  L 608C, 104–105
  L 778 Dual Spot F exposure measure, 107
Sensor definition, 419
Sensor size
  depth of field and, 48–49
  HD video shooting on digital still camera, 49
Sensors and amount of light they capture, digital, 33–34
Sepia filters, 166
Shadows
  multiple shadows and LED lighting, 396
Shooting practices formulas, 681–684
  computing exposure times, 682
  footage in feet and frames, 682
  footage versus time relationship, 681
  frames rates for miniatures, 682–683
  high speed formulas, 683
  image blur, 684–685
  running times, feet, and frames, 681
Shooting to screen time calculator handheld app, 847
Shutter angle compensator for constant exposure chart, 873

Lightning Source UK Ltd.
Milton Keynes UK
UKOW06f2320160315

247953UK00010B/97/P

9 781467 568319